STUDIES OF
WELFARE POPULATIONS

Data Collection and Research Issues

Panel on Data and Methods for Measuring the Effects of
Changes in Social Welfare Programs

Michele Ver Ploeg, Robert A. Moffitt, and Constance F. Citro,
Editors

Committee on National Statistics

Division of Behavioral and Social Sciences and Education

National Research Council

NATIONAL ACADEMY PRESS
Washington, DC

NATIONAL ACADEMY PRESS • 2101 Constitution Avenue, N.W. • Washington, DC 20418

NOTICE: The project that is the subject of this report was approved by the Governing Board of the National Research Council, whose members are drawn from the councils of the National Academy of Sciences, the National Academy of Engineering, and the Institute of Medicine. The members of the committee responsible for the report were chosen for their special competences and with regard for appropriate balance.

This study was supported by Contract No. HHS-100-98-0011 between the National Academy of Sciences and the U.S. Department of Health and Human Services. Support of the work of the Committee on National Statistics is provided by a consortium of federal agencies through a grant from the National Science Foundation (Number SBR-9709489). Any opinions, findings, conclusions, or recommendations expressed in this publication are those of the author(s) and do not necessarily reflect the views of the organizations or agencies that provided support for the project.

Library of Congress Cataloging-in-Publication Data

Studies of welfare populations : data collection and research issues :
Panel on Data and Methods for Measuring the Effects of Changes in Social
Welfare Programs / Michele Ver Ploeg, Robert A. Moffitt, and
Constance F. Citro, editors ; Committee on National Statistics, Division of
Behavioral and Social Sciences and Education, National Research Council.
    p. cm.
Includes bibliographical references and index.
  ISBN 0-309-07623-4 (pbk.)
  1. Public welfare—Statistical methods. 2. Social surveys. 3. Public
welfare—Research—Methodology. I. Ver Ploeg, Michele. II. Moffitt,
Robert A. III. Citro, Constance F. (Constance Forbes), 1942- IV. Panel
on Data and Methods for Measuring the Effects of Changes in Social
Welfare Programs (U.S.)
  HV29 .S78 2002
  362.5′8′072—dc21
                           2001005893

Additional copies of this report are available from the National Academy Press, 2101 Constitution Avenue, N.W., Lockbox 285, Washington, DC 20055; (800) 624-6242 or (202) 334-3313 (in the Washington metropolitan area); Internet, http://www.nap.edu

Suggested citation: *Studies of Welfare Populations: Data Collection and Research Issues* (2002). Panel on Data and Methods for Measuring the Effects of Changes in Social Welfare Programs, Michele Ver Ploeg, Robert A. Moffitt, and Constance F. Citro, Editors. Committee on National Statistics, Division of Behavioral and Social Sciences and Education. Washington, DC: National Academy Press.

THE NATIONAL ACADEMIES

National Academy of Sciences
National Academy of Engineering
Institute of Medicine
National Research Council

The **National Academy of Sciences** is a private, nonprofit, self-perpetuating society of distinguished scholars engaged in scientific and engineering research, dedicated to the furtherance of science and technology and to their use for the general welfare. Upon the authority of the charter granted to it by the Congress in 1863, the Academy has a mandate that requires it to advise the federal government on scientific and technical matters. Dr. Bruce M. Alberts is president of the National Academy of Sciences.

The **National Academy of Engineering** was established in 1964, under the charter of the National Academy of Sciences, as a parallel organization of outstanding engineers. It is autonomous in its administration and in the selection of its members, sharing with the National Academy of Sciences the responsibility for advising the federal government. The National Academy of Engineering also sponsors engineering programs aimed at meeting national needs, encourages education and research, and recognizes the superior achievements of engineers. Dr. Wm. A. Wulf is president of the National Academy of Engineering.

The **Institute of Medicine** was established in 1970 by the National Academy of Sciences to secure the services of eminent members of appropriate professions in the examination of policy matters pertaining to the health of the public. The Institute acts under the responsibility given to the National Academy of Sciences by its congressional charter to be an adviser to the federal government and, upon its own initiative, to identify issues of medical care, research, and education. Dr. Kenneth I. Shine is president of the Institute of Medicine.

The **National Research Council** was organized by the National Academy of Sciences in 1916 to associate the broad community of science and technology with the Academy's purposes of furthering knowledge and advising the federal government. Functioning in accordance with general policies determined by the Academy, the Council has become the principal operating agency of both the National Academy of Sciences and the National Academy of Engineering in providing services to the government, the public, and the scientific and engineering communities. The Council is administered jointly by both Academies and the Institute of Medicine. Dr. Bruce M. Alberts and Dr. Wm. A. Wulf are chairman and vice chairman, respectively, of the National Research Council.

PANEL ON DATA AND METHODS FOR MEASURING THE EFFECTS OF CHANGES IN SOCIAL WELFARE PROGRAMS

Acknowledgments

This volume is the product of the hard work of many individuals to whom we are grateful. We would first like to thank the authors of papers for their contributions and for presenting the papers at the workshop or at meetings of the panel. Each of these papers was reviewed by members of the panel and outside reviewers. Most of these reviewers were also discussants at the workshop on Data Collection for Low Income and Welfare Populations held December 16-17, 1999. We are indebted to all reviewers for their constructive comments to the authors: Sandra Berry, Rand; Harold Bloom, Manpower Demonstration Research Corporation; Mike Brick, Westat; Sheldon Danziger, University of Michigan; Betsy Martin, U.S. Census Bureau; Daniel McCaffrey, RAND; Charles Metcalf, Mathematica Policy Research; Jeffrey Moore, U.S. Census Bureau; John Karl Scholz, University of Wisconsin-Madison; Matthew Stagner, Urban Institute; William Winkler, U.S. Census Bureau; and Laura Zayatz, U.S. Census Bureau. I would also like to thank my fellow members of the Panel on Data and Methods for Measuring the Effects of Changes in Social Welfare Programs for helping to shape the topics of the papers, developing the workshop, and reviewing the papers. Graham Kalton, Westat, and Robert Groves, University of Michigan, should also be thanked for helping the panel identify authors and discussants for these papers.

I would like to thank the staff of the Committee on National Statistics for their work on this volume. I would like to thank my coeditors, Michele Ver Ploeg and Constance F. Citro, for their diligence in polishing the papers and guiding them through the review process. The production of this volume could not be possible without the efforts of Michael Siri, project assistant for the Committee on National Statistics. Michael did an excellent job on the difficult task of getting 14 papers with14 different formats into a common format for the volume. All of these papers were professionally edited by Laura Penney, to which we are also grateful. Yvonne Wise of the Division of Behavioral and Social Sciences of the National Research Council is to be thanked for her assistance in shepherding the report through the phases of production.

Finally, we are also grateful to the Office of the Assistant Secretary for Planning and Evaluation in the Department of Health and Human Services for its sponsorship of the panel that made this volume possible.

Robert A. Moffitt, *Chair*
Panel on Data and Methods for
Measuring the Effects of Changes
in Social Welfare Programs

Contents

INTRODUCTION   1
Robert A. Moffitt, Constance F. Citro, and Michele Ver Ploeg

PART I   SURVEY DATA

1   Designing Surveys Acknowledging Nonresponse   13
    Robert M. Groves and Mick P. Couper

2   Methods for Obtaining High Response Rates in Telephone Surveys   55
    David Cantor and Patricia Cunningham

3   High Response Rates for Low-Income Population In-Person Surveys   86
    Charlene Weiss and Barbara A. Bailar

4   Paying Respondents for Survey Participation   105
    Eleanor Singer and Richard A. Kulka

5   Adjusting for Missing Data in Low-Income Surveys   129
    Leyla Mohadjer and G. Hussain Choudhry

6   Measurement Error in Surveys of the Low-Income Population   157
    Nancy A. Mathiowetz, Charlie Brown, and John Bound

PART II   ADMINISTRATIVE DATA

7   Matching and Cleaning Administrative Data   197
    Robert M. Goerge and Bong Joo Lee

8   Access and Confidentiality Issues with Administrative Data   220
      Henry E. Brady, Susan A. Grand, M. Anne Powell, and
      Werner Schink

9   Measuring Employment and Income for Low-Income
      Populations with Administrative and Survey Data   275
      V. Joseph Hotz and John Karl Scholz

10 Administrative Data on the Well-Being of Children
      On and Off Welfare   316
      Richard Barth, Eleanor Locklin-Brown, Stephanie
      Cuccaro-Alamin, and Barbara Needell

PART III   QUALITATIVE DATA

11 The Right (Soft) Stuff: Qualitative Methods and the Study of Welfare
      Reform   355
      Katherine S. Newman

PART IV   WELFARE LEAVERS AND WELFARE DYNAMICS

12 Studies of Welfare Leavers: Data, Methods, and Contributions to the
      Policy Process   387
      Gregory Acs and Pamela Loprest

13 Preexit Benefit Receipt and Employment Histories and
      Postexit Outcomes of Welfare Leavers   415
      Michele Ver Ploeg

14 Experienced-Based Measures of Heterogeneity in the
      Welfare Caseload   473
      Robert A. Moffitt

Appendix: Agenda of the Workshop on Data Collection for
Low-Income and Welfare Populations   501

Index   507

STUDIES OF

WELFARE POPULATIONS

Introduction

Robert A. Moffitt, Constance F. Citro, and Michele Ver Ploeg

Academic and policy interest in the U.S. welfare system has increased dramatically over the past 15 years, an interest that has accelerated and is currently at an all-time high. Beginning in the late 1980s with welfare reform initiatives in a few states around the country and continuing in the first half of the 1990s as more states made changes in their income support programs, welfare reform culminated at the federal level with the passage of the Personal Responsibility and Work Opportunity Reconciliation Act (PRWORA) in 1996. PRWORA replaced the long-standing federal entitlement program for low-income families and children (Aid to Families with Dependent Children, AFDC) with a program financed by state-administered block grants, the Temporary Assistance for Needy Families (TANF) program. The legislation imposed several new requirements on state TANF programs, including lifetime limits on receipt of benefits, minimum work requirements, and requirements for unmarried teenage parents to reside with an adult and continue their education in order to receive benefits. Otherwise, it allowed states to configure their programs as they see fit, continuing a trend of devolving the design and control of familial assistance programs from the federal government to state governments that began earlier in the 1990s.

The enactment of PRWORA provided the impetus for a large volume of research studies aimed at studying its impact and that of changes in other federal income support programs, such as the Food Stamp Program. These studies are now yielding results and reporting new findings on an almost-daily basis. PRWORA is slated to come up for reauthorization in 2002, and it is already clear that research findings will play a significant role in the debate over the directions that welfare reform should take from here.

The Panel on Data and Methods for Measuring the Effects of Changes in Social Welfare Programs of the National Research Council was formed in 1998 to review the evaluation methods and data that are needed to study the effects of welfare reform. Sponsored by the Office of the Assistant Secretary for Planning and Evaluation (ASPE) of the U.S. Department of Health and Human Services through a congressional appropriation, the panel has issued interim and final reports (National Research Council, 1999, 2001).

Early in its deliberations, particularly after reviewing the large number of so-called "welfare leaver" studies—studies of how families who left the TANF rolls were faring off welfare—the panel realized that the database for conducting studies of welfare reform had many deficiencies and required attention by policy makers and research analysts. In its final report, the panel concluded that welfare reform evaluation imposes significant demands on the data infrastructure for welfare and low-income populations and that ". . . inadequacies in the nation's data infrastructure for social welfare program study constitutes the major barrier to good monitoring and evaluation of the effects of reform" (NRC 2001:146). The panel concluded that national-level surveys were being put under great strain for PRWORA research given their small sample sizes, limited welfare policy-related content, and, often, high rates of nonresponse (see also National Research Council, 1998). State-level administrative data sets, the panel concluded, are of much more importance with the devolution of welfare policy but are difficult to use for research because they were designed for management purposes. In addition, although they have large sample sizes, their content is limited. Surveys for specific states with more detailed content have been only recently attempted—usually telephone surveys of leavers—and the panel expressed concern about the capacity and technical expertise of state governments to conduct such surveys of adequate quality. To date, for example, many surveys of welfare leavers have unacceptably high rates of nonresponse. Overall, the panel concluded that major new investments are needed in the data infrastructure for analysis of welfare and low-income populations.

This concern led the panel to plan a workshop on data collection on welfare and low-income populations for which experts would be asked to write papers addressing in detail not only what the data collection issues are for this population, but also how the quality and quantity of data can be improved. A workshop was held on December 16-17, 1999, in Washington, DC. The agenda for the workshop is listed as an Appendix to this volume. Approximately half the papers presented at the workshop concerned survey data and the other half concerned administrative data; one paper addressed qualitative data. Altogether, the papers provide a comprehensive review of relevant types of data. The volume also contains four additional papers that were commissioned to complement the conference papers. One of them discusses methods for adjusting survey data for nonresponse. The other three papers focus on welfare leavers, a subpopulation of particular interest to Congress that a number of states have studied with grants from ASPE, as well as the importance of understanding the dynamics of the welfare caseload when interpreting findings from these studies.

After the conference, the papers were revised, following National Research Council procedures, to reflect the comments of discussants at the workshop, panel members, and outside reviewers. The additional commissioned papers also were revised in response to comments from panel members and outside reviewers. This volume contains the final versions of the papers.

In this introduction, we summarize each of the 14 papers in the volume. Together, they are intended as a guide and reference tool for researchers and program administrators seeking to improve the availability and quality of data on welfare and low-income populations for state-level, as well as national-level, analysis.

SURVEY DATA

The volume contains six papers on survey issues. They address (1) methods for designing surveys taking into account nonresponse in advance; (2) methods for obtaining high response rates in telephone surveys; (3) methods for obtaining high response rates in in-person surveys; (4) the effects of incentive payments; (5) methods for adjusting for missing data in surveys of low-income populations; and (6) measurement error issues in surveys, with a special focus on recall error.

In their paper on "Designing Surveys Acknowledging Nonresponse," Groves and Couper first review the basic issues involved in nonresponse, illustrating the problem of bias in means and other statistics, such as differences in means and regression coefficients, and how that bias is related to the magnitude of nonresponse and the size of the difference in outcomes between respondents and nonrespondents. They also briefly review methods of weighting and imputation to adjust for nonresponse after the fact. The authors then discuss the details of the survey process, including the exact process of contacting a respondent and how barriers to that contact arise, noting that welfare reform may generate additional barriers (e.g., because welfare recipients are more likely to be working and hence not at home). They also provide an in-depth discussion of the respondent's decision to participate in a survey, noting the importance of the environment, the respondent, and the survey design itself, and how the initial interaction between survey taker and respondent is a key element affecting the participation decision. They propose a fairly ambitious process of interviewer questioning, which involves contingent reactions to different statements by the respondent, a process that would require expert interviewers. They conclude with a list of 10 principles for surveys of the low-income population for improvement in light of nonresponse.

Cantor and Cunningham discuss methods for obtaining high response rates in telephone surveys of welfare and low-income populations in their paper, first identifying "best practices" and then comparing those to practices used in some welfare leaver telephone surveys. The authors note the overriding importance of recognizing language and cultural diversity among respondents and the need to take such diversity into account in designing content and deploying interviewers. They then discuss specific issues in increasing response rates, including obtaining contact information in the presurvey process (e.g., from administrative records); obtaining informed consent to gather information needed for subsequent tracking; address-related problems with mail surveys; methods for tracing hard-to-locate respondents; dealing with answering machines; the importance of highly trained interviewers, echoing the emphasis of Groves and Couper; considerations in questionnaire design, including the critical nature of the introduction; and refusal conversion. Cantor and Cunningham then review a set of telephone surveys of welfare recipients and welfare leavers. They find that response rates often are quite low and that use of the telephone alone only rarely will obtain response rates greater than 50 percent, which is a very low number by the traditional standards of survey research. They suggest that higher, acceptable response rates will almost surely require substantial in-person followup, which can move the response rate up above 70 percent. The authors note that nonresponse is mainly an issue of inability to locate respondents rather than outright refusals, which makes tracing and locating respondents of great importance. They find that many welfare records are of poor quality to assist in tracing, containing inaccurate and out-of-date locator information, and they emphasize that expertise in tracing is needed in light of the difficulties involved. Refusal conversion is also discussed, with an emphasis again on the need for trained interviewers in using this method. Finally, the authors discuss random-digit dialing telephone surveys of this population (as opposed to surveys based on list samples such as those from welfare records) and explore the additional difficulties that arise with this methodology.

The paper by Weiss and Bailar discusses methods for obtaining high response rates from in-person surveys of the low-income population. The principles are illustrated with five in-person surveys of this population conducted by the National Opinion Research Center (NORC). All the surveys drew their samples from administrative lists, provided monetary incentives for survey participation, and applied extensive locating methods. Among the issues discussed are the importance of the advance letter, community contacts, and an extensive tracing and locating operation, including field-based tracing on top of office-based tracing. The authors also provide an in-depth discussion of the importance of experienced interviewers for this population, including experience not only in administering an interview, but also in securing cooperation with the survey. The use of traveling interviewers and the importance of good field supervisory staff and site management are then addressed.

In their paper, Singer and Kulka review what is known about the effects of paying respondents for survey participation ("incentives"). Reviewing both mail and telephone surveys, the authors report that incentives are, overall, effective in increasing response rates; that prepaid incentives are usually more effective than promised incentives; that money is more important than a gift; and that incentives have a greater effect when respondent burden is high and the initial response rate is low. They also note that incentives appear to be effective in panel surveys, even when incentives are not as high in subsequent waves of interviews as they are in the initial wave. After discussing the evidence on whether incentives affect item nonresponse or the distribution of given responses—the evidence on the issue is mixed—the authors review what little is known about the use of incentives in low-income populations. The little available evidence suggests, again, that incentives are effective in this population as well. The authors conclude with a number of recommendations on the use of incentives, including a recommendation that payments to convert initial refusals to interviews be made sparingly.

Mohadjer and Choudhry provide an exposition of methods for adjusting for missing data after the fact—that is, after the data have been collected. Their paper focuses on traditional weighting methods for such adjustment and includes methods for adjustment for noncoverage of the population as well as nonresponse to the survey. The authors present basic weighting methods and give examples of how variables are used to construct weights. They also discuss the effect of using weights derived from the survey sample versus weights obtained from outside data sets on the population as a whole. For population-based weights, they discuss issues of poststratification and raking that arise. Finally, they provide a brief discussion of the bias-variance tradeoff in designing weights, which is intrinsic to the nature of weights.

Measurement error is discussed in the paper by Mathiowetz, Brown, and Bound. The paper first lists the sources of measurement error in the survey process, which include the questionnaire itself; the respondent; the interviewer; and the conditions of the survey (interviewer training, mode, frequency of measurement, etc.). The authors then review issues relating to the cognitive aspects of measurement error and provide an extended discussion of the problem of questions requiring autobiographical memory. Other topics discussed in the paper include the issue of social desirability of a particular response; errors in response to sensitive questions; and errors in survey reports of earnings and income. A number of existing studies of measurement error are reviewed, but none are focused on welfare or low-income populations per se or on populations with unstable income and employment streams. The authors point out how earnings reports need to be based on salient events and give examples in which such salience is absent. A detailed review is then provided of what is known about measurement error in reports of transfer program income, child support income, hours of work, and unemployment histories. Finally, the authors list a number of issues that should be addressed that can help reduce measurement error, including proper attention by cognitive experts to comprehension of the question by respondents, care for the process of retrieval when writing questions, the use of calendars and landmark events, and a number of other questionnaire design topics. Methods for asking socially sensitive questions also are discussed.

ADMINISTRATIVE DATA

Administrative records can be a valuable source of information about the characteristics and experiences of welfare program beneficiaries and past beneficiaries. To comply with federally mandated time limits on receipt of TANF benefits, states will need to develop the capability to track recipients over time, something not usually done in the old AFDC system. Such longitudinal tracking capability should make program records more useful for analysis; however, differences in programs across states will likely make it harder to conduct cross-state analyses. Research use of administrative records, whether TANF records or records from other systems (e.g., Unemployment Insurance) that can be used to track selected outcomes for welfare and low-income populations, poses many challenges.

Four papers on administrative data covering a wide range of different topics are included in the volume. The four address (1) issues in the matching and cleaning of administrative data; (2) issues of access and confidentiality; (3) problems in measuring employment and income with administrative data compared to survey data; and (4) the availability of administrative data on children.

Issues in the matching and cleaning of administrative data are discussed by Goerge and Lee. The authors begin by noting the importance of "cleaning" administrative data in a comprehensive sense, namely, converting what are management files into analytic files suitable for research use. They also note the importance of matching records across multiple administrative data sets (i.e., record linkage), which provides more information on respondents. A number of issues are involved in the cleaning process, many of which involve methods for assessing data quality and other aspects of the variables available in the administrative data. A number of important issues in record linkage also are discussed, perhaps the most important being the availability and accuracy of matching variables. The authors discuss deterministic and probabilistic record linkage as well as data quality issues in such linkage. The paper concludes with a number of recommendations on the cleaning and linking of administrative data.

Brady, Grand, Powell, and Schink discuss access and confidentiality issues with administrative data in their paper and propose ways for increasing researcher access to administrative data. The authors begin by noting that the legal barriers to obtaining access to administrative data by researchers often are formidable. Although laws in this area generally are intended to apply to private individuals interested in identifying specific persons, researcher access often is denied even though the researcher has no interest in identities and often intends to use the research results to help improve administration of the program. The authors provide a brief overview of the legal framework surrounding administrative data, confidentiality, and privacy, making a number of important distinctions between different types of issues and clarifying the content of several pieces of legislation—federal and state—governing access and confidentiality. They then turn to a review of how 14 ASPE-funded state welfare leaver studies have dealt with these issues and whether general lessons can be learned. The authors conclude that while success in dealing with access and confidentiality problems has been achieved in many cases, the methods for doing so are ad hoc, based on long-standing relationships of trust between state agencies and outside researchers, and not buttressed and supported by an adequate legal framework. Twelve key principles are laid out for governing data access and confidentiality. Finally, the authors recommend more use of masking methods as well as institutional mechanisms such as secure data centers to facilitate responsible researcher access to and use of confidential administrative data.

Hotz and Scholz review the measurement of employment and income from administrative data and discuss why and whether measures taken from administrative data differ from those obtained from survey data. Employment and income are, of course, two of the key outcome variables for welfare reform evaluation and hence assume special importance in data collection. They find that there often are differences in administrative and survey data reports of employment and income and that the differences are traceable to differences in population coverage, in reporting units, in sources of income, in measurement error, and in incentives built into the data-gathering mechanism. The authors provide a detailed review of the quality of employment and income data from, first, the major national survey data sets; then from state-level administrative data taken from Unemployment Insurance records; and, finally, from Internal Revenue Service records. They review what is known about differences in reports across the three as well. The authors conclude with several recommendations on reconciling potentially different results from these data sources.

Administrative data on children are discussed in the paper by Barth, Locklin-Brown, Cuccaro-Alamin, and Needell. The authors first discuss the policy issues surrounding the effects of welfare reform on children and what the mechanisms for those effects might be. They identify several domains of child well-being that conceivably can be measured with administrative data, including health, safety (child abuse and neglect), education, and juvenile justice. In each area, they find that a number of different administrative data sets could be matched, in principle, with welfare records. They identify the exact variables measured in each data set as well. The authors find that good health measures often are present in various data sets, but they are often inaccessible to researchers, while child abuse and neglect data are more often available but have many data quality issues that require careful attention. Education and juvenile justice data are the least accessible to researchers and also contain variables that would only indirectly measure the true outcomes of interest. The authors find that privacy and confidentiality barriers impose significant limitations on access to administrative data on children, similar to the finding in the paper by Brady et al.

QUALITATIVE DATA

Qualitative data increasingly have been used in welfare program evaluations and studies. Although there is a fairly long history of the use of process analysis in formal evaluations, there is less history in using direct observation of study respondents or even using focus groups. Yet in attempting to learn how current or former welfare recipients are faring, qualitative data can provide information that neither survey nor administrative data offer.

The paper by Newman discusses the use of qualitative data for investigating welfare and low-income populations. Newman notes that qualitative data can assist in helping to understand the subjective points of view of families in these populations, provide information on how recipients understand the rules of the welfare system, uncover unexpected factors that are driving families' situations, explore any unintended consequences of a policy change, and focus attention on the dynamic and constantly changing character of most families in the low-income population. The author reviews a range of methods, from open-ended questions in survey questionnaires to focus groups to detailed participant observation in the field, in each case listing the advantages and disadvantages of the method. Newman then discusses the use of qualitative data in several recent welfare reform projects to illustrate how the methods can be used. The author concludes with a recommendation that additional expertise in qualitative data be brought into state governments and that the use of these methods increase.

WELFARE LEAVERS AND WELFARE DYNAMICS

An initial focus of concern of policy makers has been the effects of PRWORA on people who left AFDC and successor TANF programs– "welfare leavers." In response to a congressional mandate, ASPE provided grant funds to states and counties to analyze administrative records and conduct surveys of two cohorts of welfare leavers. In fiscal year 1998, ASPE provided grant funds to 14 jurisdictions (10 states, the District of Columbia, and 3 counties or groups of counties) to study welfare leavers. In fiscal year 1999 it provided funds to one state to also follow welfare leavers, and to six jurisdictions (five states and one county group) to study those who were either formally or informally diverted from enrolling for TANF—"divertees."

In its interim and final report (National Research Council, 1999, 2001), the panel commented on some problems with leaver studies. These problems include differences in welfare caseload trends across states, such as faster declines in welfare rolls in some states than others and earlier program changes in states that sought AFDC waiver provisions, both of which could affect the comparability of data for cohorts of welfare leavers defined at a point in time. Also, states do not define leavers in the same way; for example, some states count "child-only cases" as leavers and others do not. (In such cases, adult members of a family are not eligible for benefits but the children are.) The panel also emphasized the need for leaver studies to categorize sample cases by their previous welfare behavior, distinguishing between people who had been on welfare for a long period or only a short period or whether they had been cyclers (i.e., alternating periods of welfare receipt with periods of nonreceipt). To illustrate the problems in welfare leaver studies and best practice in such analyses, the panel commissioned three papers.

The first paper on this topic, "Studies of Welfare Leavers: Data, Methods, and Contributions to the Policy Process" by Acs and Loprest, reviews existing welfare leaver studies, including those funded by ASPE and others. It describes the definitions, methods, and procedures used in each study and identifies their strengths and weaknesses. The paper also compares some findings of leaver studies across studies that use different methodologies to illustrate points about comparability.

The second paper, "Preexit Benefit Receipt and Employment Histories and Postexit Outcomes of Welfare Leavers" by Ver Ploeg, uses data from the state of Wisconsin to analyze welfare leavers. The analysis breaks the sample members into "long-termers," "short-termers," and "cyclers" and shows that this categorization is important for understanding outcomes for these groups. The paper also stratifies the sample by work experience prior to leaving welfare and finds that there are sizable differences in employment outcomes across groups with more work experience compared to those with less work experience and that such categorizations also can be useful in understanding outcomes of leavers.

The last paper in this section and the final paper in the collection, "Experience-Based Measures of Heterogeneity in the Welfare Caseload" by Moffitt, uses data from the National Longitudinal Survey of Youth to construct measures of heterogeneity in the welfare population based on the recipient's own welfare experience. A number of classifications of women in the U.S. population are used to characterize the amount of time they have spent on welfare, the number of welfare spells they have experienced, and the average length of their welfare spells. The same long-termer, short-termer, and cycler distinctions are used in the paper as well. The analysis of the characteristics of these groups reveals that short-termers have the strongest labor market capabilities but, surprisingly, that cyclers and long-termers are approximately the same in terms of labor market potential. More generally, the only significant indicator of labor market capability is the total amount of time a recipient has been on welfare, not the degree of turnover or lengths of spells she experiences. The analysis suggests that welfare cycling is not a very useful indicator of a recipient's labor market capability and that the nature of welfare cyclers and reasons that cycling occur are not well understood.

REFERENCES

National Research Council

    1998   *Providing National Statistics on Health and Social Welfare Programs in an Era of Change, Summary of a Workshop.* Committee on National Statistics. Constance F. Citro, Charles F. Manski, and John Pepper, eds. Washington, DC: National Academy Press.

    1999   *Evaluating Welfare Reform: A Framework and Review of Current Work.* Panel on Data and Methods for Measuring the Effects of Changes in Social Welfare Programs. Robert A. Moffitt and Michele Ver Ploeg, eds. Washington, DC: National Academy Press.

    2001   *Evaluating Welfare Reform in an Era of Transition.* Panel on Data and Methods for Measuring the Effects of Changes in Social Welfare Programs. Robert A. Moffitt and Michele Ver Ploeg, eds. Washington, DC: National Academy Press.

Part I

Survey Data

1

Designing Surveys Acknowledging Nonresponse

Robert M. Groves and Mick P. Couper

THE NATURE OF NONRESPONSE ERROR IN SURVEY STATISTICS

Sample surveys used to describe low-income populations are effective only when several things go "right." The target population must be defined well, having the geographical and temporal extents that fit the goals of the survey. The sampling frame, the materials used to identify the population, must include the full target population. The measurement instrument must be constructed in a way that communicates the intent of the research question to the respondents, ideally in their nomenclature and within their conceptual framework. The sample design must give known, nonzero chances of selection to each low-income family/person in the sampling frame. All sample persons must be contacted and measured, eliminating nonresponse error. Finally, the administration of the measurement instrument must be conducted in a manner that fulfills the design.

Rarely does everything go exactly right. Because surveys are endeavors that are (1) customized to each problem, and (2) constructed from thousands of detailed decisions, the odds of imperfections in survey statistics are indeed large. As survey methodology, the study of how alternative survey designs affect the quality of statistics, matures, it is increasingly obvious that errors are only partially avoidable in surveys of human populations. Instead of having the goal of eliminating errors, survey researchers must learn how to reduce them "within reason and budget" and then attempt to gain insight into their impacts on key statistics in the survey.

This paper is a review of a large set of classic and recent findings in the study of survey nonresponse, a growing concern about survey quality. It begins with a review of what nonresponse means and how it affects the quality of survey statistics. It notes that nonresponse is relevant to simple descriptive statistics as well as measures of the relationship between two attributes (e.g., length of time receiving benefits and likelihood of later job retention). It then reviews briefly what survey statisticians can do to reduce the impact of nonresponse after the survey is complete, through various changes in the analysis approach of the data.

After this brief overview of the basic approaches to reducing the impacts of nonresponse on statistical conclusions from the data concludes, the paper turns to reducing the problem of nonresponse. It reviews current theoretical viewpoints on what causes nonresponse as well as survey design features that have been found to be effective in reducing nonresponse rates.

Nonresponse Rates and Their Relationship to Error Properties

Sample surveys often are designed to draw inferences about finite populations by measuring a subset of the population. The classical inferential capabilities of the survey rest on probability sampling from a frame covering all members of the population. A probability sample assigns known, nonzero chances of selection to every member of the population. Typically, large amounts of data from each member of the population are collected in the survey. From these variables, hundreds or thousands of different statistics might be computed, each of which is of interest to the researcher only if it describes well the corresponding population attribute. Some of these statistics describe the population from which the sample was drawn; others stem from using the data to test causal hypotheses about processes measured by the survey variables (e.g., how length of time receiving welfare payments affects salary levels of subsequent employment).

One example statistic is the sample mean as an estimator of the population mean. This is best described by using some statistical notation in order to be exact in our meaning. Let one question in the survey be called the question, "Y," and the answer to that question for a sample member, say the $_i$th member of the population, be designated by Y_i. Then we can describe the population, mean by

$$\bar{Y} = \sum_{i=1}^{N} Y_i / N \tag{1}$$

where N is the number of units in the target population. The estimator of the population mean is often

$$\bar{Y} = (\sum_{i=1}^{r} w_i y_i) / (\sum_{i=1}^{r} w_i) \tag{2}$$

where r is the number of respondents in the sample and w_i is the reciprocal of the probability of selection of the $_i$th respondent. (For readers accustomed to equal probability samples, as in a simple random sample, the w_i is the same for all cases in the sample and the computation above is equivalent to $\sum y_i / n$.)

One problem with the sample mean as calculated here is that is does not contain any information from the nonrespondents in the sample. However, all the desirable inferential properties of probability sample statistics apply to the statistics computed on the *entire* sample. Let's assume that in addition to the r respondents to the survey, there are m (for "missing") nonrespondents. Then the total sample size is $n = r + m$. In the computation mentioned we miss information on the m missing cases.

How does this affect our estimation of the population mean, $\bar{Y}$? Let's make first a simplifying assumption. Assume that everyone in the target population is either, permanently and forevermore, a respondent or a nonrespondent. Let the entire target population, thereby, be defined as $N = R + M$, where the capital letters denote numbers in the total population.

Assume that we are unaware at the time of sample selection about which stratum each person occupies. Then in drawing our sample of size n, we will likely select some respondents and some nonrespondents. They total n in all cases, but the actual number of respondents and nonrespondents in any one sample will vary. We know that in expectation that the fraction of *sample* cases that are respondents should be equal to the fraction of *population* cases that lie in the respondent stratum, but there will be sampling variability about that number. That is, $E(r) = fR$, where f is the sampling fraction used to draw the sample from the population. Similarly, $E(m) = fM$.

For each possible sample we could draw, given the sample design, we could express a difference between the full sample mean, n, and the respondent mean, in the following way:

$$\bar{Y}_n = \left(\frac{r}{n}\right)\bar{y}_r + \left(\frac{m}{n}\right)\bar{y}_m \tag{3}$$

which, with a little manipulation, becomes

$$\bar{Y}_r - \bar{y} = \left(\frac{m}{n}\right)[\bar{y}_r - \bar{y}_m] \tag{4}$$

RESPONDENT MEAN – TOTAL SAMPLE MEAN = (NONRESPONSE RATE) *
(DIFFERENCE BETWEEN RESPONDENT AND NONRESPONDENT MEANS)

This shows that the deviation of the respondent mean from the full sample mean is a function of the nonresponse rate (m/n) and the difference between the respondent and nonrespondent means.

Under this simple expression, what is the expected value of the respondent mean over all samples that could be drawn given the same sample design? The answer to this question determines the nature of the *bias* in the respondent mean, where "bias" is taken to mean the difference between the expected value (over all possible samples given a specific design) of a statistic and the statistic computed on the target population. That is, in cases of equal probability samples of fixed size, the bias of the respondent mean is approximately

$$B(\bar{y}_r) = \left(\frac{M}{N}\right)\left(\bar{Y}_r - \bar{Y}_m\right) \qquad (5)$$

BIAS(RESPONDENT MEAN) = (NONRESPONSE RATE IN POPULATION)*
(DIFFERENCE IN RESPONDENT AND NONRESPONDENT POPULATION MEANS)

where the capital letters denote the population equivalents to the sample values. This shows that the larger the stratum of nonrespondents, the higher the bias of the respondent mean, other things being equal. Similarly, the more distinctive the nonrespondents are from the respondents, the larger the bias of the respondent mean.

These two quantities, the nonresponse rate and the differences between respondents and nonrespondents on the variables of interest, are key issues to surveys of the welfare population.

Figures 1-1a to 1-1d through show four alternative frequency distributions for respondents and nonrespondents on a hypothetical variable, y, measured on all cases in some target population. The area under the curves is proportional to the size of the two groups, respondents and nonrespondents. These four figures correspond to the four rows in Table 1-1 that show response rates, means of respondents and nonrespondents, bias, and percentage bias for each of the four cases.

The first case reflects a high response rate survey and one in which the nonrespondents have a distribution of y values quite similar to that of the respon-

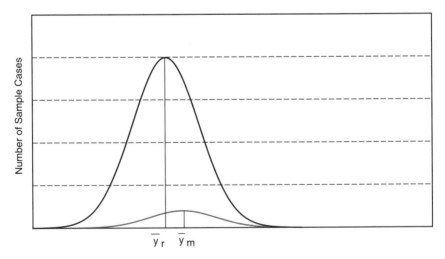

FIGURE 1-1a High response rate, nonrespondents similar to respondents.
SOURCE: Groves and Couper (1998).
NOTE: y = outcome variable of interest.

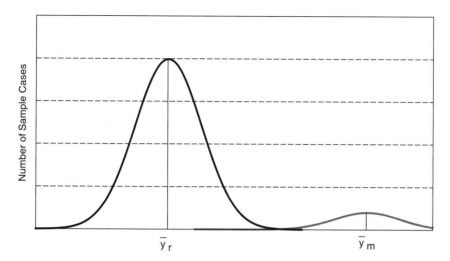

FIGURE 1-1b High response rate, nonrespondents different from respondents.
SOURCE: Groves and Couper (1998).
NOTE: y = outcome variable of interest.

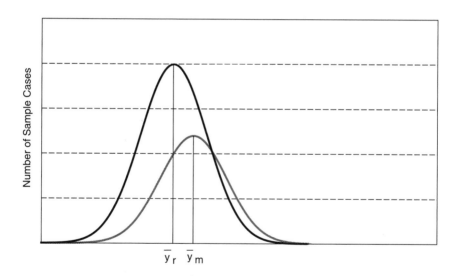

FIGURE 1-1c Low response rate, nonrespondents similar to respondents.
SOURCE: Groves and Couper (1998).
NOTE: y = outcome variable of interest.

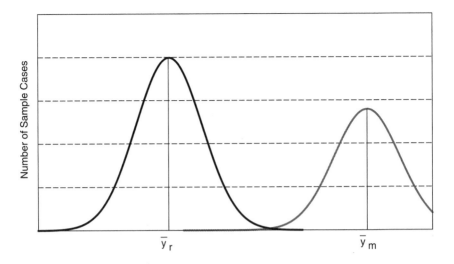

FIGURE 1-1d Low response rate, nonrespondents different from respondents
SOURCE: Groves and Couper (1998).
NOTE: y = outcome variable of interest.

dents. This is the lowest bias case; both factors in the nonresponse bias are small. For example, assume the response rate is 95 percent, the respondent mean for reported expenditures on clothing for a quarter is $201.00, and the mean for nonrespondents is $228.00. Then the nonresponse error is .05($201.00 – $228.00) = –$1.35.

The second case, like the first, is a low nonresponse survey, but now the nonrespondents tend to have much higher y values than the respondents. This means that the difference term, $(\bar{y}_r - \bar{y}_m)$, is a large negative number, meaning the respondent mean underestimates the full population mean. However, the size of the bias is small because of the low nonresponse rate. Using the same example as above, with a nonrespondent mean now of $501.00, the bias is .05($201.00 – $501.00) = –$15.00.

The third case shows a very high nonresponse rate (the area under the respondent distribution is about 50 percent greater than that under the nonrespondent—a nonresponse rate of 40 percent). However, as in the first graph, the values on y of the nonrespondents are similar to those of the respondents. Hence, the respondent mean again has low bias due to nonresponse. With the same example as mentioned earlier, the bias is .40($201.00 – $228.00) = [–$10.80].

The fourth case is the most perverse, exhibiting a large group of nonrespondents who have much higher values in general on y than the respondents. In this case, both m/n is large (judging by the area under the nonrespondent curve) and $(\bar{y}_r - \bar{y}_m)$ is large in absolute terms. This is the case of large non-

TABLE 1-1 Bias and Percentage Bias in Respondent Mean Relative to Total Sample Mean for Four Situations in Figures 1-1a-1 to 1d and Sample Size of Nonrespondents Needed to Detect the Nonresponse Bias

Response Rate	Difference	Response Rate Percentage	Respondent Mean	Nonrespondent Mean	Total Sample Mean	Bias	Bias Percentage	Required Sample Size of Nonrespondents
High	Small	95	$201	$228	$202	$1.35	−0.7	20,408
High	Large	95	$201	$501	$216	$15.00	−6.9	210
Low	Small	60	$201	$228	$212	$10.80	−5.1	304
Low	Large	60	$201	$501	$321	$120.00	−37.4	7

response bias. Using the previous example, the bias is .40($201.00 – $501.00) = –$120.00, a relative bias of 37 percent compared to the total sample mean!

These four very different situations also have implications for studies of nonrespondents. Let's imagine we wish to mount a special study of non-respondents in order to test whether the respondent mean is biased. The last column of Table 1-1 shows the sample size of nonrespondents required to obtain the same stability for a bias ratio estimate (assuming simple random sampling and the desire to estimate a binomial mean statistic with a population value of .50). The table shows that such a nonresponse study can be quite small (n = 7) and still be useful to detect the presence of nonresponse bias in a low-response-rate survey with large differences between respondents and nonrespondents (the fourth row of the table). However, the required sample size to obtain the same precision for such a nonresponse bias test in the high-response-rate case is very large (n= 20,408, in the first row). Unfortunately, prior to a study being fielded, it is not possible to have much information on the size of the likely nonresponse bias.

Nonresponse Error on Different Types of Statistics

The discussion in the previous section focused on the effect of nonresponse on estimates of the population mean, using the sample mean. This section briefly reviews effects of nonresponse on other popular statistics. We examine the case of an estimate of a population total, the difference of two subclass means, and a regression coefficient.

The Population Total

Estimating the total number of some entity is common in federal, state, and local government surveys. For example, most countries use surveys to estimate the total number of unemployed persons, the total number of new jobs created in a month, the total retail sales, and the total number of criminal victimizations. Using similar notation as previously, the population total is ΣY_i, which is estimated by a simple expansion estimator, $\Sigma w_i y_i$, or by a ratio expansion estimator, $X(\Sigma w_i y_i / \Sigma w_i x_i)$, where X is some auxiliary variable, correlated with Y, for which target population totals are known. For example, if y were a measure of the length of first employment spell of a welfare leaver, and x were a count of sample welfare leavers, X would be a count of the total number of welfare leavers.

For variables that have nonnegative values (like count variables), simple expansion estimators of totals based only on respondents always underestimate the total. This is because the full sample estimator is

$$\sum_{i=1}^{n} w_i y_i = \sum_{i=1}^{r} w_i y_i + \sum_{i=r+1}^{n} w_i y_i \qquad (6)$$

FULL SAMPLE ESTIMATE OF POPULATION TOTAL = RESPONDENT-BASED
ESTIMATE + NONRESPONDENT-BASED ESTIMATE

Hence, the bias in the respondent-based estimator is

$$-\sum_{i=r+1}^{n} w_i y_i \tag{7}$$

It is easy to see, thereby, that the respondent-based total (for variables that have
nonnegative values) always will underestimate the full sample total, and thus, in
expectation, the full population total.

The Difference of Two Subclass Means

Many statistics of interest from sample surveys estimate the difference between the means of two subpopulations. For example, the Current Population
Survey often estimates the difference in the unemployment rate for black and
nonblack men. The National Health Interview Survey estimates the difference in
the mean number of doctor visits in the past 12 months between males and
females.

Using the expressions above, and using subscripts 1 and 2 for the two subclasses, we can describe the two respondent means as

$$\bar{y}_{1r} = \bar{y}_{1n} + \left(\frac{m_1}{n_1}\right)\left[\bar{y}_{1r} - \bar{y}_{1m}\right] \tag{8}$$

$$\bar{y}_{2r} = \bar{y}_{2n} + \left(\frac{m_2}{n_2}\right)\left[\bar{y}_{2r} - \bar{y}_{2m}\right] \tag{9}$$

These expressions show that each respondent subclass mean is subject to an error
that is a function of a nonresponse rate for the subclass and a deviation between
respondents and nonrespondents in the subclass. The reader should note that the
nonresponse rates for individual subclasses could be higher or lower than the
nonresponse rates for the total sample. For example, it is common that
nonresponse rates in large urban areas are higher than nonresponse rates in rural
areas. If these were the two subclasses, the two nonresponse rates would be quite
different.

If we were interested in $\bar{y}_1 - \bar{y}_2$ as a statistic of interest, the bias in the
difference of the two means would be approximately

$$B(\bar{y}_1 - \bar{y}_2) = \left(\frac{M_1}{N_1}\right)\left[\bar{Y}_{1r} - \bar{Y}_{1m}\right] - \left(\frac{M_2}{N_2}\right)\left[\bar{Y}_{2r} - \bar{Y}_{2m}\right] \tag{10}$$

Many survey analysts are hopeful that the two terms in the bias expression
cancel. That is, the bias in the two subclass means is equal. If one were dealing
with two subclasses with equal nonresponse rates that hope is equivalent to a

hope that the difference terms are equal to one another. This hope is based on an assumption that nonrespondents will differ from respondents in the same way for both subclasses. That is, if nonrespondents tend to be unemployed versus respondents, on average, this will be true for all subclasses in the sample.

If the nonresponse rates were not equal for the two subclasses, then the assumptions of canceling biases is even more complex. For example, let's continue to assume that the difference between respondent and nonrespondent means is the same for the two subclasses. That is, assume $[\bar{y}_{r1} - \bar{y}_{m1}] = [\bar{y}_{r2} - \bar{y}_{m2}]$. Under this restrictive assumption, there can still be large nonresponse biases.

For example, Figure 1-2 examines differences of two subclass means where the statistics are proportions (e.g., the proportion currently employed). The figure treats the case in which the proportion employed among respondents in the first subclass (say, women on welfare a long time) is $\bar{y}_{r1} = 0.5$ and the proportion employed among respondents in the second subclass (say, women on welfare a short time) is $\bar{y}_{r2} = 0.3$. This is fixed for all cases in the figure. We examine the nonresponse bias for the entire set of differences between respondents and non-respondents. That is, we examine situations where the differences between respondents and nonrespondents lie between –0.5 and 0.3. (This difference applies to both subclasses.) The first case of a difference of 0.3 would correspond to

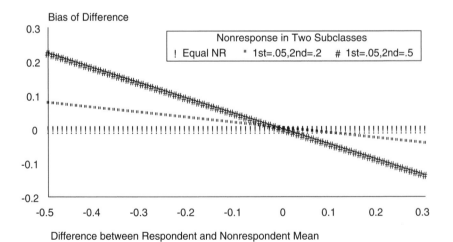

FIGURE 1-2 Illustration of nonresponse bias for difference between proportion currently employed (0.5 employed among respondents on welfare a short time versus 0.3 employed among respondents on welfare a long time), given comparable differences in each subclass between respondents and nonrespondents.
SOURCE: Groves and Couper (1998).

$$[\bar{y}_{r1} - \bar{y}_{m1}] = 0.5 - 0.2 = 0.3$$
$$[\bar{y}_{r2} - \bar{y}_{m2}] = 0.3 - 0.0 = 0.3$$

The figure shows that when the two nonresponse rates are equal to one another, there is no bias in the difference of the two subclass means. However, when the response rates of the two subclasses are different, large biases can result. Larger biases in the difference of subclass means arise with larger differences in nonresponse rates in the two subclasses (note the higher absolute value of the bias for any given $[\bar{y}_r - \bar{y}_m]$ value for the case with a .05 nonresponse rate in subclass [1 and a 0.5, in subclass 2] than for the other cases).

A Regression Coefficient

Many survey data sets are used by analysts to estimate a wide variety of statistics measuring the relationship between two variables. Linear models testing causal assertions often are estimated on survey data. Imagine, for example, that the analysts were interested in the model

$$y_1 = \beta_0 + \beta_1 x_i + \varepsilon_i \tag{11}$$

which using the respondent cases to the survey, would be estimated by

$$\hat{y}_{ri} = \hat{\beta}_{r0} + \hat{\beta}_{r1} x_{ri} \tag{12}$$

The ordinary least squares estimator of β_{r1} is

$$\hat{\beta}_{r1} = \frac{\sum\limits_{i=1}^{r}(x_i - \bar{x}_r)(y_i - \bar{y}_r)}{\sqrt{\sum\limits_{i=1}^{r}(x_1 - \bar{x}_r)^2}} \tag{13}$$

Both the numerator and denominator of this expression are subject to potential nonresponse bias. For example, the bias in the covariance term in the numerator is approximately

$$B(s_{rxy}) = \frac{M}{N}(S_{rxy} - S_{mxy}) - \left(\frac{M}{N}\right)\left(1 - \frac{M}{N}\right)(\bar{X}_r - \bar{X}_m)(\bar{Y}_r - \bar{Y}_m) \tag{14}$$

where s_{rxy} is the respondent-based estimate of the covariance between x and y based on the sample (S_{rxy} is the population equivalent) and S_{mxy} is a similar quantity for nonrespondents.

This bias expression can be either positive or negative in value. The first term in the expression has a form similar to that of the bias of the respondent mean. It reflects a difference in covariances for the respondents (S_{rxy}) and nonrespondents (S_{mxy}). It is large in absolute value when the nonresponse rate is large. If the two variables are more strongly related in the respondent set than in the nonrespondent, the term has a positive value (that is the regression coefficient tends to be overestimated). The second term has no analogue in the case of the sample mean; it is a function of cross-products of difference terms. It can be either positive or negative depending on these deviations.

As Figure 1-3 illustrates, if the nonrespondent units have distinctive combinations of values on the x and y variables in the estimated equation, then the slope of the regression line can be misestimated. The figure illustrates the case when the pattern of nonrespondent cases (designated by "O") differ from that of respondent cases (designated by "■"). The result is the fitted line on respondents only has a larger slope than that for the full sample. In this case, normally the analyst would find more support for a hypothesized relationship than would be true for the full sample.

We can use equation (14) to illustrate notions of "ignorable" and "non-ignorable" nonresponse. Even in the presence of nonresponse, the nonresponse bias of regression coefficients may be negligible if the model has a specification that reflects all the causes of nonresponse related to the dependent variable. Consider a survey in which respondents differ from nonrespondents in their employment status *because* there are systematic differences in the representation of different education and race groups among respondents and nonrespondents. Said differently, within education and race groups, the employment rates of respondents and nonrespondents are equivalent. In this case, ignoring this informa-

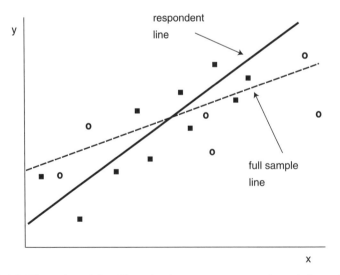

FIGURE 1-3 Illustration of the effect of unit nonresponse on estimated slope of regression line.
SOURCE: Groves and Couper (1998).

tion will produce a biased estimate of unemployment rates. Using an employment rate estimation scheme that accounts for differences in education and race group response rate can eliminate the bias. In equation (12), letting x be education and race can reduce the nonresponse bias in estimating a y, employment propensity.

Considering Survey Participation a Stochastic Phenomenon

The previous discussion made the assumption that each person (or household) in a target population either is a respondent or a nonrespondent for all possible surveys. That is, it assumes a fixed property for each sample unit regarding the survey request. They always will be a nonrespondent or they always will be a respondent, in all realizations of the survey design.

An alternative view of nonresponse asserts that every sample unit has a probability of being a respondent and a probability of being a nonrespondent. It takes the perspective that each sample survey is but one realization of a survey design. In this case, the survey design contains all the specifications of the research data collection. The design includes the definition of the sampling frame; the sample design; the questionnaire design; choice of mode; hiring, selection, and training regimen for interviewers; data collection period, protocol for contacting sample units; callback rules; refusal conversion rules; and so on. Conditional on all these fixed properties of the sample survey, sample units can make different decisions regarding their participation.

In this view, the notion of a nonresponse rate takes on new properties. Instead of the nonresponse rate merely being a manifestation of how many nonrespondents were sampled from the sampling frame, we must acknowledge that in each realization of a survey different individuals will be respondents and nonrespondents. In this perspective the nonresponse rate given earlier (m/n) is the result of a set of Bernoulli trials; each sample unit is subject to a "coin flip" to determine whether it is a respondent or nonrespondent on a particular trial. The coins of various sample units may be weighted differently; some will have higher probabilities of participation than others. However, all are involved in a stochastic process of determining their participation in a particular sample survey.

The implications of this perspective on the biases of respondent means, respondent totals, respondent differences of means, and respondent regression coefficients are minor. The more important implication is on the variance properties of unadjusted and adjusted estimates based on respondents.

Postsurvey Compensation for Nonresponse

Two principal techniques are used to account for unit nonresponse in the analysis of survey data: weighting and imputation. In computing final statistics, weighting attempts to increase the importance of data from respondents who are in classes with large nonresponse rates and decrease their importance when they are members of classes with high response rates. Imputation creates data records for nonrespondents by examining patterns of attributes that appear to co-occur among respondents, and then estimating the attributes of the nonrespondents based on information common to respondents and nonrespondents.

All adjustments to the analysis of data in the presence of nonresponse can affect survey conclusions: both the value of a statistic and the precision of the statistic can be affected.

Weighting to Adjust Statistics for Nonresponse

Two kinds of weighting are common to survey estimation in the presence of nonresponse: population-based weighting (sometimes called poststratification) and sample-based weighting. Population weighting applies known population totals on attributes from the sampling frame to create a respondent pool that resembles the population on those attributes. For example, if the Temporary Assistance for Needy Families (TANF) leavers' frame were used to draw a sample and auxiliary information were available on food stamp, general assistance, Supplemental Security Income (SSI), Medicaid, and foster care payment receipt, it would be possible to use those variables as adjustment factors. *The ideal adjustment factors are those that display variation in response rates* and *variation on key survey statistics*. To illustrate, Table 1-2 shows a survey estimating percentage of TANF leavers employed, in different categories of prior receipt status. In this hypothetical case, we are given the number of months unemployed of sample persons (both employed and unemployed). We can see that the mean number of months unemployed is 3.2 for respondents but 6.5 for nonrespondents. In this case we have available an attribute known on the entire population (the type of transfer payments received), and this permits an adjustment of the overall mean.

TABLE 1-2 Illustration of Proportion of TANF Leavers Currently Employed, by Type of Assistance Received, for Population, Sample, Respondents, and Nonrespondents

		Sample			Respondents		Nonrespondents	
Category	Population N	n	Response Rate	n	Months Unemployed	n	Months Unemployed	
General assistance only	5,000	50	.95	47	0.2	3	0.1	
Gen. asst. and food stamps	30,000	300	.90	270	0.5	30	0.4	
Gen. asst. and SSI	30,000	300	.90	270	3.2	30	3.1	
Gen. asst. and other	35,000	350	.50	175	8.1	175	8.2	
Total	100,000	1,000	.76	762	3.2	238	6.5	

The adjusted mean merely assures that the sample statistic will be based on the population distribution of the sampling frame, on the adjustment variable. In this case, the adjusted respondent mean equals 0.05*0.2 + 0.3*0.5 + 0.3*3.2 + 0.35*8.1 = 3.955. (The true mean is 3.966.)

Why does this seem to work? The adjustment variable is both correlated to the response rate and correlated to the dependent variable. In other words, most of the problem of nonresponse arises because the respondent pool differs from the population on the distribution of type of transfer payment. Restoring that balance reduces the nonresponse error. This is not always so. If the adjustment variables were related to response rates but not to the survey variable, then adjustment would do nothing to change the value of the survey statistic.

What cannot be seen from the illustration is the effects on the precision of the statistic of the adjustment. When population weights are used, the effect is usually to increase the precision of the estimate, a side benefit (Cochran, 1977). For that reason, attempting to use sampling frames rich in auxiliary data is a wise design choice in general. Whenever there are possibilities of linking to the entire sampling frame information that is correlated with the likely survey outcomes, then these variables are available for population-based weighting. They can both reduce nonresponse bias and variance of estimates.

What can be done when there are no correlates of nonresponse or the outcome variables available on all sample frame elements? The next best treatment is to collect data on all sample elements, both respondent and nonrespondent, that would have similar relationships to nonresponse likelihood and survey outcomes. For example, it is sometimes too expensive to merge administrative data sets for all sample frame elements but still possible for the sample. In this case, a similar weighting scheme is constructed, but using information available only on the sample. Each respondent case is weighted by the reciprocal of the response rate of the group to which it belongs. This procedure clearly relies on the assumption that nonresepondents and respondents are distributed identically given group membership (i.e., that nonrespondents are missing at random). Sometimes this weighting is done in discrete classes, as with the example in Table 1-2; other times "response propensity" models that predict the likelihood that each respondent was actually measured, given a set of attributes known for respondents and nonrespondents are constructed (Ekholm and Laaksonen, 1991).

Whatever is done with sample-based weights, it is generally the case that the precision of weighted sample estimates is lower than that of estimates with no weights. A good approximate of the sampling variance (square of standard error) of the adjusted mean in a simple random sample is

$$\frac{\sum w_h^2 s_{rh}^2}{r_h} + \frac{\sum w_h (\bar{y}_{rh} - \bar{y}_s)^2}{n} \tag{15}$$

where the w_h is the proportion of sample cases in a weight group with r_h respondents, y_{rh} is the mean of the respondents in that group, and y_s is the overall sample mean based on all n cases. The first term is what the sampling variance would be for the mean if the sample had come from a sample stratified by the weight classes. The second term reflects the lack of control of the allocation of the sample across the weight classes; this is the term that creates the loss of precision (as well as the fact that the total sample size is reduced from n to Σr_h, where (Σr_h/n) is the response rate.)

One good question is why weights based on the full population tend to improve the precision of estimates and why weights based on the sample reduce the precision. This rule of thumb is useful because, other things being equal, sample-based nonresponse weights are themselves based on a single sample of the population. Their values would vary over replications of the sample; hence, they tend not to add stability to the estimates but further compound the instability of estimates. Although this greater instability is unfortunate, most uses of such sample-based weights are justified by the decrease in the biasing effects of nonresponse. Thus, although the estimates may have higher variability over replications, they will tend to have averages closer to the population parameter.

Imputation to Improve Estimates in the Face of Missing Data

The second approach to improving survey estimation when nonresponse is present is imputation. Imputation uses information auxiliary to the survey to create values for individual missing items in sample data records. Imputation is generally preferred over weighting for item-missing data (e.g., missing information on current wages for a respondent) than for unit nonresponse (e.g., missing an entire interview). Weighting is more often used for unit nonresponse.

One technique for imputation in unit nonresponse is hot deck imputation, which uses data records from respondents in the survey as substitutes for those missing for nonrespondents (Ford, 1983). The technique chooses "donor" respondent records for nonrespondents who share the same classification on some set of attributes known on all cases (e.g., geography, structure type). Ideally, respondents and nonrespondents would have identical distributions on all survey variables within a class (similar logic as applies to weighting classes). In other words, nonrespondents are missing at random (MAR). The rule for choosing the donor, the size of the classes, and the degree of homogeneity within classes determine the bias and variance properties of the imputation.

More frequently imputation involves models, specifying the relationship between a set of predictors known on respondents and nonrespondents and the survey variables (Little and Rubin, 1987). These models are fit on those cases for which the survey variable values are known. The coefficients of the model are used to create expected values, given the model, for all nonrespondent cases. The expected values may be altered by the addition of an error term from a specified distribution; the imputation may be performed multiple times (Rubin, 1987) in order to provide estimates of the variance due to imputation.

Common Burdens of Adjustment Procedures

We can now see that all practical tools of adjustment for nonresponse require information auxiliary to the survey to be effective. This information must pertain both to respondents and nonrespondents to be useful. To offer the chance of reducing the bias of nonresponse, the variables available should be correlated both with the likelihood of being a nonrespondent and the survey statistic of interest itself. When the dependent variable itself is missing, strong models positing the relationship between the likelihood of nonresponse and the dependent variable are required. Often the assumptions of these models remain untestable with the survey data themselves.

Researchers can imagine more useful adjustment variables than are actually available. Hence, the quality of postsurvey adjustments are limited more often by lack of data than by lack of creativity on the part of the analysts.

DECOMPOSING THE SURVEY PARTICIPATION PHENOMENON

The phenomenon of survey participation is sequential and nested. First, the location of sample persons must be determined. Second, sample persons must be contacted. Third, they are given a request for survey information. Those not contacted make no decision regarding their participation that is known by the survey organization. Those contacted and given a survey request can cooperate, they can refuse, or they can provide information that communicates that they cannot physically or cognitively perform the respondent role. Because these are four separate processes, it is important to keep them as separate nonresponse phenomena: failure to locate, noncontact, refusals, and "other noninterview" is a common category-labeling scheme.

Locating Sample Persons

The first step in gaining contact with a sample person, when selected from a list of persons, is locating that person.[1] If the sample person has not changed address or telephone number from the time the list was prepared, this is a trivial issue. The difficulty arises when persons or households change addresses. The propensity of locating units is driven by factors related to whether or not the unit moves and the quality of contact information provided at the time of initial data collection.

A number of survey design features may affect the likelihood of locating sample units. For example, the quality of the contact information decays as time

---

[1] Gaining contact may not necessarily be the first step if the sample is not generated from a list. For example, screening households in sampled areas may be necessary to obtain sample members needed for the study.

between the initial data collection (or creation of the list) and the followup survey increases. Similarly, tracking rules affect location propensity. For cost reasons, a survey organization may track people only within a limited geographic area, such as a county or within a country. The amount and quality of information collected by the survey organization specifically for tracking movers also is driven by cost considerations. The more reliable and valid data available for tracking purposes can reduce tracking effort, and make more resources available for those units that are proving to be particularly difficult to locate.

Household characteristics also affect the likelihood of moving, and thus the propensity to locate the household or household members. Geographic mobility is related to the household or individual life stage, as well as cohort effects. For example, younger people are typically much more mobile than older persons. The number of years that a household or individual has lived at a residence, the nature of household tenure (i.e., whether the household members own or rent the dwelling), and community attachments through family and friends also determine the likelihood of moving.

Household income is strongly related to residential mobility. Using data from the Current Population Survey, we find that 19.6 percent of those with household incomes under $10,000 had moved between March 1996 and March 1997, compared to 10 percent of those with incomes above $75,000. Similarly, 25.9 percent unemployed persons age 16 or older had moved in this period, compared to 16.8 percent of those employed, and 11.1 percent not in the labor force.

Life events also are known to be related to moving likelihood. A birth in a household, a death of a significant individual, marriage, job change, crime victimization, and other events are associated with increased likelihood of moving. Furthermore, these life events may increase the difficulty of locating individuals. For example, a name change in marriage or following divorce can make it more difficult to track and locate someone who has moved. This is particularly relevant for welfare leaver studies, as this population is likely to be undergoing these very types of changes.

An important factor that can reduce the likelihood of moving, or provide more data on units that do move, is the social aspect of community attachment or connectedness. Individuals who are engaged in the civic aspects of their community or participate socially are posited to be more stable and less likely to move. Furthermore, those linked into their current community life are likely to leave many traces to their new address, and likely to be politically, socially, and economically engaged in their new community. Their lives are more public and accessible through multiple databases such as telephone directories, credit records, voter registration, library registration, membership in churches or religious organizations, or children in schools. Again, we expect that sample units in welfare leaver studies are not particularly rich in these sources of tracking information.

To the extent that the survey variables of interest are related to mobility, lifestyle changes, social isolation, or willingness to be found, nonresponse through nonlocation can lead to bias. Because these studies are primarily about changes in individual lives, failure to obtain complete data on the more mobile or those subject to lifestyle changes will underrepresent individuals with these particular characteristics in such surveys. Furthermore, the effects of disproportionate representation in the sample due to mobility or lifestyle changes may not be simply additive. For example, we expect that those who do not have a telephone and those who refuse to provide a telephone number both would be difficult to locate in subsequent waves of a survey, but for different reasons.

The Process of Contacting Sample Persons

Theoretically the process of contacting a sample household, once located, is rather straightforward. As Figure 1-4 shows, the success at contacting a household should be a simple function of the times at which at least one member of the household is at home, the times at which interviewers call, and any impediments the interviewers encounter in gaining access to the housing unit. In face-to-face surveys the latter can include locked apartment buildings, gated housing complexes, no-trespassing enforcement, as well as intercoms or any devices that limit contact with the household. In telephone surveys, the impediments include "caller ID," "call blocking," or answering machines that filter or restrict direct contact with the household.

In most surveys the interviewer has no prior knowledge about the at-home behavior of a given sample household. In face-to-face surveys interviewers report that they often make an initial visit to a sample segment (i.e., a cluster of neighboring housing units sampled in the survey) during the day in order to gain initial intelligence about likely at-home behaviors. During this visit the interviewer looks for bicycles left outside (as evidence of children), signs of difficulty of

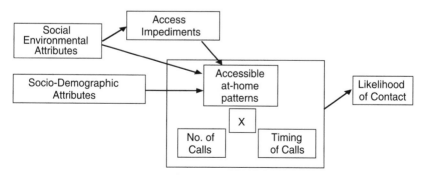

FIGURE 1-4 Influences on the likelihood of contact with a sample household.
SOURCE: Groves and Couper (1998).

accessing the unit (e.g., locked apartment buildings), small apartments in multi-unit structures (likely to be single-person units), absence of automobiles, or other signs. Sometimes when neighbors of the sample household are available, interviewers seek their advice on a good time to call on the sample unit. This process is the practical method of gaining proxy information about what call times might successfully encounter the household members at home. In telephone surveys, no such intelligence gathering is possible. The only information about at-home practices of a sample household is obtained by calling the number. (This imbalance leads to the larger number of calls required to make first contact with a household in telephone surveys; see Groves and Kahn, 1979.)

Information from time-use surveys, which ask persons to report on their activities hour by hour, has shown common patterns of at-home behavior by weekday mornings and afternoons, weekday evenings, and weekends. Those in the employed labor force are commonly out of the house, with the lowest rates of occupancy between 10 a.m. and 4:30 p.m. (Hill, 1978). Interviewers make repeated calls on households they do not contact on the first call. Their choice of time for those callbacks can be viewed as repeated samples from a day-of-week, time-of-day frame. They base their timing of successive calls on information they obtain on prior unsuccessful visits and on some sense of consistency. For example, interviewers often are trained to make a callback on a unit not contacted at the last visit on Tuesday afternoon, by visiting during an evening or weekend.

Physical impediments are sometimes so strong that they literally prevent all contact with a sample unit. For example, some higher priced multiunit structures have doormen that are ordered to prevent entrance of all persons not previously screened by a resident. Such buildings may be fully nonrespondent to face-to-face surveys. Similarly, although there is evidence that the majority of owners of telephone answering machines use them to monitor calls to their unit when they are absent, some apparently use them to screen out calls when they are at home (see Tuckel and Feinberg, 1991; Tuckel and O'Neill, 1995), thus preventing telephone survey interviewers from contacting the household.

Other impediments to contacting households may offer merely temporary barriers, forcing the interviewer to make more than the usual number of calls before first contacting the households. For example, apartment buildings whose entrance is controlled by a resident manager may require negotiations with the manager before access to sample households is given.

Is there empirical evidence regarding the model in Figure 1-4? First, let's look at the distribution of the number of calls required to make first contact with a sample household. Figure 1-5 shows the proportion of sample households contacted by calls to first contacts. This figure displays the result for several surveys at once, some telephone and some face to face. The pattern is relatively stable across the surveys, with the modal category being the first call–immediate contact with someone in the household. The proportion contacted on later calls is uniformly decreasing in subsequent calls. Rather uniformly, if the first call at-

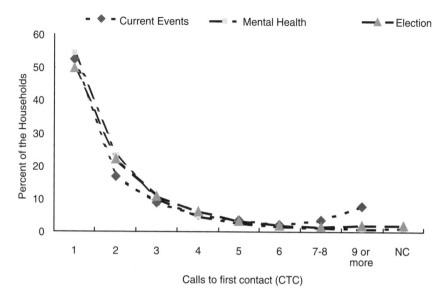

FIGURE 1-5 Percentage of eligible households contacted by calls to first contact.

tempt is unsuccessful, the likelihood of contact declines with each successive call. Does the character of sample households vary by calls to first contact? Figure 1-6 shows an increasing percentage of the households are single-person households as the number of calls to first contact increases. Single-person households tend to be more difficult to contact. Other analysis shows that the exception to this tendency is single-person households with elderly persons, which tend to be home more often than other households. Figure 1-7 shows a similar result for an access impediment in telephone surveys, the answering machine, which now is present in more than 50 percent of homes nationwide (Tuckel and O'Neil, 1995). The percentage of contacted households with answering machines increases with each succeeding category of number of calls to first contact. Households with answering machines slow down contact with household members, requiring more calls to first contact.

Other empirical results are similar to these could be presented. Households with access impediments slow down contact of interviewers with sample units. More calls are required to even deliver the survey request. Furthermore, households that are home less often require more calls; these include households where all adult members work out of the home during the day, urban versus rural households, and in telephone surveys, unlisted households.

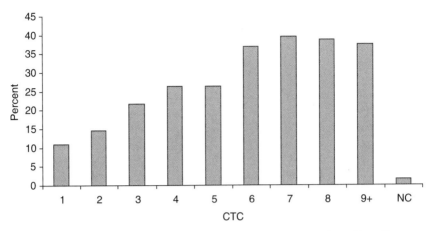

FIGURE 1-6 Percentage of contacted households with one person, by calls to first contact (National Survey of Health and Stress).

The Decision to Participate in a Survey

Once the interviewer contacts a sample household we believe that the influences on the householder's decision to participate arise from relatively stable features of their environments and backgrounds, fixed features of the survey design, as well as quite transient, unstable features of the interaction between the interviewer and the householder. This conceptual scheme is portrayed in Figure

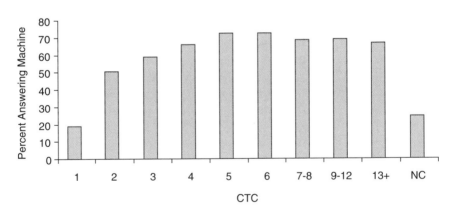

FIGURE 1-7 Percentage of contacted households with an answering machine by calls to first contact.

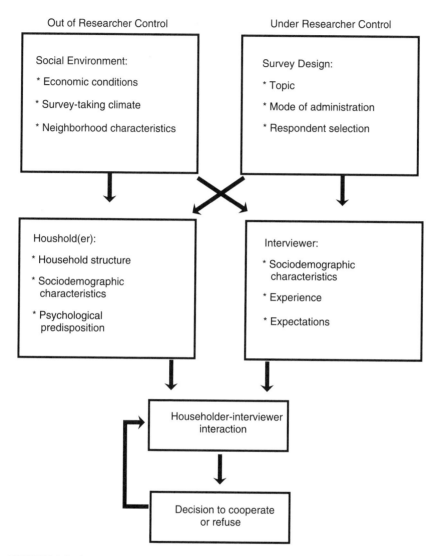

FIGURE 1-8 A conceptual framework for survey cooperation.
SOURCE: Groves and Couper (1998).

1-8, which lists influences of the social environment, householder, survey design features, interviewer attributes and behavior, and the contact-level interaction of interviewers and householders.

The influences on the left of the figure (social environment and sample household) are features of the population under study, out of control of the researcher. The influences on the right are the result of design choices by the researcher, affecting the nature of the survey requests and the attributes of the actors (the interviewers) who deliver them. The bottom of the figure, describing the interaction between the interviewer and the householder, is the occasion when these influences come to bear. Which of the various influences are made most salient during that interaction determines the decision outcome of the householder.

Social Environmental Influences on Survey Participation

Because surveys are inherently social events, we would expect that societal and group-level influences might affect their participation rates. There is a set of global characteristics in any society that affect survey participation. These factors serve to determine the context within which the request for participation takes place, and constrain the actions of both householder and interviewer. For example, the degree of social responsibility felt by a sample person may be affected by factors such as the legitimacy of societal institutions, the degree of social cohesion, and so on. Such factors influence not only the expectations that both interviewer and respondent bring to the interaction, but also determine the particular persuasion strategies (on the part of the interviewer) and decision-making strategies (on the part of the respondent) that are used. More specific to the survey-taking climate are such factors as the number of surveys conducted in a society (the "oversurveying" effect) and the perceived legitimacy of surveys.

We would expect, therefore, to the extent that societies differ on these attributes to observe different levels of cooperation for similar surveys conducted in different countries. There is evidence for this (see De Heer and Israëls, 1992), but the evidence is clouded by different design features used across countries, especially intensity of effort to reduce nonresponse. These include different protocols for advance contact with sample households, for repeated callbacks on noncontacted cases, and for dealing with initial refusals.

There are also environmental influences on survey cooperation below the societal level. For example, urbanicity is one of the most universal correlates of cooperation across the world. Urban dwellers tend to have lower response rates than rural dwellers. This contrast has been commonly observed in part because the urbanicity variable is often available from the sampling frame. The nature of urbanicity effects on response rates has been found to be related to crime rates (House and Wolf, 1978), but also may be related to population density, the type of housing structures, and household composition in urban areas. The effect also may be a function of inherent features of urban life—the faster pace, the frequency of fleeting single-purpose contacts with strangers, and the looser ties of community in such areas.

Characteristics of the Sample Householder

The factors affecting nonresponse that are most widely discussed in the survey literature are sociodemographic characteristics of the householder or sample person. These include age, gender, marital status, education, and income. Response rates have been shown to vary with each of these, as well as other, characteristics.

Other factors associated with these also have been studied for their relationship to response rates. These include household structure and characteristics, such as the number and ages of the household members and the quality and upkeep of housing, and the experience of the respondent, such as exposure to situations similar to the interview interaction or a background that provided information or training relevant to the survey topic.

We do not believe these factors are *causal* to the participation decision. Instead, they tend to produce a set of psychological predispositions that affect the decision. Some of them are indicators of the likely salience of the topic to the respondent (e.g., socioeconomic indicators on income-related surveys); others are indicators of reactions to strangers (e.g., single-person households).

The sociodemographic factors and household characteristics all may influence the householder's psychological predispositions. Feelings of efficacy, embarrassment, or helpfulness and moods of depression, elation, or anger all will be affected by these factors. All of these characteristics will then influence the cognitive process that will occur during the interaction with the interviewer.

Few householders appear to have strongly preformed decisions about survey requests. Rather, these decisions are made largely at the time of the request for participation. Much social and cognitive psychological research on decision making (e.g., Eagly and Chaiken, 1984; Petty and Cacioppo, 1986) has contrasted two types of processes. The first is deep, thorough consideration of the pertinent arguments and counterarguments of the costs and benefits of options. The second is shallower, quicker, more heuristic decision making based on peripheral aspects of the options. We have a very specific meaning of "heuristic" in this context—use of general rules of behavior (e.g., strange men at the telephone are to be avoided) to guide the survey decision rather than judgments based on the specific information provided about the survey.

We believe the survey request situation most often favors a heuristic approach because the potential respondent typically does not have a large personal interest in survey participation and, consequently, is not inclined to devote large amounts of time or cognitive energy to the decision of whether or not to participate. Furthermore, little of the information typically provided to the householder pertains to the details of the requested task. Instead, interviewers describe the purpose of the survey, the nature of the incentive, or the legitimacy of the sponsoring organization. All of these in some sense are peripheral to the respondent's task of listening to the interviewer's questions, seriously considering alternative answers, and honestly reporting one's judgment.

Cialdini (1984) has identified several compliance principles that guide some heuristic decision making on requests and appear to be activated in surveys. These include reciprocation, authority, consistency, scarcity, social validation, and liking. We review these briefly there (see also Groves et al., 1992) and link them to other concepts used in the literature.

Reciprocation. This heuristic suggests that a householder should be more willing to comply with a request to the extent that compliance constitutes the repayment of a perceived gift, favor, or concession. Thus, one may choose to participate in a survey based on a perceived sense of obligation to the organization making the request, or to the broader society it represents. On a narrower level, more periph- eral features of the request (e.g., incentives, interviewer compliments) may be sufficient to invoke the reciprocity heuristic.

Reciprocation, as a concept, is closely related to sociological notions of *social exchange*. Social exchange theories tend to focus on long-run relationships between individuals and groups, but contain the same influence of past favors given by another influencing similar actions by a focal person or group.

Authority. People are more likely to comply with a request if it comes from a properly constituted authority, someone who is sanctioned by the society to make such requests and to expect compliance. In the survey interview context, the immediate requester is typically not the authority figure but is seen as represent- ing some sponsoring organization that can be judged to have varying degrees of authority status. Survey organizations with greater legitimacy (e.g., those repre- senting federal government agencies) are more likely to trigger the authority heuristic in influencing the householders' decision to participate.

Notions of *social isolation*, the perception by people that they are not part of the larger society or bound by its norms, may be useful here. Socially isolated groups include both those believing they have suffered historical inequities at the hands of major institutions or groups and those identifying quite strongly with a distinct subculture. These types of groups may be guided by the same norms of reciprocation or influences of authority during interactions involving institutions of the majority culture, but in such cases the effect on cooperation may be nega- tive.

We have found concepts of reciprocation and authority very important to understanding the behavior of sample persons. In addition, however, four other compliance heuristics described by Cialdini (1984) are relevant to surveys: con- sistency, scarcity, social validation, and liking.

Consistency. The consistency heuristic suggests that, after committing oneself to a position, one should be more willing to comply with requests for behaviors that are consistent with that position. This is the likely explanation for the foot-in-the-door effect in surveys (e.g., Freedman and Fraser, 1966), where compliance with a small initial request leads to greater willingness to accede to a larger request.

Scarcity. This heuristic notes that one should be more willing to comply with requests to secure opportunities that are scarce. To the extent that the survey request is perceived as a rare opportunity to participate in an interesting and/or important activity, the scarcity principle may lead to greater likelihood of acceptance of the request.

Social validation. Using this heuristic, one would be more willing to comply with a request to the degree that one believes similar others are likely to do so. If householders believe that most people like themselves agree to participate in surveys, they may be more inclined to do so themselves.

Liking. Put simply, one should be more willing to comply with the requests of liked others. A variety of factors (e.g., similarity of attitude, background, or dress; praise) have been shown to increase liking of strangers, and these cues may be used to guide the householder's decision in evaluating the interviewer's request.

Although we believe these heuristics often come to the fore when a householder is confronted with a request to participate in a survey, other factors more closely associated with a rational choice perspective also may influence their decision.

For example, a common finding in research on attitude change (see, for example, Petty and Cacioppo, 1986) is that when the topic of discussion is highly salient to laboratory subjects, they tend to give careful consideration to the arguments pro and con concerning the topic. Similarly, we think that saliency, relevance, and interest in the survey topic are relevant to the householder's decision process. That is, when the survey topic is highly relevant to the well-being or for other reasons of interest to the householders, they might perform a more thorough analysis of the merits of cooperating with the survey request.

However, in contrast to the laboratory experiments in the attitude change literature, largely based on willing and motivated subjects, the survey setting probably limits cost-benefit examination of a survey request. Calls by interviewers to sample households generally are unscheduled events. The amount of discretionary time perceived to be possessed by the householders at the time of contact also will affect their tendency to engage in deliberate, careful consideration of the arguments to participate in the survey. Householders who see themselves as burdened by other obligations overwhelmingly may choose heuristic shortcuts to evaluate the survey request.

Attributes of the Survey Design

Much survey research practice is focused on reducing nonresponse by choosing features of the survey design that generate higher participation rates. These by and large are fixed attributes of the request for an interview that are applied to all cases. This section discusses those features in an indirect manner, by identifying and elaborating the concepts that underlie their effectiveness.

Many of the survey design features aimed at gaining cooperation use one or more of the compliance heuristics reviewed earlier. For example, the reciprocation heuristic probably underlies the large literature on the effects of incentives on survey participation rates. Consistent with the concept of reciprocation, there appear to be larger effects of incentives provided prior to the request for the survey, compared to those promised contingent on the completion of the interview (Berk et al., 1987; Singer et al., 1996).

The concept also underlies the common training guideline in some surveys for interviewers to emphasize the potential benefits of the survey to the individual respondent. For example, in the Consumer Expenditure Survey, used as part of the Consumer Price Index of the United States, interviewers often tell elderly householders that their government Social Security payments are affected by the survey.

One implication of the consistency principle for survey design is that an interviewer who can draw a connection between the merits of particular (or general) survey participation and the respondent's committed beliefs, attitudes, and values (e.g., efficiency in government, advancement of knowledge) is likely to be more successful in gaining compliance.

Evoking authority is a common tool in advance mailings in household surveys and in the introductory script of interviewers. Advance letters often are crafted to use stationery that evokes legitimate authority for the information collection; the letters are signed, whenever possible, by persons with titles conveying power and prestige. Some social surveys (e.g., studies of community issues) seek the endorsement of associations or organizations that would aid the communication of legitimate authority to collect the data. Furthermore, interviewers often are trained to emphasize the sponsor of their survey when the sponsor generally is seen as having legitimate authority to collect the information (e.g., government or educational institutions), but rarely to do so when that is less likely (e.g., certain commercial organizations).

The scarcity principle may underlie the interviewer tactics of emphasizing the value to a respondent of "making your voice heard" or "having your opinion count" while noting that such an opportunity is rare (e.g., "We only contact one person in every 30,000"). This principle may also help explain the decline of survey participation in Western society that has coincided with the proliferation of surveys. People may no longer consider the chance to have their opinions counted as an especially rare, and therefore valuable, event. Consequently, at the end of the interviewing period, some interviewers are known to say that "There are only a few days left. I'm not sure I'll be able to interview you if we don't do it now"—a clear attempt to make the scarcity principle apply.

Similarly, survey organizations and interviewers may attempt to invoke social validation by suggesting that "Most people enjoy being interviewed," or "Most people choose to participate," or by evincing surprise at the expression of reluctance by a householder.

The use of race or gender matching by survey organizations may be an attempt to invoke liking through similarity, as well as reducing the potential threat to the householder.

Other survey design features do not fit nicely into the compliance heuristics conceptualized by Cialdini. Indeed, these are much more closely aligned with rational choice, cost versus benefit tradeoff decisions. For example, there is some evidence that longer questionnaires require the interviewer to work harder to gain cooperation. In interviewer-assisted surveys some of the disadvantages can be overcome by interviewer action, but more work is required. Thus, other things being equal, choosing a short survey interview may yield easier attainment of high participation.

Related to burden as measured by time is burden produced by psychological threat or low saliency. Survey topics that ask respondents to reveal embarrassing facts about themselves or that cover topics that are avoided in day-to-day conversations between strangers may be perceived as quite burdensome. For example, surveys about sexual behaviors or income and assets tend to achieve lower cooperation rates, other things being equal, than surveys of health or employment. On the other hand, when the topic is salient to the householders, when they have prior interest in the topic, then the perceived burden of answering questions on the topic is lower. This probably underlies the finding of Couper (1997) that householders who express more interest in politics are interviewed more easily than those with no such interests.

Attributes of the Interviewer

Observable attributes of the interviewer affect participation because they are used as cues by the householder to judge the intent of the visit. For example, consider the sociodemographic characteristics of race, age, gender, and socioeconomic status. At the first contact with the interviewer, the householder is making judgments about the purposes of the visit. Is this a sales call? Is there any risk of physical danger in this encounter? Can I trust that this person is sincere? Assessments of alternative intentions of the caller are made by matching the pattern of visual and audio cues with evoked alternatives. All attributes of the interviewer that help the householder discriminate the different scripts will be used to make the decision about the intent of the call. Once the householder chooses an interpretation of the intent of the call—a "cognitive script" in Abelson's (1981) terms—then the householder can use the script to guide his or her reactions to the interviewer.

The second set of influences from the interviewer is a function of the householders' experience. To select an approach to use, the interviewer must judge the fit of the respondent to other respondent types experienced in the past (either through descriptions in training or actual interaction with them). We believe that experienced interviewers tend to achieve higher levels of cooperation because they carry with them a larger number of combinations of behaviors proven to be effective for one or more types of householders. A corollary of this is that interviewers experiencing diverse subpopulations are even more resourceful and are valuable for refusal conversion work. We can also deduce that the initial months and years of interviewing offer the largest gains to interviewers by providing them with new persuasion tools.

The third set of attributes might be viewed as causally derivative of the first two, interviewer expectations regarding the likelihood of gaining cooperation of the householder. Research shows that interviewers who believe survey questions are sensitive tend to achieve higher missing-data rates on them (Singer and Kohnke-Aguirre, 1979). Interviewers report that their emotional state at the time of contact is crucial to their success: "I do not have much trouble talking people into cooperating. I love this work and I believe this helps 'sell' the survey. When I knock on a door, I feel I'm gonna get that interview!" We believe these expectations are a function of interviewer sociodemographic attributes (and their match to those of the householder), their personal reactions to the survey topic, and their experience as an interviewer.

Respondent-Interviewer Interaction

When interviewers encounter householders, the factors discussed come to bear on the decision to participate. The strategies the interviewer employs to persuade the sample person are determined not only by the interviewer's own ability, expectations, and other variables, but also by features of the survey design and by characteristics of the immediate environment and broader society. Similarly, the responses that the sample person makes to the request are affected by a variety of factors, both internal and external to the respondent, and both intrinsic and extrinsic to the survey request.

We have posited that most decisions to participate in a survey are heuristically based. The evidence for this lies in the tendency for refusals to come quickly in the interaction; for interviewers to use short, generally nonoffensive descriptors in initial phases of the contact; and for respondents to only rarely seek more information about the survey. This occurs most clearly when participation (or lack thereof) has little personal consequence. With Brehm (1993) we believe that the verbal "reasons" for refusals—"I'm too busy," "I'm not interested"—partially reflect these heuristics, mirroring current states of the householder but, in contrast to Brehm, we believe they are not stable under alternative cues presented to the householder. We believe there are two constructs regarding interviewer behavior during the interaction with a householder that underlie which heuristics will dominate in the householder's decision to participate. These are labeled "tailoring" and "maintaining interaction."

Tailoring. Experienced interviewers often report that they adapt their approach to the sample unit. Interviewers engage in a continuous search for cues about the attributes of the sample household or the person who answers the door, focusing on those attributes that may be related to one of the basic psychological principles reviewed previously. For example, in poor areas, some interviewers choose to drive the family's older car and to dress in a manner more consistent with the neighborhood, thereby attempting to engage the liking principle. In rich neighborhoods, interviewers may dress up. In both cases, the same compliance principle—similarity leads to liking—is engaged, but in different ways.

In some sense, expert interviewers have access to a large repertoire of cues, phrases, or descriptors corresponding to the survey request. Which statement they use to begin the conversation is the result of observations about the housing unit, the neighborhood, and immediate reactions upon first contact with the person who answers the door. The reaction of the householder to the first statement dictates the choice of the second statement to use. With this perspective, all features of the communication are relevant—not only the words used by the interviewer, but the inflection, volume, pacing (see Oksenberg et al., 1986), as well as physical movements of the interviewer.

From focus groups with interviewers, we found that some interviewers are aware of their "tailoring" behavior: "I give the introduction and listen to what they say. I then respond to them on an individual basis, according to their response. Almost all responses are a little different, and you need an ability to intuitively understand what they are saying." Or "I use different techniques depending on the age of the respondent, my initial impression of him or her, the neighborhood, etc." Or "From all past interviewing experience, I have found that sizing up a respondent immediately and being able to adjust just as quickly to the situation never fails to get their cooperation, in short being able to put yourself at their level be it intellectual or street wise is a must in this business…".

Tailoring need not occur only within a single contact. Many times contacts are very brief and give the interviewer little opportunity to respond to cues obtained from the potential respondent. Tailoring may take place over a number of contacts with that household, with the interviewer using the knowledge he or she has gained in each successive visit to that household. Tailoring also may occur across sample households. The more an interviewer learns about what is effective and what is not with various types of potential respondents encountered, the more effectively requests for participation can be directed at similar others. This implies that interviewer tailoring evolves with experience. Not only have experienced interviewers acquired a wider repertoire of persuasion techniques, but they are also better able to select the most appropriate approach for each situation.

Maintaining interaction. The introductory contact of the interviewer and householder is a small conversation. It begins with the self-identification of the interviewer, contains some descriptive matter about the survey request, and ends with the initiation of the questioning, a delay decision, or the denial of permission to continue. There are two radically different optimization targets in developing an introductory strategy—maximizing the number of acceptances per time unit (assuming an ongoing supply of contacts), and maximizing the probability of each sample unit accepting.

The first goal is common to some quota sample interviewing (and to sales approaches). There, the supply of sample cases is far beyond that needed for the desired number of interviews. The interviewer behavior should be focused on gaining speedy resolution of each case. An acceptance of the survey request is preferred to a denial, but a lengthy, multicontact preliminary to an acceptance can be as damaging to productivity as a denial. The system is driven by number of interviews per time unit.

The second goal, maximizing the probability of obtaining an interview from each sample unit, is the implicit aim of probability sample interviewing. The amount of time required to obtain cooperation on each case is of secondary concern. Given this, interviewers are free to apply the "tailoring" over several turns in the contact conversation. How to tailor the appeal to the householder is increasingly revealed as the conversation continues. Hence, the odds of success are increased as the conversation continues. Thus, the interviewer does *not* maximize the likelihood of obtaining a "yes" answer in any given contact, but minimizes the likelihood of a "no" answer over repeated turntaking in the contact.

We believe the techniques of tailoring and maintaining interaction are used in combination. Maintaining interaction is the means to achieve maximum benefits from tailoring, for the longer the conversation is in progress, the more cues the interviewer will be able to obtain from the householder. However, maintaining interaction is also a compliance-promoting technique in itself, invoking the commitment principle as well as more general norms of social interaction. That is, as the length of the interaction grows, it becomes more difficult for one actor to summarily dismiss the other.

Figure 1-9 is an illustration of these two interviewer strategies at work. We distinguish between the use of a general compliance-gaining strategy (e.g., utilizing the principle of authority) and a number of different (verbal and nonverbal) arguments or tactics within each strategy (e.g., displaying the ID badge prominently, emphasizing the sponsor of the survey). The successful application of tailoring depends on the ability of the interview to evaluate the reaction of the householder to his or her presence, and the effectiveness of the arguments pre-

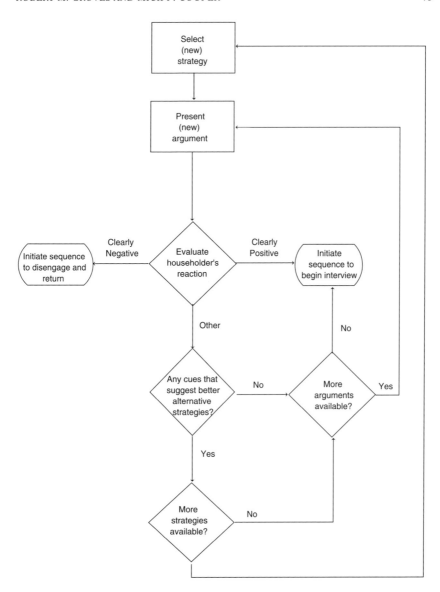

FIGURE 1-9 Interviewer behavior during interaction with householders.
SOURCE: Groves and Couper (1998).

sented. Note that the interviewer's initial goal is to maintain interaction (avoiding pushing for the interview) as long as the potential respondent's reaction remains neutral or noncommittal. An interviewer will continue to present different arguments until the householder is clearly receptive to an interview request, or there are no more arguments to present. For inexperienced interviewers the latter may occur before the former, forcing the interviewer to (prematurely in some cases) initiate the interview request.

There is some support from training procedures that the "maintaining interaction" model operates as theorized. First, interviewers typically are warned against unintentionally leading the householder into a quick refusal. If the person appears rushed or preoccupied by some activity in the household (e.g., fighting among children), the interviewer should seek another time to contact the unit. A common complaint concerning inexperienced interviewers is that they create many "soft refusals" (i.e., cases easily converted by an experienced interviewer) by pressing the householder into a decision prematurely. Unfortunately, only rarely do interviewer recruits receive training in the multiturn repartee inherent in maximizing the odds of a "yes" over all contacts. Instead, they are trained in stock descriptors of the survey leading to the first question of the interview.

We note how similar the goals of a quota sample interviewer are to those of any salesperson, but how different are those of the probability sample interviewer. Given this, it is not surprising that many attempts to use sales techniques in probability sample surveys have not led to large gains in cooperation. The focus of the salesperson is on identifying and serving buyers. The "browser" must be ignored when a known buyer approaches. In contrast, the probability sample interviewer must seek cooperation from both the interested and uninterested.

At the same time that the interviewer is exercising skills regarding tailoring and maintaining interaction, the householder is engaged in a very active process of determining whether there has been prior contact with the interviewer, what is the intent of the interviewer's call, whether a quick negative decision is warranted, or whether continued attention to the interviewer's speech is the right decision. Figure 1-10 describes this process.

The process has various decision points at which the householder can make positive or negative decisions regarding participation in the survey. These arise because the householder misinterprets the visit as involving some unpleasant nonsurvey request; that is, the householder chooses the wrong script. They arise if there are very high opportunity costs for the householder to continue the interaction with the interviewer. They arise if any of the heuristics point to the wisdom of a negative or positive decision.

DESIGNING SURVEYS ACKNOWLEDGING NONRESPONSE

The previous discussions review various theoretical perspectives on nonresponse. These theoretical perspectives have two implications for survey design:

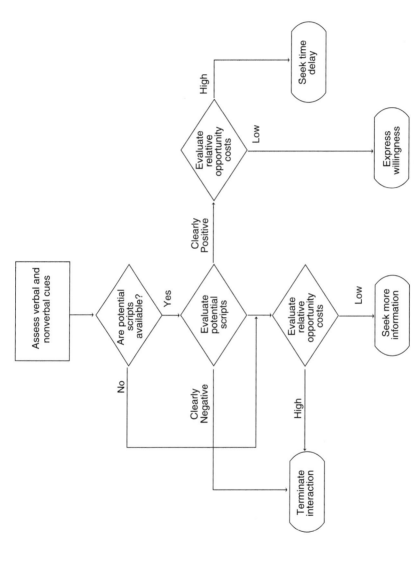

FIGURE 1-10 Householder behavior during interactions with the interviewer.
SOURCE: Groves and Couper (1998).

(1) contact and interviewer protocols should be chosen to be consistent with the diverse influences, and (2) no single survey design will achieve 100-percent response rates and defenses to nonresponse error should be built into the chosen survey design.

The Value of Rich Sampling Frames

The list of the target population (or the materials used to construct a list) is a tool to assure that a probability sample will offer a useful description of the full population. When the designer acknowledges that nonresponse inevitably will occur in the survey, the frame takes on new value. When the designer has a choice of frames (e.g., a list frame from a social welfare agency containing data about the person's prior income and employment experience, an area frame, a random digit dial frame), evaluation of the frame must include both coverage and nonresponse issues. Coverage, the extent to which the frame includes all target population elements and nothing else, is an important attribute.

Sampling frames that contain information beyond simple identifiers can help reduce nonresponse error. If the frames include data on prior addresses, then those with a history of moves might be identified as likely movers, with higher than expected locating effort. If frames contain data on use of agency services in the past, the data might be used to customize approaches to sample persons in an effort to address potential interests and concerns about survey participation (e.g., having interviewers explain the importance of the survey to measuring the well-being of former food stamp recipients). Sometimes data exists that are correlates of key survey variables (e.g., participation in types of programs [higher corre-lated with current statuses like work training programs]). Such data might be useful in assessing nonresponse errors and building weighting adjustment or imputation models.

Collecting Additional Information to Enhance Data Collection

Sometimes interviewers can observe that sample persons have certain at-tributes that are related to certain concerns about survey participation. Followup efforts to persuade the sample person to be interviewed can use this information creatively to improve response rates. This has included treating sample numbers generating answering machine responses as candidates for calling at different times of the day, attempting to avoid times when the machine is activated. It includes interviewer observation about any concerns regarding the legitimacy of the survey request, followed by special mailings or communications demonstrat-ing the sponsorship and purpose of the survey. It includes, in face-to-face sur-veys, observations of housing units for entrance impediments (e.g., locked apart-ment buildings, locked gates, security guards), leading to more intensive calling patterns on those sample units versus others.

Collecting Information Valuable in Postsurvey Adjustment

Several studies (Purdon et al, 1999; Groves and Couper, 1998; Brehm, 1993) now demonstrate that the utterances of sample persons during their interactions with interviewers contain some information regarding motivations for their reaction to the survey request and the likelihood of eventual cooperation with the survey request. The evidence comes more from face-to-face surveys than from telephone surveys, although Couper and Groves (1995) find some support for links between the utterances and the final outcome in telephone surveys as well. These become useful predictors in response-propensity models sometimes used in postsurvey adjustment.

Another set of variables involves fixed attributes of the housing unit, best observed in face-to-face surveys. For example, the Consumer Expenditure Survey uses observations from the interviewer about whether the unit is owned or rented in postsurvey adjustments based on the belief that the consumption patterns are relatively homogeneous in the two groups. Similarly, observations of multiple-person households (through records on who answered the telephone) the presence of children, etc. are possible in some designs. These too can be useful in forming postsurvey adjustment weighting classes.

Two-Phase Sampling to Acquire Information About Nonrespondents

When survey data are used in legal or policy settings, the credibility of results is sometimes enhanced by mounting separate studies concerning nonresponse. There are two possible foci: experimental comparisons of different protocols and two-phase sample surveys of nonrespondents. An example of the first study is a mixed-mode design based on a list frame sample of prior recipients, one mode using telephone matching and telephone survey requests; and the other uses address locating and face-to-face interviews. For cost reasons the face-to-face mode might use a smaller sample size than the telephone mode. The telephone mode is likely to have lower response rates than the face-to-face mode. The sample sizes might be fixed to determine the magnitude of mode differences at some prior specified standard error. The total cost of the survey per unit measured lies between the telephone and face-to-face modes, but the additional information purchased with the mixed-mode design is protection against large-mode effects on key survey conclusions.

A two-phase sample design for nonresponse studies begins after the main survey has completed its work. The intent under perfect conditions is that a probability subsample of nonrespondents to the first phase of the survey can yield evidence regarding the likelihood of large nonresponse errors in the first-phase estimates. The "perfect" conditions yield 100 percent response rates on the second-phase cases, thus providing unbiased estimates of the characteristics of the nonrespondent pool. Although such designs have a long history (Deming, 1953;

Hansen and Hurwitz, 1958), they never inevitably achieve the perfect conditions in practice. They are used, however, when some information on the nonrespondents is judged to be of crucial importance. For example, a second-phase sample of nonrespondents was taken on the National Survey of American Families, using a radically reduced telephone interview, relaxed respondent rules, and an incentive offer. Among the nonrespondent cases to the first-phase effort (spanning many months and repeated refusal conversion efforts), 36 percent of screener nonrespondents and 58 percent of full interview nonrespondents complied with the second-phase request (Groves et al., 1999). Those responding were found not to have large socioeconomic status differences from the respondent group (what differences did exist suggested higher income households were more likely to be nonrespondents).

JUDGMENTS REGARDING DESIRABLE DESIGN FEATURES FOR SURVEYS OF THE U.S. LOW-INCOME POPULATION

As survey methodology matures, it is increasingly finding that the process of survey participation is subject to diverse causes across different subgroups. In short, what "works" for some groups does not for others. Furthermore, in free societies 100 percent compliance is not to be expected; survey designers should incorporate nonresponse concerns into every aspect of their designs.

What follows is a listing of the top 10 lessons from the survey methodology literature regarding nonresponse in studies of the low-income population. *These are current judgments of the authors of this paper based on experience and study of the field.*

1. No record system is totally accurate or complete.

Using a record system as a sampling frame generally asks more of the record than it was designed to provide. Surveys demand accurate, up-to-date, personal identifiers. They demand that the person sampled can be located.

2. Choose sample sizes that permit adequate locating, contacting, and recruitment efforts.

Sample surveys suffer from the tyranny of the measurable, with sampling errors dominating design decisions because they can be measured more easily than nonresponse errors. It is tempting to assume the absence of nonresponse error and to maximize sample size to achieve low reported sampling errors. It is important to note that the larger the sample size, the greater the proportion of total error likely to come from nonresponse bias, other things being equal. (Sampling errors can be driven down to a trivial amount, but nonresponse biases may remain the same.)

3. Assume nonresponse will occur; prepare for it.

In practice no sample survey avoids nonresponse completely. Assuming at the design stage that it will not occur leaves the researcher unprepared to deal with it at the estimation stage. Whenever possible use interviewers to collect information that can be used either to reduce nonresponse (e.g., utterances of the sample person suggesting reasons for nonresponse, useful later in tailoring refusal conversion protocol) or to adjust for nonresponse (e.g., observations about respondents and nonrespondents related to propensities to respond).

4. Consider relationships with the sponsoring agency as sources of nonresponse error.

Sample persons with prior experiences or relationships with the sponsoring agency for the survey make decisions based partially on how they evaluate those relationships. This may underlie the tendency for those persons dependent on programs to respond at higher levels. It also underlies the findings of those with relatively low trust in government to respond at lower rates to some government surveys. Mixed-mode designs and alternative sponsoring organizations may act to reduce these sources of differential nonresponse.

5. Do not script interviewers; use flexible interviewer behaviors.

The research literature is increasingly strong on the conclusion that effective interviewers need to be trained to deliver information relevant to a wide variety of concerns that different sample persons may have. Stock phrases and fixed approaches defeat the need to address these diverse concerns. Once interviewers can classify the sample person's utterances into a class of concerns, identify a relevant piece of information to convey to the person, and deliver it in the native language of the sample person, cooperation rates can be higher.

6. Consider incentives, especially for the reluctant.

Incentives have been shown to have disproportionately large effects on those who have no other positive influence to respond. Although not completely clear from the literature, the value of a given incentive may be dependent on relative income/assets of the sample person. If greater effects pertain to low-income populations, then incentives might be more attractive to studies of that population.

7. Give separate attention to location, noncontact, refusal; each has different causes and impacts on error.

Sample persons not interviewed because of failure to locate are dispropor-tionately movers. All the correlates of residential mobility (rental status, small households, relative youth, few extended family ties), if relevant to the survey measures, make nonlocation nonresponse a source of error. Noncontacts and refusals may have very different patterns of correlates. Treating nonresponse rates as an undifferentiated source of nonresponse error is thus naive. Separate tracking of these nonresponse rates is needed.

8. Mount special studies of nonrespondents.

The higher the nonresponse rate, the higher the risk of nonresponse error, other things being equal. With higher than desired nonresponse rates, the investi-gators have an obligation to assure themselves that major nonresponse errors are not present, damaging their ability to draw conclusions from the respondent-based statistics. Special studies of nonrespondents are appropriate in these cases, using auxiliary data from records, followback attempts at samples of respon-dents, and other strategies.

9. Perform sensitivity analyses on alternative postsurvey adjustments.

Postsurvey adjustments (weighting and imputation) entail explicit or implicit assumptions about the relationships between propensity to respond to the survey and survey variables. Insight is sometimes gained into the dependence on non-response adjustments of substantive conclusions by varying the assumptions, using different postsurvey adjustments, and comparing their impact on conclu-sions.

10. Involve the target population.

Using focus groups and other intensive qualitative investigations can offer insights into how the target population might receive the survey request. Such insights are rarely native to research investigators who are members of different subcultures.

REFERENCES

Abelson, R.P.
  1981   Psychological status of the script concept. *American Psychologist* 36(7):715-729.
Berk, M.L., N.A. Mathiowetz, E.P. Ward, and A.A. White
  1987   The effect of prepaid and promised incentives: Results of a controlled experiment. *Jour-nal of Official Statistics* 3(4):449-457.

Brehm, J.
1993	*The Phantom Respondents: Opinion Surveys and Political Representation.* Ann Arbor: University of Michigan Press.
Cialdini, R.B.
1984	*Influence: The New Psychology of Modern Persuasion.* New York: Quill.
1988	*Influence: Science and Practice.* Glenview, IL: Scott, Foresman and Company.
Cochran, W.G.
1977	*Sampling Techniques.* Third Edition, New York: Wiley and Sons.
Couper, M.P.
1997	Survey introductions and data quality. *Public Opinion Quarterly* 61(2):317-338.
Couper, M.P., and R.M. Groves
1995	Introductions in Telephone Surveys and Nonresponse. Unpublished paper presented at the Workshop on Interaction in the Standardized Survey Interview, Amsterdam.
De Heer, W.F., and A.Z. Israëls
1992	Response Trends in Europe. Unpublished paper presented at the Joint Statistical Meetings of the American Statistical Association, Boston.
Deming, W.E.
1953	On a probability mechanism to attain an economic balance between the resultant error of response and the bias of nonresponse. *Journal of the American Statistical Association* 48(264):743-772.
Eagly, A.H., and S. Chaiken
1984	Cognitive theories of persuasion. Pp. 267-359 in *Advances in Experimental Social Psychology Volume 17*, L. Berkowitz, ed. San Diego: Academic Press.
Ekholm, A., and S. Laaksonen
1991	Weighting via response modeling in the Finnish household budget survey. *Journal of Official Statistics* 7(3):325-337.
Ford, Barry
1983	An overview of hot-deck procedures. Pp. 185-209 in *Incomplete Data in Sample Surveys*, W. Madow, I. Olkin, and D. Rubin, eds. New York: Academic Press.
Freedman, J.L., and S.C. Fraser
1966	Compliance without pressure: The foot-in-the-door technique. *Journal of Personality and Social Psychology* 4:195-202.
Groves, R.M., R.B. Cialdini, and M.P. Couper
1992	Understanding the decision to participate in a survey. *Public Opinion Quarterly* 56(4):475-495.
Groves, R.M., and M.P. Couper
1998	*Nonresponse in Household Interview Surveys.* New York: Wiley and Sons.
Groves, R.M., and R.L. Kahn.
1979	*Surveys by Telephone: A National Comparison with Personal Interviews.* New York: Academic Press.
Groves, R.M., D. Wissoker, and E. Singer
1999	*Early Nonresponse Studies of the 1997 National Survey of America's Families.* Washington, DC: Urban Institute.
Hansen, M.H., and V.M. Hurwitz
1958	The problem of nonresponse in sample surveys. *Journal of the American Statistical Association* (December) 517-529.
Hill, D.H.
1978	Home production and the residential electric load curve. *Resources and Energy* 1:339-358.

House, J.S., and S. Wolf
   1978   Effects of urban residence on interpersonal trust and helping behavior. *Journal of Person-
           ality and Social Psychology* 36(9), 1029-1043.
Keeter, S., C. Miller, A. Kohut, R. Groves, and S. Presser
   2000   Consequences of reducing nonresponse in a national telephone survey. *Public Opinion
           Quarterly,* 64, 125-148.
Little, R., and D.B. Rubin
   1987   *Statistical Analysis with Missing Data.* New York: Wiley and Sons.
Oksenberg, L., L. Coleman, and C.F. Cannell
   1986   Interviewers' voices and refusal rates in telephone surveys. *Public Opinion Quarterly*
           50(1):97-111.
Petty, R.E., and J.T. Caccioppo
   1986   *Communication and Persuasion: Central and Peripheral Routes to Attitude Change.* New
           York: Springer-Verlag.
Purdon, S., P. Campanelli, and P. Sturgis
   1999   Interviewers' calling strategies on face-to-face interview surveys. *Journal of Official Sta-
           tistics* 15(2):199-216.
Rubin, D.B.
   1987   *Multiple Imputation for Nonresponse in Surveys.* New York: Wiley and Sons.
Singer, E., and L. Kohnke-Aguirre
   1979   Interviewer expectation effects: A replication and extension. *Public Opinion Quarterly*
           43(2):245-260.
Singer, E., N. Gebler, T. Raghunathan, J. Van Hoewyk, and K. McGonagle
   1996   The Effects of Incentives on Response Rates in Personal, Telephone, and Mixed-Mode
           Surveys: Results from a Meta Analysis. Unpublished paper presented at the Annual Con-
           ference of the American Association of Public Opinion Research, Salt Lake City.
Tuckel, P., and B.M. Feinberg
   1991   The answering machine poses many questions for telephone survey researchers. *Public
           Opinion Quarterly* 55(2):200-217.
Tuckel, P., and H. O'Neil
   1995   A profile of answering machine owners and screeners. Pp. 1157-1162. In *Proceedings of
           the Section on Survey Research Methods.* Alexandria, VA: American Statistical Associa-
           tion.

2

Methods for Obtaining High Response
Rates in Telephone Surveys

David Cantor and Patricia Cunningham

The purpose of this paper is to review methods used to conduct telephone surveys of low-income populations. The motivation for this review is to provide information on "best practices" applicable to studies currently being conducted to evaluate the Personal Responsibility and Work Opportunity Reconciliation Act of 1996 (PRWORA—hereafter referred to as "Welfare Reform"). The National Academy of Sciences panel observed that many of the states are conducting telephone surveys for this purpose and that it would be useful to provide them with information on the best methods for maximizing response rates. The information provided in this paper is intended to assist these individuals, as well as others, to either conduct these studies themselves or to evaluate and monitor contractors conducting the studies.

We have divided the telephone surveys into two types. The first, primary, method is to sample welfare recipients or welfare leavers from agency lists. This can take the form of a randomized experiment, where recipients are randomly assigned to different groups at intake, with a longitudinal survey following these individuals over an extended period of time. More commonly, it takes the form of a survey of those leaving welfare during a particular period (e.g., first quarter of the year). These individuals are then followed up after "X" months to assess how they are coping with being off welfare.

The second type of telephone survey is one completed using a sample generated by random digit dialing methods (RDD). In this type of study, telephone numbers are generated randomly. The numbers then are called and interviews are completed with those numbers that represent residential households and that agree to participate in the interview. To effectively evaluate welfare reform, this type of survey would attempt to oversample persons who are eligible and/or who are participating in welfare programs.

The issues related to these two types of telephone surveys, one from a list of welfare clients and one using RDD, overlap to a large degree. The following discussion reviews the common issues as well as the unique aspects related to each type of survey. In the next section, we discuss methods to increase response rates on telephone surveys, placing somewhat more emphasis on issues related to conducting surveys from lists of welfare clients. We chose this emphasis because this is the predominant method being used by states to evaluate welfare reform. The third section reviews a number of welfare studies that have been implemented recently. In this section we discuss how the methods that are being used match up with the "best practices" and how this may relate to response rates. The fourth section provides an overview of issues that are unique to RDD surveys when conducting a survey of low-income populations. To summarize the discussion, the final section highlights practices that can be implemented for a relatively low cost but that could have relatively large impacts.

METHODS TO INCREASE RESPONSE RATES

In this section we discuss the methods needed to obtain high response rates in a telephone survey. These methods include locating, contacting, and obtaining the cooperation of survey subjects. The review applies to all types of telephone surveys, but we have highlighted those methods that seem particularly important for conducting surveys from lists of welfare clients. A later section provides issues unique to RDD.

The Importance of Language

The methods discussed in the following sections should be considered in terms of the language and cultural diversity of the state being studied. The percentage of non-English speakers ranges from as high as a third in California to a quarter in New York and Texas, down to a low of 4 to 5 percent in South Carolina, Missouri, and Georgia (1990 Census). Spanish is the most common language spoken by non-English speakers. Again these percentages vary a great deal by state, with 20 percent of the population in California and Texas speaking Spanish at home and only 2 percent in South Carolina. These variations imply that surveys may have to be prepared to locate and interview respondents in languages other than English and Spanish. Moreover, language barriers are greater among low-income households, and low-income households are more likely to be isolated linguistically, where no one in the household speaks English.

The need for bilingual staff as well as Spanish (and perhaps other languages) versions of all questionnaires and materials is crucial, particularly in some states.

It is important to keep in mind that many people who do not speak English also may not be literate in their native language, so they may not be able to read materials or an advance letter even if it is translated into a language they speak. In some situations it might be useful to partner with social service agencies and community groups that serve and have special ties with different language and culture communities. Such groups may be able to vouch for the legitimacy of the survey, provide interviewers or translators with special language skills, and assist in other ways. Representatives of respected and trusted organizations can be invaluable in communicating the purpose of the study and explaining to prospective respondents that it is in the community's best interest to cooperate.

Locating Respondents

Locating survey subjects begins with having sufficient information to find those that moved from their latest residence. Low-income households move at higher rates than the general population, and it seems reasonable to assume that within this group, "welfare leavers" will be the most mobile. Therefore, if surveys are going to become a routine part of the evaluation process, agencies should consider future evaluation needs in all their procedures. This includes changing intake procedures to obtain additional information to help locate subjects in the future and designing systems to allow access to other state administrative records. In the sections that follow, these presurvey procedures are discussed in more detail. This is followed by a description of the initial mail contact, which provides the first indication of whether a subject has moved. The section ends with a discussion of some tracing procedures that might be implemented if the subject is lost to the study.

Presurvey Preparations

As part of the intake process, or shortly thereafter (but perhaps separately from the eligibility process), detailed contact information should be obtained for at least two other people who are likely to know the subject's whereabouts and who do not live in the same household as the subject. In addition to name, address, and telephone number, the relationship of the contact to the subject should be determined along with his or her place of employment. We believe this step is crucial to obtaining acceptable response rates. This step also may be difficult to achieve because, in some situations, it may require a change in the intake system.

It is also useful to consider obtaining the subject's informed consent as needed to access databases that require consent at the same time as contact information is obtained. It is hard to state when and how consent might be used given the differences in state laws, but we assume that, at a minimum, state income tax records fall into this category (if they are assessable at all, even with consent). This is a common procedure on studies that track and interview drug users and criminal populations (Anglin et al., 1996).

Data to Be Provided to the Contractor with the Sample

In addition to the subject's name, address, telephone number, Social Security number, and all contact information, consideration should be given to running the subject through other state administrative databases (Medicaid, food stamps, etc.) prior to the survey. This may be particularly useful if the information in the sample file from which the sample is drawn is old or if the information in the files is different. Initial contacts should always start with the most recent address and telephone number. The older information is useful if a subject needs to be traced. The advantage of using the older information is that it might help to avoid unnecessary calls and tracing.

If the field period extends for a long period of time, it might be necessary to update this information for some subjects during the course of the survey.

Contacting Survey Subjects by Mail

Sending letters to prenotify the subject is accepted practice when conducting surveys (Dillman, 1978). It serves the dual purpose of preparing the subject for the telephone interview and identifying those subjects whose address is no longer valid. It is always iterative in a survey of this type. That is, each time a new address is located for a subject (through tracing as discussed later), an advance letter is sent prior to telephone contact.

If an envelope is stamped "return service requested," for a small fee, the U.S. Postal Service will not forward the letter, but instead will affix the new address to the envelope and return it to the sender. This only works if (1) the subject has left a forwarding address and (2) the file is still active, which is usually just 6 months. If the letter is returned marked "undeliverable," "unknown," insufficient address," etc., additional tracing steps must be initiated.

Because the post office updating procedure is only active for 6 months, it is important to continue mail contacts with survey subjects if they are to be interviewed at different points in time. These mail contacts can be simple and include thoughtful touches such as a birthday card or perhaps a newsletter with interesting survey results.

Mailings should include multiple ways for the subject to contact the survey organization, such as an 800 number and a business reply post card with space to update name, address, and telephone numbers. Some small percentage will call and/or return the post card, negating the need for further tracing.

One of the problems with first-class letters is that the letters often do not reach the subject. The address may be out of date and not delivered to the correct household (e.g., Traugott et al., 1997), the letter may be thrown out before anyone actually looks at it, or the subject may open but not read the letter. To increase the chances that the subject does read the letter, consideration should be given to using express delivery rather than first-class mail. This idea is based on the logic that express delivery will increase the likelihood that the package will be opened by potential respondents and the contents perceived to be important. Express delivery may also provide more assurance that the letter has actually reached the household and the subject, particularly if a signature is required. However, requiring a signature may not produce the desired result if it becomes burdensome for the subject, for example, if the subject is not home during the initial delivery and needs to make special arrangements to pick it up. The annoyance may be lessened if, in addition to the letter, an incentive is enclosed.

Because express delivery is costly (but less than in-person contacts), it should be saved for those prenotification situations in which other means of contact have not been fruitful. For example, if first-class letters appear to be delivered, yet telephone contact has not been established, and tracing seems to indicate the address is correct, an express letter might be sent. It also might be used if the telephone number is unlisted or if the subject does not have a telephone. In these situations an express letter with a prepaid incentive might induce the subject to call an 800 number to complete the interview by telephone.

Tracing

Tracing is costly. Tracing costs also vary quite a bit by method. As a general rule, it is best to use the least costly methods first when the number of missing subjects is greatest, saving the costlier methods for later when fewer subjects are missing. Database searches are generally the least costly at a few pennies a "hit," while telephone and in-person tracing can cost hundreds of dollars a hit.

Two key components of a tracing operation are: (1) a comprehensive plan that summarizes the steps to be taken in advance, and (2) a case management system to track progress. The case management system should maintain the date and result of each contact or attempt to contact each subject (and each lead). The system should provide reports by subject and by tracing source. The subject reports provide "tracers" with a history and allow the tracer to look for leads in the steps taken to date. The reports should provide cost and hit data for each method to help manage the data collection effort. In the end it helps to determine those methods that were the most and least cost effective for searching for the population of interest, and this knowledge can be used for planning future surveys. Each of the tracing sources is discussed briefly in the following paragraphs.

Directory assistance (DA). Several DA services are now available. Accuracy of information from these services is inconsistent. DA is useful and quick, however, when just one or two numbers are needed. If the first DA attempt is not successful it may be appropriate to try again a few minutes later (with a different operator) or to try a different service. These calls are not free and the rates vary widely. Costs also include the labor charges of the interviewer/tracer making the calls.

Telephone lookup databases. There are several large telephone lookup services that maintain telephone directory and information from "other" sources in a database. These data are available by name, by address, or by telephone number. The search is based on a parameter determined by the submitter, such as, match on full name and address, match on last name and address, match on address only, or match on last name in zip code. Early in the tracing process the criteria should be strict, with matches on address only and/or address with the last name preferred. Later in the process broader definitions may be incorporated. Charges for database lookups are generally based on the number of matches found, rather than the total number of submissions. The cost is usually a few cents. These lookups are quick, generally requiring less than 48 hours, with many claiming 24-hour turnaround. However, the match rate is likely to be low. In a general population survey the match rate might be as high as 60 percent, and of those, some proportion will not be accurate. For a highly mobile, low-income population, where only those whose numbers are known to have changed are submitted, the hit rate is likely to be quite low. However, given the relatively low cost, even a very low match rate makes this method attractive.

Several companies provide this information, so one might succeed where another might fail. There also may be regional differences, with data in one area being more complete than in others. In California, for example, telephone numbers are often listed with a name and city, but no address. This limits the data's usefulness, especially for persons with common last names.

Specialized databases. These include credit bureaus and department of motor vehicles (DMV) checks where permitted. Checks with one or more of the credit bureaus require the subject's Social Security number, and they are more costly than other database searches. Charges are based on each request not the outcome of the request. More up-to-date information will be returned if the subject has applied for credit recently, which is less likely with a low-income population than the general population. DMV checks in many states, such as California, require advance planning to obtain the necessary clearances to search records.

Other databases. Proprietary databases available on the Internet and elsewhere contain detailed information on large numbers of people. Access to the databases is often restricted. However, these restrictions are often negotiable for limited searches for legitimate research purposes. Like credit bureaus, these files often are compiled for marketing purposes and low-income populations may not make the purchases necessary to create a record. Records on people often are initiated by simple acts such as ordering a pizza or a taxi.

Telephone tracers. For the purpose of this discussion, it is assumed that each telephone number and address that has been obtained for the subject has led to a dead end. This includes all original contact information and results from all database searches. At this point tracing becomes expensive. Tracers receive special training on how to mine the files for leads. People who have done similar work in the past, such as "skip tracing" for collection agencies, tend to be adept at this task. Tracers need investigative instincts, curiosity, and bullheadedness that not all interviewers possess. Tracers usually are paid more than regular interviewers.

The tracers' task is to review the subject's tracing record, looking for leads, and to begin making telephone calls in an attempt to locate the subject. For example, online criss-cross directories and mapping programs might be used to locate and contact former neighbors; if children were in the household, neighborhood schools might be called; and employers, if known, might be contacted. Of course, all contact must be carried out discreetly. Some of these techniques are more productive in areas where community members have some familiarity with one another, generally places other than the inner cities of New York, Chicago, and Los Angeles. Nonetheless, even in urban areas, these techniques sometimes work.

Cost control is crucial in this process because much of the work is limited only by the imagination of the tracer (and tracers sometimes follow the wrong trail). Perhaps a time limit of 15 or 20 minutes might be imposed. At that time limit, the tracers work could be reviewed by a supervisor to determine if further effort seems fruitful, if another approach might be tried, or the case seems to have hit a dead end.

In-person tracing. This is the most expensive method of tracing, and it is most cost effective if it is carried out in conjunction with interviewing. Like telephone tracing, in-person tracing requires special skills that an interviewer may not possess and vice versa. For this reason it might be prudent to equip tracers with cellular telephones so that the subject, when located, can be interviewed by telephone interviewers. The tracer can thus concentrate on tracing.

Tracing in the field is similar to telephone tracing except that the tracer actually visits the former residence(s) of the subject and interviews neighbors, neighborhood businesses, and other sources. Cost control is more of a problem because supervisory review and consultation is more difficult but just as important.

Contacting Subjects

When a telephone number is available for either a subject or a lead, the process of establishing contact becomes important. An ill-defined calling protocol can lead to significant nonresponse. In this section we discuss some of the issues related to contact procedures.

Documenting Call Histories and Call Scheduling

Telephone calls need to be spread over different days of the week and different times of the day in order to establish contact with the household (not necessarily the subject). If contact with the household is established, it is possible to learn if the subject can be contacted through that telephone number, and if so, the best time to attempt to call. If the subject is no longer at the number, questions can be asked to determine if anyone in the household knows the subject's location.

If the telephone is not answered on repeated attempts, an assessment must be made of the utility of further attempts against the possibility that the number is no longer appropriate for the subject. In other words, how many times should a nonanswered telephone be dialed before checking to make sure it is the correct number for the respondent? It is important to remember that this is an iterative process applicable to the initial number on the subject's record as well as to each number discovered through tracing, some of which will be "better" than others. The issue is assessing the tradeoffs between time and cost.

Many survey firms suggest making seven calls over a period of 2 weeks—on different days (two), evenings (three), and weekends (two)—before doing any further checking (e.g., checking with DA; calling one or more of the contacts; or searching one of the databases). Other firms suggest doubling the number of calls, theorizing that the cost of the additional calls is less than the cost of the searches. Unfortunately, there is no definitive answer because much depends on the original source of the number being dialed, the time of year, the age of the number, and other factors. Very "old" numbers are less likely to be good, and perhaps fewer calls (perhaps seven) should be made before moving to a tracing mode. If contact information is available, checking with the contact may be cost effective earlier in the process. In the summer or around holidays, more calls (perhaps 10 to 12) might be prudent.

Call histories, by telephone number, for the subject (and lead) should be documented thoroughly. This includes the date, time, outcome, as well as any comments that might prove useful as a lead should tracing be necessary.

Message Machines

Message machines are now present in an estimated 60 to 70 percent of U.S. households (*STORES*, 1995; Baumgartner et al., 1997). As more households obtain machines, there has been a growing concern that subjects will use them to screen calls and thereby become more difficult to contact. However, empirical evidence to date has not shown message machines to be a major impediment to contacting respondents. Oldendick and Link (1994) estimate that a maximum of 2 to 3 percent of respondents may be using the machine in this way.[1]

A related issue has been the proper procedure to use when an interviewer reaches an answering machine. Should a message be left? If so, when should it be left? Survey organizations differ on how they handle this situation. Some organizations leave a message only after repeated contacts fail to reach a respondent on the phone (as reported by one of the experts interviewed). Other organizations leave a message at the first contact and do not leave one thereafter. The latter procedure has been found to be effective in RDD studies relative to not leaving any message at all (Tuckel et al., 1996; Xu et al., 1993). The authors favor leaving messages more often (perhaps with every other call with a maximum of four or five) than either of these approaches. We believe, but cannot substantiate empirically, that if the goal is to locate and interview a particular person, then the number of messages left might signal the importance of the call to the person hearing the message and might induce that person to call the 800 number. Even if the caller says the subject does not live there, that is useful information. However, leaving too many messages may have a negative effect.

Obtaining Cooperation

In this section we highlight some of the standard survey procedures for obtaining high cooperation rates once contact with the subject has been established. These can be divided into issues of interviewer training, the questionnaire, and the treatment of refusals.

Interviewer Materials and Training

Interviewer experience has been found to be related to obtaining high respondent cooperation (Groves and Fultz, 1985; Dillman et al., 1976). The theory is that experience makes interviewers familiar with many questions reluctant respondents may have about cooperating (Collins et al., 1988), and allows them to respond in a quick and confident manner. Showing any type of hesitation or lack of confidence is correlated with high refusal rates.

This finding suggests that intense training of interviewers on how to handle reluctant respondents may provide them with increased confidence, as well as the necessary skills, to handle difficult situations. Groves and Couper (1998) present results from an experiment on an establishment survey that shows significant improvement in cooperation rates once interviewers are provided with detailed training on how to handle reluctant respondents. This training consisted of drill-

---

[1] A related concern is whether respondents are using caller ID in a similar way.

ing interviewers, through a series of role plays, on providing quick responses to respondent concerns about participating in the study. Because this study was done in an establishment survey, the applicability to a survey of low-income respondents is not clear. Respondents to establishment surveys are more willing to converse with the interviewer, which allows for more time to present arguments on why the respondent should participate in the study.

Nevertheless, this suggests that interviewers must have the skills to answer the subject's questions, to overcome objections, and to establish the necessary rapport to conduct the interview. Training in these areas is crucial if refusals are to be avoided. Answers to Frequently Asked Questions (FAQs) must be prepared and practiced so that the "answers" sound like the interviewer's own words rather than a script that is being read. Interviewers also must be trained to know when to accept a refusal, leaving the door open for future conversion by a different interviewer who might have more success. This type of training is more difficult than training that is centered on the content of questions, but it is also vital if refusals are to be avoided.

Questionnaire Design

Several areas related to the design of the questionnaire could impact response rates. These include: (1) the length of the questionnaire, (2) the introduction used, and (3) the type and placement of the questions. Each of these has been hypothesized to affect the ability of the interviewer to obtain a high response rate. Interestingly, for each of these characteristics, there is some belief that the effects are primarily on the interviewer's perception of the task, rather than concerns the respondent may have with the procedure. If interviewers perceive the task to be particularly difficult to complete, their confidence levels may go down and their performance might be affected.

Pretests of the questionnaire should be conducted as part of any research design. Pretests, and accompanying debriefings of the interviewers often uncover problems that are easily corrected prior to interviewing the sample subjects. More elaborate pretesting methods also should be considered. These include, for example, "cognitive interviews," as well as review of the questionnaire by a survey research professional who has experience in conducting structured interviews.

Questionnaire length. Although it is commonly believed that the length of the questionnaire is related to response rates, very little empirical evidence shows that this, in fact, is true. Much of the evidence that does show a relationship between length and response rates concerns mail surveys, where respondents get visual cues on how long the interview may be (Bogen, 1996). The length of a telephone interview may not be mentioned unless the respondent asks, so the respondent may not know how long it will take. This fact further confuses the relationship between interview length and response rates.

Two exceptions to this are studies by Collins et al. (1988) and Sobal (1982). Both found a relationship between how long the interviewer told the respondent the interview would take and the response rate. Collins et al. (1988) found a modest effect of approximately 2 percent, while Sobal (1982) found a much larger reduction of 16 percent when comparing a 5-minute interview to a 20-minute interview. These studies, however, are difficult to generalize to other studies because they do not compare the effects of different descriptions of the length of the interview to one that does not state the length at all. This makes it unclear what the overall effect of interview length might be in the context of another survey, which does not state the length of the interview (unless asked).

This research does suggest, however, that significantly shortening the interview to 5 minutes may increase response rates to some degree. If the interview were shortened to this length, then it might be advantageous to state the length of the interview in the introduction to the survey. One would assume that cutting the interview to just 5 minutes is not an efficient way to increase the response rate. The loss of information needed for analyses will be much larger than anticipated gains in the response rate. For this reason, it might be useful to consider shortening the interview only for a special study of refusers. If this strategy significantly increases the number of persons who are converted after an initial refusal, more information might be obtained on how respondents differ from nonrespondents.

Survey introduction. A natural place to start redesigning the questionnaire to improve response rates is the introduction. Many respondents refuse at this point in the interview. This is especially the case for an RDD survey, where interviewers do not have the name of the respondent and the respondent does not recognize the voice on the other end of the call. For this reason, it is important to mention anything that is seen as an advantage to keeping the respondent on the line. Advantages generally are believed to be: (1) the sponsor of the study, (2) the organization conducting the interviews, (3) the topic of the survey, and (4) why the study is important.

Research in an RDD survey context has not found any general design parameters for the introduction that are particularly effective in increasing response rates. Dillman et al. (1976), for example, find no effects of offering respondents results from the survey or statements about the social utility of the survey. Similarly, Groves et al. (1979) find variations in the introduction do not change response rates. Exceptions to this are a few selected findings that: (1) government sponsorship seems to increase response rates (Goyder, 1987), (2) university sponsorship may be better than private sponsorship, and (3) making a "nonsolicitation statement" (e.g., "I am not asking for money") can help if the survey is not sponsored by the government (Everett and Everett, 1989).

The most widely agreed-on rule about introductions is that they need to be as short as possible. Evidence that shorter is better is found in Dillman et al. (1976), as well as our own experience. Because the interviewer may not have the full attention of the respondent at the initial outset of the call, it is better to simply state the best points of the survey and get the respondent to react to the first question. Interviewers also generally prefer short introductions, because they provide a greater opportunity to involve the respondent in the conversation (less opportunity to hang up). By increasing interviewer confidence, the response rate should be affected positively. It is important to balance the informational requirements with the need to be brief and simple. Long explanations, going into great detail about the survey, may turn respondents off more than motivate them to participate. The best approach is to provide the respondent with a broad set of statements to capture their attention at this point in the interview. Once rapport and trust have built up a bit, more details about the study can be presented.

Type/placement of questions. Sensitive questions have higher rates of nonresponse and should be placed later in the questionnaire but still positioned logically so that the flow from one topic to the next is smooth. Sensitive information includes topics such as income, detailed household composition (e.g., naming everyone in the household), participation in social programs, and child care. Careful placement allows these questions to be asked after rapport has been established. This is especially true with initial contacts into the household. Asking sensitive questions within the first few minutes of the initial contact may turn respondents off unnecessarily.

Refusal Conversion

If a respondent refuses to participate, it is important for the interviewer to indicate the level of hostility, if any. It may not be desirable (nor cost effective) to try to convert subjects who are extremely hostile (e.g., one in which the respondent is abusive). Other subjects might be recontacted in an attempt to have them reconsider their decision. This recontact should take place several days (7 to 21) after the initial contact to allow the respondent time to reconsider.

Prior to refusal conversion, a letter should be sent to try to convince the respondent to participate. This letter has been shown to be particularly effective if: (1) an incentive is enclosed, and (2) express delivery is used for mailing (Cantor et al., 1999). Comparisons between the use of express delivery to a first class refusal conversion letter show a difference of 10 percentage points in conversion rates on an RDD study and a difference of 15 to 20 percentage points if an incentive is enclosed. These results are not likely to be as dramatic for a survey of welfare leavers. However, this strategy has been applied in this context and is believed to be effective.

Based on work related to personal interviews (Couper et al., 1992), it is possible to create specialized letters for refusal conversion based on what the respondent said at the time of the refusal. A procedure adopted for the National

Survey of America's Families (NSAF) was to have the interviewer provide a recommendation on the type of letter that would be sent to the respondent after the refusal occurred. Because most refusals fall into two or three categories (e.g., "no time," "not interested"), special letters could be developed that emphasized particular arguments why the respondent should cooperate (e.g., "no time"— emphasize the length of the interview; can do the interview in several calls). The problem with this procedure is that for most refusals, the interviewer has little information on which to base a good decision on the reason for refusal. A large number of respondents hang up before providing detailed feedback to the interviewer. As a result, a large majority of the mailouts for the refusal conversion are done using the "general" letter, which does not emphasize anything in particular.

However, in a survey of welfare leavers, where the interviewer may have more information about the reason for refusal, tailoring the letters to the respondent's concerns may be useful. This would depend on the amount of information the interviewer is able to collect on the reason for the nonresponse.

Refusal conversion calls are best handled by a select group of handpicked interviewers who are trained to carry out this type of work. They must be trained to analyze the reason for the refusal and be able to prepare answers for different situations.

STUDIES OF WELFARE LEAVERS

Table 2-1 summarizes the procedures discussed previously. It is organized around the three primary activities required to conduct a study: (1) locating the subject, (2) contacting the subject, and (3) obtaining cooperation.

In this section we discuss how these "best practices" have been applied in a number of surveys that have been conducted to evaluate welfare reform in different states. The purpose of this review is to provide a picture of the range of practices that have been used and how these practices relate to results.

Description of Methods Used in Recent Studies

To better understand the methods that have been implemented in recent studies of welfare reform, we collected information on a small sample of state surveys. The largest portion of our sample of studies is from the group of Assistant Secretary for Planning and Evaluation (ASPE) grantees funded in FY99 (9 of the 13 studies). The remaining studies were chosen by networking or referral by colleagues. Information was collected through interviews with the director of the research team and any reports that were available. These studies are meant to represent what the current practice is for welfare-leaver studies.

A summary of key characteristics for these 13 surveys is shown in Table 2-2. In 12 of the 13 surveys for which we collected information, a mixed-mode,

TABLE 2-1 Summary of Best Practices for Conducting Telephone Surveys of Welfare Leavers

Task	Method	Comment
Locate Respondent		
• Accurate address and telephone number	Collect at intake and update regularly	Try to collect consent to search other databases
• Contact for persons not living with subject		
• Use other sources to locate subject	Use available administrative databases (e.g., food stamps, Medicaid, driver's licenses); use commercially available sources (reverse directories, credit bureaus)	Start with the least expensive methods
• Telephone tracing; in-person tracing	Review tracing record and follow leads	Very expensive and requires specialized skills
• In-person tracing		
Contacting Subjects		
• Prenotification	Send letter prior to making contact	Use express delivery if possible
• Incentives and continued contact	Repeated mailings to subjects	
• Call scheduling	Spread out calls over day/night; weekdays/weekends	
Obtaining Cooperation		
• Interviewer training and experience	Provide interviewers with answers to common questions	Try to use experienced interviewers with good records
• Questionnaire design	Minimize redundant questions Keep length as short as possible	Pretest questions and allow for time to revise after the pretest
• Survey introduction	Keep initial introduction as short as possible	
• Refusal conversion	Prenotify with express mail and incentives	

two-step, approach was used. First, as many telephone interviews as possible were conducted using information accessible to home office staff. Respondents were contacted initially using information available from the administrative records from the sample frame. Advance letters were sent out. For those persons who do not have a phone number, the letter asked for the subject to call an 800 number to do the interview or set up an appointment.

If the telephone number did not lead to the subject, tracing was done from the home office. This typically included using directory assistance, reverse directories to find other addresses and free services on the Internet. Other methods implemented by most of the studies included:

• Searches of credit databases: These include databases such as Transunion, CBI/Equifax and TRW. Stapulonis et al. (1999) report the use of an unnamed database that seemed to add information above and beyond these.

• Searches of other databases across agencies: These included food stamps, unemployment insurance, child support enforcement, motor vehicles, Medicaid, employment training, Social Security, vital records, and state ID cards.

The ability to search the "other databases" was possible because in all cases the research organizations had the Social Security number of the respondent.

In discussions with different organizations, we got a clear sense that the original contact information was not of high quality. One study reported, for example, that 78 percent of the original phone numbers did not lead directly to subjects. This may be, in part, because there is very little need for agency representatives to maintain contact with recipients over the telephone. In one state, for example, recipients are paid using a debit card that is continually re-valued at the beginning of a payment period. Thus, the address and telephone number information is not used on a frequent basis. In a study conducted by Westat several years ago, a similar result was found when trying to locate convicted felons (Cantor, 1995). Contact information provided by probation officers was found to be accurate about 50 percent of the time.[2]

If the subject cannot be located with available contact information, the case is sent out into the field. In some instances, the field interviewer is expected to both locate and interview the subject. In other instances the interviewer asked the subject to call a central interviewing facility. If the subject does not have a telephone, the interviewer provides them with a cellular telephone to call the facility. Several organizations reported that having the respondent call into the central office allowed for more specialization in the field tracing task. Interviewers would not be required to administer the interview. When hiring field person-

---

[2]This rate is surprisingly low, given that probation officers should be in regular contact with probationers.

TABLE 2-2 Results of Interviews with 14 Selected Telephone Surveys of Welfare or Ex-Welfare Recipients

Study Number	Advance Letter/ Incentives	Telephone Tracking Sources	Field Tracking	Refusal Conversion	Response Rate %	Field Period
1	Yes/Yes	Directory assistance Reverse directory	No	No	30	3 months
2	Yes/Yes	Directory assistance Reverse directory Specialized tracking firm Motor vehicle/ID records	Yes Exp. staff	Yes	51	9 months+
3	Yes/Yes	Directory assistance Credit databases Other welfare offices	Yes Exp. staff	Yes	Total: >70 Tel: 50	5 months
4	Yes/Yes	Directory assistance Credit databases Other welfare offices	Yes Exp. staff	Yes	Total: >70 Tel: 50	5 months
5	Yes/Yes	DK	Yes Unknown Exp.	DK	52	DK
6	No/No	Directory assistance Other agency database	Yes Exp. staff	No	Total: 78 Tel: 66	4 months
7	Yes/Yes	Directory assistance Credit databases Motor vehicle Other agency databases	Yes Exp. staff No exp.	Yes	Total: 72 Tel: 25 - 30	60 months

8	Yes/Yes	Reverse directory Other agencies	Yes No exp.	no	Total: 46 Tel: 40	DK
9	DK	Directory assistance Tracing contact Credit databases Other agencies	Yes Exp. staff	DK	Total: 80 Tel: 50	DK
10	Yes/Yes	Directory assistance Credit databases Other agencies	Yes Exp. staff	DK	Total: 75	DK
11	Yes/Yes	Directory assistance Credit databases Other agencies	Yes Exp. staff	Yes	Total: 81*	DK
12	Yes/Yes	Directory assistance Credit databases Other agencies	No	DK	Total: 40	4 months
13	Yes/Yes	Directory assistance Other agencies	Yes Exp. staff	No	Total: 72	DK
14++	Yes/Yes**	Directory assistance Other agencies	Yes No Exp	No	Total: 72 Tel: >65	2 months

DK = Don't Know

* Response rate after 5 years.

** Used nonmonetary incentive.

+ Interviewing period was 3 months. Used 6 months before interviewing period to establish contact information and find respondents.

++ Did extensive tracing over the telephone with highly experienced personnel.

nel, therefore, the agency should be able to recruit individuals who are especially adept at tracking and tracing.

Empirical Results and Relation to Best Practice

These 14 studies provide some data on the possibilities and limitations related to conducting welfare-leaver studies. Many of these studies are implementing the "best practices" summarized in Table 2-1. These include, for example, advance letters, incentives, tracking/tracing, and refusal conversion. Resulting response rates ranged from a low of 30 percent to a high of 80 percent. Many studies are in the 40 to 50 percent range.

It is clear from these data, as well as from the authors' collective experience, that no single design feature guarantees a high response rate. The effectiveness of particular methods varies by situation and a number of methods are needed to maximize response rates. A useful illustration is a survey that was completed in Iowa of current and former Temporary Assistance for Needy Families recipients (Stapulonis et al, 1999). This was a mixed-mode survey that implemented all of the methods discussed earlier, including: (1) repeated mailings to respondents, (2) use of telephone interviewers experienced in tracking respondents over the phone, (3) incentive payments, (4) specialized database searches, and (5) use of field staff to trace and interview respondents. As reported by Stapulonis et al. (1999), no single method produced a high response. A response rate of approximately 25 to 30 percent was achieved through the use of the telephone. At the end of 16 weeks, a 48-percent response rate was achieved by offering an incentive of $10 and sending cases into the field. The remainder of the 60-week field period was used to increase the rate to 72 percent. During this interim period, numerous methods were instituted, such as increasing incentive payments, remailings (using express mail) to households, field tracing, and using more specialized tracing sources and methods. The latter included using highly experienced trackers in the telephone center and the field.

The data in Table 2-2 seem to indicate that the mixed-mode approach, at least as currently implemented by most of these states, is necessary to achieve response rates of at least 50 percent. The data also indicate that for many studies, use of only the telephone yields a response rate of approximately 30 to 40 percent. The clearest example of this is study #1 and #2. These two studies were completed in the same state by the same organizations. In study #1, where a 30-percent response rate was obtained, only telephone and limited tracking was done from a central office. Study #2 instituted a number of additional tracing steps, but also added a field component. Similarly, study #7 reported a 25 to 30-percent response rate before going into the field and study #8 reported a 40-percent response rate before releasing cases to the field. The major exceptions to these patterns are the few studies that report final response rates of at least 70 percent. In these instances, the response rate obtained over the telephone is at least 50 percent and, in one case, 66 percent. Study #14 had a response rate of 72 percent and reported very poor experiences with their field tracers. Effectively, most of their cases were completed using the telephone. A few of these higher rates were achieved as part of planned experiments, where contact was initiated while the recipient was in the program. Other successes may be attributed more to the quality of the information available at the start of the study. Overall, we believe that if response rates of at least 50 percent are desired, it would seem important to use both telephone and field personnel to trace and locate respondents.

This pattern is consistent with our general experience in working with low-income populations. Although it is possible, using proper procedures and preparation, to complete a significant number of interviews via mail and telephone, a proportion of this group simply does not respond to anything but in-person contacts. This may be related to this group's mobility rate, the intermittent availability of the telephone, or simply busy work schedules. Whatever is the case, it is unlikely that achieving extremely high response rates (e.g., 70 percent or above) for welfare leavers can be achieved by simply the use of mail or telephone interviews.

Tracking Respondents

As one might expect, the primary source of nonresponse in these studies is noncontact, rather than refusals. For example, of the 25-percent nonresponse in the study #6, approximately 17 percent is from not being able to locate respondents and 8 percent is from refusals. For surveys that have lower response rates (e.g., around 50 percent), the percent of nonlocatables is even higher. This suggests that improving response rates has to do most with improving tracking.

Given this, an important component to pushing response rates above 50 percent is to improve the ability to find subjects. This relates to both the type of staff and the type of information available for finding the subjects. Study #6, with a 78-percent response rate, is a good illustration of the importance of experienced staff. This study did not implement many of the procedures discussed previously, including prenotification letters, refusal conversion, or incentives. The staff doing the interviewing and tracing, however, were program quality assurance personnel. Because part of their job is to find and interview welfare recipients to conduct audits, they were highly experienced in finding this population. In addition, the supervisor seemed to have very strong oversight of the interviewers' progress. Similarly, study #14 completed all interviews over the telephone and achieved a 72-percent response rate. The study did not offer a monetary incentive and did not conduct refusal conversion. The success of this survey was attributed to the interviewers, who were also part of the quality assurance program.

Alternatively, a number of survey directors reported that the major barriers they encountered were related to inexperienced staff, either in the phone center or in the field, in tracking and tracing subjects. Stapulonis et al. (1999) report failure of a field effort because of inexperienced field trackers, as did the survey director for study #8. In the latter case, the telephone interviewers were asked to conduct field interviewing.

Our experience has been very similar to this profile and it applies to in-person interviewing as well as tracking from a central telephone facility. The ability to look over case records, find leads, and followup on those leads requires the ingenuity of a detective, as well as a personality that gains trust when calling neighbors or other community members.

Having solid information from which to trace subjects is also essential to finding them eventually. As noted previously, most survey directors commented on the poor quality of the information contained in the original sample records. In many cases, the information is quite old (e.g., up to 6-9 months) and, in many cases, of questionable accuracy. Because this is a highly mobile population, the age of the records limits the utility of the information quickly. Study #2 attempted to minimize this problem by beginning the tracking process as soon as subjects came off the welfare records. Although this may lead to tracking too many people,[3] it provided a way to maintain contact with subjects until the field interviewing started 6 months later. The success of this process is yet to be evaluated, but this method may provide a way to keep the information about sampled persons as up to date as possible.

All the studies had Social Security numbers for subjects, as well as access to databases in other parts of the government (e.g., motor vehicle registrations, food stamps, child support enforcement, Medicaid, unemployment insurance). These provide a powerful set of tools to find respondents. However, only two of the studies have tracing contact information, containing the names and phone numbers of at least one person, preferably someone who the subject does not live with, who is likely to know where the person is at any point in the future. These two studies both achieved response rates above 75 percent. Both studies were experiments, set up in advance to sample clients at intake and collect this information at that time.

The availability of tracing contacts would not only improve the tracking rates for these studies, but it would reduce the amount of time devoted to tracing. In fact, our experience, has shown that with good tracing contacts, as well as occasional interim contacts with subjects (e.g., every 6 months), little in-person tracking has to be done. Respondents can be located by interviewers making update phone calls. This is what many longitudinal surveys do as part of their routine activities for staying in touch with respondents. As a point of illustration, Westat recently completed a feasibility study that located 85 percent of subjects 3

---

[3]Most studies had, as an eligibility criteria, that leavers had to stay off the welfare program for at least 2 months. Sampling within a month of leaving the program, therefore, eventually results in having to drop subjects because they return to the program within 2 months.

years after their last contact with the study. These subjects were high-risk youth who had been diverted into a family counseling program in 1993 and were last contacted in 1996. At that time, tracing contact information had been collected. This population lived in highly urbanized, poor neighborhoods and could be considered comparable to those being traced in the welfare-leaver studies discussed previously. Approximately 67 percent of the population was found through the use of mail and telephone contacts. The remaining 18 percent were found by field tracing.

Increasing Cooperation

Pushing response rates higher also can be done through selective adoption of other methods related to making the response task easier. Some percentage of the persons classified as nonlocatable are really tacit refusers. That is, some of those individuals that "can't be located" are explicitly avoiding contact with the interviewer or field tracer because of reluctance to participate in the survey. This reluctance may be because the person does not want to take the time to do the survey or it may be more deep-seated and related to a general fear of being found by anyone who happens to be looking for them.

Several of the studies found that repeated mailings to the same addresses over time did result in completed interviews. This approach seemed to be especially effective when these mailings were tied to increased incentives. This approach would tend to support the idea that at least some portion of the "noncontacts" are actually persons who are tacitly refusing to do the interview, at least the first few times around. Express mail was also used for selected followup mailings, although it is unclear whether this method of delivery was particularly effective.

As noted in Table 2-2, a number of the studies do not implement any type of refusal conversion. The reluctance stems from fear that this would be viewed as coercive, because the agency conducting the research is the same agency responsible for providing benefits on a number of support programs. Other survey groups, however, reported confidence in conducting refusal conversion activities, as long as they were convinced the interviewers were well trained and understood the line between trying to directly address respondents' concerns and coercion. In fact, many initial refusals are highly situational. The interviewer may call when the kids are giving the parent an especially difficult time or at a time when the subject just came home from an exhausting day at work. In another situation, the respondent may not have understood the nature of the survey request. In all of these cases, calling back at another time, with an elaborated explanation of the survey, is useful. In fact, one study director reported that about 50 percent of the initial refusers in the study were eventually converted to final completed interviews. This is not out of line with refusal conversion rates found on other studies, either of the general or low-income populations.

SPECIAL ISSUES FOR RDD SURVEYS OF
LOW-INCOME POPULATIONS

In many ways, RDD surveys pose a much different set of challenges than those for list-based samples, especially on issues related to nonresponse. For surveys of welfare clients, the target population is identified clearly and quality issues have to do with finding sample members to conduct the interview. For RDD surveys, the primary issues have to do with efficiently identifying low-income subjects and, once identified, convincing them to participate in a survey.

Response Rates on RDD Surveys

To provide some perspective on the level of response achieved on RDD surveys, Massey et al. (1998) presented results of a study that reviewed the response rates of a large number of RDD surveys conducted for government agencies or as part of a large survey effort. Their results found a median response rate 60 to 64 percent with about 20 percent of the surveys exceeding 70 percent. The overall perception among survey analysts is that the trend is for this rate to decrease over time. That is, achieving high response rates for RDD surveys is becoming more difficult.

An RDD survey of low-income populations faces several hurdles relative to achieving a high response rate. The first is the need to screen all households on the basis of income. This leads to two types of problems. The first is that it adds an opportunity for someone to refuse to do the survey. A screener written to find low-income households has to include a number of questions that respondents are sensitive to, including information on who lives in the households, and some type of income measure. Much of the nonresponse on RDD surveys occur at this point in the process. For example, on the NSAF, a national RDD survey that over-samples low-income groups, the screener response rate was in the high 70s. Once a respondent within the household was selected, the response rate to do the extended interview was in the 80s. Nonetheless, the combination of the two rates, which form the final response rate, resulted in a rate in the mid-60s (Brick et al., 1999).

Low response rates on RDD surveys are partly an issue of credibility. Relative to a survey of welfare leavers, the issue of credibility places more emphasis on design features that motivate respondents to participate in the survey (vis-à-vis trying to locate respondents). For example, research on methods to increase RDD response rates has shown that prenotification prior to the call, methods of delivery of prenote letters, and use of incentives can provide important boosts above those normally achieved when implementing many of the other important design features reviewed earlier. All three of these increase response rates in the context of an RDD survey (Camburn et al., 1995; Brick et al., 1997; Cantor et al, 1999).

In addition, refusal conversion is particularly important for an RDD survey, because such a large proportion of the nonresponse is from refusals. Refusal to the screener could be from almost any member of the household, because most screeners accept responses from any adult who answers the phone. Calling the household a second time provides an opportunity to obtain another person in the household (who may be more willing to participate) or reach the same respondent who may not be as difficult to convince to participate in a short screening instrument. Refusal to the extended interview may be more difficult to turn around. Refusal conversion strategies at this level are amenable to more traditional "tailoring" methods (e.g., Groves and Couper, this volume: Chapter 1), because respondents at this stage of the process may be more willing to listen to the interviewer.

Efficiently Sampling Low-Income Populations

A second issue related to conducting RDD surveys of low-income populations is the ability to actually find and oversample this group. Screening for persons of low-income has been found to have considerable error. This has been assessed when comparing the poverty status reported on the initial screener and the income reported when using more extensive questions in the longer, extended interview. For example, on the NSAF approximately 10 to 15 percent of those who report being below 200 percent of poverty on the longer interview initially tell the screener they are above this mark. Alternatively, 20 to 30 percent of those reporting themselves as above 200 percent of poverty on the extended interview initially screen in as above this mark (Cantor and Wang, 1998). Similar patterns have been observed for in-person surveys, although the rates do not seem to be as extreme. This reduces the overall efficiency of the sample design. This, in turn, requires increasing sample sizes to achieve the desired level of precision.

To date, the problem has not had a clear solution. In-person surveys have developed more extensive screening interviews to allow predicting income status at the point of the screener (Moeller and Mathiowetz, 1994). This approach also might be taken for RDD screeners, although there is less opportunity to ask the types of questions that are needed to predict income. For example, asking detailed household rosters, or collecting information on jobs or material possessions likely would reduce the screener response rate.

A second issue related to sample design on an RDD survey is the coverage of low-income households. Although only 6 percent of the national population is estimated to be without a telephone (Thornberry and Massey, 1988), about 30 percent of those under poverty are estimated to be in this state. For an RDD survey of a low-income populations, therefore, it is important to decide how coverage issues will be approached. One very expensive approach would be to introduce an area frame into the design. This would include screening for nontelephone households in person and then conducting the extended interviews either in person or over the telephone.[4]

Over the past few years, a new method, based on an imputation method, has been tested that does not require doing in-person interviews (Keeter, 1995). The premise of the method is based on the idea that for a certain segment of the population, having telephone service is a dynamic, rather than stable, characteristic. Consequently, many of the people who do not have service at one point in time may have service shortly thereafter. This implies that one might be able to use persons that have a telephone, but report interrupted service, as proxies for those who do not have telephones at the time the survey is being conducted. Based on this idea, telephone surveys increasingly are including a question that asks respondents if they have had any interruptions in their telephone service over an extended period of time (e.g., past 12 months). If there was an interruption, they are asked how long they did not have service. This information is used in the development of the survey weights. Those reporting significant interruptions of service are used as proxies for persons without a telephone.

Recent evaluations of this method as a complete substitute for actually conducting in-person interviews has shown some promise (Flores-Cervantes et al., 1999). Initial analysis has shown that the use of these questions significantly reduces the bias for key income and other well-being measures when compared to estimates that use in-person interviewing. This is not always the case, however. For certain statistics and certain low income subgroups, the properties of the estimator are unstable. This may be due, in part, to developing better weighting strategies than currently employed. Nonetheless, the use of these questions seems to offer a solution that, given the huge expense involved with doing in-person interviews, may offer significant advantages.

The use of this method also may be of interest to those conducting telephone surveys with persons from a list of welfare clients. Rather than being viewed as a way to reduce coverage error, however, they could be used when trying to impute missing data for high nonresponse rates.

HIGHLIGHTING LOW-COST ACTIONS

This paper has attempted to provide information on methods to achieve high response rates on telephone surveys of low-income populations. We have concentrated much of the review on studies that start with a list of welfare recipients, but we also have provided information for persons conducting RDD interviews. The second section of this paper provided a list of best practices that should be considered when conducting telephone surveys. The third section provided examples of what is currently being practiced in recently completed welfare-leaver

---

[4]Telephone interviews would be conducted by having the respondent call into a central facility using a cellular telephone.

studies and how these practices relate to results. The fourth section provided special issues related to RDD surveys. In this section we concentrate on highlighting suggestions that seem practical and relatively low cost.

Improve Tracking and Tracing

Clearly one primary theme taken from our review is the need to improve the ability of studies to find subjects. Most agencies face similar situations—the information used to track respondents is both relatively old (6–9 months) and limited. The age of the information could be addressed partly through methods such as those mentioned earlier—start contacting respondents immediately after they leave the program. Maintain this contact until the time to conduct the interview (e.g., 6 months after leaving). This approach, however, is relatively expensive to implement. Following subjects over extended periods of time can be labor intensive. Furthermore, the information provided when exiting the program may not have been updated for quite some time. This constraint is difficult to get around.

A more effective and cost-efficient method to improve contact information is to collect tracing contacts when the subjects initially enter the program. This type of information does not go out of date nearly as fast as a single name and address. Even if they go out of date, the names and addresses can provide additional leads that can be followed up by trackers. When collecting this information, it is important that the names are of persons who do not live with the subject. This decreases the possibility that if the subject moves, the contact person would have moved as well.

Another potentially rich source of information is case history documentation. Many of the studies reviewed above reported using information from other government databases, such as motor vehicles or other recipiency programs, to collect updated addresses and phone numbers. Examination of hardcopy case folders, if they exist, would be one way to supplement this information. One study reported doing this and found it was a good source for tracing contact information. Subjects, at some point, could have provided information on references, employers and friends as part of the application process. This information, if confidentiality issues can be addressed, can be examined to locate further leads to find and track those people who cannot be found.

To provide some perspective on the impact that tracing might have on the cost of a survey, we developed estimates of cost under two scenarios, one in which contact information is available and another in which it is not available. Costs for surveys of this type are difficult to estimate because so much depends on the ability of the data collector to monitor the process; the availability of skilled staff to carry out the tracing; and the nature and quality of information that is available at the start. The first two factors rest with the data collector while the latter depends on information obtained about each subject (and his or her accessibility) by the agency. If the data are not current or not complete, tracing is difficult and costly regardless of the controls the data collector has in place.

Under the assumptions described in Table 2-3, we estimate that approximately 600 fewer hours are required to trace 1,000 subjects if tracing contact information is available. Contact information, for this example, would have been obtained during the intake process and delivered to the data collector with the sample. The table may be somewhat deceptive because, for purposes of illustration, we have forced the two samples to have approximately the same location rate in order to compare the level of effort. In reality, the location rate (and consequently the response rate) for those with contact data would be higher than for those without.

In creating Table 2-3, we assumed the following times for each level of tracing. In practice, most of the welfare leaver studies have used both telephone and in-person surveys:

- 20 minutes for calling through the contacts
- 20 minutes for calls to the hits of database searches
- 1 hour for intense telephone tracing
- 7 hours for in-person tracing

Although these estimated times are reasonable, they also can be misleading. For example, if several databases are used (e.g., agency, credit bureau, DMV,

TABLE 2-3 Comparison of Tracing Hours, by Availability of Contact Information

	(a) No Tracing	(b) Calling Contacts	(c) Database Search	(d) Intense Telephone Follow-up	(e) In-person Tracing	(f) Total
Tracing Time Per Sample Unit (minutes)	0	20	20	60	420	
With Contact Information						
Sample size	1,000	700	490	343	240	1,000
Percent of cases located	0.30	0.30	0.30	0.30	0.15	0.80
Number located	300	210	147	103	36	796
Estimated number of hours	0	233	163	343	1,681	2,420
Without Contact Information						
Sample size	1,000	N/A	700	469	314.23	1,000
Found rate	0.30		0.33	0.33	0.33	0.79
Number found	300		231	154.77	104	789
Estimated number of hours	0		233	469	2,200	2,902

commercial) each can produce a hit and require followup, so it is likely that more than one followup call might be carried out for some sample members, and none for others. In organizing a hit, care must be taken to make sure it is genuine and not a duplicate of an earlier hit that already has been invalidated. This adds time, though the process can be aided by a case management system.

The level of interviewer/tracer effort is only one dimension of cost. Supervisory hours will range between 20 to 40 percent of interviewer hours, depending on the activity, with the highest percentage needed for the intense tracing. Other variable labor costs include all clerical functions related to mailing and maintaining the case management system, and all direct nonlabor costs. These include, but are not limited to charges from database management companies to run files, directory assistance charges, telephone line charges, field travel expenses, and postage/express delivery charges.

Fixed costs include the management costs to coordinate the activities and the programming functions to develop a case management system; preparing files for data searches; updating files with results of data searches; and preparing labels for mailing.

A second important point to remember for agencies operating on a limited budget is to hire supervisory and interviewing staff who are experienced at locating subjects. Prudent screening of personnel, whether internal employees or external contractors, potentially have a big payoff with respect to maximizing the response rate. Strong supervisors are especially important because they can teach new interviewers methods of finding particular cases. They also can provide guidance and new ideas for experienced interviewers. The supervision has to be done on an interviewer-by-interviewer basis. Supervisors should review each case with interviewers on a frequent basis (e.g., every week) and provide feedback/advice on how to proceed with each one. This includes making sure the interviewer is following up with the leads that are in hand, as well as discussing ideas on how to generate more leads.

Effective locating and management of a survey cannot be learned on the job. Therefore, sponsoring agencies should gather evidence that the personnel involved have the appropriate experience and successful track record to complete the work successfully. This advice applies if using personnel within the sponsoring agency or through a contractor. When considering a contractor, the sponsoring agency should ask for hard evidence that a study like this has been conducted, and check references and evaluate success rates. Questions should be asked about the availability of experienced staff to complete the work. If the work is to be done by telephone, then some information on the track record of telephone tracers should be requested. For in-person contacts, information on the experience of personnel who reside in the local area where the study is to be conducted should be collected.

Improving Methods to Contact and Obtain Cooperation

First and foremost in any survey operation is the need to develop an infrastructure that maintains control over cases as they move from the initial prenotification letter to call scheduling and case documentation. Understanding what stage each case is in and what has been tried already is critical to making sure each case goes through all possibilities. These basics are not particularly expensive to implement and can yield a large payoff in terms of completed interviews. For example, supervisory staff should be reviewing telephone cases as they move to different dispositions, such as "ring, no answer," "initial refusal," or "subject not at this number." As with tracing, supervisors should review cases and make case-by-case determinations on the most logical next step.

Monitoring of the call scheduling also should ensure that different times of the day and different days are used when trying to contact respondents. This is one big advantage of a centralized computer-assisted telephone interview (CATI). The computer "deals" cases at the appropriate times and pretty much ensures that the desired calling algorithms are followed. However, if the study is being done with paper and pencil, then a system to document and monitor call history should be in place to ensure that this occurs.

Prenotification is being used extensively for the studies reviewed earlier. Low-income populations are particularly difficult to reach by mail. For this reason, some attention to the form and content of this correspondence is likely worth a small investment of professional time. This includes, for example, the way the letters are addressed (e.g., labels, computer generated, hand written), the method of delivery (express delivery versus first-class mail) and the clarity of the message. The contents of the letter should be structured to be as clear and as simple as possible. One study reviewed earlier noted an improvement (although not experimentally tested) when formatting letters with large subheadings and minimal text. The details surrounding the study were relegated to a question-and-answer sheet. We also have found this to be an improvement over the standard letter-type format. Similarly, use of express delivery, at least when there is some confidence in the validity of the respondent's address, may also be a cost-effective way to provide respondents with information about the survey that would eventually increase their motivation to participate.

Incentives are also being used in the studies mentioned previously. We have not elaborated on this much, partly because another paper will be presented on just this topic. One pattern we did notice for the studies reviewed earlier was that all incentives are "promised" for completion of the interview. Amounts generally ranged from $15 to $50, with the largest amounts being paid at the end of field periods to motivate the most reluctant respondents. Research has found that prepaid incentives are more effective than promised incentives. Research we have done in an RDD context has shown, in fact, that not only is more effective, but the amount of money needed to convince people to participate is much smaller. It may be worth experimenting with prepayments that are considerably smaller than the current promised incentives (e.g., $5) to see if there is a significant improvement in the ability to locate and interview respondents.

In conclusion, conducting a telephone survey of low-income populations is a task that requires careful preparation and monitoring. The surveys implemented by states to this point have been discovering this as they attempt to locate and interview respondents. Improving response rates will require attention to increasing the information used to locate respondents, as well as making it as easy as possible for respondents to participate. This paper has provided a thumbnail sketch of some important procedures to consider to achieve this goal. It will be interesting to see how future surveys adapt or innovate on these procedures to overcome the barriers they are currently encountering.

REFERENCES

Anglin, D.A., B. Danila, T. Ryan, and K. Mantius
  1996 *Staying in Touch: A Fieldwork Manual of Tracking Procedures for Locating Substance Abusers for Follow-Up Studies.* Washington, DC: National Evaluation Data and Technical Assistance Center.
Bogen, K.
  1996 The effect of questionnaire length on response rates—A review of the literature. In *Proceedings of the Section on Survey Research Methods.* Alexandria, VA: American Statistical Association.
Brick, J.M., M. Collins, and K. Chandler
  1997 *An Experiment in Random Digit Dial Screening.* Washington, DC: U.S. Department of Education, National Center for Education Statistics.
Brick, J.M., I. Flores-Cervantes, and D. Cantor
  1999 *1997 NSAF Response Rates and Methods Evaluation, Report No. 8.* NSAF Methodology Reports. Washington, DC: Urban Institute.
Camburn, D.P., P.J. Lavrakas, M.P. Battaglia, J.T. Massey, and R.A. Wright
  1995 Using Advance Respondent Letters in Random-Digit-Dialing-Telephone Surveys. Unpublished paper presented at the American Association for Public Opinion Research Conference; May 18-21, 1995; Fort Lauderdale, FL, May.
Cantor, D.
  1995 *Prevalence of Drug Use in the DC Metropolitan Area Juvenile and Adult Offender Populations: 1991.* Washington, DC: National Institute on Drug Abuse.
Cantor, D., P. Cunningham, and P. Giambo
  1999 The use of pre-paid incentives and express delivery on a Random Digit Dial Survey. Unpublished paper presented at the International Conference on Survey Nonresponse. Portland, October.
Cantor, D., and K. Wang
  1998 Correlates of Measurement Error when Screening on Poverty Status for a Random Digit Dial Survey. Unpublished paper presented at the meeting of American Statistical Association, Dallas, August.
Collins, M., W. Sykes, P. Wilson, and N. Blackshaw
  1988 Non-response: The UK experience. Pp. 213-232 in *Telephone Survey Methodology*, R.M. Groves, P.P. Biermer, L.E. Lyberg, J.T., Massey, W.L. Nicholls, and J. Waksberg, eds. New York: John Wiley and Sons.

Couper, M., R.M. Groves, and R.B. Cialdini
  1992   Understanding the decision to participate in a survey. *Public Opinion Quarterly* 56:475-
          495.
Dillman, D.
  1978   *Mail and Telephone Surveys: The Total Design Method.* New York: John Wiley and
          Sons.
Dillman, D., J.G. Gallegos, and J.H. Frey
  1976   Reducing refusal rates for telephone interviews. *Public Opinion Quarterly* 40:66-78.
Everett, S.E., and S.C. Everett
  1989   Effects of Interviewer Affiliation and Sex Upon Telephone Survey Refusal Rates. Paper
          presented at the Annual Conference of the Midwest Association for Public Opinion Re-
          search, Chicago.
Flores-Cervantes, I., J.M. Brick, T. Hankins, and K. Wang
  1999   Evaluation of the Use of Data on Interruption in Telephone Service. Unpublished paper
          presented at the meeting of American Statistical Association in Baltimore, August 5-12.
Frankel, M.R., K.P. Srinath, M.P. Battaglia, D.C. Hoaglin, R.A. Wright, and P.J. Smith
  1999   Reducing nontelephone bias in RDD surveys. Pp. 934-939 in *Proceedings of the Section
          on Survey Research Methods.* Alexandria, VA: American Statistical Association.
Goyder, J.
  1987   *The Silent Minority, Nonrespondents on Sample Surveys.* Cambridge, Eng.: Polity Press.
Groves, R., D. Cantor, K. McGonagle, and J. Van Hoewyk
  1997   Research Investigations in Gaining Participation from Sample Firms in the Current Em-
          ployment Statistics Program. Unpublished paper presented at the Annual Meeting of the
          American Statistical Association, Anaheim, CA, August 10-14.
Groves, R.M., and M.P. Couper
  1998   *Nonresponse in household interview surveys.* New York: John Wiley & Sons.
Groves, R., and N. Fultz
  1985   Gender effects among telephone interviewers in a survey of economic attributes. *Socio-
          logical Methods and Research* 14:31-52.
Groves, R.M., C. Cannell, and M. O'Neil
  1979   Telephone interview introductions and refusal rates: Experiments in increasing respon-
          dent cooperation. Pp. 252-255 in *Proceedings of the Section on Survey Research Meth-
          ods.* Alexandria, VA: American Statistical Association.
Keeter, S.
  1995   Estimating telephone noncoverage bias with a telephone survey. *Public Opinion Quar-
          terly* 59:196-217.
Massey, J., D. O'Connor, K. Krotki, and K. Chandler
  1998   An investigation of response rates in random digit dialing (RDD) telephone surveys. In
          Proceedings of the Section on Survey Research Methods. Alexandria, VA: American
          Statistical Association.
Moeller, J.F., and N.A. Mathiowetz
  1994   Problems of screening for poverty status. *Journal of Official Statistics* 10:327-337.
Oldendick, R.W., and M.W. Link
  1994   The answering machine generation: Who are they and what problem do they pose for
          survey research? *Public Opinion Quarterly* 58:264-273.
Sobal, J.
  1982   Disclosing information in interview introductions: Methodological consequences of in-
          formed consent. *Sociology and Social Research* 66:349-361.
Stapulonis, R.A., M. Kovac, and T.M. Fraker
  1999   *Surveying Current and Former TANF Recipients in Iowa.* Unpublished paper presented at
          the 21st Annual Research Conference of the Association for Public Policy Analysis and
          Management, Washington, DC: Mathematica Policy Research, Inc.

STORES
1995 Answering machines hold off voice mail challenge. *STORES* 77(11):38-39.

Thornberry, O.T., and J.T. Massey
1988 Trends in United States telephone coverage across time and subgroups. Pp. 25-50 in *Telephone Survey Methodology*, R.M. Groves, P.P. Biemer, L.E. Lyberg, J.T., Massey, W.L. Nicholls, J. Waksberg, eds. New York: Wiley.

Traugott, M., J. Lepkowski, and P. Weiss
1997 An Investigation of Methods for Matching RDD Respondents with Contact Information for Validation Studies. Unpublished paper presented at the Annual Meeting of the American Association for Public Opinion Research, Norfolk, VA, May 15-17.

Tuckel, P.S., and B.M. Feinberg
1991 The answering machine poses many questions for telephone survey researchers. *Public Opinion Quarterly* 55:200-217.

Tuckel, P., and H. O'Neil
1996 New technology and nonresponse bias in RDD surveys. Pp. 889-894 in *Proceedings of the Section on Survey Research Methods*. Alexandria, VA: American Statistical Association.

Xu, M., B. Bates, and J.C. Schweitzer
1993 The impact of messages on survey participation in answering machine households. *Public Opinion Quarterly* 57:232-237.

3

High Response Rates for Low-Income
Population In-Person Surveys

Charlene Weiss and Barbara A. Bailar

In this paper we will look at the context of interviewing low-income populations and the unique challenges presented to survey practitioners. Within that context, we will explore what data collection approaches can increase the likelihood of success in the pursuit of high response rates while staying within the limits of a project's budget and schedule. Finally, we will make some recommendations for future efforts in this arena.

THE CONTEXT

In the *Best Practices* booklet published by the American Association of Public Opinion Research (1997a) 1 of the 12 named "best practices" is to maximize cooperation or response rates within the limits of ethical treatment of human subjects (p. 5). In surveys concentrated on low-income populations, high response rates are especially important. In the past few years, there has been a great deal of interest in finding out what is happening to people after they leave the welfare rolls. Outside of the usual concern about nonrespondents causing a potential bias, there is often the need to stratify populations by their relationship to welfare systems. For example, though those that leave welfare are of great interest, so are the stayers, as are potential applicants diverted from programs or those who do not apply. If samples are to be large enough to make meaningful comparisons among groups, then nonresponse must be kept to a minimum.

Low-income populations are of special interest to survey practitioners. Whether one is doing a survey of employment, crime victimizations, health conditions, or health insurance status, the low-income population has an abundance of people who are having difficulty. In its most recent report on poverty, the U.S. Census Bureau reported that people who worked at any time during 1998 had a lower poverty rate than nonworkers (6.3 percent compared with 21.1 percent). The Census Bureau also recently reported that 16.3 percent of all people in the United States were without health insurance for the entire year of 1998, but that 32.3 percent of poor people were in that category (Campbell, 1999).

Of interest to the survey community are the statistics cited by Federal Communications Commission Chairman Reed Hundt about access to communication services in the United States. Of households on food stamps, roughly 30 percent have telephone service. In 1993, 27 percent of households with children and below the poverty line did not have phone service. About 12 percent of unemployed adults did not have phone service.

This lack of telephone service shows the importance of expanding the mode of data collection for low-income persons beyond telephone surveys. Nonresponse rates by income type show that refusals are lowest for low-income populations (Groves and Couper, 1998). However, those who are not contacted in surveys are clustered among those who are in the low-income groups. Groves and Couper show that in areas of high population density, more than 6 percent of the population were not contacted. In central cities, 7.2 percent were not contacted. When homeownership was below 48.5 percent, 4.9 percent were not contacted. In areas where minorities made up more than 8 percent of the population, the noncontact rate was 3.6 percent or higher. Therefore, when looking at income distributions, the high end would be underrepresented primarily because of refusals and the low income would be underrepresented because of noncontacts. If the low-income population is approached only by telephone, the nonresponse rates would be even higher because of the lower incidence of telephones among this population.

In-person efforts will be critical to achieving high response rates for people who have no usual residence, those who move frequently, those who have no telephones, and those who need some immediate gratification before they agree to be interviewed. Often, concepts and ideas can be explained easier when face to face.

The low-income populations of interest in surveys present some special challenges. They are often hard to find. Though they may have lived at a fixed address at one time, low-income people move often, mostly within the same neighborhood, but not always. Sometimes they live in regular housing until their money runs out, then live on the streets until the next influx of money. A survey organization must be prepared to spend resources locating respondents. Low-income respondents are often suspicious of strangers and the government. Often they do not want to be found. Names are not always given freely, nor are responses to where people can be found. In National Opinion Research Center (NORC) surveys, a common problem is that it is hard to make and keep appointments with potential respondents.

In addition, because of high immigration in the past 15 years, many people in the population do not speak English. In many surveys, people who do not speak English or Spanish are excluded. However, in surveys of low-income populations, these people with language barriers may be extremely important. Thus, a survey organization must be ready to find interviewers who speak the needed languages, and have a facility for translating questionnaires. Using a questionnaire translated into other languages brings additional problems. The translated version needs pretesting to make sure that the correct meaning is used and that the basic concepts have not been lost. To make these situations work, it is important to collaborate with the ethnic communities and enlist their help. This collaboration also can be helpful in gaining access to the communities so that respondents will cooperate. Some interesting work at the Census Bureau in a series of ethnographic studies (de la Puente, 1995) shows how a difference in meaning that affects responses can occur when there is not collaboration.

These special issues that arise in interviewing low-income populations all have appropriate solutions. Which of these solutions can be applied for a given survey will be dependent on budget, schedule, and Institutional Review Board (IRB) and Office of Management and Budget (OMB) constraints. NORC has conducted several studies of low-income populations and has been successful in interviewing them. This paper reviews the methods leading to success.

All the surveys referenced for this paper are list samples. (Note that the D.C. Networks Study used targeted chain referral sampling to build its list sample.) Five NORC surveys will be referenced to illustrate methods for finding and interviewing these populations. Response rates for the five surveys were all 75 percent or above. Indeed, in follow-up surveys of the same populations, rates higher than 90 percent were achieved in most instances.

To be most relevant for State grantees who are conducting or planning to conduct surveys of low-income and welfare populations, studies with the following characteristics are discussed: respondents are primarily from low-income and/or welfare populations; the sample is clustered within one area rather than being national; paper and pencil interviewing (PAPI) is the mode for all but one of the studies, which is computer-assisted personal interviewing (CAPI); extensive locating is required; and respondents are offered an incentive for participation. Note that the issues related to survey materials being available in multiple languages will not be addressed in this paper; only one of the studies referenced here offered Spanish-language materials, New York Minority Youth.

Each of the five studies used to illustrate NORC's approach to obtaining high response rates with low-income populations is based on a list sample and involves follow-up interviews. These seem most appropriate for people who wish to survey low-income and welfare populations. The lists came from a variety of sources, one of them compiled in the mid-1960s (Woodlawn Studies). List samples illustrate the importance of good methods of locating respondents, many of whom have moved. Each of the studies is confined to a specific area. Though

PAPI was used for four of the five studies, CAPI was used for one (D.C. Networks Study). The rationale behind the use of PAPI was either cost or speed. Some people fear that carrying laptops into areas where low-income people live is too dangerous, but NORC has not experienced problems. Laptop surveys in big cities are routinely conducted year-round. (Table 3-1 provides some basic information about the studies we will reference in the paper as: the Seattle Study, the Woodlawn Studies, the New York Minority Youth Study, and the D.C. Networks Study.)

NORC has adopted the following protocol outline for obtaining high response rates. It includes measures we have developed to: (1) locate and contact the sample; (2) staff and train interviewers; (3) optimize field support and communications; and (4) control budget and quality.

The following is a compilation of input regarding this topic from NORC's top field management team members who were actively involved in carrying out these studies successfully.

THE SAMPLE

List

Ideally, the sample list will be up to date, comprehensive, and accurate. However, most often it contains aged information provided by the client based on administrative records. The standard information—including full name, most recent address and phone number, and date of birth—can be enhanced by researching other ancillary information. This includes maiden name for women, driver's license or state identification number, employers, schools or training programs attended, military service, prison records, and persons likely to know where the sample member can be found (a parent, grandparent, close friend, or neighbor). Once obtained, it is essential that this augmenting information and its source be documented accurately for future reference.

Advance Letter

The initial correspondence to the respondent is a critical step toward gaining cooperation. It sets the tone of the survey and must compel participation. The advance letter should be straightforward and brief. Proprietary terms and legal jargon should be avoided. The letter explains the study and certifies that the interview: (1) will be strictly confidential; (2) is voluntary; and (3) will be conducted by a properly identified and trained interviewer. If a respondent fee will be provided it should be mentioned, and if such a fee can be exempt from income reporting by virtue of the client obtaining a waiver, that should be mentioned too. (A respondent fee is strongly recommended as a method of assuring maximum response rates.) A toll-free telephone number is supplied in the letter to permit the respondent to ask questions and/or set up an interview.

TABLE 3-1 Listing of Representative Surveys of Low-Income Population

Study Name and Dates of Data Collection Activities	Location	Sample	Questionnaire Length	Percentage of Response Rates	Respondent Incentives	Mode
Seattle Study 1996-1999	King County, Washington	571 for baseline list sample	45-60 minutes	75 baseline 90-97 on each of four follow-ups	$40-interview $5-urine specimen	PAPI
Woodlawn Study 1992-1993	Lived in Woodlawn neighborhood of Chicago in 1966 and 1967	1,242 African American respondents list sample	90 minutes (avg.)	85	$25	PAPI, some telephone interviews
Woodlawn Mothers 1996-1997	Subsample of mothers of original 1966-67 sample	1,026 African American mothers list sample	90 minutes (avg.)	79	$25	PAPI, some telephone interviews
New York Minority Youth 1994-1996	East Harlem area of New York City; respondents were 7th-10th graders in 1990	1,330 youth, 666 mothers; African American and Puerto Rican list sample	75 minutes-youth 75 minutes-mother	92	$25-youth $25-mother	PAPI
D.C. Networks Study 1997-present	Washington, D.C., area	500 cases; targeted chain referral sampling for baseline, now list sample	90-120 minutes (CAPI) 30-180 minutes (ethnographic)	86 baseline 82 and 62 on follow-ups one and two	$20-CAPI $20-ethnographic interview	CAPI and ethnographic interviews

The advance letter serves another valuable purpose: to update preliminary locating information. The envelope is marked "Address Service Requested." This statement will result in the post office providing information about the address/person; if the post office forwards the mail to another address, it will provide notification of that new address. For all other mail that does not go directly to the addressee, the mail is sent back with the reason for return, such as a missing apartment number, transposed street numbers, or lack of forwarding address. If one prefers that the letter not be forwarded, the envelope can be marked "Do Not Forward" and it will be returned, allowing it to be remailed to the correct address. Names and addresses from returned letters can be submitted in batch mode through the National Change of Address if time allows. Recent experience shows that this latter approach is more useful when the sample is quite outdated, namely 5 years or more. When time and budget allow, it also helps to work the "unlocatables" through centralized database searches. The sample file should be updated with any leads obtained through this prefield stage; releasing the sample to interviewers without having made the updates will result in extra costs caused by duplicated efforts.

Community Authority Contacts

Informing and/or gaining the support of influential community leaders can be pivotal to the success of the survey. Letters to the local police, Better Business Bureau, ethnic leaders in the National Association for the Advancement of Colored People (NAACP) or Hispanic Council, housing authorities, and others serve two important purposes. They provide a sense of security to the interviewer, who then knows that appropriate officials have been notified. Respondents can be shown the letter as a reenforcement measure. The leaders, in turn, often supply essential strategic information regarding places to avoid, whether an escort is justified, and safest times to interview. The letter to community authorities should explain the survey, in addition to how and by whom the interviews will be conducted. It assures them that interviewers will wear photo identification badges.

Locating

NORC has established and maintains a locating protocol that documents, in order of cost, the basic steps involved in locating people. The locating effort, critical to any project's success, is influenced by budget, schedule, IRB and/or OMB constraints, and the locating skills of the project's assigned staff. Therefore, emphasis is placed on centralizing the process before employing the more costly means of in-field locating. Depending on available resources, the centralization of locating can be in a central/home office or in the field (if locating experts equipped with computers that can access the relevant databases and the Internet are available). Centralizing this locating effort allows efficient access to the resources to do the preliminary work of checking phone directories, mailing addresses, contact names, employers, and other information. Field staff are then called on to personally visit the last known address and talk to neighbors, the mail carrier, and others. Interviewers document the results of each locating step on a Record of Calls. Many projects provide the field interviewers with a job aid, referred to as a Locating Checklist. It identifies the steps to be taken by the field in locating a respondent, listing the steps in order of cost. This greatly reduces duplication of effort.

The Seattle Study Experience

The respondents in the Seattle Study were first interviewed in their final month of eligibility for drug-addicted or alcoholic Supplemental Security Income (SSI). The baseline sample information included the identity of a payee to whom the prospective respondent's SSI check was sent. Because many of the payees were agency staff, the interviewers often were able to work directly with the payee to determine when the respondent would be coming in to pick up the check. The agency often let the interviewer have space to interview the respondent at the time of that visit.

However, because of the nature of the sample, there were large numbers of respondents who were homeless. The field manager obtained a list of all the agencies that serviced the homeless and went in person to each place with a list of names. Interviewers made daily visits to many of these locations and eventually found many respondents. The field staff worked diligently to identify the extensive homeless network in the area; they asked homeless people questions such as where they slept, where they got their meals, and where they kept their belongings. This effort proved beneficial during the baseline interview as well as during the follow-ups, which were done at 6-month intervals to examine the effects of the program's termination on former recipients. During this process, the field staff found it is important to learn a respondent's "street" name, because many of them do not go by their legal, given names out in the community. Field staff on this study believed it would be helpful, if possible, to obtain IRB/OMB approval for the interviewer to take a snapshot of the respondent that could be used during subsequent locating efforts.

Also, because all the respondents were in the study because their alcohol- and/or drug-related SSI benefits had been discontinued, another potential locating source was expected to be area taverns. The field manager in charge organized night-time locating trips into the areas of Seattle where the homeless gather. Two or three field interviewers would travel with the field manager into the core area of the city searching for respondents among those waiting in line for entrance into a shelter for the night, or among those patrons in the taverns and bars frequented by street people. These "pub crawls," as the field interviewers called them, were very helpful in locating homeless respondents.

Prisons and jails were another valuable source for locating respondents. On the Seattle Study, a census of all the jails was available. Interviewers checked the list regularly looking for names that matched the pending sample list. Some interviewers were able to obtain special IDs after agreeing to a background check done by the jail. These IDs allowed the interviewers to come and go just as lawyers do, and their visits did not impact on the respondent's allowed number of visitations. To access prisons, in some cases, the client for the Seattle Study had to complete the requisite paperwork before the interviewers could approach incarcerated respondents. On the D.C. Networks Study, a significant effort was made to gain access to the prison system by working closely with the D.C. Department of Corrections. One experienced field person on that study who was particularly effective was a private investigator before joining the interviewer and field management staff at NORC. Protocols related to working in jails and prisons vary considerably by state, so it is important to determine the kinds of access that interviewers will be allowed at the outset of the data collection period. Many states now have a Web site and/or telephone number for locating inmates.

On the Woodlawn Studies in which the original respondents were first graders enrolled in elementary school in an inner-city, predominantly African American urban neighborhood in 1966 and 1967, the locating challenges were enormous. The client had made interim contacts with some respondents, but much of the sample information was very old, so the field staff relied on intensive locating efforts in the neighborhood. They went to the neighborhood and tried to locate the oldest residents on the block, visited neighborhood churches to talk with long-time members, called people with the same last name living in the place of birth to look for relatives of the respondent, and mailed letters to every old address and every new address they found. With regard to the last step, they mailed again and again if not returned by the post office; their persistence often paid off as many respondents moved back to their hometown during the course of the fieldwork.

On the New York Minority Youth Study, a useful locating resource was the schools that respondents had attended. Because the baseline data were collected in the school setting, the client contacted the schools to obtain permission to contact them for locating information. The follow-up interviews were with a sample of inner-city African American and Puerto Rican adolescents and their mothers. Prison contacting was also helpful for this population.

On the D.C. Networks Study, where 62 percent of the respondents have a monthly income of $500 or less, 63 percent have been drug injectors for more than 21 years, and only 50 percent have lived in an apartment or house during the past 6 months—the locating challenges for follow-up have been intense. This is a study in which two outreach workers who are "street wise" and know a lot about the locations where drugs are sold and used, identify respondents in the streets and bring them into the site office to be interviewed. The experienced field staff on the study (four interviewers, a locating expert, and a field site manager) also work on the case, locating by phone or in the field, but they leave the locating in "drug areas" to the outreach workers.

TABLE 3-2 Locating Methods Used

Locating Effort/Source	Seattle Study	Woodlawn Studies	N.Y. Minority Youth	D.C. Networks Study
Probation/parole officers	x			x
Doormen/guards at building complexes				x
Known contacts, such as family members, case workers	x	x	x	x
Last known address	x	x	x	x
Jails/detention centers/prisons	x	x	x	x
Halfway houses	x			x
Clinics	x			x
Hospitals, regular and rehabilitation	x			x
Drug treatment centers	x			x
Known geographical areas for drug purchase/use	x			x
Homeless shelters	x			x
Schools			x	x
Churches	x	x		
Food banks	x			
Old neighborhood	x	x	x	x
Needle exchanges	x			

Table 3-2 indicates some of the specific locating resources that were used during these representative studies.

STAFFING AND TRAINING

Data Collection Plan

Optimum results are more likely to be achieved when the data collection plan reflects both the theoretical underpinnings of the client's research goals and data needs and the best practices of the data collection contractor. Such a plan should be preapproved by the client and precisely match the resources available. This avoids any misunderstanding of what can reasonably be provided by the contractor within the time and budget allowed. Also, as the work proceeds it is important to be in close contact with the client, to share successes and obstacles encountered. Contingency planning within the constraints of the research goals must be addressed in a timely manner.

For example, the Seattle Study was tasked to begin on short notice, with no flexibility on the start date. It had to be started before the respondent's SSI benefits ended, then completed as quickly as possible. A data collection plan was rapidly developed and approved by all parties, thus avoiding any ensuing disagreements regarding production results.

On the Woodlawn Studies, the client was very supportive and even helped with gaining access to some records for locating purposes. She met with the field staff whenever she was in Chicago if her schedule permitted. When production was low, she remained optimistic and reminded the staff how important their efforts were to her research. The sense of team camaraderie on these projects has been unrivaled on other studies and contributed to an outcome that was satisfactory to the client, even though more time than originally projected was needed to reach the final completion rates of 85 percent on the Woodlawn Study and 79 percent on the Woodlawn Mothers.

Recruitment

Key to assigning interviewers who are appropriate to low-income and welfare populations is the recognition that unique attributes are needed. Not all interviewers, even experienced ones, are equally effective in this environment. Screening prospective interviewers begins in the help wanted ad. It must specifically state that the job entails interviewing low income persons in their residences or elsewhere out in the field. The fact that the work will require some evenings and weekends must be understood. Supplying this information beforehand will avoid any misconceptions that may occur later.

During the job interview, it is important that applicants be evaluated on their ability to be nonjudgmental in the situations to which they may be exposed. If the content of the questionnaire is sensitive, it is useful to show candidates a sample of the questions. Some candidates will eliminate themselves, knowing they would be uncomfortable asking these kinds of questions. Successful candidates, both experienced and new to interviewing, will be comfortable with the gaining cooperation aspect of the job. When conducting exit interviews with interviewers who have left a project, one of the frequently mentioned reasons for leaving relates to the "door-to-door sales" aspect of interviewing; they often did not realize how difficult that preinterview step could be and were not up for the challenge or the rejection that can be associated with slammed doors or hung-up phones.

NORC experience with studies involving hard-to-reach populations and/or sensitive topics supports the findings by Groves and Couper that experienced interviewers are more adept at gaining cooperation than inexperienced interviewers. Those who thrive in the interviewing environment see these situations as personal challenges to which they apply their skills gained from earlier experiences.

> To select an approach to use, the interviewer must judge the fit of the respondent to other respondent types experienced in the past (either through descriptions in training or actual interaction with them). We believe that experienced interviewers tend to achieve higher levels of cooperation because they carry with them a larger number of combinations of behaviors proven to be effective for one or more types of householders. (Groves and Couper, 1988:36)

On the D.C. Networks Study, all the interviewers have had experience working in difficult neighborhoods or previous studies in the D.C. area. The experienced locating specialist has been helping them to gain access to prisons and has been doing a great deal of street locating.

Training

Interviewers must be well versed in basic interviewing techniques, including reading questions as worded, neutral probing, "training" the respondent, and confidentiality. At NORC, these basic topics are covered in an eight hour general interviewing techniques training session, which is required of all interviewers new to NORC. In the recent literature on obtaining high response rates, Sullivan et al. (1966) put forth a retention protocol for conducting longitudinal studies with mobile populations that includes three phases, the first of which is relevant to training. In Phase I of their retention protocol (which relates to setting the stage for future contacts with the respondents) Sullivan et al. refer to the importance of establishing trust between the researcher and the respondent (1996:266). To accomplish this, interviewers need to be able to convey to respondents why the survey is needed and how it might impact others in similar circumstances, stress confidentiality of data, and so on. Ensuring that interviewers understand these basics is important to the quality of the data being collected.

Project-specific training then focuses on the purpose of the study, the questionnaire, the informed consent procedure, gaining cooperation, sensitivity, safety, production goals, and other areas. When a project has unique protocols for locating, such as in a study of battered women conducted by Sullivan and colleagues, this is the forum where such procedures would be covered. They had the respondent sign "a Release of Information form indicating that she gave her permission to the alternate contact to give us her address and phone number. Each participant receiving governmental assistance was also asked to sign a release form for the government agency handling her case." This is a protocol that has been used successfully at NORC, primarily on drug study follow-up interviews. Contacts are more comfortable knowing (by actually seeing the respondent's signature on the form) that the respondent has given permission to help locate them.

Training on gaining respondent cooperation is essential on all types of studies, and is best provided when woven throughout the training session, rather than just being covered directly in a module of its own. The ultimate goal in this type of training is to enhance the interviewer's abilities to tailor his or her reaction to the respondent and to maintain interaction with the respondent long enough to gain cooperation. (See Groves and Couper, 1998, Chapter 9, for elaboration on the concepts of tailoring and maintaining interaction.) During training, interviewers practice their approach to gaining cooperation through role playing. They are encouraged to rely on all "tools" provided by the study. For example, each of the five NORC studies referenced in this paper offered an important tool for gaining cooperation, namely, respondent incentives (see Table 3-1). Interviewers report that when a survey involves a long questionnaire that focuses on sensitive topics, as each of these surveys did, incentives make their task of gaining cooperation/ averting refusals significantly easier.

Sensitivity training often is appropriate to prepare interviewers for the situations they may encounter. It is designed to help them respond respectfully to the respondents with whom they will interact and to make them "unshockable." Sensitivity training typically covers some background information about the kinds of situations likely to be encountered. The presentation of this information can be done by the principal investigator, an outside expert, or an experienced senior-level field manager. On a study of the terminally ill, for example, the principal investigators talked with the interviewers at training; the interviewers saw a videotape about terminal illness and its effect on the respondent and his or her family; and grief counseling was available to field staff during the course of data collection. In addition to providing interviewers with substantive background, the training often provides opportunities to help the trainees to deal with the emotional responses they are likely to experience themselves and to handle those reactions in the interview situation. On some studies, the field staff are invited to attend special conference sessions prior to the study's implementation. For example, field staff working on the D.C. Networks Study, attended an HIV conference to make them more aware of the types of situations facing potential respondents.

Traveling Interviewers

Supplementing local interviewers with a team of highly experienced traveling interviewers is a strategy that has been successful and cost effective on these studies. This is especially true when the sample is clustered and therefore requires a large number of newly hired interviewers. It is also particularly valuable if the data collection period is very short. On the Seattle Study, several experienced travelers came in at the start of the data collection period. When some of them had to leave, others came in to assume their assignments. Throughout the data collection period, the local field staff worked together with the travelers. NORC experience shows that seasoned travelers can focus on weak data collection areas and apply their proven skills in locating, refusal conversion, and strong production. They also help to motivate and train local interviewers, providing role models of success for new interviewers to emulate. This modeling is especially important when the number of refusals from respondents grows during the field period. Experienced interviewers can describe and/or demonstrate (in the field and/or in role plays) how they prepare for and approach respondents who have refused at least once. They help the less experienced interviewers to move beyond experiencing refusals as personal attacks and turn the focus back onto the importance of the study, the production goals, and how to use the information obtained and recorded in the call notes for each case. Successful interviewers see each problem case as a personal challenge and help convey that state of mind to less experienced interviewers.

SUPPORT AND COMMUNICATIONS

Supervision

Supporting and motivating field staff on low-income studies can differ markedly from the traditional methods used on a national study with a mixed sample. Assigning strong, experienced supervisors with field interviewing expertise is key to achieving high response rates. Interviewers need continual support, brainstorming opportunities, motivation, locating assistance, and morale boosting from involved and caring supervisors. Supervisors must:

(1) Communicate by phone with interviewers no less than twice a week, or more often if indicated.

(2) Discuss numbers, projections, costs, and disposition codes for cases during one call, and have a completely separate call for problem solving. The second call is for question-and-answer periods and problem solving, uninterrupted by the administrative process.

(3) Offer to do locating through central office or Internet sources or to help convert refusals. Managers sometimes can do phone interviews for interviewers on projects that allow it.

(4) Pair up new interviewers or ones hesitant to interview during late hours with experienced interviewers or escorts. (For example, traveling interpreters worked with interviewers who needed to interview Chinese, Vietnamese, and other ethnic groups on the recent Media Use Study.)

(5) Readily transfer cases around once the interviewers have established a work pattern. Supervisors must be quick to recognize procrastinators and replace them with more effective interviewers. This also helps to motivate less productive persons to improve and increase their efforts. Some interviewers prove to be more effective on the telephone than in person, so flexibility is key.

Supervisors also should be adept at refusal aversion, refusal conversion, and locating in order to help interviewers strategize effectively.

Site Office

A centrally located site office, whether for the duration of the study or just during the startup and the final crunch phase of the data collection effort, has proven beneficial. On the Woodlawn Studies, the field management staff were based at an office at NORC's University of Chicago location. This office was set up with multiple telephone lines to allow for centralized locating and some telephone interviewing by the field staff. On the New York Minority Youth Study, the office was set up in client-provided space at Columbia University. On the D.C. Networks Study, a permanent office is set up in a storefront centrally located to the sample members. On the Seattle Study, the site office was set up at the hotel where training was held and the travelers stayed; for the baseline interviewing it was maintained and staffed for the entire data collection period, whereas for the other rounds of interviewing it was set up for training and maintained for the first couple of weeks of data collection. After that the interviewers were supervised remotely, although the supervisor visited at least a few times to meet with field interviewers. There were travelers (experienced interviewers) in for the entire data collection period, although they were not the same individuals during the entire time.

In many studies the site office served to make interviewers more responsible and provided supervisors with greater flexibility to transfer cases and assignments when necessary. Interviewers were required to submit their Time & Expense Reports in person together with their completed cases. This closely tied pay to production and receipt control. Site offices also permitted supervisors to review Records of Calls and do the strategy planning face to face with interviewers.

On the New York Minority Youth Study, the front-line field manager believed that having a site office for the field interviewers helped in many ways. The respondent population was very transient, presenting multiple locating, refusal aversion, and conversion problems. Having a site itself lent a "helping hand" to interviewers who were not strong in these areas. The site office also provided a physical opportunity to brainstorm and share successful approaches with peers. Where one interviewer may have been unsuccessful with a certain case, the field manager could have another interviewer share his or her experience with similar cases or transfer that case for another approach. The field manager believed another benefit of the site office was in the team pressure it created. Interviewers had the opportunity to "shine" in person when they had a great week, and those who were not as successful felt pressured to perform better the following week.

Communications

Field managers on all projects know they are expected to be available to their interviewers 7 days a week. However, on some of these studies that expectation was intensified. On the Seattle Study, for example, a communication link between the field manager and the interviewers was needed 7 days a week and 24 hours a day. Respondents were given a toll-free number that was staffed by the senior field manager in charge who could page any of the interviewers if a respondent called and wanted an appointment. On this study, all interviewers had pagers, and the toll-free number was set up with three-way calling, caller ID, call waiting, and other features. This allowed the supervisor to contact an interviewer while she had a respondent on the phone and set up an appointment on the spot. Cellular phones would have been even more efficient, but at the time they were too costly to rent.

Teamwork

Support also comes in the form of working together in teams, during either the interviewing or the locating phases. The team could include a field supervisor or experienced traveler who can model an effective approach at the door and gain cooperation when new interviewers are unsure of themselves. It also can involve sending both a male and a female interviewer to an area where the female interviewer alone might be uncomfortable. The team effort also can be invoked for a "blitz" when all of the interviewers and supervisors work together to finish up specific cases.

BUDGET CONTROL/QUALITY CONTROL

Successful containment of costs requires strict measures and frequent monitoring. Senior field staff are involved in developing the proposal and the associated budget. During this process, alternative options and tradeoffs are discussed until all are in agreement on priorities and budget caps. Contingency plans, in keeping with the client's objectives, must be in place. Field staff are then provided with a budget they helped formulate and are given the responsibility to manage it.

During the Woodlawn Studies, when the locating became more time consuming than expected, the client extended the field period to give the field staff more time. When extending the data collection period may not be feasible, as was the case during the baseline interviewing for the Seattle Study, other contingencies were adopted, such as keeping the travelers on site longer than anticipated originally. Others included the need for attrition training if interviewers dropped out for one reason or another, lowering targeted response goals, and so on.

The pressures imposed on the interviewers in a study characterized by a short field period, low budget, and difficult-to-locate respondents increase the importance of quality control efforts. It is essential to conduct validation interviews for at least 10 percent of each interviewer's cases, sampling from completed cases as well as noninterviews. If possible, especially if there is a site office, plan to have supervisors observe some of the interviewing. This step displays their interest in quality control.

RECOMMENDATIONS

The protocol described in this paper for obtaining high response rates in in-person surveys of low-income and welfare populations (summarized in Box 3-1) includes, but goes beyond, the factors identified by Gordon et al. as being important in follow-up surveys of low-income populations: initial contact information; updating of contact information; sophisticated tracking methods; mixed-mode interviewing; and respondent payments (Gordon et al., 1992). To those factors, the NORC approach adds effective field staffing; training with appropriate emphasis placed on the gaining cooperation tasks; and strong field support. Without identifying and deploying the resources to collect the data in the most supportive manner, even the best sample information will not result in a completed interview. The people involved in the actual data collection tasks are key, from the field interviewers to the field supervisors to the support staff in the home office. Groves and Couper's (1998) concepts of tailoring and maintaining interaction support our recommendations. In terms of the staffing approach, the most effective field staff are expert at tailoring their approach to respondents; staffing as many experienced field interviewers as possible and/or supplementing a staff of less experienced interviewers with experienced travelers is important. On the training front, it is important to cover issues related to training the respondent and gaining cooperation, along with examples and opportunities for practice, throughout the course of training. On the field support front, having a site office where interviewers and field managers can interact in person and brainstorm and allow early intervention if a problem is developing further supports the opportunities for interviewers to learn how important tailoring and maintaining interaction can be.

Finally, because of cost constraints, we recognize that face-to-face interviewing is not going to be affordable in many cases. Therefore, we strongly recommend that more focus be given to planned mixed-mode studies, acknowledging that high response rates by mail or telephone are very difficult and potentially miss key parts of this population, such as the homeless and other respondents who move frequently or those who lack phones. Part of a successful mixed-mode model would include approaches such as collaborative locating efforts with agency staff to help cut locating costs; adaptation of a Release of Information form for use with locating contacts (Sullivan et al., 1996:267); use of respondent incentives; and perhaps even "piggybacking" of some data collection that could offer a more cost-effective way to obtain additional data.

BOX 3-1
Key Elements in Obtaining High Response Rates in In-Person Studies

Locating and Contacting the Sample

Quality of the list sample: Prior to fielding the sample, make any effort possible to update the list. Collaboration with the client often can be very beneficial.

Use of advance letter: Interviewers report that an advance letter sent to the respondent helps to emphasize the legitimacy and importance of the survey, thus becoming a "tool" in their gaining cooperation kit.

Community authority contacts: Interviewers feel supported and safer when a project alerts community authorities of the study and their presence in the community.

Locating: Resources devoted to locating efforts, both centralized and in the field, are essential for obtaining high completion rates with low-income populations. Putting together a cost-effective locating protocol is key because it is easy to spend a great deal on these efforts.

Staffing and Training Interviewers

Data collection plan: It is important that the researchers and data collection staff consult about the feasibility of any proposed data collection strategies.

Recruiting field interviewers: Careful screening and selection criteria applied by experienced field recruiters are critical. Not all interviewers, even those who are experienced, are effective working with low-income populations.

Training: Training for interviewers should cover basic interviewing techniques, project-specific topics, and sensitivity training. It should be ongoing throughout data collection and focus on the needs that emerge, such as dealing with refusals.

REFERENCES

American Association for Public Opinion Research
   1997a   Best Practices for Survey and Public Opinion Research. Available: http://www.aapor.org/ethics/best.htmlc
   1997b   Survey Practices That AAPOR Condemns. Available: http://www.aapor.org/ethics/condemn.html and end of data collection, it can be a positive impact on production.
Breakwell, Glynis M., Sean Hammond, and Chris Fife-Schaw, eds.
   1995   *Research Methods in Psychology.* London: Sage Publications.
Campbell, J.
   1999   Health insurance coverage. *Current Population Reports,* P-60(208):1-8.
Day, Neil Atherton, David Dunt, and Susan Day
   1995   Maximizing response to surveys in health program evaluation at minimum cost using multiple methods. *Evaluation Review* 19(4):436-450.

Use of experienced, traveling interviewers: Although this may seem counterintuitive on a survey with limited data collection funds, NORC's experience has shown that such a strategy can be cost effective if planned from the outset and managed carefully.

Optimizing Field Support and Communication

Field supervision: Use experienced field supervisors who have experience working successfully with low-income populations. Make sure the budget allows for close supervision, not just taking reports.

Site office: When the sample is clustered, setting up a site office can be very effective for motivating interviewers to stay on task. Even when the site is set up only temporarily, such as at the beginning and end of data collection, it can be a positive impact on production.

Communications: Be available to interviewers beyond regular business hours. Depending on the schedule and sample, consider use of beepers, cell phones, and other communications methods.

Teamwork: Interviewers are more likely to be successful if they feel they are part of a team and have contact with that team during the data collection period, even if just via conference calls.

Controlling Budget and Quality

Budget: Review the budget on a regular basis.

Contingency plans: Have contingency plans ready for implementation in case original budget assumptions don't hold.

Quality control: Don't skimp on quality control; be sure to validate a percentage of each interviewer's cases, both completes and noninterviews.

de la Puente, Manuel
   1995   Using ethnography to explain why people are missed or erroneously included by the census: Evidence from small-area ethnographic studies. In *Proceedings of the Section on Survey Research Methods.* Alexandria, VA: American Statistical Association.
Gordon, Anne, Jonathan Jacobson, and Thomas Fraker
   1996   Approaches to Evaluating Welfare Reform: Lessons from Five State Demonstrations. Unpublished report submitted to Office of the Assistant Secretary for Planning and Evaluation at the U.S. Department of Health and Human Services by Mathematica Policy Research, Inc. Contract #06587-005.
Groves, Robert M., and Mick P. Couper
   1998   *Non-Response in Household Interview Surveys.* New York: John Wiley and Sons.
Lannon, Larry
   1995   *Telephony* 229(22):76.

National Governors' Association, National Conference of State Legislatures, and the American Public Human Services Association

    1998   Tracking Welfare Reform: Designing Follow-Up Studies of Recipients Who Leave Welfare. Issue brief based on Conference on Tracking and Follow-up Under Welfare Reform, Falls Church, VA, February. Prepared by the Center for Best Practices. Available: http://www.nga.org/Pubs/IssueBriefs/1998/980519TrackingWelfare.asp [Accessed August 2, 1999].

Oueulette, T.

    1999   Conducting Surveys with Welfare Leavers. Unpublished paper provided as background to the Fall 1999 Welfare Outcomes Grantee Meeting of the U.S. Department of Health and Human Services, Office of the Assistant Secretary for Planning and Evaluation, Washington, DC, October 25-26.

Rennison, Callie

    1999   *Bureau of Justice Statistics, National Crime Victimization Survey, Criminal Victimization 1998, Changes 1997-98 with Trends 1993-98.* Washington, DC: U.S. Department of Justice.

Sullivan, Cris, Maureen Rumptz, Rebecca Campbell, Kimberly Eby, and William Davidson, II

    1996   Retaining participants in longitudinal community research: A comprehensive protocol. *Journal of Applied Behavioral Science*, 32(3):262-276.

Wisconsin Department of Workforce Development

    1999   Tracing and Representativeness of Responses. Unpublished paper prepared for the Fall 1999 Welfare Outcomes Grantee Meeting of the U.S. Department of Health and Human Services, Office of the Assistant Secretary for Planning and Evaluation, Washington, DC, October 25-26.

4

Paying Respondents for Survey Participation

Eleanor Singer and Richard A. Kulka

THE PROBLEM: SURVEYING LOW-INCOME POPULATIONS

To evaluate the effects of recent changes in welfare policy on the lives of people living at or below the poverty level, it is often necessary to survey a representative sample. As the chapter in this volume by Groves and Couper makes clear, achieving such a representative sample can be problematic both because members of low-income groups are hard to locate—they are more mobile, more likely to live in multifamily households, and less likely than the more affluent to have telephones—and because they may not be highly motivated to participate in surveys. Incentives—especially monetary incentives—are particularly useful in countering the second difficulty, as a supplement or complement to other efforts at persuasion. In this paper, we briefly consider why people participate in surveys (or fail to do so) and then review the use of incentives in counteracting certain kinds of nonresponses. We also review separately those findings that appear to be particularly relevant for low-income populations. Finally, we consider two special issues: The potential consequences of refusal conversion payments for respondents and interviewers, and the cost effectiveness of prepaid incentives.

Why Do People Participate in Surveys?

Porst and von Briel (1995) point out that although a great deal is known about survey respondents—their demographic characteristics, as well as their answers to thousands of different survey questions—little is known about why they choose to participate. Based on a content analysis of open-ended responses, their study of 140 participants in 5 waves of a German Methods Panel identifies 3 pure types of participants: (1) those who respond for altruistic reasons (e.g., the survey is useful for some purpose important to the respondent, or the respondent is fulfilling a social obligation—31 percent of respondents); (2) those who respond for survey-related reasons (e.g., they are interested in the survey topic, or find the interviewer appealing—38 percent); and (3) those who cite what the authors call personal reasons (e.g., they promised to do it—30 percent). In reality, of course, most people participate for a variety of reasons.

More recently, Groves et al. (2000) outlined a theory describing the decision to participate in a survey as resulting from a series of factors—some survey specific, such as topic and sponsorship, others person specific, such as concerns about privacy, still others specific to the respondent's social and physical environment—each of which may move a particular person toward or away from cooperation with a specific survey request. Furthermore, these factors assume different weights for different persons, and they become salient for a specific individual—the potential respondent—when an interviewer calls to introduce the survey and request participation.

From this perspective, monetary as well as nonmonetary incentives are an inducement offered by the survey designer to compensate for the relative absence of factors that might otherwise stimulate cooperation—for example, interest in the survey topic or a sense of civic obligation. Although other theoretical frameworks such as social exchange theory (cf. Dillman, 1978), the norm of reciprocity (Gouldner, 1960), and economic exchange (e.g., Biner and Kidd, 1994) also can be used to explain the effectiveness of incentives, the present perspective is able to account for the differential effects of incentives under different conditions (e.g., for respondents with differing interest in the survey topic or with different degrees of community activism) in a way that other theories cannot easily do.

Incentives and Hard-to-Reach Populations

As indicated above, members of a group may be hard to interview both because they are difficult to locate or to find at home and because they have little motivation to participate in a survey. There is no empirical evidence that incentives are helpful in overcoming the first problem in a random digit dial (RDD) survey, nor any theoretical justification for believing that they would or should be. Thus, if the primary problem is one of finding people at home for such a survey, incentives may not be very useful. However, an experiment by Kerachsky and Mallar (1981) with a sample of economically disadvantaged youth suggests that prepayment may be helpful in locating members of a *list* sample, especially in later waves of a longitudinal survey. One reason, apparently, is that prepayment (and perhaps promised incentives from a trusted source) may be useful in persuading friends or relatives to forward the survey organization's advance letter or to provide interviewers with a current telephone number for the designated respondent.

The remainder of this chapter is devoted to reviewing the evidence pertaining to the second reason for survey nonresponse—namely, the situation in which the respondent has little intrinsic motivation to respond to the survey request. This situation is likely to characterize many low-income respondents, especially those who no longer receive welfare payments because of changes in federal and state legislation. Hence, the findings reported in this chapter about the effectiveness of prepaid monetary incentives are especially likely to apply to this population.

WHAT DO WE KNOW ABOUT THE EFFECTS OF INCENTIVES?

In this section we review what is known about the *intended* effects of incentives on response rates in mail as well as interviewer-mediated surveys, drawing on two existing meta- analyses (Church, 1993; Singer et al., 1999a) as well as subsequent work by the same and other authors. We specifically consider the usefulness of lotteries as an incentive and the use of incentives in panel studies. We also review what is known about *unintended* consequences of incentives such as effects on item nonresponse and response bias.

Effects on Response Rates

In an effort to counter increasing tendencies toward noncooperation, survey organizations are offering incentives to respondents with increasing frequency, some at the outset of the survey, as has been done traditionally in mail surveys, and some only after the person has refused, in an attempt to convert the refusal.

The use of incentives has a long history in mail surveys (for reviews, see Armstrong, 1975; Church, 1999; Cox, 1976; Fox et al.,1988; Heberlein and Baumgartner, 1978; Kanuk and Berenson, 1975; Levine and Gordon, 1958; Linsky, 1975; Yu and Cooper, 1983). In such surveys, incentives are one of two factors, the other being number of contacts, that have been found to increase response rates consistently.

A meta-analysis of the experimental literature on the effects of incentives in mail surveys by Church (1999) classifies incentives along two dimensions: whether the incentive is a monetary or nonmonetary reward, and whether it is offered with the initial mailing or made contingent on the return of the questionnaire. Analyzing 38 mail surveys, Church concluded that:

• Prepaid incentives yield higher response rates than promised incentives;
• The offer of contingent (promised) money and gifts does not significantly increase response rates;

- Prepaid monetary incentives yield higher response rates than gifts offered with the initial mailing; and
- Response rates increase with increasing amounts of money.

Studies using prepaid monetary incentives yielded an average increase in response rates of 19.1 percentage points, representing a 65-percent average increase in response. Gifts, on the other hand, yielded an average increase of only 7.9 percentage points. The average value of the monetary incentive in the *mail surveys* analyzed by Church was $1.38 (in 1989 dollars); the average value of the gift could not be computed, given the great diversity of gifts offered and the absence of information on their cost. Reports similar to those of Church are reported by Hopkins and Gullikson (1992).

Incentives are also used increasingly in telephone and face-to-face surveys, and the question arises as to whether their effects differ from those found consistently in mail surveys. A meta-analysis of 39 experiments by Singer et al. (1999a) indicates that they do not, although the percentage point gains per dollar expended are much smaller, on average (and the levels of incentives paid significantly higher), than those reported by Church. Their main findings are as follows:

- Incentives improve response rates in telephone and face-to-face surveys, and their effect does not differ by mode of interviewing. Each dollar of incentive paid results in about a third of a percentage point difference between the incentive and the zero-incentive condition. As in the analyses by Church (1999) and Yu and Cooper (1983), the effects of incentives are linear: within the range of incentives used, the greater the incentive, the greater the difference in response rates between the lowest and the higher incentive conditions.
- Prepaid incentives result in higher response rates than promised incentives, but the difference is not statistically significant. However, prepaid monetary incentives resulted in significantly higher response rates in the four studies in which it was possible to compare prepaid and promised incentives within the same study.
- Money is more effective than a gift, even controlling for the value of the incentive.
- Increasing the burden of the interview increases the difference in response rates between an incentive and a zero-incentive condition. However, incentives have a significant effect even in low-burden studies.
- Incentives have significantly greater effects in surveys where the response rate without an incentive is low. That is, they are especially useful in compensating for the absence of other motives to participate. They are also most effective in the absence of other persuasion efforts. A number of studies have found that the difference in response rates between the group that received the incentive and the group that did not receive an incentive diminished after repeated follow-up attempts.

Lotteries as Incentives

Some researchers, convinced of the value of incentives but reluctant to use prepaid incentives for all respondents, have advocated the use of lotteries as an incentive for stimulating response. This might be thought desirable, for example, in surveys of women on welfare in those states where incentives are counted against the value of the benefits they receive. The studies reported in the literature—all mail surveys or self-administered questionnaires distributed in person—have yielded inconsistent findings (e.g., positive effects by Balakrishnan et al., 1992; Hubbard and Little, 1988; Kim et al., 1995; and McCool, 1991; no effects in four studies reviewed by Hubbard and Little, 1988, or in the experiment by Warriner et al., 1996). A reasonable hypothesis would seem to be that lotteries function as cash incentives with an expected value per respondent (e.g., a $500 prize divided by 10,000 respondents would amount to an incentive of 5 cents per respondent), and that their effect on response rates would be predicted by this value. Thus, the effect of lotteries would generally be small, both because the expected value per respondent is small, and because they are essentially promised, rather than prepaid, incentives.

Incentives in Panel Studies

Many studies of welfare leavers are panel studies—that is, they reinterview the same household, or the same respondent, more than once over a period of time. Assuring participation is especially important for panel studies because participation at baseline usually sets a ceiling for the retention rate over the life of the panel.[1] For this reason, investigators often advocate using sizable incentives at the first wave of a panel study. An incentive experiment was carried out at Wave 1 of the 1996 Survey of Income and Program Participation (SIPP), a longitudinal survey carried out by the U.S. Census Bureau to provide national estimates of sources, amounts, and determinants of income for households, families, and persons. SIPP primary sample units were divided into three groups to receive $0, $10, and $20. James (1997) found that the $20 incentive significantly lowered nonresponse rates in Waves 1 to 3 compared with both the $10 and the $0 conditions, but the $10 incentive showed no effect relative to the zero-incentive group. Mack et al. (1998) reported on the results through Wave 6 using cumulative response rates, including an analysis of the effects of incentives on households differing by race, poverty status, and education in Wave 1. They found that an incentive of $20 reduced household, person, and item (gross wages) nonresponse rates in the initial interview and that household nonresponse rates

---

[1]Some investigators (see, e.g., Presser, 1989) recommend attempting to interview in later waves the nonrespondents to an earlier wave, but often this is not done. Even when it is, cooperation on a subsequent wave is generally predicted by prior cooperation.

remained significantly lower, with a cumulative 27.6 percent nonresponse rate in the $0 incentive group, 26.7 percent in the $10 group, and 24.8 percent in the $20 group at Wave 6, even though no further incentive payments were made. (The SIPP does not attempt to reinterview households that do not respond in Wave 1 or that have two consecutive noninterviews.) Differences between the $10 incentive and the no-incentive group were not statistically significant. A subsequent experiment with paying incentives in Waves 8 and 9 of the 1996 SIPP to all Wave 7 and 8 nonrespondents (Martin et al., 2001) found that both a $20 and a $40 prepayment significantly increased the response rate above that in the $0 group; there was no significant difference between the two incentive groups. (Differential responsiveness to incentives by respondents differing in economic status is discussed in the later section on Findings for Low-Income Populations.)

Research on the Health and Retirement Survey (HRS) suggests that respondents who are paid a refusal conversion incentive during one wave do not refuse at a higher rate than other converted refusers when reinterviewed during the next wave (Lengacher et al., 1995). Unlike the SIPP, all respondents to the HRS receive an incentive at each wave, but these are much lower than the refusal conversion payments.

In sum, although the evidence currently available is still quite limited, that which is available suggests that the use of incentives in panel studies to increase initial response rates, convert refusals, and reduce subsequent attrition can be quite effective. Moreover, although in this context it is often assumed that once incentives are paid one must continue to offer them in all subsequent waves of data collection, these studies suggest that the effects of incentives on nonresponse and attrition in panel surveys can be sustained, even when incentives are not paid in subsequent waves of the study.

Effects on Respondents or Effects on Interviewers?

Are the consistent effects of incentives in telephone and face-to-face interviews attributable to their effect on respondents, or are they, perhaps, mediated by their effect on interviewers? Clearly this question does not arise with respect to mail surveys, where incentives also have been consistently effective, but it seems important to try to answer it with respect to interviewer-mediated surveys. It is possible, for example, that interviewers expect respondents who have received an incentive to be more cooperative, and that they behave in such a way as to fulfill their expectations.[2] Or they may feel more confident about approaching

---

[2]For evidence concerning interviewer expectation effects, see Hyman (1954); Sudman et al. (1977); Singer and Kohnke-Aguirre (1979); Singer et al. (1983); and Hox (1999). Lynn (1999) reports an experiment in which interviewers believed respondents who had received an incentive responded at a lower rate, whereas their response rate was in fact significantly higher than those who received no incentive. However, these interviewer beliefs were measured after, rather than before, the survey.

a household that has received an incentive in the mail, and therefore be more effective in their interaction with the potential respondent.

To separate the effects of incentives on interviewers from their effects on respondents, Singer et al. (2000) randomly divided all sample numbers in an RDD survey that could be linked to addresses into three groups. One third of the group was sent an advance letter and $5; interviewers were kept blind to this condition. Another third also received a letter plus $5, and still another third received the letter only. Interviewers were made aware of these last two conditions by information presented on their Computer-Assisted Telephone Interview (CATI) screens.

The results of this experiment are shown in Table 4-1. Large differences were observed between the letter-only and the letter-plus-incentive conditions, but there is no evidence that this is due to the effect of incentives on interviewers. Only one of the differences between the conditions in which interviewers were aware of the incentive and those in which they were not aware reaches statistical significance, and here the results are in a direction opposite of that hypothesized. Thus prepayment of a $5 incentive substantially increases cooperation with an RDD survey, and the incentive appears to exert its effect directly on the respondent rather than being mediated through interviewer expectations. This conclusion is in accordance with research by Stanley Presser and Johnny Blair, at the University of Maryland, who also found substantial increases in response rates as a result of small prepayments to respondents to which interviewers were blind (personal communication, n.d.).

UNINTENDED CONSEQUENCES OF INCENTIVES

Effects on Item Nonresponse

One question often raised about the use of incentives in surveys is whether they bring about an increase in the response rate at the expense of response quality. This does not appear to be the case. On the contrary, what evidence there is suggests that the quality of responses given by respondents who receive a prepaid or a refusal conversion incentive does not differ from responses given by those who do not receive an incentive. They may, in fact, give better quality answers, in the sense that they have less item-missing data and provide longer open-ended responses (Baumgartner et al., 1998; Singer et al., 2000; Shettle and Mooney, 1999; but cf. Wiese, 1998). Experiments reported by Singer et al. (2000) indicate that promised and prepaid incentives *reduce* the tendency of older people and nonwhites to have more item-missing data, resulting in a net reduction in item nonresponse.

Findings reported by Mason and Traugott (1999) suggest that persistent efforts to persuade reluctant respondents to participate may produce more re-spondents at the price of more missing data. But these authors did not use incen-

TABLE 4-1 Response and Cooperation Rates by Advance Letters and Letters Plus Prepaid Incentive, Controlling for Interviewer Expectations

	Response Rate[a,b]		Cooperation Rate[b,c]	
	Interviewed %	Not Interviewed % (n)	Interviewed %	Not Interviewed % (n)
May 1998				
Letter only	62.9	37.1 (62)	68.4	31.6 (57)
Letter + $5, interviewers blind	75.4	24.6 (69)	86.7	13.3 (60)
Letter + $5, interviewers not blind	78.7	21.3 (61)	82.8	17.2 (58)
Ltr only vs. ltr + $5	X^2=4.13, df=1, p<.05		X^2=6.27, df=1, p<.05	
Blind vs. not blind	*n.s.*		*n.s.*	
June 1998				
Letter only	58.2	41.8 (55)	62.8	37.2 (51)
Letter + $5, interviewers blind	73.8	26.2 (61)	86.5	13.5 (52)
Letter + $5, interviewers not blind	74.6	25.4 (59)	83.0	17.0 (53)
Ltr only vs. ltr + $5	X^2=4.52, df=1, p<.05		X^2=9.56, df=1, p<.01	
Blind vs. not blind	*n.s.*		*n.s.*	
July 1998				
Letter only	61.8	38.2 (55)	72.3	27.7 (47)
Letter + $5, interviewers blind	81.3	18.6 (59)	87.3	12.7 (55)
Letter + $5, interviewers not blind	69.6	30.4 (56)	72.2	27.8 (54)
Ltr only vs. ltr + $5	X^2=3.47, df=1, p=.06		*n.s.*	
Blind vs. not blind	*n.s.*		X^2=5.83, df=1, p<.10	
August 1998				
Letter only	63.8	36.2 (58)	69.8	30.2 (53)
Letter + $5, interviewers blind	75.0	25.0 (68)	81.0	19.0 (63)
Letter + $5, interviewers not blind	76.7	23.3 (60)	85.2	14.8 (54)
Ltr only vs. ltr + $5	X^2=2.85, df=1, p=.09		X^2=3.75, df=1, p=.05	
Blind vs. not blind	*n.s.*		*n.s.*	

SOURCE: Singer et al. (2000).
[a]Includes noncontacts in denominator.
[b]After refusal conversion.
[c]Excludes noncontacts from denominator.

tives, and motivational theory suggests that people who are rewarded for their participation would continue to give good information, whereas those who feel harassed into participation may well retaliate by not putting much effort into their answers. However, there is no evidence about the effect of incentives on validity or reliability, and this is an important research question.

Effects on Response Distributions

Even more troubling, potentially, than an effect on item missing data is the effect of incentives on the distribution of responses. Does offering or paying incentives to people who might otherwise refuse affect their answers to the survey questions?

It is useful to think about the reasons why effects on response distributions might occur. One is that the use of incentives brings into the sample people whose characteristics differ from those who otherwise would be included, and their answers differ because of those differing characteristics. If that is the case, the apparent effect on response distributions is really due to a change in the composition of the sample, and should disappear once the appropriate characteristics are controlled. An example of the first process is presented by Berlin et al. (1992), who demonstrate that the apparent effect of a monetary incentive on literacy scores can be accounted for by the disproportionate recruitment of respondents with higher educational levels into the zero-incentive group. There was no significant relationship between incentive level and the proportion of items attempted, indicating that the incentive influenced the decision to participate, but not performance on the test. Another example is presented by Merkle et al. (1998) in their report of an experimental effort to increase the response rate to exit polls by having interviewers in a random sample of precincts carry clipboards and folders clearly identifying them as associated with the major media and handing out pens with the same logo. Although the response rate was increased by these methods (not necessarily by the incentive alone), the responses were actually distorted because a greater number of Democratic voters were brought into the sample—apparently as a result of the clearer identification of the poll with the media. Effects of incentives on sample composition are discussed further in the following section.

A second reason incentives might influence responses is if they influence people's opinions directly, or at any rate the expression of those opinions. A striking example of such influence (not, however, involving an incentive) is reported by Bischoping and Schuman (1992) in their analysis of discrepancies among Nicaraguan preelection polls in the 1990 election and the failure of many to predict the outcome of the election accurately. Bischoping and Schuman speculate that suspicions that preelection polls had partisan aims may have prevented many Nicaraguans from candidly expressing their voting intentions to interviewers. They tested this hypothesis by having interviewers alternate the use of three different pens to record responses: one carried the slogan of the Sandinista party; another, that of the opposition party; the third pen was neutral. The expected distortions of responses were observed in the two conditions that clearly identified the interviewers as partisan. Even in the third, neutral, condition, distortion occurred. The authors claim that polls apparently were not perceived as neutral by many respondents. In the Nicaraguan setting, after a decade of Sandinista rule, a poll lacking partisan identification was evidently regarded as likely to have an FSLN (Sandinista) connection (p. 346); the result was to bias the reporting of vote intentions, and therefore the results of the preelection polls, which predicted an overwhelming Sandinista victory when in fact the opposition candidate won by a large majority.

Still a third way in which incentives might affect responses is suggested by theory and experimental findings about the effects of mood (Schwarz and Clore, 1996). If incentives put respondents in a more optimistic mood, then some of their responses may be influenced as a result. Using 17 key variables included in the Survey of Consumer Attitudes, Singer et al. (2000) looked at whether the response distributions varied significantly by (1) the initial incentive or (2) refusal conversion payments, controlling for demographic characteristics.[3]

The offer of an initial incentive was associated with significantly different response distributions (at the .05 level) on 4 of the 17 variables; a refusal conversion payment also was associated with significantly different response distributions on 4 of them. One variable was affected significantly by both types of incentives.[4] In five of these cases, the responses given with an incentive were more optimistic than those given without an incentive; in two cases, they were more pessimistic. In the remaining case, respondents who received an incentive were somewhat more likely to respond good *and* bad, and somewhat less likely to give an equivocal reply. Thus, there is a suggestion that respondents to the Survey of Consumer Attitudes who receive an incentive *may give somewhat more optimistic responses* than those who do not. Similar findings have been reported by Brehm (1994) and James and Bolstein (1990). However, such effects were not observed by Shettle and Mooney (1999) in their experimental investigation of incentives in a survey of college graduates, which found only 8 significant differ-

---

[3]They used the multinomial logit specification in CATMOD, which allows researchers to perform modeling of data that can be represented by a contingency table. CATMOD fits linear models to functions of response frequencies and can use linear modeling, log-linear modeling, logistic regression, and repeated measurement analysis. A more complete description can be found in: SAS Institute Inc., 1989, *SAS/STAT Users Guide, Version 6, Fourth Edition, Volume 1*, Cary, NC: SAS Institute Inc.

[4]These counts are based on the bivariate distributions, without controls for demographic characteristics. The effects do not disappear with such controls; indeed, three additional variables show such effects with demographic controls.

ences (at the .05 level) in response distributions to 148 questions—a number that does not differ from that expected on the basis of chance.

EFFECTS IN SURVEYS OF LOW-INCOME POPULATIONS

The question of particular interest to this audience is how effective monetary and other incentives are in recruiting and retaining members of low-income populations. In a 1995 paper presented to a Council of Professional Associations on Federal Statistics (COPAFS) workshop, Kulka reported some evidence suggesting that monetary incentives might be especially effective in recruiting into the sample low-income and minority respondents, groups that ordinarily would be underrepresented in a probability sample. Reviewing a number of experimental studies that provided evidence on the issue of sample composition, including the studies discussed by Kulka, Singer et al. (1999a) found that in three studies, there was an indication that paying an incentive might be useful in obtaining higher numbers of respondents in demographic categories that otherwise tend to be underrepresented in sample surveys (e.g., low-income or nonwhite race).[5] Five other studies reported no significant effects of incentives on sample composition, and in one study the results were mixed.

Since then, additional evidence has accumulated suggesting that monetary incentives can be effective in recruiting and retaining minority respondents. Mack et al. (1998) found that the use of a $20 incentive in the first wave of a SIPP panel was much more effective in recruiting and retaining black households and households in poverty than it was in recruiting and retaining nonblack and nonpoverty households.[6] Martin et al. (2001) found that $20 was more effective in converting black and "other race" nonrespondents than in converting white respondents. These results agree with findings reported by Juster and Suzman (1995). They report that a special Nonresponse Study, in which a sample of people who refused normal refusal conversion efforts on the Health and Retirement Survey were offered $100 per individual or $200 per couple to participate,[7] brought into the sample a group of people distinctly different from other participants: they were more likely to be married, in better health, and, particularly, they had about 25 percent more net worth and a 16 percent higher income than other refusal conver-

---

[5]To our knowledge, however, no high-quality studies are available yet that explore potential differences in the effectiveness of incentives by ethnicity or language per se.

[6]However, Sundukchi (1999) reports that an incentive paid in Wave 7 to all low-income households that had received an incentive in Wave 1 reduced the nonresponse rate among nonblack low-income households, but not among black low-income households.

[7]In that study, all nonrespondents were sent the incentive offer by FedEx mail; hence, it was not possible to separate the effect of the monetary incentive from the special mailing. In a subsequent small-scale experiment, money had a significant effect on converting refusals, whereas a FedEx mailing did not (Daniel Hill, personal communication n.d.).

sion households or those who never refused. Finally, analyses by Singer et al. (2000) indicate that a $5 incentive paid in advance to a random half of RDD households for which an address could be located brought a disproportionate number of low-education respondents into the sample; there were no significant differences on other demographic characteristics.

In other words, these studies suggest that, while monetary incentives are effective with all respondents, less money is required to recruit and retain low-income (and minority) groups than those whose income is higher, and for whom the tradeoff between the time required for the survey and the incentive offered may be less attractive when the incentive is small. It should be noted that few, if any, of these studies (Mack et al., 1998, is a notable exception) have explicitly manipulated both the size of the incentive and the income level of the population; the findings reported here are based on ex post facto analyses for different subgroups, or on analyses of the composition of the sample following the use of incentives.

A number of other studies also have reported on the effects of incentives on sample composition. In some of these, it appears that incentives can be used to *compensate for lack of salience of, or interest in,* the survey by some groups in the sample. For example, the survey reported on by Shettle and Mooney (1999), the National Survey of College Graduates, is believed to be much more salient to scientists and engineers than to other college graduates, and in the 1980s the latter had a much lower response rate. Although this was also true in the 1992 pretest for the 1993 survey, the bias was less in the incentive than in the nonincentive group (7.1 percentage-point underreporting, compared with 9.8 percentage points), though not significantly so.[8] Similar findings are reported by Baumgartner and Rathbun (1997), who found a significant impact of incentives on response rate in the group for which the survey topic had little salience, but virtually no impact in the high-salience group, and by Martinez-Ebers (1997), whose findings suggest that a $5 incentive, enclosed with a mail questionnaire, was successful in motivating less satisfied parents to continue their participation in a school-sponsored panel survey. Berlin et al. (1992) found that people with higher scores on an assessment of adult literacy, as well as people with higher educational levels, were overrepresented in their zero-incentive group. Groves et al. (2000) reported a similar result; in their study, the impact of incentives on response rates was significantly greater for people low on a measure of community involvement than for those high on community involvement, who tend to participate at a higher rate even without monetary incentives. In these studies, incentives function by raising the response rate of those with little interest, or low civic involvement; they do

---

[8]Shettle and Mooney (1999) conclude that the incentive does not reduce nonresponse bias in their study. It is true that after extensive followups, there is no difference at all between the incentive and the no-incentive groups. Nevertheless, the trends prior to phone followup are in the expected direction.

not reduce the level of participation of the highly interested or more altruistic groups.

In these studies, certain kinds of dependent variables would be seriously mismeasured if incentives had not been used. In the case of Groves et al. (2000), for example, the conclusions one would reach about the distribution of community involvement would be in error if drawn from a survey that did not use incentives. Nevertheless, questions remain about how representative of their group as a whole those brought into the sample by incentives are, and this is true for low-income and minority respondents, as well. In other words, low-income respondents brought into the sample by the lure of an incentive may well differ from those who participate for other reasons. But even if prepaid incentives simply add more respondents to the total number interviewed, without reducing the nonresponse bias of the survey, they still may prove to be cost effective if they reduce the effort required to achieve a desired sample size. The theory of survey participation outlined at the beginning of this paper (Groves et al. 2000) suggests that the representativeness of the sample will be increased by using a *variety* of motivational techniques, rather than relying on a single one.

ISSUES IN THE USE OF DIFFERENTIAL INCENTIVES

Some of the research reported in the previous section suggests that it may make economic sense to offer lower incentives to people with lower incomes and higher incentives to those who are economically better off. Another instance of differential incentives is the use of refusal conversion payments, in which respondents who have expressed reluctance, or who have actually refused, are offered payment for their participation whereas cooperative respondents are not. In both of these situations, the question arises how respondents who received lower, or no, rewards would feel if they learned of this practice, and how this might affect their future participation in this or another survey.

Effects of Disclosure of Differential Incentives on Perceptions of Fairness

From an economic perspective, the fact that some people refuse to be interviewed may be an indication that the survey is more burdensome for them and that therefore the payment of incentives to such respondents (but not others) is justified. Nevertheless, some researchers are concerned that using incentives in this way will be perceived as inequitable by cooperative respondents, and that if they learn of the practice, this will adversely affect their willingness to cooperate in future surveys (Kulka, 1995).

These unintended consequences were the focus of two studies (Singer et al., 1999b; Groves et al., 1999). The first was conducted as part of the Detroit Area Study (DAS), using face-to-face interviews, and the second was done in the laboratory with community volunteers, using self-administered responses to videotaped vignettes.

In the first study, respondents were asked a series of questions concerning their beliefs about survey organization practices with respect to incentives. Three-quarters believed that such organizations offer monetary incentives to respondents to encourage participation (8.9 percent said they did not know). Those who received a prepaid $5 incentive (a random two-thirds of the survey sample) were significantly more likely than those who received no such payment to say that at least some survey organizations use incentives. Indeed, beliefs about this practice appeared to increase with the total amount ($0, $5, $25, or $30) of the incentive the respondent received or was offered, with 94 percent of those who received $30 expressing the belief that at least some survey organizations use incentives.[9]

All respondents also were asked the following question: "Some people do not want to be interviewed. However, to get accurate results, everyone chosen for the survey needs to be interviewed. Otherwise, the data may mislead people in the government who use the conclusions to plan important programs that affect everyone. Do you think it's fair or unfair for people who refuse to be interviewed to receive money if other people don't?" Despite the extensive justification for differential payment included here, 74 percent said they considered the practice unfair.

Near the end of the survey, in a more stringent test of whether the payment of differential incentives was perceived as fair or unfair, a random half of the respondents were informed that because of the importance of including everyone in the sample, some of those who had expressed reluctance to participate had been offered $25, while others had received nothing; they were asked whether they considered this practice fair or unfair. Again, almost three-quarters (72.4 percent) said they considered the practice unfair.

Effects of Disclosure of Differential Incentives on Willingness to Participate

Singer et al. (1999b) hypothesized that those to whom the payment of differential incentives was disclosed would be less willing to participate in a future survey.

---

[9]The finding that respondent beliefs about survey organization practices are affected by their own experience parallels findings reported elsewhere (Singer et al. 1998c). In that Singer et al. study, 31 percent of respondents to the Survey of Consumer Attitudes who had not been offered any incentives 6 months earlier said, in 1997, that respondents should get paid for participating in that type of survey; 51 percent of those offered $5 said, 6 months later, that they thought respondents should get paid; and 77 percent of respondents who received $20 or $25 as a refusal conversion payment said respondents should get paid.

In the laboratory study described in the previous section, subjects were significantly more likely to say they would not be willing to participate in a survey where some respondents received a payment for participating but others did not. However, the difference was reduced to insignificance when an explanation for the payment was offered by the interviewer.

In the field study, there were no differences in expressed willingness to participate between those to whom differential payments had been disclosed and those to whom they had not. About a quarter of each group said they definitely would be willing to participate in another survey by the same organization. Even those to whom differential incentive payments were disclosed *and who perceived these payments as unfair* did not differ significantly in their expressed willingness to participate in a subsequent survey by the same organization, although the trend in responses was as predicted: 25.8 percent versus 32.8 percent expressed such willingness.[10] The investigators speculated that rapport with the interviewer might have mitigated the deleterious effects of disclosing differential incentives that previously had been observed in the laboratory experiment (Groves et al. 1999).

A little more than a year later, all the original DAS respondents for whom an address could be located were sent a mail questionnaire on the topic of assisted suicide, ostensibly from a different survey organization. There were no significant differences in participation between those to whom differential payments had been disclosed a year earlier and those to whom they had not.

Thus, the data indicate that most respondents believe survey organizations are currently using incentives to encourage survey participation; that these beliefs are affected by personal experience; that only half of those who are aware of the use of incentives believe that payments are distributed equally to all respondents; and that a large majority of respondents perceive the practice of paying differential incentives as unfair. However, disclosure of differential payments had no significant effect on expressed willingness to participate in a future survey, nor were respondents to whom differential incentives had been disclosed significantly less likely to respond to a new survey request, from an ostensibly different organization a year later, although again the differences were in the hypothesized direction.

---

[10]However, as we would expect, the perception of fairness is directly and significantly related to whether or not respondents had themselves received a refusal conversion payment. Among those who did *not* receive such a payment, 74.5 percent (of 200) considered this practice unfair. Among those who *did* receive a refusal conversion payment, only 55 percent (of 20) considered the practice unfair; this difference is significant at the .06 level.

ARE PREPAID INCENTIVES COST EFFECTIVE?

For a variety of reasons, including those discussed in the previous section, prepaid incentives to everyone in the sample may be preferable to refusal conversion or other differential payments.

One reason is that interviewers like them. Knowing the household is in receipt of an advance payment, modest though it may be, interviewers feel entitled to ask the respondent to reciprocate with an interview. Furthermore, prepaid incentives are equitable. They reward equally everyone who happens to fall into the sample, and they reward them for the right behavior—that is, for cooperation, rather than refusal. Both of these advantages are likely to make modest prepaid incentives an attractive alternative to refusal conversion payments in many types of surveys. There is also indirect evidence that the use of refusal conversion payments to persuade reluctant respondents leads to increasing reliance on such payments within an organization, in all likelihood because of their effects on interviewer expectations.

Still, the question arises whether such incentives are cost effective. It would appear that paying a small number of refusal conversion payments to reluctant respondents would be cheaper than paying everyone, even if those initial payments are smaller.

Several studies have concluded that prepaid incentives are cost effective in mail surveys. For such surveys, the comparison ordinarily has been among incentives varying in amount or in kind, or in comparison with no incentive at all, rather than with refusal conversion payments. Two recent investigations of cost effectiveness, by James and Bolstein (1992) and by Warriner et al. (1996), have included information on the relative effectiveness of various incentives. James and Bolstein (1992) found that a prepaid incentive of $1 was the most cost effective, yielding nearly as high a return as larger amounts for about one-quarter of the cost. Warriner et al. (1996:9) conclude that for their study, a $5 prepaid incentive was the optimal amount, resulting in a saving of 40 cents per case (because the same response rate could be achieved as in a no-incentive, two-follow-up condition). The $2 incentive resulted in costs per case only a dollar less than the $5 incentive, while yielding a response rate 10 percentage points lower. Similar findings have been reported by Asch et al. (1998) in a mail survey of physicians.

For interviewer-mediated studies, as noted earlier, the comparison is much more likely to be with refusal conversion payments. The answer is likely to depend on the nature of the study and the importance of a high response rate, on how interesting the study is to respondents (i.e., how many of them are willing to participate even without a prepaid incentive), on whether prepaid incentives reduce the effort required, and on a variety of other factors.

Several face-to-face surveys have reported that promised monetary incentives are cost effective. Berlin et al. (1992), for example, reported that use of a

$20 promised incentive in a field-test experiment with the National Adult Literacy Survey, which entails completion of a test booklet by the respondent, resulted in cost savings on a per interview basis when all field costs were taken into account. Similarly, Chromy and Horvitz (1978) reported (in a study of the use of monetary incentives among young adults in the National Assessment of Educational Progress) that when the cost of screening for eligible respondents is high, the use of incentives to increase response rates actually may reduce the cost per unit of data collected.

Singer, Van Hoewyk, and Couper[11] investigated this problem in the Survey of Consumer Attitudes (SCA). They found that a $5 incentive included with an advance letter significantly reduced the number of calls required to close out a case (8.75 calls when an incentive was sent, compared with 10.22 when it was not; p=.05), and significantly reduced the number of interim refusals (.282 refusals when an incentive was sent, compared with .459 when it was not). As expected, there was no significant difference between the incentive and the no-incentive condition in calls to first contact. The outcome of the first call indicates that compared with the letter only, the addition of a $5 incentive results in more interviews, more appointments, and fewer contacts in which resistance is encountered.

Given the size of the incentive and the average cost per call aside from the incentive, sending a prepaid incentive to respondents for whom an address could be obtained was cost effective for the SCA. However, as we have tried to indicate, this conclusion depends on the size of the incentive as well as the structure of other costs associated with a study for a given organization, and should not be assumed to be invariant across organizations and incentives.

An argument that can be raised against the use of prepaid incentives is that they may undermine more altruistic motives for participating in surveys. Indeed, we have found that prepaid incentives have smaller effects on survey participation for people who score high on a measure of community activism (Groves et al., 2000) than on people who score low on this characteristic. But this is because groups high in community activism already respond at a high rate. There is no evidence (because we did not test this hypothesis) that people high on community activism who are offered a prepaid incentive respond at a *lower* rate than they would have had they *not* been offered the incentive, nor do we know whether such an effect would appear on a later survey. Although anecdotal evidence shows that some people are offended by the offer of an incentive, going so far as to return the incentive to the survey organization, by all accounts such negative reactions are few.

---

[11]This discussion is based on unpublished analyses by Van Hoewyk, Singer, and Couper of data from the Survey of Consumer Attitudes during 8 months in 1998.

Prepaid incentives have been common in mail surveys for many years, although the amounts used are ordinarily quite modest (see Church, 1999). We suspect that the use of such incentives will increase in interviewer-mediated surveys as well. Such incentives are likely to be especially appropriate when other reasons that might move potential respondents to participate are weak or lacking, and when the names and addresses (or telephone numbers) of such potential respondents are known.

RECOMMENDATIONS AND CONCLUSIONS

The workshop for which this chapter was prepared is focused specifically on collecting better data from low-income and welfare populations, and one of the clear challenges associated with surveying such populations is how to achieve high enough levels of participation to minimize bias due to nonresponse. Increasingly, respondent incentives have been proposed as a valuable tool in achieving this goal. Thus, the basic question addressed in this chapter is whether the payment of respondent incentives is indeed an effective means of reducing nonresponse, both for surveys in general and, especially, in surveys conducted with low-income and welfare populations.

As noted in the paper, a substantial research literature consistently has demonstrated the value of incentive payments to survey respondents for increasing cooperation and improving speed and quality of response in a broad range of data collection efforts, most notably in mail surveys. Because mail surveys are of limited utility in studies of welfare reform or low-income populations, experiments involving the use of incentives in face-to-face or telephone interviews are of greatest relevance to answering this basic question. These experiments are more recent in vintage, sparser in coverage, and not entirely consistent in their findings.[12]

Thus, although it is tempting to generalize from the findings presented here, it is important to note that many of the results are based on only a few studies and may not apply to other populations or situations, including especially those of particular interest here (i.e., surveys of low-income and welfare populations on questions related to welfare reform). Thus, if at all possible, we urge pretesting of the particular incentive plan proposed with the population targeted by one's

---

[12]Such inconsistencies are *not* largely due to differences in sample sizes, that is an inability to detect significant differences between incentive and nonincentive groups (or other relevant comparisons) because the sample sizes in these studies were too low. Sample sizes were provided for each of the studies cited in their original reports. Although we have not repeated them here, they were, with very few exceptions, adequate to detect reasonable expected differences between experimental groups.

survey and the instrumentation and other survey methods to be employed, rather than relying exclusively on this research literature.

Nevertheless, with these cautions, a few basic conclusions, guidelines, and recommendations can be gleaned from the evidence accumulated to date:

1. Consistent with an extensive literature on the use of incentives with mail surveys, prepaid monetary incentives seem to be useful in recruiting low-income and minority respondents into interviewer-mediated surveys, even when the burden imposed on participants is relatively low. The use of incentives probably should be part of the design and strategy for all such surveys. However, they should not be used as substitutes for other best-practice persuasion strategies designed to increase participation, such as explanatory advance letters, endorsements by people or organizations important to the population being surveyed, assurances of confidentiality, and so on.

2. How much money to offer respondents in these circumstances is not at all clear from the evidence currently available. Less money appears to be needed to recruit lower income respondents into a survey than those with higher incomes, but the optimal amount likely will depend on factors such as the length of the interview and the salience of the topic, and may also change over time. To determine the appropriate incentive amount for a given study, we reiterate our prior admonition that there is no real substitute for a careful pretest of various incentive amounts within the specific population and design context proposed for a given survey.

3. Although it is tempting to speculate on this issue, and we often have been asked to venture an educated guess on what an appropriate range might be for incentives in studies of welfare and low-income populations, we believe that doing so would not be prudent for a number of reasons. In particular, as we have noted, the experimental literature that provides evidence directly relevant to this question is relatively sparse, idiosyncratic, and inconsistent, and the dynamics associated with providing incentives to these populations quite likely are both fluid and in large part specific to location, economy, and even cultural factors.

As a general guideline, the Office of Management and Budget (OMB) has most recently approved the use of respondent incentives in the $20-$30 range based on empirical experimental tests conducted with specific target populations similar to those of interest here, but incentive amounts both higher and lower than these also have been approved and successfully implemented.

4. Prepaid respondent incentives are especially important in panel surveys (a design favored by many studies of low-income populations and studies of welfare reform because of the questions of particular interest in such studies) because of the critical need to recruit a high proportion of the eligible population into the initial round of measurement. When it is possible to send payment in advance to

at least a portion of the sample, the amount of cash interviewers must carry with them is reduced. Although such concerns have not been systematically validated either empirically or by anecdotal evidence from survey practitioners (see Kulka, 1995), the potential for putting either respondents or interviewers at increased risk of crime through the use of incentives is at least partially offset by this approach, along with accruing the well-established benefits of prepayment.

5. For a number of practical reasons, including restrictions on the use of state and federal monies to compensate survey participants (especially those receiving state aid), the use of lotteries as an incentive strategy has considerable appeal. However, lotteries rather consistently appear to be less effective than individual prepaid incentives in stimulating survey response.

6. It is possible that the use of prepaid incentives will change responses to at least some questions by affecting a respondent's mood (i.e., making the respondent more optimistic about the survey's content). Although evidence of this phenomenon is mixed, it is worth evaluating this possibility empirically through an experiment whenever it is feasible to do so.

7. Although the use of incentives strictly or primarily for refusal conversion is fairly widespread in current survey practice, incentives should be used sparingly as a refusal conversion technique. Respondents regard this practice as unfair or inequitable, although there is no evidence that such differential payments reduce future willingness to participate in surveys, including termination of payments in subsequent waves of a panel survey in which an incentive was previously provided. However, there are suggestions that the routine use of refusal conversion payments may condition interviewers to expect (and depend on) them, and that this may have a negative impact on overall interviewer performance.

8. Finally, several issues broadly related to the protection of human subjects are sometimes raised in connection with using respondent incentives. First, specific to welfare populations is the issue of whether incentives count against the value of benefits received. Although the legislative and regulatory bases for such restrictions vary by state, and there is at least anecdotal evidence that some states have been reluctant to authorize the use of incentives in their surveys for this reason, such restrictions do not yet appear to be widespread, and researchers and officials in some states have indicated that such restrictions can be waived by the state in any case.

Second, it is well known that the OMB has had a longstanding policy that has strongly discouraged the use of incentives in federal statistical surveys. Although these policies are currently in review, recent drafts of OMB's Implementing Guidance prepared to support the Paperwork Reduction Act of 1995 provide more specific guidelines to federal agencies on the use of incentives, when incentives might be justified, and the types of documentation or evidence required to support a request for incentives. Specifically, these guidelines make clear that: (1) incentives are not intended to pay respondents for their time; (2) noncash or monetary incentives of modest size ($20-$30) are preferred; and (3) one must demonstrate empirically that such payments will significantly increase response rates (and the resulting reliability and validity of the study), although the potential need for and efficacy of incentives for certain purposes and circumstances is clearly acknowledged.

Third, some welfare reform researchers have noted a recent and potentially growing problem with Institutional Review Boards (IRBs), some of which have argued that the use of incentives (especially large incentives) may be regarded as coercive, especially among low-income respondents, thereby posing a credible threat to truly informed consent. That is, having been offered (or paid) an incentive to participate in a study, potential respondents feel they cannot really refuse, even if they are reluctant to do so for other reasons. Although assessing this potential human subject threat is clearly within the purview of IRB review, most incentive payments used to date have in fact been fairly modest in size. These are often characterized as tokens of appreciation rather than compensation for time spent. Most IRBs to date have determined that these token incentives are not so large as to constitute coercion, provided that such incentives are not cited as part of informed consent or as one of the benefits of participation in the study.

REFERENCES

Armstrong, J.S.
  1975   Monetary incentives in mail surveys. *Public Opinion Quarterly* 39:111-116.
Asch, D.A., N.A. Christakis, and P.A. Ubel
  1998   Conducting physician mail surveys on a limited budget: A randomized trial comparing $2 vs. $5 incentives. *Medical Care* 36(1):95-99.
Balakrishnan, P.V., S.K. Chawla, M.F. Smith, and B.P. Micholski
  1992   Mail survey response rates using a lottery prize giveaway incentive. *Journal of Direct Marketing* 6:54-59.
Baumgartner, Robert, and Pamela Rathbun
  1997   Prepaid Monetary Incentives and Mail Survey Response Rates. Unpublished paper presented at the Annual Conference of the American Association of Public Opinion Research, Norfolk, VA, May 15-18.
Baumgartner, Robert, Pamela Rathbun, Kevin Boyle, Michael Welsh, and Drew Laughlan
  1998   The Effect of Prepaid Monetary Incentives on Mail Survey Response Rates and Response Quality. Unpublished paper presented at the Annual Conference of the American Association of Public Opinion Research, St. Louis, May 14-17.
Berlin, Martha, Leyla Mohadjer, Joseph Waksberg, Andrew Kolstad, Irwin Kirsch, D. Rock, and Kentaro Yamamoto
  1992   An experiment in monetary incentives. Pp. 393-398 in *Proceedings of the Section on Survey Research Methods.* Alexandria, VA: American Statistical Association.
Biner, Paul M., and Heath J. Kidd
  1994   The interactive effects of monetary incentive justification and questionnaire length on mail survey response rates. *Psychology and Marketing* 11:483-492.
Bischoping, Katherine, and Howard Schuman
  1992   Pens and polls in Nicaragua: An analysis of the 1990 preelection surveys. *American Journal of Political Science* 36:331-350.

Brehm, John
    1994   Stubbing our toes for a foot in the door? Prior contact, incentives and survey response. *International Journal of Public Opinion Research* 6(1):45-63.
Chromy, James R., and Daniel G. Horvitz
    1978   The Use of Monetary Incentives in National Assessment Household Surveys. *Journal of the American Statistical Association* 73(363):473-78.
Church, Allan H.
    1999   Estimating the effect of incentives on mail survey response rates: A meta-analysis. *Public Opinion Quarterly* 57:62-79.
Cox, Eli P.
    1976   A cost/ benefit view of prepaid monetary incentives in mail questionnaires. *Public Opinion Quarterly* 40:101-104.
Dillman, Don A.
    1978   *Mail and Telephone Surveys: The Total Design Method.* New York: John Wiley and Sons.
Fox, Richard J., Melvin Crask, and Kim Jonghoon
    1988   Mail Survey Response Rate: A Meta-Analysis of Selected Techniques for Inducing Response. *Public Opinion Quarterly* 52:467-491.
Groves, Robert M., Eleanor Singer, Amy D. Corning, and Ashley Bowers
    1999   A laboratory approach to measuring the effects on survey participation of interview length, incentives, differential incentives, and refusal conversion. *Journal of Official Statistics* 15:251-268.
Groves, Robert M., Eleanor Singer, and Amy D. Corning
    2000   Leverage-salience theory of survey participation: Description and an illustration. *Public Opinion Quarterly* 64:299-308.
Heberlein, Thomas A., and Robert Baumgartner
    1978   Factors affecting response rates to mailed questionnaires: A quantitative analysis of the published literature. *American Sociological Review* 43:447-462.
Hopkins, K.D., and A.R. Gullickson
    1992   Response rates in survey research: A meta-analysis of monetary gratuities. *Journal of Experimental Education* 61:52-56
Hox, Joop
    1999   The influence of interviewer's attitude and behavior on household survey nonresponse: An international comparison. Unpublished paper presented at the International Conference on Survey Nonresponse, Portland, OR, October 28-31.
Hubbard, Raymond, and Eldon L. Little
    1988   Promised contributions to charity and mail survey responses: Replication with extension. *Public Opinion Quarterly* 52:223-230.
Hyman, Herbert H.
    1954   *Interviewing in Social Research.* Chicago: University of Chicago Press.
James, Jeannine M., and Richard Bolstein
    1990   The effect of monetary incentives and follow-up mailings on the response rate and response quality in mail surveys. *Public Opinion Quarterly* 54:346-361.
    1992   Large monetary incentives and their effect on mail survey response rates. *Public Opinion Quarterly* 56:442-453.
James, Tracy
    1997   Results of the Wave 1 incentive experiment in the 1996 survey of income and program participation. Pp. 834-839 in *Proceedings of the Section on Survey Research Methods.* Alexandria, VA: American Statistical Association.

Juster, F. Thomas, and Richard Suzman
1995   An overview of the health and retirement study. *The Journal of Human Resources* 30(5):S7-S56.
Kanuk, L., and C. Berenson
1975   Mail surveys and response rates: A literature review. *Journal of Marketing Research* 12:440-453.
Kerachsky, Stuart J., and Charles D. Mallar
1981   The effects of monetary payments on survey responses: Experimental evidence from a longitudinal study of economically disadvantaged youths. Pp. 258-263 in *Proceedings of the Section on Survey Research Methods*. Alexandria, VA: American Statistical Association.
Kim, K., C. Lee, and Y. Whang
1995   The effect of respondent involvement in sweepstakes on response rates in mail surveys. Pp. 216-220 in *Proceedings of the Section on Survey Research Methods*. Alexandria, VA: American Statistical Association.
Kulka, Richard A.
1995   The use of incentives to survey hard-to-reach respondents: A brief review of empirical research and current practice. Pp. 256-299 in *Seminar on New Directions in Statistical Methodology* (Statistical Policy Working Paper 23), Part 2 of 3. Washington, DC: Federal Committee on Statistical Methodology, Statistical Policy Office, Office of Information and Regulatory Affairs, Office of Management and Budget.
Lengacher, Jennie E., Colleen M. Sullivan, Mick P. Couper, and Robert M. Groves
1995   Once Reluctant, Always Reluctant? Effects of Differential Incentives on Later Survey Participation in a Longitudinal Study. Unpublished paper presented at the Annual Conference of the American Association for Public Opinion Research, Fort Lauderdale, FL, May 18-21.
Levine, S., and G. Gordon
1958   Maximizing returns on mail questionnaires. *Public Opinion Quarterly* 22:568-575.
Linsky, Arnold S.
1975   Stimulating responses to mailed questionnaires: A review. *Public Opinion Quarterly* 39:82-101.
Lynn, Peter
1999   Is the Impact of Respondent Incentives on Personal Interview Surveys Transmitted via the Interviewers? Unpublished manuscript. Institute for Social and Economic Research, University of Essex, Colchester.
Mack, Stephen, Vicki Huggins, Donald Keathley, and Mahdi Sundukchi
1998   Do monetary incentives improve response rates in the survey of income and program participation? Pp. 529-534 in *Proceedings of the Section on Survey Research Methods*. Alexandria, VA: American Statistical Association.
Martin, Elizabeth, Denise Abreu, and Franklin Winters
2001   Money and motive: Effects of incentives on panel attrition in the Survey of Income and Program Participation. *Journal of Official Statistics* 17:267-284.
Martinez-Ebers, Valerie
1997   Using monetary incentives with hard-to-reach populations in panel surveys. *International Journal of Public Opinion Research* 9:77-86.
Mason, Robert, Virginia Lesser, and Michael W. Trangott
1999   Impact of missing values from converted refusals on nonsampling error. Unpublished paper presented at the International Conference on Survey Nonresponse, Portland, OR, October 28-31.

McCool, Steven F.
1991   Using probabilistic incentives to increase response rates to mail return highway intercept diaries. *Journal of Travel Research* 30:17-19.
Merkle, Daniel, Murray Edelman, Kathy Dykeman, and Chris Brogan
1998   An Experimental Study of Ways to Increase Exit Poll Response Rates and Reduce Survey Error. Unpublished paper presented at the Annual Conference of the American Association of Public Opinion Research, St. Louis, May 14-17.
Porst, Rolf, and Christa von Briel
1995   Waren Sie vielleicht bereit, sich gegenebenfalls noch einmal befragen zu lassen? Oder: Gründe für die Teilnahme an Panelbefragungen. In *ZUMA-Arbeitsbericht*, Nr. 95/04. Mannheim, Germ.
Presser, Stanley
1989   Collection and design issues: Discussion. Pp. 75-79 in *Panel Surveys*, D. Kasprzyk, G. Duncan, G. Kalton, and M. Singh, eds. New York: Wiley.
Schwarz, N., and G.L. Clore
1996   Feelings and phenomenal experiences. Pp. 433-465 in *Social Psychology: Handbook of Basic Principles*, E.T. Higgins and A. Kruglanski, eds. New York: Guilford.
Shettle, Carolyn, and Geraldine Mooney
1999   Monetary incentives in government surveys. *Journal of Official Statistics* 15:231-250.
Singer, Eleanor, Martin R. Frankel, and Marc B. Glassman
1983   The effect of interviewers' characteristics and expectations on response. *Public Opinion Quarterly* 47:68-83.
Singer, Eleanor, Nancy Gebler, Trivellore Raghunathan, John Van Hoewyk, and Katherine McGonagle
1999a The effect of incentives in interviewer-mediated surveys. *Journal of Official Statistics* 15:217-230.
Singer, Eleanor, Robert M. Groves, and Amy D. Corning
1999b Differential incentives: Beliefs about practices, perceptions of equity, and effects on survey participation. *Public Opinion Quarterly* 63:251-260.
Singer, Eleanor, and Luane Kohnke-Aguirre
1979   Interviewer expectation effects: A replication and extension. *Public Opinion Quarterly* 43:245-260.
Singer, Eleanor, John Van Hoewyk, and Mary P. Maher
1998   Does the payment of incentives create expectation effects? *Public Opinion Quarterly* 62:152-164.
2000   Experiments with incentives in telephone surveys. *Public Opinion Quarterly* 64:171-188.
Sudman, Seymour, Norman M. Bradburn, Ed Blair, and Carol Stocking
1977   Modest expectations: The effects of interviewers' prior expectations on responses. *Sociological Methods and Research* 6:171-182.
Sundukchi, M.
1999   SIPP 1996: Some results from the Wave 7 incentive experiment. Unpublished document, January 28, U.S. Census Bureau.
Warriner, Keith, John Goyder, Heidi Gjertsen, Paula Hohner, and Kathleen McSpurren
1996   Charities, No, Lotteries, No, Cash, Yes: Main Effects and Interactions in a Canadian Incentives Experiment. Unpublished paper presented at the Survey Non-Response Session of the Fourth International Social Science Methodology Conference, University of Essex, Institute for the Social Sciences, Colchester, UK, October 6-8.
Wiese, Cheryl J.
1998   Refusal conversions: What Is Gained? *National Network of State Polls Newsletter* 32:1-3
Yu, Julie, and Harris Cooper
1983   A quantitative review of research design effects on response rates to questionnaires. *Journal of Marketing Research* 2036-2044.

5

Adjusting for Missing Data in Low-Income Surveys

Leyla Mohadjer and G. Hussain Choudhry

Partly as a consequence of the recent significant changes in welfare programs and policies, many states are conducting or sponsoring surveys to investigate the effect of changes in welfare policy on the well-being of people living at or below the poverty level. Under ideal circumstances, every low-income person (or family) in the state would have a chance of selection for such a survey, would be located and agree to participate in the survey, and would provide correct answers to all questions asked. In practice, these circumstances are not realized in any population survey. This paper focuses on the problems of missing data in surveys arising from a failure to give all members of the target population a chance of selection for the survey and a failure to obtain the survey data from some of those sampled. The following sections indicate how missing data can lead to biased survey estimates and describe some widely used methods to reduce this effect.

Missing data in surveys can be divided usefully into three classes:

- **Noncoverage.** Noncoverage occurs when persons (or families) in the target population of interest are not included in the sampling frame from which the sample is selected. In the case of a survey of a state's low-income population, noncoverage could, for instance, occur if the list from which the sample was drawn was out of date, and hence failed to include those most recently enrolled.

The authors are grateful to Graham Kalton, Joseph Waksberg, Robert Moffitt, and the referees for their valuable comments and suggestions that led to improvements in this paper.

- **Unit nonresponse.** Unit nonresponse occurs when a sampled unit (person or family) fails to participate in the survey. Unit nonresponse can occur, for example, because the sampled person cannot be located, refuses to participate, is too ill to participate, cannot participate because of language or hearing problems, or is away from the area for the period of the survey fieldwork.

- **Item nonresponse.** Item nonresponse occurs when a sampled unit participates in the survey but fails to provide responses to one or more of the survey questions. This failure may occur because the respondent refuses to answer a question on the grounds that it is too sensitive or personal, or because he or she does not know the answer to the question. Item nonresponse also occurs when an interviewer fails to ask a question or record the answer and when recorded responses are deleted in editing a questionnaire because the response is inconsistent with the answers recorded for other questions.

There is a potential for bias whenever sampled persons who did not participate in the survey have different characteristics than those who did. For some important characteristics, the respondents may be substantially different from those with missing data. In fact, if such differences exist and no attempt is made to adjust for them in the analyses, estimates or inferences for the target population may be misleading. The potential for bias is particularly great when nonresponse rates are high. Thus, for example, if those recently enrolled are not included on the sampling frame for enrollees in a state's welfare program, the survey clearly will produce biased estimates of the distribution of length of time on the program, and any other associated estimates. Similarly, in a survey of welfare leavers, it may be that those who participate in the survey have had appreciably different experiences than those who do not, and thus, estimates based on the respondents will be biased. Suppose that families with positive outcomes (those who successfully made the transition from welfare) are easier to locate and more willing to respond than families with negative outcomes. In fact, policy makers are concerned that this situation does exist and that nonresponding and nonlocatable families and those whose current status is no longer reflected in administrative data are worse off and at greater risk than families for whom data are available (U.S. General Accounting Office, 1999). This situation can result in estimates with large nonresponse bias.

The standard method of attempting to reduce the potentially biasing effect of noncoverage and of unit nonresponse is a "weighting adjustment." Weighting adjustments for these two sources of missing data are described in this paper. Because some state surveys have experienced high nonresponse rates, nonresponse weighting adjustments are likely to be particularly important.The intent of this paper is to describe how they may be applied.

All methods for handling missing data aim to reduce their potential biasing effects, but these methods cannot be expected to eliminate the effects of missing data. The best protection against potential nonresponse bias is to plan and implement field procedures that maintain a high level of cooperation. A wide variety of tools and strategies are available to improve survey response rates. Some examples include an advance letter to sampled cases, effective callback or followup strategies, reductions in the length of the questionnaire or the interview, improved interviewer training, and payment of incentives. The literature includes an extensive discussion on methods for obtaining high response rates in surveys. Cantor and Cunningham (this volume), Weiss and Bailar (this volume), and Singer and Kulka (this volume) describe such methods for low-income surveys. However, even with the best strategies, some nonresponse occurs.

The standard method of attempting to reduce the potentially biasing effect of noncoverage and of unit nonresponse is a "weighting adjustment." Weighting adjustments for these two sources of missing data are described in this paper. Because some state surveys have experienced high nonresponse rates, nonresponse weighting adjustments are likely to be particularly important.[1] The intent of this paper is to describe how they may be applied.

The usual method for handling item nonresponse is some form of imputation, that is, assigning a value for the missing response based on the responses given to other questions in the survey and usually conducted within classes of sample persons with similar characteristics. If done well, imputation usually can reduce bias in survey estimates. It is nearly always preferable to impute missing items rather than treating them as randomly missing data at the analysis stage because confining analyses to nonmissing responses to questionnaire items may lead to biased estimates. But bias reduction depends on the suitability of the assumptions made in the imputation. When imputations are performed separately on different variables, the bias may be reduced for univariate statistics, but multivariate relationships among variables could become distorted. Also, researchers may treat the resulting data set as if it were complete, thus affecting the variances of the estimates. An extensive body of literature currently exists for compensating for item nonresponse in surveys. Readers are referred to Kalton and Kasprzyk (1986) and Brick and Kalton (1996).

This paper focuses on the standard weighting adjustment methods used to compensate for noncoverage and unit nonresponse in survey research. These methods are general-purpose strategies that automatically adjust all analyses of the survey data, at a low cost. Other available procedures are more complex and may produce somewhat better results when analysts have a specific model they plan to estimate. Because these procedures have only limited applicability in multipurpose surveys, they have not been included here. Refer to Little and Rubin (1987) for information about these methods.

---

[1]Nonresponse adjustments are usually conducted by creating a factor or a "nonresponse adjustment weight" for each respondent in the sample. In the final survey analysis, the nonresponse weight may be used with additional adjustment factors that serve other purposes, including sometimes compensating for noncoverage.

Studies of low-income populations involve various methods of data gathering. We begin with a brief description of two alternative types of low-income studies. We then provide a brief discussion of noncoverage and unit nonresponse in low-income surveys. Sample weighting is then described, followed by a review of the most common general-purpose nonresponse adjustment procedures. Finally, we include a brief summary of the paper. The procedures are illustrated using examples that we carry throughout the paper.

LOW-INCOME POPULATION STUDIES

We begin this discussion about nonresponse adjustments with a review of two different types of studies often conducted by state welfare agencies. Studies of the low-income population (such as studies of the current welfare population or studies of those who have left welfare rolls) mainly rely on two types of data collection: one collects data directly from administrative records and the other collects data directly from a sample of eligible persons. Some studies use a combination of administrative data and data from survey respondents.

States' welfare systems generally collect administrative data on the demographic characteristics of welfare recipients, the number of adults and children in the welfare case, and the receipt and value of welfare benefits. Many research studies use administrative records, and researchers frequently match the records to data from sources such as the Food Stamp Program and Medicaid. The state Unemployment Insurance files also are used to collect information about employment and earnings for families who have left welfare. Some studies rely on information available in administrative records, and thus do not require any contact with the subjects of the study.

Some states collect data through surveys. These are most often telephone interviews, although some states also conduct in-person interviews to ensure that families without telephones are included. Surveys usually collect information from respondents that is not available in administrative data.

Both types of studies of low-income populations usually suffer from some form of missing data. For example, in studies that include only administrative data collection, persons or families for whom no information is included in the administrative list (used as the sampling frame) have no chance of being included in the sample, and thus will not be represented in the results of the study. In addition, a number of sampled persons, or families, may not have the required data because they were not matched correctly or had no record in other administrative files used to collect outcome data (e.g., earnings data from Unemployment Insurance records). Similarly, surveys that collect data from sampled persons also are subject to underrepresentation due to sampling from incomplete or outdated lists, as well as missing information due to nonresponse. Later, we describe, in more detail, the sources of missing data in the two types of low-income studies.

As mentioned earlier, this paper describes the common procedures used to adjust for nonresponse and noncoverage. These procedures rely on the auxiliary data available for both respondents and nonrespondents. In general, the greater the amount of auxiliary data that can be used for adjustment, the better the adjustment is likely to be. To evaluate the availability and the amount of such data for low-income surveys, we contacted a number of states to inquire about the content and the quality of their administrative data. The main focus of this inquiry was the availability and quality of demographic, socioeconomic, and geographic variables. The results of this survey are provided in a later section. In general, we found that many states have high-quality data for demographic variables such as age, gender, race/ethnicity, and number of children. Welfare income and length of time on welfare seemed to be among the socioeconomic variables of high quality, and county name and zip code were the geographic variables with good-quality data for the states that responded to our survey. In a later section, we show how this information (or any other data source available to states) can be used to adjust for nonresponse in state surveys.

NONCOVERAGE AND NONRESPONSE IN SURVEYS

A fundamental objective in the design of any state survey is to adequately represent the targeted population; for the state surveys under consideration here, this usually consists of low-income persons. However, the target population is not completely represented by the sample when either some persons or families are not included in the sampling frame (e.g., the administrative records if used for sampling) or information cannot be obtained for some eligible sampled persons. The term "noncoverage" refers to situations where some units in the target population have no chance of selection into the sample. The following subsection provides more detail on reasons for survey noncoverage. The term "nonresponse" in surveys refers to failure to obtain data for those eligible units that were selected into the sample. The subsection after that provides a summary of various sources of nonresponse in sample surveys.

Survey Noncoverage

Most population surveys are subject to some noncoverage. Surveys of low-income populations are no exception. One source of noncoverage is the use of incomplete or outdated administrative files as sampling frames, resulting in the omission of a part of the population of interest. Similarly, noncoverage occurs when telephone interviewing is the only vehicle for data collection, because those without telephones have no chance of being selected and thus will not be covered in the survey.

In many survey applications, the omitted part of the population differs in many ways from the part that is included in the sampling frame. For example, if the objective of the study is to obtain information about the postreform status of all low-income families, families eligible for Temporary Assistance for Needy Families (TANF) who did not become welfare recipients will not be included in the welfare records. These families are not covered in the administrative file used for sampling, and thus they will not be covered in the sample.

The following example[2] illustrates the potential effect of the choice of sampling frame on survey noncoverage. Assume that a survey is designed to evaluate, in two states, the impact of the loss of Supplemental Security Income (SSI) benefits by individuals whose low-income status was caused by substance abuse. SSI benefit termination for this population was mandated by federal legislation (Public Law 104-121) in 1996. After SSI benefits were terminated, some of the past SSI recipients applied to Referral and Monitoring Agencies (RMA), funded by the Center for Substance Abuse Treatment (CSAT). Refer to Tonkin et al. (in press) for more details on the methodology for the CSAT study.

One of the first steps in designing a survey is to define the study population of interest. Assume that the target population consists of all individuals between the ages of 21 and 59 who were receiving SSI as a result of substance abuse and who had an active case on or before July 1, 1996. Although the population of interest is all individuals receiving benefits because of substance abuse, assume that the two states (State A and State B) used different frames for sample selection; State A used the RMA client rosters, which covered only 66 percent of the target population, and State B used the Social Security Administration client roster, which was a complete frame.

In the State A sample, individuals not included in the RMA lists of active cases (i.e., 34 percent of individuals) had no chance of being selected into the sample. This is a potential source of bias if the characteristics of interest (e.g., drug abuse) are different for individuals not covered by the RMA frame compared to those on the RMA frame. The potential for noncoverage bias increases as the frame coverage rate decreases.

Survey Nonresponse

Unit nonresponse in surveys occurs for various reasons, including the failure to locate sampled persons and the refusal of sampled persons to be interviewed. In some cases, collected data may be lost during data transmission stages. In welfare studies that collect outcome data from administrative files, nonresponse can occur because of inability to match the sampled case to the administrative file that includes the outcome data. Statistics derived from survey data may be biased if the missed persons are different, with respect to the variable of interest to the survey, from those who participated in the survey.

---

[2]The example is hypothetical but is based on actual surveys conducted in a number of counties across the United States.

LEYLA MOHADJER AND G. HUSSAIN CHOUDHRY

In the SSI benefit example, assume that the response rate was 67 percent for the State A sample and 92 percent for the State B sample. The lower response rate for State A is another source of potential bias. If those who did not participate differ in important ways from those who did, the bias due to nonresponse could be substantial.

The marginal population distributions of demographic variables—age, gender, and race—usually are available, and these can be used to examine the potential for noncoverage and nonresponse biases, as shown in the following text. Tables 5-1 and 5-2 provide the marginal distributions of the demographic vari-

TABLE 5-1 Hypothetical Population and Sample Distribution for State A

	SSI Population (%)	State A Sample (%)	State A Respondents (%)
Factor 1: Age			
Less than 40	30	26	31
40-49	44	44	47
50 or over	26	30	22
Factor 2: Gender			
Male	65	66	58
Female	35	34	42
Factor 3: Race			
White	30	38	40
Black	34	12	10
Others	36	50	50

NOTE: SSI = Supplemental Security Income.

TABLE 5-2 Hypothetical Population and Sample Distribution for State B

	SSI Population (%)	State B Sample (%)	State B Respondents (%)
Factor 1: Age			
Less than 40	37	39	40
40-49	40	38	40
50 or over	23	23	20
Factor 2: Gender			
Male	71	72	70
Female	29	28	30
Factor 3: Race			
White	7	7	6
Black	88	89	90
Others	5	4	4

NOTE: SSI = Supplemental Security Income.

ables age, gender, and race for the assumed target population (SSI only); the enrollment sample; (State A and State B selected samples), and the respondents for the two states.[3]

We observe that for State A, in spite of 34-percent noncoverage, the sample distribution is not distorted for the variable gender. However, blacks are underrepresented and the race category "others" is overrepresented in the State A sample. For State B, where a complete frame was available for sampling, the sample distributions are similar to the SSI population distributions for all three variables.

The State A sample had a moderately low response rate, resulting in a distortion in the distributions for respondents by gender and age. This obviously would bias the results if the outcome characteristics of males and females are different, or if the age distribution affects the outcome. The response rate for State B was high, and the sample distributions and the respondent distributions of all three demographic variables are very similar to the population distributions. This suggests a lower potential for substantial nonresponse and noncoverage bias.

The hypothetical samples for States A and B are examples of the impact of noncoverage and nonresponse in survey outcome. In the following subsection, we provide a general formula that attempts to quantify the bias associated with noncoverage and nonresponse.

Nonresponse Bias

The size of the nonresponse bias depends on the amount of nonresponse and the difference between the respondent and nonrespondent mean values of the study variables. For example, in an equal probability sample (a description of an unequal probability sample is provided in the section on base weights) of size n selected from a population of N families, let n_1 stand for the number of respondents and let n_2 stand for the nonrespondents where $n_2(= n - n_1)$. Let y be the study variable (e.g., family income) with $\bar{y}_1$ as the respondent mean and $\bar{y}_2$ as the mean for nonrespondents (where $\bar{y}_2$ is unknown). The sample mean $\bar{y}$ for the total sample can be expressed as (see, for example, Groves, 1989)

$$\bar{y} = \frac{1}{n}(n_1\bar{y}_1 + n_2\bar{y}_2).$$ [1]

Because $\bar{y}_2$ is unknown, analysts use $\bar{y}_1$ to estimate $\bar{y}$ for the target population. When no nonresponse adjustments are made, the bias can be estimated as

---

[3]Note that in the SSI example, samples were selected from the associated frames with equal probability. For cases where sampling involves unequal probabilities of selection, "weighted" sample distributions should be compared to the associated frame distributions. Refer to the section that discusses weighting for unequal probabilities of selection.

$$bias(\bar{y}_1) = \frac{n_2}{n}(\bar{y}_1 - \bar{y}_2).$$ [2]

Therefore, the extent of bias is a function of both the nonresponse rate (n_2/n) and the difference between the respondent and nonrespondent means ($\bar{y}_1 - \bar{y}_2$).

For example, assume that a survey of 820 low-income families has been carried out and that the variable of interest is the average monthly family income. Table 5-3 provides examples of the amount of bias in the estimate of variable of interest (i.e., average monthly family income) for various levels of nonresponse and average incomes for respondents and nonrespondents.

The level of bias in Table 5-3 is a function of both the variable response rates and the difference in the mean income for respondents and nonrespondents.

Some part of differences in average income between respondents and nonrespondents is usually due to differences in their demographic composition (e.g., race, age, as in the States A and B examples) and the fact that income tends to vary among these demographic groups. The bias resulting from this distortion of the respondent sample can be reduced considerably by devising adjustment factors and applying them to the responding units data. Adjustment factors typically vary among demographic groups, and their purpose is to establish a data set whose sample representation has been adjusted to compensate for the missing nonrespondent data. (We used the term "demographic groups" because race, age,

TABLE 5-3 Level of Bias by Nonresponse Rate and Differences in Average Income of Respondents and Nonrespondents

	Example 1		Example 2		Example 3	
	Sample Size	Average Income	Sample Size	Average Income	Sample Size	Average Income
Respondents	600	$1,500	410	$1,500	600	$2,000
Nonrespondents	220	$1,100	410	$1,100	220	$1,100
Survey estimate with no nonresponse adjustment	$1,500		$1,500		$2,000	
Estimated population value	$1,393		$1,300		$1,759	
Bias	$ 107		$ 200		$ 241	

NOTE: The data used for the Family Income Survey (FIS) example is hypothetical.

gender, and other factors, are most frequently known for the population of interest. However, sometimes additional information such as income in a recent time
period or employment status also is available for both respondents and nonrespondents. Adjustment factors can, of course, be developed for these variables
as well as the demographic variables.) The underlying assumption for these adjustments is that respondents are similar to nonrespondents within the adjustment
subgroups (or classes); that is, the data are missing at random (MAR)[4] and
nonresponse is ignorable within the nonresponse adjustment group (Little and
Rubin, 1987). Because respondents are not fully representative of nonrespondents
(the MAR assumption does not hold perfectly), some unknown bias remains,
even after conducting weighting adjustments.

The adjustments for nonresponse described in this report are designed to
eliminate the part of the bias arising from the distortion in the respondent sample,
but they have little effect on other causes of bias, which are usually independent
of the sample composition. (Among possible reasons are that many persons who
cannot be located have obtained jobs outside the area and have moved and that
nonrespondents are in some ways psychologically different from the general
population and the differences affect their ability to find employment.) Unfortunately, the extent to which these causes affect the result of a particular survey are,
in most cases, not known, and consequently there is the possibility of significant
bias when high nonresponse rates exist. Although we strongly recommend the
adjustment procedures, they should not be considered replacements for a vigor-
ous effort to achieve the highest response rate possible. They are an adjunct to
such an effort.

A later section provides a summary of the general-purpose nonresponse
adjustment methods currently used in many social surveys. The nonresponse
adjustment factors are incorporated into the survey weights. The next section
reviews the properties of sampling weights in preparation for the discussion of
nonresponse adjustment procedures.

WEIGHTING SURVEY DATA

Sample weighting is carried out to accomplish a number of objectives, including adjustments for nonresponse. The purpose of weighting the survey data is
to permit analysts to produce estimates of statistics for the total target population.
For example, state surveys usually involve the selection of a random sample of

---

[4]A more relaxed assumption is where data are missing completely at random (MCAR). The MCAR
model assumes that nonresponse occurs completely at random and does not depend on the characteristics of nonrespondents (Little and Rubin, 1987). In most surveys, however, the MCAR assumption
is not realistic, as is shown in many nonresponse bias analyses conducted for state and national
surveys (for example, see U.S. General Accounting Office (1999).

low-income persons from an existing administrative data file. Sampling weights produced for such surveys can be considered as estimated measures of the number of persons in the target population that the particular sampled low-income individual represents. Weighting takes into account several features of the survey: the specific probabilities of selection of individuals in the sample (as described in the following subsection), as well as nonresponse and differences between the sample of low-income persons and the total low-income population. Differences between the sample and the population may arise because of sampling variability, differential noncoverage in the survey among population subgroups, and possibly other types of response errors, such as differential response rates or misclassification errors.

In summary, sample weighting in surveys is carried out to accomplish the following objectives:

• To enable the production of tabulations that provide estimates of the number of persons (or families) in the population for the various categories tabulated;
• To compensate for disproportionate sampling of various subgroups in the sample;
• To reduce biases arising from the fact that nonrespondents may be different from those who participate;
• To compensate, to the extent possible, for noncoverage in the sample due to inadequacies in the sampling frame or other reasons for noncoverage; and
• To reduce variances in the estimation procedure by using auxiliary information that is known with a high degree of accuracy if the auxiliary variables are highly correlated with the study variables.

We start with a description of base weights because the adjustments are applied to these weights.

Base Weights

The base weight for a sample unit (e.g., a sampled low-income family) is defined as the reciprocal of the probability of including the unit in the sample. The base weight for the i-th unit in the sample is given by

$$w_i = \frac{1}{\pi_i},$$ [3]

where π_i is the known probability of including unit i in the sample. If the sample units are selected with equal probability, the probability of selection is $\pi_i = n/N$ for all sample units, where n is the sample size and N is the number of units in the sampling frame. The base weight, therefore, is $w_i = N/n$ for all sampled units. In this case, $\sum_{i=1}^{n} w_i = N$. In the family income survey (FIS) example given earlier, assume that a sample of $n = 820$ families was selected with equal probabilities of selection from a population of $N = 41,000$ families. Then the probability of selection for each unit in the sample is equal to $n/N = 820/41,000$, and the base weight would be equal to $N/n = 50$ for each sampled family. Thus, each family selected into the sample represents 50 families in the administrative file used for sampling.

State surveys may be designed to provide an equal probability sample (similar to the previous example) or a disproportionate sample of low-income persons with respect to a selected set of characteristics (e.g., demographic characteristics). In an equal-probability sample, the distribution of the sample is expected to be similar to the administrative frame. For example, if the administrative frame in state S includes 10 percent Hispanics and 90 percent non-Hispanics, an equal probability sample is expected to include about 10 percent Hispanics and 90 percent non-Hispanics. However, if state S is interested in analyzing the well-being of the low-income Hispanic population, the survey is likely to include an oversampling of low-income Hispanic persons. The oversampling can be accomplished by stratifying the frame into two strata, Hispanics and non-Hispanics, and applying a larger sampling rate to Hispanics. In this case, the sample will contain a disproportionate representation of Hispanics. When disproportionate sampling is applied in stratified sampling, different weights (referred to as base weights) are used to compensate for the unequal representation in the sample. Otherwise, estimates will be biased. Returning to the FIS example, assume that Hispanic families are sampled at a rate of 1 in 30 and that non-Hispanics are sampled at a rate of 1 in 60. Then the base weight for the Hispanics is equal to 30, and the base weight for non-Hispanics is equal to 60. Thus, each sampled Hispanic family represents 30 Hispanic families in the population, and each non-Hispanic family in the sample represents 60 non-Hispanic families in the population. For more information on disproportionate sampling, refer to Kish (1992).

Although the base weights are theoretically unbiased weights that "inflate" the sample observations to population levels, in practice, most survey practitioners find it useful to modify the base weights. Nonresponse in the survey, for example, results in losses in the sample data that can be partially compensated for by adjusting the weights of the respondents. If the sampling frame is deficient because it is outdated or its coverage of certain population subgroups is inadequate, further adjustment of the weights may be desirable to compensate for these deficiencies. The following section provides brief descriptions of various weight adjustment procedures commonly used in large-scale surveys.

COMMON NONRESPONSE ADJUSTMENT
METHODS IN SURVEYS

In spite of the best strategies for collecting data from sampled units, non-response nearly always occurs in population surveys, including those of low-income families. A "nonrespondent" is any sampled unit that is eligible for the study but for which data are not obtained for any reason. Failure to match the sample cases with the administrative files used to gather outcome data, refusal to participate in the survey, or situations such as "not-at-home after multiple calls," "language problems," and "knowledgeable person not available" are some of the reasons why an eligible sampled unit may not participate in a survey. On the other hand, sampled units that are ineligible for the survey are not considered nonrespondents, even though they do not provide survey data. As discussed later in this section, nonrespondents and ineligibles are treated differently in the nonresponse adjustment process.

When nonresponse is present, a weight adjustment can partially compensate for the loss of data. This weight adjustment increases the weights of the sampled cases for which data were collected. The first step in adjusting for nonresponse is the construction of weighting classes. As discussed in the following text, within each weighting class, the base weights are inflated by the inverse of the response rate so that the sum of the adjusted base weights for respondents is equal to the sum of the base weights for the total eligible sample selected in the weighting class. Returning to the FIS example, assume that 160 families were selected (with equal probability) within a weighting class and that 77 families responded to the survey. Because the weight for each family is equal to 50 (as shown earlier), the nonresponse-adjusted weight is about 104 (i.e., 50 multiplied by 160/77). Thus, after nonresponse adjustment each responding family in the sample represents about 104 families in the population within the weighting class.

The effectiveness of nonresponse adjustment procedures in reducing non-response bias is directly related to the ability to construct appropriate nonresponse adjustment classes. The following subsection provides a brief summary of two procedures commonly used to construct adjustment classes. The next subsection discusses sample-based adjustment procedures that are commonly used to compensate for nonresponse. Then we describe population-based adjustment procedures (poststratification and raking) that are widely used for noncoverage adjustment, or sometimes used to correct simultaneously for both nonresponse and noncoverage. Additional benefits of population-based adjustments include reduction in the sampling errors of the sample estimates as well as achieving consistency with the known population counts. In poststratification and raking, respondents are categorized according to one or more variables (e.g., age, gender, race, or income level) at a recent point in time, and the survey estimates are benchmarked to the known population totals. For a general review of weighting for nonresponse, refer to Elliot (1991). Finally, we provide a discussion of the importance of balancing bias and variance when adjusting survey data.

Construction of Nonresponse Adjustment Classes

Implementing nonresponse adjustment procedures requires the specification of appropriate weighting classes or cells. Survey responses generally are correlated with certain characteristics of the sample units, and it would be desirable to form classes based on these characteristics. Often, little is known about the nonrespondents. Relevant information about each sampled unit sometimes can be obtained through data retrieval efforts to collect limited data about the nonrespondents or by interviewer observation (if applicable). The availability of this information would enhance the effectiveness of the nonresponse adjustment.

Data used to form classes for nonresponse adjustments must be available for both respondents and nonrespondents. In state low-income surveys, the administrative files used to select the sample are good sources of information for forming weighting classes. In a recent survey, we contacted a number of states to inquire about the availability and the quality of their administrative data, including the following variables:

- Demographic
    Age
    Gender
    Race/ethnicity
    Marital status
    Number of children
- Socioeconomic
    Education
    Employment
    Earned income
    Welfare income
    Housing subsidy
    Length of time on welfare
- Geographic
    Urban/rural
    Metropolitan/nonmetropolitan status
    County code
    Zip code

Thirteen states completed our questionnaire. All states reported having data on age, gender, race/ethnicity, number of children, and length of time on welfare. Most states also have data on earned income, welfare income, employment, county code, zip code, and marital status. About 50 to 60 percent of states reported having data on education, housing subsidies, metropolitan/nonmetropolitan status, and urbanicity. The 13 states that responded to the questionnaire on auxiliary data also indicated their assessments of the quality of the administrative data that their state maintains. We observed that the quality of data on demographic variables was quite high, with less than 1 percent missing values. For the socioeconomic variables, the only two variables with high-quality data are "welfare income" and "length of time on welfare," where length of time on welfare is measured for the most recent episode. Data on employment and earned income, if applicable, were obtained by matching with quarterly wage records. The only geographic variables of high quality are county and zip codes. We encourage state welfare program administrators to look for other potential data sources that could be used as auxiliary variables for nonresponse and/or noncoverage adjustments, such as wages and employment data sources. The above variables are usually good candidates for use in nonresponse adjustment. However, missing data on items used for nonresponse adjustment can present problems for postsurvey adjustments. If a substantial amount of data are missing for an item on the sampling frame, this variable is probably not appropriate for the purpose of nonresponse adjustments.

The variables used to form weighting classes should be effective in distinguishing between subgroups with different response rates. They are most useful when survey responses are roughly similar for respondents and nonrespondents within a class. If this implicit assumption holds, the estimates are effectively unbiased. In establishing the nonresponse adjustment classes, the following should be kept in mind:

• The variables used in nonresponse adjustment should be available for both respondents and nonrespondents;
• Response rates should be different among the nonresponse adjustment classes;
• Survey responses are expected to be different among the classes; and
• The adjustment classes should respect a balance between bias and variance (refer to the section entitled "Balancing Bias and Variance When Adjusting for Nonresponse" for a discussion of balancing bias and variance when creating adjusted sampling weights).

As mentioned earlier, knowledge of the likely behavior of persons in various demographic and socioeconomic classes can be used to construct weighting classes. A preliminary analysis of response rates in these classes can refine the classification further.

Returning to the FIS example provided earlier, assume that nonresponse evaluation research has identified the gender and race (white/nonwhite) of the head of family as the best predictors of nonresponse. Then, the sample is divided into four classes, as shown in Table 5-4. Note that mean income and the non-

TABLE 5-4 Nonresponse Adjustment Classes for the FIS* Example

Adjustment Class	Head of Family's Gender and Race	Sample Size	Respondent Mean Income ($)	Respondents	Nonresponse Rate (%)
	Male				
1	White	160	1,712	77	52
2	Nonwhite	51	1,509	35	31
	Female				
3	White	251	982	209	17
4	Nonwhite	358	911	327	9
	Total	820	1,061	648	21

NOTE: *Family Income Survey = FIS.

response rate are both quite variable across the four classes. This suggests that the adjustments have the potential to reduce the nonresponse bias.

More sophisticated methods also are available. We discuss two commonly used procedures (referred to as modeling response propensity) for defining weighting classes using data on auxiliary variables. The first method involves classification or segmentation based on a categorical search algorithm. The second method is based on logistic regression modeling. Software is available to perform the computations required for both procedures.

The first class of methods divides a population into two or more distinct groups based on categories of the "best" predictor of a dependent variable. The dependent variable is a categorical variable with two categories: respondents and nonrespondents. The predictor variable with the highest significance level is used to split the sample into groups. It then splits each of these groups into smaller subgroups based on other predictor variables. This splitting process continues until no more statistically significant predictors can be found, or until some other stopping rule is met (e.g., there are too few observations for further splitting). The result is a tree-like structure that suggests which predictor variable may be important.[5] It is a highly efficient statistical technique for segregation, or tree growing, with many different versions currently available, as described in Breiman et al., (1993).

The second approach models the response status of the sampled units using predictor variables that are known for both respondents and nonrespondents from

---

[5]The above cell creation can be carried out using SPSS AnswerTree. For more information about SPSS AnswerTree, visit http://www.spss.com.

the sampling frame. Most commonly, the prediction approach is based on a logistic or probit regression model effectively using auxiliary variables, such as demographic, socioeconomic, and geographic variables, to predict the probability of response. For more information on logistic response propensity modeling, refer to Little and Rubin (1987), Brick and Kalton (1996), and Iannacchione et al. (1991).

Sample-Based Adjustment Procedures

Sample-based nonresponse adjustments make use of information that is available for the sample, and thus do not require any external population counts. In effect, sample-based nonresponse adjustments distribute the base weights of the nonresponding units to the responding sampled units so that the sum of the adjusted weights over the responding units equals the sum of the base weights for the entire sample.

The basic form of the sample-based nonresponse adjustments is a ratio of sums of base weights where the sums extend over specified subsets of the sample defined by response status. The particular form of the adjustment depends on whether the eligibility status of the nonresponding units can be ascertained. First, we describe the nonresponse adjustment under the assumption that every sampled unit can be assigned to one of the following three response status groups:

Group 1: **Respondents.** This group consists of all eligible sample units that participated in the survey (i.e., provided usable survey data).

Group 2: **Nonrespondents.** This group consists of all eligible sample units that did not provide usable survey data.

Group 3: **Ineligible or out of scope.** This group consists of all sample units that were ineligible or out of scope for the survey.

In this particular case, it is assumed that all of the nonrespondents (Group 2) in the sample have been determined to be eligible for the survey and that all of those in Group 3 have been determined to be ineligible for the survey. If eligibility is unknown for some of the selected cases, the usual approach is to distribute proportionally the weights of those with unknown eligibility to those for which eligibility was determined. In the FIS example, let's assume that 850 families originally were selected from an administrative file. However, it was determined later that 30 families were ineligible because the administrative frame was outdated, for example. The total number of eligible families is 820, and 648 responded to the survey. In this case, Group 1 = 648, Group 2 = 172, and Group 3 = 30. The corresponding sample-based nonresponse adjustment factor $A^{(nr)}$ is defined to be the ratio of sums:

$$A^{(nr)} = \frac{\sum\limits_{i \in R} w_i + \sum\limits_{i \in N} w_i}{\sum\limits_{i \in R} w_i}, \qquad [4]$$

where w_i is the base weight for the sampled unit i, R represents survey respondents (Group 1), and N represents nonrespondents (Group 2). The adjustment factor $A^{(nr)}$ is applied only to the base weights of the respondents (Group 1) in the sample; that is, the nonresponse-adjusted weight w_i^* is computed as

$w_i^* = 0$, if unit i is nonrespondent (Group 2).
$w_i^* = w_i$, if unit i is out of scope (Group 3).
$w_i^* = A^{(nr)}w_i$, if unit i is an eligible respondent (Group 1).

In practice, the nonresponse adjustment, $A^{(nr)}$, is calculated within specified weighting or adjustment classes. The procedures for forming appropriate weighting classes for this purpose were discussed earlier.

Table 5-5 shows the nonresponse adjustment factors and adjusted weights for the FIS example. Because the base weights are equal to N/n (=50) for each sampled family (as shown in an earlier section on base weights), the nonresponse adjustment factors in column 4 are simply equal to the ratio of column 2 to column 3. The base weights would be adjusted by multiplying the base weights by the nonresponse adjustment factors i.e., column 1 multiplied by column 4.

TABLE 5-5 Nonresponse Adjustment Factors and the Adjusted Weights for the FIS* Example

Head of Family's Gender and Race	Base Weight (1)	Sample Size (2)	Respondents (3)	Nonresponse Adjustment Factor (4)	Adjusted Weight** (5)
Male					
White	50	160	77	2.08	104
Nonwhite	50	51	35	1.46	73
Female					
White	50	251	209	1.20	60
Nonwhite	50	358	327	1.10	55
Total		820	648		

NOTES:
*Family Income Survey
**For presentation purposes, we have rounded up the adjustment factors (to two decimals) and the adjusted weights (to whole numbers). The calculations, however, carry all the decimals.

That is, the adjusted weight for each of the respondents in the four cells created by gender and race is equal to the weight given in column (5).

Population-Based Adjustments

In applications where external control counts are available for weighting, the usual practice is to first calculate sample-based nonresponse-adjusted weights and then to further adjust these weights through population-based adjustments. Population-based adjustment tends to reduce the effects of noncoverage (e.g., incomplete frames) and improve the representation of the sample. Sometimes, it is convenient or necessary to bypass the intermediate step of calculating the sample-based nonresponse-adjusted weights. In this case, the base weights would be ratio adjusted directly to known control totals in a single step. For example, if the classes used for nonresponse adjustment also are used for population-based adjustments, the two-step procedure of first adjusting for nonresponse and then adjusting to known control totals is equivalent to the single population-based adjustment procedure discussed in this section. Separate nonresponse adjustments are necessary when the nonresponse weighting classes are different from those planned for the population-based adjustments. This is usually, although not always, the case because different sources of data are available for each adjustment. In the following sections, we briefly describe the two most commonly used population-based adjustment procedures.

The term "calibration" is used in the literature to cover a variety of techniques used in benchmarking the weights to known external totals. In this paper, we focus our attention on the two procedures most commonly used in general surveys: poststratification and raking.

Poststratification

Poststratification is a popular estimation procedure in which the weights of the respondents are adjusted further so that the sums of the adjusted weights are equal to known population totals for certain subgroups of the population. For example, take the case where the population totals of subgroups (referred to as poststrata) defined by age, gender, and race/ethnicity are known from the sampling frame (or other external sources), and they also can be estimated from the survey. Poststratification adjusts the survey weights so that the distribution by subgroups (when weighted by the poststratified weights) is the same as the population distribution from the survey frame or external sources.

Let N_g denote the population count in the poststratum denoted by g as obtained from the sampling frame or an external source, and let $\hat{N}_g$ be the corresponding survey estimate obtained by using the nonresponse-adjusted weights. Then the ratio $N_g / \hat{N}_g$ is the poststratification adjustment factor for subgroup g.

The main advantage of poststratification is that the procedure reduces the bias from some types of noncoverage and nonresponse. An additional advantage of poststratification is the improvement in the reliability of the survey estimates for variables that are highly correlated with the variables used for post-stratification. Generally, the poststratified weights are the final survey weights, and these would be used to tabulate the survey results. Occasionally, an additional weighting factor, called a "trimming factor," is used to protect against extremely high variances. A brief description of trimming procedures used in practice is provided in a later section. If a trimming factor is calculated for a survey data file, it should be incorporated into the final weight as another multiplication factor.

Earlier, we illustrated the nonresponse adjustment procedure by assuming that the number of families in the population was 41,000 and that there was no noncoverage. We continue the FIS example, assuming that the number of families in the population was actually 46,000 and that the sampling frame contained only 41,000 families because information necessary for locating respondents was missing for 5,000 families. However, some limited demographic and other socio-economic information was available in the data files for all 46,000 families. Suppose further that the noncoverage rate varies within the four cells defined by the cross-classification of employment status (employed/not employed) and education (high school diploma/no high school diploma) of the head of the family. Poststratification adjustment can be applied to reduce the bias arising from non-coverage.

The poststratification adjustment factor for a poststratification cell is the ratio of the known family count within the poststratification cell to the corresponding estimate of the family count from the survey. The estimate of the family count within a poststratification cell is obtained by summing the nonresponse-adjusted weights of the families (as shown in Table 5-5) in the poststratification cell. Because the base weights were adjusted to account for the nonresponse (as given in Table 5-5), these adjusted weights would vary by poststratified adjustment classes. Therefore, Table 5-6 gives the count and the adjusted weight for the 16 cells defined by the cross-classification of nonresponse adjustment classes (4 classes) and poststrata (4 cells).

Column 2 is the nonresponse adjusted weight for each family in the gender/race/employment/education class. The initial estimate of total number of families in each class (taking nonresponse into account) is the product of colums 1 and 2 and is given in column 3. The total of the nonresponse-adjusted weights (column 3) can be used to estimate the number of families by poststrata defined by employment status and education of the head of the family. Table 5-7 provides the estimates of the family count and the corresponding known family count from external sources by poststrata. The table also gives the poststratification adjust-

TABLE 5-6 Distribution of Nonresponse-Adjusted Weights by Gender, Race, Employment, and Education for the FIS* Example

Head of family			Respondent Count (1)	Nonresponse-Adjusted Weight** (2)	Initial Estimated No. of Families (3)
Gender and Race	Employment	Education			
Male					
White	Employed	HS***	38	104	3,948
Nonwhite	Employed	HS	15	73	1,093
White	Employed	No HS	11	104	1,143
Nonwhite	Employed	No HS	6	73	437
White	Unemployed	HS	12	104	1,247
Nonwhite	Unemployed	HS	5	73	364
White	Unemployed	No HS	16	104	1,662
Nonwhite	Unemployed	No HS	9	73	656
Female					
White	Employed	HS	101	60	6,065
Nonwhite	Employed	HS	158	55	8,649
White	Employed	No HS	30	60	1,801
Nonwhite	Employed	No HS	47	55	2,573
White	Unemployed	HS	33	60	1,982
Nonwhite	Unemployed	HS	51	55	2,792
White	Unemployed	No HS	45	60	2,702
Nonwhite	Unemployed	No HS	71	55	3,887
Total			648		41,000

NOTES:
*Family Income Study
**For presentation purposes, adjusted weights are rounded to whole numbers. The calculations, however, carry all the decimals.
***HS = high school diploma.

ment factors, defined as the ratio of the known family count and the survey estimate.

The final survey weights are defined as the product of the base weight and the adjustment factors for nonresponse and poststratification. Table 5-8 includes the final weights for the FIS example. The final weight in column 5 is equal to the product of the base weight in column 1 and the nonresponse adjustment in column 3 and the poststratification factor in column 4.

It is not always possible to use poststratification because it requires data on the cross-classification of categorical variables that are used to define poststrata. Either the cell-level population counts may not be available or the sample sizes

TABLE 5-7 Poststratification Adjustment Factors for the FIS* Example

Poststratum	Initial Survey Estimate*	Known Auxiliary Total	Adjustment Factor**
Employed			
HS***	19,757	22,125	1.12
No HS	5,955	6,313	1.06
Unemployed			
HS	6,385	6,966	1.09
No HS	8,908	10,596	1.19

NOTES:
  *Family Income Study
  **For presentation purposes, we have rounded up the adjustment factors (to two decimals) and the adjusted weights (to whole numbers). The calculations, however, carry all the decimals.
  ***HS = high school diploma.

for some of the cells in the poststrata may not be adequate (for a discussion of adequate cell sample sizes, refer to the following section entitled "Balancing Bias and Variance When Adjusting for Nonresponse"). In such situations, survey practitioners frequently use a more complex poststratification method, referred to as a raking procedure, which adjusts the survey estimates to the known marginal totals of several categorical variables.

Raking Procedure

This methodology is referred to as raking ratio estimation because an iterative procedure is used to produce adjustment factors that provide consistency with known marginal population totals. Typically, raking is used in situations where the interior cell counts of a cross-tabulation are unknown or the sample sizes in some cells are too small for efficient estimation (refer to the following section for more information about sufficient cell sample size).

Raking ratio estimation is based on an iterative proportional fitting procedure developed by Deming and Stephan (1940). It involves simultaneous ratio adjustments of sample data to two or more marginal distributions of the population counts. With this approach, the weights are calculated such that the marginal distribution of the weighted totals conforms to the marginal distribution of the targeted population; some, or all, of the interior cells may differ.

The raking procedure is carried out in a sequence of adjustments. The base weights (or nonresponse-adjusted weights) are first adjusted to produce one marginal distribution, the adjusted weights are used to produce a second marginal distribution, and so on, up to the number of raking dimensions. One sequence of adjustments to the marginal distributions is known as a cycle or iteration. The sequence of adjustments is repeated until convergence is achieved, meaning that

TABLE 5-8 Final Poststratified Weights for the FIS* Example

Poststratum — Head of Family's Gender and Race	Employment	Education	Base Weight (1)	Respondents (2)	Nonresponse Adjustment (3)**	Poststrat. Adjustment (4)**	Final Weight (5)**	Final Estimate of No. of Families (6)
Male								
White	Employed	HS***	50	38	2.08	1.12	116	4,422
Nonwhite	Employed	HS	50	15	1.46	1.12	82	1,224
White	Employed	No HS	50	11	2.08	1.06	110	1,212
Nonwhite	Employed	No HS	50	6	1.46	1.06	77	463
White	Unemployed	HS	50	12	2.08	1.09	113	1,360
Nonwhite	Unemployed	HS	50	5	1.46	1.09	80	397
White	Unemployed	No HS	50	16	2.08	1.19	124	1,978
Nonwhite	Unemployed	No HS	50	9	1.46	1.19	87	780
Female								
White	Employed	HS	50	101	1.20	1.12	67	6,793
Nonwhite	Employed	HS	50	158	1.10	1.12	62	9,687
White	Employed	No HS	50	30	1.20	1.06	64	1,910
Nonwhite	Employed	No HS	50	47	1.10	1.06	58	2,728
White	Unemployed	HS	50	33	1.20	1.09	65	2,162
Nonwhite	Unemployed	HS	50	51	1.10	1.09	60	3,046
White	Unemployed	No HS	50	45	1.20	1.19	71	3,215
Nonwhite	Unemployed	No HS	50	71	1.10	1.19	65	4,624
Total				648				46,000

NOTES:

*Family Income Survey

**For presentation purposes, we have rounded up the adjustment factors (to two decimals) and the adjusted weights (to whole numbers). The calculations, however, carry all the decimals.

*** HS = high school diploma.

the weights no longer change with each iteration. In practice, the raking procedure usually converges, but the number of iterations may be large when there are many marginal distributions involved in raking.

The final weights are produced automatically by the software that implements raking. The raking procedure only benchmarks the sample to known marginal distributions of the population; it should not be assumed that the resulting solution is "closer to truth" at the cross-classification cell level as well. The final solution from a raking procedure may not reflect the correlation structure among different variables. For a more complete discussion of raking, refer to Kalton and Kasprzyk (1986).

As noted earlier, raking is one of a range of related methods known as calibration methods. One specific calibration method is GREG (Generalized REGression). GREG is not as commonly used as poststratification and raking because of its rather complex application and some of its limitations. Refer to Särndal et al. (1992) and Valliant et al. (2000) for a description of GREG.[6] For information about calibration techniques, refer to Deville and Särndal (1992) and Theberge (2000).

The weighting system is implemented by assigning weights to each person (or family) in the sample, inserting the weight into the computer record for each person, and incorporating the weights in the estimation process using software created for survey data analysis.

Balancing Bias and Variance When Adjusting for Nonresponse

The fundamental objective of the design of any survey sample is to produce a survey data set, that, for a given cost of data collection, will produce statistics that are nearly unbiased and sufficiently precise to satisfy the goals of the expected analyses of the data. In general, the goal is to keep the mean square error (MSE) of the primary statistics of interest as low as possible. The MSE of a survey estimate is

$$\text{MSE} = \text{Variance} + (\text{Bias})^2. \qquad [5]$$

The purpose of the weighting adjustments discussed in this paper is to reduce the bias associated with noncoverage and nonresponse in surveys. Thus, the application of weighting adjustments usually results in lower bias in the associated survey statistics, but at the same time adjustments may result in some increases in variances of the survey estimates.

The increases in variance result from the added variability in the sampling weights due to nonresponse and noncoverage adjustments. Thus, the analysts

---

[6]GREG and some similar procedures are available in GES (Generalized Estimation Systems), developed by Statistics Canada. For more information about GES, refer to Estevao et al. (1995).

who create the weighting adjustment factors need to pay careful attention to the variability in the sampling weights caused by these adjustments. The variability in weights will reduce the precision of the estimates. Thus, a tradeoff should be made between variance and bias to keep the MSE as low as possible. However, there is no exact rule for this tradeoff because the amount of bias is unknown.

In general, weighting class adjustments frequently result in increases in the variance of survey estimates when (1) many weighting classes are created with a few respondents in each class, and (2) some weighting classes have very large adjustment factors (possibly due to much higher nonresponse or noncoverage rates in these classes). To avoid such situations, survey statisticians commonly limit the number of weighting classes created during the adjustment process. In general, although exact rules do not exist for minimum sample sizes or adjustment factors for adjustment cells, statisticians usually avoid cells with fewer than 20 or 30 sample cases or adjustment factors larger than 1.5 to 2. Refer to Kalton and Kasprzyk (1986) for more information on this topic.

Occasionally, the procedures used to create the weights may result in a few cases with extremely large weights. Extreme weights can seriously inflate the variance of survey estimates. "Weight trimming" procedures are commonly used to reduce the impact of such large weights on the estimates produced from the sample.

Weight trimming refers to the process of adjusting a few extreme weights to reduce their impact on the weighted estimates (i.e., increase in the variances of the estimates). Trimming introduces a bias in the estimates; however, most statisticians believe that the resulting reduction in variance decreases the MSE. The inspection method, described in Potter (1988, 1990), is a common trimming method used in many surveys. This method involves the inspection of the distribution of weights in the sample. Based on this inspection, outlier weights are truncated at an acceptable level (the acceptable level is derived based on a tradeoff between bias and variance). The truncated weights then are redistributed so that the total weighted counts still match the weighted total before weight trimming.

Analysts should pay attention to the variability of the weights when working with survey data, even though all measures (such as limits on adjustment cell sizes, and weight trimming) may have been taken to keep the variability of weights in moderation. Analysts should keep in mind that large variable values in conjunction with large weights may result in extremely influential observations, that is, observations that dominate the analysis.

Analyzing Weighted Survey Data

Because estimates will be based on sample data, they will differ from figures that would have been obtained from complete enumeration of the universe. Results are subject to both sampling and nonsampling errors. Nonsampling errors include biases because of inaccurate reporting, measurement and processing errors, as well as errors because of nonresponse and incomplete sampling frames. Inaccurate or incomplete responses can occur due to misunderstanding or the misinterpretation of questions. Errors can also occur when responses are coded, edited, and entered into the database. Generally, the nonsampling errors cannot be measured readily but a number of quality assurance techniques are employed to reduce the frequency of such errors.

For the computation of sampling errors, most standard techniques used in statistical packages (e.g., SAS, SPSS, and others) assume that observations are independent and drawn using simple random sampling (SRS) selection methods and that all sampled cases participated in the survey. The estimates of variances for complex survey designs computed using standard statistical software packages that assume simple random sampling and a 100-percent response rate are biased. Once a sample departs from SRS and in the presence of nonresponse (especially in cases where nonresponse is rather high), new computational procedures are required in order to take into account the impact of survey design and nonresponse on statistical estimation. Two common approaches available for estimation of variances for complex survey data are Taylor linearization and replication. Using these procedures, factors such as stratification and the use of differential sampling rates to oversample a targeted subpopulation, and adjustments for nonresponse, can be reflected appropriately in estimates of sampling error. Wolter (1985) is a useful reference on the theory underlying variance estimation using replication and Taylor linearization methods. For information about relevant survey analysis software, visit http://www.amstat.org/srms/links.html.

SUMMARY

The occurrence of missing data—whether for a unit or an item and whether due to nonresponse or noncoverage—creates the potential for bias. The potential for bias is particularly great in the presence of high nonresponse rates. In this paper, we provided brief descriptions of the methods most commonly used to adjust for unit nonresponse and noncoverage in general-purpose surveys. However, it is also very important to pay attention to nonresponse rates for each item in the questionnaire, and data analysts should consider using imputation procedures to compensate for missing items in the state surveys.

As discussed earlier, studies of the low-income population usually suffer from missing data. In studies that include only administrative data, noncoverage bias can result from using an incomplete administrative frame of eligible persons, and nonresponse occurs because of an inability to match the sample with the administrative file that includes the outcome data. Surveys are also subject to both underrepresentation due to nonresponse and frame noncoverage. Descriptions of nonresponse and frame noncoverage also are provided.

We also summarize the most commonly used procedures for nonresponse adjustments in multipurpose surveys. There are basically two types of adjustments, sample-based and population-based adjustments. The first group is based on procedures that use only sample information to reduce the nonresponse bias. The second approach uses external data to reduce the effects of both nonresponse and noncoverage. These adjustments are applied to respondents' records after the sample has been divided into a number of subgroups, called nonresponse adjustment classes. Adjustment methods for unit nonresponse involve deriving adjustment factors to be incorporated into sampling weights. A brief description of sample weighting is given in a previous section. When data are collected as part of a survey and sample weights are created, special procedures are needed to analyze the survey data. The previous section provides a brief review of the current procedures used to analyze weighted survey data.

Nonresponse adjustment methods can serve to reduce nonresponse bias. However, the total elimination of such bias generally is not possible, because within any weighting class the respondents ordinarily will not be fully representative of the nonrespondents. The impact of nonresponse bias is usually small in surveys with low nonresponse rates when nonresponse-adjusted weights are used along with the survey data. Although sample weighting cannot take all differences between respondents and nonrespondents into account, the weighting cells that are usually used appear, in general, to reduce the effect of any potential differences between respondents and nonrespondents.

The potential for bias is particularly great in the presence of high nonresponse rates. Thus, analysts are advised to take survey nonresponse rates and effects on the reliability of data into account when analyzing and reporting survey data. Analysis based on data from surveys with low nonresponse rates can be reported with a much higher level of confidence than those coming from surveys with high nonresponse rates.

REFERENCES

Breiman, L., J.H. Friedman, R.A. Olshen, and C.J. Stone
  1993   *Classification and Regression Trees.* New York: Chapman & Hall.
Brick, J.M., and G. Kalton
  1996   Handling missing data in survey research. *Statistical Methods in Medical Research* 5:215-238.
Deming, W.E., and F.F. Stephan
  1940   On a least square adjustment of a sampled frequency table when the expected marginal totals are known. *Annals of Mathematical Statistics* 11:427-444.
Deville, J.C., and C.E. Särndal
  1992   Calibration estimators in survey sampling. *Journal of the American Statistical Association* 74:911-915.
Elliot, D.
  1991   *Weighting for Non-Response: A Survey Researcher's Guide.* London, England: Office of Population Censuses and Surveys, Social Survey Division.

Estevao, V., M. Hidiroglou, and C.E. Särndal
   1995   Methodological principles for a generalized estimation system at Statistics Canada. *Journal of Official Statistics* 11:181-204.
Groves, R.M.
   1989   *Survey Errors and Survey Costs.* New York: Wiley.
Iannacchione, V.G., J.G. Milne, and R.E. Folsom
   1991   Response probability weight adjustments using logistic regression. Pp. 637-642 in *Proceedings of the Section on Survey Research Methods, American Statistical Association.* Alexandria, VA: American Statistical Association.
Kalton, G., and D. Kasprzyk
   1986   The treatment of missing survey data. *Survey Methodology* 12(1):1-16.
Kish, L.
   1992   Weighting for unequal P_i. *Journal of Official Statistics* 8:183-200.
Little, R.J.A., and D.B. Rubin
   1987   *Statistical Analysis with Missing Data.* New York: Wiley.
Potter, F.
   1988   Survey of procedures to control extreme sampling weights. Pp. 453-458 in *Proceedings of the Section on Survey Research Methods, American Statistical Association.* Alexandria, VA: American Statistical Association.
   1990   A study of procedures to identify and trim extreme sampling weights. Pp. 225-230 in *Proceedings of the Section on Survey Research Methods, American Statistical Association.* Alexandria, VA: American Statistical Association
Särndal, C.-E., B. Swensson, and J. Wretman
   1992   *Model-Assisted Survey Sampling.* New York: Springer-Verlag.
Theberge, A.
   2000   Calibration and restricted weights. *Survey Methodology* 26(1):99-107.
Tonkin, P., J. Swartz, and J. Baumohl
   in   The Methodology of CSAT's Study of the Termination of Supplement Security Income
   press   Benefits for Drug Addicts and Alcoholics—Contemporary Drug Problems.
U.S. General Accounting Office
   1999   *Welfare Reform, Information on Former Recipients' Status.* (GAO/HFHS–99-48). Washington, DC: U.S. Government Printing Office.
Valliant, R., A. Dorfman, and R. Royall
   2000   *Finite Populations Sampling and Reference: A Prediction Approach.* New York: Wiley.
Wolter, K.
   1985   *Introduction to Variance Estimation.* New York: Springer-Verlag.

6

Measurement Error in Surveys of the Low-Income Population

Nancy A. Mathiowetz, Charlie Brown, and John Bound

The measurement of the characteristics and behavioral experience among members of the low-income and welfare populations offers particular challenges with respect to reducing various sources of response error. For many of the substantive areas of interest, the behavioral experience of the welfare populations is complex, unstable, and highly variable over time. As the behavioral experience of respondents increases in complexity, so do the cognitive demands of a survey interview. Contrast the task of reporting employment and earnings for an individual continuously employed during the past calendar year with the response task of someone who has held three to four part-time jobs. Other questionnaire topics may request that the respondent report sensitive, threatening, socially undesirable, or perhaps illegal behavior. From both a cognitive and social psychological perspective, there is ample opportunity for the introduction of error in the reporting of the events and behaviors of primary interest in understanding the impacts of welfare reform.

This paper provides an introduction to these sources of measurement error and examines two theoretical frameworks for understanding the various sources of error. The empirical literature concerning the quality of responses for reports of earnings, transfer income, employment and unemployment, and sensitive behaviors is examined, to identify those items most likely to be subjected to response error among the welfare population. The paper concludes with suggestions for attempting to reduce the various sources of error through alternative questionnaire and survey design.

SOURCES OF ERROR IN THE SURVEY PROCESS

The various disciplines that embrace the survey method, including statistics, psychology, sociology, and economics, share a common concern with the weakness of the measurement process, the degree to which survey results deviate from "those that are the true reflections of the population" (Groves, 1989). The disciplines vary in the terminology used to describe error as well as their emphasis on understanding the impact of measurement error on analyses or the reduction of the various sources of error. The existence of these terminological differences and our desire to limit the focus of this research to *measurement error* suggests that a brief commentary on the various conceptual frameworks may aid in defining our interests unambiguously.

One common conceptual framework is that of mean squared error, the sum of the variance and the square of the bias. Variance is the measure of the variable error associated with a particular implementation of a survey; inherent in the notion of variable error is the fundamental requirement of replication, whether over units of observation (sample units), questions, or interviewers. Bias, as used here, is defined as the type of error that affects all implementations of a survey design, a constant error, within a defined set of essential survey conditions (Hansen et al., 1961). For example, the use of a single question to obtain total family income in the Current Population Survey (CPS) has been shown to underestimate annual income by approximately 20 percent (U.S. Bureau of the Census, 1979); this consistent underestimate would be considered the extent of the bias related to a particular question for a given survey design.

Another conceptual framework focuses on errors of observation as compared to errors of nonobservation (Kish, 1965). Errors of observation refer to the degree to which individual responses deviate from the true value for the measure of interest; as defined, they are the errors of interest for this research, to be referred to as measurement errors. Observational errors can arise from any of the elements directly engaged in the measurement process, including the questionnaire, the respondent, and the interviewer, as well as the characteristics that define the measurement process (e.g., the mode and method of data collection). Errors of nonobservation refer to errors related to the lack of measurement for some portion of the sample and can be classified as arising from three sources, coverage: nonresponse (both unit and item nonresponse), and sampling. Errors of nonobservation are the focus of other papers presented in this volume (see, for example, Groves and Couper, this volume).

Questionnaire as Source of Measurement Error

Ideally a question will convey to the respondent the meaning of interest to the researcher. However, several linguistic, structural, and environmental factors affect the interpretation of the question by the respondent. These factors include the specific question wording, the structure of each question (open versus closed), and the order in which the questions are presented. Question wording is often seen as one of the major problems in survey research; although one can standardize the language read by the respondent or the interviewer, standardizing the language does not imply standardization of the meaning. In addition, a respondent's perception of the intent or meaning of a question can be shaped by the sponsorship of the survey, the overall topic of the questionnaire, or the environment more immediate to the question of interest, such as the context of the previous question or set of questions or the specific response options associated with the question.

Respondent as Source of Measurement Error

Once the respondent comprehends the question, he or she must retrieve the relevant information from memory, make a judgment as to whether the retrieved information matches the requested information, and communicate a response. The retrieval process is potentially fraught with error, including errors of omission and commission. As part of the communication of the response, the respondent must determine whether he or she wishes to reveal the information. Survey instruments often ask questions about socially and personally sensitive topics. It is widely believed, and well documented, that such questions elicit patterns of underreporting (for socially undesirable behaviors and attitudes) as well as overreporting (for socially desirable behaviors and attitudes).

Interviewers as Sources of Measurement Error

For interviewer-administered questionnaires, interviewers may affect the measurement processes in one of several ways, including:

- Failure to read the question as written;
- Variation in interviewers' ability to perform the other tasks associated with interviewing, for example, probing insufficient responses, selecting appropriate respondents, or recording information provided by the respondent; and
- Demographic and socioeconomic characteristics as well as voice characteristics that influence the behavior and responses provided by the respondent.

The first two factors contribute to measurement error from a cognitive or psycholinguistic perspective in that different respondents are exposed to different stimuli; thus variation in responses is, in part, a function of the variation in stimuli. All three factors suggest that interviewer effects contribute via an increase in variable error across interviewers. If all interviewers erred in the same direction (or their characteristics resulted in errors of the same direction and magnitude), interviewer bias would result. For the most part, the literature indicates that among well-trained interviewing staff, interviewer error contributes to the overall variance of estimates as opposed to resulting in biased estimates (Lyberg and Kasprzyk, 1991).

Other Essential Survey Conditions as Sources of Measurement Error

Any data collection effort involves decisions concerning the features that define the overall design of the survey, here referred to as the essential survey conditions. In addition to the sample design and the wording of individual questions and response options, these decisions include:

- Whether to use interviewers or to collect information via some form of self-administered questionnaire;
- The means for selecting and training interviewers (if applicable);
- The mode of data collection for interviewer administration (telephone versus face to face);
- The choice of respondent rule, including the extent to which the design permits the reporting of information by proxy respondents;
- The method of data collection (paper and pencil, computer assisted);
- The extent to which respondents are encouraged to reference records to respond to factual questions;
- Whether to contact respondents for a single interview (cross-sectional design) or follow respondents over time (longitudinal or panel design);
- For longitudinal designs, the frequency and periodicity of measurement;
- The identification of the organization for whom the data are collected; and
- The identification of the data collection organization.

No one design or set of design features is clearly superior with respect to overall data quality. For example, as noted, interviewer variance is one source of variability that obviously can be eliminated through the use of a self-administered questionnaire. However, the use of an interviewer may aid in the measurement process by providing the respondent with clarifying information or by probing insufficient responses.

MEASUREMENT ERROR ASSOCIATED WITH AUTOBIOGRAPHICAL INFORMATION: THEORETICAL FRAMEWORK

Three distinct literatures provide the basis for the theoretical framework underlying investigations of measurement error in surveys. These theoretical foundations come from the fields of cognitive psychology, social psychology, and to a lesser extent, social linguistics.[1] Although research concerning the existence, direction, magnitude as well as correlates of response error have provided insight into the factors associated with measurement error, there are few fundamental principles that inform either designers of data collection efforts or analysts of survey data as to the circumstances, either individual or design based, under which measurement error is most likely to be significant or not. Those tenets that appear to be robust across substantive areas are outlined in the following sections.

Cognitive Theory

Tourangeau (1984) as well as others (see Sudman et al., 1996, for a review) have categorized the survey question-and-answer process as a four-step process involving comprehension of the question, retrieval of information from memory, assessment of the correspondence between the retrieved information and the requested information, and communication. In addition, the encoding of information, a process outside the control of the survey interview, determines a priori whether the information of interest is available for the respondent to retrieve from long-term memory.

Comprehension of the interview question is the "point of entry" to the response process. Does the question convey the concept(s) of interest? Is there a shared meaning among the researcher, the interviewer, and the respondent with respect to each of the words as well as the question as a whole? The comprehension of the question involves not only knowledge of the particular words and phrases used in the questionnaire, but also the respondent's impression of the purpose of the interview, the context of the particular question, and the interviewer's behavior in the delivery of the question.

The use of simple, easily understood language is not sufficient for guaranteeing shared meaning among all respondents. Belson (1981) found that even simple terms were subject to misunderstanding. For example, Belson examined respondents' interpretation of the following question: "For how many hours do you usually watch television on a weekday? This includes evening viewing." He found that respondents varied in their interpretation of various terms such as "how many hours" (sometimes interpreted as requesting starting and stopping times of viewing), "you" (interpreted to include other family members), "usually," and "watch television" (interpreted to mean being in the room in which the television is on).

---

[1]Note that although statistical and economic theories provide the foundation for analysis of error-prone data, these disciplines provide little theoretical foundation for understanding the source of the measurement error nor the means for reducing measurement error. The discussion presented here will be limited to a review of cognitive and social psychological theories applicable to the measures of interest in understanding the welfare population.

Much of the measurement error literature has focused on the retrieval stage of the question-answering process, classifying the lack of reporting of an event as retrieval failure on the part of the respondent, comparing the characteristics of events that are reported to those that are not reported. One of the general tenets from this literature concerns the length of the recall period; the greater the length of the recall period, the greater the expected bias due to respondent retrieval and reporting error. This relationship has been supported by empirical data investigating the reporting of consumer expenditures and earnings (Neter and Waksberg, 1964); the reporting of hospitalizations, visits to physicians, and health conditions (e.g. Cannell et al., 1965); and reports of motor vehicle accidents (Cash and Moss, 1969), crime (Murphy and Cowan, 1976); and recreational activities (Gems et al., 1982). However, even within these studies, the findings with respect to the impact of the length of recall period on the quality of survey estimates are inconsistent. For example, Dodge (1970) found that length of recall was significant in the reporting of robberies but had no effect on the reporting of various other crimes, such as assaults, burglaries, and larcenies. Contrary to theoretically justified expectations, the literature also offers several examples in which the length of the recall period had no effect on the magnitude of response errors (see, for example, Mathiowetz and Duncan, 1988; Schaeffer, 1994). These more recent investigations point to the importance of the complexity of the behavioral experience over time, as opposed to simply the passage of time, as the factor most indicative of measurement error. This finding harkens back to theoretical discussions of the impact of interference on memory (Crowder, 1976).

Response errors associated with the length of the recall period typically are classified as either telescoping error, that is the tendency of the respondent to report events as occurring earlier (backward telescoping) or more recently (forward telescoping) than they actually occurred, or recall decay, the inability of the respondent to recall the relevant events occurring in the past (errors of omission). Forward telescoping is believed to dominate recall errors when the reference period for the questions is of short duration, while recall decay is more likely to have a major effect when the reference period is of long duration. In addition to the length of the recall period, the relative salience of the event affects the likelihood of either telescoping or memory decay. For example, events that are unique or that have a major impact on the respondent's life are less likely to be forgotten (error of omission) than less important events; however, the vividness of the event may lead respondents to recall the event as occurring more recently than is true (forward telescoping).

Another tenet rising from the collaborative efforts of cognitive psychologists and survey methodologists concerns the relationship between true behavioral experience and retrieval strategies undertaken by a respondent. Recent investigations suggest that the retrieval strategy undertaken by the respondent to provide a "count" of a behavior is a function of the true behavioral frequency. Research by Burton and Blair (1991) indicate that respondents choose to count events or items (episodic enumeration) if the frequency of the event/item is low and they rely on estimation for more frequently occurring events. The point at which respondents switch from episodic counting to estimation varies by both the characteristics of the respondent and the characteristics of the event. As Sudman et al. (1996) note, "no studies have attempted to relate individual characteristics such as intelligence, education, or preference for cognitive complexity to the choice of counting or estimation, controlling for the number of events" (p. 201). Work by Menon (1993, 1994) suggests that it is not simply the true behavioral frequency that determines retrieval strategies, but also the degree of regularity and similarity among events. According to her hypotheses, those events that are both regular and similar (brushing teeth) require the least amount of cognitive effort to report, with respondents relying on retrieval of a rate to produce a response. Those events occurring irregularly require more cognitive effort on the part of the respondent.

The impact of different retrieval strategies with respect to the magnitude and direction of measurement error is not well understood; the limited evidence suggests that errors of estimation are often unbiased, although the variance about an estimate (e.g., mean value for the population) may be large. Episodic enumeration, however, appears to lead to biased estimates of the event or item of interest, with a tendency to be biased upward for short recall periods and downward for long recall periods.

A third tenet springing from this same literature concerns the salience or importance of the behavior to be retrieved. Sudman and Bradburn (1973) identify salient events as those that are unique or have continuing economic or social consequences for the respondent. Salience is hypothesized to affect the strength of the memory trace and subsequently, the effort involved in retrieving the information from long-term memory. The stronger the trace, the lower the effort needed to locate and retrieve the information. Cannell et al. (1965) report that those events judged to be important to the individual were reported more completely and accurately than other events. Mathiowetz (1986) found that short spells of unemployment were less likely to be reported than longer (i.e., more salient) spells.

The last maxim concerns the impact of interference related to the occurrence of similar events over the respondent's life or during the reference period of interest. Classical interference and information-processing theories suggest that as the number of similar or related events occurring to an individual increases, the probability of recalling any one of those events declines. An individual may lose the ability to distinguish between related events, resulting in an increase in the rate of errors or omission. Inaccuracy concerning the details of any one event also may increase as the respondent makes use of general knowledge or impressions concerning a class of events for reconstructing the specifics of a particular occurrence. Interference theory suggests that "forgetting" is a function of both the number and temporal pattern of related events in long-term memory. In addition, we would speculate that interference also contributes to the misreporting of information, for example, the reporting of the receipt of Medicare benefits rather than Medicaid benefits.

Social Psychology: The Issue of Social Desirability

In addition to asking respondents to perform the difficult task of retrieving complex information from long-term memory, survey instruments often ask questions about socially and personally sensitive topics. Some topics are deemed, by social consensus, to be too sensitive to discuss in "polite" society. This was a much shorter list in the 1990s than in the 1950s, but most would agree that topics such as sexual practices, impotence, and bodily functions fall within this classification. Some (e.g., Tourangeau et al., 2000) hypothesize that questions concerning income also fall within this category. Other questions may concern topics that have strong positive or negative normative responses (e.g., voting, the use of pugnacious terms with respect to racial or ethnic groups) or for which there may be criminal retribution (e.g., use of illicit drugs, child abuse).

The sensitivity of the behavior or attitude of interest may affect both the encoding of the information as well as the retrieval and reporting of the material; little of the survey methodological research has addressed the point at which the distortion occurs with respect to the reporting of sensitive material. Even if the respondent is able to retrieve accurate information concerning the behavior of interest, he or she may choose to edit this information at the response formation stage as a means to reduce the costs, ranging from embarrassment to potential negative consequences beyond the interview situation, associated with revealing the information.

Applicability of Findings to the Measurement of Economic Phenomena

One of the problems in drawing inferences from other substantive fields to that of economic phenomena is the difference in the nature of the measures of interest. Much of the assessment of the quality of household-based survey reports concerns the reporting of discrete behaviors; many of the economic measures that are the subject of inquiry with respect to the measurement of the welfare population are not necessarily discrete behaviors or even phenomena that can be linked to a discrete memory. Some of the phenomena of interest could be considered trait phenomena. Let's consider the reporting of occupation. We speculate that the cognitive process by which one formulates a response to a query concerning current occupation is different from the process related to reporting the number of doctor visits during the past year.

For other economic phenomena, we speculate that individual differences in the approach to formulating a response impact the magnitude and direction of error associated with the measurement process. Consider the reporting of current earnings related to employment. For some respondents, the request to report current earnings requires little cognitive effort—it may be almost an automatic response. For these individuals, wages may be considered a characteristic of their self-identity, a trait related to how they define themselves. For other individuals, the request for information concerning current wages may require the retrieval of information from a discrete episode (the last paycheck), the retrieval of a recent report of the information (the reporting of wages in an application for a credit card), or the construction of an estimate at the time of the query based on the retrieval of information relevant to the request.

Given both the theoretical and empirical research conducted within multiple branches of psychology and survey methodology, what would we anticipate are the patterns of measurement error for various economic measures? The response to that question is a function of how the respondent's task is formulated and the very nature of the phenomena of interest. For example, asking a respondent to provide an estimate of the number of weeks of unemployment during the past year is quite different from the task of asking the respondent to report the starting and stopping dates of each unemployment spell for the past year. For individuals in a steady state (constant employment or unemployment), neither task could be considered a difficult cognitive process. For these individuals, employment or unemployment is not a discrete event but rather may become encoded in memory as a trait that defines the respondent. However, for the individual with sporadic spells of unemployment throughout the year, the response formulation process most likely would differ for the two questions. Although the response formulation process for the former task permits an estimation strategy on the part of the respondent, the latter requires the retrieval of discrete periods of unemployment. For the reporting of these discrete events, we would hypothesize that patterns of response error evident in the reporting of events in other substantive fields would be observed. With respect to social desirability, we would anticipate patterns similar to those evident in other types of behaviors: overreporting of socially desirable behaviors and underreporting of socially undesirable behaviors.

Measurement Error in Household Reports of Income

As noted by Moore et al. (1999), the reporting of income by household respondents in many surveys can be characterized as a two-step process: the first involving the correct enumeration of sources of household income and the second, the accurate reporting of the amount of the income for the specific source. They find that response error in the reporting of various sources and amounts of income may be due to a large extent to cognitive factors, such as "definitional issues, recall and salience problems, confusion, and sensitivity" (p. 155). We return to these cognitive factors when considering alternative means for reducing measurement error in surveys of the low-income population.

Earnings

Empirical evaluations of household-reported earnings information include the assessment of annual earnings, usual earnings (with respect to a specific pay period), most recent earnings, and hourly wage rates. These studies rely on various sources of validation data, including the use of employers' records, administrative records, and respondents' reports for the same reference period reported at two different times.

With respect to reports of annual earnings, mean estimates appear to be subject to relatively small levels of response error, although absolute differences indicate significant overreporting and underreporting at the individual level. For example, Borus (1970) focused on survey responses of residents in low-income census tracts in Fort Wayne, Indiana. The study examined two alternative approaches to questions concerning annual earnings: (1) the use of two relatively broad questions concerning earnings, and (2) a detailed set of questions concerning work histories. Responses to survey questions were compared to data obtained from the Indiana Employment Security Division for employment earnings covered by the Indiana Unemployment Insurance Act. Borus found that the mean error in reports of annual earnings was small and insignificant for both sets of questions; however, more than 10 percent of the respondents misreported annual earnings by $1,000 (based on a mean of $2,500). Among poor persons with no college education, Borus found that the broad questions resulted in more accurate data than the work history questions.

Smith (1997) examined the reports of earnings data among individuals eligible to participate in federal training programs. Similar to the work by Borus (1970), Smith compared the reports based on direct questions concerning annual earnings to those responses based on summing the report of earnings for individual jobs. The decomposition approach, that is, the reporting of earnings associated with individual jobs, led to higher reports of annual earnings, attributed to both an increase in the reporting of number of hours worked as well as an increase in the reporting of irregular earnings (overtime, tips, and commissions). Comparisons with administrative data for these individuals led Smith to conclude that the estimates based on adding up earnings across jobs led to overreporting, rather than more complete reporting.[2]

Duncan and Hill (1985) sampled employees from a single establishment and compared reports of annual earnings with information obtained from the employer's records. The nature of the sample, employed persons, limits our ability

---

[2]An alternative interpretation of the findings might suggest that the decomposition approach was more accurate and that the apparent overestimation, when compared to administrative records, is because of underreporting of income in the administrative records rather than overreporting of earnings using the decomposition method.

to draw inferences from their work to the low-income population. Respondents were interviewed in 1983 and requested to report earnings and employment-related measures for calendar years 1981 and 1982. For neither year was the mean of the sample difference between household-based reports and company records statistically significant (8.5 percent and 7 percent of the mean, respectively), although the absolute differences for each year indicate significant underreporting and overreporting. Comparison of measures of change in annual earnings based on the household report and the employer records indicate no difference; interview reports of absolute change averaged $2,992 (or 13 percent) compared to the employer-based estimate of $3,399 (or 17 percent).

Although the findings noted are based on small samples drawn from either a single geographic area (Borus) or a single firm (Duncan and Hill), the results parallel the findings from empirical research comprised of nationally representative samples. Bound and Krueger (1991) examined error in annual earnings as reported in the March, 1978 CPS. Although the error was distributed around approximately a zero mean for both men and women, the magnitude of the error was substantial.

In addition to examining bias in mean estimates, the studies by Duncan and Hill and Bound and Krueger examined the relationship between measurement error and true earnings. Both studies indicate a significant negative relationship between error in reports of annual earnings and the true value of annual earnings. Similar to Duncan and Hill (1985), Bound and Krueger (1991) report positive autocorrelation (.4 for men and .1 for women) between errors in CPS-reported earnings for the 2 years of interest, 1976 and 1977.

Both Duncan and Hill (1985) and Bound and Krueger (1991) explore the implications of measurement error for earnings models. Duncan and Hill's model relates the natural logarithm of annual earnings to three measures of human capital investment: education, work experience prior to current employer, and tenure with current employer, using both the error-ridden self-reported measure of annual earnings and the record-based measure as the left-hand-side variable. A comparison of the ordinary least squares parameter estimates based on the two dependent variables suggests that measurement error in the dependent variable has a sizable impact on the parameter estimates. For example, estimates of the effects of tenure on earnings based on interview data were 25 percent lower than the effects based on record earnings data. Although the correlation between error in reports of earnings and error in reports of tenure was small (.05) and insignificant, the correlation between error in reports of earnings and *actual* tenure was quite strong (–.23) and highly significant, leading to attenuation in the estimated effects of tenure on earnings based on interview information.

Bound and Krueger (1991) also explore the ramifications of an error-ridden left-hand-side variable by regressing error in reports of earnings with a number of human capital and demographic factors, including education, age, race, marital status, region, and standard metropolitan statistical area (SMSA). Similar to

Duncan and Hill, the model attempts to quantify the extent to which the correlation between measurement error in the dependent variable and right-hand-side variables biases the estimates of the parameters. However, in contrast to Duncan and Hill, Bound and Krueger conclude that mismeasurement of earnings leads to little bias when CPS-reported earnings are on the left-hand side of the equation.

The reporting of annual earnings within the context of a survey is most likely aided by the number of times the respondent has retrieved and reported the information. For some members of the population, we contend that the memory for one's annual earnings is reinforced throughout the calendar year, for example, in the preparation of federal and state taxes or the completion of applications for credit cards and loans. To the extent that these requests have motivated the respondent to determine and report an accurate figure, such information should be encoded in the respondent's memory. Subsequent survey requests therefore should be "routine" in contrast to many of the types of questions posed to a survey respondent. Hence we would hypothesize that response error in such situations would result from retrieval of the wrong information (e.g., annual earnings for calendar year 1996 rather than 1997; net rather than gross earnings), social desirability issues (e.g., overreporting among persons with low earnings related to presentation of self to the interviewer), or privacy concerns, which may lead to either misreporting or item nonresponse.

Although the limited literature on the reporting of earnings among the low-income population indicates a high correlation between record and reported earnings (Halsey, 1978), we hypothesize that for some members of the population— such as low-income individuals for whom there are fewer opportunities to retrieve and report annual earnings information—a survey request would not be routine and may require very different response strategies than for respondents who have regular opportunities to report their annual earnings. Only two studies cited here, Borus (1970) and Smith (1997), compared alternative approaches to the request for earnings information among the low-income population. Borus found that the broad-based question approach led to lower levels of response error than a work history approach and Smith concluded that a decomposition approach led to an overestimation of annual earnings. The empirical results of Borus and Smith suggest, in contrast to theoretical expectations, that among the lower income populations, the use of broad questions may result in more accurate reports of income than detailed questions related to each job. Despite these findings, we speculate that for the low income population, those with loose ties to the labor force, or those for whom the retrieval of earnings information requires separate estimates for multiple jobs, the use of a decomposition approach or some type of estimation approach may be beneficial and warrants additional research.

In contrast to the task of reporting annual earnings, the survey request to report weekly earnings, most recent earnings, or usual earnings is most likely a relatively unique request and one that may involve the attempted retrieval of information that may not have been encoded by the respondent, the retrieval of information that has not been accessed by the respondent before, or the calculation of an estimate "on the spot." To the extent that the survey request matches the usual reference period for earnings (e.g., weekly pay), we would anticipate that requests for the most recent period may be well reported. In contrast, we would anticipate that requests for earnings in any metric apart from a well-rehearsed metric would lead to significant differences between household reports and validation data.

A small set of studies examined the correlation between weekly or monthly earnings as reported by workers and their employer's reports (Keating et al., 1950; Hardin and Hershey, 1960; Borus, 1966; Dreher, 1977). Two of these studies focus on the population of particular interest, unemployed workers (Keating et al., 1950) and training program participants (Borus, 1966). All four studies report correlations between the employee's report and the employer's records of .90 or higher. Mean reports by workers are close to record values, with modest overreporting in some studies and underreporting in others. For example, Borus (1966) reports a high correlation (.95) between household and employer's records of weekly earnings, small mean absolute deviations between the two sources, and equal amounts of overreporting and underreporting.

Carstensen and Woltman (1979), in a study among the general population, compared worker and employer reports, based on a supplement to the January, 1977 CPS. Their survey instruments allowed both workers and employers to report earnings in whatever time unit they preferred (e.g., annually, monthly, weekly, hourly). Comparisons were limited to those reports for which the respondent and the employer reported earnings using the same metric. When earnings were reported by both worker and employer on a weekly basis, workers under-reported their earnings by 6 percent; but when both reported on a monthly basis, workers overreported by 10 percent.

Rodgers et al. (1993)[3] report correlations of .60 and .46 between household reports and company records for the most recent and usual pay, respectively, in contrast to a correlation of .79 for reports of annual earnings. In addition, they calculated an hourly wage rate from the respondents' reports of annual, most recent, and usual earnings and hours and compared that hourly rate to the rate as reported by the employer; error in the reported hours for each respective time period therefore contributes to noise in the hourly wage rate. Similar to the findings for earnings, correlation between the employer's records and self-reports were highest when based on annual earnings and hours (.61) and significantly lower when based on most recent earnings and hours and usual earnings and hours (.38 and .24, respectively).

---

[3]Based on the Panel Study of Income Dynamics validation study, a survey conducted among a sample of employees at a single establishment and comparing their responses to those obtained from company records. The data from the first wave of this two-wave study were the basis for the study reported by Duncan and Hill (1985).

Hourly wages calculated from the CPS-reported earnings and hours compared to employers' records indicate a small but significant rate of underreporting, which may be due to an overreporting of hours worked, an underreporting of annual earnings, or a combination of the two (Mellow and Sider, 1983). Similar to Duncan and Hill (1985), Mellow and Sider examined the impact of measurement error in wage equations; they concluded that the structure of the wage determination process model was unaffected by the use of respondent- or employer-based information, although the overall fit of the model was somewhat higher with employer-reported wage information.

As noted earlier, one of the shortfalls with the empirical investigations concerning the reporting of earnings is the lack of studies targeted at those for whom the reporting task is most difficult—those with multiple jobs or sporadic employment. Although the empirical findings suggest that annual earnings are reported more accurately than earnings for other periods of time, the opposite may be true among those for whom annual earnings are highly variable and the result of complex employment patterns.

One of the major concerns with respect to earnings questions in surveys of Temporary Assistance for Needy Families (TANF) leavers is the reference period of interest. Many of the surveys request that respondents report earnings for reference periods that may be of little salience to the respondent or for which the determination of the earnings is quite complex. For example, questions often focus on the month in which the respondent left welfare (which may have been several months prior to the interview) or the 6 month period prior to exiting welfare. The movement off welfare support would probably be regarded as a significant and salient event and therefore be well reported. However, asking the respondent to reconstruct a reference period prior to the month of exiting welfare is most likely a cognitively difficult task. For example, consider the following question:

- During the six months you were on welfare before you got off in MONTH, did you ever have a job which paid you money?

For this question, the reference period of interest is ambiguous. For example, if the respondent exited welfare support in November 1999, is the 6-month period of interest defined as May 1, 1999, through October 31, 1999, or is the respondent to include the month in which he or she exited welfare as part of the reference period, in this case, June 1999-November 1999? If analytic interest lies in understanding a definitive period prior to exiting welfare, then the questionnaire should explicitly state this period to the respondent (e.g., "In the 6 months prior to going off welfare, that is, between May 1 and October 31, 1999") as well as encourage the respondent to use a calendar or other records to aid recall. The use of a calendar may be of particular importance when the reference period spans 2 calendar years. If the analytic interest lies in a more diffuse measure of employment in some period prior to exiting welfare, a rewording of the question so as to not imply precision about a particular 6 months may be more appropriate.

TRANSFER PROGRAM INCOME AND CHILD SUPPORT

For most surveys, the reporting of transfer program income is a two-stage process in which respondents first report recipiency (or not) of a particular form of income and then, among those who report recipiency, the amount of the income. One shortcoming of many studies that assess response error associated with transfer program income is the design of the study, in which the sample for the study is drawn from those known to be participants in the program. Responses elicited from respondents then are verified with administrative data. Retrospective or reverse record check studies limit the assessment of response error, with respect to recipiency, to determining the rate of underreporting; prospective or forward record check studies that only verify positive recipiency responses are similarly flawed because by design they limit the assessment of response error only to overreports. In contrast, a "full" design permits the verification of both positive and negative recipiency responses and includes in the sample a full array of respondents. Validation studies that sample from the general population and link all respondents, regardless of response, to the administrative record of interest represent full study designs.

We focus our attention first on reporting of receipt of a particular transfer program. Among full design studies, there does appear to be a tendency for respondents to underreport receipt, although there are also examples of over-reporting recipiency status. For example, Oberheu and Ono (1975) report a low correspondence between administrative records and household report for receipt of Aid to Families with Dependent Children (AFDC)—monthly and annual—and food stamps (disagreement rates exceeding 20 percent), but relatively low net rates of underreporting and overreporting. Underreporting of the receipt of general assistance as reported in two studies is less than 10 percent (e.g., David, 1962). In a study reported by Marquis and Moore (1990), respondents were asked to report recipiency status for 8 months (in two successive waves of Survey of Income and Program Participation [SIPP] interviews). Although Marquis and Moore report a low error rate of approximately 1 percent to 2 percent, the error rate among true recipients is significant, in the direction of underreporting. For example, among those receiving AFDC, respondents failed to report receipt in 49 percent of the person-months. Underreporting rates were lowest among Old-Age and Survivors Insurance and Disability Insurance (OASDI) beneficiaries, for which approximately 5 percent of the person-months of recipiency were not reported by the household respondents. The mean rates of participation based on the two sources differed by less than 1 percentage point for all income types. However, because some of these programs are so rare, small absolute biases mask high rates of relative underreporting among true participants, ranging from

+1 percent for OASDI recipiency to nearly 40 percent for AFDC recipiency. In a followup study, Moore et al. (1996) compared underreporting rates of known recipients to overreporting rates for known nonrecipients and found underreporting rates to be much higher than the rate of false positives by nonrecipients. They also note that underreporting on the part of known recipients tends to be due to failure to *ever* report receipt of a particular type of income rather than failure to report specific months of receipt.

In contrast, Yen and Nelson (1996) found a slight tendency among AFDC recipients to overreport receipt in any given month, such that estimates based on survey reports exceeded estimates based on records by approximately 1 percentage point. Oberheu and Ono (1975) also note a net overreporting for AFDC (annual) and food stamp recipiency (annual), of 8 percent and 6 percent, respectively. Although not investigated by these researchers, one possible explanation for apparent overreporting on the part of the respondent is confusion concerning the source of recipiency, resulting in an apparent overreporting of one program coupled with an underreporting of another program. Because many of the validity studies that use administrative records to confirm survey reports are limited to verification of one or two particular programs, most response error investigations have not addressed this problem.

Errors in the reporting of recipiency for any given month may be attributable to misdating the beginning and end points of a spell, as opposed to an error of omission or confusion concerning the source of support. The "seam effect" refers to a particular type of response error resulting from the misdating of episodic information in panel data collection efforts (Hill, 1987). A seam effect is evident when a change in status (e.g., from receipt of AFDC to nonreceipt of AFDC) corresponds to the end of a reference period for Wave x and the beginning of a reference period for Wave x+1. For example, a respondent may report receipt of AFDC at the end of the first wave of interviewing; at the time of the second wave of interviewing, he or she reports that no one in the family has received such benefits for the entire reference period. Hence it appears (in the data) as if the change in status occurred on the day of the interview.

With respect to the direction and magnitude of estimates concerning the amount of the transfer, empirical investigations vary in their conclusions. Several studies report a significant underreporting of assistance amount (e.g., David, 1962; Livingston, 1969; Oberheu and Ono, 1975; Halsey, 1978) or significant differences between the survey and record reports (Grondin and Michaud, 1994). Other studies report little to no difference in the amount based on the survey and record reports. Hoaglin (1978) found no difference in median response error for welfare amounts and only small negative differences in the median estimates for monthly Social Security income. Goodreau et al. (1984) found that 65 percent of the respondents accurately report the amount of AFDC support; the survey report accounted for 96 percent of the actual amount of support. Although Halsey (1978) reported a net bias in the reporting of unemployment insurance amount of −50 percent, Dibbs et al. (1995) conclude that the average household report of unemployment benefits differed from the average true value by approximately 5 percent ($300 on a base of $5,600).

Schaeffer (1994) compared custodial parents' reports of support owed and support paid to court records among a sample of residents in the state of Wisconsin. The distribution of response errors indicated significant underreporting and overreporting of both the amount owed and the amount paid. The study also examined the factors contributing to the absolute level of errors in the reports of amounts owed and paid; the findings indicate that the complexity of the respondent's support experience had a substantial impact on the accuracy of the reports. Characteristics of the events (payments) were more important in predicting response error than characteristics of the respondent or factors related to memory decay. The analysis suggests two areas of research directed toward improving the reporting of child support payments: research related to improving the comprehension of the question (specifically clarifying and distinguishing child support from other transfer payments) and identifying respondents for whom the reporting process is difficult (e.g., use of a filter question) with follow-up questions specific to the behavioral experience.

Hours Worked

The number of empirical investigations concerning the quality of household reports of hours worked are few in number but consistent with respect to the findings. Regardless of whether the measure of interest is hours worked last week, annual work hours, usual hours worked, or hours associated with the previous or usual pay period, comparisons between company records and respondents' reports indicate an overestimate of the number of hours worked. We note that none of the empirical studies examined in the following text focuses specifically on the low-income or welfare populations.

Carstensen and Woltman (1979) assessed reports of "usual" hours worked per week. They found that compared to company reports, estimates of the mean usual hours worked were significantly overreported by household respondents: 37.1 hours versus 38.4 hours, respectively, a difference on average of 1.33 hours, or 3.6 percent of the usual hours worked. Similarly, Mellow and Sider (1983) report that the mean difference between the natural log of worker-reported hours and the natural log of employer-reported hours is positive (.039). Self-reports exceeded employer records by nearly 4 percent on average; however, for approximately 15 percent of the sample, the employer records exceeded the estimate provided by the respondent. A regression explaining the difference between the two sources indicates that professional and managerial workers were more likely to overestimate their hours, as were respondents with higher levels of education and nonwhite respondents. In contrast, female respondents tended to underreport usual hours worked.

Similar to their findings concerning the reporting of earnings, Rodgers et al. (1993) report that the correlation between self-reports and company records is higher for annual number of hours worked (.72) than for either reports of hours associated with the previous pay period (.61) or usual pay period (.61). Barron et al. (1997) report a high correlation between employers' records and respondents' reports of hours last week, .769. Measurement error in hours worked is not independent of the true value; as reported by Rodgers et al. (1993), the correlation between error in reports of hours worked and true values (company records) ranged from –.307 for annual hours worked in the calendar year immediately prior to the date of the interview to –.357 for hours associated with the previous pay period and –.368 for hours associated with usual pay period.

Examination of a standard econometric model with earnings as the left-hand-side variable and hours worked as one of the predictor variables indicates that the high correlation between the errors in reports of earnings and hours (ranging from .36 for annual measures to .54 for last pay period) seriously biases parameter estimates. For example, regressions of reported and company record annual earnings (log) on record or reported hours, age, education, and tenure with the company provide a useful illustration of the consequences of measurement error. Based on respondent reports of earnings and hours, the coefficient for hours (log hours) is less than 60 percent of the coefficient based on company records (.41 versus 1.016) while the coefficient for age is 50 percent larger in the model based on respondent reports. In addition, the fit of the model based on respondent reports is less than half that of the fit based on company records (R^2 of .352 versus .780).

Duncan and Hill (1985) compare the quality of reports of annual hours worked for two different reference periods, the prior calendar year and the calendar year ending 18 months prior to the interview. The quality of the household reports declines as a function of the length of the recall period, although the authors report significant overreporting for each of the two calendar years of interest. The average absolute error in reports of hours worked (157 hours) was nearly 10 percent of the mean annual hours worked for 1982 (μ=1,603) and nearly 12 percent (211 hours) of the mean for 1981 (μ=1,771). Comparisons of changes in hours worked reveal that although the simple differences calculated from two sources have similar averages, the absolute amount of change reported in the interview significantly exceeds that based on the record report.

In contrast to the findings with respect to annual earnings, we see both a bias in the population estimates as well as a bias in the individual reports of hours worked in the direction of overreporting. This finding persists across different approaches to measuring hours worked, regardless of whether the respondent is asked to report on hours worked last week (CPS) or account for the weeks worked last year, which then are converted to total hours worked during the year (Panel Study of Income Dynamics [PSID]). Whether this is a function of social desirability or whether it is related to the cognitive processes associated with formulating a response to the questions measuring hours worked is something that can only be speculated on at this point. One means by which to attempt to repair the overreporting of hours worked is through the use of time-use diaries, where respondents are asked to account for the previous 24-hour period. Employing time-use diaries has been found to be an effective means for reducing response error associated with retrospective recall bias as well as bias associated with the overreporting of socially desirable behavior (Presser and Stinson, 1998).

Unemployment

In contrast to the small number of studies that assess the quality of household reports of hours worked, there are a number of studies that have examined the quality of unemployment reports. These studies encompass a variety of unemployment measures, including annual number of person-years of unemployment, weekly unemployment rate, occurrence and duration of specific unemployment spells, and total annual unemployment hours. Only one study reported in the literature, the PSID validation study (Duncan and Hill, 1985; Mathiowetz, 1986; Mathiowetz and Duncan, 1988), compares respondents' reports with validation data; the majority of the studies rely on comparisons of estimates based on alternative study designs or examine the consistency in reports of unemployment duration across rounds of data collection. In general, the findings suggest that retrospective reports of unemployment by household respondents underestimate unemployment, regardless of the unemployment measure of interest. Once again, however, these studies focus on the general population; hence our ability to draw inferences to the low income or welfare populations is limited.

The studies by Morganstern and Bartlett (1974), Horvath (1982), and Levine (1993) compare the contemporaneous rate of unemployment as produced by the monthly CPS to the rate resulting from retrospective reporting of unemployment during the previous calendar year.[4] The measures of interest vary from study to study; Morganstern and Bartlett focus on annual number of person-years of unemployment as compared to average estimates of weekly unemployment (Horvath) or an unemployment rate, as discussed by Levine. Regardless of the

---

[4]The CPS is collected each month from a probability sample of approximately 50,000 households; interviews are conducted during the week containing the 19th day of the month: respondents are questioned about labor force status for the previous week, Sunday through Saturday, which includes the 12th of the month. In this way, the data are considered the respondent's current employment status, with a fixed reference period for all respondents, regardless of which day of the week they are interviewed. In addition to the core set of questions concerning labor force participation and demographic characteristics, respondents interviewed in March of any year are asked a supplemental set of questions (hence the name March supplement) concerning income recipiency and amounts, weeks employed, unemployed and not in the labor force, and health insurance coverage for the previous calendar year.

measure of interest, the empirical findings from the three studies indicate that when compared to the contemporaneous measure, retrospective reports of labor force status result in an underestimate of the unemployment rate.

Across the three studies, the underreporting rate is significant and appears to be related to demographic characteristics of the individual. For example, Morganstern and Bartlett (1974) report discrepancy rates in the range of around 3 percent to 24 percent with the highest discrepancy rates among women (22 percent for black women; 24 percent for white women). Levine compared the contemporaneous and retrospective reports by age, race, and gender. He found the contemporaneous rates to be substantially higher relative to the retrospective reports for teenagers, regardless of race or sex, and for women. Across all of the years of the study, 1970-1988, the retrospective reports for white males, ages 20 to 59, were nearly identical to the contemporaneous reports.

Duncan and Hill (1985) found that the overall estimate of mean number of hours unemployed in years t and $t-1$ based on employer reports and company records did not differ significantly. However, microlevel comparisons, reported as the average absolute difference between the two sources, were large relative to the average amount of unemployment in each year, but significant only for reports of unemployment occurring in 1982.

In addition to studies examining rates of unemployment, person-years of unemployment, or annual hours of unemployment, several empirical investigations have focused on spell-level information, examining reports of the specific spell and duration of the spell. Using the same data as presented in Duncan and Hill (1985), Mathiowetz and Duncan (1988) found that at the spell level, respondents failed to report more than 60 percent of the individual spells. Levine (1993) found that 35 percent to 60 percent of persons failed to report an unemployment spell one year after the event. In both studies, failure to report a spell of unemployment was related, in part, to the length of the unemployment spell; short spells of unemployment were subject to higher rates of underreporting.

The findings suggest (Poterba and Summers, 1984) that, similar to other types of discrete behaviors and events, the reporting of unemployment is subject to deterioration over time. However, the passage of time may not be the fundamental factor affecting the quality of the reports; rather the complexity of the behavioral experience over longer recall periods appears to be the source of increased response error. Both the microlevel comparisons as well as the comparisons of population estimates suggest that behavioral complexity interferes with the respondent's ability to accurately report unemployment for distant recall periods. Hence we see greater underreporting among population subgroups who traditionally have looser ties to the labor force (teenagers, women). Although longer spells of unemployment appear to be subject to lower levels of errors of omission, a finding that supports other empirical research with respect to the effects of salience, at least one study found that errors in reports of duration were associated negatively with the length of the spell. Whether this is indicative of an error in cognition or an indication of reluctance to report extremely long spells of unemployment (social desirability) is unresolved.

Sensitive Questions: Drug Use, Abortions

A large body of methodological evidence indicates that embarrassing or socially undesirable behaviors are misreported in surveys (e.g., Bradburn, 1983). For example, comparisons between estimates of the number of abortions based on survey data from the National Survey of Family Growth (NSFG) and estimates based on data collected from abortion clinics suggest that fewer than half of all abortions are reported in the NSFG (Jones and Forrest, 1992). Similarly, comparisons of survey reports of cigarette smoking with sales figures indicates significant underreporting on the part of household respondents, with the rate of underreporting increasing over time, a finding attributed by the authors as a function of increasing social undesirability (Warner, 1978).

Although validation studies of reports of sensitive behaviors are rare, there is a growing body of empirical literature that examines reports of sensitive behaviors as a function of mode of data collection, method of data collection, question wording, and context (e.g., Tourangeau and Smith, 1996). These studies have examined the reporting of abortions, AIDS risk behaviors, use of illegal drugs, and alcohol consumption. The hypothesis for these studies is that, given the tendency to underreport sensitive or undesirable behavior, the method or combination of essential survey design features that yields the highest estimate is the "better" measurement approach.

Studies comparing self-administration to interviewer-administered questions (either face to face or telephone) indicate that self-administration of sensitive questions increases levels of reporting relative to administration of the same question by an interviewer. Increases in the level of behavior have been reported in self-administered surveys (using paper and pencil questionnaires) concerning abortions (London and Williams, 1990), alcohol consumption (Aquilino and LoSciuto, 1990), and drug use (Aquilino, 1994). Similar increases in the level of reporting sensitive behaviors have been reported when the comparisons focus on the difference between interviewer-administered questionnaires and computer-assisted self administration (CASI) questionnaires.

One of the major concerns with moving from an interviewer-administered questionnaire to self-administration is the problem of limiting participation to the literate population. Even among the literate population, the use of self-administered questionnaires presents problems with respect to following directions (e.g., skip patterns). The use of audio computer-assisted self-interviewing (ACASI) techniques circumvents both problems. The presentation of the questions in both written and auditory form (through headphones) preserves the privacy of a self-administered questionnaire without the restriction imposed by respondent literacy. The use of computers for the administration of the questionnaire eliminates two problems often seen in self-administered paper and pencil questionnaires—missing data and incorrectly followed skip patterns. A small but growing body of literature (e.g., O'Reilly et al., 1994; Tourangeau and Smith, 1996) finds that ACASI methods are acceptable to respondents and appear to improve the reporting of sensitive behaviors. Cynamon and Camburn (1992) found that using portable cassette players to administer questions (with the respondent recording answers on a paper form) also was effective in increasing reports of sensitive behaviors.

Methods for Reducing Measurement Error

As we consider means for reducing measurement error in surveys of the low-income population, we return to the theoretical frameworks that address the potential sources of error: those errors associated with problems of cognition and those resulting from issues associated with social desirability.

REPAIRS FOCUSING ON PROBLEM OF COGNITION

Comprehension

Of primary importance in constructing question items is to assure comprehension on the part of the respondent. Although the use of clear and easily understood language is a necessary step toward achieving that goal, simple language alone does not guarantee that the question is understood in the same manner by all respondents.

The literature examining comprehension problems in the design of income questions indicates that defining income constructs in a language easily understood by survey respondents is not easy (Moore et al., 1999). Terms that most researchers would consider to be well understood by respondents may suffer from differential comprehension. For example, Stinson (1997) found significant diversity with respect to respondents' interpretations of the term "total family income." Similarly, Bogen (1995) reported that respondents tend to omit sporadic self-employment and earnings from odd jobs or third or fourth jobs in their reports of income due to the respondents' interpretations of the term "income." These findings suggest the need for thorough testing of items among the population of interest to assess comprehension.

Comprehension of survey questions is affected by several factors, including the length of the question, the syntactical complexity, the degree to which the question includes instructions such as inclusion and exclusion clauses, and as the use of ambiguous terms. Consider, for example, the complexity of the following questions:

NANCY A. MATHIOWETZ, CHARLIE BROWN, AND JOHN BOUND 179

Example 1: Since your welfare benefits ended in (FINAL BENEFIT MONTH), did you take part for at least one month in any Adult Basic Education (ABE) classes for improving your basic reading and math skills, or General Education Development (GED) classes to help you prepare for the GED test, or classes to prepare for a regular high school diploma?

Example 2: In (PRIOR MONTH), did you have any children of your own living in the household? Please include any foster or adopted children. Also include any grandchildren living with you.

Example 3: Since (FINAL BENEFIT MONTH), have you worked for pay at a regular job at all? Please don't count unpaid work experience, but do include any paid jobs, including paid community service jobs or paid on-the-job training.

Each of these items is cognitively complex. The first question requires the respondent to process three separate categories of education, determine whether the conditional phrase "at least one month" applies only to the adult basic education classes or also to the GED and regular high school classes, and also attribute a reason for attending ABE ("improving reading and math skills") or GED classes. Separating example 1 into three simple items, prefaced by an introductory statement concerning types of education, would make the task more manageable for the respondent. Examples 2 and 3 suffer from the problem of providing an exclusion or inclusion (or in the case of example 3, both) clause after the question. Both would be improved by defining for the respondent what the question concerns and then asking the question, so that the last thing the respondent hears is the question. Example 2 may be improved by simply asking separate questions concerning own children, foster children, and grandchildren. Although questionnaire designers may be reluctant to add questions to an instrument for fear of longer administration times, we speculate that the administration of several well-designed short questions actually may be shorter than confusing compound questions that may require repeating or clarification.

With respect to question length, short questions are not always better. Cannell and colleagues (Cannell et al., 1977; Cannell et al., 1981) demonstrated that longer questions providing *redundant* information can lead to increased comprehension, in part because the longer question provides additional context for responding as well as longer time for the respondent to think about the question and formulate a response. On the other hand, longer questions that introduce new terms or become syntactically complex will result in lower levels of comprehension.

Comprehension can suffer from both lexical and structural ambiguities. For example, the sentence "John went to the bank" could be interpreted as John going to a financial institution or the side of a river. Lexical problems are inherent in a language in which words can have different interpretations. Although difficult to fix, interpretation can be aided through context and the respondent's usual use of the word (in this case, most likely the financial institution interpretation). Note that when constructing a question, one must consider regional and cultural differences in language and avoid terms that lack a clearly defined lexical meaning (e.g., "welfare reform"). Structural ambiguities arise when the same word can be used as different parts of speech—for example, as both a verb or an adjective in the sentence "Flying planes can be dangerous." Structural ambiguities most often can be repaired through careful wording of the question.

Questionnaire designers often attempt to improve comprehension by grouping questions so as to provide a context for a set of items, writing explicit questions, and, if possible, writing closed-ended items in which the response categories may aid in the interpretation of the question by the respondent. In addition, tailoring questions to accommodate the language of specific population subgroups is feasible with computer-assisted interviewing systems.

Comprehension difficulties are best identified and repaired through the use of selected pretesting techniques such as cognitive interviewing or expert panel review (e.g., Presser and Blair, 1994; Forsyth and Lessler, 1991). Requesting respondents to paraphrase the question in their own words often provides insight into different interpretations of a question; similarly, the use of other cognitive interviewing techniques such as think-aloud interviews or the use of vignettes can be useful in identifying comprehension problems as well as offer possible alternative wording options for the questionnaire designer.

Retrieval

Many of the questions of interest in surveying the welfare population request that the respondent report on retrospective behavior, often for periods covering several years or more (e.g., year of first receipt of AFDC benefits). Some of these questions require that the respondent date events of interest, thus requiring episodic retrieval of a specific event. Other questions request that respondents provide a numeric estimate (e.g., earnings from work last month); in these cases the respondent may rely on episodic retrieval (e.g., the more recent pay-check), reconstruction, an estimation strategy, or a combination of retrieval strategies to provide a response. As noted earlier, response strategies are often a function of the behavioral complexity experienced by the respondent; however, the strategy used by the respondent can be affected by the wording of the question.

Although both responses based on episodic enumeration and estimation are subject to measurement error, the literature suggests that questions which direct the respondent toward episodic enumeration tend to suffer from errors of omissions (underreports) due to incomplete memory searches on the part of the respondent, whereas responses based on estimation strategies result in both inclusion and exclusion errors, resulting in greater variance but unbiased population estimates (Sudman et al., 1996). The findings from Mathiowetz and Duncan (1986) illustrate the difference in reports based on estimation strategies as compared to episodic enumeration. In their study, population estimates of annual hours of unemployment for a 2-year reference period based on respondents' reports of unemployment hours were reasonably accurate. In contrast, when respondents had to report the months and years of individual spells of unemployment (requiring episodic enumeration) more than 60 percent of the individual spells of unemployment were not reported.

Several empirical investigations have identified means by which to improve the reporting of retrospective information for both episodic enumeration and estimation-based reports. These questionnaire design approaches include:

Event History Calendar. Work in the field of cognitive psychology has provided insight into the structure of autobiographic information in memory. The research indicates that "certain types of autobiographical memories are thematically and temporally structured within an hierarchical ordering" (Belli, 1998). Event history calendars have been found to be effective in reducing response error related to the reporting of what, when, and how often events occurred (Freedman et al., 1988). Whereas traditional survey instruments ask for retrospective reports through a set of discrete questions (e.g., "In what month and year did you last receive welfare payments?"), thereby emphasizing the discrete nature of events, event history calendars emphasize the relationship between events within broad thematic areas or life domains (work, living arrangements, marital status, child bearing and rearing). Major transitions within these domains such as getting married or divorced, giving birth to a child, moving into a new house, or starting a job, are identified by the respondent and recorded in such ways as to facilitate "an extensive use of autobiographical memory networks and multiple paths of memory associated with top-down, sequential, and parallel retrieval strategies" (Belli, 1998). If the question items of interest require the dating of several types of events, the literature suggests that the use of event history calendars will lead to improved reporting. For example, event history calendars could prove to be beneficial in eliciting accurate responses to questions such as "What was the year and month that you first received welfare cash assistance as an adult?"

Landmark Events. The use of an event history calendar is most beneficial if the questionnaire focuses on the dating and sequencing of events and behaviors across several life domains. In some cases, the questionnaire contains a limited number of questions for which the respondent must provide a date or a correct sequence of events. In these cases, studies have indicated that the use of landmark dates can improve the quality of reporting by respondents (Loftus and Marburger, 1983). Landmark events are defined as either public or personal landmarks; for some of these, the respondent can provide an accurate date (personal landmark such as birthday, anniversary) whereas public landmarks can be dated accurately by the researcher. Landmarks are effective for three reasons: (1) landmark dates make effective use of the cluster organization of memory; (2) landmark dates may convert a difficult absolute judgment of recency to an easier relative judgment; and (3) landmark dates may suggest to the respondent the need to pay attention to exact dates and not simply imprecise dates. One way to operationalize landmark dates is to begin the interview with the respondent noting personal and/ or public landmark dates on a calendar that can be used for reference throughout the interview.

Use of Records. If the information has not been encoded in memory, the response quality will be poor no matter how well the questions have been constructed. For some information, the most efficient and effective means by which to improve the quality of the reported data is to have respondents access records. Several studies report an improvement in the quality of asset and income information when respondents used records (e.g., Maynes, 1968; Grondin and Michaud, 1994; Moore et al., 1996). Two factors often hinder questionnaire designers from requesting that respondents use records: interviewers' reluctance and mode of data collection. Although in some cases interviewers have been observed discouraging record use (Marquis and Moore, 1990), studies that request detailed income and expenditure information such as the SIPP and the National Medical Expenditure Survey, have both reported success in encouraging respondents to use records (Moore et al., 1996). Record use by respondents is directly related to the extent to which interviewers have been trained to encourage their use by respondents. For telephone interviews, the fear is that encouraging record use may encourage nonresponse; a small body of empirical literature does not support this notion (Grondin and Michaud, 1994). One form of record to consider is the prospective creation of a diary that is referenced by the respondent during a retrospective interview.

Recall versus Recognition. Any free-recall task, such as the enumeration of all sources of income, is a cognitively more difficult task than the task of recognition, such as, asking the respondent to indicate which of a list of income sources is applicable to his or her situation. Consider the two approaches taken in examples 1 and 2:

> Example 1: In (PRIOR MONTH), did you receive any money or income from any other source? This might include (READ SLOWLY) unemployment insurance, workers' compensation, alimony, rent from a tenant or boarder, an income tax refund, foster child payments, stipends from training programs, grandparents' Social Security income, and so on.

Example 2:   Next, I will read a list of benefit programs and types of support and I'd like you to tell me whether you or someone in your home gets this.
Food stamps
Medicaid
Child-care assistance
Child support from a child's parent
Social Security

In the first example, the respondent must process all of the items together; most likely after the first or second item on the list was read, the respondent failed to hear or process the remaining items on the list. Hence the list does not provide an effective recognition mechanism. In the second example, the respondent is given time to process each item on the list individually (the entire list consists of 20 items).

Complex Behavioral Experience. Simple behavioral experiences are relatively easy to report even over long reference periods whereas complex behavioral experiences can be quite difficult to reconstruct. For example, the experience of receiving welfare benefits continuously over a 12-month period is quite different from the experience of receiving benefits for 8 of the 12 months. The use of filter questions to identify those for whom the behavioral experience is complex would permit the questionnaire designer to concentrate design efforts on those respondents for whom the task is most difficult. Those with complex behavioral experiences could be questioned using an event history calendar whereas those for whom the recent past represents a steady state could be asked a limited number of discrete questions.

Recall Strategies. When respondents are asked to report a frequency or number of times an event or a behavior occurred, they draw on different response strategies to formulate a response. The choice of response strategy is determined, in part, by the actual number or frequency as well as the regularity of the behavior. Rare or infrequent events often are retrieved through episodic enumeration in which the respondent attempts to retrieve each occurrence of the event. Such strategies are subject to errors of omission as well as misdating of the event by the respondent. When the event or behavior of interest occurs frequently, respondents often will use some form of estimation strategy to formulate a response. These strategies include rule-based estimation (recall a rate and apply to time-frame of interest), automatic estimation (drawn from a sense of relative or absolute frequency), decomposition (estimate the parts and sum), normative expectations, or some form of heuristic, such as availability heuristic (based on the speed of retrieval). All estimation approaches are subject to error, but a well-designed questionnaire can both suggest the strategy for the respondent to use and attempt to correct for the expected biases. For example, if the behavior or event of interest is expected to occur on a regular basis, a question that directs the respondent to retrieve the rule, and apply the rule to the time frame of interest, and then probes to elicit exceptions to the rule may be a good strategy for eliciting a numeric response.

Current versus Retrospective Reports. Current status most often is easier to report, with respect to cognitive difficulty, than retrospective status, so it is often useful to consider beginning questions concerning current status. Information retrieved as part of the reporting of current status also will facilitate retrieval of retrospective information.

REPAIRS FOCUSING ON PROBLEMS
RELATED TO SOCIAL DESIRABILITY

Questions for which the source of the measurement error is related to perceived sensitivity of the items or the socially undesirable nature of the response often call for the use of question items or questionnaire modes that provide the respondent within greater sense of confidentiality or even anonymity as a means for improving response quality. The questionnaire designer must gauge the level of sensitivity or threat (or elicit information on sensitivity or threat through developmental interviews or focus groups) and respond with the appropriate level of questionnaire modifications. The discussion that follows attempts to provide approaches for questions of varying degrees of sensitivity, moving from slightly sensitive to extremely sensitive or illegal behaviors.

Reducing Threat Through Question Wording

Sudman and Bradburn (1982) provide a checklist of question approaches to minimize threat from sensitive questions. Among the suggestions made by the authors are the use of open questions as opposed to closed questions (so as to not reveal extreme response categories), the use of longer questions so as to provide context and indicate that the subject is not taboo, the use of alternative terminology (e.g., street language for illicit drugs), and embedding the topic in a list of more threatening topics to reduce perceived threat, because threat or sensitivity is determined in part by the context.

Alternative Modes of Data Collection

For sensitive questions, one of the most consistent findings from the experimental literature indicates that the use of self-administered questionnaires results in higher reports of threatening behavior. For example, in studies of illicit drug use, the increase in reports of use was directly related to the perceived level of sensitivity, greatest for the reporting of recent cocaine use, less profound but still significant with respect to marijuana and alcohol use. Alternative modes could involve the administration of the questions by an interviewer, with the respondent completing the response categories using paper and pencil, or administration of the questionnaire through a portable cassette and self-recording of responses. More recently, face-to-face data collection efforts have experimented with CASID in which the respondent reads the questions from the computer screen and directly enters the responses and ACASI, in which the questions can be heard over headphones as well as read by the respondent. The latter has the benefit of not requiring the respondent to be literate; furthermore, it can be programmed to permit efficient multilingual administration without requiring multilingual survey interviewers. In addition, both computer-assisted approaches offer the advantage that complicated skip patterns, not possible with paper and pencil self-administered questionnaires, can be incorporated into the questionnaire. Similar methods are possible in telephone surveys, with the use of push-button or voice recognition technology for the self-administered portion of the questionnaire.

Randomized Response and Item Count Techniques

Two techniques described in the literature provide researchers with a means of obtaining a population estimate of an event or a behavior but not information that can be associated with the individual. Both were designed initially for use in face-to-face surveys; it is feasible to administer an item count approach in a telephone or self-administered questionnaire. The randomized response technique is one in which two questions are presented to the respondent, each with the same response categories, usually yes and no. One question is the question of interest; the other is a question for which the distribution of the responses for the population is known. Each question is associated with a different color. A randomized device, such as a box containing beads of different colors, indicates to the respondent which of the questions to answer, for which he or she simply states to the interviewer either "yes" or "no." The probability of selecting the red bead as opposed to the blue bead is known to the researcher. An example is as follows: A box contains 100 beads, 70 percent of which are red, 30 percent of which are blue. When shaken, the box will present to the respondent one bead (only seen by the respondent). Depending on the color, the respondent will answer one of the following questions: (Red question) Have you ever had an abortion? and (Blue question) Is your birthday in June? In a survey of 1,000 individuals, the expected number of persons answering "yes" to the question about the month of the birthday is approximately 1,000(.30)/12 or 25 persons (assuming birthdays are equally distributed over the 12 months of the year). If 200 persons said "yes" in response to answering either the red or blue questions, then 175 answered yes in response to the abortion item, yielding a population estimate of the percent of women having had an abortion as 175/(1000*.70) or 25 percent.

The item count method is somewhat easier to administer than the randomized response technique. In the item count method, two nearly identical lists of behaviors are developed; in one list k behaviors are listed and in the other list, $k +1$ items are listed, where the additional item is the behavior of interest. Half of the respondents are administered the list with k items and the other half are offered the list with the $k +1$ behaviors. Respondents are asked to simply provide the number of behaviors in which they have engaged (without indicating the specific behaviors). The difference in the number of behaviors between the two lists provides the estimate of the behavior of interest.

The major disadvantage of either the randomized response technique or item count method is that one cannot relate individual characteristics of the respondents with the behavior of interest; rather one is limited to a population estimate.

CONCLUSIONS

The empirical literature addressing response errors specifically among the low-income or welfare population is limited. However, if we couple those limited findings with results based on studies of the general population, some principles of questionnaire design to minimize response error emerge. At the risk of appearing to provide simple solutions to complex problems, we speculate on some guidelines to assist in the construction of questionnaires targeted at the low-income or welfare populations.

• Complex versus simple behavioral experience. One finding that is consistent throughout the literature indicates that complex behavioral experiences are more difficult to retrieve and report accurately than simple behavioral experiences. Despite this, questionnaire designers tend to treat all potential respondents the same, opting for a single set of questions for many questions, such as a single question or set of questions concerning annual earnings or amount of program support. One means by which to attempt to improve the reporting for those persons for whom the task is most difficult is to adopt, as suggested by Schaeffer (1994), the use of filter questions to determine the complexity of the experience, offering different follow-up questions for those with simple and complex behavior. For example, the person who has been employed continuously at a single job or unemployed continuously during a particular reference period easily can be identified and directed toward a different set of questions concerning earnings than the individual who has held several jobs, either concurrently or sequentially. Similarly, one can ask the respondent whether the amount of income from a particular income support program varies from month to month, with follow-up questions based on the response. Although this approach to questionnaire design deviates from the desire to "standardized" the measurement process, it acknowledges the need to be flexible within a standardized measurement process so as to maximize the quality of the final product.

- Simple, single-focus items often are more effective than complex, compound items. Whenever possible, a question should attempt to address a single concept. Questions that include the use of "and" or "or" or that end with exclusion or inclusion clauses often can be confusing to respondents. Although these questions often are constructed so as to minimize the number of questions read to the respondent (and therefore minimize administration time), we speculate that the use of several shorter questions is more effective, both from the perspective of administration time as well as the quality of the data. As an example, let's return to an earlier example:

Since your welfare benefits ended in (FINAL BENEFIT MONTH), did you take part for at least one month in any Adult Basic Education (ABE) classes for improving your basic reading and math skills, or GED classes to help you prepare for the GED test, or classes to prepare for a regular high school diploma?

One means to improve this item would be as follows:

Since (FINAL BENEFIT MONTH) have you taken any of the following classes?
a. An Adult Basic Education class for improving basic reading and math skills? YES/NO
b. A GED class to prepare for the GED test? YES/NO
c. A class or classes to prepare for a regular high school diploma? YES/NO

If the "one month" qualifier offered in the original question was important analytically, each "yes" response could be followed up with a probe directed at the length of the class.

- Reduce cognitive burden whenever possible. Regardless of the population of interest, we know that, from a cognitive perspective, some tasks are easier to perform than others. Several means by which this can be accomplished include:
- Phrase tasks in the form of recognition rather than free recall. For example, asking the respondent to answer the question "Did you receive income from any of the following sources?" followed by a list of income sources is easier than asking the respondent to identify all income sources for the reference period of interest. Note that in asking a recognition question such as the one described, the ideal format would be to have the respondent respond "yes/no" to each income source, so only one item needs to be processed.
- Request information that requires estimation rather than episodic recall. For example, asking for the total number of jobs held during the reference period of interest requires less cognitive effort than asking for the starting and ending date of each job. If the latter information is needed to address analytic needs,

preceding the request with an estimation question may aid the respondent's retrieval of individual episodes.

• Request information in the format or metric used by the respondent. For example, earning information may be best reported when the most salient or most rehearsed metric is used by the respondent. For example, the findings by Borus (1970) and Smith (1997) that indicated a single broad-based question yielded a more accurate reporting by low-income respondents than a series of questions that required event-history type reconstruction of earnings simply may indicate that annual earnings are well rehearsed and more easily accessible to respondents than earnings related to any one job. One means by which to determine whether to ask the respondent about annual earnings, monthly earnings, or hourly earnings is to ask the respondent how he or she is best able to respond. Once again, this implies that tailoring the questionnaire to the respondent's circumstances may result in higher quality data.

• Focus on reference periods that are salient to the respondent. The 6-month period prior to exiting welfare may not necessarily be a particularly salient reference period, even though the date of termination of benefits may be quite salient. For reference periods that may not be salient to the respondent, the use of calendars or other records coupled with the identification of landmark events within the reference period may aid retrieval of information and the dating of events and behaviors.

• Provide the respondent with assistance in how to perform the task. For the most part, respondents rarely perform the task we are asking them to tackle. Instructions and feedback throughout the process can clarify the task for the respondent as well as provide feedback for appropriate respondent behavior. Instructions indicating that the questionnaire designer is interested in all spells of unemployment, including short spells lasting less than a week, provides an instruction to the respondent as well as additional time for the respondent to search his or her memory. Should the respondent provide such information, appropriate feedback would indicate that such detailed information is important to the study. Other forms of instruction could focus the respondent on the use of a calendar or other types of records.

In addition, we know from the literature that use of additional probes or cues stimulates the reporting of additional information. When there is interest in eliciting information from the respondent concerning short spells of employment or unemployment or odd or sporadic sources of income, repeated retrieval attempts by the respondent in response to repeated questions may be the most effective approach.

In some cases, the provision of some information may be preferable to no information from the respondent. Consider the case in which the respondent reports "don't know" in response to a question concerning earnings. One approach that has been effective is the use of broad-based followup questions in response to "don't know" items, for example, asking the respondent if his or her earnings were more than or less than a specific amount, with subsequent followup items until the respondent can no longer make a distinction (see Hurd and Rodgers, 1998).

• Comprehension. The concepts of interest for many surveys of the low-income and welfare populations are fairly complex, for example, distinguishing among the various income support programs or determining whether sporadic odd jobs count as being employed. As indicated in several of the studies reviewed, research directed toward improving the comprehension of survey questions is greatly needed. For those developing questionnaires, this implies the need for iterative testing and pretesting, focusing on the interpretation of questions among members of the population of interest.

The empirical literature provides evidence of both reasonably accurate reporting of earnings, other sources of income, and employment as well as extremely poor reporting of these characteristics on the part of household respondents. The magnitude of measurement error in these reports is in part a function of the task as framed by the question. Careful questionnaire construction and thorough testing of questions and questionnaires can effectively identify question problems and reduce sources of error.

REFERENCES

Aquilino, W.
  1994 Interview mode effects in surveys of drug and alcohol use. *Public Opinion Quarterly* 58:210-240.
Aquilino, W., and L. LoSciuto
  1990 Effect of interview mode on self-reported drug use. *Public Opinion Quarterly* 54:362-395.
Barron, J., M. Berger, and D. Black
  1997 *On the Job Training.* Kalamazoo, MI: W.E. Upjohn Institute for Employment Research.
Belli, R.
  1998 The structure of autobiographical memory and the event history calendar: Potential improvements in the quality of retrospective reports in surveys. *Memory* 6(4):383-406.
Belson, T.
  1981 *The Design and Understanding of Survey Questions.* Aldershot, Eng.: Gower Publishing Company.
Bogen, K.
  1995 Results of the Third Round of SIPP Cognitive Interviews. Unpublished manuscript, U.S. Bureau of the Census.
Borus, M.
  1966 Response error in survey reports of earnings information. *Journal of the American Statistical Association* 61:729-738.
  1970 Response error and questioning technique in surveys of earnings information. *Journal of the American Statistical Association* 65:566-575.
Bound, J., and A. Krueger
  1991 The extent of measurement error in longitudinal earnings data: Do two wrongs make a right? *Journal of Labor Economics* 9:1-24.

Bradburn, N.
    1983   Response effects. In *Handbook of Survey Research*, P. Rossi, J. Wright, and A. Anderson, eds. New York: Academic Press.
Burton, S., and E. Blair
    1991   Task conditions, response formation processes, and response accuracy for behavioral frequency questions in surveys. *Public Opinion Quarterly* 55:50-79.
Cannell, C., G. Fisher, and T. Bakker
    1965   Reporting of hospitalization in the health interview survey. *Vital and Health Statistics, Series 2, No. 6.* Washington, DC: U.S. Public Health Service.
Cannell, C., K. Marquis, and A. Laurent
    1977   A summary of studies of interviewing methodology. *Vital and Health Statistics, Series 2, No. 69.* Washington, DC: U.S. Public Health Service.
Cannell, C., P. Miller, and L. Oksenberg
    1981   Research on interviewing techniques. In *Sociological Methodology*, S. Leinhardt, ed. San Francisco: Jossey-Bass.
Carstensen, L., and H. Woltman
    1979   Comparing earnings data from the CPS and employers' records. In *Proceedings of the Section on Social Statistics*. Alexandria, VA: American Statistical Association.
Cash, W., and A. Moss
    1969   Optimum recall period for reporting persons injured in motor vehicle accidents. In *Vital and Health Statistics, Series 2, No. 50.* Washington, DC: U.S. Department of Health and Human Services.
Crowder, R.
    1976   *Principles of Learning and Memory.* Hillsdale, NJ: Lawrence Erlbaum Associates.
Cynamon, M., and D. Camburn
    1992   Employing a New Technique to Ask Questions on Sensitive Topics. Unpublished paper presented at the annual meeting of the National Field Directors Conference, St. Petersburg, FL, May, 1992.
David, M.
    1962   The validity of income reported by a sample of families who received welfare assistance during 1959. *Journal of the American Statistical Association* 57:680-685.
Dibbs, R., A. Hale, R. Loverock, and S. Michaud
    1995   *Some Effects of Computer Assisted Interviewing on the Data Quality of the Survey of Labour and Income Dynamics.* SLID Research Paper Series, No. 95-07. Ottawa: Statistics Canada.
Dodge, R.
    1970   Victim Recall Pretest. Unpublished memorandum, U.S. Bureau of the Census, Washington, DC. [Cited in R. Groves (1989).]
Dreher, G.
    1977   Nonrespondent characteristics and respondent accuracy in salary research. *Journal of Applied Psychology* 62:773-776.
Duncan, G., and D. Hill
    1985   An investigation of the extent and consequences of measurement error in labor-economic survey data. *Journal of Labor Economics* 3:508-532.
Forsyth, B., and J. Lessler
    1991   Cognitive laboratory methods: A taxonomy. In *Measurement Error in Surveys*, P. Biemer, S. Sudman, and R.M. Groves, eds. New York: John Wiley and Sons.
Freedman, D., A. Thornton, D. Camburn, D. Alwin, and L. Young-DeMarco
    1988   The life history calendar: A technique for collecting retrospective data. In *Sociological Methodology*, C. Clogg, ed. San Francisco: Jossey-Bass.

Gems, B., D. Gosh, and R. Hitlin
  1982   A recall experiment: Impact of time on recall of recreational fishing trips. In *Proceedings of the Section on Survey Research Methods*. Alexandria, VA: American Statistical Association.
Goodreau, K., H. Oberheu, and D. Vaughan
  1984   An assessment of the quality of survey reports of income from the Aid to Families with Dependent Children (AFDC) program. *Journal of Business and Economic Statistics* 2:179-186.
Grondin, C., and S. Michaud
  1994   Data quality of income data using computer assisted interview: The experience of the Canadian Survey of Labour and Income Dynamics. In *Proceedings of the Section on Survey Research Methods*. Alexandria, VA: American Statistical Association.
Groves, R.
  1989   *Survey Errors and Survey Costs*. New York: Wiley and Sons.
Halsey, H.
  1978   Validating income data: lessons from the Seattle and Denver income maintenance experiment. In *Proceedings of the Survey of Income and Program Participation Workshop-Survey Research Issues in Income Measurement: Field Techniques, Questionnaire Design and Income Validation*. Washington, DC: U.S. Department of Health, Education, and Welfare.
Hansen, M., W. Hurwitz, and M. Bershad
  1961   Measurement errors in censuses and surveys. *Bulletin of the International Statistical Institute* 38:359-374.
Hardin, E., and G. Hershey
  1960   Accuracy of employee reports on changes in pay. *Journal of Applied Psychology* 44:269-275.
Hill, D.
  1987   Response errors around the seam: Analysis of change in a panel with overlapping reference periods. Pp. 210-215 in *Proceedings of the Section on Survey Research Methods*. Alexandria, VA: American Statistical Association.
Hoaglin, D.
  1978   Household income and income reporting error in the housing allowance demand experiment. In *Proceedings of the Survey of Income and Program Participation Workshop-Survey Research Issues in Income Measurement: Field Techniques, Questionnaire Design and Income Validation*. Washington, DC: U.S. Department of Health, Education, and Welfare.
Horvath, F.
  1982   Forgotten unemployment: recall bias in retrospective data. *Monthly Labor Review* 105:40-43.
Hurd, M., and W. Rodgers
  1998   The Effects of Bracketing and Anchoring on Measurement in the Health and Retirement Survey. Institute for Social Research, University of Michigan, Ann Arbor, MI.
Jones, E., and J. Forrest
  1992   Underreporting of abortions in surveys of U.S. women: 1976 to 1988. *Demography* 29:113-126.
Keating, E., D. Paterson, and C. Stone
  1950   Validity of work histories obtained by interview. *Journal of Applied Psychology* 34:6-11.
Kish, L.
  1965   *Survey Sampling*. New York: John Wiley and Sons.

Levine, P.
   1993   CPS contemporaneous and retrospective unemployment compared. *Monthly Labor Review* 116:33-39.
Livingston, R.
   1969   Evaluation of the reporting of public assistance income in the Special Census of Dane County, Wisconsin: May 15, 1968. In *Proceedings of the Ninth Workshop on Public Welfare Research and Statistics.*
Loftus, E., and W. Marburger
   1983   Since the eruption of Mt. St. Helens, has anyone beaten you up? Improving the accuracy of retrospective reports with landmark events. *Memory and Cognition* 11:114-120.
London, K., and L. Williams
   1990   A Comparison of Abortion Underreporting in an In-Person Interview and Self-Administered Question. Unpublished paper presented at the Annual Meeting of the Population Association of America, Toronto, April.
Lyberg, L., and D. Kasprzyk
   1991   Data collection methods and measurement error: An Overview. In *Measurement Error in Surveys*, P. Biemer, S. Sudman, and R.M. Groves, eds. New York: Wiley and Sons.
Marquis, K., and J. Moore
   1990   Measurement errors in SIPP program reports. In *Proceedings of the Annual Research Conference.* Washington, DC: U.S. Bureau of the Census.
Mathiowetz, N.
   1986   The problem of omissions and telescoping error: New evidence from a study of unemployment. In *Proceedings of the Section on Survey Research Methods.* Alexandria, VA: American Statistical Association.
Mathiowetz, N., and G. Duncan
   1988   Out of work, out of mind: Response error in retrospective reports of unemployment. *Journal of Business and Economic Statistics* 6:221-229.
Maynes, E.
   1968   Minimizing response errors in financial data: The possibilities. *Journal of the American Statistical Association* 63:214-227.
Mellow, W., and H. Sider
   1983   Accuracy of response in labor market surveys: Evidence and implications. *Journal of Labor Economics* 1:331-344.
Menon, G.
   1993   The effects of accessibility of information in memory on judgments of behavioral frequencies. *Journal of Consumer Research* 20:431-440.
   1994   Judgments of behavioral frequencies: Memory search and retrieval strategies. In *Autobiographical Memory and the Validity of Retrospective Reports*, N. Schwarz and S. Sudman, eds. New York: Springer-Verlag.
Moore, J., K. Marquis, and K. Bogen
   1996   The SIPP Cognitive Research Evaluation Experiment: Basic Results and Documentation. Unpublished report, U.S. Bureau of the Census, Washington, DC.
Moore, J., L. Stinson, and E. Welniak
   1999   Income reporting in surveys: Cognitive issues and measurement error. In *Cognition and Survey Research*, M. Sirken, D.J. Herrmann, S. Schechter, and R. Tourangeau, eds. New York: Wiley and Sons.
Morganstern, R., and N. Bartlett
   1974   The retrospective bias in unemployment reporting by sex, race, and age. *Journal of the American Statistical Association* 69:355-357.

Murphy, L., and C. Cowan
  1976   Effects of bounding on telescoping in the national crime survey. In *Proceedings of the Social Statistics Section*. Alexandria, VA: American Statistical Association.

Neter, J., and J. Waksberg
  1964   A study of response errors in expenditure data from household interviews. *Journal of the American Statistical Association* 59:18-55.

Oberheu, H., and M. Ono
  1975   Findings from a pilot study of current and potential public assistance recipients included in the current population survey. In *Proceedings of the Social Statistics Section*. Alexandria, VA: American Statistical Association.

O'Reilly, J., M. Hubbard, J. Lessler, P. Biemer, and C. Turner
  1994   Audio and video computer assisted self-interviewing: Preliminary tests of new technology for data collection. *Journal of Official Statistics* 10:197-214.

Poterba, J., and L. Summers
  1984   Response variation in the CPS: Caveats for the unemployment analyst. *Monthly Labor Review* 107:37-42.

Presser, S., and J. Blair
  1994   Survey pretesting: Do different methods produce different results? *Sociological Methodology*. San Francisco: Jossey-Bass.

Presser, S., and L. Stinson
  1998   Data collection mode and social desirability bias in self-reported religious attendance. *American Sociological Review* 63:137-145.

Rodgers, W., C. Brown, and G. Duncan
  1993   Errors in survey reports of earnings, hours worked, and hourly wages. *Journal of the American Statistical Association* 88:1208-1218.

Schaeffer, N.
  1994   Errors of experience: Response errors in reports about child support and their implications for questionnaire design. In *Autobiographical Memory and the Validity of Retrospective Reports*, N. Schwarz and S. Sudman, eds. New York: Springer-Verlag.

Smith, J.
  1997   Measuring Earning Levels Among the Poor: Evidence from Two Samples of JTPA Eligibles. Unpublished manuscript, University of Western Ontario.

Stinson, L.
  1997   The Subjective Assessment of Income and Expenses: Cognitive Test Results. Unpublished manuscript, U.S. Bureau of Labor Statistics, Washington, DC.

Sudman, S., and N. Bradburn
  1973   Effects of time and memory factors on response in surveys. *Journal of the American Statistical Association* 68:805-815.
  1982   *Asking Questions: A Practical Guide to Questionnaire Design*. San Francisco: Jossey-Bass.

Sudman, S., N. Bradburn, and N. Schwarz
  1996   *Thinking About Answers: The Application of Cognitive Processes to Survey Methodology*. San Francisco: Jossey-Bass.

Tourangeau, R., and T. Smith
  1996   Asking sensitive questions: The impact of data collection mode, question format, and question context. *Public Opinion Quarterly* 60:275-304.

Tourangeau, R., L. Rips, and K. Rasinski
  2000   *The Psychology of Survey Response*. Cambridge, Eng.: Cambridge University Press.

U.S. Bureau of the Census
   1979   Vocational school experience: October, 1976. In *Current Population Reports Series P-70, No. 343*. Washington, DC: Department of Commerce.
Warner, K.
   1978   Possible increases in the underreporting of cigarette consumption. *Journal of the American Statistical Association* 73:314-318.
Yen, W., and H. Nelson
   1996   Testing the Validity of Public Assistance Surveys with Administrative Records: A Validation Study of Welfare Survey Data. Unpublished paper presented at the Annual Conference of the American Association for Public Opinion Research, May.

Part II

Administrative Data

7

Matching and Cleaning Administrative Data

Robert M. Goerge and Bong Joo Lee

This paper addresses the cleaning and linking of individual-level administrative data for the purposes of social program research and evaluation. We will define administrative data as that collected in the course of programmatic activities for the purposes of client-level tracking, service provision, or decision making—essentially, nonresearch activities. Although some data sets are collected with both programmatic and research activities in mind—birth certificates are a good example—researchers usually think of administrative data as a secondary data source in contrast to surveys that are conducted solely for research purposes.

When we refer to administrative data to be used for research and evaluation of social programs, we are referring primarily to data from management information systems designed to assist in the administration of participant benefits, including, income maintenance, food stamps, Medicaid, nutritional programs, child support, child protective services, childcare subsidies, Social Security programs, and an array of social services and public health programs. Because the focus of the research is often on individual well-being, most government social programs aimed at individuals could be included.

Before these administrative data can be used for research purposes, cleaning the data is a major activity as it is in conducting and using any large social surveys. Cleaning is necessary because there are numerous sources of potential error in the data and because the data are not formatted in a way that is easily analyzed by social scientists. We take a broad view of cleaning. It is not just correcting "dirty" data; it is producing a clean data set from a messy assortment of data sets. In this paper, cleaning refers to the entire process of transforming the data as it exists in the information system into an analytic data set.

Record linkage is a major activity in the use of administrative data, especially if the research is longitudinal—and, by definition, evaluation nearly always is. Record linkage is the process of determining that two data records belong to the same individual. Being able to track an individual from one time to the next or across numerous data sets is nearly always necessary when using administrative data, especially because, in most cases, one does not have access to the independent sources of data that can assure that a time 1 measurement and time 2 measurement are of the same person or that an agency 1 record and agency 2 record are for the same individual.[1]

Data cleaning and record linkage are closely related activities. At its most simple level, record linkage is necessary to determine if any duplicate records exist for a single individual or case in a particular data set. Record linkage is used to produce clean, comprehensive data sets from single program data sets. Without accurate record linkage, it is likely that the data on an individual will be incomplete or contain data that do not belong to that individual. And, to do accurate record linkage, the data fields necessary to perform the linkage, typically individual identifiers, must be accurate and in a standardized format across all the data sets to be linked.

ADVANTAGES AND DISADVANTAGES
OF ADMINISTRATIVE DATA

The advantages and disadvantages of administrative data can be identified most easily when they are compared with survey data. However, the comparison of these two types of data collection is a straw man. The research questions that are appropriately addressed are qualitatively different from those appropriately addressed by surveying a subset of the general population. The type of data that one should use for answering a particular research question should be determined by the question. If a comprehensive study of a particular issue requires a survey of a population not covered by administrative data or if important variables are unavailable, other data collection is necessary. However, it is almost always the case that a rich study of a particular issue that identifies or rules out multiple potential causes or correlates of a particular phenomena requires data from multiple sources.

Administrative data, in most cases, are superior to other data sources for identifying program participation—what benefits were provided to whom, when, and in what amount. (The exact reason why people are participating is often missing.) Administrative data are collected on an entire population of individuals

---

[1]Because of problems with recall, often the individual cannot confirm his or her participation at a particular point in time (see Kalil et al., 1998).

or families participating in a given program. This is advantageous for two reasons. First, it is possible to study low-incidence phenomena that may be expensive to uncover in a survey of the general population. Second, and related to the first, it is possible to study the spread of events over a geographical area; this is even easier if extensive geographical identifiers are available on the data record. Given that information about events is usually collected when the events happen, there is much less opportunity for errors because of faulty recall.

Using administrative data is also advantageous for uncovering information that a survey respondent is unlikely to provide in an interview. In our work, we were relatively certain that families would underreport their incidence of abuse or neglect. The same issue exists for mental health or substance abuse treatment. Although survey methods have progressed significantly in addressing sensitive issues, administrative data can prove to be an accurate source of indicators for phenomena that are not easily reported by individuals—if one can satisfactorily address issues of accessing sensitive or confidential data.

Because the data record for an individual or case is likely viewed often by the program staff, opportunities exist for correcting and updating the data fields. The value of this is even greater when the old information is maintained in addition to the updates. A major problem with administrative data archiving and storing is that when data are updated, the old information is lost when it is overwritten.

As noted, the disadvantages of administrative data are often listed as a contrast to the characteristics of survey data. Although this may be a straw man argument, other legitimate concerns should be addressed when using administrative data. The concerns are related to the choice-, event-, or participation-based nature of the data; the reliability of administrative data for research purposes; the lack of adequate control variables; and the facts that all outcomes of interest are not measured (e.g., some types of indicators of well-being) that data are available only for the periods that the client is in the program, and that the level of reliability of administrative data is uncertain. Also, the data are difficult to access because of confidentiality issues (as far as getting informed consent) and because of bureaucratic issues in obtaining approval. When the data will be available, therefore, is often unpredictable.

Finally, there is often a lack of documentation and information about quality. One must do ethnographic research to uncover "qualitative" information about the condition of the data. There is no shortcut for understanding the process behind the collection, processing, and storage of the administrative data.

ASSESSING THE QUALITY OF THE DATA AND CLEANING THE DATA FOR RESEARCH PURPOSES

In this section, we present strategies for determining if a particular administrative data set can be used to answer a particular question. Researchers seldom go directly to the online information system itself to assess its quality—although this may be one step in the process. Typically, government agencies give researchers both inside and outside the agency an extract of the information system of interest. This file may be called a "pull" file. It is a selection of data fields, never all of them, typically on all individuals in the information system during a specified period of time created for a particular purpose, usually not specified each time a request for data is made. Any one actual pull refers to a time period that corresponds to some administrative time period—for example, month or fiscal year. These cross-sectional pulls are very useful for agency purposes because they describe the point-in-time caseload for which an agency is responsible. As we will explain, this approach is not ideal for social research or evaluation.

The programming for a pull file is often a time-consuming task that is done as part of the system design based on the analytic needs at the time of the design. Even a small modification to the pull file may be costly or impossible given the capacity of the state or county agency information systems division. The advantage of this practice is that multiple individuals usually have some knowledge of the quality of the pull file—they may know how some of the fields are collected and how accurate they are. The disadvantage is that it probably requires additional cleaning to answer a particular set of research questions.

We cannot stress enough the importance of assessing data sets individually for each new research project undertaken. A particular data set may be ideal for one question and a disaster for another. Some fields in a database that may be perfectly reliable because of how the agencies collect or audit these fields, while other fields may almost seem to contain values entered in a random manner. Also, a particular programmatic database may have certain fields that are reliable at one point in time and not at other points. Needless to say, one field may be entered reliably in one jurisdiction and not in another.

For example, income maintenance program data are ideal for knowing the months in which families received Aid to Families with Dependent Children (AFDC) or Temporary Assistance for Needy Families (TANF) grants. However, because they rely on the reporting of grantees for employment information and there are often incentives for providing inaccurate information, addressing questions about the employment of TANF recipients using income maintenance program data is not ideal. Furthermore, information about the grantee, such as marital status or education, may only be collected at case opening and therefore is more likely to be inaccurate the longer the time since the case opening. Undertaking these tasks of assessing data quality is quite time consuming and resource intensive. The resource requirements are similar to those of cleaning large survey data sets, however, where to go to get information to do the cleaning is often unclear. Often documentation is unavailable and the original system architects have moved to other projects. Therefore, cleaning administrative data is often a task that goes on for many years as more is learned about the source and maintenance of the particular database.

In the following paragraphs, we provide some of the strategies and methods that we use to assess and address issues of data quality in the use of administrative data. The most basic, and perhaps best, of these is to compare the data with another source on the same event or individual. We will end with a discussion of that strategy.

Assessing Data Quality

Initially, the researcher would want to assess if the data entry were reliable, which would include knowing whether the individual collecting the data had the skill or opportunity to collect reliable information. The questions that should be asked are as follows:

• What is the motivation for collecting the data? Often a financial or contractual motivation produces the most reliable data. When reimbursement is tied to a particular data field, both the payer and the payee have incentives to ensure that neither party is provided with an additional benefit. The state agency does not want to pay more TANF that it needs to pay, and a grantee (or his or her advocate) wants to ensure that the family gets all to which they are entitled. Also, an agency may have a legal requirement to track individuals and their information. Properly tracking the jail time of incarcerated individuals would seem to be one such activity for which one could be fairly certain of the data accuracy—although not blindly so.

• Is there a system for auditing the accuracy of the data? Is there a group of individuals who sample the data and cross-check the accuracy of the data with another source of the information? In some agencies, the computer records will be compared to the paper files.

• Are the data entered directly by the frontline worker? Adding a step to the process of entering the data—having a worker filling out a paper form and then passing it on to a data entry function—allows another opportunity for error and typically also excludes the opportunity for the worker to see the computerized record in order to correct it.

• Do "edit checks" exist in the information system? If there is no direct audit of the data or the data are not entered or checked by a frontline worker, having edit checks built into the data entry system may address some errors. These checks are programmed to prevent the entry of invalid values or not entering anything into a field. (This is similar to the practice of programming skip patterns or acceptable values for data entry of survey instruments.) For example, an edit check can require that a nonzero dollar amount is entered into a current earnings field for those individuals who are labeled as employed.

• What analyses have been done with these data in the past? There is no substitute for analyzing the data—even attempting to address some of the research questions—in the process of assessing the quality, especially when the administrative data have not been used extensively. A good starting point for such analysis is examining the frequencies of certain fields to determine if there are any anomalies, such as values that are out of range; or examining inexplicable variation by region, suggesting variation in data entry practices; or seeking missing periods of the time series. Substantive consistency of the data is an important starting point as well. One example of this with which we have been wrestling is why 100 percent of the AFDC caseload were not eligible for Medicaid. We were certain that we had made some error in our record linkage. When we conferred with the welfare agency staff, they also were stymied at first. We eventually discovered that some AFDC recipients are actually covered by private health insurance through their employers. With this information, we are at least able to explain an apparent error.

   • Finally, are the items in the data fields critical to the mission of the program? This issue is related to the first noted issue above. Cutting checks is critical for welfare agencies. If certain types of data are required to cut checks, the data may be considered to be accurate. For example, if a payment cannot be made to an individual until a status that results in a sanction is addressed, one typically expects that the sanction code will be changed so payment can be made. On the other hand, if a particular assessment is not required for a worker to do his or her job or if an assessment is outside the skill set of the typical worker doing the assessment, one should have concerns about the accuracy (Goerge et al., 1992). For example, foster care workers have been asked to provide the disability status of the child on his or her computerized record. This status in the vast majority of the cases has no impact on the decision making of the worker. Therefore, even if there is an edit check that requires a particular set of codes, one would not expect the coding to be accurate.

   We will continue to give examples of data quality issues as we discuss ways to address some of them. The following examples center on the linking of an administrative data set with another one in order to address inadequacies in one set for addressing a particular question.

   The choice-based nature of administrative data can be addressed in part by linking the data to a population-based administrative data set. Such linkages allows one to better understand who is participating in a program and perhaps how they were selected or selected themselves into the program. There are some obvious examples of choice-based linking data to population-based data. In analyzing young children, it is possible to use birth certificate data to better understand what children might be selected into programs such as Women, Infants and Children (WIC), Early, Periodic, Screening, Diagnosis And Treatment Program (EPSDT), and foster care. If geographic identifiers are available, administrative data can be linked to census tract information to provide additional information on the context as well as the selection process. For example, knowing how many poor children live in a particular census tract and how many children participate in a welfare program can address whether the welfare population is representative of the entire population of those living at some fraction of the poverty level.

If one is interested in school-age children, computerized school data provide a base population for understanding the selection issues. One example is to link the 6- to 12-year-old population and their School Lunch Program (SLP) information to Food Stamp administrative data to understand who uses Food Stamps and what population the administrative data actually represent. Because SLP eligibility is very similar to Food Stamps (without the asset test), such data could provide a very good idea of Food Stamp participation. The criticism that administrative data only tracks individuals while they are in the program is true. Extending this a bit, administrative data, in general, only track individuals while they are in some administrative data set. Good recent examples of addressing this issue are the TANF leaver studies being conducted by a number of states. They are linking records of individuals leaving TANF with UI and other administrative data, as well as survey data, to fill in the data that welfare agencies typically have on these individuals—data from the states' FAMIS or MMIS systems. Especially when we are studying welfare or former welfare recipients, it is likely that these individuals appear in another administrative data set—Medicaid, Food Stamps, child support, WIC, or child care, to name a few. Although participation in some of these is closely linked to income maintenance, as we have learned in the recent past, there is also enough independence from income maintenance programs to provide useful post-participation information. Finally, if they are not in any of these social programs databases, they are likely to be in the income tax return databases or in credit bureau databases, both now becoming data sets used more commonly for social research (Hotz et al., 1999).

A more thorny problem may be situations in which an individual or a family leaves the jurisdiction where administrative data were collected. We may be "looking" for them in other databases when they may have moved out of the county or state (or country) in which the data were collected. The creation of national-level data sets may help to address this problem simply through a better understanding of mobility issues, if not actually linking data from multiple states to better track individuals or families.

It is certainly possible that two administrative databases will label an individual as participating in two programs that should be mutually exclusive. For example, in our work in examining the overlap of AFDC or TANF and foster care, we find that children are identified as living with their parents in an income maintenance case when they are actually living with foster parents. Although these records eventually may be reconciled for accounting purposes (on the income maintenance side), we do need to accurately capture the date that living in an AFDC grant ended and living in foster care began. Foster care administrative data typically track accurately where children live on a day-to-day basis. Therefore, in studying these two programs, it is straightforward to truncate the AFDC record when foster care begins. However, one would want to "overwrite" the

AFDC end date so that one would not use the wrong date if one were to analyze the overlap between AFDC and another program, such as WIC, where the participation date may be less accurate than in the foster care program.

Basic reliability issues also arise. For example, some administrative databases do a less than acceptable job of identifying the demographic characteristics of an individual. At a minimum, data entry errors may occur in entering gender or birth dates (3/11/99, instead of 11/3/99). Also, data on workers' determination of race/ethnicity might not be self-reported, or race/ethnicity might not be critical to the business of the agency, although this is often a concern of external parties. In some cases, when one links two administrative data files, the race/ethnicity codes for an individual do not agree. This discrepancy may be a particular problem when the data files cover time periods that are far apart, because some individuals do change how they label themselves and the labels used by agencies may change (Scott, 2000). Linking administrative data with birth certificate data—often computerized for decades in many states—or having another source of data can help address these problems. We will discuss this issue below when we discuss record linkage in detail (Goerge, 1997).

Creating Longitudinal Files

As mentioned earlier, the pull files provided by government agencies are often not cumulative files and most often only span a limited time period. For most social research, longitudinal data are required, and continuous-time data—as opposed to repeated, cross-sectional data—are preferred, again depending on the question. Although these pull files may contain some historical information, this is often kept to a minimum to limit the file size. The historical information is typically maintained for the program's unit of administration. For TANF, this is the family case. For Food Stamps, it is the household case. In either program, the historical data for the individual member of the household or family are not kept in these pull files. The current status typically is recorded in order to accurately calculate the size of the caseload. Therefore, to create a "clean" longitudinal file at the individual level, one must read each monthly pull file in order to recreate the individual's status history. Using a case history for an individual would be inaccurate. An example is the overlap between AFDC and foster care discussed earlier. The case history for the family—often that of the head of the household, and which may continue after the child enters foster care—would not accurately track the child's income maintenance grant participation. More on this topic is discussed in the following sections.

Linking Administrative Data and Survey Data

The state of the art in addressing the most pressing policy issues of the day is to use administrative data and survey methods to obtain the richest, most accurate data to answer questions about the impact and implementation of social programs. The TANF leaver studies mentioned earlier, which use income maintenance administrative data to select and weight samples and TANF and other programmatic databases to locate former TANF participants, provide certain outcome measures (e.g., employment and readmission) and characteristics of the grantees and members of the family. Survey data are used to obtain perceptions about employment and fill in where the administrative data lack certain information. Administrative lists have also been used to generate samples for surveys that intend to collect data not available in the administrative data.

Such studies can be helpful in understanding data quality issues when the two sources of data overlap. For example, we worked with other colleagues to compare reports of welfare receipt with administrative data and were able to gauge the accuracy of participant recall. We have some evidence for situations in which it is quite defensible to use surveys when administrative data are too difficult or time consuming to obtain. For example, although childcare utilization data may be available in many states, the data often are so decentralized that bringing them together into a single database may take many more resources than a survey. Of course, this depends on the sample size needed. However, much more needs to be done in this vein to understand when it is worthwhile to take on the obstacles that are more the rule than the exception in using administrative data.

ADMINISTRATIVE DATA RECORD LINKAGE

A characteristic of administrative data that offers unique opportunities for researchers is the ability to link data sets in order to address research questions that have otherwise been difficult to pursue because of lack of suitable data.[2] For example, studying the incidence of foster care placement, or any low-incidence event, among children who are receiving cash assistance requires a large sample of children receiving cash assistance given that foster care placement is a rare event. The resources and time required to gather such data using survey methods can be prohibitive. However, linking cash assistance administrative data and foster care data solves the problem of adequate sample size in a cost-effective way. Linking administrative data sets is also advantageous when the research

---

[2]Our discussion of record linkage focuses on its application at the individual level, where research interests require individual-level linkage as opposed to aggregate population overlap statistics. In other words, we address the need to follow the outcome of interest at the individual level, focusing on research questions dealing with temporal data on timing and sequence. Utility of statistical techniques that are developed to estimate aggregate population overlap among different data sets without doing individual-level record linkage, such as the probabilistic population estimation method, is beyond the scope of our discussion in this paper. (For further information on such a technique, refer to Pandiani et al., 1998.)

interest is focused in one particular service area. For example, if one is interested in studying the multiple recurrences of some event, such as multiple reentries to cash assistance, recurring patterns of violent crime, or reentries to foster care, the size of the initial baseline sample must be large enough to observe an adequate number of recurrences in a reasonable time period. Linking administrative data over time at the population level for each area of concern is an excellent resource for pursuing such research questions without large investments of time and financial resources.

When the linked administrative data sets are considered as an ongoing research resource, it is preferable to have data from the entire population from each source database that are linked to each other and maintained. Given the large number of cases needed to be processed during record linkage, the idea of working with data from the entire population could overwhelm the researcher. However, because most data processing now is done using computers, the sheer size of the data files needed to be linked is typically not a major factor in the time and resources needed. On the other hand, the importance of having good programmers with necessary analytic and programming skills cannot be overemphasized for achieving successful record-linking results. Because the amount of skilled programming for a sample file may be equal to the amount needed for an entire large file, the additional cost involved in linking the entire files rather than samples is justifiable in computerized record-linking situations. The advantages that arise from having population data (as opposed to samples from each system or some systems) far exceed the costs involved. When tracking certain outcomes of a base population using linked data, one needs at least the population-level data from the data source that contains information about the outcome of interest.

For example, suppose one is interested in studying the incidence of receiving service X among a 10 percent random sample of a population in data set A. The receipt of service X is recorded in data set B. Because the researcher must identify *all* service X receipt for the 10 percent sample in data set A, the sample data must be linked to the entire population in data set B. Suppose the researcher only has a 10 percent random sample of data set B. Linking the two data samples would provide, at best, only 10 percent of the outcomes of interest identified in the 10 percent sample of the base population A. Furthermore, the "unlinked" individuals in the sample would be a combination of those who did not receive service X and those who received service X but were not sampled from data set B. Because one cannot distinguish the two groups among the "unlinked" individuals, any individual-level analysis becomes impossible (see Deming and Glasser, 1959, for a discussion of the issue of linking samples and the difficulty associated with it).

Research Applications of Data Linking

There are four different research applications of linked data sets. Each represents a different set of issues and challenges. The four types of linking applications can be broadly defined as: (1) linking an individual's records within a service system over time, (2) linking different information system data sets across service areas, (3) linking survey data to administrative data sets when the survey sample is drawn from an administrative data set, and 4) linking sample data to administrative data sets when the sample is drawn independent of administrative data.

The first type of linking application is the most common. Typically researchers take advantage of administrative data's historical information for various longitudinal analyses of service outcomes. Often this type of research requires linking data on individuals across several cross-sectional extracts from an agency's information system. Many agency information systems only contain information on the most recent service activities or service populations. Some information systems were designed that way because the agency's activity is defined as delivering services to a caseload at a given point in time or at some intervals. A good example would be a school information system in which each school year is defined as the fixed service duration, and each school year population is viewed as a distinct population. In this case, there is typically no unique individual ID in the information system across years because every individual gets a new ID each year—one that is associated with the particular school year. Even in a typical state information system on cash assistance, case status information is updated (in other words, overwritten) in any month when the status changes. To "reconstruct" the service histories, as discussed in the earlier section on cleaning, one must link each monthly extract to track service status changes.

At times, the information system itself is longitudinal, and no data are purged or overwritten. Even when the database is supposedly longitudinal, a family or an individual can be given multiple IDs over time. For example, many information systems employ a case ID system, which includes a geographic identifier (such as county code or service district code) as part of a unique individual ID. In this instance, problems arise when a family or an individual moves and receives a different ID. Our experience suggests that individuals are often associated with several case IDs over time in a single agency information system. Sometimes individuals may have several agency IDs assigned to them either because of a data entry error or a lack of concerted effort to track individuals in information systems. In any situation outlined here, careful examination of an explicit linking strategy is necessary.

The second type of linking application most often involves situations in which different agency information systems do not share a common ID. Where the funding stream and the service delivery system are separate and categorical in nature, information systems developed to support the functions of each agency are not linked to other service information systems. In some instances, information systems even in a single agency do not share a common ID. For example, many child welfare agencies maintain two separate legacy information systems; one tracks foster care placement and payments and the other records child maltreatment reports. Although following the experiences of children from a report of abuse or neglect to a subsequent foster care event is critical for child welfare agencies, the two systems were not designed to support such a function. Obviously, where there is no common ID, linking data records reliably and accurately across different data sources is an important issue. Also, as in the case of linking individual records over time in a single information system, there is always a possibility of incorrect IDs, even when such a common ID exists. In fact, a reliable record linking between the two information systems that contain a common ID on a regular basis could provide a means to "correct" such incorrect IDs. For example, when the data files from the two systems are properly linked by using data fields other than the common ID, such as names and birth dates, the results of such a link could be compared to the common IDs in the information systems to identify incorrectly entered IDs.

The third type of linking application is when a sample of individuals recorded in administrative data is used as the study population. In such a study, researchers employ survey methods to try to collect information not typically available in administrative data. Items such as unreported income, attitude, and psychological functioning are good examples of information that is unavailable in administrative data. Most often, this type of application is not readily perceived as a linking application. However, when researchers use administrative data to collect information about the service receipt history of the sample, either retrospectively or prospectively, they face the same issues as one faces in linking administrative data in a single information system or across multiple systems. Also, if researchers rely on the agency ID system to identify the list of "unique" individuals when the sampling frame is developed, the quality of the agency ID has important implications for the representativeness of the sample. The degree of multiple IDs for the same individuals should be ascertained and the records unduplicated at the individual level for the sampling frame.

The fourth type of linking application involves cases in which researchers supplement the information collected through survey methods with detailed service information; they do this by linking survey data to service system administrative data after the survey is completed. Because the sample is drawn independent of the administrative data, no common ID is designated between the sample and the administrative data. Here the major concern is the kinds of identifying information that are available for linking purposes from both data sources. In particular, whether and how much identifying information—such as full names, birth dates, and Social Security numbers (SSNs)—is available from the survey data is a critical issue. When the identifying information is collected, data confidentiality issues might prohibit researchers from making information available for linking purposes.

TECHNICAL ISSUES IN LINKING

Two Methods of Linking:
Probabilistic and Deterministic Record-Linkage Methods

Linking data records reliably and accurately across different data sources is key to the success in the four applications outlined. In this section, we focus on the data linkage methods. Our main purpose is to provide basic concepts for practitioners rather than to present a rigorous theoretical method. Our discussion focuses on two methods of record linkage that are possible in automated computer systems: deterministic and probabilistic record linking.

Deterministic Record Linkage

Deterministic linkage compares an identifier or a group of identifiers across databases; a link is made if they all agree. For example, relying solely on an agency's common ID when available for linking purposes is a type of deterministic linking. When a common ID is unavailable, standard practice is to use alternative identifiers—such as SSNs, birth dates, and first and last names of individuals—that are available in two sets of data. Researchers also use combinations of different pieces of identifying information in an effort to increase the validity of the links made. For example, one might use SSN and the first two letters of the first and last names. In situations where an identifier with a high degree of discriminating power (such as SSN) is unavailable, a combination of the different pieces of identifying information must be used because many people have the same first and last names or birth dates. What distinguishes deterministic record linkage is that when two records agree on a particular field, there is no information on whether that agreement increases or decreases the likelihood that the two records are from the same individual. For example, the two situations in which, on last name, Goerge matches Goerge, and where Smith matches Smith, would be treated with similar matching power, even though it is clear that because there are few Goerges and many Smiths, these two matches mean different things.

Probabilistic Record Linkage

Because of the problems associated with deterministic linking, and especially when there is no single identifier distinguishing between truly linked records (records of the same individual) in the data sets, researchers have developed a set of methods known as probabilistic record linkage.[3] Probabilistic record

---

[3]Presentation of the detailed mathematical process of probabilistic record linkage method is beyond the scope of this paper. Readers interested in the theory should refer to references cited in this section of the paper.

linking is based on the assumption that no single match between variables common to the source databases will identify a client with complete reliability. Instead, the probabilistic record-linking method calculates the probability that two records belong to the same client by using multiple pieces of identifying information. Such identifying data may include last and first name, SSN, birth date, gender, race and ethnicity, and county of residence.

The process of record linkage can be conceptualized as identifying matched pairs among all possible pairs of observations from two data files. For example, when a data file A with A observations and a data file B with B observations are compared, the record-linkage process attempts to classify each record pair from the A by B pairs into the set of true matches (M set) and the set of true nonmatches (U set). First introduced by Newcombe et al. (1959) and further developed by Fellegi and Sunter (1969), the two probabilities for each field that are needed to determine if a pair belongs to M or U are m and u probabilities. Each field that is being compared in the record-linking process has m and u probabilities. The m probability is the probability that a field agrees given that the record pair being examined is a matched pair. The m probability is a measure of validity of the data field used in the record-linkage process because it is essentially one minus the error rate of the field. Thus, one can see that a more reliable data field will provide greater m probability. The u probability is the probability that a field agrees given that the record pair being examined is not a matched pair. This is a chance probability that a field agrees at random. For example, if the population has the same number of males and females, the u probability will be .5 because there is a 50 percent chance the gender field will match when the pair being examined is not a matched pair. Accordingly, a variable such as SSN will have a very low u probability because it is very unlikely that different individuals have the same SSN. Although there are many methods to calculate M and U probabilities, recent studies show that maximum-likelihood-based methods such as the Expectation-Maximization (EM) algorithm is the most effective of those developed and tested (Winkler, 1988; Jaro, 1989).

Using m and u probabilities, Fellegi and Sunter (1969) define weights that measure the contribution of each field to the probability of making an accurate classification of each pair into M or U sets. The "agreement" weight when a field agrees between the two records being examined is calculated as $log2(m/u)$. The "disagreement" weight when a field does not agree is calculated as $log2((1-m)/(1-u))$. These weights indicate how powerful a particular variable is in determining whether two records are from the same individual. These weights will vary based on the distribution of values of the identifiers. For example, a common last name match will provide a lower agreement weight than a match with a very uncommon name because u probability for such a common name will be greater than the uncommon name.

Fellegi and Sunter (1969) further showed that a composite weight could be calculated by summing the individual data field's weights. Using the composite weights, one can classify each pair of records into three groups: a link when the composite weight is above a threshold value (U), a non link when the composite weight is below another threshold value (L), and a possible link for clerical review when the composite weight is between U and L. Furthermore, the threshold values can be calculated given the accepted probability of false matches and the probability of false nonmatches (Fellegi and Sunter, 1969; Jaro, 1989). This contrasts favorably with the link or non link dichotomy in deterministic linkage.

Since the seminal work by Fellegi and Sunter (1969), the main focus of record linkage research has been how to determine the threshold values of U and L to improve the accuracy of determining what the threshold weight is for a certain link, as well as the threshold value for a certain non link. Recent development in improving record linkage allows us to take advantage of the speed and cost that computerized and automated linkage confer, such as deterministic matching, while allowing a researcher to identify at which "level" a match would be considered to be a true one (see for example; Jaro, 1989; Winkler, 1993, 1994, 1999).

Standardization and Data-Cleaning Issues in Record Linking

Regardless of which method of deterministic linking is used, entry errors, typographical errors, aliases, and other data transmission errors can cause problems. For example, one incorrectly entered digit of a Social Security number will produce a nonmatch between two records for which all other identifying information is the same. Names that are spelled differently across different systems also cause a problem. A first name of James that is recorded in one system as Jim and in the other as James will produce a nonmatch when the two records, in fact, belong to the same individual. The data cleaning in the record linkage process often involves (1) using consistent value-states for the data fields used for linking, (2) parsing variables into components that need to be compared, (3) dealing with typographical errors, and (4) unduplicating each source file for linkage.

Because record linking typically involves data sets from different sources, the importance of standardizing the format and values of each variable is used for linking purposes cannot be overemphasized. The exact coding schemes of all the variables from different source files used in the matching process should be examined to make sure all the data fields have consistent values. For example, males coded as "M" in one file and "1" in another file should be standardized into a same value. In the process, missing and invalid data entries also should be identified and coded accordingly. For example, a birth year 9999 should be recognized as a missing value before the data set is put into the record-linking process. Otherwise, records with a birth year 9999 from the two data sets can be linked because they have the "same" birth year. We also find that standardization of names in the matching process is important because names are often spelled differently or misspelled altogether across agency information systems. For example, a first name of Bob, Rob, and Robert should be standardized into a same first name such as Robert to achieve better record-linking results.

The data cleaning and standardization in matching process often requires parsing variables into a common set of components that can be compared. Names may have to be split or parsed into first name, middle initial, and last name and suffix (e.g., Junior). In using geographic information, street names and the form of the addresses must be standardized. This may mean parsing the address into number (100), street prefix (West), street name (Oak), and street suffix (Boulevard).

Because of typographical errors, an exact character-by-character comparison for certain fields used in a record-linking process may miss many "true" matches. A good example is variant spellings of names. For example, character-by-character comparison of a last name spelled as "Goerge" in one data file to a misspelled name "George" in another file would cause disagreement in the last name comparison even though "George" in the second file was a misspelling. In some situations, these types of typological errors can be a serious problem in record linkage. Winkler and Thibaudeau (1991) and Jaro (1989) describe how researchers at the U.S. Bureau of the Census reported that about 20 percent of last names and 25 percent of first names disagreed character by character among true matches in the Post Enumeration Survey. In recent years researchers in the field of record linkage have made substantial progress in developing algorithms to deal with such problems in character-by-character comparisons. As a result, some complex string comparator algorithms also have been developed to determine how close two strings of letters or numbers are to each other that account for insertions, deletions, and transpositions (Jaro, 1985, 1989; Winkler, 1990; Winkler and Thibaudeau, 1991).

In the record linkage process, one critical data cleaning process is to "unduplicate" each source data set before any two data sets are linked. As discussed earlier, often individuals are associated with several IDs because of data entry errors or a lack of concerted effort to track individuals in agency information systems. Obviously, multiple records for the same individual in each data set being linked produce uncertain links because the process must deal with N to N link situations. Unduplication of the records in a single data set can be thought as "self-match" of the data set. Once a match has been determined, a unique number is assigned to the matched records so that each individual can be uniquely identified. The end result of the unduplication process is a "person file," which contains the unique number assigned during unduplication and the individual's identifying data (name, birth date, race/ethnicity, gender, and county of residence) with a "link file" that links the unique individual ID to all the IDs assigned by an agency. Once each data set is unduplicated in such a way, the unduplicated person files can be used for cross-system record links.

Accuracy of Record Linking

Regardless of which method is used, the ultimate concern is in the degree of validity and accuracy of the links made. Whether it is a deterministic or probabilistic record-linkage technique that is used, the linking process essentially involves making an educated guess about whether two records belong to the same individual. Because the decision is a guess, it might be wrong. These errors in record linkage can be viewed as making false-positive and false-negative errors. A false-positive error occurs when the match is made between the two records when the two records, in fact, do not belong to the same individual. This type of error is comparable to a Type I error in statistical hypothesis testing. A false-negative error occurs when the match is not made between the two records when they, in fact, belong to the same individual. The type of error is comparable to a Type II error in statistical hypothesis testing.

As with Type I and Type II errors, although the probability of making a false-positive error can be easily ascertained in the linking process, determining the probability of a false negative error is more complex. Because the "weights" calculated in the probabilistic record-linkage method are essentially relative measures of the probability of a match, the weights can be converted to an explicit probability that a record pair is a true match (i.e., 1-false positive error rate). Belin and Rubin (1995) introduced a method for estimating error rates for cutoff weight values in the probabilistic record-linkage process. Many developments also have been made in dealing with linkage errors in post-linkage analysis stages (such as a regression analysis using linked files) (see Scheuren and Winkler, 1993). In the case of deterministic record linkage, an audit check on the matched pairs could provide an estimate of false-positive errors. Estimating the false-negative error rate is much more complex because it conceptually requires knowing the true matches prior to the linking and comparing the linking results to the true matches.

Adding to the complexity, as one tries to reduce one type of error, the other type of error increases. For example, in an effort to reduce false-positive errors, one might use a stringent rule of labeling the compared matches as matched pairs only when they are "perfect" matches. In the process, a slight difference in identifying information (such as one character mismatch in the names) might cause a non link when, in fact, the two records belong to the same individual. Hence, false-negative error rates increase. In the opposite scenario, one might accept as many possible matches as true matches, thereby relaxing the comparison rule by reducing false-negative errors. In this case, false-positive errors increase.

An Example

In practice, it would be useful to consider false-positive and false-negative error rates as a means to compare different methods of record linkage. One practical issue researchers face is determining which linkage method to use, especially when an ID variable such as SSN is available in the two data sets to be linked. Although most experts agree that probabilistic record linkage is a more reliable method than deterministic linking, it requires extensive programming or the purchase of software, which can be quite expensive. If one does not have ready access to suitable commercial record-linkage software, it may be sufficient for a good programmer to write a quick deterministic linkage program that matches a good deal of the records. There are other situations where there is no apparent common ID and the quality of identifying information in the data is questionable (such as many typographical errors in certain data fields), so that only using probabilistic record-linkage methods will yield acceptable linking results.

We present some empirical data comparing the two methods in the following paragraphs and corresponding tables. The methods compared are a deterministic record link using SSN and a probabilistic link using SSN, full name, birth date, race/ethnicity, and county of residence. We use data from the Client Database and the Cornerstone Database from the Illinois Department of Human Services. The Client Database records receipt of AFDC/TANF and Food Stamps and documents all those who are registered as eligible for Medicaid from 1989 to the present. The Cornerstone database contains WIC and case management service receipt at the individual level. There is no common ID between the two systems, while SSN and other identifying information are available in both systems.

Because both systems serve mainly low-income populations and contain data for a long period of time, we expected a high degree of overlap between the two populations. When the existence of SSN in both systems is examined, we find that about 38 percent of the Cornerstone records have missing SSNs while the Client Database identifies nearly 100 percent of the SSNs. In our first analysis, we excluded the records with missing SSNs from the Cornerstone data. Table 7-1 compares the number of matched and unmatched Cornerstone data records to the Client Database records comparing the deterministic match using SSN and

TABLE 7-1 Comparison of SSN Match (Deterministic) Versus Probabilistic Match (Without Missing SSN)

		Probabilistic Matching Number			Probabilistic Matching Percent		
		Nonmatch	Match	Total	Nonmatch	Match	Total
SSN	Nonmatch	74,496	45,987	120,483	61.8	38.2	100.0
Matching	Match	5,849	438,959	444,808	1.3	98.7	100.0
	Total	80,345	484,946	565,291	14.2	85.8	100.0

the probabilistic match using all other identifying information, including SSN. As shown in Table 7-1, the probabilistic match identified about 86 percent of non-SSN-missing Cornerstone record links to the Client Database. The SSN deterministic method identified about 84 percent of the matches.

Although the percentage of overall matches is similar, the distribution of error types is quite different, as shown in Table 7-1. The false-negative error rate of using the SSN deterministic record-linking method when compared to the results from the probabilistic match is about 38 percent. On the other hand, the false positive error rate is about 1 percent. We checked the results of the probabilistic link from random samples of the disagreement cells (i.e., probabilistic match/SSN no match and probabilistic nonmatch/SSN match) to verify the validity of the probabilistic match. We found that the probabilistic match results are very reliable. For example, we found that most of the pairs in the probabilistic match/SSN no match cell involve typographical errors in SSN with the same full name and birth date. Also, we found that most of the pairs in the probabilistic nonmatch/SSN match involve entirely different names or birth dates. Although the findings might be somewhat different when applied to different data systems, our finding suggests that employing a probabilistic record-linkage method helps to reduce both false-negative and false-positive errors. The findings also show that the benefit of employing probabilistic record linkage is greater in reducing false-negative errors (Type II errors) than in reducing false-positive errors (Type I errors) when compared with a deterministic record-linkage method using SSN.

Next, we included the Cornerstone records with missing SSN in the analysis. The findings are presented in Table 7-2. As one might expect, the probabilistic record-linkage method significantly enhances the results of the match by linking many more records. Compared with the results presented in Table 7-1, the number of matches from the probabilistic match increases by about 210,000 records, representing about 62 percent of matches made among the records with missing SSNs. Again, most of the benefit of using the probabilistic linkage method is in reducing false-negative errors. With about 30 percent of the records showing

TABLE 7-2 Comparison of SSN Match Versus Probabilistic Match (With Missing SSN)

		Probabilistic Matching Number			Probabilistic Matching Percent		
		Nonmatch	Match	Total	Nonmatch	Match	Total
SSN	Nonmatch	199,442	260,720	460,162	43.3	56.7	100.0
Matching	Match	5,782	444,540	475,537	1.3	98.7	100.0
	Total	205,224	699,478	904,702	22.7	77.3	100.0

missing SSNs, the false-negative error rate of the SSN deterministic link method is about 57 percent. From the above results, one can conclude that when SSN information is nearly complete in the two data sets, the added benefit of using probabilistic linking is relatively smaller (although quite significant) and the benefit comes largely from identifying false-negative errors. As the number of records with missing SSN increases, the benefit of employing a probabilistic record-linkage method increases.

Very often in practice, being able to link different data sources involves many other issues than that of the linking method. A key issue is data confidentiality, especially when full names are needed for linking purposes in the absence of a common ID. One possible solution to the confidentiality issue is the use of Soundex codes. Even though Soundex is not a complete method to preserve confidentiality, it provides added protection compared to using actual full names. The Soundex system is a method of indexing names by eliminating some letters and substituting numbers for other letters based on a code. Although experts disagree on what should be the authoritative Soundex system, the most familiar use of Soundex is by the U.S. Bureau of the Census, which uses it to create an index for individuals listed in the Census. Because it is impossible to derive an exact name from a Soundex name, the system can be used to conceal the identity of an individual to some extent. (For example, similar sounding but different names are coded to a same Soundex name.)

The issue in probabilistic linking, however, is how valid a Soundex name is alone compared to using full names. We examine this issue by comparing the two methods involving the same data sets with the other identifying information fixed. The other identifying information variables are SSN, birth date, race/ethnicity, and county of residence. Table 7-3 presents the results of such an exercise. The agreement rate between the Soundex-only method and the full-name method is very high—close to 100 percent. The results suggest that Soundex coded names work equally as well as full names in a probabilistic match. In situations in which full names cannot be accessed for linking purposes, Soundex

TABLE 7-3 Comparison of Full Name Match Versus Soundex Code Match

		Full Name Matching Number			Full Name Matching Percent		
		Nonmatch	Match	Total	Nonmatch	Match	Total
Soundex	Nonmatch	256,628	221	256,849	99.9	0.1	100.0
Matching	Match	40	43,111	43,151	0.1	99.9	100.0
	Total	256,668	43,332	300,000	85.6	14.4	100.0

names might be a good alternative while providing a better means of protecting individual identities.[4]

CONCLUSION

Recommendations

We recommend a number of activities in the cleaning of administrative data for research use. These include:

- Examining the internal consistency of the data;
- Examining how the data were collected, processed, and maintained before delivery to the researcher;
- Taking every opportunity to compare with other data sets, either survey or administrative, through record linkage; and,
- Most important, getting to know the operations of the program, not just the collection of administrative data, but also how services are provided so that inconsistencies in the data might be understood better.

We also recommend using probabilistic record linkage and not relying on any one identifier for linking records. We believe our analysis above makes this case. The golden rule of record linkage is that there is no such thing as a unique identifier, because individuals can match on many identifiers. In many cases the same SSN has been provided to two or more individuals.

Developments in Information Technology That May Improve Administrative Data

Much of what is discussed previously is required because public policy organizations are still, for the most part, in their first generation of information systems. These "legacy" systems are typically a decade or older mainframe installations that do not take advantage of much of today's technology. Data entry in the legacy systems, for example, is often quite cumbersome and requires a specialized data entry function. Frontline workers are typically not trained to do this or do not have the time or resources to take on the data entry task. An exception is in entitlement programs in some jurisdictions, where the primary activity for eligibility workers is collecting information from individuals and entering it into a computerized eligibility determination tool. The development of new graphical user interfaces that are more worker friendly—in that the screens

---

[4]Popular software programs such as SAS provide a simple method of converting names to Soundex codes.

flow in a way that is logical to a worker—is likely to have a positive effect on data entry both because of the ease of entry and because the worker may be able to retrieve information more easily. If this is the case, the worker will have a greater stake in the quality of the data.

The development of integrated online information systems, where a worker can obtain information on a client's use of multiple programs, also may have a positive effect on the quality of the data. First, the actual job of linking across the programs will likely be an improvement over the after-the-fact linking of records. For example, if an integrated system already exists, when a mental health case is opened for an individual with Medicaid eligibility, his or her records should be linked immediately. This, of course, requires an online record-linkage process for the one case or individual. Even though a researcher would still want to check whether an individual has multiple IDs, the process at the front end will greatly improve the quality of the analytic database.

Many states are now creating data warehouses in order to analyze many of the issues of multiple-program use and caseload overlap. These data warehouses "store" data extracts from multiple systems and link records from individuals across programs. If states are successful in creating comprehensive, well-implemented data warehouses, researchers may not have to undertake many of the cleaning or linking activities discussed in this paper. Government will have already done the data manipulations. The researchers, just as is typically done with survey data, will have to verify that the warehouse was well built. Although this may require some confidential information, it should make it easier to access administrative data.

REFERENCES

Belin, T.R., and D.B. Rubin
   1995   A method for calibrating false-match rates in record linkage. *Journal of the American Statistical Association* 90(June):694-707.
Deming, W., R. Edwards, and G. Glasser
   1959   One the problem of matching lists by samples. *Journal of the American Statistical Association* 54(June):403-415.
Fellegi, I.P., and A.B. Sunter
   1969   A theory for record linkage. *Journal of the American Statistical Association* 64:1183-1210.
Goerge, R.M.
   1997   Potential and problems in developing indicators on child well-being from administrative data. In *Indicators of Children's Well-Being*, R.M. Hauser et al., eds. New York: Russell Sage Foundation.
Goerge, R.M., J. Van Voorhis, S. Grant, K. Casey, and M. Robinson
   1992   Special education experiences of foster children: An empirical study. *Child Welfare* 71:5.
Hotz, V.J., C. Hill, C.H. Mullin, and J.K. Scholz
   1999   EITC Eligibility, Participation and Compliance Rates for AFDC Households: Evidence from the California Caseload. Working Paper 102. Joint Center for Poverty Research, University of Maryland and University of Michigan.

Jaro, M.A.
  1985   Current record linkage research. In *Proceedings of the Section on Statistical Computing.* Alexandria, VA: American Statistical Association.
  1989   Advances in record-linkage methodology as applied to matching the 1985 census of Tampa, Florida. *Journal of the American Statistical Association* 84(June):414-420.
Kalil, A., P.L. Chase-Lansdale, R. Coley, R. Goerge, and B.J. Lee
  1998   Correspondence between Individual and Administrative Reports of AFDC Receipt. Unpublished paper presented at the Annual Workshop of the National Association for Welfare Research and Statistics, Chicago, August 2-5.
Pandiani, J., S. Banks, and L. Schacht
  1998   Personal privacy versus public accountability: A technical solution to an ethical dilemma. *Journal of Behavioral Health Services and Research* 25:456-463.
Scheuren, F., and W.E. Winkler
  1993   Regression analysis of data files that are computer matched. *Survey Methodology* 19:39-58.
Scott, C.
  2000   Identifying the race/ethnicity of SSI recipients. In *Turning Administrative Systems into Administrative Systems.* Washington, DC: U.S. Department of the Treasury, Internal Revenue Service.
Winkler, W. E.
  1988   Using the EM algorithm for weight computation in the Fellegi-Sunter model of record linkage. In *Proceedings of the Section on Survey Research Methods.* Alexandria, VA: American Statistical Association.
  1990   String comparator metrics and enhanced decision rules in the Felligi-Sunter model of record linkage. In *Proceedings of the Section on Survey Research Methods.* Alexandria, VA: American Statistical Association.
  1993   Matching and record linkage. In *Statistical Research Division Report 93/08.* Washington, DC: U.S. Bureau of the Census.
  1994   Advanced methods for record linkage. In *Statistical Research Division Report 94/05.* Washington, DC: U.S. Bureau of the Census.
  1999   The state of record linkage and current research problems. In *Statistical Research Division Report 99/04.* Washington, DC: U.S. Bureau of the Census.
Winkler, W.E., and Y. Thibaudeau
  1991   An application of the Fellegi-Sunter model of record linkage to the 1990 U.S. decennial census. In *Statistical Research Division Report 91/09.* Washington, DC: U.S. Bureau of the Census.

8

Access and Confidentiality Issues with Administrative Data

Henry E. Brady, Susan A. Grand, M. Anne Powell,
and Werner Schink

The passage of welfare reform in 1996 marked a significant shift in public policy for low-income families and children. The previous program, Aid to Families with Dependent Children (AFDC), provided open-ended cash assistance entitlements. The new program, Temporary Assistance for Needy Families (TANF), ended entitlements and provided a mandate to move adult recipients from welfare to work within strict time limits. This shift poses new challenges for both monitoring and evaluating TANF program strategies. Evaluating the full impact of welfare reform requires information about how TANF recipients use TANF, how they use other programs—such as child support enforcement, the Food Stamp Program, employment assistance, Medicaid, and child protective services—and how they fare once they enter the job market covered by the Unemployment Insurance (UI) system.

Administrative data gathered by these programs in the normal course of their operations can be used by researchers, policy analysts, and managers to measure and understand the overall results of the new service arrangements occasioned by welfare reform. Often these data are aggregated and made available as caseload statistics, average payments, and reports on services provided by geographic unit. These aggregate data are useful, but information at the individual and case levels from TANF and other programs is even more useful, especially if it is linked with several different sets of data so that the histories and experiences of people and families can be tracked across programs and over time. Making the best use of this individual level information will require major innovations in the techniques of data matching and linking for research and evaluation.

Even more challenging, however, are the complex questions about privacy and confidentiality that arise in using individual-level data. The underlying concern motivating these questions is the possibility of inappropriate disclosures of personal information that could adversely affect an individual or a family. Such fear is greatest with respect to disclosure of conditions that may lead to social stigma, such as unemployment, mental illness, or HIV infection.

In this paper we consider ways to facilitate researchers' access to administrative data collected about individuals and their families in the course of providing public benefits. In most cases, applicants to social welfare programs are required to disclose private information deemed essential to determining eligibility for those programs. Individuals who are otherwise eligible for services but who refuse to provide information may be denied those services. Most people forgo privacy in these circumstances; that is, they decide to provide personal information in order to obtain public benefits. They believe that they have little choice but to provide the requested information. Consequently, it is widely agreed that the uses of this information should be limited through confidentiality restrictions to avoid unwanted disclosures about the lives of those who receive government services.

Yet this information is crucial for evaluating the impacts of programs and for finding ways to improve them. Making the 1996 welfare reforms work, for example, requires that we know what happens to families as they use TANF, food stamps, the child support enforcement system, Medicaid, child protective services, and employment benefits such as the UI system. In this fiscally conservative political environment, many program administrators feel using administrative data from these programs is the only way to economically carry out the required program monitoring. Program administrators believe that they are being "asked to do more with less" and that administrative data are an inexpensive and reliable substitute for expensive survey and other primary data collection projects.

How, then, should we use administrative data? Guidance in thinking about the proper way to use them comes from other circumstances in which individuals are required to forgo a certain degree of privacy in order to collect important information. These situations include the decennial census, public health efforts to control the spread of communicable diseases, as well as the information collected on birth certificates. Underlying each of these situations is a determination that the need for obtaining, recording, and using the information outweighs the individual's privacy rights. At the same time, substantial efforts go into developing elaborate safeguards to prevent improper disclosures.

Administrators of public programs must, therefore, weigh the public benefits of collecting and using information versus the private harms that may occur from its disclosure. The crucial questions are the following: What data should be collected? Who should have access to it? Under what conditions should someone have access? Answering these questions always has been difficult, but the need for answers was less urgent in the days of paper forms and files. Paper files made it difficult and costly to access information and to summarize it in a useful form. Inappropriate disclosure was difficult because of the inaccessibility of the forms. It was also unlikely because the forms were controlled directly by public servants with an interest in the protection of their clients.

Computer technology has both increased the demand for data by making it easier to get and increased the dangers of inappropriate disclosure because of the ease of transmitting digital information. Continued advances in computer technology are providing researchers and others with the capabilities to manipulate multiple data sets with hundreds of thousands (in some cases, millions) of individual records. These data sets allow for sophisticated and increasingly reliable evaluations of the outcomes of public programs, and nearly all evaluations of welfare reform involve the extensive use of administrative data. The benefits in terms of better programs and better program management could be substantial. At the same time, the linking of data sets necessitates access to individual-level data with personal identifiers or other characteristics, which leads to an increased risk of disclosure. Thus, the weighing of benefits versus harms must now contend with the possibilities of great benefits versus substantial harms.

The regulatory and legal framework for dealing with privacy and confidentiality has evolved enormously over the past 30 years to meet some of the challenges posed by computerization, but it has not dealt directly with the issues facing researchers and evaluators. There is a good deal of literature on the laws and regulations governing data sharing for program administration, much of which presupposes limiting access to these data for just program administration in order to avoid or at least limit unwanted disclosures. Unfortunately, little has been said in the literature regarding the use of such data for research and evaluation, particularly in circumstances where these analyses are carried out by researchers and others from "outside" organizations that have limited access to administrative data. Because research and evaluation capabilities generally are limited by tight staffing at all levels of government, researchers and evaluators from universities and private nonprofit research organizations are important resources for undertaking evaluations and research on social programs. Through their efforts, these organizations contribute to improving the administration of social welfare programs, but they are not directly involved in program administration. Therefore, these organizations may be prevented from obtaining administrative data by laws that only allow the data to be used for program administration.

The problem is even more complex when evaluations require the use of administrative data from other public programs (e.g., Medicaid, Food Stamp Program, UI) whose program managers are unable or unwilling to share data with social welfare program administrators, much less outside researchers. To undertake evaluations of social welfare programs, researchers often need to link individual-level information from multiple administrative data sets to understand how people move from one situation, such as welfare, to another, such as work. But unlike program administrators, credit card companies, investigative agencies, or marketing firms, these researchers have no ultimate interest in the details of individual lives. They do, however, need to link data to provide the best possible evaluations of programs. Once this linking is complete, they typically expunge any information that can lead to direct identification of individuals, and their reports are concerned with aggregate relationships in which individuals are not identifiable. Moreover, these researchers have strong professional norms against revealing individual identities.

Problems arise, however, because the laws developed to protect confidentiality and to prevent disclosure do so by limiting access to administrative data to only those involved in program administration. Even though researchers can contribute to better program administration through their evaluations, they may be unable to obtain access to the data they need to evaluate a program.

Ironically, evaluations have become harder to undertake just as new policy initiatives—such as those embodied in federal welfare reform—require better and more extensive research to identify successful strategies for public programs. Evaluations have become more difficult because disclosures of individual information—fears driven by considerations having virtually nothing to do with research uses of the data—have led to legislation making it difficult to provide the kinds of evaluations that would be most useful to policy makers.

Against this background, this paper considers how researchers can meet the requirements for confidentiality while gaining greater access to administrative data. In the next section of the paper, we define administrative data, provide an overview of the concepts of privacy and confidentiality, and review current federal laws regarding privacy and confidentiality. We show that these laws have developed absent an understanding of the research uses of administrative data. Instead, the laws have focused on the uses of data for program administration where individual identities are essential, with lawmakers limiting the use of these data so that information about individuals is not used inappropriately. The result is a legal framework restricting the use of individual level information that fails to recognize that for some purposes, such as research, identities only have to be used at one step of the process for matching data and then can be removed from the data file.

After a relatively brief overview of the state regulatory framework for privacy and confidentiality in which we find a mélange of laws that generally mimic federal regulations, the paper turns to an extended discussion, based on information from a survey of 14 Assistant Secretary for Planning and Evaluation (ASPE)-funded welfare leavers studies, of how states have facilitated data matching and linkage for research despite the many obstacles they encountered. Based on our interviews with those performing studies that involve data matching, we identify and describe 12 principles that facilitate it. We show that states have found ways to make administrative data available to researchers, but these methods often are ad hoc and depend heavily on the development of a trusting and long-term relationship between state agencies and outside researchers. We end by arguing that these fragile relationships need to be buttressed by a better legal framework and the development of technical methods such as data masking and institutional mechanisms such as research data centers that will facilitate responsible use of administrative data.

ADMINISTRATIVE DATA, CONFIDENTIALITY, AND PRIVACY: DEFINITIONS AND LEGAL FRAMEWORK

Administrative Data, Matched Data, and Data Linkage

Before defining privacy and confidentiality, it is useful to define what we mean by administrative data, matched data, and data sharing. Our primary concern is with administrative data for operating welfare programs—"all the information collected in the course of operating government programs that involve the poor and those at risk of needing public assistance" (Hotz et al., 1998:81). Although not all such information is computerized, more and more of it is, and our interest is with computerized data sets that typically consist of individual-level records with data elements recorded on them.

Records can be thought of as "forms" or "file folders" for each person, assistance unit, or action. For example, each record in Medicaid and UI benefit files is typically about one individual because eligibility and benefit provisions typically are decided at the individual level. Each record in TANF and Food Stamp Program files usually deals with an assistance unit or case that includes a number of individuals. Medicaid utilization and child protective services records typically deal with encounters in which the unit is a medical procedure, a doctor's visit, or the report of child abuse.

Records have information organized into data elements or fields. For individuals, the fields might be the name of the person, his or her programmatic status, income last month, age, sex, and amount of grant. For encounters, the information might be the diagnosis of an illness, the type and extent of child abuse, and the steps taken to solve the problem, which might include medical procedures or legal actions.

It is important to distinguish between statistical and administrative data. Statistical data are information collected or used for statistical purposes only. Data gathered by agencies such as the U.S. Census Bureau, Bureau of Labor Statistics, Bureau of Justice Statistics, and the National Center for Health Statistics is statistical data. Administrative data are information gathered in the course of screening and serving eligible individuals and groups. The data gathered by, for example, state and local welfare departments are an example of administrative data. Administrative data can be used for statistical purposes when they are employed to describe or infer patterns, trends, and relationships for groups of respondents and not for directing or managing the delivery of services.

Administrative data, however, are used primarily for the day-to-day operation of a program, and they typically only include information necessary for current transactions. Consequently, they often lack historical information such as past program participation and facts about individuals, such as educational achievement that would be useful for statistical analysis. In the past, when welfare programs were concerned primarily with current eligibility determination, historical data were often purged and data from other programs were not linked to welfare records. Researchers who used these data to study welfare found that they had to link records at the individual or case level over time to develop histories of welfare receipt for people. In addition, to make these data even more useful, they found it was worthwhile to perform data matches with information from other programs such as UI wage data; vital statistics on births, deaths, and marriages: and program participation in Medicaid, the Food Stamp Program, and other public programs. Once this matching was completed, researchers expunged individual identities, and they analyzed the data to produce information about overall trends and tendencies. Matched files are powerful research tools because they allow researchers to determine how participation in welfare varies with the characteristics of recipients and over time. They also provide information on outcomes such as child maltreatment, employment, and health.

Matched administrative data are becoming more and more widely used in the evaluation and management of social programs. In February 1999, UC Berkeley's Data Archive and Technical Assistance completed a report to the Northwestern/ University of Chicago Joint Center for Poverty Research that provided an inventory of social service program administrative databases in 26 states[1] and an analysis of the efforts in these states to use administrative data for monitoring, evaluation, and research. Unlike other studies that have dealt with data sharing in general, this study was concerned primarily with the use of administrative data for research and policy analysis.

The UC study found that the use of administrative data for policy research was substantial and growing around the country. More than 100 administrative data-linking projects were identified in the study sample. Linkages were most common within public assistance programs (AFDC/TANF, Food Stamp Program, and Medicaid), but a majority of states also had projects linking public assistance data to Job Opportunities and Basic Skills, UI earnings, or child support data.

---

[1]The 26 states inventoried in the report included the 10 states with the largest populations plus a random selection of at least four states from the northeast, south, west, and midwestern regions of the nation. These states comprise four-fifths of the U.S. population and more than five-sixths of the welfare population. This report can be viewed at http://ucdata.berkeley.edu.

Approximately a third of the states had projects linking public assistance data to child care, foster care, or child protective services. Four-fifths of the states used outside researchers to conduct these studies, and about half of all the projects identified were performed outside of state agencies. The vast majority of projects were one time, but there is a small, and growing, trend toward ongoing efforts that link a number of programs.

Figure 8-1 indicates the likelihood of finding projects that linked data across eight programs. Programs that are closer on this diagram are more likely to have been linked. Arrows with percentages of linkage efforts are included between every pair of programs for which 35 percent or more of the states had linkage projects. Percentages inside the circles indicate the percentage of states with projects linking data within the program over time. AFDC/TANF, Food Stamp Program, and Medicaid eligibility are combined at the center of this diagram

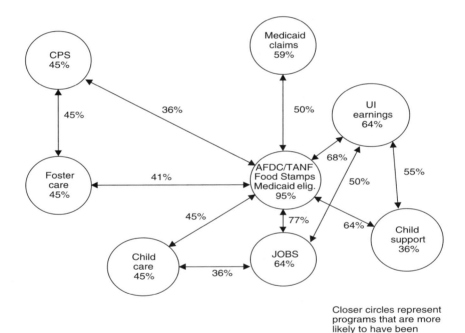

fig 8-1

FIGURE 8-1 Percent of states with projects linking data from social service programs.
SOURCE: U.C. Data Archive and Technical Assistance (1999).

because they were the major focus of the study and because they are often combined into one system. The diagram clearly shows that there are many linkage projects across data sets from many different programs, frequently involving sensitive information.

Data Sharing

Matched data and data linkage should be distinguished from data sharing[2], which implies a more dynamic and active process of data interchange. Data sharing among agencies refers to methods whereby agencies can obtain access to one another's data about individuals, sometimes immediately but nearly always in a timely fashion. Data sharing offers a number of benefits. If different agencies collect similar data about the same person, the collection process is duplicative for both the agencies and the person. Data sharing therefore can increase efficiencies by reducing the paperwork burden for the government and the individual because basic information about clients only needs to be obtained once. Improved responsiveness is also possible. Data sharing enables agencies and researchers to go beyond individual program-specific interventions to design approaches that reflect the interactive nature of most human needs and problems, reaching beyond the jurisdiction of one program or agency. For example, providing adequate programs for children on welfare requires data about the children from educational, juvenile justice, and child welfare agencies. Data sharing is one way to ensure better delivery of public services and a "one-stop" approach for users of these services. Preis (1999) concluded, in his analysis of California efforts to establish integrated children's mental health programs, that data sharing is essential to good decision making and a prerequisite for service coordination. In fact, "if data cannot be exchanged freely among team members an optimal service and support plan cannot be created" (Preis, 1999:5).

Although data sharing has many benefits, it raises issues regarding privacy and confidentiality. Should data collected for one program be available to another? What are the dangers associated with having online information about participants in multiple programs? Who should have access to these data? How can confidentiality and privacy rights be protected while gaining the benefits of linking program data?

When agencies engage in data sharing, the technical problems of getting matched data for research and policy analysis are easily surmounted because information from a variety of programs is already linked. But matched and linked data sets for research and policy analysis can be created without data sharing, and data matching poses far fewer disclosure risks than data sharing because identifi-

---

[2]Note that we are using the term "data sharing" in a fashion that is much narrower than its colloquial meaning.

ers only need to be used at the time when data are merged. As soon as records are matched, the identifiers are no longer needed and can be removed. The merged data can be restricted to a small group of researchers, and procedures can be developed to prohibit any decisions from being made about individuals based on the data. Nevertheless, even data matching can lead to concerns about invasions of privacy and breaches of confidentiality.

Both data sharing and data matching require the careful consideration of privacy issues and techniques for safeguarding the confidentiality of individual level data. The starting place for understanding how to attend to these considerations is to review the body of law about privacy and confidentiality and the definitions of key concepts that have developed in the past few decades. After defining the concepts of privacy, disclosure, confidentiality, and informed consent, we then briefly review existing federal privacy and confidentiality laws.

Privacy

The right to privacy is the broadest framework for protecting personal information. Based on individual autonomy and the right to self-determination, privacy embodies the right to have beliefs, make decisions, and engage in behaviors limited only by the constraint that doing so does not interfere unreasonably with the rights of others. Privacy is also the right to be left alone and the right not to share personal information with others. Privacy, therefore, has to do with the control that individuals have over their lives and information about their lives.

Data collection can intrude on privacy by asking people to provide personal information about their lives. This intrusion itself can be considered a problem if it upsets people by asking highly personal questions that cause them anxiety or anguish. However, we are not concerned with that problem in this paper because we only deal with information that has already been collected for other purposes. The collection of this information may have been considered intrusive at the time, but our concern begins after the information has already been collected. We are concerned with the threat to privacy that comes from improper disclosure.

Disclosure

Disclosure varies according to the amount of personal information that is released about a person and to whom it is released. Personal information includes a broad range of things, but it is useful to distinguish among three kinds of information. *Unique identifiers* include name, Social Security number, telephone number, and address. This information is usually enough to identify a single individual or family. *Identifying attributes* include sex, birth date, age, ethnicity, race, residential address, occupation, education, and other data. Probabilistic matching techniques use these characteristics to match people across datasets when unique identifiers are not available or are insufficient for identification.

Birth date, sex, race, and location are often enough to match individual records from different databases with a high degree of certainty. Finally, there is information about *other attributes* that might include program participation status, disease status, income, opinions, and so on. In most, but not all cases, this information is not useful for identification or matching across data sets. But there are some instances, as with rare diseases, that this other information might identify a person. These three categories are not mutually exclusive, but they provide a useful starting place for thinking about information.

Identity disclosure occurs when someone is readily identifiable on a file, typically through unique identifiers. It can also occur if there are enough identifying characteristics. *Attribute disclosure* occurs when sensitive information about a person is released through a data file. *Inferential disclosure* occurs when "released data make it possible to infer the value of an attribute of a data subject more accurately than otherwise would have been possible" (National Research Council and Social Science Research Council, 1993:144). Almost any release of data leads to some inferential disclosure because some of the general facts about people are better known once the data are published. For example, when states publish their welfare caseloads, it immediately becomes possible to say something precise about the likelihood that a random person in the state will be on welfare. Consequently, it would be unrealistic to require "zero disclosure." "At best, the extent of disclosure can be controlled so that it is below some acceptable level" (Duncan and Lambert, 1986:10).

One fallback position might be to say that the publication of data should not lead to absolute certainty regarding some fact about a person. This would rule out the combination of identity and attribute disclosure to an unauthorized individual.[3] This approach, however, may allow for too much disclosure because data could be published indicating a high probability that a person has some characteristic. If this characteristic is a very personal matter, such as sexual orientation or income, then disclosure should be limited further.

Disclosure, then, is not all or nothing. At best it can be limited by making sure that the amount of information about any particular person never exceeds some threshold that is adjusted upward as the sensitivity of the information increases. In the past 20 years, statisticians have begun to develop ways to measure the amount of information that is disclosed by the publication of data (Fellegi, 1972; Cox, 1980; Duncan and Lambert, 1986). Many complexities have been identified. One is the issue of the proper baseline. If everyone knows some sensitive facts from other sources, should researchers be allowed to use a set of

---

[3]Bethlehem et al. (1990:38) define disclosure in this way when they say that "Identification is a prerequisite for disclosure. *Identification* of an individual takes place when a one-to-one relationship between a record in released statistical information and a specific individual can be established." It seems to us that this is a sufficient condition for improper disclosure to have occurred, but it is not clear that it is a necessary condition.

data that contains these facts? For example, if firms in some industry regularly publish their income, market share, and profit, should data files that contain this information be considered confidential? Another problem is the audience and its interest in the information. Disclosure of someone's past history to an investigative agency is far different from disclosure to a researcher with no interest in the individual. Finally, there is the issue of incremental risks. In many instances, hundreds and even tens of thousands of individuals are authorized to access administrative data. As such, access by researchers represents an incremental risk for which appropriate safeguards are available and practical.

Because disclosure is not all or nothing, we use the phrase "improper disclosure" throughout this paper.[4] Through this usage we mean to imply that disclosure is inevitable when data are used, and the proper goal of those concerned with confidentiality is not zero disclosure unless they intend to end all data collection and use. Rather, the proper goal is a balance between the harm from some disclosure and the benefits from making data available for improving people's lives.

Confidentiality

Confidentiality is strongly associated with the fundamental societal values of autonomy and privacy. One definition of confidentiality is that it is "a quality or condition accorded to information as an obligation not to transmit that information to an unauthorized party" (National Research Council and Social Science Research Council, 1993:22). This definition leaves unanswered the question of who defines an authorized party. Another definition of confidentiality is more explicit about who determines authorization. Confidentiality is the agreement, explicit or implicit, made between the data subject and the data collector regarding the extent to which access by others to personal information is allowed (National Research Council and Social Science Research Council, 1993:22). This definition suggests that the data subject and the data collector decide the rules of disclosure.

Confidentiality rules ensure that people's preferences are considered when deciding with whom data will be shared. They also serve a pragmatic function, encouraging participation in activities that involve the collection of sensitive information (e.g., medical information gathered as a part of receiving health care). Guarantees of confidentiality are also considered essential in encouraging

---

[4]Most of the literature on statistical data collection (e.g., National Research Council and Social Science Research Council, 1993) assumes that disclosure in and of itself is a bad thing. This presumption developed because most of this literature deals with a very specific situation where statistical agencies have collected data under the promise that they will not share it with anyone and where disclosure refers to information that can be readily attached to an individual. Because we deal with a much broader class of situations, we find it useful to distinguish between disclosure and improper disclosure where impropriety may vary with the circumstances of data collection and data use.

participation in potentially stigmatizing programs, such as mental health and substance abuse treatment services, and HIV screening programs.

Confidentiality limits with whom personal information can be shared, and confidentiality rules are generally found in program statutes and regulations. Varying levels of sensitivity are associated with different data. Accordingly, variations in privacy and confidentiality protections can be expected.

Confidentiality requires the development of some method whereby the limits on data disclosure can be determined. In most situations, the data collection organization (which may be a governmental agency) and the source of the information should be involved in determining this method. In addition, as the government, as the representative of the general public, has an obvious interest in regulating the use of confidential information. There are several ways that these parties can ensure confidentiality, including anonymity, informed consent, and notification.

Anonymity

Anonymity is an implicit agreement between an individual and a data collector based on the fact that no one can identify the individual. Privacy can be protected by not collecting identifying information so that respondents are anonymous. Anonymity is a strong guarantor of protection, but it is sometimes hard to achieve. As noted earlier, even without names, Social Security numbers, and other identifying information, individuals sometimes can be identified when enough of their characteristics are collected.

Informed Consent and Notification

The strongest form of explicit agreement between the data subject and the data collector regarding access to the personal information collected is informed consent. An underlying principle of informed consent is that it should be both informed and voluntary. In order for consent to be informed, the data subject must understand fully what information will be shared, with whom, how it will be used, and for how long the consent remains in effect. Consent requires that the subject indicate in some way that he or she agrees with the use of the information.

Consent can be written, verbal, or passive. Written consent occurs when a data subject reads and signs a statement written by the data collector that explains the ways information will be used. Verbal consent occurs when a data subject verbally agrees to either a written or verbal explanation of how information will be used. Verbal consent is often used when data subjects are contacted over the telephone, when they are illiterate, or when written consent might create a paper trail that might be harmful to the subject.

Passive informed consent is similar to, but distinct from, notification. Passive consent occurs when people have been notified about the intent to collect or use data and told that their silence will be construed as consent. They can, however, object and prevent the collection or use of the data. With notification the elements of choice and agreement are absent. People are simply informed that data will be used for specified purposes. Notification may be more appropriate than informed consent when data provided for stated purposes are mandatory (such as information required for participation in a public program).

Some privacy advocates believe that conditioning program participation on the completion of blanket information release consent forms is not voluntary (Preis, 1999). Without choice, it is argued that the integrity of the client-provider relationship is compromised. As a result, many confidentiality statutes and regulations provide a notification mechanism so that the subjects of data being released can be informed of the release (e.g., Privacy Act), or they provide a mechanism for data subjects to decide who will be allowed access to their personal information (e.g., Chapter 509, California Statutes of 1998).

One of the difficulties facing data users in attempting to gain informed consent is that it is often very hard to describe the ultimate uses to which information will be put, and blanket descriptions such as "statistical purposes" are often considered too vague by those who regulate the use of data. It is also possible that data users may want to use the data for reasons not previously anticipated when the data were originally collected and, hence, not described when informed consent was initially granted from data providers. In such cases, data users may need to recontact data providers to see if providers are willing to waive confidentiality or data access provisions covering their data for the new uses of the data. However, the legality of these waivers is still being sorted out. See NRC (1993) for an example of a case where such waivers were not considered sufficient to cover the public release of collected data.

Confidentiality and Administrative Data

Administrative data are often collected with either no notification or some blanket notification about the uses to which the information will be put. As a result, legislatures and administrative agencies are left with the problem of determining the circumstances under which program participation records, drivers' license data, or school performance data should be considered private information and treated confidentially. One solution is to release only anonymous versions of these data through aggregation of the data or removal of identifying information. Anonymity, however, is not always feasible, especially when researchers want to link individual-level data across programs. In this case, should the collecting agency regulate the use of the information to ensure confidentiality when the individual has not been notified or has not provided informed consent? Can the government or some other regulatory body regulate the use of information and substitute for informed consent? What constitutes notification or informed consent? In the next section, we provide a quick overview of how the federal government has dealt with some of these issues.

FEDERAL PRIVACY AND CONFIDENTIALITY LAWS

Fair Information Practices

Several important bodies of federal law and regulation protect privacy and confidentiality of individuals served by one or more government programs, and about which government collects information. These laws reflect the Fair Information Practice Principles that were voluntarily developed and adopted by several government groups and privacy sector organizations in the 1970s. In 1973, the U.S. Department of Health, Education, and Welfare's (HEW's) Advisory Committee on Automated Personal Data Systems, Records, Computers and the Rights of Citizens published these principles in the report, *Records, Computers, and the Rights of Citizens*. These principles have served as the basis for formulation of the federal Privacy Act of 1974, the Freedom of Information Act, and subsequent federal laws and regulations. The Committee recommended five basic information principles for governing the use of personal information:

1. There must be no personal data record-keeping systems whose very existence is secret.

2. There must be a way for a person to find out what information about the person is in a record and how it is used.

3. There must be a way for a person to prevent information about the person that was obtained for one purpose from being used or made available for other purposes without the person's consent.

4. There must be a way for a person to correct or amend a record of identifiable information about the person.

5. Any organization creating, maintaining, using, or disseminating records of identifiable personal data must assure the reliability of the data for their intended use and must take precautions to prevent misuses of the data.

These principles were clearly developed to regulate situations where data would be used to learn about individuals or to make decisions about them.[5] Rules

---

[5]Other commissions and organizations developed similar codes of fair information practice that appear to limit severely the availability of data. Hotz et al. (1998) summarizes the common themes as follows:
- Promote openness.
- Provide for individual participation.
- Limit the collection of personal information.
- Encourage accurate, complete, and current information.
- Limit the use of information.
- Limit the disclosure of information.
- Ensure the information is secure.
- Provide a mechanism for accountability.

1, 2, and 4 require that individuals know about databases and can correct faulty information. These are important principles for agencies that collect information, but they have little relevance for researchers who want to use these data. Rules 3 and 5, however, propose strict ground rules for researchers' use of data. Under the strictest construction, they might require researchers to get prior consent from subjects for the use of administrative data. In reality, federal law has been somewhat less restrictive than this construction might imply.

Numerous federal privacy and confidentiality laws have been enacted in recent decades that elaborate on the Fair Information Practices. These include the Privacy Act of 1974 and the Data Matching and Privacy Protection Act of 1988.[6]

Privacy Act of 1974

The Privacy Act of 1974 was born out of the Watergate scandal in response to public outcry against the many invasions of privacy that occurred in that case. The concern was focused on the government's collection and disclosure of personal information. The Privacy Act places information disclosure limitations on the federal government, providing that certain records cannot be disclosed without the permission of the individual who is the subject of the record.

The act establishes certain responsibilities and conditions for information collection, maintenance, use, and dissemination. The information gathered must be relevant and necessary to the agency's mission. It should be collected directly from the individual to the greatest extent possible. The individual subjects of the data have to be informed of (1) the purpose of data collection, (2) whether participation in the collection of data is voluntary or mandatory, (3) the planned uses for the data, and (4) the consequences to an individual who does not provide the information.[7]

Third-party disclosure by a federal agency is also regulated by the Privacy Act. Data may be disclosed only when (1) the data subject has provided written consent authorizing the disclosure and (2) the disclosure in question is altogether exempted by the Act or it falls within an exception that allows for certain types of disclosures without consent.

The Fair Information Practices and the requirements of the Privacy Act of 1974 would seem to make research use impossible in the typical case where data are used by researchers in unanticipated ways after they have been collected and where contacting individuals at that point is nearly always prohibitively expensive. Research has, however, proceeded by using the "routine use" exemptions of

---

[6]Other important laws include the Freedom of Information Act (enacted in 1966), the Family Education Rights and Privacy Act of 1974, the Confidentiality of Alcohol and Drug Abuse Patient Records Act, the Right to Financial Privacy Act of 1978, and the Drivers Privacy Protection Act of 1994.

[7]U.S.C.S. §552a(e).

the Privacy Act and similar legislation that serve as the legal basis for disclosing information to a state agency that operates a parallel benefits program.[8] This exemption requires that (1) the use is compatible with the purposes for which the information was collected, and (2) the agency places notices about its information disclosure plans in the Federal Register and provides a 30-day opportunity for interested persons to comment on any new or intended use of the agency's data. The act also provides that consent is not required when the recipient of data provides the agency with written assurance that the data will be used solely as a statistical record and will be transferred in a form that is not identified individually.

The Privacy Act establishes limitations on what can be done with personal information collected by federal agencies, but the act itself is not the primary source of protection at the agency level. Separate federal laws and regulations have been promulgated that govern federally funded programs, and the provisions of the Privacy Act frequently have been included in them, thus extending its protections down to the state and local governments and other nongovernmental entities that administer and deliver these federally funded services. Thus, the Privacy Act provides a good starting place for understanding the legal issues associated with data sharing, but a thorough understanding requires examining informational privacy, confidentiality, and consent provisions for each specific federal program and agency.

Data Matching and Privacy Protection Act of 1998

In response to concerns about computer matching and perceived attempts by government agencies to circumvent the Privacy Act, Congress passed the Computer Matching and Privacy Protection Act of 1988 (and amendments to this new Act in 1990). Although no new standard is established by this Act, it creates procedural requirements for agencies that engage in computer matching. Matching agreement contracts are required between source and recipient agencies in a data-sharing program. The agreement must specify the purpose, justification, and procedures for the intended matching program. Although there are no criteria for determining when matching is appropriate, these agreements do provide notice and regulate the behavior of each party to the agreement. Matching agreements must describe the procedure by which applicants and recipients of federal assistance will be notified that information they provide may be subject to verification via a matching program. In addition, there must be procedures for verification and the opportunity of data subjects to contest findings.

The Computer Matching and Privacy Protection Act also adds new oversight provisions to the Privacy Act. Specifically, Data Integrity Boards are required for

---

[8]U.S.C.S. §552a(b)(3).

federal agencies that are involved in computer matching activities. These boards, composed of senior agency officials, have responsibility for reviewing matching agreements and programs for compliance with federal privacy laws. They also serve a clearinghouse and reporting function.

These acts and practices create a regulatory framework for the collection and use of data. For researchers, there are exemptions from requiring informed consent in which recipients did not give their consent when the data were collected initially. Agencies, for example, can forego informed consent when the use of the data is compatible with the purposes for which the information was collected and when the agency provides notice of its intentions in the Federal Register. They can also use data when the data will be used solely as a statistical record and will be transferred in a form that is not individually identifiable. In most cases, these procedures were not designed specifically to facilitate research, but they have been used for that purpose.

Common Rule—Institutional Review Boards

Concerns about the conduct of research have led to the development of Institutional Review Boards (IRBs) at universities, at government agencies, and at private organizations that conduct federally sponsored research involving human subjects. IRBs play an increasingly important role in the regulation of organizations that undertake social policy research using administrative data.

The federal "Common Rule," adopted in 1991, governs nearly all research involving human subjects that is conducted or supported by any federal department or agency.[9] Researchers and their institutions must comply with safeguards that ensure that individuals freely consent to participate in such research. Researchers also must ensure that the research employs procedures that are consistent with sound research design and that do not pose unnecessary risk to the research subjects. Finally, there must be adequate provisions to protect the privacy of research subjects and to maintain the confidentiality of individually identifiable private information.

The review of all federally funded research by IRBs is the principal mechanism by which these safeguards are implemented, and informed consent is the primary way that IRBs ensure that human subjects are protected. However, an IRB may waive some or all elements of informed consent under a number of circumstances.[10] Research involving the use of educational testing, surveys, and interviews is entirely exempt from review if individual identities cannot be established from the information so obtained. Research involving analysis of existing data is exempt if the information is either publicly available or recorded in a

---

[9]45 CFR Part 46.

[10]In an effort to simplify the complex regulations governing IRBs, we conflate waiver of informed consent (which does not necessarily mean exemption from IRB review) with exemptions.

manner such that individuals cannot be identified either directly or through identifiers linked to individuals. Also exempt from the rule is research that is designed to evaluate public benefit or service programs and that is conducted by or subject to the approval of federal department or agency heads. Finally, a waiver of informed consent may be given if the research involves no more than minimal risk to the subjects, the waiver will not adversely affect the rights and welfare of the subjects, and the research could not practicably be carried out without the waiver.

As with the Privacy Act, IRBs place a great emphasis on informed consent, although there are some provisions for waiving consent when anonymity can be assured, when risk is minimal, or when public benefit programs are being evaluated. The emphasis on informed consent is not surprising because IRBs were established initially to oversee medical research which often involves medical procedures. The need for informed consent regarding the procedure to be performed is obvious in this case because of the great potential for harm. Moreover, there may be no other way to protect subjects except through informed consent.

The role of informed consent is somewhat different in the conduct of most social science research, which involves acquiring information about subjects. It is possible, of course, to do harm through the collection of social science data by asking questions that provoke great anxiety or consternation, but the major danger is undoubtedly the possibility that private information will be revealed. In this case, confidentiality may be the primary concern, and some method for controlling the *use* of the data may be much more important than informed consent regarding its *collection*. Informed consent is one way to control the use of data, but it is not the only way. Anonymity potentially provides even better protection than informed consent. Other methods for protecting confidentiality also might provide the protections that are needed. For example, the confidentiality of administrative data might be protected without informed consent through the development of procedures such as the Data Integrity Boards and other mechanisms created by the Privacy Act and the Computer Matching and Privacy Protection Act. At the moment, however, IRBs rely heavily on informed consent, and they typically have only a limited understanding of the intricacies of matching administrative data and the laws regarding confidentiality.

Summary of Federal Legislation

Federal legislation has been built on a concern about disclosure of information about individuals. It has been done without much thought about the needs of researchers who only care about individual identities when they match data sets. At the moment, the federal regulatory environment for data is characterized by a multiplicity of laws, cross-cutting jurisdictions (e.g., Data Integrity Boards and IRBs), and some incoherence. The emphasis on informed consent in many laws would appear to limit severely the use of administrative data, but agencies have used the provisions for statistical analysis and for "routine use" to allow researchers to use administrative data. All in all, the legal situation is highly ambiguous for researchers, and no one has come to grips with what should be done with data when informed consent is not possible and when researchers need identities solely for the interim stage of data matching.[11]

STATE PRIVACY AND CONFIDENTIALITY CONSIDERATIONS

It would be useful to conduct a state-by-state analysis of how privacy, confidentiality, and consent laws affect research and to compare the results with the impacts of federal laws and regulations. This analysis would contribute significantly to achieving a more complete and substantial understanding of how state and federal requirements interact with one another. However, this task is far beyond what we can do here. Instead, we make some comments based on the secondary literature.

State constitutional privacy protections are very diverse. For example, in California, privacy protections are expressly mentioned in the constitution, while Washington state's constitution requires that certain information—such as who receives welfare—be publicly available. In addition to state constitutional provisions regarding privacy and confidentiality, every state has enacted numerous privacy protection laws principally drafted in response to a specific perceived problem. The result is many narrow prescriptions, rather than a coherent statement of what information is private, when it can be collected, and how it can be used. Consequently, it is hard to know exactly what information is protected, and how it is protected. In addition, many privacy laws have exceptions and exemptions that make them hard to understand, hard to apply, and subject to divergent interpretations (Stevens, 1996). The resulting laws have been described as "reactive, ad-hoc, and confused" (Reidenberg and Gamet-Pol, 1995).

There are two broad classes of laws, those dealing with privacy in general and those that mention privacy and confidentiality in the process of establishing programs. The general privacy laws deal with computer crime, medical records, the use of Social Security numbers, access to arrest records, and other issues. Table 8-1 indicates the presence of general state privacy protections for the states in which there are ASPE welfare leavers studies (Smith, 1999).[12] It shows that state privacy laws cover a broad range of issues from arrest records to wiretaps,

---

[11]The recent National Academy Press publication, *Improving Access to and Confidentiality of Research Data* (National Research Council, 2000) is directed to this exact set of concerns.

[12]Basic information about state privacy laws in all states is available in *Compilation of State and Federal Privacy Laws* (Smith, 1999). We have focused on states with ASPE leavers studies to complement the survey described later.

TABLE 8-1 Privacy Laws in States with Welfare Leavers Studies

	AZ	CA	DC	FL	GA	IL	MD	MA	MO	NJ	NY	NC	OH	PA	SC	TX	WA	US
Arrest records	x	x	x	x	x	x	x	x	x	x	x		x	x	x		x	
Computer crime	x	x		x	x	x	x	x	x	x	x	x	x	x	x	x	x	x
Credit	x	x		x	x		x	x		x	x		x			x	x	x
Criminal justice	x	x		x	x	x	x	x		x			x	x		x	x	x
Employment		x	x	x	x	x	x	x		x	x	x	x	x			x	x
Government data banks	x	x	x	x			x	x	x	x	x	x	x	x	x			x
Insurance	x	x	x	x	x	x	x	x	x	x		x	x		x			x
Medical	x	x	x	x	x	x	x	x	x	x	x		x	x		x	x	x
Polygraphing	x	x	x		x	x	x	x			x			x	x	x	x	x
Privacy statutes	x	x		x	x	x		x		x	x	x		x	x	x	x	x
Privileges				x		x	x	x	x	x	x	x	x			x	x	
School records	x	x		x		x	x	x		x	x		x			x	x	x
Social Security numbers		x		x	x						x	x				x	x	
Tax records	x			x		x	x			x	x	x		x		x	x	
Testing				x			x	x			x	x	x			x		
Wiretaps	x	x	x	x	x	x	x	x		x	x	x	x	x		x	x	x
Miscellaneous		x		x		x		x			x							x

NOTE: An x indicates that the state law covers the subject (but not necessarily that the law affords a great deal of privacy protection).

and that some topics, such as arrest records, computer crime, medical records, and wiretaps, have led to more legislative activity by states than other topics such as the uses of Social Security numbers, credit information, or tax records. Moreover, some states, such as California, Florida, Maryland, Massachusetts, Ohio, and Washington, have laws that cover many more areas of concern than other states such as Missouri, South Carolina, or Texas. These laws affect researchers when they seek to utilize Social Security numbers for matching or to obtain school, arrest, or tax records.

Programmatic laws regulate the collection and uses of information as part of the social program's legislation at the federal and state levels. Harmon and Cogar (1998) found that federal program statutes and regulations provide substantial privacy protections similar to that in the federal Privacy Act. Explicit limits on disclosure within the statutes authorizing federal programs and agencies are common, as is the imposition of informational privacy protections on states via federal program regulations. Harmon and Cogar (1998) also found that—as with the provisions of the Privacy Act—federal regulations do not clearly specify penalties or the consequences of violating the regulations by state or local personnel or contractors. Their study of five states found state information privacy laws to be similar to federal protections.

Most of the state and federal laws regarding the collection and use of data for programs are quite restrictive, but they typically have a clause, similar to the "routine use" provisions in the federal Privacy Act, that allows agencies to use data to achieve the "program's purpose." Researchers and others who want access to the data use this clause in the same way as the "routine use" clause of the Privacy Act. Harmon and Cogar (1998) suggest that federal agencies often label their data uses as "routine" without determining if the use is consistent with the purpose for which the information was collected. Some state agencies follow a similar practice, although standards vary dramatically from state to state and agency to agency.

In their report about experiences in five states, "The Protection of Personal Information in Intergovernmental Data-Sharing Programs," Harmon and Cogar (1998) describe the complexity of the information protection provisions that apply to individuals under the U.S. Department of Agriculture (USDA) Food Stamp Program's Electronic Benefit Transfer (EBT) project and the HHS Child Support Enforcement Program's Federal Parent Locator Service/National Directory of New Hires project. None of the states reported major violations of privacy in the operation of the Child Support Enforcement and EBT programs, but the significant variation in regulation of information across the states could prove a significant barrier to the overall data-sharing responsibilities of the systems and for researchers who want to use the data. Moreover, most of the states, with the exception of Maryland, paid little heed to researchers' needs. Maryland's statutes specifically authorize public agencies to grant researchers access to personal information under specified conditions. This statute appears as Appendix 8-A as an example of model legislation that authorizes researcher access to data.[13]

UC Berkeley's Data Archive and Technical Assistance also explored confidentiality issues in its inventory (UC Data Archive and Technical Assistance, 1999) of social service administrative databases in 26 states. This study found that researchers and administrators from other programs who seek access to social service data must negotiate with the owners of the data, and they must demonstrate that they meet the legal criteria for access. Legislation and regulations were characterized as generally requiring the party petitioning for access to the data to identify: (1) the benefits associated with release of the data, (2) how the research will benefit administration of the programs, and (3) how confidentiality of the data will be protected from unauthorized disclosure.

In most cases, a formal contract or interagency agreement was required, and often these agreements are required because of legislative mandates. Apart from the legal issues of gaining access to confidential data, there are often coordination issues that affect the transfer of information from one agency to another. Only

[13]We also include Washington state's statute, which provides for researchers having access to administrative data.

about half of the states surveyed for this report had specific, well-outlined policies and procedures for sharing confidential administrative data.

The use of administrative data for research purposes has not been considered in the development of most federal and state legislation. The major purpose of most federal and state confidentiality and privacy legislation has been to regulate the use and disclosure of information about individuals.[14] As a result, a strict interpretation of most laws might preclude research uses that require data matching even though identifiers are removed before data analysis and researchers have no interest in individual information. This outcome would be mostly inadvertent. In their desire to protect individuals, lawmakers typically have written legislation that makes no distinction between research uses and disclosure of information about individuals. State and federal agencies sometimes have overcome restrictions on research by accommodating researchers through the use of the routine use and program purpose clauses. This accommodation is fitful and uncertain because it depends on each agency's interpretation of these clauses and its overall interest in allowing researcher access to administrative data.

ACCESS TO CONFIDENTIAL DATA IN PRACTICE: INTERVIEWS WITH RESEARCHERS CONDUCTING WELFARE LEAVERS STUDIES

The legal basis for the use of social program administrative data by nongovernmental researchers is ambiguous. Consequently, governmental agencies that are inclined to provide data to researchers usually can find a legal way to do so through a broad interpretation of the statutory "routine use" or "program purposes" clauses, while agencies that are inclined to block researcher uses can also do so by interpreting these clauses narrowly. From the research perspective, the best solution to this problem would be that privacy and confidentiality legislation take into account the significantly fewer risks posed by research uses of data and develop clearcut regulatory mechanisms tailored to the needs of researchers. We discuss this possibility later (Guiding Principle 12), but it is worth knowing that in the absence of a favorable regulatory environment, many researchers and program administrators have found ways to undertake research with administrative data. Because it may be difficult to get better legislation, the methods used by these program administrators and researchers deserve careful consideration.

To identify these methods, we interviewed researchers and state administrators working in federally funded welfare leavers projects. Because of the complexity of the lives of individuals leaving welfare, these studies require diverse

---

[14]Basic information about state privacy laws is available in a recent publication, *Compilation of State and Federal Privacy Laws* (Smith, 1999).

BOX 8-1
Welfare Leavers Studies: States/Localities Interviewed

- Arizona
- California (San Francisco Bay Area Counties; Los Angeles County)
- Florida
- Georgia
- Illinois
- Missouri
- New York
- Ohio (Cuyahoga County)
- Massachusetts
- South Carolina
- Texas
- Washington State
- Washington, D.C.
- Wisconsin

---

types of data, including multiple sources of confidential administrative data. In this section, we discuss information from 14 welfare leavers studies.[15] These include projects that received fiscal year 1998 ASPE grants to study the outcomes of individuals and families who left the TANF program, and Texas.[16] (We refer to this group of projects as "Welfare Leavers Studies".)

This research began by reviewing the findings from the inventory of research uses of social services administrative data in 26 states that UC DATA completed in 1999. A series of questions then was developed as the basis for telephone interviews with the state officials and researchers conducting ASPE-funded Welfare Leavers Studies. Officials and researchers working on these studies were queried about their experiences with confidentiality and data access. More than 20 individuals in the 14 locations listed in Box 8-1 were interviewed in winter 1999/2000.

In the course of our interviews with Welfare Leavers Studies representatives, we identified 12 guiding principles or practices we believe to be at the heart of successfully overcoming issues of data confidentiality and privacy. We found repeated examples of these principles or practices being put into action across the country in varying ways. They are listed in Box 8-2. The principles, the keys to data collaboration, fell naturally into four categories that are discussed in more detail later: the characteristics of the requesting organization, the characteristics of the organization providing the data, the characteristics of the requesting organization, the "contract" process itself, and the legal framework.

---

[15]Fall 1999.

[16]Texas was not an ASPE Fiscal Year 1998 welfare leavers study grantee.

BOX 8-2
Twelve Guiding Principles of Data Access and Confidentiality

The Characteristics of the Organization With the Data
1. Strong political or administrative leadership
2. Designation of a "Data Steward" in the department and structuring staffing levels and responsibilities to cover data access requests.
3. Develop a written confidentiality and security procedure—keep a catalog of written documents: contracts, memorandums of understanding (MOU's), personal security agreements.
4. The agency architecture encompasses all "providing" agencies as in "super agencies."
5. A central clearinghouse negotiates or assists in legal and/or technical issues.
6. Plan for data access in the development of information systems.

The Characteristics of the Requesting Organization
7. The reputation and integrity of the requesting organization engenders trust.
8. Trust between organizations, a history of working together, and strong personal relationships.
9. Develop a confidentiality/security procedure and keep a catalog of exemplary written contracts, MOUs, and personal security agreements.

The "Contract" Process
10. Put in writing mechanisms for monitoring confidentiality and security and for sanctioning breaches.
11. Congruence of research agency goals: demonstrated benefits to participating organizations.

The Legal or Statutory Authority
12. Statutory language authorizes or is broadly interpretable to authorize data access for researchers.

The specific principles range from the obvious—"Put Procedures and Contracts in Writing"—to the sublime—Find Strong Leadership." We discuss each of the principles in detail and give illustrative examples of these principles. See Table 8-2 for a complete listing of examples of the principles in the Welfare Leavers Study sites.

Data Access Principles Regarding the Organization with the Data

Principle 1: Strong Political or Administrative Leadership

We found that many new and established data-matching projects were successful because they had the interest or patronage of well-connected or inspiring

TABLE 8-2 Twelve Guiding Principles of Data Access and Confidentiality Examples from Interviews with Welfare Leavers Study Researchers (Fall 1999)

The Characteristics of Donor Organization	Examples
1. Strong leadership	California: California Department of Social Services (CDSS), Employment Development Department (EDD) Illinois Missouri: Governor Mel Carnahan, Missouri Training & Employment Commission New York: Federal Department of Labor Texas: Federal Department of Labor
2. Staff levels or responsibilities	California: Labor Market Information Division Illinois: Bureau of Program Design & Evaluation Missouri: "Administrative Data Guardian" Washington State: Office of Planning & Research Wisconsin: Data Stewardship
3. Written confidentiality/ security procedure	California Illinois: Dept. of Human Services Wisconsin: Data Stewardship
4. Agency architecture	Arizona: Arizona Department of Economic Security (ADES) Illinois: Dept. of Human Services
5. Central clearinghouse	Arizona: ADES Data Mart Florida: Florida Education & Training Program Placement Information Program Illinois: Chapin Hall, University of Chicago South Carolina: Budget & Contracts Board Texas: State Occupational Information Coordinating Committee Washington State: Internal Review Board
6. Plan for data sharing in development of information systems	California: Family Health Outcomes Project
The Characteristics of Requesting Organization	
7. Reputation and/or integrity	California: RAND Illinois: Chapin Hall, University of Illinois Massachusetts: Center for Survey Research at University of Massachusetts-Boston Ohio: Manpower Demonstration Research Program (MDRC)

TABLE 8-2 Continued

8. History of working together, personal relationships	California: UC Data & CDSS Georgia: Georgia State University & Department of Children and Family Services (DFCS) Illinois: Chapin Hall at University of Chicago, Illinois & Department of Children and Family Services, Department of Employment Security & Illinois Department of Human Services Missouri: University of Missouri & state agencies New York: Office of Transitional and Disability Assistance (OTDA) and Department of Labor (DOL) Ohio: Case Western University (CWRU) and Bureau of Employment Services (BES), CWRU and DSS, and CWRU and MDRC Washington, DC: Urban Institute & Department of Human Services
9. Written confidentiality/ security procedure	California: UC Data, RAND Ohio: Case Western Reserve University
The "Contract" Process 10. Put in place mechanisms for monitoring confidentiality and security and/or sanctioning breaches. contracts in writing	California Georgia Illinois Missouri New York Ohio South Carolina Washington State Washington, DC Wisconsin
11. Congruence of research to agency goals– demonstrated benefits to participating organizations	Arizona California CalWORKs California Leavers Studies Florida Georgia Illinois Massachusetts Missouri New York Ohio South Carolina Washington State Washington, DC Wisconsin

continues

TABLE 8-2 Continued

The Legal or Statutory Authority	
12. Statutory language authorizes or is broadly interpreted to authorize data access	California
	Georgia
	Illinois
	Missouri
	New York
	Ohio
	South Carolina
	Washington State

leaders. This, in and of itself, comes as no surprise. However, the sources of this leadership are diverse.

In some cases, this leadership was political in nature. For example, the University of Missouri at Columbia Department of Economics began its long collaboration with the Missouri Department of Social Services at the request of Governor Mel Carnahan. In January 1997, the university was asked to begin an analysis of the workforce development system for the Governor's Training and Employment Council. Because of the high-profile support for this project, the agencies providing data were forthcoming so as not to appear to be hindering the effort. A governor's directive can be powerful.

Another example of political leadership can be found in the moving force behind the Texas State Occupational Information Coordinating Committee (SOICC). The SOICC was mandated by the U.S. Congress via the federal Job Training Partnership Act (JTPA) and the Carl D. Perkins Vocational Education Act of 1976. The Texas SOICC receives no state general revenue funding and is supported by the U.S. Department of Labor through the national network organization National Occupational Information Coordinating Committee.

Data linking is facilitated when those at the top make it clear that they want to know about the impacts governmental programs are having on clients. Governors can provide this kind of leadership. More commonly, and perhaps most effectively, this leadership can be found among program administrators, bureau chiefs, and agency heads. For example, California found valuable leadership in the California Department of Social Services (CDSS) Research Branch. Staff in the Research Branch made use of many years of experience in service to the state to forge data-sharing coalitions between CDSS and the California Employment Development Department. In Illinois, the decisions to link data were made by Department of Human Services administrators who were supporting the Welfare Leavers Study.

Principle 2: Designation of a "Data Steward" in the Department and Structuring Staffing Levels and Responsibilities to Cover Data Access Requests

Adequate staffing is essential for ironing out the issues of data access. Data-linking requests require extensive administrative and analytic effort. In fact, as the rapid growth of information technology makes privacy and security policies de rigueur, information security officers in many states are requiring the completion of more and more complicated data security and confidentiality procedures for data linking.

Information security offices are not solely responsible for the time and effort it takes to get a data-linking project approved. Each state department often requires approval by a contracts office, a legal office, and the program with the data. In addition, many projects are required to submit their project for review by the state's human subjects committee. Each of these approvals can take from a few days to a few weeks, or even months in some cases.

Success in data-linking projects requires staff dedicated to shepherding data requests through the complexities of confidentiality requirements and data access issues. Although lawyers are often assigned these tasks because of their knowledge of statutorily defined notions of confidentiality, experienced government staff with a research bent must be involved as well in order to explain the technical aspects of data linking. In fact, agency staff with a strong investment in data linking and a belief in the benefits of research can overcome exaggerated fears about data linking and overly narrow interpretations of the law.

A delicate balance must be reached here. The law regarding the use of administrative data is typically sufficiently ambiguous that beliefs about the usefulness of a research project, about the risks from data matching, and about the trustworthiness of researchers can determine the outcome of a data request. It is easy for lawyers to assume that research is not very useful, that the risks of data matching are great, and that researchers cannot be trusted with the data. Yet we found in our interviews that research staff believe data matching provides extraordinary opportunities for high-quality and relatively inexpensive evaluations. Moreover, researchers can make the case that the risks from data matching for research purposes typically are quite low—certainly much lower than the risks from many other kinds of data matching projects. What is needed is a balance of agency staff committed to both the appropriate protection of data and the appropriate sharing of data for research and evaluation. We were told in our interviews that there are plenty of staff people, legal and otherwise, who are zealously "protecting" data in the name of confidentiality, but there are not enough with strong investments in data linking and a belief in the benefits of research to their department to make the case for data matching.

Our interviews provide examples. One respondent in Missouri referred to himself as the administrative data "guardian." He saw himself as the data shepherd, the person who saw that the data got to where it needed to go and got there safely. He facilitated data access, safeguarded data confidentiality, and educated researchers about the complexities of the data. Other Missouri respondents reported this administrator to be knowledgeable and helpful. In the Washington State Department of Social and Health Services, staff in the Office of Planning and Research blazed new trails of data access through state divisions that were unfamiliar with, if not uncomfortable with, providing data to researchers. One respondent from Wisconsin reported an environment of data "stewardship" coming about in the state, an environment of making data available in a responsible manner. The California Employment Development Department, Labor Market Information Division has designated a Confidential Data Coordinator. In Illinois, the Bureau of Program Design and Evaluation in the Department of Human Services frequently negotiates data access arrangements.

Principle 3: Develop a Written Confidentiality and Security Procedure—Keep a Catalog of Written Documents: Contracts, Memorandums of Understanding (MOU's), Personal Security Agreements.

A written policy of confidentiality and security is a must. This document should make explicit the data security procedures required of the data requesting organizations by the agencies with the data. This written policy should include detailed standards to maintain the privacy of individual data subjects. Another necessary document is a written guideline to obtaining data. This document can be provided to data requesters to assist them in applying for access to confidential data. The confidentiality and security manual and the guideline to obtaining data can provide assurance to data-providing agencies that proper consideration will be given to maintaining the confidentiality of their data in advance of the data being requested of them. They will also reassure data-providing organizations that their staff will not waste precious staff time fielding fly-by-night data requests.

In addition to these documents, there should be an archive of exemplary memorandums of understanding, letters of understanding, contracts for goods and services, data access agreements, and confidentiality agreements for use among state agencies or between state agencies and nongovernmental organizations. These documents should have explicit sections on the maintenance of data security and confidentiality, similar to the protocol described. The archive should also contain statements regulating individual behaviors, commonly known as "personal security agreements" or "statements of confidentiality". These documents require each individual staff person on the project to acknowledge procedures required for maintaining confidentiality and penalties for a breach of these procedures. An archive promotes quick and thorough contract negotiations, and it avoids the nuisance of having to start from scratch with every data request.

The California Department of Social Services Research Branch has prepared two such model documents: "The CDSS Confidentiality and Security Policy" and "The Guidelines for the Preparation of A Protocol." Also, in the new environment of "Data Stewardship," Wisconsin is developing templates and exemplar agreements.

Principle 10, "Put in Writing Mechanisms for Monitoring Confidentiality and Security and for Sanctioning Breaches," discusses briefly which confidentiality and security procedures one might want to include in a contract and therefore in the archive of documents.

Principle 4: The Agency Architecture Encompasses All "Providing" Agencies as in "Super Agencies"

In some cases, a "super agency" organization can facilitate sharing of data among departments within the agency. For example, in response to the latest welfare reforms, some states combined state agencies under an umbrella organization. In most cases, administrative data are considered to be owned by this overarching agency. Although this does not eliminate the need for appropriate bureaucratic negotiation on data access, in most cases it makes the process easier.

One respondent referred to the Illinois Department of Human Services as a "super agency." The department handles data for AFDC/TANF, the Food Stamps Program, Substance Abuse, Mental Health, Special Supplemental Nutrition Program for Women, Infants, and Children (WIC) (family case management), Medicaid, and Child Care programs (and their data). Gaining access to some of these data was reported to be easier because of the "super agency" structure. It was reported that gaining access to data from Substance Abuse and WIC (family case management), although by no means easy, would have been even harder had not the agencies been part of this "super agency."

The Arizona Department of Economic Security (ADES) also can be considered a super agency. ADES covers a broad range of programs, including AFDC/TANF, Food Stamp Program, Medicaid, Child Welfare, Child Care, *and* Child Support Enforcement *and* Unemployment Insurance. A respondent reported that no interagency data access agreements were necessary with *any* of these programs because of this all-encompassing administrative structure.

Principle 5: A Central Clearinghouse Negotiates or Assists in Legal and/or Technical Issues

A centrally located institution or center can help facilitate data access. This center can be placed in the state government or outside, and it can serve a number of purposes.

First, a central organization can serve as a *data archive or data warehouse* that actually stores data from multiple state agencies, departments, and divisions.

In some cases, data archives match the data and provide data requesters with match-merged files. In other cases, data archives provide a place where data from multiple agencies are stored so that data requesters can obtain the data from one source and match the data themselves.

Second, a central organization can serve as a *data broker*. This organization does not actually store data from other agencies but "brokers" or "electronically mines" data from other agencies on an ad hoc or regular basis. This organization then performs analyses on these data and reports results back to the requesting agency. The data are stored only temporarily at the location of the data broker, before they are returned to the providing agency or destroyed.

Third, a central organization can serve another very important purpose, as a *clearinghouse for legal issues around confidentiality*. Organizations like this are sometimes called internal review boards. They maintain exemplar or template agreements, contracts, documents, as described earlier.

For example, the South Carolina Budget and Control Board (SC BCB) serves all three functions—data archive, data broker, and internal review board. The SC BCB plays a key role in the general management of state government. This institution is unique to South Carolina and oversees a broad array of central administrative and regulatory functions. In our interview with staff from the Welfare Leavers Study grantee in South Carolina, we learned of the office of Research and Statistics in the SC BCB. The office gathers, analyzes, and publishes data vital to the social, and economic well-being and health of residents of South Carolina. These data are used by other state agencies and by local governments to guide planning, management, and development decisions. The office also works with other agencies to prevent overlap and duplication of data-gathering activities. The Welfare Leavers Study grantee (South Carolina Department of Social Services) negotiated data access through the SC BCB and conducted their analysis inhouse. However, one South Carolina respondent noted that despite the central location of this clearinghouse, it was still necessary to obtain legal authorization to data access on an agency-by-agency basis.

The Arizona Department of Economic Security is in the process of building a data warehouse, referred to as the "data mart." The data mart will automatically receive and link data from all the programs covered by ADES. The Welfare Leavers Study researchers used this resource to access data. At this point, the data mart provides only data-archiving and data-matching functions. However, eventually the data mart will include front-end data analysis functions.

The Texas State Occupational Information Coordinating Committee (SOICC) serves as a data broker. SOICC does not archive or store data at all. Our respondent reported that SOICC "mines data electronically" from relevant agencies, conducts analysis, and provides requesters with results of these analyses.

In Florida, the Florida Education and Training Placement Information Program (FETPIP) serves a data brokerage role by archiving data and providing analysis. However, our respondent reported that FETPIP did not archive data or provide analyses for the Florida Welfare Leavers Study grantee.

The Chapin Hall Center for Children at the University of Chicago has developed an extensive archive of child welfare and family welfare data. The center uses these data to assess the impacts of welfare reform and other programs on child well-being. Chapin Hall's archive of data on children's welfare is called the Integrated Database on Children's Services in Illinois (IDB). Built from administrative data collected over two decades by Illinois human services programs, the IDB allows researchers to create a comprehensive picture of the interactions children and their families have with social programs offered by the state. One respondent cited this database as an absolutely invaluable resource.

The University of Missouri at Columbia Department of Economics is another example of a center that archives and analyzes data. Here data from multiple state agencies are matched, merged, and analyzed. The archive contains data from five state agencies: the Department of Economic Development, the Department of Social Services, the Department of Labor and Industrial Relations, the Department of Elementary and Secondary Education, and the Department of Higher Education. The staff provide research and analysis for many of the separate agencies on an ad hoc and a contractual basis.

In Washington State, the Institutional Review Board serves a role as a central place to resolve legal issues of data access. The IRB assisted the Welfare Leavers Study grantee in ironing out legal issues. The IRB serves as a human subjects review board and maintains exemplar documents.

Principle 6: Plan for Data Access in the Development of Information Systems

It would be difficult to include all the requirements for the development of information systems in a single principle. The development of information systems requires a set of its own guiding principles, including, but not limited to, adoption of common identifiers and establishment of standardized data definitions.

Rather than try to list all of the relevant principles, we cite the following example from California: The Family Health Outcomes Project (FHOP). It is a joint project of the Department of Family and Community Medicine and the Institute for Health Policy Studies (both at the University of California at San Francisco). Initiated in 1992, FHOP is a planning and training effort to streamline and standardize the administrative aspects of state child and family health programs in California.

FHOP has developed an information structure for an extremely fragmented and difficult-to-access system—health care and health-related services for women and children in California. California has many categorical health and social service programs serving women, children, and families. Each has a separate application and eligibility process, although all require similar application information. Clients must complete an application for each service they wish to receive, often at different times and in different locations. To bring these programs "together," FHOP has developed CATS, a "Common Application Transaction System." CATS addresses the need for a uniform, accessible application and eligibility determination process and provides aggregate data for state and local planning and management.

CATS is a methodology for integrating registration and eligibility determination across numerous state-funded family health programs. CATS establishes unique client identification through the use of core data elements (birth name, birth date, birth place, mother's first name, and gender) and confirmatory data elements (social security number, other client number, father's name, mother's maiden name, current name/client alias/nickname, county of client's residence, and zip code of client's residence). Utilizing probabilistic matching and relative weighting of the core data elements, CATS can uniquely identify clients and find duplicate records for the same client.

Health care providers can link local automated registration systems to the state CATS hub, which can then return eligibility and demographic information. The CATS goal is to simplify the eligibility process so that the necessary demographic and self-declared financial information need only be collected and entered once.

In summary, CATS includes a standardized approach to collecting demographic, race, ethnic, and financial eligibility information; standardized confidentiality procedures and informed consent for sharing information; information on client eligibility status for Medi-Cal, Family Planning, Healthy Families Children's Health Insurance Program (CHIP), and Children's Medical Services; methods for the discovery of duplicate client records for tracking and case management; and a secure Internet connection option for community clinics and private providers. By providing a common method for collecting information on participation in state child and family health programs, CATS makes it possible to identify clients across programs, track them over time, and monitor outcomes. From a researcher's perspective, systems such as CATS make matching data across data systems much simpler.

Data Access Principles That Have to Do With the Characteristics of Requesting Organization

Principle 7: The Reputation and Integrity of the Requesting Organization Engenders Trust

In many cases, we found that the reputation of the requesting agency was a major factor in successfully obtaining approval for the use of administrative data.

This reputation can be technical, academic, or professional. We found that some of our respondents were reassured by the sheer prominence of the requesting organization.

However, in most cases, feelings of confidence were firmly based on the earned substantive reputation of the requesting organization. Most of the examples we found were organizations that had established a reputation through extensive experience with similar types of research and therefore provided key expertise. For example, Chapin Hall has a well-deserved reputation for its extensive technical expertise in the complex issue of matching administrative data from child and family welfare systems. In fact, Chapin Hall's reputation is so great that the Illinois Department of Human Services believes that it could do no better than subcontract with Chapin Hall when doing any matching of children's and families' services data.

Another example comes from Massachusetts, where the Department of Transitional Assistance contracted with the Center for Survey Research at the University of Massachusetts, Boston, to field the survey of former TAFDC (Transitional Aid to Families with Dependent Children) households. The Department of Transitional Assistance provided the Center for Survey Research with confidential data necessary for developing a sample of welfare leavers. It was reported that the department chose the center in large part because of the center's local reputation for expertise and competence.

Principle 8: Trust Between Organizations, a History of Working Together, and Strong Personal Relationships

Of all the guiding principles, trust between organizations appears to make the most wide-ranging contribution to successful data access. In our interviews with Welfare Leavers Study grantees, and in discussions with other researchers and state and nongovernmental staff, we learned of countless longstanding relationships between departments, between organizations, and between individuals. These relationships played a large and very important role in establishing the trust and confidence necessary for smooth contract negotiation and productive collaboration in the Welfare Leavers Studies.

The separation of Principle 7, "Reputation," and Principle 8, "Trust," does not mean these two are mutually exclusive, but it is meant to imply they are somewhat different. Past projects may have been established because of the requesting organization's reputation, but future projects depend heavily on the development of trust. In many cases, the established association was continued because the projects went well. In some cases, however, it was reported that the past project was not entirely successful, but that the association was continued, it seems, merely based on personal friendships or the force of one or more personalities (not necessarily friendships). Whatever the case, these prior relationships were a major factor in the success of the majority of the data access efforts we examined, including projects in California (San Francisco Bay area counties), Washington, DC, Georgia, Illinois, Missouri, New York, Ohio, and South Carolina.

Obviously, this phenomenon is not limited to welfare leavers projects. California, New York, Missouri, Arizona, and Texas respondents all reported knowledge of data access projects that were facilitated because of personal relationships. Indeed, it should be noted here that many of these longstanding relationships were the result of Principle 1, Strong Leadership.

Principle 9: Develop a Confidentiality/Security Procedure and Keep a Catalog of Exemplary Written Contracts, MOU's, and Personal Security Agreements.

This principle is parallel to Principle 3 except that it applies to the requesting organization. Every data-requesting organization should maintain a file of data access and confidentiality documents. Such a resource provides reassurance to the providing agency that the requester has given appropriate consideration to the issues of data access. In fact, one state administrator said they do not take seriously organizations that do not have a written procedure. Furthermore it allows the requesting agency to respond quickly to data access opportunities without having to reinvent the wheel. UC Data Archive and Technical Assistance at the University of California, at Berkeley has a Manual on Confidentiality and Security, which includes exemplar contracts, personal security agreements, and description of extensive data security procedures.

Principle 10 discusses briefly what confidentiality and security procedures one might want to include in a contract and therefore in the archive of documents.

Data Access Principles That Have to Do with the "Contract" Process

Principle 10: Put in Writing Mechanisms for Monitoring Confidentiality and Security and for Sanctioning Breaches

A contract between the requesting organization and the department providing the data makes accessing administrative data much easier. In a contract, confidentiality and security measures or requirements are clarified and put in writing. Written provisions to uphold confidentiality and security provide a vehicle for action if a breach of confidentiality occurs. Nearly all our respondents reported that their collaboration was governed by a written contract.

Contracts should include clauses that contractually provide for data security and maintenance of confidentiality. The following list provides examples of provisions that should be specified in any written contract governing access to confidential data. This list, although not intended to be exhaustive, illustrates most of the procedures requested by state agencies for protecting the confidentiality of individuals in research projects using administrative microdata files:

- Prohibition on redisclosure or rerelease.
- Specification of electronic data transmission (e.g., encryption methods for network access).
- Description of storage and/or handling of paper copies of confidential data.
- Description of storage and/or handling of electronic media such as tapes or cartridges.
- Description of network security.
- Requirement for notification of security incidents.
- Description of methods of statistical disclosure limitation.
- Description of the disposition of data upon termination of contract.
- Penalties for breaches.

Furthermore, contracts should include references to statutes that provide for explicit sanctions of breaches of confidentiality. For example, California State Penal Code, Section 502, included in contracts, states that:

...(c) Except as provided in subdivision (h), any person who commits any of the following acts is guilty of a public offense:

(1) Knowingly accesses and without permission alters, damages, deletes, destroys, or otherwise uses any data, computer, computer system, or computer network in order to either (A) devise or execute any scheme or artifice to defraud, deceive, or extort, or (B) wrongfully control or obtain money, property, or data.

(2) Knowingly accesses and without permission takes, copies, or makes use of any data from a computer, computer system, or computer network, or takes or copies any supporting documentation, whether existing or residing internal or external to a computer, computer system, or computer network.

....

(4) Knowingly accesses and without permission adds, alters, damages, deletes, or destroys any data, computer software, or computer programs which reside or exist internal or external to a computer, computer system, or computer network.

(5) Knowingly and without permission disrupts or causes the disruption of computer services or denies or causes the denial of computer services to an authorized user of a computer, computer system, or computer network.

....

(d) (1) Any person who violates any of the provisions of paragraph (1), (2), (4), or (5) of subdivision (c) is punishable by a fine not exceeding ten thousand dollars ($10,000), or by imprisonment in the state prison for 16 months, or two or three years, or by both that fine and imprisonment, or by a fine not exceeding five thousand dollars ($5,000), or by imprisonment in a county jail not exceeding one year, or by both that fine and imprisonment.

All staff members who have access to the confidential data should sign a document agreeing to uphold the required confidentiality measures. This is sometimes called a "personal security agreement," a "confidentiality agreement," or a "disclosure penalty document." This agreement should notify the employee of the penalties for disclosure of the personal identities of the individuals of the data and requires that the employee acknowledge and understand the penalties. This task can be time consuming, but it is worth the effort. It is simplified if files of exemplar documents are maintained (Principles 3 and 9).

If money cannot flow between the requesting organization and the providing organization, then a no-cost contract can be put in place, which puts the requesting agency under the confidentiality constraints.

Principle 11: Congruence of Research Agency Goals: Demonstrated Benefits to Participating Organizations

Successful collaborations occur when all the parties perceive benefits for themselves. Requesting organizations should make sure that the goals of their research contribute to the goals of the organization providing the data. All our respondents reported that this was an important factor is easing the data access process. The importance of studying welfare leavers and the federal funding of the studies helped to facilitate data access. More generally, researchers find that they have greater access to data when there is obvious congruence between their research goals and the agency's need to comply with federal or state requirements, e.g., waiver demonstrations, reporting of performance measures, or completing of specified grant-related evaluations.

But the benefits are not always obvious and can come in many forms. For example, researchers can provide briefings, presentations, or technical assistance on special analyses to state administrators and staff on research completed with the administrative data. Researchers who have successfully obtained administrative data with confidential identifiers can return merged, cleaned, and enhanced databases to their state colleagues. As part of completing their research with the administrative data, researchers often clean and enhance the data. They may eliminate questionable outliers, identify likely biases, develop ways of dealing with the biases, and enhance the data by geocoding addresses. Researchers often develop high levels of expertise with certain types of administrative data. Sometimes researchers develop software applications to do their own analyses of the data which, if provided to the agency, would allow the agency to conduct their own analyses more efficiently. When this expertise comes back to the agency, in the form of briefing, technical assistance, software applications, or other format, the agency sees the benefits to them of sharing these data.

Also, researchers from the academic and nonprofit research fields can serve on and can often provide great benefit to the agencies' ad hoc or standing expert panels. These panels give guidance to the agencies on research methodologies, data analysis, software development, reports or products produced by contractors, development of information systems, public policies, technical administrative procedures, and legislative solutions.

Requesting organizations must seriously consider including services like these to the data-providing agencies in their contracts and requests to state departments. They not only provide state officials with something for the trouble of making data available, but they also provide proof to legislators and the general public that data access provides substantial public benefits.[17]

Data Access Principles That Have to Do with the Legal or Statutory Authority

Principle 12: Statutory Language Authorizes or Is Broadly Interpretable to Authorize Data Access for Researchers

As discussed earlier, lawmakers have written legislation that protects the privacy of individuals but makes no distinction between research uses and disclosure of personal information. State agencies sometimes have overcome the legislative restrictions by accommodating researchers through a broad interpretation of the statutory "routine use" and/or "program purposes" clauses.

In our interviews, we learned that many state agencies interpret evaluation and research to be an integral part of the performance of their duty. Respondents reported knowledge of statutory language that was being broadly interpreted to allow diverse data-linking projects, such as "administration of programs under this title," "eligibility determination," "performance of the agency's duty," "implementation of state policy," "routine use," "direct benefit to the public," and "research into employment and training programs." For example, one contract stated that data were "being shared pursuant to Section 1704 of the Unemployment Insurance Act which states in pertinent part that 'The Director shall take all appropriate steps to assist in the reduction and prevention of unemployment...and to promote the reemployment of unemployed workers throughout the State in every feasible way...'" (820 ILCS 405/1704). It was reported that the New York Department of Labor has had access to welfare data and employment-related data for 5-6 years under statutorily approved language to "monitor employment and training programs."

---

[17]The U.S. Census Bureau "Research Data Centers Programs" is entirely based on the strong belief that researchers can help the Bureau improve the quality of its data, and researchers are required, by law and regulation, to develop strong rationales for why their work will improve census data.

Conclusions

In a very ambiguous and unclear legal environment, states nevertheless have found ways to provide researchers with data, but it is a difficult process requiring strong leadership, adequate staff, extensive negotiations over confidentiality and security, and trust between the data-requesting and data-providing organizations. It also requires that data-providing organizations believe that they are obtaining substantial benefits from providing their data to researchers. In some cases, the benefits follow because the state has contracted with the researchers, but in other cases researchers must find ways to convince agencies that their research will be helpful to the agency itself.

All in all, the situation for research uses of administrative data is precarious. The laws are unclear about whether data can be used for research. Agencies are only sometimes convinced that research is in their best interests. Coordinating and convincing many different agencies is a difficult task. An obvious solution would be to develop a better legal framework that would recognize the smaller risks of data disclosure from datalinking for research, but before this can be done, researchers have to develop a menu of technical and institutional solutions to the problems of data confidentiality.

TECHNICAL AND INSTITUTIONAL SOLUTIONS

There are two basic ways to limit disclosure, data alteration, and restricted access to data. The recent National Research Council (2000) report on "Improving Access to and Confidentiality of Research Data" notes the strengths and weaknesses of each method:

> Data alteration allows for broader dissemination, but may affect researchers' confidence in their modeling output and even the types of models that can be constructed. Restricting access may create inconveniences and limit the pool of researchers that can use the data, but generally permits access to greater data detail (29).

"Anonymizing" data by removing identifying information is one method of data alteration, but this procedure may not limit disclosure enough. Data alteration can be thought of as a more versatile and thorough collection of methods for reducing the risk of disclosure.

Requiring informed consent for the use of data can be thought of as an institutional method for restricting access, but it may be impractical or it may be inadequate in many cases. Once data have been collected in an administrative system, it is nearly impossible to go back and obtain informed consent, but perhaps more importantly, informed consent might not really serve the purposes of individuals who cannot easily judge the costs and benefits of the various ways data might be used. We discuss some institutional methods such as Confidential

Research Data Centers that can protect individual privacy and ensure confidentiality while making data available to researchers.

Data Alteration

Cross tabulations. One way to avoid unwanted disclosure is to present only aggregate data in the form of tables. In many cases, this amply limits disclosure, although at the cost of losing the analytical power that comes from being able to analyze individual-level data. Moreover, in some cases, the identification of individuals, families, firms, or other specific units can still be inferred from the tables themselves. One way to guard against this is to require a minimum number of reporting units, for example, five individuals in each cell of the table. This goal can be achieved starting with tables developed from unadjusted microdata through aggregation, suppression, random rounding, controlled rounding, and confidentiality edits (see Cox, 1980; Duncan and Pearson, 1991; Office of Management and Budget, 1994, 1999; Jabine, 1999; Kim and Winkler, no date).

Aggregation involves reducing the dimensionality of tables such that no individual cells violate the rules for minimum reporting. For example, data for small geography such as census block groups might be aggregated to census tracks for sparsely represented areas.

Suppression is the technique of not providing any estimate where cells are below a certain prespecified size. As row and column totals generally are provided in tabular data, there is a further requirement when suppressing cells to identify complementary cells that are also suppressed to ensure that suppressed data cannot be imputed. The identification of complementary cells and ensuring that suppressed cells cannot be imputed generally requires judgments of which potential complementary cells are least important from the vantage of data users. It also requires statistical analyses to ensure that suppressed cells cannot be estimated.

Random rounding is a technique whereby all cells are rounded to a certain level, such as to multiples of 5. The specific procedure provides that the probability for rounding up or down is established on the initial cells value. For example, the number 2 would not automatically be rounded to 0 but instead would be assigned a 60-percent probability of rounding down and a 40- percent probability of rounding up, and the final rounded value would be based on these random probabilities. Similarly, 14 would have an 80-percent probability of rounding to 15 and a 20-percent probability of rounding to 10. A problem with random rounding is that row and column cell totals will not necessarily equal reported actual totals.

Controlled rounding is a process using linear programming or other statistical techniques to adjust the value of rounded cells so that they equal published (actual) totals. Potential problems with this approach include (1) the need for more sophisticated tools, (2) for some situations there may not be any solution, and (3) for large tables the process may be computationally intensive.

Confidentiality edit is a process whereby the original microdata are modified. One confidentiality edit procedure called "swapping" is to identify households in different communities that have a certain set of identical characteristics and swap their records. The Census Bureau used this procedure in developing some detailed tabulations of the 100-percent file. Another edit procedure called "blank and impute" involves selecting a small sample of records and blanking them out and refilling with imputed values.

Tables of magnitude data. An additional problem arises with magnitude data such as total employees or revenue for a firm. For example, where a single firm is dominant, the publication of data on the industry may allow a fairly accurate estimate of the firm's data. In this case rules need to be established, for instance that no single firm can account for more than 80 percent of the cell total, to provide protection. This rule can be generalized in the form of "no fewer than n (a small number) of firms can contribute more than k percent of the cell total." These rules are used to identify "sensitive cells" that require suppression. The process of suppression requires complementary suppression, as discussed.

Unfortunately, all of these methods lead to a loss of significant amounts of information. Published tables, because they generally only provide cross-tabulations of two or three data elements, often do not provide the precise analysis that a researcher needs, and they are usually not useful for multivariate analysis. In these cases, researchers need to obtain microdata.

Masking public use microdata[18] Although microdata provide extraordinary analytical advantages over aggregated data, they also pose substantial disclosure problems for two reasons. Microdata sets, by definition, include records containing information about individual people or organizations, and micro-datasets often include many data elements that could be used to identify individuals. Although it is very unlikely that an individual could be identified on a data set by age group, size category, the combination of these three items might be enough to identify at least some people (Bethlehem et al, 1990:40). In fact:

> In every microdata set containing 10 or more key variables, many persons can be identified by matching this file with another file containing the key and names and addresses (disclosure matching). Furthermore, response knowledge (i.e., knowing that the person is on the file) nearly always leads to identification (disclosure by response knowledge), even on a low-resolution key. Finally, analysis showed that on a key consisting of only two or three identifiers, a considerable number of persons are already unique in the sample, some of them "rare persons" and therefore also unique in the population" (p. 44).

---

[18]See "Report on Statistical Disclosure and Limitation Methodology" prepared by the Subcommittee on Disclosure Limitation Methodology and published by the Office of Management and Budget in 1994.

A variety of methods can be used to mask the identity of individuals or households in microdata, although it is harder to mask the identities of firms because of the small number of firms and the high skew of establishment size in most business sectors. Units can be masked by providing only sample data, not including obvious identifiers, limiting geographical detail, and limiting the number of data elements in the file. High-visibility elements can be masked by using top or bottom coding, recoding into intervals or rounding, adding noise, and swapping records.

- *Sampling* provides a means of creating uncertainty about the uniqueness of individuals or households.
- *Eliminating obvious identifiers* involves removing items such as name, address, and Social Security number or other variables that would allow for identification of individuals or households.
- *Limiting geographical detail* creates a greater pool and reduces the chance of identification of records with unique characteristics. For example, the Census Bureau restricted the geography for the Public Use Microdata Sample for the 1990 Census to areas with populations of at least 100,000.
- *Limiting the number of data elements* in a file reduces the probability that an individual can be uniquely identified.
- *Top and bottom coding* provide a means of eliminating disclosure risk. Top coding establishes an upper bound on continuous data, for example, 85 years and older would be coded as 85. Bottom coding is similar and might be used for old housing units.
- *Recoding into intervals and rounding* are a means of taking continuous data and grouping the data. In each case unique information can be modified to mask identity. For example, data of birth might be transformed into age groups.
- *Random noise* can be added to microdata by adding or multiplying values by a randomly determined factor. This process can be useful in preventing individuals from attempting to match the public use database with other databases where identity is known.
- *Swapping, blanking and imputing, and blurring* are techniques used to modify the original data but not significantly change the statistical properties of the database. Swapping is identifying matching records based on key fields and swapping the detailed data. Blanking and imputing is to blank out certain data on selected records and statistically impute new values. Blurring is to replace exact values with mean values of all records meeting certain profiles.

Many of these methods are now commonly used when microdata are released to the public. Researchers, however, worry that the loss of information from data alteration may make it difficult or even impossible to do many kinds of analysis, and some statisticians have suggested that these methods do not provide sufficient disclosure protection (Bethlehem et al., 1990). These worries have led some to propose even more radical alterations of the data that would amount to creating "simulated data."

Simulated data can be created from the original microdata by using variants of imputation methods (see Rubin, 1987, 1993; Little and Rubin, 1987, Kennickell, 1997, 1998) to impute entirely new values of every variable for every case. The resulting data set is composed entirely of "made-up" people, and it may be possible to do analysis that is almost as good with these data as with the original information. Developing these methods is an active research area.

Some researchers, however, are wary of these methods, and in a recent seminar run by the Committee on National Statistics, Richard Suzman of the National Institute on Aging (NIA) reported that "all leading researchers currently supported by NIA are opposed to the imposition of synthetic data" (National Research Council, 2000:32). The solution may be to turn to institutional solutions, as suggested by Bethlehem et al. (1990:45):

> Therefore, if microdata are released under the conditions that the data may be used for statistical purposes only and that no matching procedures may be carried out at the individual level, any huge effort to identify and disclose clearly shows malicious intent. In view of the duty of a statistical office to disseminate statistical information, we think disclosure protection for this kind of malpractice could and should be taken care of by legal arrangements, and not by restrictions on the data to be released.

Institutional Methods for Restricted Access

If data alteration is not the final answer (and there is substantial disagreement about this given some of the technical possibilities), then some new institutional forms need to be created to protect confidentiality. Many approaches are possible, but we shall discuss two especially useful ones, research data centers and licensing combined with substantial penalties for misuse.

Research data centers. The U.S. Census Bureau has been working with other federal agencies for the past few years to create Census Research Data Centers (CRDCs) in several locations around the country (Boston, California, Chicago, Pittsburgh, and North Carolina) where researchers can go to work with nonpublic census data under strict supervision and after a stringent application process. The goal of the CRDCs is to improve the quality of census data by getting researchers to use the data in new ways that push the data to their limits. The centers are locked and are secure facilities where researchers can come to work on microdata, but only after they have developed a proposal indicating how their work will help to improve the data and signed a contract promising to meet all the obligations to protect it required of Census Bureau employees. Once they have passed these hurdles, they can work with the data in the CRDC facility, but they can only remove output once it has undergone disclosure analysis from an on-site Census Bureau employee.

The CRDC model has worked well for some innovative projects, but it has its drawbacks. It is costly, requiring several hundred thousand dollars a year to cover space, equipment, the Census Bureau employee salary, and other needs, and it is not clear how these costs can be covered in the long run even though fees have been charged to researchers. Although the CRDCs have improved access for some researchers, others still must travel some distance to the nearest site. The approval process takes time, and the outcome is uncertain. Data availability often depends on the ability of Census Bureau employees to devote time to projects that may not be their first priority. There is some concern on the part of the Census Bureau about having microdata located away from the Census Bureau itself. Universities have concerns about storing confidential data on-site.

Despite these problems, something like these centers seems to be an inevitable result of researchers' desires for data and the confidentiality concerns of the governmental agencies that own the data. In our discussion of principle 5, "A central clearinghouse negotiates or assists in legal and technical issues," we noted that organizations such as the University of Chicago's Chapin Hall, the South Carolina Budget and Control Board, and the University of Missouri at Columbia's Department of Economics are developing variants of these centers. We can imagine many different approaches to these centers depending on where they are located (state governments or universities), how they are funded, how they determine access to data, and what types of responsibilities and limitations are placed on researchers.

Licensing and increased penalties for misuse—The great drawbacks of the RDC model are the costs and the need to travel to specific locations to do research. For some data sets, another approach might make more sense. Since 1991, the National Center for Educational Statistics (NCES) has issued nearly 500 licenses for researchers to use data from NCES surveys (National Research Council, 2000:44). As part of the licensing process, researchers must describe their research and justify the need for restricted data, identify those who will have access to the data, submit affidavits of nondisclosure signed by those with this access, prepare and execute a computer security plan, and sign a license agreement binding the institution to these requirements. Criminal penalties can be invoked for confidentiality violations. This model easily could be extended to other data, and it would work especially well for discouraging disclosure matching in cases where unique identifiers, but not all key identifiers, have been removed from the data.

Summary of Alternatives for Ensuring Confidentiality

Both data alteration and institutional restrictions hold promise for making data accessible while protecting confidentiality. Both approaches are still in their infancy, and much needs to be learned. It is possible that combinations of the two will work best. Simulated data sets might be released to the public to allow researchers to learn about the data and to test preliminary hypotheses. When the researcher feels ready, he or she could go to a research data center for a relatively short period of time to finish the analysis.

SUMMARY AND RECOMMENDATIONS

Summary

Matching and linking administrative data can be a great boon to researchers and evaluators trying to understand the impacts of welfare reform, but researchers sometimes find that they cannot access administrative data because of concerns about individual privacy, the ambiguity of statutory authority, and agency fears about public scrutiny.

Concerns about individual privacy and the desire to protect confidential data have grown dramatically in the past decade. Data matching often raises the Orwellian threat of a big brother government that knows all about its citizens' lives. The result has been a welter of laws that have often reacted to the worst possibilities that can be imagined rather than to realistic threats. Researchers, we have argued, do not pose the worst threats to data confidentiality, but they have had to cope with laws that assume data users will try to identify individuals and use sensitive information in inappropriate ways. In fact, researchers have only a passing interest in individual identifiers and microlevel data. They want to be able to do analysis that employs the full power of individual level data and to link data using identifiers to create even more powerful data sets. But as researchers they have no interest in information about individuals.[19] At worst, researchers pose only a moderate risk of disclosure.

Nevertheless, agencies with data must deal with an ambiguous legal environment that makes it hard to know whether and under what circumstances information can be shared with another agency or with researchers. Many agencies are hesitant to share information because of the lack of clear-cut statutory authority about who can access and use data. Others prefer the current situation, viewing ambiguous laws as providing greater flexibility and latitude. The downside of this ambiguity is that much is left to the individual judgments of agency managers who must deal with fears of legislative and public scrutiny. Although providing greater access to information potentially increases public knowledge and understanding about the agency, this information may cause others to second-

---

[19]The exception is when researchers want to contact individuals listed in an administrative file. The human subject risks are greater here, and they require greater scrutiny.

guess the agency. The result is a skeptical and suspicious posture toward researchers' requests for data.

Overcoming these obstacles requires experience, leadership, the development of trust, and the availability of resources.[20]

Most data requesters and potential data providers are just beginning to gain experience with the rules governing research uses of administrative data. Most requesters are unfamiliar with the relevant laws and with agencies' concerns about confidentiality. Many agencies with administrative data have not had much experience with researchers, and they lack the relatively long time horizon required to wait for research to pay off. This is especially true of those parts of the agency that control administrative data. As a result, data requestors are impatient with procedures and find it hard to proceed. Agencies, faced with the unknown, delay providing data because they prefer to attend to their day-to-day problems. Leadership is essential for overcoming these problems.

Trust is also important. Trust may be hard to establish because of fears about how the data will be used and worries about whether the data will be protected against inappropriate disclosure. The "providing" agency must trust that the "receiver" will both protect confidentiality and not use the information in a way that compromises the basis on which the providing agency collected the information. The data provider also must believe it will receive some payoff for it from providing the data.

Even with experience, leadership, and trust, enough resources may not be available to overcome the many obstacles to providing data. Requesters may run out of steam as they encounter complicated requirements and seemingly endless meetings and negotiations. Providers may balk at the requester's requests for documentation and technical assistance in using the data. Adequate resources, also are essential for successful projects. There must be staff members who can help prepare data requests and the data themselves. There must be resources to fund the facilities (such as data archives or research data centers) that facilitate data access.

We found many instances where administrative data were used successfully, but the legal, technical, and institutional situation is parlous. Laws and regulations continue to be enacted with virtually no consideration of the needs of researchers. Technical advances offer some hope of making data available while protecting confidentiality, but technical advances such as the Internet and powerful computers also threaten data security. Institutional arrangements are precarious, often perched on nothing more than the leadership and trust developed by a few individuals.

---

[20]There are also technical obstacles to using administrative data, but we do not believe these are the major difficulties faced by most researchers. These obstacles include hardware and software incompatibility and lack of common standards. Fortunately, technological advances increasingly are addressing these issues, and they are less and less important compared to other difficulties.

Recommendations

Against this backdrop, our recommendations fall naturally into three categories: legal, technical, and institutional. Interestingly, in our interviews and in those reported in another study[21] we found differences of opinion about the proper set of prescriptions. One perspective is that the only way that data access will work is if there is a specific legislative mandate requiring it. Otherwise, it is argued, agencies will have no incentives to solve the many problems posed by efforts to make data more accessible. The other perspective suggests that just requiring public agencies to engage in making data available does not mean they will have the capacity or the ability to actually implement it. Rather, the priority should be on providing the tools and resources necessary to support research access to administrative data, with sparing use of statutory mandates. There seems to be some truth in both perspectives, and we make recommendations on both sides.

Legal Issues

Two sets of legal issues seem most pressing to us:

1. *Develop model state legislation allowing researchers to use administrative data.* Although we have some models for legislation that would help researchers gain access to data, we do not have a thoroughgoing legal analysis of what it would take to facilitate access while protecting confidentiality. We strongly suspect, for example, that such legislation must carefully distinguish research from other uses by developing a suitable definition of what is meant by research. In addition, it must describe how researchers could request data, who would decide whether they can have access, how data would be delivered to them, and how the data would be safeguarded. At the federal level, H.R. 2885, "The Statistical Efficiency Act of 1999" appears to provide an important means for improving researcher access to confidential data.

2. *Clarify the legal basis for research and matching with administrative data, with special attention to the role of informed consent and Institutional Review Boards*—Most of the projects using administrative data have relied on "routine use" and "program purposes" clauses to obtain access to the data, but IRBs prefer to base permissions to use data on informed consent, which is typically not obtained for administrative data. These approaches are somewhat at

---

[21]Landsbergen and Wolken (1998) interviewed officials in five states about barriers to establishing, maintaining and evaluating informational data sharing policies and practices. Although this study focused on data sharing and these five states' experiences with regard to environmental programs, the conclusions clearly extend to data access in other topical areas.

odds, and they have already started to collide in some circumstances where IRBs have been leery of allowing researchers access to data because of the lack of informed consent. Yet informed consent may not be the best way to protect administrative data because of the difficulty of ensuring that subjects are fully informed about the benefits and risks of using these data for research. At the same time, "routine use" and "program purpose" clauses may not be the best vehicle either. Some innovative legal thinking about these issues would be useful. This thinking might provide the basis for implementing our first recommendation.

Technical Issues

New techniques may make it easier to protect data making the data accessible to researchers:

3. *Develop better methods for data alteration, especially "simulated" data.* Although there are differences of opinion about the usefulness of simulated data, there is general agreement that simulated data would at least help researchers get a "feel" for a data set before they go to the time and trouble of gaining access to a confidential version. It would be very useful to develop a simulated dataset for some state administrative data, then see how useful the data are for researchers and how successfully they protect confidentiality.

4. *Develop "thin-clients" that would allow researchers access to secure sites where research with confidential data could be conducted.* Another model for protecting data is to provide access through terminals—called "thin-clients"— that are linked to special servers where confidential data reside. The linkages would provide strong password protection, and ongoing monitoring of data usage. All data would reside on the server, and the software would only allow certain kinds of analysis. As a result, agencies would have an ongoing record of who accessed what data, and they would be able to block some forms of sensitive analysis such as disclosure matching.

Institutional Issues

The primary lesson of our interviews with those doing Welfare Leavers Studies is that institutional factors can contribute enormously to the success or failure of an effort to use administrative data:

5. *Support agency staff who can make the case for research uses of administrative data.* There is a large and growing infrastructure to protect data, but there is no corresponding effort to support staff who can make the case for research uses of administrative data. Without such staff, agencies may find it much easier to reject data requests, even when they are justified on legal and practical grounds.

6. *Support the creation of state data archives and data brokers who can facilitate access to administrative data.* One way to get a critical mass of people who can help researchers is to develop data archives and data brokers whose job is to collect data and make the data available within the agency and to outside researchers. In our presentation of Data Access Principle 5, we described several models for what might be done to create central clearinghouses that negotiate and assist in legal and technical issues related to data access. A *data archive or data warehouse* stores data from multiple state agencies, departments, and divisions. In some cases, an archive matches the data and provides data requesters with match-merged files. In other cases, data archives provide a place where data from multiple agencies are stored so that data requesters can obtain the data from one source and match it for themselves. *Data brokers* do not actually store data from other agencies but "brokers" or "electronically mines" data from other agencies on an ad hoc or regular basis. These organizations then perform analyses on the data and report results back to the requesting agency. The data are stored only temporarily at the location of the data broker, before being returned to the providing agency or destroyed.

7. *Support the creation of university-based research data centers.* Another model worth exploring is university-based research data centers modeled after the Census Bureau's Research Data Centers. These centers, located around the country, provide a site where researchers can use nonpublic Census data to improve the quality of census data by getting researchers to evaluate new ways to push the data to their limits. The centers are locked and secure facilities where researchers can come to work on microdata, but only after they have developed a proposal indicating how their work will help to improve the data and signed a contract promising to meet all the obligations to protect it required of Census Bureau employees. Once they have passed these hurdles, they can work with the data in the CRDC facility, but they can only remove output once it has undergone disclosure analysis from an on-site Census Bureau employee. A similar model could be developed for administrative data.

8. *Use contract law to provide licenses and criminal and civil law to provide penalties for misuse of data.* Licensing arrangements would allow researchers to use data at their own workplace. Researchers would describe their research and justify the need for restricted data, identify those who will have access to the data, submit affidavits of nondisclosure signed by those with this access, prepare and execute a computer security plan, and sign a license agreement binding themselves to these requirements. Criminal penalties could be invoked for confidentiality violations. This model would work especially well for discouraging matching in cases where unique identifiers, but not all key identifiers, have been removed from the data.

REFERENCES

Bethlehem, J.G., W.J. Keller, and J. Pannekoek
   1990   Disclosure control of microdata. *Journal of the American Statistical Association* 85(March):38-45.
Cox, Lawrence H.
   1980   Suppression methodology and statistical disclosure control. *Journal of the American Statistical Association* 75 (June):377-385.
Duncan, G.T., and D. Lambert
   1986   Disclosure-limited data dissemination. *Journal of the American Statistical Association* 18 (March):10-18.
Duncan, G.T., and R.W. Pearson
   1991   Enhancing access to microdata while protecting confidentiality: Prospects for the future. *Statistical Science* 6(August):219-232.
Fellegi, I.P.
   1972   On the question of statistical confidentiality. *Journal of the American Statistical Association* 67(March):7-18.
Harmon, J.K., and R. N. Cogar
   1998   *The Protection of Personal Information in Intergovernmental Data-Sharing Programs: A Four-Part Report on Informational Privacy Issues in Intergovernmental Programs.* Electronic Commerce, Law, and Information Policy Strategies, Ohio Supercomputer Center, Columbus, OH, June.
Hotz, V. Joseph, Robert George, Julie Balzekas, and Francis Margolin.
   1998   *Administrative Data for Policy-Relevant Research: Assessment of Current Utility and Recommendations for Development.* Chicago: Joint Center for Poverty Research.
Jabine, Thomas B.
   1999   Procedures for restricted data access. *Journal of Official Statistics* 9(2):537-589.
Kennickell, Arthur B.
   1997   *Multiple Imputation in the Survey of Consumer Finances.* Washington, DC: Federal Reserve Bank.
   1998   Multiple Imputation in the Survey of Consumer Finances. Unpublished paper Prepared for the Joint Statistical Meetings, Dallas, Texas.
Kim, Jay J., and W.E. Winkler
   no   Masking Microdata Files. Unpublished Bureau of the Census discussion paper.
   date
Landsbergen, D., and G. Wolken
   1998   *Eliminating Legal and Policy Barriers to Interoperable Government Systems.* Electronic Commerce, Law, and Information Policy Strategies, Ohio Supercomputer Center, Columbus, OH.
Little, Roderick, and Donald B. Rubin
   1987   *Statistical Analysis with Missing Data.* New York. John Wiley and Sons.
National Research Council
   2000   *Improving Access to and Confidentiality of Research Data: Report of a Workshop,* Christopher Mackie and Norman Bradburn, eds. Commission on Behavioral and Social Sciences and Education, Committee on National Statistics. Washington, DC: National Academy Press.
National Research Council and Social Science Research Council
   1993   Private Lives and Public Policies: Confidentiality and Accessibility of Government Statistics. G.T. Duncan, T.B. Jabine, and V.A. de Wolf, eds. Commission on Behavioral and Social Sciences and Education, Committee on National Statistics. Washington, DC: National Academy Press.

Office of Management and Budget
1994   Report on Statistical Disclosure and Limitation Methodology. Statistical Policy Working Paper 22. Prepared by the Subcommittee on Disclosure Limitation Methodology, Federal Committee on Statistical Methodology, May.
1999   Checklist on Disclosure Potential of Proposed Data Releases. Prepared by the Interagency Confidentiality and Data Access Group: An Interest Group of the Federal Committee on Statistical Methodology, July.

Preis, James
1999   *Confidentiality: A Manual for the Exchange of Information in a California Integrated Children's Services Program.* Sacramento: California Institute for Mental Health.

Reamer, F.G.
1979   Protecting research subjects and unintended consequences: The effect of guarantees of confidentiality. *Public Opinion Quarterly* 43(4):497-506.

Reidenberg and Gamet-Poll
1995   The fundamental role of privacy and confidence in the network. *Wake Forest Law Review* 30(105).

Rubin, Donald B.
1987   *Multiple Imputation for Nonresponse in Surveys.* New York: John Wiley and Sons.
1993   Discussion of statistical disclosure limitation. *Journal of Official Statistics* 9(2):461-468.

Smith, R. E.
1999   *Compilation of State and Federal Privacy Laws with 1999 Supplement.* Providence: Privacy Journal.

Stevens, D.
1996   *Toward an All Purpose Confidentiality Agreement: Issues and Proposed Language.* Baltimore, MD: University of Baltimore.

UC Data Archive and Technical Assistance
1999   *An Inventory of Research Uses of Administrative Data in Social Service Programs in the United States 1998.* Chicago: Joint Center for Poverty Research.

U.S. Department of Health, Education, and Welfare, Advisory Committee on Automated Personal Data Systems, Records, Computers and the Rights of Citizens
1973   *Records, Computers, and the Rights of Citizens.* Washington, DC: U.S. Department of Health, Education, and Welfare.

APPENDIX 8-A

State Statutes Providing Researcher Access to Data

MARYLAND:

This Maryland statute is a model for what might be done in other states.

Government Code. §10-624. Personal records

(c) Access for research.—The official custodian may permit inspection of personal records for which inspection otherwise is not authorized by a person who is engaged in a research project if:

(1) the researcher submits to the official custodian a written request that:

(i)   describes the purpose of the research project;

(ii) describes the intent, if any, to publish the findings;

(iii) describes the nature of the requested personal records;

(iv) describes the safeguards that the researcher would take to protect the identity of the persons in interest; and

(v)   states that persons in interest will not be contacted unless the official custodian approves and monitors the contact;

(2) the official custodian is satisfied that the proposed safeguards will prevent the disclosure of the identity of persons in interest; and

(3) the researcher makes an agreement with the unit or instrumentality that:

(i)   defines the scope of the research project;

(ii) sets out the safeguards for protecting the identity of the persons in interest; and

(iii) states that a breach of any condition of the agreement is a breach of contract.

WASHINGTON:

The following statute from Washington state also provides language for model legislation that authorizes researcher access to data.

Revised Code of Washington (RCW). Chapter 42.48. Release of Records for Research

RCW 42.48.010 Definitions.

For the purposes of this chapter, the following definitions apply:

(1) "Individually identifiable" means that a record contains information which reveals or can likely be associated with the identity of the person or persons to whom the record pertains.

(2) "Legally authorized representative" means a person legally authorized to give consent for the disclosure of personal records on behalf of a minor or a legally incompetent adult.

(3) "Personal record" means any information obtained or maintained by a state agency which refers to a person and which is declared exempt from public disclosure, confidential, or privileged under state or federal law.

(4) "Research" means a planned and systematic sociological, psychological, epidemiological, biomedical, or other scientific investigation carried out by a state agency, by a scientific research professional associated with a bona fide scientific research organization, or by a graduate student currently enrolled in an advanced academic degree curriculum, with an objective to contribute to scientific knowledge, the solution of social and health problems, or the evaluation of public benefit and service programs.

This definition excludes methods of record analysis and data collection that are subjective, do not permit replication, and are not designed to yield reliable and valid results.

(5) "Research record" means an item or grouping of information obtained for the purpose of research from or about a person or extracted for the purpose of research from a personal record.

(6) "State agency" means: (a) The department of social and health services; (b) the department of corrections; (c) an institution of higher education as defined in RCW 28B.10.016; or (d) the department of health.
[1989 1st ex.s. c 9 § 207; 1985 c 334 § 1.] NOTES: Effective date — Severability — 1989 1st ex.s. c 9: See RCW 43.70.910 and 43.70.920.

RCW 42.48.020 Access to personal records.

(1) A state agency may authorize or provide access to or provide copies of an individually identifiable personal record for research purposes if informed written consent for the disclosure has been given to the appropriate department secretary, or the president of the institution, as applicable, or his or her designee, by the person to whom the record pertains or, in the case of minors and legally incompetent adults, the person's legally authorized representative.

(2) A state agency may authorize or provide access to or provide copies of an individually identifiable personal record for research purposes without the informed consent of the person to whom the record pertains or the person's legally authorized representative, only if:

(a) The state agency adopts research review and approval rules including, but not limited to, the requirement that the appropriate department secretary, or the president of the institution, as applicable, appoint a standing human research review board competent to review research proposals as to ethical and scientific soundness; and the review board determines that the disclosure request has scientific merit and is of importance in terms of the agency's program concerns, that the research purposes cannot be reasonably accomplished without disclosure of the information in individually identifiable form and without waiver of the informed consent of the person to whom the record pertains or the person's legally authorized representative, that disclosure risks have been minimized, and that remaining risks are outweighed by anticipated health, safety, or scientific benefits; and

(b) The disclosure does not violate federal law or regulations; and

(c) The state agency negotiates with the research professional receiving the records or record information a written and legally binding confidentiality agreement prior to disclosure. The agreement shall:

(i) Establish specific safeguards to assure the continued confidentiality and security of individually identifiable records or record information;

(ii) Ensure that the research professional will report or publish research findings and conclusions in a manner that does not permit identification of the person whose record was used for the research. Final research reports or publications shall not include photographs or other visual representations contained in personal records;

(iii) Establish that the research professional will destroy the individual identifiers associated with the records or record information as soon as the purposes of the research project have been accomplished and notify the agency to this effect in writing;

(iv) Prohibit any subsequent disclosure of the records or record information in individually identifiable form except as provided in RCW 42.48.040; and

(v) Provide for the signature of the research professional, of any of the research professional's team members who require access to the information in identified form, and of the agency official authorized to approve disclosure of identifiable records or record information for research purposes.
[1985 c 334 § 2.]

RCW 42.48.030 Charge for costs of assistance.

In addition to the copying charges provided in RCW 42.17.300, a state agency may impose a reasonable charge for costs incurred in providing assistance in the following research activities involving personal records:

(1) Manual or computer screening of personal records for scientific sampling purposes according to specifications provided by the research professional;

(2) Manual or computer extraction of information from a universe or sample of personal records according to specifications provided by the research professional;

(3) Statistical manipulation or analysis of personal record information, whether manually or by computer, according to specifications provided by the research professional.

The charges imposed by the agency may not exceed the amount necessary to reimburse the agency for its actual costs in providing requested research assistance.

RCW 42.48.050 Unauthorized disclosure—Penalties.

Unauthorized disclosure, whether wilful [sic] or negligent, by a research professional who has obtained an individually identifiable personal record or record information from a state agency pursuant to RCW 42.48.020(2) is a gross misdemeanor. In addition, violation of any provision of this chapter by the research professional or the state agency may subject the research professional or the agency to a civil penalty of not more than ten thousand dollars for each such violation.

RCW 42.48.060 Exclusions from chapter.

Nothing in this chapter is applicable to, or in any way affects, the powers and duties of the state auditor or the joint legislative audit and review committee. [1996 c 288 § 34; 1985 c 334 § 6.]

RCW 42.48.900 Severability — 1985 c 334.

If any provision of this act or its application to any person or circumstance is held invalid, the remainder of the act or the application of the provision to other persons or circumstances is not affected. [1985 c 334 § 8.]

9

Measuring Employment and Income for Low-Income Populations with Administrative and Survey Data

V. Joseph Hotz and John Karl Scholz

With passage of the Personal Responsibility and Work Opportunity Reconciliation Act (PRWORA) of 1996 and the expansions of the Earned Income Tax Credit (EITC) over the past decade, increasing attention has been paid to the employment experiences, labor market earnings, and transfer income received by disadvantaged individuals and households. This attention, prompted by explicit performance goals in PRWORA and implicit goals of the EITC expansions, focuses on whether low-income households can achieve self-sufficiency without resorting to Temporary Assistance for Needy Families (TANF) for other public assistance programs. Although income and employment levels are only partial indicators of the well-being of households, they continue to be ones most often used to assess the consequences, intended and unintended, of welfare reform.

More broadly, good measures of income and employment for low-income families are necessary to (1) assess the well-being and labor market attachment of low-income and welfare populations at the national, state, and local levels; (2) evaluate welfare reform and learn the effects of specific policies, such as time limits and sanctions; and (3) meet reporting requirements under TANF and aid in the administration of welfare programs.

There are two data sources for measuring employment and incomes of the disadvantaged: survey data and administrative. Surveys have been the mainstay of evaluating welfare programs and of monitoring changes in income and employment for decades. These include national surveys—such as the U.S. Censuses of Population, the Current Population Survey (CPS), the Survey of Income and Program Participation (SIPP), the National Longitudinal Surveys (NLS), and the Panel Study of Income Dynamics (PSID)—and more specialized surveys that gather data for targeted groups, such as current or former welfare recipients, and at the state or local level.[1] Although survey data continue to be important, the use of administrative data sources to measure income and employment has grown dramatically over the past 30 years. Data on wages and salaries from state Unemployment Insurance (UI) systems, for example, have been used to measure the earnings and employment of individuals that participated in state AFDC/TANF programs, manpower training, and other social programs. Data on earnings (and employment) from Social Security Administration (SSA) records have been linked with the records of welfare and social program participants.

What type of data one uses to measure income and employment among current and past welfare participants and welfare-eligible households may have important consequences for implementing and evaluating recent welfare reforms. Recent debates between the states and the federal government, for example, over employment targets and associated sanctions mandated under PRWORA hinged crucially on exactly how the fraction of a state's caseload that is employed would be measured. Furthermore, the conclusions of several recent assessments of the impacts of welfare reform and caseload decline appear to depend on how income and employment of welfare leavers and welfare-eligible populations are measured.[2]

In this paper we assess the strengths and weaknesses of using survey or administrative data to measure the employment and income of low-income populations. We review a number of studies, most of which have been conducted in the past 10-15 years,[3] that assess the comparability of income and employment measures derived from surveys and administrative records. Clearly the primary criterion for evaluating data sources is their *accuracy* or *reliability*. Ideally one would compare the income and employment measures derived from either surveys or administrative data sources with their true values in order to determine which source of data is the most accurate.

Unfortunately this ideal is rarely achieved. One seldom, if ever, has access to the true values for any outcome at the individual level. At best, one only can determine the *relative differences* in measures of a particular outcome across data sources. In this paper, we try to summarize the evidence on these relative differ-

---

[1]Often these samples are gathered in the context of evaluations of specific welfare or training programs.

[2]See, for example, studies by Primus et al. (1999), Cancian et al. (1999), and Rolston (1999) for a flavor of how this debate hinges on measurement issues.

[3]Several earlier studies compared employment measures for low-income populations across alternative data sources, most notably the study by Greenberg and Halsey (1983) with data from the SIME/DIME Experiments. Given changes over time in such things as Unemployment Insurance coverage and response rates in surveys, we focus on the most recent studies available to maximize the relevance of our findings for the measurement of these outcomes for current and future studies.

ences and the state of knowledge as to why they differ. These studies point to several important dimensions along which surveys and administrative records differ and, as such, are likely to account for some, if not all, of the differences in the measures of income and employment derived from each. These include the following:

- *Population Coverage:* Surveys generally sample the population while administrative data typically cover the population of individuals or households who are enrolled in some program. In each case issues arise about the sizes of samples at state or substate levels and sample designs that may limit the issues that can be examined.
- *Reporting Units:* Different data sources focus on individuals, households, tax-filing units, or case units. Differences in reporting units hinder the ability to move across data sources to obtain measures of income and complicate efforts to evaluate the differential quality of income data across data sets. Furthermore, differences in reporting units may have important consequences for the comprehensiveness of income measures, an issue especially relevant when attempting to assess the well-being, and changes in the well-being, of disadvantaged populations.
- *Sources of Income:* Data sources differ in the breadth of the sources of individual or household income they collect. Surveys such as the CPS and, especially, the SIPP, attempt to gather a comprehensive set of income elements, including labor earnings, cash benefits derived from social programs, and income from assets. In contrast, administrative data sources often contain only information on a single type of income (as in the case of UI earnings) or only those sources of income needed for the purposes of a particular record-keeping system.
- *Measurement Error:* Different data sources may be subject to different sources of measurement problems, including item nonresponse, imputation error, and measurement error with respect to employment and income (by source). Furthermore, issues such as locating respondents, respondent refusals, and sample attrition are important in conducting surveys on low-income populations.
- *Incentives Associated with Data-Gathering Mechanisms:* Data sources also may differ with respect to the incentives associated with the gathering of information. In the case of surveys, respondents' cooperation may depend on a comparison of the financial remuneration for a survey with the respondent "burden" associated with completing it. In the case of administrative data, the incentives relate to the administrative functions and purposes for which the information is obtained. What is important is attempting to anticipate the potential for and likelihood of biases in measures of income and employment that may result from such incentives.

The importance of various strengths and weaknesses of different data sources for measuring employment and income generally will depend on the purpose to which these measures are put. We note five considerations. First, when conducting an experimental evaluation of a program, the criteria for judging data sources is whether they yield different estimates of program impact, which generally depends on *differences* in income (employment) between treatment and control groups. In this case, errors in measuring the level of income between treatment and control groups could have little effect on the evaluation. Alternatively, suppose one's objective is to describe what happened to households who left welfare. In this case, researchers will be interested in the average *levels* of postwelfare earnings (or employment). We discuss results from Kornfeld and Bloom (1999) where UI data appear to understate the level of income and employment of treatments and controls in an evaluation of the Job Training Partnership Act (JTPA), but *differences* between the two groups appear to give accurate measures of program impacts. Depending on the question of interest, the UI data may be suitable or badly biased.

Second, surveys, and possibly tax return data, can provide information on family resources while UI data provide information on individual outcomes. When assessing the well-being of case units who leave welfare, we often are interested in knowing the resources available to the family. When thinking about the effects of a specific training program, we often are interested in the effects on the individual who received training.

Third, data sets differ in their usefulness in measuring outcomes over time versus at a point in time. UI data, for example, make it relatively straightforward to examine employment and earnings over time, while it is impossible to do this with surveys unless they have a longitudinal design.

Fourth, sample frames differ between administrative data and surveys. Researchers can not use administrative data from AFDC/TANF programs, for example, to examine program take-up decisions because the data only cover families who already receive benefits. Surveys, on the other hand, generally have representative rather than targeted or "choice-based" samples.

Fifth, data sources are likely to have different *costs*. These include the costs of producing the data and implicit costs associated with gaining access. The issue of access is often an important consideration for certain sources of administrative data, particularly data from tax returns.

The remainder of this paper is organized as follows: We characterize the strengths and weaknesses of income and employment measures derived from surveys, with particular emphasis on national surveys, from UI wage records, and from tax returns. For each data source, we summarize the findings of studies that directly compare the income and employment measures derived from that source with measures derived from at least one other data source. We conclude the paper by identifying the "gaps" in existing knowledge about the survey and administrative data sources for measuring income and employment for low-income and welfare-eligible populations. We offer several recommendations for future research that might help to close these gaps.

USING SURVEY DATA TO MEASURE EMPLOYMENT AND INCOME

In this section, we discuss the strengths and weaknesses of measuring income and employment status for low-income populations using survey data. Most of our analysis focuses on the use of national surveys—CPS and SIPP in particular—because of the availability of several high-quality studies that compare their income and employment measures to other data sources. Where available, we also summarize studies that assess income and employment measurement with more targeted surveys.

TABLE 9-1 Key Features of Selected National Surveys That Report
Employment and Income Status of Individuals and Households

Feature	Current Population Survey (CPS)	Survey of Income and Program Participation (SIPP)	Panel Study of Income Dynamics (PSID)	National Longitudinal Survey of Youth, 1979 (NLSY79)
Nationally representative sample?	Yes	Yes	Only at sample inception in 1968	No, but representative for cohorts covered at sample inception
Primary unit of analysis	Household	Household	Household	Individual
Longitudinal data?	No	Yes	Yes	Yes
Typical sample size	60,000 households	21,000 households	8,700 households	11,400 individuals
Capacity for state and local Analysis	For all but small states	For large states only	Limited	Limited
Coverage of income sources	Broad	Very broad	Broad	Very broad
Accuracy of earnings data[a]	97%	92%	—	—
Accuracy of AFDC data[b]			—	—
Timeliness of data	Several months	2+ years	2-year lag	1-2 year lag

[a]For 1990, See Table 9-3.

[b]AFDC = Aid to Families with Dependent Children, for 1990, see Tables 9-2 and 9-3.

The key features of the national surveys for the purposes of this paper are summarized in Table 9-1.

Potential Strengths

The CPS and SIPP are vital data sets for understanding the functioning of low-wage labor markets and the effects of antipoverty programs. These data get high marks on many of the concerns mentioned in the introduction. They have a national sampling frame covering program participants and nonparticipants that make these data valuable for developing a broad perspective on developments in low-wage labor markets. An example of this type of study is Primus et al. (1999), which uses CPS data to show that AFDC/TANF and Food Stamp Program participation rates have declined considerably faster than poverty rates between 1993 and 1997. They further report that incomes of poor single mothers fell between 1995 and 1997 (after rising between 1993 and 1995), and that the safety net is lifting fewer children from poverty than in the past. Concerns arise with this study, some of which are mentioned in the text that follows. Nonetheless, the CPS and the SIPP are the only data sets that would allow analysts to address the important issues that Primus et al. examine on a national scale.

The other national data sets that have been used to analyze the employment and income status of low-income populations are the National Longitudinal Survey (particularly the National Longitudinal Survey of Youth 1979) and the PSID. Both of these data sets have the additional feature that they are longitudinal surveys so that one can obtain information on earnings and employment status over time for the same person (and household).[4] The PSID has surveyed, until very recently, its respondents and the "splitoffs" of initial respondent households on an annual basis since 1968. Similarly, until 1994 the NLSY79 conducted annual surveys of a random sample of individuals who were 14-21 years of age in 1979. Both of these surveys gathered detailed information on labor market earnings and employment status of respondents, earnings and some employment information on other adult household members, and some information on other sources of income, including income from various public assistance programs. One of the advantages of longitudinal data sets such as SIPP, PSID, and NLSY is that they allow one to monitor the entry into and exit from welfare or other social programs and the factors related to welfare dynamics, including changes in earnings and family structure.

The CPS, SIPP, and PSID, in addition to having nationally representative samples, focus on households as the unit of analysis, and include information on all adult household members.[5] Given the general presumption that families pool

---

[4]Each wave of the SIPP is a longitudinal survey with between 2.5 and 4 years of data on the residents of a sample housing unit. Surveys to these respondents are asked every 4 months.

[5]The NLSY79 focuses on the original respondent, but it gathers a considerable amount of information on the respondent's spouse and/or cohabiting partner.

resources, data sets that focus on families or households (and include information on cohabiting partners) are valuable. A calculation in Meyer and Cancian (1998) illustrates the usefulness of having data on family, as well as individual, incomes. Their study examines the economic well-being of women in the 5 years after leaving AFDC. They show that in the first year upon exit from AFDC, 79 percent of the women have incomes below the poverty line, but when family income is considered, a smaller number, 55.5, have income below the (correspondingly larger) poverty line. After 5 years, 64.2 percent of the women still have incomes below the poverty line, while only 40.5 percent of the broader family unit had income below the poverty line.

The nationally representative surveys provide information on multiple sources of income, especially in the SIPP, either through separate questions or prompting of specific income sources. By asking specific questions about, for example, welfare receipt or food stamps, the data identify participants and (eligible) nonparticipants, so the data can be used to study program entry effects.

The national surveys also measure income and employment in a comparable fashion both over time and across geographical locations, though in January 1994 the way that earnings information was elicited in the CPS was changed (Polivka, 1997).[6]

Another strength of the nationally representative surveys is that questions can be modified to reflect changing circumstances. For example, the U.S. Census Bureau periodically conducts cognitive interviews of respondents to the CPS in order to assess how they responded to different CPS income- and welfare-related questions. Such studies are used to determine which of the CPS questions were confusing and how respondents interpreted questions. Results from these cognitive interviews are used to improve the way questions are asked, with the goal of improving the quality of the data on key variables such as income and program participation.[7] Typically, this sort of sophisticated assessment can only be done on large-scale, national surveys.

To summarize, there are several potential strengths of using survey data to measure income and employment. These include the following:

• Surveys can provide representative samples for specific populations and generally include data for other family members.

---

[6]Previously, earnings had to be reported in weekly amounts, and amounts over $2,000 per week were truncated. Now earnings can be reported over any interval and the data (to Bureau of Labor Statistics) are not truncated. Studies that use repeated cross-sections of the CPS that span 1994 risk misinterpreting results if they fail to account for the redesign. Polivka provides adjustment factors for earnings (at the 10th, median, and 90th percentiles) reported prior to 1994 to make the series comparable. She also shows that top-coded values that are imputed using a Pareto distribution do a good job of fitting the distribution of data that are not top coded.

[7]See Bogen et al. (1997) and Bogen (1998).

• Surveys typically provide demographic data and data on other character-istics of households (such as educational attainment). They also may gather de-tailed information on many distinct income sources.

• National surveys provide consistent information across states and locali-ties.

• Surveys can be flexible, so their developers can control what information is collected about income and employment, and this information can be improved over time

Potential Weaknesses

Three general concerns arise with the nationally representative surveys that keep them from being the solution, or "core" data, for understanding the effects of welfare reform. The most important issue is that sample sizes and sampling frames are such that these data cannot be used to examine certain subpopulations of interest, such as welfare recipients in a particular state (perhaps with the exception of the largest states, such as California, New York, and Texas). A distinguishing feature of welfare reform is that program responsibility now largely rests with states and even counties within a state. The nationally representative data sets do not have sample designs and sample sizes that allow analysts to examine behavior at a level that corresponds to where program decisions are being made.

Second, there appear to be systematic changes in the coverage of low-in-come populations in the CPS. Studies have found that AFDC and Food Stamp Program benefits and the number of recipients in the CPS have declined over time relative to estimates of participants from administrative records. This issue of coverage is a serious concern for studies that use the CPS for measuring the income of welfare populations.[8] In Table 9-2, we reproduce comparisons of aggregate AFDC/TANF and Food Stamp Benefits Program between CPS and administrative data sources from the Primus et al. (1999) study. It shows there has been a sharp decline between 1990 and 1997 in the percentage of AFDC/TANF and Food Stamp Program benefits reported in the CPS compared to amounts reported in administrative data.[9] The reduction in coverage of AFDC/

---

[8]Roemer (1999) suggests the reduction in coverage could be related to PRWORA—the March 1997 survey did not use state-specific labels for TANF benefits in 14 states that had abolished AFDC. Benefit estimates were 4.5 percentage points lower than the benchmark in states that had abolished AFDC than in states that had not. The delivery mechanism of benefits in some circum-stances (for example, through employers), an enhanced sense of stigma, and caseload reductions that exacerbate recall errors may also contribute to underreporting.

[9]Primus et al. adjust the CPS data proportionately to account for the decline in benefits over time, but the value of this adjustment depends on the patterns of discrepancies in the data. Unfortunately, we know little about the factors associated with the underrepresentation of program participants in the CPS or the SIPP.

TABLE 9-2 AFDC/TANF and Food Stamp Aggregate Benefits Paid Based on Administrative Data Compared to Estimates from Current Population Survey (CPS) (in billions of dollars)

	AFDC/TANF Benefits			Food Stamp Benefits		
	CPS Data	Administrative Data	Ratio (%)	CPS Data	Administrative Data	Ratio (%)
1990	14.259	18.855	75.6	10.335	13.556	76.2
1991	15.554	20.804	74.8	12.373	16.551	74.8
1992	15.362	22.258	69.0	13.394	20.014	66.9
1993	17.540	22.307	78.6	15.010	22.253	67.5
1994	17.145	22.753	75.4	15.317	22.701	67.5
1995	15.725	21.524	73.1	14.542	22.712	64.0
1996	13.494	19.710	68.5	14.195	22.440	63.3
1997	10.004	15.893	62.9	12.274	19.570	62.7

SOURCE: Primus et al. (1999:65), which in turn gives the sources, as Health and Human Services and U.S. Department of Agriculture administrative records and Center on Budget and Policy Priorities tabulations of CPS data.

TANF (or family assistance) benefits also is consistent with Roemer's (2000: Table 3b) calculations from the CPS for 1990 through 1996. Interestingly, the apparent decline in AFDC/TANF coverage does not show up in the SIPP, though the SIPP appears to capture only about three-quarters of aggregate benefits.

Polivka (1998) compares the monthly average number of AFDC recipients in the March CPS to the monthly average reported to the Department of Health and Human Services (prior to quality control). She finds there has been a modest decrease in the proportion of total months on AFDC as measured in the CPS. The ratio of the CPS estimated to the administrative count (excluding Guam, the Virgin Islands, and Puerto Rico) is 83.0 (1989), 86.7 (1990), 86.0 (1991), 82.5 (1992), 84.2 (1993), 78.5 (1994), 75.5 (1995), and 79.6 (1996). The timing of the drop in the ratio corresponds to changes in the March CPS survey instrument. Taken together, the Primus et al. (1999) and Polivka (1998) results suggest that the decline in benefits reported in the CPS results from both a reduction in the coverage of families receiving AFDC and from an underrepresentation of benefits conditional on receipt, though the second factor seems quantitatively more important than the first.

The third potential weakness of national surveys is that there is little or no "cost" to respondents of misreporting of income, employment, or other circumstances.[10]

[10]Shroder and Martin (1996), for example, show subsidized housing (broadly defined) is badly reported on surveys, including the American Housing Survey (and presumably the SIPP). An underlying problem is that the phrase "public housing" means different things to different people, ranging from only projects to any kind of subsidized housing.

Some specific potential weaknesses associated with the PSID and NLSY79 are of potential relevance for obtaining information on the income and employment status of low-income populations. Most notable is the fact that they are not, by design, representative of the general population over time. Both data sets began with samples that were representative of their targeted groups—young adults in the case of the NLSY79 and the national population as of 1968 in the case of the PSID—but are not designed to be representative of the national population, or even of the age group covered in the NLSY79, in subsequent years. This feature can result in biased measures of summary statistics on income and employment vis-à-vis the nation as a whole in more recent years.

The other feature of the NLSY79 and PSID relevant for assessing the income and employment status of low-income populations is their respective sample sizes. The original sample for the NLSY79 was 12,686 young men and women, from which approximately 90 percent of the original sample remains today. The original sample in the PSID was 5,000 U.S. households in 1968 and, because of its growth through the accumulation of additional households through splitoffs from original households, it contained more than 8,700 in 1995. Although these are not small sample sizes, the sizes of low-income samples at a point in time are relatively small compared to both the CPS (which contains some 60,000 households at a point in time) and most waves of the SIPP (which, in its larger waves, contains data on 21,000 households). The sizes of the low-income or welfare subsamples in the NLSY79 and PSID for even the largest states are generally too small to derive reliable measures on income and employment, let alone other outcomes.

To summarize, there are two primary potential weaknesses with using national survey data to measure income and employment of low-income populations. They are the following:

• Sample sizes in national surveys often are small for studies that focus on welfare or low-income populations, or that wish to examine specific targeted groups, such as current or former welfare recipients.
• There appears to be falling coverage (of both recipients and benefits) in national surveys.

Direct Assessments of Income and Employment Measures from Survey Data

Moore et al. (1997) conducted a general survey of income reporting in the CPS and SIPP, and Roemer (2000) assesses trends in SIPP and CPS income reporting between 1990 and 1996.[11] A central finding in Moore et al. (1997) and

---

[11]There are no comprehensive assessments of the quality of income and employment measurements for either the NLSY79 or the PSID. Roemer (1999) and Nelson et al. (1998) update the CPS

Roemer (2000) is that there is underreporting of many types of income in surveys. The reasons for this and, hence, solutions in the design of effective surveys are complex. The magnitudes of CPS and SIPP underreporting for selected years are given in Tables 9-3a and 9-3b, taken from the two papers. (Note that differences may be the result of flawed benchmarks rather than flawed surveys.)

Surveys of Income Reporting in the SIPP and CPS

The understatement of certain types of income, such as interest and dividend receipts, is probably not critical for low-income populations because low-income families typically receive small amounts of income from these sources. Based on the evidence presented in Tables 9-3a and 9-3b, it appears that wages and salaries are fairly accurately reported in the CPS, although less accurately in the SIPP. But Moore et al. (1997) note that 26.2 percent (35,205,000 out of 134,135,000 total weighted cases) of the wage and salary "responses" in CPS surveys are imputed from cases where the respondent did not give an answer, replied "don't know," or refused to answer the question. They also report that 7 to 8 percent of households refuse to participate in the CPS, so imputations and imputation quality is clearly a critical element in survey quality.

The apparent accuracy of wage and salary reporting in Tables 9-3a and 9-3b does not fully resolve concerns that we have about data accuracy for low-income populations, because we do not know much about the characteristics of families that underreport their incomes. If, for example, most of the underreporting of income occurs among the disadvantaged, the findings of Moore et al. (1997) and Roemer (2000) on wage and salary reporting in the CPS and SIPP may be of little comfort. Roemer, for example, shows there are significantly more aggregate dollars reported below family income of $25,000 in the SIPP relative to the March CPS. He suggests that the SIPP does a better job than the CPS of capturing the incomes of low earners and a worse job of capturing the incomes of high earners. Learning more about the nature of underreporting would appear to be a high priority for future research.

Matching Studies of Wage and Salary Income

Roemer (2000) examines the accuracy of CPS wage and salary reports by matching CPS data to Internal Revenue Service (IRS) tax returns in selected years for the first half of the 1990s. The sample is limited to nonjoint returns and selected joint returns where each filer matches a March CPS person. The sample is restricted further to observations with no imputed wages in the CPS. He finds that in the middle of the income distribution (from $15,000 to $150,000), at least

---

calculations to 1996. Roemer (2000) also provides a nice discussion of adjustments that need to be made to compare aggregate SIPP and CPS totals to National Income and Product Account data.

TABLE 9-3a Ratio of SIPP and CPS March Income Supplement Aggregate
Income Estimates to Independent Aggregate Income Estimates for 1984 and
1990

	1984			1990		
Source of Income	Indep. Estimate (billions $)	SIPP (%)	CPS (%)	Indep. Estimate (billions $)	SIPP (%)	CPS (%)
Employment:						
Wages and salaries	1,820.1	91.4	97.3	2,695.6	91.8	97.0
Self-employment	192.6	103.1	70.2	341.4	78.4	66.8
Asset:						
Interest	244.8	48.3	56.7	282.8	53.3	61.1
Dividends	59.3	65.9	51.8	126.3	46.1	31.3
Rents and royalties	19.4	211.3	95.4	44.1	102.9	87.8
Govt. transfer:						
Social Security	160.5	96.2	91.9	225.5	98.3	93.0
Railroad retirement	5.6	96.4	71.4	6.9	95.7	66.7
SSI	9.9	88.9	84.8	13.6	94.9	89.0
AFDC	13.9	83.5	78.4	19.7	70.1	71.6
Other cash welfare	2.0	135.0	120.0	2.9	86.2	80.2
Unemployment Ins.	16.3	76.1	74.8	17.7	84.2	80.2
Workers' Comp.	14.1	56.7	48.2	14.6	86.3	94.5
Vets' pension and comp.	13.9	82.0	59.7	13.8	84.1	77.5
Retirement:						
Private pensions	65.2	63.8	57.2	70.2	107.1	110.8
Federal employee pension	20.3	98.0	84.7	30.4	73.4	82.6
Military retirement	15.6	105.1	98.1	20.4	92.2	89.2
S&L employee pension	21.9	88.1	71.7	36.1	75.1	80.1
Miscellaneous:						
Alimony	2.7	100.0	81.5	2.5	116.0	124.0

SOURCE: These figures are adapted from Coder and Scoon-Rogers (1996).

half the CPS and tax reports are within 10 percent of each other. Anywhere from
60 to 80 percent of the observations are within 15 percent of one another. Discrepancies appear much larger in the bottom and very top of the income distribution. Below $10,000 and above $150,000, at least half the observations have
discrepancies exceeding 20 percent, and most are larger than that. Discrepancies
are both positive and negative, though, as expected, CPS incomes tend to be
larger than incomes reported on tax returns in the bottom of the income distribution, and CPS incomes tend to be smaller than incomes reported on tax returns in
the top of the income distribution.

Beyond the cited studies, there appears to be little recent work on the accuracy of the wage and salary income in the SIPP, CPS, or related national sur-

TABLE 9-3b Ratio of SIPP and CPS March Income Supplement Aggregate Income Estimates to Independent Aggregate Income Estimates for 1990 and 1996

	1990			1996		
Source of Income	Indep. Estimate (billions $)	SIPP (%)	CPS (%)	Indep. Estimate (billions $)	SIPP (%)	CPS (%)
Employment:						
Wages and salaries	2,727.7	90.1	95.9	3,592.3	91.0	101.9
Self-employment	333.5	85.1	68.5	475.9	69.1	52.6
Asset:						
Interest	258.5	56.7	67.1	187.1	50.2	83.8
Dividends	96.8	65.8	40.9	129.4	51.0	59.4
Rents and royalties	45.6	113.1	85.0	76.2	82.0	58.6
Govt. transfer:						
Social Security and railroad retirement	283.4	97.1	90.6	332.2	87.9	91.7
SSI	15.3	83.1	78.9	26.5	101.4	84.2
Family assistance	18.9	75.6	74.4	19.8	76.3	67.7
Other cash welfare	2.9	81.9	85.6	3.4	114.0	80.5
Unemployment Ins.	17.9	77.5	79.9	21.6	69.4	81.6
Workers' Comp.	15.4	67.8	89.5	17.0	71.7	62.7
Vets' pens. and comp.	14.5	83.1	73.9	17.8	72.9	89.6
Retirement:						
Private pensions	68.5	91.8	98.3	98.7	98.1	93.1
Federal employee pension	30.5	75.9	82.7	38.8	75.6	80.8
Military retirement	21.4	87.4	85.6	28.3	101.6	58.2
S&L employee pension	36.9	76.8	78.7	66.0	67.8	57.3

SOURCE: These figures are from Roemer (2000). The independent estimates are the mean values of the implied independent estimates from the SIPP and the CPS (from Tables -2a, 2b, 3a, and 3b in Roemer, 2000).

veys.[12] The dates of the citations for American work on this topic (there also is one Canadian study) are 1958, 1970, and 1980. In each case there seemed to be a small (on the order of 5 percent) incidence of non-reporting of wage and salary income.[13] Coder (1992) compares a restricted set of SIPP households with tax data (married couples with valid Social Security numbers who file joint returns

---

[12]Abraham et al. (1998) conclude, "There is some evidence that CPS hours worked are overreported, that this overreporting may have worsened over time.... Given the paucity of data on hours worked, we view our conclusions on this subject as suggestive rather than definitive" (p. 319).

[13]Moore et al. (1997) also provide a brief discussion of income data collected as part of the Gary Negative Income Tax Experiment (from the late 1960s and early 1970s). They note that the income

and have positive wage and salary income in either the SIPP or on tax returns) and finds a roughly 5-percent discrepancy in the existence of wage and salary income. Moore et al. (1996) examine a sample of SIPP households working for specific employers and find that respondents sometimes drop months of wage and salary receipt over a 4-month interview cycle, though virtually all accurately reported the presence of a job during the wave.

Several other studies assess the quality of income and earnings measurement based on matching survey data with various types of administrative data. Bound and Krueger (1991) match CPS data from 1977 and 1978 with SSA earnings records and find essentially zero net bias in CPS income reports for those whose incomes did not exceed the SSA's earnings maximum cutoff. In fact, more than 10 percent of the CPS sample matched their Social Security reported earnings to the dollar, and 40 percent were within 2.5 percent. Second, Rodgers et al. (1993) examine wage records in the PSID for unionized men working fulltime at an hourly rate in one specific durable goods manufacturing firm in 1983 and 1987. These authors examine three common measures of earnings: earnings from the previous week, from the previous year, and "usual" earnings. They find annual earnings are reported fairly reliably, but this is less true for the other two measures. They also find for each measure that there is a tendency for workers with lower than average earnings to overreport and for workers with higher than average earnings to underreport.[14]

Studies of Program Participation and Transfer Income

The previous discussion focused on income reporting. There are also several studies of transfer program reporting in surveys, though the cited studies are old (dates for the citations are 1940, 1962, 1969, 1969, 1971, 1975, 1978, 1980, and 1984). These are not "complete" design studies, in that they typically focus on a sample of recipients and examine whether or not they report benefits. Complete designs also would look at nonrecipients and see if they falsely report receipt. More recent studies do the latter. Most, but not all, of these studies find fairly substantial underreporting of transfer program receipt.

---

data in this experiment, gathered through surveys of respondents, was not very reliable. In the Seattle and Denver Income Maintenance experiments, there was evidence of statistically significant underreporting of wage and salary amounts. But the magnitude of underreporting was only 2 to 4 percent, leading Halsey (1978) to conclude that they were not large enough to be important economically. The correlation between administrator records and reported values was .9, also indicating high reliability.

[14]They also examine several measurement error assumptions that challenge standard practice in empirical economics.

Marquis and Moore (1990), using two waves of the 1994 SIPP panel, did a comprehensive study of the accuracy of reporting of transfer program participation. They discuss evidence of substantial underreporting of program participation among true program participants, on the order of 50 percent for Workers' Compensation and AFDC, 39 percent for UI and 23 percent for food stamps and Supplemental Security Income. Overall participation rates for transfer programs, however, were quite close to what would be expected from administrative controls.

Subsequent work by Moore et al. (1996) on a sample of households from Milwaukee found smaller underreporting among true recipients, and found that most error, when it exists, is due to participants' failures to report the sources of income, rather than a failure to report all months of participation.

Bollinger and David (2001) give a detailed examination to food stamp underreporting in the 1984 SIPP panel. They find that the high rate of underreporting for food stamps arises in part from failures to locate the person legally certified within the household. About half of the underreports within a household were offset by an overreport from another household member. The net effect was underreporting of food stamps receipt of 12 to 13 percent in the 1984 SIPP panel. Bollinger and David also (2001) document the important point that nonresponse and false answers are correlated across survey waves in the SIPP.

Finally, Yen and Nelson (1996) examine survey and administrative records from Washington state and find that 93 percent of the nearly 49,000 person-months are reported correctly, and net overreports roughly equal net underreports.

Assessment of Income and Transfer Program Reporting in National Surveys

Moore et al. (1997:12) conclude their survey of what is known about income measurement in surveys by stating that:

> Wage and salary income response bias estimates from a wide variety of studies are generally small and without consistent sign, and indicators of unreliability (random error) are quite low. Bias estimates for transfer income amount reporting vary in magnitude but are generally negative, indicating underreporting, and random error also is an important problem.

They conclude, "in general we find that the additional data continue to support the conclusion of very little bias in survey reports of wage and salary income, and little random error as well." They conclude that studies that match administrative records of transfer programs and survey data "suggest a general tendency for transfer program income to be at least modestly—and in some instances substantially—under reported" (p. 16).

Based on our review of available assessments of income and employment measurement in national surveys, we think the above quotation is still correct. The CPS, SIPP, NLS, and PSID surveys provide:

• Valuable information on the behavior of the low-income population (and many other issues). They have national samples, and broad and fairly accurate measures of income, and their focus on families as the unit of analysis and their ease of access greatly enhance their value.

• The value of these data sets for evaluating welfare reform is severely limited, however. With the devolution of responsibility for TANF, the CPS and SIPP sampling frames and sample sizes mean that, at best, they can be only supplementary data sources for understanding the effects of welfare reform at the state and local levels. The apparent decline in program coverage in the CPS is also worrisome.[15]

UNEMPLOYMENT INSURANCE WAGE RECORDS DATA
TO MEASURE INCOME AND EMPLOYMENT
FOR LOW-INCOME POPULATION

We now consider the evidence on using UI wage records to measure the income and employment status of low-income populations. UI wage records contain the earnings reported by employers (on a quarterly basis) to state UI agencies for each employee. As we noted above, UI data often are linked to information on targeted samples, such as participants in evaluations of specific welfare or training programs. Thus, the populations for which UI wage data are used to measure their income and employment varies with the particular investigation being conducted. We report on several of these studies, attempting to draw some general conclusions about the strengths and weaknesses of this data source.

Potential Strengths

Using UI wage records to measure income and employment has several potential advantages. The first is that wages reported to state UI programs are thought to include most of the wage earnings of individuals. By law, any employer paying $1,500 in wages during a calendar quarter to one or more employees is subject to a state UI tax and, hence, must report quarterly what is paid to each employee, including regular earnings, overtime, and tips and bonuses. Agricultural employers must report earnings if they have either a quarterly payroll of at least $20,000 or have hired 10 or more employees in each of 20 or more weeks

---

[15]We were not able to find a comparable study of trends in program participation for the SIPP. U.S. Department of Commerce, Bureau of the Census (1998) compiles summaries of an extensive, long-running research program on SIPP quality. It starts with an overview of SIPP design, and then describes sample selection, data collection, nonresponse and measurement error, data preparation, weighting, sampling error, evaluation of estimates from the 1984 to 1993 panels, and the 1996 redesign of the SIPP.

during the preceding calendar year. Employers of paid household help must report wages if they pay at least $1,000 in cash wages during any quarter. In a study of the use of UI wage records to measure the post enrollment earnings of JTPA recipients, Baj et al. (1991) claim that, "Virtually all jobs that most observers would consider appropriate targets for JTPA terminee placement are covered by the UI reporting system." (More on this study follows.)

A second potential advantage of UI wage data is their presumed accuracy. Hill et al. (1999), for example, made the following, perhaps incorrect argument. "Employers are liable for taxes up to an earnings threshold. Because this threshold is quite low, there appears to be little incentive for employers to underreport earnings for most employees. Moreover, employers' reports are used to determine unemployment benefits. Discrepancies between employer and employee reports upon application of unemployment benefits can result in employer sanctions." Baj, Trott and Stevens (1991:10) write, "The accuracy of the reporting of money wages is unknown. However, relatively few corrections occur in the routine processing of individual unemployment insurance claims. In addition electronic payroll processing is increasing, electronic cross-matching capabilities are expanding, and new revenue quality control practices have been introduced. Thus, there is reason to think that the accuracy of UI data is higher than that of most self-reported sources of earnings information. Intentional underreporting of wages constitutes fraud, which is subject to sanctions. Unintentional misreporting is subject to penalty payments."

A third presumed advantage of using UI data to measure employment and wage income of individuals is its ready availability, at least for certain authorized studies, and the ability to link this data with information from other administrative or survey data sources. (Note that state UI authorities control access to UI wage records and the Social Security numbers necessary to link these data to other data sources for individuals, in order to safeguard the confidentiality of this information.) UI wage records are commonly used in state-level evaluations of welfare reform and other social programs. As Baj et al. (1991) conclude in their study of the feasibility of using UI wage data from different states to monitor the post training earnings outcomes of individuals who received training services in JTPA:

> The findings from the first phase of this project indicate that JTPA and *any other program* [emphasis added] whose goal is to increase the employment and earnings of participants can use UI wage-record data with confidence. Obtaining post-program information from state UI systems is not only a viable option, it is far more cost-effective than the current practice of gathering this information through contact with participants. Furthermore, UI data are of higher quality than corresponding survey-based information. (p. 30)

They found, for example, that the response rate to the survey was 70.2 percent for those who were employed at termination compared to 49.6 percent for those who were not. Based on these results, they concluded that using UI wage data was preferred to obtaining data via surveys, especially given the cost of conducting surveys on this population.

To summarize, using UI wage records to measure income and employment has several potential strengths. These include the following:

- UI data are available at the state level and can be matched to individuals in existing samples at relatively low cost (as long as Social Security numbers are available).
- It is straightforward to do follow-up analyses on income and employment for workers that remain in the state.
- Data are timely in that they become available with roughly a two-quarter lag.
- For most workers the reporting of wage and salary income appears to be accurate; however, concerns are noted in the following section.

Potential Weaknesses

Relying on UI wage records to measure employment and income for low-income populations has two potentially serious weaknesses. The first arises because UI wage records do not cover all forms of employment. In particular, state UI systems typically do not cover the employment of self-employed persons, most independent contractors, military personnel, federal government workers, railroad employees, some part-time employees of nonprofit institutions, employees of religious orders, and some students employed by their schools. Therefore, wage earnings from these types of employment are not contained in state UI wage records.

The importance of these exemptions is unclear. In at least two places in the literature, an assertion is made that 90 percent of workers in the U.S. economy are in jobs covered by the UI system (Baj et al., 1991; Kornfeld and Bloom, 1999).[16] As noted in the following paragraphs, this statistic is challenged by the results of Blakemore et al. (1996) and Burgess et al. (1998), but even if true, it is not clear how comforting it should be if the topic of interest is low-wage labor markets. If, for example, 8 percent of all jobs are missing from UI wage records, but all 8 percent are low-income workers (which in turn is a much larger fraction of all low-income workers), the usefulness of UI data in monitoring the effects of welfare reform would be severely eroded.

Blakemore et al. (1996) and Burgess et al. (1998) report results of a fascinating study of 875 Illinois employers from 1987 that were subjected to detailed

---

[16]Despite our efforts, we have not found documentation for this particular statistic.

audits of their UI reports. As part of the data set, routine information such as the employment size of the firm, the statutory UI tax rate for each firm, one-digit Standard Industrial Classification codes, and UI reporting punctuality were compiled. They also have unique audit information on unreported workers, under-reported total and taxable wages, and UI taxes due on these unreported wages. They also merged information on the total number of independent contractors that each firm reported to the IRS. The data set does not attempt to identify employers who are part of the underground economy.

If the results for Illinois are projected nationally,[17] employers failed to report the presence of 11.1 million UI-eligible workers and $70.6 billion in wages to state UI agencies in 1987. This is 13.6 percent of all workers. Some of the undercoverage arose from failure to report casual or part-time workers, and failure to report tips, bonuses, or other types of irregular compensation. By far the largest problem (accounting for roughly 50 percent of the discrepancy), however, was with independent contractors. Issues surrounding independent contractors are among the most vexing in tax administration and labor law. In brief (and at the risk of oversimplification), in tax law there is a somewhat subjective, 20-part test to define a worker as a regular employee or independent contractor. Elements of the test include (from IRS Publication 15A: Employer's Supplemental Tax Guide) whether the business has "behavioral control" of the worker (does the business give instructions and train the worker?); financial control (can the worker make a profit or loss, does the worker have unreimbursed business expenses, or does the worker make services available to a broad market?); and type of relationship (does the job have benefits, is it permanent, are the tasks a key aspect of the regular business of the company?). If a worker is treated as an independent contractor, an employer does not have to withhold income taxes, withhold and pay Social Security and Medicare taxes, or pay UI taxes.

It is not clear if the issues raised in the Illinois UI audits are associated strictly with independent contractors (in the technical sense) or more broadly with flexible staffing arrangements. Houseman (1999) provides a nice introduction to issues associated with flexible staffing arrangements. She reports data from the February 1997 CPS Supplement on Contingent and Alternative Work Arrangements showing that 6.7 percent of workers were "independent contractors," 1 percent were "agency temporaries," 1.6 percent were "on-call or day laborers," .6 percent were "contract company workers," and 2.6 percent were "other direct-hire temporaries." These categories compose 12.5 percent of the workforce. The use of flexible staffing arrangements appears to have been grow-

---

[17]Clearly strong assumptions are needed to make this projection, but the size and industrial composition of the Illinois sample is not sharply different from national statistics. The Illinois UI system is typical of what is observed nationally, and, if anything, Midwestern states tend to have lower rates of income and payroll tax noncompliance than other states.

ing sharply over time, but detailed information on its growth is not available. Houseman (1999) reports that the IRS estimates it loses billions in tax revenues each year due to misclassification of employees.

Houseman (1999) also reports information on the incomes of "flexible workers" drawn from the February 1995 CPS Supplement on Contingent and Alternative Work Arrangements, matched to the March 1995 CPS. Of "regular" employees 7.5 percent had incomes below 125 percent of poverty. The corresponding figures for agency temporaries was 21.7 percent; 16.2 percent for on-call or day laborers; 10.8 percent for independent contractors; 11.5 percent for contract company workers; and 15.1 percent for other short-term direct hires. Consequently, a failure of UI data to fully capture workers in flexible staffing arrangements could be a major problem for studies that rely exclusively on UI data to measure the income and employment of low-income workers.

In many industries, employers have considerable flexibility in designating the status of workers. At least in the Illinois audit study, employers aggressively overused the independent contractor designation. In all, 45 percent of employers make some underreporting error. This includes nearly 500,000 cases in which workers were excluded erroneously, which resulted in $2.6 billion in wages being underreported. Smaller firms were estimated to underreport 14 percent of their taxable wages and 56 percent of their UI-covered workforce. In statistical models, the percentage of workers on the payroll who are independent contractors and the turnover of the firms' workers are two key explanatory variables. The effective tax rate, while related to turnover, also appears to be positively associated with compliance. The characteristics of firms that make errors on UI reports would appear to be positively correlated with the type of employers who disproportionately hire workers with low levels of human capital.

Hence, we view the Blakemore et al. (1996) and Burgess et al. (1998) studies as raising a serious concern about the coverage of UI data, and hence its suitability as the *exclusive* source of data with which to evaluate welfare reform. In our conclusions, we recommend that at least one additional study be conducted along the lines of the Illinois study to assess UI coverage. It is our impression, based on casual, anecdotal evidence, that the use of independent contractors has increased fairly substantially over time, and thus the work based on 1987 Illinois data may understate the problem.

The second potentially major weakness with using UI data for evaluating welfare reform is that they contain limited accompanying demographic information on individuals, and, more importantly, may not allow one to form an accurate measure of family income. In assessing the impacts of welfare reform, many argue that it is important to assess how these changes affect the well-being of children and the families in which they reside. As such, families constitute the natural "unit of analysis" for such assessments and family income often is used as an indicator of this unit's well-being.

The potential problem of relying on earnings data from UI wage records when the objective is to assess the level of family resources in studying the impact of welfare reform recently has been highlighted by Rolston (1999). Based on past research, Rolston notes that changes in individual income account for only 40 to 50 percent of exits from welfare. Thus, to have a complete picture of the effects of welfare reform, analysts need information on other economic and demographic changes occurring in the family. Given this, the problem is clear. Income as reported: through UI records fails to include sources of nonemployment income and income of partners that is available to a family. Income sources that are not UI data may result in a family not receiving cash assistance or being ineligible.

The calculations from Meyer and Cancian (1998) suggest the concern raised by Rolston (1999) is economically important. Recall that Meyer and Cancian found, for example, that 5 years after leaving welfare, 64.2 percent of the women still have incomes below the poverty line, while, when considering the broader family unit, only 40.5 percent have income below the poverty line. In a related calculation, however, Primus et al. (1999) do an analysis that shows "for most single-mother families, including the income of unrelated male individuals does not materially change the picture drawn of a decline in overall disposable income between 1995 and 1997." More needs to be learned about the importance of the issue raised by Rolston in assessing the level and trend in family well-being following welfare reform.

To summarize, using UI wage records to measure income and employment has two potential weaknesses. These are as follows:

• UI data do not cover all workers, including the self-employed, military, federal employees, independent contractors, and other employment arrangements. Some evidence shows that gaps in coverage may be significant.
• UI data follow individuals, so one cannot get information on incomes of other family members, at least without Social Security numbers of other household members. UI data also provide limited demographic and background information on workers.

Direct Comparisons of UI Wage (and Employment) Data with Income and Employment Measures from Surveys

In this section, we review two sets of studies that make direct comparisons of income and employment measurements across several data sources for the same individual and/or family. We first consider the results of a comparison of measures of income and employment gathered from UI records in 11 states and from a survey for a sample of 42,564 adults who left JTPA programs during the 1986 program year. The findings from this study are described in Baj et al. (1991) and

Baj et al. (1992).[18] Of those terminees, 27,721 responded to all three of the questions that were mandatory for "terminees" of JTPA-sponsored programs, giving an overall response rate of 65.1 percent. The investigators had access to separate data files containing UI wage records for the full sample of terminees, where the latter information was drawn from the UI systems for the 11 Midwestern states included in this study. Baj et al. (1991) drew the following conclusions about estimating the post enrollment incomes of these JTPA terminees with these two alternative data sources:

> There are two major conclusions to be drawn from these analyses. First, there is ample evidence to suggest that the post-program survey data is substantially affected by the presence of non-response bias. While this conclusion is based largely on the examination of post-program employment experiences, it is suspected that the same conclusion would hold if the focus was on post-program earnings. The second conclusion is that the major source of this bias, i.e., the different post-program employment experiences of respondents and non-respondents who were employed at termination, is not addressed through current non-response adjustment procedures. The implication of these findings is that the estimates of post-program performance based on the information gathered through the post-program survey are not a true reflection of the actual post-program experiences of all JTPA terminees. (p. 35)

The survey they examined was not constructed in a way that allows comparisons of earnings reports. Instead, the presence of employment in a given quarter was compared across the survey and UI data. To do this, they sharply restrict the sample to people leaving Title II-A (JTPA) a week prior to the week containing the starting date of a fiscal quarter. For data reasons three states also were dropped from the sample.[19] This left 1,285 participants, of which 863 responded to the survey. Even with these sample restrictions, employment comparisons are not completely straightforward because UI earnings are reported for the quarter in which they are paid, not the quarter in which they are earned. With these issues in mind, Table 9-4 shows the result of the comparisons.

The diagonal elements in Table 9-4 show that 81.7 percent (72.8 percent + 8.9 percent) of the UI-survey observations are in agreement on employment status. The lower off diagonal element indicates that 5.1 percent of the matched sample report that they were unemployed during the quarter, yet they had UI earnings. One might think welfare recipients would be reluctant to report earnings, but they were only slightly (5.4 percent) more likely to not report earnings (when they had positive UI earnings) than nonrecipients (4.4 percent). This result has two potential explanations. First, respondents may have earned the UI wages reported for the quarter during the previous quarter and subsequently lost their

---

[18]Stevens et al. (1994) is a similar study that focuses on Maryland.

[19]Title II-A is the nation's employment and training program for low-income adults and out-of-school youth with significant barriers to employment.

TABLE 9-4 Comparison of the Employment Status Results for the 13-Week Program Survey and UI Wage Record Data. Title II-A Adult Survey Population

Post Program Survey Status	First Quarter UI Status		Total
	Employed	Unemployed	
Employed	628 (72.8%)	114 (13.2%)	742 (86%)
Unemployed	44 (5.1%)	77 (8.9%)	121 (14%)
Total	672 (77.9%)	191 (22.1%)	863 (100%)

SOURCE: Baj et al. (1992:39).

jobs. Second, respondents may have provided inaccurate reports. Given that many of these 44 cases were employed at the time they left JTPA, Baj et al. (1991) suggest the second explanation is more likely than the first.

The upper diagonal element shows that 13.2 percent of the sample report being employed yet have no UI wages.[20] Again, it is possible that the timing of UI wage reports can partially account for this discrepancy, though most of these people were employed at the time they left JTPA, so this again is an unlikely explanation. Instead, it is likely that some of these people were employed out of state, and that others had jobs that were not covered by UI.[21]

Baj et al. (1992) update the Baj et al. (1991) calculations and provide more detail on the potential sources of discrepancy between UI data and the survey that was administered. In 1987, 11.3 percent of the sample report being unemployed for the quarter but have UI data (the corresponding figure from the earlier study was 5.1 percent), and 9.1 percent have no UI record but report they are employed (the corresponding figure from the earlier study was 13.2 percent). Baj et al. (1992) discuss three possible reasons to explain cases that claim to be employed but show no UI record.[22] The respondent may have been employed out-of-state or employed in the quarter but have wages that were not paid until the next quarter, or are employed in a job not covered by UI or where the employer fails to report UI wages.

[20]Although this figure would appear to be comparable to Blakemore et al. (1996), it actually suggests a much smaller gap in coverage. This study found a 13.6-percent gap for the total workforce, while the Baj et al. (1991) study found that the corresponding gap is 13.2 percent for a JTPA sample.

[21]Tabulations from the Wisconsin Department of Workforce Development (1999) suggest that as many as 16 percent (60/375) of a small sample of recent welfare recipients have missing employment episodes in UI data.

[22]They do not discuss independent contractor issues that are the focus of Blakemore et al. (1996). Instead, these would be grouped into the last category.

TABLE 9-5 Causes for Mismatches: Participants Employed at Termination With No UI Record for the Quarter of Termination, Illinois Program Year 1987, Title II-A Adult Population

Reason for Mismatch	Number of Cases	Percent
Employed out of state	517	15.3
Self-employed	51	1.5
Federal employment	172	5.1
Within program UI record	81	2.4
1st-quarter UI record	608	18.0
2nd-quarter UI record	93	2.7
No related UI record	1,865	55.0
No UI record	1,325	39.1
Mismatched employers	540	15.9
Total	3,387	100.0

SOURCE: Baj et al.(1992:142).

To look at these factors, the authors used data from the Illinois JTPA management information system, which gives detailed information on the employment status at termination of the program and compares that to UI status at termination. The analysis focuses on 3,387 cases (13.1 percent of the sample) that reported that JTPA participants were employed at termination, but there was no UI record for the termination quarter. Table 9-5 suggests some explanations for the mismatches (at the termination quarter). The table shows that out-of-state employment accounts for 15.3 percent of the discrepancies (line 1). Identifiable employment in uncovered (self-employed and federal appointments) sectors accounts for 6.6 percent of the discrepancy (lines 2 and 3). The next three rows of the table—the within, first-quarter, and second-quarter UI entries—are supposed to reflect timing differences in the data. Collectively these account for 23.1 percent of the discrepancy (lines 4, 5, and 6). Another 15.9 percent of the discrepancies seem to result from name mismatches between employers that could be reconciled fairly easily. This still leaves 39.1 percent of the remaining sample unexplained. Of this group of 1,325 participants, there were 1,108 different employers. The potential explanations for the discrepancy that Baj et al. (1992) offer include: errors in reporting the Social Security number on the JTPA or UI data systems, an employer's neglect of UI reporting requirements, and reporting errors by JTPA operators.

Baj et al. (1991) and Baj et al. (1992) examine the existence of employment in survey and UI data, but do not provide comparisons of earnings as their survey did not elicit information on earnings. Kornfeld and Bloom (1999) look at both employment and earnings. They describe their study as attempting "to determine whether wage records reported by employers to state unemployment insurance agencies provide a valid alternative to more costly retrospective sample surveys of individuals as the basis for measuring the impacts of employment and training programs for low-income persons" (p. 168). Kornfeld and Bloom (1999) is based on data covering 12,318 people from 12 sites around the country in which an experimental evaluation of JTPA training programs was conducted. For each site, they had access to data from both UI wage records and follow-up surveys of experimental (received JTPA services) and control (did not receive JTPA services) group members. In their analysis, they dropped observations with missing or imputed data, but included observations where earnings were recorded as zeros in the follow-up surveys.

Another, and slightly different, comparison of measurement of employment status and wage income across two different data sources for a sample of individuals who were provided access to JTPA services is found in Kornfeld and Bloom (1999). They assess how UI and survey data differ, where the latter was conducted as part of the National JTPA Study, in estimating the *levels* of earnings and the *differences* in mean earnings and employment rates between experimental and control group members, where control group members were denied access to JTPA services. Although the primary objective of the Kornfield and Bloom (1999) is how to assess how the estimated impacts of JTPA services on income and employment status vary by data source—they found virtually no difference in the estimates of impact by data source—we shall focus on what they found with respect to differences in levels of earnings across the two sources of income and employment data available to them.

Table 9-6, drawn from their study, shows that employment rates calculated from the two data sources are quite close. The discrepancies between employment data derived from their survey versus from UI records range anywhere from employment being 1 percent lower in surveys to being 11 percent more. At the same time, Kornfeld and Bloom find that the discrepancies in the *level* of earnings for JTPA participants are much greater. In particular, they consistently find that the level of earnings from survey data is higher than those found in UI data. The nature of this discrepancy in earnings measures is different from the one raised in Rolston (1999). Recall that Rolston is concerned that using UI wage data to measure the earnings of welfare leavers tends to be biased because such data do not include the income of other family members. Rolston argues that this lack of inclusion of the earnings of other family members is important given evidence that suggests that many exits from welfare are coincident with changes in family structure. The comparison in Table 9-6 from Kornfeld and Bloom (1999) focuses on only earnings reports for individuals. It documents systematic discrepancies of UI and survey data, where income reported by UI data is always substantially lower (in one case, by half) than that reported in survey data. Because the employment rates are comparable, Kornfeld and Bloom conclude that the earnings differences must reflect either differences in hours of work for JTPA participants who are recorded as being employed in a quarter, differences in the rate of pay recorded for this work, or both.

TABLE 9-6 Comparison of Quarterly Earnings and Employment Rates from UI and Survey Data

	Treatment Earnings ($)	Control Earnings ($)	Treatment Employment Rate (%)	Control Employment Rate (%)
Adult women (4,943; 18,275; 8,916)				
Survey data	1,294	1,141	59.2	54.5
UI data	1,048	922	57.6	54.1
Ratio (survey UI)	1.23	1.24	1.03	1.01
Adult men (3,651; 13,329; 6,482)				
Survey data	1,917	1,824	65.8	63.5
UI data	1,456	1,398	61.7	60.7
Ratio (survey/UI)	1.32	1.30	1.07	1.05
Female youth (2,113; 9,452; 4,316)				
Survey data	951	949	51.3	50.6
UI data	701	700	50.6	51.2
Ratio (survey/UI)	1.36	1.36	1.01	0.99
Male youths without a prior arrest (1,225; 5,009; 2,442)				
Survey data	1,556	1,655	65.5	69.3
UI data	1,015	1,103	61.3	63.2
Ratio (survey/UI)	1.53	1.50	1.07	1.10
Male youths with a prior arrest (386; 1,646; 705)				
Survey data	1,282	1,531	58.0	61.3
UI data	759	760	52.8	55.0
Ratio (survey/UI)	1.69	2.01	1.10	1.11

SOURCE: Kornfeld and Bloom (1999), Tables 1 and 2. Numbers after each panel heading reflect the number of persons represented (4,943 adult women) with the number of person-quarters in the treatment and control groups.

Kornfeld and Bloom (1999) also condition on whether a JTPA participant was receiving AFDC benefits during a particular quarter and find that, while the level of earnings is lower, the discrepancy between survey and UI data is strikingly similar. Survey earnings reports for adult women and female youth are 24 to 34 percent higher than reported UI earnings levels. There was also wide variation across JTPA sites in the size of earnings discrepancies between survey and UI data, but the survey always yielded larger numbers than did the UI data. The "ratio range" was 1.15 to 1.40 for adult women, 1.16 to 1.72 for adult men, 1.16 to 1.76 for female youth and even larger for male youth. Whatever the mechanism is generating these discrepancies, it exists across all 12 geographically diverse JTPA sites.

The dispersion of earnings discrepancies is very large, so the means mask large variations, across earnings reports. We do not know, of course, which measure of earnings more closely resembles the truth. If survey data tend to be more accurate, however, the discrepancies shown in Table 9-7 would be reason

TABLE 9-7 Distribution of Mean Individual-Level Differences Between
Survey and UI-Reported Quarterly Earnings

Mean Survey - Mean UI	Adult Women	Adult Men	Female Youth	Male Youth No Arrest	Male Youth With Arrest
$2,001 +	3.5	9.9	2.0	8.7	9.3
1,001–2,000	7.7	11.1	7.7	15.0	16.1
601-1,000	7.9	9.4	9.1	12.4	13.2
401-600	6.8	5.9	8.3	8.2	7.3
201-400	10.4	8.6	13.0	11.9	9.6
1-200	17.3	12.7	20.6	13.2	14.8
0	14.3	8.1	10.0	3.8	5.7
–$1 - –$200	16.2	13.2	17.3	10.8	11.1
–201- –400	6.2	6.2	5.3	5.6	6.0
–401 - –600	3.3	4.2	3.3	3.4	1.6
–601 - –1,000	3.4	4.6	2.0	4.5	3.4
–1,001 - –2,000	2.3	4.1	1.1	1.7	1.6
–2,001 -	0.9	2.0	0.2	0.8	0.5
Mean diff ($)	228	451	256	547	605

SOURCE: Table 5 from Kornfeld and Bloom (1999).

for one to give pause in using UI data to assess the economic well-being of families following welfare reform. It shows that more than 10 percent of women and 20 percent of men have discrepancies that exceed $1,000 in a quarter.[23]

Kornfeld and Bloom (1999) also examine those JTPA participants for whom they found positive earnings in one data source but not the other. "When only the survey reported employment (and UI data presumably missed it), mean earnings were more than twice what they were when only UI data reported employment (and the surveys presumably missed it). This suggests that surveys are more likely to miss 'low earnings' quarters, perhaps because respondents forget about minor, or short-term, jobs. In contrast, UI data appear more likely to miss 'average earnings' quarters—where mean earnings are similar to when both data sources report employment. This might be due to random errors in matching UI wage records, out-of-state jobs, jobs that are not covered by UI, and/or earnings that are 'off the books.'" (p. 184)

The above-noted discrepancies could arise between the data sources because some jobs are uncovered, some jobs may be located out of state, some payments may go unreported because of unintentional or intentional noncompliance, or

[23]All zeros in the table correspond to people without earnings in both data sets. No observations with positive earnings agreed exactly.

Social Security numbers may be misreported. To provide further insight, Kornfeld and Bloom compare the earnings reports that employers make about their employees to state UI systems with those they make to the IRS. Although employers have an incentive to underreport earnings to the UI system (and hence avoid paying UI taxes), they have no incentive to conceal earnings when reporting to the IRS, because wages are a business expense that will lower tax payments. The sample for doing this comparison is smaller than the previous samples because each observation needs to be there for 4 consecutive quarters, corresponding to the calendar year. The ratio of mean IRS earnings to mean UI earnings ranged from 1.14 for adult women to 1.25 for male youth, so UI wage records clearly are missing earnings from some jobs.

Based on their analysis, Kornfeld and Bloom draw the following conclusions from their investigation.[24] Approximately half of the survey-UI earnings difference reflects earnings that are missing from UI wage records (by making use of the IRS data). Out-of-state jobs do not explain why UI wage records reported lower earnings than sample surveys. Uncovered jobs account for only a small part of the survey/UI earnings difference. There is little evidence consistent with recall bias in the survey data. There is no evidence that large survey discrepancies result from survey reports of "unusually good" jobs or weird reports of industry of employment. Survey discrepancies also do not appear to be driven by overtime or odd pay periods.

From the direct comparisons of the data sources used to measure income and employment status found in the studies reviewed above, we draw the following tentative conclusions about the differences between using survey versus UI data:

• Earnings in UI data generally appear be lower than earnings reported in survey data. The UI data may miss earnings from second or casual jobs. At the same time, surveys may *overstate* earnings. Smith (1997) provides a thorough comparison of a dataset of JTPA-eligible nonparticipants at 4 of the 16 JTPA training centers with data from the SIPP. He provides evidence that his JTPA survey may be biased upward, due to nonresponse bias (lower earners are not covered in the survey) and upward-biased measures of overtime and usual hours in the survey.

---

[24]A third comparative study assessing differences in income and employment across data sources was conducted by the Rockefeller Institute of Government (Primus et al., 1999). This study summarizes (in its Table 2) six studies that compare UI data and survey data. The studies include five that we do not review in this paper and those from Kornfeld and Bloom (1999), which we do review. The results from the Rockefeller Institute study differ somewhat from the Kornfeld and Bloom results. One of two other studies finds UI earnings are lower than survey data (though one found them nearly identical), like Kornfeld and Bloom. Several other studies suggest that employment rates from surveys were significantly higher (on the order of 20 percent) than employment rates from UI data, unlike the Kornfeld and Bloom evidence. We have not assessed the quality of these other studies.

• Employment rates derived from UI data are comparable to lower than those that result from survey data. We expect UI-based employment rates to be lower because of coverage problems with flexible workers and independent contractors. Surveys also suffer from nonresponse, however, so undercounts in both data sources may be comparable, making the UI-based rates similar to survey-based rates.

Overall Assessment of Using UI Administrative Data to Measure Income and Employment

Our review of the literature has pointed to three critical concerns that arise with using UI data to measure the earnings and employment of low-income and welfare-eligible populations. The concerns are as follows:

• First, earnings are available only for individuals, while changes in family composition upon exit from welfare have been shown to have a large bearing on economic well-being. UI data do not allow us to track these changes.

• Second, there appears to be a substantial problem with some workers being classified as independent contractors, and hence not entering the UI system. Overall gaps in coverage appear to be at least 13 percent and may be significantly higher.

• Third, even when wages are reported, they appear to be understated by at least 11 to 14 percent (based on the Kornfeld and Bloom comparisons with IRS data) and perhaps more than twice that (based on their comparisons with survey data). Smith (1997) shows, however, that survey responses also can be biased upward.

DATA FROM FEDERAL (AND STATE) INCOME TAX RETURNS

Although not widely used in past evaluations, wage and salary data from federal and state income tax returns represent an alternative to UI data for measuring the income and employment of low-income populations. Here we outline the potential strengths and weaknesses of these data sources and briefly summarize a recent comparison of UI wage and tax return data for a disadvantaged population drawn from the AFDC caseload in California.

Potential Strengths

Compared to using surveys or UI records, using tax return data for measuring the income and employment has at least two potential advantages. These are the following:

- The data are accurate. Taxpayers provide information under the threat of audit and there is third-party information reporting, so employers as well as recipients are reporting wage and salary information.
- The definition of income that is reported is broader than that provided by unemployment insurance data, including, most importantly, self-employment income and in cases where a person is married and they file a joint return, spousal income.[25]

Potential Weaknesses

Several potential weaknesses are associated with using tax returns data to measure income and employment. We summarize several: Note that some of these weaknesses apply to the general population, while others are more relevant for low-income populations. First, the access by researchers to tax returns data is extremely limited and constrained because of Section 6103 of the Internal Revenue Code. Section 6103 explicitly states that tax data cannot be released, except to organizations specifically designated in Section 6103(j). The exceptions are the Department of Commerce, but only as it relates to the Census and National Income Accounts, the Federal Trade Commission, the Department of the Treasury, and the Department of Agriculture (for conducting the Census of Agriculture). Penalties for unauthorized disclosure are severe, including jail terms of up to 5 years.

Second, tax return data also contain only limited information on demographic characteristics of taxpayers. For example, the tax system does not collect information on the race or education of tax filers.

Third, tax-filing units differ from both families and individuals. Married couples can file either a joint return or separate returns (as "married filing separate"). Cohabiting couples, even if fully sharing resources, will file separate returns as individuals or head of household (generally meaning the filer is a single parent with dependents). In general we believe families pool resources so families are the best unit of analysis for assessing economic well-being. Hence, case units probably are the most useful unit of analysis.

Fourth, there also are differences between tax return data and other data sources in the frequency of reporting. Unemployment insurance wages are reported quarterly. Transfer program information is reported monthly. Tax returns are filed annually. Because shorter periods can be aggregated into longer ones and there can be major changes in family composition over time, the annual frequency of tax reporting is less appealing than monthly or quarterly reporting in other data sets. To the extent that family structure changes over these intervals, problems may arise when trying to link different data sets to assess well-being.

---

[25]It also will include interest and dividend income, farm income, capital gains and losses, and gambling winnings, and indicate recipients of government transfers and Social Security benefits.

A fifth concern relates to the incidence and accuracy of tax filing by individuals and households, especially among low-income populations. This concern takes two forms: (1) whether people file any tax return, and (2) if they file, whether they report all sources of income to the IRS (or state taxing authorities).[26] We consider each in turn.

If large fractions of low-income taxpayers do not file tax returns, then tax return data have very limited value. Unfortunately, there is not a lot of information on the filing propensities of people with low income. Information from the early 1990s (Scholz, 1994) suggests that 14 to 20 percent of those entitled to the earned income tax credit at the time failed to receive it, meaning that they failed to file tax returns.[27] Later, we discuss one recent study on the tax filing propensities of a low-income population that sheds some preliminary light on this issue.

Among filing units, it is also possible that their members do not report all of their sources of income on their tax returns. For example, individuals may fail to file income received as independent contractors. Although firms or individuals who use independent contractors are obligated to report payments to such contractors to the IRS, failures to do this generally are difficult to detect. Again, we know little about the incidence of underreporting of various income sources for low-income populations.

To summarize, using tax return data to measure income and employment has several potential weaknesses. These are the following:

- Gaining access to tax returns is difficult.
- The data provide limited information on demographic and other characteristics.
- Some low-income workers may not file, despite being eligible for the earned income tax credit, or may not report all their income.

Comparison of Income Reporting from UI Wage and IRS Tax Filings Data for a Low-Income Population

In a recent study of the EITC for a sample of assistance units on the California caseload, Hill et al. (1999) compared UI wage data with linked data from the

---

[26]If one is just interested in enumerating the population (as opposed to knowing incomes associated with families and individuals within the population), IRS data appear to be comprehensive. Sailer and Weber (1999) report that the IRS population count is 95.4 percent of the Census population count. The consistency is fairly good across gender, age, and state. Unfortunately, for many of the people enumerated, the IRS does not know anything about them other than that they exist.

[27]Cilke (1998) uses a CPS-IRS exact match file to examine the characteristics of people who are not required to file tax returns and actually did not file tax returns. The entire paper is presented as proportions, however, so it does not provide information on the absolute number of low-income families with earnings who fail to file.

sample members' IRS tax returns. The study used data from the California Work Pays Demonstration Project (CWPDP), which was conducted in four counties (Alameda, Los Angeles, San Bernardino, and San Joaquin) starting in 1992. The data consisted of two sets of assistance units drawn from the caseloads in these counties. One set, which is used for the sample in Table 9-8, consisted of a random sample drawn from a caseload at a particular date in 1992. Although this sample is representative of the caseload at that time, recall that the study by Bane and Ellwood (1983) showed that random samples from the existing caseload of AFDC are disproportionately made up of assistance units that are "welfare dependent."

The second set of assistance units, which is the sample used for Table 9-9, is a random sample of new entrants to the caseload in 1993. Bane and Ellwood (1983) and others have found that a significant proportion of new entrants remain on welfare for only a relatively short period.[28] Furthermore, Gritz and MaCurdy (1991) find that most new entrants exit from AFDC to employment. We also break both samples up into female-headed households (Aid to Families with Dependent Children-Family Group AFDC-FG cases) and two-parent households (AFDC-U). We report on annual earnings information for the year after the samples were drawn, that is, 1993 for the random sample of the caseload and 1994 for the new entrants sample.[29]

The first two lines of each panel of each table give estimates of the employment rates of each sample of AFDC recipients. As expected, employment rates of the point-in-time caseload (Table 9-8) are lower than the sample of new entrants (Table 9-9). Employment rates of one-parent cases (AFDC-FG) are lower than the employment rates of two-parent cases (Aid to Families with Dependent Children-Unemployed Parent [AFDC-U]). What is striking and not necessarily expected, however, is that the implied employment rates using UI data and using tax return data are nearly identical. From Table 9-8, employment rates of the point-in-time AFDC-FG caseload were 26 percent using UI data and 22 percent using tax return data. The corresponding rates for AFDC-U cases were 31 percent for both data sources. Employment rates were 37 percent using UI data for the new entrant sample and 33 percent using tax returns. Employment rates were 48 percent using UI data for the AFDC-U new entrants and 49 percent using tax returns.

---

[28]For example, Bane and Ellwood (1983) estimate that 65 percent of new entrants leave the caseload in 2 years.

[29]Through an interagency agreement between the California Department of Social Services (CDSS) and the state's taxing authority, the Franchise Tax Board (FTB), UI wages and wages and adjusted gross income (AGI) from tax returns were merged by the FTB. The researchers were able to specify computer runs on these merged files. Assistance units in the study could, and did, leave AFDC after they were enrolled in this study. Nonetheless, wage and income data from UI records and tax returns were available for all of the original assistance units in the CWPDP study.

TABLE 9-8 Random Sample from Caseload in 1992, Information for Tax
Year 1993

	Those Filing Tax Returns	Full Sample
AFDC-FG cases		
% of households with UI earnings		26
% of households that filed tax returns		22
Average UI earnings ($) of adults in household	4,514	1,242
Average adjusted gross earnings ($) on tax returns	10,589	2,378
Average wage & salary earnings ($) on tax returns (Line 7)	9,748	2,189
Average income ($) reported to AFDC	1,222	360
% of households with No UI earnings, but filed tax return		5.89
% of households with UI earnings, but filed no tax return		11.41
% of households for which AGI < UI wages		12.61
% of households for which AGI = UI wages		78.59
% of households for which AGI > UI wages		8.80
% of households for which AGI < UI wages, for UI wages > 0		3.39
% of households for which AGI > UI wages, for AGI > 0		40.47
Self-employment income ($) reported on tax returns		
Fraction of filers reporting any	0.06	
Average amount reported	357	
AFDC-U Cases		
% of households with UI earnings		31
% of households that filed tax returns		31
Average UI earnings ($) of adults in household	5,223	1,792
Average adjusted gross earnings ($) on tax returns	8,482	2,595
Average wage & salary earnings ($) on tax returns (line 7)	7,554	2,311
Average income ($) reported to AFDC	2,513	894
% of households with no UI earnings, but filed tax return		7.07
% of households with UI earnings, but filed no tax return		8.21
% of households for which AGI < UI wages		9.26
% of households for which AGI = UI wages		78.39
% of households for which AGI > UI wages		12.05
% of households for which AGI < UI Wages, for UI Wages > 0		3.97
% of households for which AGI > UI wages, for AGI > 0		40.53
Self-employment income ($) reported on tax returns		
Fraction of filers reporting any	0.12	
Average amount reported	562	

SOURCE: Hill et al. (1999).

Although tax return data and UI data would give similar perspectives about
employment patterns of the 4-county California sample, it is clear that each
sample covers workers that the other misses. For example, in the top panel of
Table 9-8 (AFDC-FG cases from the point-in-time sample), roughly one-quarter

TABLE 9-9 Random Sample of New Entrants to AFDC Caseload in 1993, Information for Tax Year 1994

	Those Filing Tax Returns	Full Sample
AFDC-FG cases		
% of households with UI earnings		37
% of households that filed tax returns		33
Average UI earnings ($) of adults in household	6,769	2,868
Average adjusted gross earnings ($) on tax returns	13,185	4,342
Average wage & salary earnings ($) on tax returns (Line 7)	12,575	4,141
Average income ($) reported to AFDC	1,625	709
% of households with no UI earnings, but filed tax return		8.34
% of households with UI earnings, but filed no tax return		13.55
% of households for which AGI < UI wages		15.69
% of households for which AGI = UI wages		71.31
% of households for which AGI > UI wages		13.00
% of households for which AGI < UI wages, for UI wages > 0		4.21
% of households for which AGI > UI wages, for AGI > 0		39.88
Self-employment income ($) reported on tax returns		
Fraction of filers reporting any	0.04	
Average amount reported	95	
AFDC-U cases		
% of households with UI earnings		48
% of households that filed tax returns		49
Average UI earnings ($) of adults in household	8,516	5,138
Average adjusted gross earnings ($) on tax returns	12,970	6,360
Average wage & salary earnings ($) on tax returns (Line 7)	11,421	5,601
Average income ($) reported to AFDC	3,264	1,831
% of households with no UI earnings, but filed tax return		10.45
% of households with UI earnings, but filed no tax return		7.94
% of households for which AGI < UI wages		11.77
% of households for which AGI = UI wages		64.71
% of households for which AGI > UI wages		23.51
% of households for which AGI < UI wages, for UI Wages > 0		6.12
% of households for which AGI > UI wages, for AGI > 0		46.83
Self-employment income ($) reported on tax returns		
Fraction of filers reporting any	0.11	
Average amount reported	512	

SOURCE: Hill et al. (1999).

of people (5.89/22) who filed tax returns had no corresponding UI record.[30] Over 40 percent (11.41/26) of those with positive UI earnings did not file taxes.[31] Of

---

[30]We took great care in the analysis to make sure the comparison samples did not have changes in marital status and had a full four quarters of UI data (including zero quarters).

[31]Households with low earnings are not obligated to file tax returns. For example, a married

those with both UI and tax return earnings, more than 40 percent reported more earnings on tax returns than would be expected based on UI data. Similar figures apply to each other group, though for AFDC-U cases, only about 20 percent of the cases with UI earnings do not file tax returns.

The fact that across all four groups (two samples, and AFDC-FG and AFDC-U cases), tax return income exceeded UI income in at least 40 percent of the cases with positive earnings from both sources, is consistent with households from this welfare-based population having earnings that are not from covered employment. The fact does not seem to be explained by people leaving welfare (through changes in family structure). Among AFDC-FG cases, only 1 to 13 percent of these households had no months on AFDC during the tax reference year and between 56 and 83 percent were on welfare for 9 to 12 months during that year. There is also little evidence that self-employment income plays an important role in earnings differences between tax return and UI income.

Based on comparisons between UI and tax return data, we offer several tentative conclusions:

• Tax return and UI data appear to give very similar information on employment rates of the four-county California caseload. There are good reasons, however, to think that both data sources will lead to underestimates. UI data will miss independent contractors and possibly other "flexible workers." Tax return data will miss families who do not file tax returns.

• The two data sources appear highly *complementary*. Each appears to capture a significant number of families that the other misses. Using them together, therefore, should result in more accurate measures of the employment experiences of the caseload than using either separately.

• Tax return data have a broader definition of income and, if the household unit is married, will cover both spouses and hence are likely to offer more accurate income information.

• UI data are much easier to access than tax returns.

RECOMMENDATIONS

Taking into account all of the features of a data source, including not only its accuracy but also its cost and ease of access, it appears that no single source can be declared "preferred." The inability to find a preferred data source is inevitable given the differences in the desired uses of data, the constraints imposed by budgets for data collection, and the access limitations to data. The fact that UI

---

couple, is not required to file if their income is below the standard deduction and two exemptions ($12,200 in 1997), regardless of how many children they have. Hill et al. (1999) also show that most of these non filers had very low levels of UI earnings ($2,500 or less in annual covered earnings).

wage data are inexpensive, timely to obtain, and available at the state level, for example, implies that they will continue to be a focal data set for state-level evaluations of welfare reform. But our review raises a number of serious questions about UI data. In the remainder of this paper, we highlight selected issues that we believe need further attention in the hopes of encouraging future research on at least some of them.

Certain questions related to welfare reform can only be answered with nationally representative data sets, such as the CPS or SIPP. While Moore et al. (1990) and Roemer (1999a) conclude that income, especially labor earnings, are measured well in the CPS and SIPP, there are, in our view, several important questions that remain with respect to income and employment measurements for low-income populations with national surveys. The questions are as follows:

• First, none of these studies, to our knowledge, focus on the reporting of income by disadvantaged, welfare-eligible, and/or welfare-prone populations.
• Second, as noted in Primus et al. (1999), participation in welfare programs is underreported in the CPS (and the SIPP). Moreover, this underreporting appears to have increased over time. This is a troubling problem, especially as one looks to the future when TANF programs become state specific, with different names.

Recommendation 1: We would like to see further work on the sources of antipoverty program underreporting and its origins in nationally representative survey data.

Plans are under way for some of the needed work. Professor Hotz is a principal investigator on a project recently approved by the U.S. Census Bureau to match data from UI wage records and administrative data on AFDC/TANF participation for the California subsamples of several waves of the SIPP.[32] The work of this project should yield some more recent information on both the welfare participation underreporting and income reporting issues. This study—or comparable ones done with matches of the SIPP with administrative data for the subsamples from other states— also may provide some insight into the impact of changes in family structure on income reporting for welfare leavers by exploiting the (limited) panel structure of the SIPP.

Further research also is needed on the use of UI wage records to measure the income of low-income and welfare-prone populations. While the Kornfeld and Bloom (1999) evaluation suggested that UI wage data and survey data produced similar estimates of the impact of a social program (i.e., JTPA-funded training programs) on earnings and employment, their study also found that average earnings of JTPA-eligible individuals were consistently lower than those based

[32]The other investigators on this project are in collaboration with David Card, Andrew Hildreth, and Michael Clune at University of California-Berkeley and Robert Schoeni at RAND.

on survey data. Furthermore, the study by Hill et al. (1999) also found that UI wage data produced substantially lower estimates of earnings than did tax returns data for a welfare-based population drawn from the California AFDC caseload. Learning more about the quality of this data source for measuring income is extremely important because UI wage data presumably will continue to be a core resource in state and local evaluations of the effects of welfare reform.

Several issues related to UI wage data appear to need further scrutiny. First, the studies by Burgess and his coauthors raises important concerns about the "coverage" of UI and tax returns, particularly for the low-income population.

Recommendation 2: It would be extremely useful to follow the helpful lead of the various Burgess studies to closely examine the coverage and trends in coverage of low-income populations with UI data. Such an examination could be aided by using a match of UI data with respondents in a national survey, such as the SIPP, so that one could learn more about the demographic characteristics of individuals (and households) that report labor market earnings on a survey that are not recorded in UI wage records data.

• States may be able to augment UI data used for evaluation of welfare reform by collecting supplemental information on the degree to which employers are designating workers as independent contractors. Additional work at the state level to assess the overall coverage of UI data also would be valuable.

Second, more work is needed to understand the extent to which UI wage data provide a misleading measure of the earnings available to low-income *households*. This problem arises in short- and long-term follow-up analyses of earnings for welfare samples drawn from state caseloads. One can use UI data to measure subsequent earnings for individuals who were in assistance units as long as they remain on welfare. However, as noted by Rolston (1999), one may not be able to accurately measure household income *after* assistance units leave the rolls because it is difficult to keep track of the identities of household members. The evidence provided in the Meyer and Cancian (1998) and Hill et al. (1999) studies suggest that this *may* be a serious problem.

Recommendation 3: To learn more about family well-being, it will be necessary to continue to rely on targeted follow-up surveys to monitor samples of welfare leavers. Unfortunately surveys are expensive. We recommend that a pilot study be undertaken to devise a survey that is designed just to obtain Social Security numbers of other adults in a household, which can then be used to obtain UI wage earnings for these family members.

• It might be useful for state TANF agencies to analyze the methods that their JTPA agencies use to gather follow-up earnings data on terminees from their programs. Such follow-up assessments are required under JTPA, and many states have contracted with firms and/or universities to gather these follow-up data.

• Tax returns data also may be useful to learn more about whether the discrepancies between UI wage data and income measures from tax returns noted in that study are the result of differences in family composition and the "composition" of income reported on tax returns.

A third issue relates to the possibility that wage earnings are missed because individuals move out of the state from which UI wage data are drawn or because workers earn part of their income in other states. Again, comparisons of UI wage data with data from federal tax returns may help us to assess the importance of this problem and, more importantly, the biases that it imparts on measures of individual and household income. To learn more, it may be useful to take a closer look at what is known about the interstate mobility of disadvantaged and welfare-prone populations, such as the work done on movements of welfare populations in response to "welfare magnets," as in Meyer (1999) and the citations therein, and the implications this mobility has for the coverage of low-income workers in UI data.

REFERENCES

Abraham, Katherine G., James R. Spletzer, and Jay C. Stuart
   1998   Divergent trends in alternative wage series. Pp. 293-324 in *Labor Statistics Measurement Issues*, J. Haltiwanger, M. Manser, and R. Topel, eds. National Bureau of Economic Research Studies in Income and Wealth, Volume 60. University of Chicago Press.
Baj, John, Sean Fahey, and Charles E. Trott
   1992   Using unemployment insurance wage-record data for JTPA performance management. In Chapter 4 of Research Report 91-07. Chicago: National Commission for Employment Policy.
Baj, John, Charles E. Trott, and David Stevens
   1991   A Feasibility Study of the Use of Unemployment Insurance Wage-Record Data as an Evaluation Tool for JTPA: Report on Project Phase 1 Activities. Chicago: National Commission on Employment Policy, January.
Bane, Mary Jo, and David T. Ellwood
   1983   *The Dynamics of Dependence: The Routes to Self-Sufficiency*. Prepared for the U.S. Department of Health and Human Services, Office of the Assistant Secretary for Planning and Evaluation. Cambridge, MA: Urban Systems Research and Engineering, Inc.
Blakemore, Arthur E., Paul L. Burgess, Stuart A. Low, and Robert D. St. Louis
   1996   Employer tax evasion in the unemployment insurance program. *Journal of Labor Economics* 14(2):210-230.
Bogen, Karen, Meredith Lee, Julia Klein Griffiths, and Anne Polivka
   1997   Income Supplement—Summary and Recommendations from Cognitive Interviews, Unpublished paper, Bureau of the Census, Bureau of Labor Statistics, September.

Bogen, Karen
  1998   Once Upon a Time, There Was Welfare Reform: Evaluating the New March CPS Welfare-Related Questions: Results from the 1998 Respondent Debriefing. Unpublished paper, Bureau of the Census, June.
Bollinger, Christopher R., and Martin H. David
  2001   Estimation with response error and non-response: Food stamp participation in the SIPP. *Journal of Business and Economic Statistics* 19(a):129-141.
Bound, John, and Alan B. Krueger
  1991   The extent of measurement error in longitudinal earnings data: Do two wrongs make a right? *Journal of Labor Economics* 9(1):1-24.
Burgess, Paul L., Arthur E. Blakemore, and Stuart A. Low
  1996   Using statistical profiles to improve unemployment insurance tax compliance. *Research in Employment Policy* 1:243-2711.
Cancian, Maria, Robert Haveman, Thomas Kaplan, and Barbara Wolfe
  1999   *Post-Exit Earnings and Benefit Receipt Among Those Who Left AFDC in Wisconsin.* Institute for Research on Poverty, Special Report No. 75. Madison, WI: University of Wisconsin.
Cilke, Jim
  1998   A Profile of Non-Filers. OTA Paper #78, Office of Tax Analysis, U.S. Department of Treasury, Washington, DC.
Coder, J., and L.S. Scoon-Rogers
  1996   Evaluating the Quality Income Data Collection in the Annual Supplement to the March Current Population Survey and the Survey of Income and Program Participation. SIPP Working Paper 96-04.
Coder, John
  1992   Using administrative record information to evaluate the quality of the income data collected in the SIPP. Pp. 295-306 in *Proceedings of Statistics Canada Symposium 92: Design and Analysis of Longitudinal Surveys*, Ottawa: Statistics Canada.
Goodreau, K., H. Oberheu, and D. Vaughan
  1984   An assessment of the quality of survey reports of income from the Aid to Families with Dependent Children (AFDC) program. *Journal of Business and Economic Statistics* 2:179-186.
Greenberg, David, and Harlan Halsey
  1983   Systematic misreporting and the effects of income maintenance experiments on work effort: Evidence from the Seattle-Denver experiment. *Journal of Labor Economics* 1:380-407.
Gritz, R.M, and T. MaCurdy
  1991   *Patterns of Welfare Utilization and Multiple Program Participation Among Young Women.* Report to the U.S. Department of Health and Human Services under Grant 88-ASPE 198A.
Halsey, Harlan
  1978   Validating income data: Lessons from the Seattle and Denver income maintenance experiment, pp. 21-51 in *Proceedings of the Survey of Income and Program Participation Workshop*, U.S. Department of Health, Education and Welfare, Washington, DC.
Hill, Carolyn, V.J. Hotz, Charles Mullin, and John Karl Scholz
  1999   EITC Eligibility, Participation and Compliance Rates for AFDC Households: Evidence from the California Caseload. Report submitted to the California Department of Social Services, April.

Houseman, Susan N.
  1999   Flexible Staffing Arrangements: A Report on Temporary Help, On-Call, Direct-Hire Tem-
          porary, Leased, Contract Company, and Independent Contractors Employment in the
          United States, August. Available: http://www.dol.gov/asp/futurework/conference/staffing/
          intro.htm [September 7, 2001]
Internal Revenue Service
  1996   *Federal Tax Compliance Research: Individual Income Tax Gap Estimates for 1985, 1988,
          and 1992.* Publication 1415 (Rev. 4-96). Washington, DC.
Kornfeld, Robert, and Howard S. Bloom
  1999   Measuring program impacts on earnings and employment: Do unemployment insurance
          wage reports from employers agree with surveys of individuals? *Journal of Labor Eco-
          nomics* 17(January):168-197.
Lamas, E., T. Palumbo, and J. Eargle
  1996   The Effect of the SIPP Redesign on Employment and Earnings Data. SIPP Working
          Paper 9606.
Lamas, E., J. Tin, and J. Eargle
  1994   The Effect of Attrition on Income and Poverty Estimates from the Survey of Income and
          Program Participation (SIPP). SIPP Working Paper 190.
Marquis, K.H., and C.J. Moore
  1990   Measurement errors in SIPP program reports. Pp. 721-745 in *Proceedings of the Bureau
          of the Census 1990 Annual Research Conference.*
Meyer, Daniel R., and Maria Cancian
  1998   Economic well-being following an exit from Aid to Families with Dependent Children.
          Journal of Marriage and the Family 60(2):479-492.
Meyer, Bruce D.
  1999   Do the Poor Move to Receive Higher Welfare Benefits? Unpublished paper, Northwest-
          ern University Economics Department, October.
Moore, J., K. Marquis, and K. Bogen
  1996   The SIPP Cognitive Research Evaluation Experiment: Basic Results and Documentation.
          Bureau of the Census, January.
Moore, Jeffrey C., Linda L. Stinson, and Edward J. Welniak, Jr.
  1997   Income Measurement Error in Surveys: A Review. Statistical Research Report. U.S. Cen-
          sus Bureau.
Nelson, Charles T., Marc I. Roemer, Daniel H. Weinberg, and Edward J. Welniak, Jr.
  1998   Fifty Years of United States Income Data from the Current Population Survey. Unpub-
          lished paper, Housing and Household Economics Statistics Division, Bureau of the Cen-
          sus. December.
Polivka, Anne P.
  1997   Using Earnings Data from the Current Population Survey After the Redesign. Unpub-
          lished paper. Bureau of Labor Statistics.
  1998   Note on the Possible Effects of Welfare Reform on Labor Market Activities: What Can
          Be Gleaned from the March CPS. Unpublished paper, Bureau of Labor Statistics. Decem-
          ber 1.
Primus, Wendell, Lynette Rawlings, Kathy Larin, and Kathryn Porter
  1998   After Welfare: A Study of Work and Benefit Use After Case Closing in New York State.
          Revised interim report submitted to the Office of the Assistant Secretary for Planning and
          Evaluation, U.S. Department of Health and Human Services, December.
  1999   *The Initial Impacts of Welfare Reform on the Incomes of Single-Mother Families.* Wash-
          ington, DC: Center for Budget and Policy Priorities.Rockefeller Institute of Government.

Rodgers, Willard L., Charles Brown, and Greg J. Duncan
   1993   Errors in survey reports of earnings, hours worked, and hourly wages. *Journal of American Statistical Association* 88(December):1208-1218.
Roemer, Marc
   1999   Assessing the Quality of the March Current Population Survey and the Survey of Income and Program Participation Income Estimates, 1990-1996. Unpublished paper, Income Statistics Branch, Bureau of the Census, June 16.
   2000   Reconciling March CPS Money Income with the National Income and Product Accounts: An Evaluation of CPS Quality. Unpublished paper, Income Statistics Branch, Bureau of the Census, August 10.
Rolston, Howard
   1999   The Income of Former Welfare Recipients. Unpublished paper, Administration on Children and Families, U.S. Department of Health and Human Services, September 21.
Sailer, Peter, and Michael Weber
   1999   The IRS population count: An Update. Pp. 85-89, In *Turning Administrative Systems into Information Systems.*
Scholz, John Karl
   1994   The earned income tax credit: Participation, compliance and anti-poverty effectiveness. *National Tax Journal* (March):59-81.
Shroder, Mark, and Marge Martin
   1996   New Results from Administrative Data: Housing the Poor, or, What They Don't Know Might Hurt Somebody. Unpublished paper, Office of Policy Development and Research, U.S. Department of Housing and Urban Development.
Smith, Jeffrey
   1997   Measuring Earnings Levels Among the Poor: Evidence from Two Samples of JTPA Eligibles. Unpublished paper, Department of Economics, University of Western Ontario, June.
Stevens, David W., Liping Chen, and Jinping Shi
   1994   The Use of UI Wage Records for JTPA Performance Management in Maryland. Unpublished paper, The Jacob France Center at the University of Baltimore, September 19.
U.S. Department of Commerce, Bureau of the Census
   1998   SIPP Quality Profile, 1998. SIPP Working Paper Number 230, Third Edition.
Wisconsin Department of Workforce Development
   1999   Differences Between AFDC and W-W Leavers Survey Data for January-March 1998 and Wisconsin's UI Wage Records for 1998. DWD MEP Folio Brief 01-99, October 19.
Yen, W., and H. Nelson
   1996   Testing the Validity of Public Assistance Surveys with Administrative Records: A Validation Study of Welfare Survey Data, unpublished manuscript, May 1996.

10

Administrative Data on the Well-Being of Children On and Off Welfare

Richard Barth, Eleanor Locklin-Brown, Stephanie Cuccaro-Alamin, and Barbara Needell

The Personal Responsibility and Work Opportunity Reconciliation Act of 1996 (PRWORA) significantly altered the way the United States provides assistance to its neediest citizens. The act eliminated the federal entitlement to services that existed under the Aid to Families with Dependent Children (AFDC) program and replaced it with the block grant program Temporary Assistance for Needy Families (TANF). TANF provides temporary financial assistance while recipients make the mandatory transition from welfare to work. These efforts to move adult recipients toward self-sufficiency may have consequences for the well-being of their children (Collins and Aber, 1996; Zaslow et al., 1998). Potential implications include changes in children's health, safety, education, and social competence.

Whether these consequences are positive or negative depends on how reforms impact family income, parenting practices or parental stress, and access to services (Collins and Aber, 1996; Zaslow et al., 1998). For example, economic hardship related to loss of benefits or other supports may complicate families' efforts to provide supportive environments for their children (Knitzer and Bernard, 1997). Increased parental stress related to economic, employment, or child care difficulties also may lead to poor parent/child interactions or exacerbate existing mental health conditions such as depression or substance abuse, thereby increasing the risk of negative outcomes (Knitzer and Bernard, 1997; Zaslow et al., 1998). Child health and safety also might be compromised if TANF alters access to non-TANF services such as health and childcare.

In contrast, positive changes in these areas may be beneficial to children and families (Collins and Aber, 1996; Zaslow et al., 1998). Specifically, policy changes might lead to improved outcomes for children whose parents become employed successfully. Children might benefit from access to more comprehensive health care, opportunities to observe parents coping effectively with work demands, higher educational aspirations and achievement, and exposure to parental peers who are engaged in more prosocial activities.

PRWORA currently is being praised by some, and criticized by others, for moving nearly 1.7 million recipients from welfare to work. However, until the impact of these reforms on child well-being is known, such celebrations are premature. Even if reforms succeed in moving mothers from welfare to work, if this in turn has negative consequences for children, its effectiveness will need to be reevaluated in light of these costs.

Prior to passage of welfare-to-work legislation, more than 40 states received waivers to experiment with welfare-to-work programs. Experimental evaluations of these initiatives now under way will provide valuable information about possible effects of certain aspects of PRWORA. Most, however, focus primarily on adult outcomes such as changes in income, employment, family formation, and attitude, and cover only a limited number of child outcomes (Research Forum on Children, Families, and the New Federalism, 1999; Yaffe, 1998). Additionally, those child outcomes "typically lack depth and uniformity" (Yaffe, 1998). Several states (e.g., Connecticut, Florida, Iowa, and Minnesota) are looking at child outcomes resulting from parental participation in AFDC waiver conditions that approximate TANF and that eventually will yield child-level outcome data. The Administration for Children and Families (ACF), Office of the Assistant Secretary for Planning and Evaluation (ASPE) in the Department of Health and Human Services has implemented the Project on State-Level Child Outcomes to assist waiver states in using administrative data to expand these child outcome measures and make them comparable across states. Although this uniformity will allow for the assessment of different state models, their utility is limited by their small sample sizes. In particular, small sample sizes make subgroup comparisons difficult and prohibit evaluation of rare events such as foster care placement or child mortality. Current evaluations of state welfare-to-work initiatives under PRWORA suffer from similar limitations. Given these limitations, researchers increasingly are turning to administrative data to try to gauge the relationship between receiving income assistance services under TANF and child well-being.

The purpose of this paper is to assist researchers in addressing the following questions:

• What are the key policy issues and related domains of child well-being associated with the impact of PRWORA?
• What are the opportunities and challenges in using administrative data to measure the impact of PRWORA on children?

KEY POLICY ISSUES AND CHILD WELL-BEING

Data about social welfare programs for children are fragmented and incomplete and lack a cohesive framework or policy ownership. Given this, it is important to identify the priority of policy issues and the specific research questions about PRWORA and child well-being when research is conducted. These early steps will assist in then defining the population of interest, the appropriate methodology, and the data sources available (National Research Council, 1999).

Key Policy Issues

Several key policy issues have been identified for states examining the impact of welfare reform (Child Trends, 2000a; National Conference of State Legislators, 1999). First is the need to understand the specific components of an individual state's welfare reform program. This is especially important given the diversity across states in the implementation of PRWORA and corresponding use of TANF funds. Specific components left up to the states include mandated work, time limits, and sanctions. The implementation of these components may impact the outcomes for families and children; for example, mandated work without childcare may lead to cases of child neglect. Also needed is an examination of the interaction between welfare reform—that is, the change from AFDC to TANF—and other social welfare programs such as Medicaid, Children's Health Insurance Program (CHIP), the Food Stamps Program, Special Supplemental Nutrition Program for Women, Infants, and Children (WIC), Child Protective Services, and foster care, which also may be undergoing changes. Although efforts over the past two decades have sought to delink AFDC to other social welfare programs, in practice and for individual families these programs remain interwoven. The eligibility, availability, and accessibility of these supplemental services can impact family outcomes in conjunction with, or separate from, TANF enrollment, exit, and reentry. Understanding TANF's impact on children requires thoughtful specification of the child well-being outcomes TANF might influence so that investigators can fashion data collection efforts to maximize measurement of the predicted impact. Research about child outcomes can guide questions about current implementation and future programming using the flexibility of TANF funds.

Domains of Child Well-Being

Child Trends, a nonprofit, nonpartisan research center, along with colleagues at the federal and state levels participating in the Project on State-Level Child Outcomes, have offered a conceptual framework that organizes and clarifies the pathways through which welfare reform can impact children. This framework is displayed in Figure 10-1.

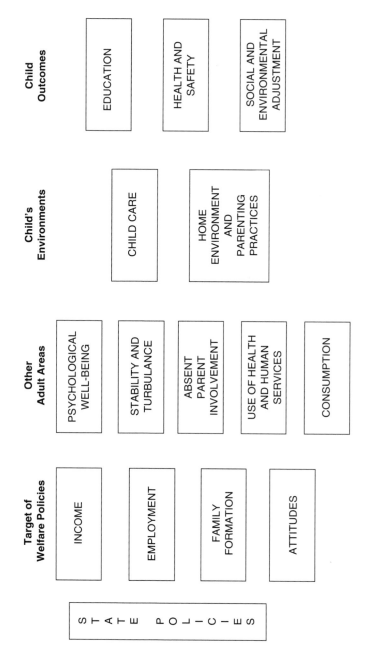

FIGURE 10-1 Child Trends, Inc. conceptual framework for child well-being—how welfare policies might affect children.
SOURCE: Child Trends (1999).

In this conceptual framework, state policies regarding **PRWORA** will directly effect family income, employment, family formation outcomes such as marriage or out-of-wedlock births, and attitudes of the adults in the case, such as self-esteem or feelings of being in control of one's life. Changes in these four areas will further influence the family and child's psychological well-being, the stability of the child's home, involvement of the absent parent (through child support enforcement), use of health and human services, and consumption of goods and services spent on the child. As a single mother copes with job training, new employment, transportation problems, childcare dilemmas, and confusion about eligibility for supplemental services, the child's physical home environment, relationship to the parent, and time with the parent can be expected to change. Such changes in the capacity and day-to-day schedule of maternal caretaking very likely will, in turn, impact the child's educational experiences, health and safety, and social and emotional adjustment.

This conceptual framework evinces the multifaceted ways that welfare programs can influence a range of child outcomes. The framework offers a critical organizing logic about how welfare reform impacts children, one that can be used to shape research agendas and frame research questions. The framework was developed to guide survey researchers studying about welfare, but it also serves as a useful reference for the inclusion of administrative data in research initiatives. Administrative data are far more useful for estimating some components of this model than others. Specifically, administrative data rarely contain in-depth information about parental psychological well-being or home environment, parenting practices, or social and emotional adjustment of children. Survey research is much better suited to these components. Administrative data can, however, be used to estimate family stability and turbulence through the inclusion of information about household changes and movement in and out of foster care. Administrative data also can help explain the changes in the utilization of supplemental health and human services—especially Medicaid, CHIP, Food Stamps, or WIC—which could be an indirect result of welfare changes. Finally, administrative data have the potential to measure health and safety outcomes, including abuse and neglect, injury, and mortality.

The remaining sections of this paper are developed to assist researchers in defining indicators for domains of child well-being and to clarify substantive issues that must be considered in applying these indicators toward addressing key evaluation questions about the impact of welfare reform. The paper is divided into sections roughly corresponding to the constructs and domains of child well-being offered by Child Trends (1999): (1) health, (2) safety (child welfare), (3) education, and (4) social and emotional adjustment (juvenile justice). For each domain we will identify information that directly describes or reflects on child well-being. Each section also includes a description of key data that are available to inform us about children's outcomes. For each domain we discuss exemplary efforts to use these data for evaluation of welfare reform. Finally, we conclude by discussing some of the scientific sensibilities that should be respected in the use of such data during research on welfare reform, including a discussion of linkages between population surveys and administrative data.

CHILD HEALTH

Access to health care services is a central consideration in the assessment of welfare reform, as these reforms change existing relationships among income, employment, and insurance of health care services for poor families and children (Child Trends, 2000a; Darnell and Rosenbaum, 1997; Moffitt and Slade, 1997; Schorr, 1997). Measures of child health typically emphasize access to care as an important measure, recognizing that health care is necessary but not sufficient for positive child health outcomes (Gortmaker and Walker, 1984; Margolis et al., 1997; Andrulis, 1998).

Parents access health care for their children through several paths. Many children receive health insurance provided by their parent's employer. However, some children of working parents may not have employer-sponsored health plans, and children of nonworking parents certainly do not have this benefit. These children of low-income or nonworking parents are eligible for services paid by publicly funded programs such as Medicaid or the new CHIP. The PRWORA legislation did not significantly alter Medicaid eligibility, and CHIP is designed to reach more of these uninsured children. Yet in July 1999 an estimated 4.7 million uninsured children were eligible for Medicaid but not enrolled (Families USA, 1999). Many states are beginning to track children's enrollment in Medicaid and CHIP, implement outreach efforts to increase CHIP enrollment, and expand Medicaid and CHIP income-level guidelines (Families USA, 1999; Children's Defense Fund, 1998).

The actual health services the child receives are also major determining factors in child health status. Examples of services may include (1) preventive care such as immunizations or dental care; (2) diagnostic screening such as vision and hearing screening, or weight for height measures; and (3) treatment for chronic conditions and disability, with corresponding risk of secondary disability. State policies about welfare reform have the potential to change, positively or negatively, the family environment where health behaviors and health decisions are carried out (Willis and Kleigman, 1997; O'Campo and Rojas-Smith, 1998; Brauner and Loprest, 1999). For example, even if a child is enrolled in Medicaid or CHIP, PRWORA work requirements may constrain a parent's ability to access health care. When access to health care services is limited, either through limited availability or limited utilization of services, children's health could suffer. Alternatively, the work requirements could encourage the parent to secure a job that includes health insurance (gaining access to health care), which may mean the family is able to utilize more services.

Access and utilization of services are interesting for evaluation purposes because they are believed to contribute to the actual health of the child. However, direct measures of child health outcomes are also needed to measure the effects of welfare reform on children. Direct measures of child health outcomes are scarce, however. Often researchers have to rely on indicators of health status. Recent discussions about welfare reform and health suggest some indicators to measure child health status. Children in poverty are more likely to be undernourished, iron deficient, or lead exposed (Geltman et al., 1996). Several measures such as infant mortality, injury, and the use of preventive medical services can be good indicators of child health status (Pappas, 1998). Starfield's Child Health and Illness Profile (Starfield et al., 1993) combines several of these indicators into a bio psycho social developmental assessment but is not found in administrative data sets. Even in survey research, questions about child health status may be limited to asking parents to rate their child's health from excellent to poor (Child Trends, 2000b). Thus, when using administrative data about child health status, it is often necessary to use measures of health services as markers for positive outcomes such as immunizations, enrollment in health plans, or preventive screening, along with indicators of actual outcomes such as infant mortality, low birthweight, blood lead levels, or adolescent substance abuse.

Our purpose here is to identify a reasonably comprehensive set of child health indicators available in at least some administrative data that are relevant to changes in welfare policy because they address health access or status of children. Healthy People 2000, an initiative begun in 1990 by the U.S. Department of Health and Human Services, set health objectives for the nation, including child health status objectives (National Center for Health Statistics, 1996). Over the years, the initiative has prompted state and local communities to develop their own similar objectives and indicators of progress toward achieving them. As a result, the Healthy People 2000 effort has created a set of fairly common measurements of child health across a range of public and private health programs. For example, one of the Healthy People objectives is to reduce infant mortality. This supports the inclusion of infant mortality reduction as part of most state health objectives, and as part of many state and local programs targeted toward women and children. At the federal level, the Maternal and Child Health Bureau (MCHB) identified 18 of the Healthy People 2000 objectives that specifically relate to women and children. Of these, 15 are child health status indicators that can be used to measure impact of welfare reform (Maternal and Child Health Bureau, 1996). Table 10-1 presents these indicators, along with several others, as recommendations for measuring utilization of health services as well as child health status. For each indicator, we describe whether data generally are available at the individual level or aggregated to some larger population. We also identify suggested data sources for these indicators. Many of these data sources are being used in current research about child health (Vermont Agency of Human Services, 2000; Child Trends, 1999).

TABLE 10-1 Suggested Child Health Indicators

Indicator	Level	Data Sources
Medicaid eligibility/enrollment/services	Individual	Medicaid data files
CHIP eligibility/enrollment/services	Individual	CHIP data files
Number/percent uninsured	Population	State dept. of insurance
SSI benefits	Individual	SSA data
Infant mortality	Individual	Vital statistics
Low birth weight	Individual	Vital statistics
HIV infection among women with live births	Individual	Vital statistics
Prenatal care	Individual	Vital statistics
Newborn screening	Individual	Vital statistics
		Birth defects registry
		State data system for newborn screening
Early and Periodic Screening, Diagnosis, and Treatment (EPSDT)	Population	Medicaid services/payment data
Identification of hearing impairments	Individual	State data system for newborn screening
	Population	Program evaluation data
Immunizations	Individual	Medicaid, state immunization registry
	Population	Program evaluation data
Blood lead levels	Individual	EPSDT, clinic record
	Population	Program evaluation data
Dental caries	Individual	Medicaid
		Public health department
Unintentional injuries	Individual	Vital statistics, hospital discharge
		School-based health centers
Child homicide	Individual	Vital statistics
Adolescent suicides	Individual	Vital statistics
Adolescent substance use rates	Individual	Vital statistics
	Population	Hospital discharge/health department
		School-based health centers
		Program evaluation data
STD rates among youth	Population	Hospital discharge
		Program evaluation data
		School-based health centers
Adolescent pregnancy rates	Individual	Vital statistics

Of the data sources identified in Table 10-1, the core indicators come from Medicaid and vital statistics. The following two sections discuss these two sources of data, how they can be used in studies of welfare reform outcomes on children, and some methodological issues in their use.

Medicaid Data

Data from Medicaid eligibility, enrollment, and claims and the new state CHIP can be linked to provide longitudinal tracking of a child or family's health care services or lack of services. For example, a state could track the Medicaid or CHIP enrollment of a child whose mother left AFDC. Since it is unlikely that many families leaving TANF will promptly go to jobs with sufficient health benefits or wages above the Medicaid and CHIP guidelines, that is, 200 percent of the federal poverty level in most states but 350 percent of the federal poverty level in some Medicaid expansion programs, lack of Medicaid coverage of a child in an AFDC/TANF leaver family may indicate that the child is at risk of having no health care coverage. If Early and Periodic Screening and Diagnostic Testing (EPSDT) services also are recorded in the Medicaid files, similar linkages with welfare data will allow tracking of the utilization of preventive services for these low-income children. Linked administrative data from AFDC/TANF and Medicaid have also been used as the sample frame for complementary survey research, which can gather indicators of health status or measures of health care utilization and provide more in-depth measures. For example, the Next Generation, a project conducted by Manpower Demonstration Research Corporation (2000), will use survey data from 10 studies to obtain a more comprehensive perspective about the effects of welfare reform on health outcomes. Variables about health will be measured through survey questions, but the project also will include the existing administrative data used in each of the 10 studies.

Using administrative data from Medicaid and CHIP (or other health-related supplemental services such as the Food Stamps Program or WIC) requires attention to a variety of considerations.

One must consider the populations in the data sets in relation to the population of interest for the study. Specifically:

• Determining what cases are to be included in the population of study. Study populations that can be drawn from Medicaid or CHIP files include: applicants, eligible cases, open cases, closed cases, cases closed with high risk, time-limited or sanctioned cases, or reentry cases.

• Within the group of eligible children are several subgroups that might be of interest. One group for Medicaid is those children actually enrolled. This subgroup of enrolled children includes a second subgroup of children receiving services. This group is not representative of all children enrolled, or all children eligible, or all low-income children in need of health care.

• Medicaid data can be used to extend the analysis of the impact of welfare reform beyond the TANF population because the Medicaid eligibility pool is larger than the TANF eligibility pool. For example, California uses data files on Medicaid recipients as the core of its data sharing/data integration initiatives (National Conference of State Legislators, 1999). This strategy can allow evaluators to track service provided across time and programs to low-income children and families.

- However, Medicaid administrative data can provide data on some of these populations, but not all (i.e. Medicaid administrative data do not represent the entire population of children eligible for Medicaid).
- Public services data tend to overrepresent families at greatest risk. Findings must be interpreted with this in mind. If a family or child leaves TANF and does not appear on Medicaid enrollment files, this does not necessarily mean the child does not have access to health care as they could be covered by private insurance (Child Trends, 2000a).
- Beyond data on eligibility and enrollment, the actual Medicaid or CHIP benefits within a state also should be considered part of the evaluation. State CHIP programs can vary by age, geographic area, disability status, or calculation of income.

A thorough understanding of the administrative data being used is necessary.

- One consideration is whether historical AFDC or Medicaid data were defined the same way across the years.
- In a cross-state context, one must consider possible differences in programs, definitions of data, caseload characteristics, and take-up rates in each state. Within state differences in each of these are also possible.
- The dynamics of changing caseloads to determine whether changes are due to differences in entries to health services or differences in lengths of stay in those services need to be clarified (Greenberg, 1998).
- Administrative data systems for Medicaid often are inadequately automated, even though provision of Medicaid benefits to needy families and children are highly dependent on automated systems. These systems may erroneously terminate a family from Medicaid. Also, eligibility systems typically are not part of the Medicaid division's information system, but reside elsewhere in state government. Because current technology dollars are being spent on TANF automated data systems, there may be some migration away from more archaic Medicaid data (Ellwood, 1999).
- When designing research about children's access to health care services, it is important to remember that a family or adult parent can be dropped from Medicaid but the child can remain eligible.

Data linkage and confidentiality issues also arise:

- How cases in the two files are linked requires the establishment of clear decision rules that are appropriate to specific research questions. There are inherent challenges to linking welfare data to Medicaid data because welfare data are

case based (and can include a family or group of siblings) and Medicaid data are individual based (Ellwood, 1999).
- It is useful to maximize the use of common health identifiers. In some states, such as North Carolina, a common health identifying number is used across a range of data sets, from vital statistics to disease registries (North Carolina State Center for Health Statistics, 1997). Where the health identifying number and social services number can be linked together, one can evaluate a child's experiences and outcomes with both health and social service programs.
- Examining claims data under Medicaid or CHIP requires that issues of confidentiality are responsibly addressed. Many states, such as California, Maryland, Kentucky, and Tennessee, are already addressing these concerns through data sharing and data warehousing projects: (National Conference of State Legislators, 1999).

In addition to these concerns about administrative data, identification of the relevant research questions is critical in guiding the analysis plan and selection of relevant data sets. The question of whether regulations make health care services available to all children who need them could be answered with eligibility data. The question of whether children leaving TANF continue to get needed health services cannot be answered with eligibility or enrollment data. That question only can be answered with service utilization data. The question of whether children exiting TANF are continuing to get timely immunizations could be answered by Medicaid services data or by separate immunization registries within a state (Child Trends, 1999).

Another relevant research question to include would be whether the population of cases had changed since PRWORA was enacted. Will you study AFDC populations before PRWORA, or just those TANF cases after the legislation was implemented? This would require including AFDC and TANF cases in the research. Beyond analysis of the data about AFDC/TANF and Medicaid, the Food Stamps Program, or WIC, research should include questions about barriers to supplemental services for families exiting welfare. One possible barrier is the continued linking of welfare to these supplemental services, despite efforts over the past decade to delink regulations about the programs. In practice, and for individual families, these programs remain interwoven. Another barrier is the complicated eligibility rules for services to support families leaving TANF and the media about the program that might affect whether families think they are eligible or not (Ellwood, 1999). Finally, a research question of interest would be "Upon exiting TANF, do families drop supplemental services, add supplemental services, or maintain existing levels?"

Vital Statistics

As a second predominant type of administrative data, vital statistics systems also can be linked to welfare data sets to provide a range of child health data. Issues of interest in using birth and death certificate files are described as follows:

- Although obtaining access to birth records varies in difficulty depending on many state characteristics, birth records carry information of at least three kinds: the timing and nature of the birth (e.g., family size, birth spacing); services and the payment source for the birth (e.g., prenatal care used and whether the birth was covered by private pay, Medicaid, or medically indigent funds); the family (e.g., marital status); and the well-being of the child at the time of birth (e.g., birthweight, length of hospital stay, 5- and 10-minute scores, and the presence of congenital abnormalities).

- Birth and death records increasingly are being maintained in electronic form, with greatly improved systems for updating this information in a more timely manner and linking these data for research purposes.

- Child death is another indicator that can show differences as a result of services received (Barth and Blackwell, 1998). Although preventing child death is not the primary or sole responsibility of public assistance programs alone, child death rates are sensitive to conditions affected by public assistance, including poverty and lack of supervision. For example, if TANF programs increase the likelihood of home visits by caseworkers who also look for dangerous conditions in the home, if they result in changes in parental substance abuse, if they change access to health care, if they lead to longer spells in which a child is not supervised, changes in death rates from accidents, illnesses, and overdoses could result. Thus, death rates and types of deaths that comprise that rate can change for program users, nonusers, and former users.

- A variety of relevant outcomes can be captured using death records, including adolescent suicide, adolescent homicide, many kinds of accidental deaths, deaths caused by injuries, deaths from abuse and neglect, and deaths caused by substance abuse (if overdose is the cause of death).

- Death records are in the public domain and are available at the state level as well as from the National Death Index (NDI)—a central computerized index of death record information on file in state vital statistics offices. Investigators also can obtain data at the state level and make arrangements with the appropriate state offices to obtain copies of death certificates or specific statistical information such as cause of death.

- Several public welfare agencies have matched child deaths against their welfare caseloads to better understand the vulnerability of their populations. Children who participate in AFDC, Medicaid, or Food Stamp Programs may experience an overall death rate greater than or different than that for other children (Maine Department of Human Services, 1983). Parents on welfare in

Maine did not have mortality that was significantly higher than other children in poverty, although some types of mortality were high among welfare recipients; for example, the risk ratio for children whose parents were on welfare had a five times greater risk of experiencing a death from nonmotor vehicle accidents than other children in poverty. In a more recent study (Philips et al., 1999), mortality related to homicide, suicide, and automobile accidents (when substance abuse was mentioned on the death certificates) was shown to be substantially higher in the first week of the month—probably related to the greater availability of discretionary income following the arrival of government assistance checks and pay checks.

• Evaluations of the relationship between deaths and welfare changes need to assess the type and timing of the deaths. Because child mortality is relatively rare—even among high-risk populations—studies of welfare populations may need to combine these mortality data with injury data and incarceration data (discussed later in this paper) to obtain an overall assessment of significant threats to well-being.

Other data sets may not be as easily linked to welfare data sets, yet they should be considered. Twenty-one states have comprehensive databases on hospital discharges (Pappas, 1998). These data can provide information about a wide variety of health concerns, such as child injuries, acute illnesses, and emergency room visits. These data sets may include measures of income, payment authorization, or actual welfare status. Injury data can be linked to welfare participation for individual-level analyses if they can be obtained from local hospital organizations.

Data from school-based health centers are available in fewer places, but could be expected to become more useful as school-based health clinics expand their reach. Although not yet widely available, school-based health centers are growing in coverage and in some states now blanket the state. Some states, such as Massachusetts, have initiated statewide systems of maintaining school health data. School-based clinics often are under the umbrella of a local hospital, and can serve as Medicaid providers under managed care contracts. These data will be most useful when they cover a large proportion of all youth in the area under study and when they provide additional information not available in the Medicaid data. This is the case in Colorado and Connecticut, which have extensive school-based health center networks (Koppelman and Lear, 1998).

Another source of data is programs funded under Title V, the Maternal and Child Health Block Grant (MCHB), which requires performance measurement for contracting and evaluation. State welfare reform evaluators should collaborate with Title V program staff to explore data linkage, inclusion of common data elements of welfare status and health across data sets, and other ways to share data and evaluate child health in the era of reform. For example, several states, including Kansas and Arizona, are implementing performance measurement systems in their Title V maternal and child health programs (Gabor et al., 1997; Grason and Nachbar, 1997). In a pilot project involving seven states, sponsored by the MCHB in 1998, core performance measurements are monitored. These measurements include: needs assessments, percentage of Medicaid-eligible children enrolled, standards of care for women and children, health insurance coverage, and cooperative agreements among state Medicaid, WIC, and other human service agencies. An emphasis on information systems development is also part of these pilot programs and should be explored for linkage with welfare reform evaluation. In another example, the Institute for Child Health Policy at the University of Florida, Gainesville is currently evaluating enrollment in its Healthy Kids programs of outreach to uninsured children, as well as the quality of services in the program for children with special health care needs (Reiss, 1999; Shenkman, 1999).

Efforts to promote and monitor state health objectives should include indicators of children's health according to welfare, employment, and/or income status. As state and local communities plan for future Healthy People 2010 objectives, the impact of continuing welfare reform should be part of future health objectives. Where monitoring systems exist or are planned, they should include either linkage to state and local welfare data sets or common data elements that would provide for evaluation. For example, child health status measures could be monitored regularly according to the following categories: employed families with private health coverage, employed families with Medicaid or CHIP coverage, employed families with no coverage, unemployed families with Medicaid or CHIP, unemployed families with no coverage. These categories could be applied across a range of child health measures: prenatal care, infant mortality, low birthweight, immunizations, hearing and vision screening, specialist care for children with special health care needs, injuries, or teen pregnancy.

The Aspen Roundtable on Comprehensive Community Based Initiatives has addressed the issue of using administrative data and identified several useful sources for conducting small-area analysis (Coulton and Hollister, 1999). These data include Head Start records, emergency medical service records, immunization registries, and hospital discharge records. Aggregate data at the neighborhood level, combined with comparable welfare data aggregated to the same level, can answer research questions about selected high-risk neighborhoods within a county, within major metropolitan areas, or across a state. Table 10-2 lists several Web sites of organizations conducting these types of neighborhood-level analyses using small-area analysis (Child Trends, 2000,b).

Examples of current research using administrative data on Medicaid use, health care access, and other health outcomes to evaluate the impact of welfare reform on children's health are increasing. In spring 2000, a three-state study about children's movement among AFDC, Medicaid, and foster care was released by the Assistant Secretary for Planning and Evaluation (ASPE) of the U.S. Department of Health and Human Services. The study was conducted by Chapin

TABLE 10-2 Small Area Analysis Using Administrative Data: Web Sites

Web Sites for Local Research in Welfare Reform	
United Way of Chittenden County, Vermont www.unitedwaycc.org	Chapin Hall Center for Children at the University of Chicago www.chapin.uchicago.edu
Social Assets and Vulnerabilities Indicators for Central Indiana (SAVI) www.savi.org	Center for the Study of Social Policy www.cssp.og
United Way of Central Indiana www.unitedwaycc.org	Community Building Resource Exchange of the Aspen Institute www.commbuild.org/aspen
National Governors' Association www.nga.org	Aspen Institute Roundtable on Comprehensive Community Initiatives www.aspenroundtable.org
Urban Strategies Council Oakland, CA www.urbanstrategies.org	Zero Population Growth www.zpg.org

The Center on Urban Poverty and Social
  Change at Case Western Reserve
  University
Povertycenter.cwru.edu/	

SOURCE: Child Trends (2000b).

Hall Center for Children at the University of Chicago, Center for Social Services Research at the School of Social Welfare of the University of California at Berkeley, the University of North Carolina School of Social Work at Chapel Hill, and the American Institutes for Research (2000). The study used administrative data from 1995 to 1996 from AFDC, Medicaid, and child welfare programs, obtained through close collaboration with state agencies responsible for these program areas. A baseline population was identified and entry cohorts for each program were used to track experiences of children over the period just prior to PRWORA. The study focused on research questions about transitions from AFDC, including:

- Percentage of AFDC cohort that leave AFDC, by 1 year.
- Percentage of AFDC cohort that after 1 year transition to Medicaid only.
- Percentage of AFDC cohort that after 1 year exit the system (AFDC, Medicaid, and foster care)
- Among AFDC exiters at 1 year, the percentage who use Medicaid.

Wide variation was found in these measures across Illinois, California, and North Carolina. Differences also were identified for the four measures across children's age groups. This study provides an example of (1) the need to collaborate with other state agencies when using administrative data; (2) the importance of defining the population of study, in this case entry cohorts for 1 year prior to PRWORA with no AFDC/TANF enrollment in the previous 2 years; and (3) the difficulty of generalizing across local areas when studying the characteristics and consequences of welfare programs.

South Carolina has also developed linking capacity of administrative data called CHILD LINK (South Carolina Department of Social Services 1999). This state system links the following data sets: AFDC/TANF, food stamps, Medicaid eligibility, Medicaid payments, work support program data, child protective services, foster care, juvenile justice, alcohol and substance abuse, and wage data. The purpose is to better understand the Medicaid utilization for children after a parent becomes employed and to determine whether, after a client leaves welfare, they use other services to help them through the transition period.

Finally, an inventory of administrative data sets was prepared by UC Data Archive and Technical Assistance of the University of California at Berkeley (1999). This inventory was the result of surveying 26 states about their use of administrative data sets and their capacity to link them. Ninety-five percent of the 26 states were linking AFDC/TANF, Medicaid eligibility, and Food Stamp Program data. Fifty percent were linking AFDC/TANF, Medicaid claims, Medicaid eligibility, and Food Stamp Program data.

CHILD ABUSE AND NEGLECT

The considerable overlap between welfare and child welfare service populations is well documented. Children from welfare families account for as much as 45 percent of those served by the child welfare system (American Humane Association, 1984). The strong association between welfare and child maltreatment may be due to a number of factors, including the stresses associated with poverty, the existence of concurrent risk factors such as mental illness and illicit drugs, and welfare recipients' more frequent contact with public authorities (Coulton et al., 1995; Gelles, 1992; Gil, 1971; Giovannoni and Billingsley, 1970; Wolock and Magura, 1996; Zuravin and DiBlasio, 1996).

Given the documented association between welfare and child maltreatment, a number of authors have reflected on the possible impacts of welfare reform on child welfare (Aber et al., 1995; Haskins, 1995; Meezan and Giovannoni, 1995; Wilson et al., 1995; Zaslow et al., 1995). Essentially all conclude that efforts to induce welfare mothers to self-sufficiency may impact rates of child maltreatment. Again, whether this impact is positive or negative depends in part on what effect reforms have on family income, parental stress, and access to services (Collins and Aber, 1996). For example, loss of benefits or other income supports such as Supplemental Security Income may strain a family's abilities to provide basic necessities such as food and shelter, causing increased neglect and homelessness, even abandonment (Collins, 1997; Knitzer and Bernard, 1997; Shook, 1998). Increased parental stress related to economic, employment, or childcare difficulties may also lead to increased rates of abuse (Knitzer and Bernard, 1997; Meezan and Giovannoni, 1995).

In contrast, positive changes in these areas may be favorable to children and families. For example, rates of abuse and neglect may decline if reforms reduce family's economic hardship. Additionally, gainful employment might improve the mental health of single mothers thereby decreasing the risk of child maltreatment (Garfinkel and McLanahan, 1986). Better access to mental health and drug services also might have similar effects. In addition to impacting the actual rates of maltreatment, the increased scrutiny by public authorities faced by TANF participants and their families might result in greater detection of previously unreported abuse and neglect. Whether positive or negative, these changes likely will be reflected in the number and types of maltreatment reports, the number of case investigations and substantiations, and the number of children placed in foster care.

Welfare reform also may affect the experiences of the children served by the child welfare system. With the passage of PRWORA, a family's economic circumstances become a critical component of the child welfare decision-making process. In particular, parental TANF status could influence the decision to remove a child from a sanctioned parent without any legitimate source of income, and if removed, the TANF status of potential kin caregivers might alter the subsequent placement decision (Zeller, 1998). For example, the proportion of kin placements might decline because kin caregivers might not be exempt from TANF requirements (Berrick et al., 1999; Geen and Waters, 1997; Boots and Green, 1999). Economic factors also might influence children's length of stay in foster care, placement stability, as well as their rates and types of exits from the system. Specifically, parental TANF status might facilitate or stall reunification efforts impacting the duration of children's out-of-home placements. Children placed with kin might experience placement disruptions if their TANF status changes. Although the impact of TANF noncompliance on reunification efforts is clear, compliance also might be problematic, with work making it difficult for parents to meet child welfare timelines such as visitation and court appearances (Knitzer and Bernard, 1997).

In addition to these potential impacts on exit rates, changes in a family's TANF status following reunification might lead to an increased likelihood of reabuse and child welfare system recidivism. Recent research on the child welfare experiences of families in Cleveland suggests that families that go on and off of welfare are more likely to fail in their attempts with reunification of their children than families that continuously receive welfare during the reunification period (Wells and Guo, in press). This, along with data from California (Needell et al., 1999) showing that AFDC families with breaks in AFDC receipt are more likely to become involved with child welfare services, suggests the substantial sensitivity of welfare families to changes in service circumstances.

Unlike the domain of child health, child welfare data traditionally have offered little uniform program participation data. Relevant data are collected only by state child protective service and foster care service departments. In some states (e.g., California) all child welfare administrative data are now entered into one data system. In most states, however, child abuse and neglect reporting and investigation data are gathered separately from data about foster care and adoption. The following section provides an overview of different configurations of these data sources that can be utilized to assess the impact of welfare reform on child maltreatment rates and children's experiences in and exits from the child welfare system. Access and confidentiality issues loom large when using such data to study vulnerable children. Readers should consult Brady and his colleagues (1999, this volume) for an in-depth review of these important topics.

Child Welfare Services Indicators

Most administrative data in the child welfare domain is composed of service event types and dates that can be configured to construct a variety of outcome indicators. The two most common configurations are descriptions of caseloads at a point in time (or several points in time) and longitudinal data analyses of individual service careers over time. In addition to program participation data, demographic data for the children and families under study (e.g., birthdate, ethnicity, home address or location) are also common elements found in these databases. When combined with these demographic data, caseload and longitudinal indicators can provide a source for estimating system performance and client status.

Caseload data provide a snapshot of welfare and child welfare at a specific point in time. They are usually used for program management purposes and can contribute to the assessment of system impacts by indicating covariation between subpopulations in welfare and child welfare. Broadly, for instance, caseload indicators of how many children of a certain age are leaving welfare and how many children of a certain age are entering foster care can provide some indication of whether the welfare exits *might be* contributing to increases in foster care. However, given the large size of the welfare caseload and the small numbers of children entering foster care, this relationship could not be adequately understood without individual-level data that linked welfare and child welfare histories.

Recently the ACF's Child Welfare Outcomes and Measures Project developed a set of outcome measures using point-in-time data from the Adoption and Foster Care Analysis and Reporting System (AFCARS) to assess state performance in operating child welfare programs. Outcomes include annual incidence of child maltreatment, types of exits from the child welfare system, timing of exits, and placement stability. Although point-in-time data also can be used to measure case status outcomes such as foster care length of stay; the resulting statistics are biased because they overrepresent children with longer stays in care and are not very sensitive to changes in entries to foster care because the new-comers to care are just a portion of the overall population. Thus, although point-in-time estimates are the easiest and least expensive configuration of administrative data, this inherent bias limits their usefulness until the individual records comprising these caseload data are reconfigured into longitudinal data.

Administrative data typically can be reconfigured into event-level files that record program participation histories. Depending on the scope of available data, these events may be restricted to foster care spells or placements, or may more broadly include child abuse reports, investigations, and services provided in the home. Working with entry cohorts provides the clearest evidence of changes in patterns of care that might be associated with changes in welfare programs be-cause the interpretation of the outcomes does not have to disentangle the contri-butions of different service programs (e.g., AFDC and TANF). Using data that can be subset into entry cohorts captures the dynamics of both system entries and exits, and therefore provides a more accurate assessment of outcomes than caseload. Although free from the biases of point-in-time data, longitudinal data analyses often are preceded by considerable programming to reconfigure data into an even-level, longitudinal format, and to link welfare and child welfare files.

The Multistate Foster Care Data Archive provides an illustration of the com-plexity as well as promise that longitudinal data offer researchers trying to under-stand child welfare careers (and how they might be influenced by TANF). The archive is an initiative by the Children's Bureau of the U.S. Department of Health and Human Services that is designed to foster increased collaboration among states regarding administrative data collection in the child welfare services arena. Administered by the Chapin Hall Center for Children at the University of Chi-cago, the archive currently includes data from child welfare agencies in 11 states. The archive processes state data to make them comparable across state systems. To ensure data comparability, the project focuses on "a limited set of characteris-tics and events that have clear meaning in all jurisdictions" (Wulczyn et al., 1999:1). The core of the archive is two databases—one consisting of child records, including unique identifiers and demographic information, and a second event-level field that stores information on child welfare events of interest. This struc-ture allows researchers to use the data in a longitudinal format to capture children's spells in child welfare as well as other experiences. Additionally, data can be configured to provide traditional point-in-time estimates of caseload flow over time.

A sufficiently comprehensive set of outcome indicators is shown in Box 10-

1 (note that some indicators have a clearer theoretical relationship to welfare reform than others).

Depending on the purpose of the analysis, indicators can be derived from either point-in-time or longitudinal data. Indicators can be expressed as rates based on the number of people at risk in a state, county, and even zip code of the underlying populations, such as the foster care incidence (entry) rates and prevalence (caseload) rates by age and ethnicity. Benchmarks can be set for both caseload and longitudinal indicators, such as prevalence rate over time, or number and proportion of children who experience reabuse within a year of being reunified from foster care.

Measuring Impact

In anticipation of later analyses of the effects of welfare reform, researchers in several states have undertaken projects using linked longitudinal AFDC and child welfare data to better understand the overlap between these two programs. These projects serve as models of what will be possible with post-TANF data. In one such endeavor, the Child Welfare Research Center at the University of California at Berkeley undertook an analysis to identify the characteristics of poor families at risk of child maltreatment. Using data from the California Children's Services Archive, researchers constructed a longitudinal database of children entering AFDC between 1988 and 1995 using MediCal data in 10 counties. Probability-matching software was employed to link AFDC histories for these children with birth records, statewide foster care data, and child maltreatment reporting data. Results revealed substantial overlap between the welfare and child welfare populations, with approximately 27 percent of all 1990 child AFDC entrants having child welfare contact, within 5 years and 3 percent entering foster care. This indicates that the overlap between welfare and child protective services is large enough to allow modeling of changes over time and across program types, although analyses of transitions to foster care may be too few to allow

---

BOX 10-1
Minimum Child Welfare Services Indicators

Child maltreatment reports (with reason for report)
Case investigation (with reason for not investigating)
Case substantiations (with reasons for providing services or not)
In-home services (duration and frequency of provisions)
Foster care placements (with placement dates and type of placement)
Placement moves
Foster care exits (with type of exit)
Reentry to foster care (with reason for reentry)

powerful modeling. Both total time on aid as well as the number of spells on aid were associated with child welfare contact. Children who transitioned to the child welfare system were more likely to come from single-parent families, larger families, have low birthweight and late or no prenatal care (Needell et al., 1999).

A similar analysis was undertaken in Illinois at the University of Chicago's Chapin Hall Center for Children. Using linked longitudinal data from the state Department of Children and Family Services and the Division of Financial Support Services, Shook (1998) set out to identify baseline rates of maltreatment among children in the Illinois AFDC program between 1990 and 1995. She also identified risk factors for child welfare contact among this population. Risks were higher for children on nonparent cases, children from single-parent families, and white children. Of particular interest were the findings that transitions were more likely among children with sanctioned family grants, because child removals for neglect, lack of supervision, or risk of harm were more likely among sanctioned cases. In addition to helping to identify possible implications of TANF sanctions, the research highlights the use of linked administrative data in assessing the impact of welfare reform on child welfare.

Administrative data from child welfare records also have been combined with qualitative survey data to study the impact of welfare reform. For example, a study currently under way (a collaborative effort by The Urban Institute and The University of California at Berkeley's Center for Social Services Research and UC Data Archive and Technical Assistance, funded by the Stuart Foundation) will combine qualitative data of welfare recipients with data from their administrative welfare records and any available data on children in the home that exist in child welfare administrative data records. This "marriage" between administrative data and qualitative data holds great promise. Specifically, although administrative data can provide information to answer questions such as "How many? What proportion? How long?", other methods can shed some light as to "Why?"

The Center for Social Services Research at the University of California at Berkeley routinely has used child welfare administrative data to draw representative samples to study children using other research methods. For example, counties in the Bay Area Social Services Consortium have funded research to understand the educational needs of children in foster care. A random sample of caregivers drawn from administrative data records is being interviewed to gather detailed information about the children in their care. Similarly, case records of children have been reviewed to look at concurrent planning in child welfare. (Concurrent planning is the provision of an alternative permanent plan, such as adoption, simultaneously with efforts to return a child to his or her birthparent.) In both cases, the samples were drawn from administrative data. Such methods easily could be adapted to provide more in-depth analysis of critical welfare reform issues.

Despite the wide variety of outcome indicators that can be configured from child welfare administrative data, like all services data, child welfare data cover only those who receive services. Because child welfare data are available only for those abused and neglected children who come to the attention of public systems of care, changes to the undetected abuse rate that may result from welfare program changes cannot be assessed. Despite the hurdles associated with linking welfare and child welfare data, given the established association between poverty and maltreatment, child welfare advocates and policy makers must examine the impact of welfare reform on child welfare services. In particular, whether these changes increase the likelihood of maltreatment has important consequences for both the TANF families and children as well as the general social good. In addition to the immediate risk of physical harm and even death maltreated children face, longer term consequences include deficits in emotional and physical health, cognitive development, and socialization difficulties (Ammerman et al., 1986; Couch and Milner, 1993). Furthermore, observed relationships between childhood maltreatment and later criminal activity or abusive behavior also increase future consequences for both children and society (Gray, 1988; Jonson-Reid and Barth, 2000).

EDUCATION

Educational success is a key indicator of a child's well-being and clearly is related to current and future economic and physical well-being (Barnett, 1998; Card and Krueger, 1998). Educational success can be affected by educational histories, parental work, and targeted efforts to address parents' educational needs. Indeed, some welfare programs (i.e., Job Opportunities and Basic Skills [JOBS]) have more provisions directed at parental education than others (i.e., TANF). Because of the strong relationship between education of parents and children, when welfare programs help recipients to improve their educational skills (Boudett and Friedlander, 1997), they can be expected to have an influence on the learning of their children.

Certainly, improved educational performance of children is one hope of TANF. Because TANF does not pay for substantial educational programs for parents, the benefits for the education of children would have to be by more indirect means. This process may take several forms. For example, if parents' employment efforts result in relocation to communities that have schools with higher achievement for low-income children, this could result in educational achievement. Or, by witnessing their parents' success at the worksite, children could be inspired to have higher standards for their own achievement.

A limited set of pre-TANF research studies indicates there may not be a simple, sizable effect of welfare participation on children's educational attainment. Hill and O'Neill (1994) found that parental AFDC participation has no effect on children's scores on a standardized test of vocabulary, given income.

Currie and Duncan (1995) confirmed that their results hold up even when sibling comparisons are used to account for unobserved maternal background characteristics. Yet a recent analysis of National Longitudinal Study of Youth data that included access to other mother and child services found a relationship between program participation and children's learning (Yoshikawa, 1999). Although the evidence base for research on educational outcomes and welfare reform primarily comes from surveys, there is good reason to suggest the importance of using administrative records to study this relationship. This will be particularly fruitful as the availability and meaningfulness of educational records continue to improve.

Measures of educational success include data elements that describe the child's achievement as well as their receipt of services. Many of these data are now in electronic databases in the school districts, but the automation of educational records tends to begin with the high schools and trickle down to the elementary schools. Thus, elementary school grades are not as likely to be automated as middle school or high school grades. Standardized statewide test scores are now quite routinely required of all students, as are periodic achievement test scores during certain sentinel years. The variety and repetition of tests is becoming quite extensive. (As an illustration, Box 10-2 includes the testing schedule for students in North Carolina schools.)

Most, but not all, students take these tests. Exemptions may be given to students in special education, as determined by their Individual Education Program teams. Exemptions also may be given to students who are not following a standard course of study, such as those in alternative education or adolescent parenting programs.

Grade retention histories usually are available (or can be inferred from birthdates and grade levels). Educational reform is making grade retention data more valuable. Although widespread adherence to the principles of social promotion have dominated the nation's public schools for many years, legislation in

---

BOX 10-2
Educational Tests Routinely Used In North Carolina

End-of-grade tests (grades 3 - 8)
Writing assessment (grades 4, 7, 10)
Norm-referenced testing (grades 5, 8; sampled)
Open-ended assessment (grades 4, 8)
Computer Skills Proficiency (grade 8)
Reading and Mathematics competency testing (screen in grade 8; must pass for diploma by grade 12)
End-of-course tests in Algebra, Biology, English, and U.S. History

---

BOX 10-3
Minimum Educational Indicators

Academic achievement (T scores from standardized tests)
Absences and dates of absences (full day and part day)
Suspensions and dates of suspensions (with reasons)

---

many states (e.g., California, New York, North Carolina) is now discouraging social promotion. In the future, grade retention may indicate a child's true performance, not just a school's educational strategy regarding social promotion.

School services data also are obtainable, although the lack of standardization makes it difficult to assess change when students also change schools during the period under study. School attendance data also is likely to be automated, although comparisons across schools and, especially, unified school districts must be done with care because of different ways of administering the statewide definitions of attendance. Schools also have data about student's disciplinary actions—nearly always including suspensions or expulsions, but also including a variety of other disciplinary actions that are less severe. But caution is also needed in making comparisons about disciplinary actions in school. This is particularly true of suspensions, as some schools use them routinely and some schools use them only after considerable effort to mediate the problematic situation. Further, different rules typically apply to children receiving special education services and the proportion of children receiving special education services is, in turn, quite variable across schools. To assess the effects of welfare reform on the educational outcomes of children, even a minimum data set that included measures of academic achievement, absences, and suspensions would be useful (see Box 10-3).

Access to School Records Data

A major impediment to using educational data to estimate the well-being of children is the Family Educational Rights and Privacy Act (FERPA). First enacted in 1974, FERPA gives parents the right to inspect and review their children's education records, request amendment of the records, and have some control over the disclosure of information from the records. At age 18, this right is transferred to the student. The act also restricts the release of school records or information from those records that could identify the student. Before releasing such records or information to a party outside the school system, the school first must obtain the consent of the student's parent. FERPA offers a key exception to the prior consent requirement. Specifically, educators may disclose information without prior consent if the disclosure is being made to organizations conducting studies for, or on behalf of education agencies or institutions in order to develop tests, administer student aid, or improve instruction (§99.31(a)(6) of FERPA regulations). To meet this requirement, the researcher must have an agreement with the educational institution that the researcher is working on the institutions' behalf and that the study will create information that will improve instruction. Additionally, FERPA was amended in 1994 to permit nonconsensual disclosures of education records to officials in the state juvenile justice system and under certain special circumstances. Despite some loosening of restrictions, FERPA remains a significant barrier to data access for researchers.

Because educational attainment represents one of the few unambiguous outcomes that can be assessed with administrative records, substantial legislative efforts need to be taken to make this critical source of information about child well-being more available to researchers. Consideration should be given to amend FERPA to not require parental signatures for the routine use of administrative data in research in cases where students' rights to privacy are not jeopardized.

More must be done to allow educational data to be used by researchers to better understand the educational implications of other social programs. This would be a low-cost way to try to assist our highest risk children—who are most likely to be involved in multiple systems of care. FERPA has been revised to make it possible for schools to share information with correctional agencies. Under FERPA, schools may disclose information from law enforcement unit records (see §99.3 and §99.8 of FERPA regulations) without the consent of the parents or eligible students. This enables schools to give information to social services or juvenile justice agencies as long as the school district first creates and maintains a "law enforcement unit" that is officially authorized to (1) enforce federal, state, or local law, or (2) maintain the physical security and safety of schools in the district. Although this is a modest amendment of FERPA that may not have direct relevance to most researchers endeavoring to use administrative educational data (perhaps unless they are also studying law enforcement issues), it does suggest the willingness of Congress to modify FERPA for good cause. The "Solomon Amendment" of 1999 also limited the unintended implications of FERPA in order to deny aid to schools that either prohibit or prevent the Secretary of Defense from obtaining, for military recruiting purposes, access to directory information on students. The needs of researchers and policy makers to have good information about the educational outcomes of welfare reform (and other social programs) also are worthy of a FERPA amendment.

Perhaps because of the obstacles created by FERPA, there has been little work matching administrative records to welfare data to assess possible relationships between educational progress and welfare program participation. There are a few examples, however. Orthner and Randolph (1999) examined the impact of parental work and continuity of welfare receipt on the dropout rates of high school students in families in poverty. This work was accomplished by matching individual records of children who were enrolled in the JOBS program in Mecklenburg County with the administrative records from the Mecklenburg Unified School District. Some case record checking also was done of the paper school district records. Using event history analysis, they examined the risk of dropping out of school in light of potential effects on subsequent social and economic well-being. The data indicate that that consistency in parental employment (i.e., parents who worked in all quarters) and transitions off welfare are associated with lower rates of dropping out of high school. Longer spells on public assistance are associated with higher dropout rates.

Some community colleges have merged their data with the public welfare data to better understand the overlap between their student population and the welfare population (Community College Involvement in Welfare; www.aacc. nche.edu/research/welfare.htm/11/6/99). In a survey of 1,124 community colleges conducted by the American Association of Community Colleges, about 32 percent track students on public assistance. Among the primary reasons given for not tracking students were student confidentiality and privacy issues. Yet the disruption in the educational careers of welfare recipients that may occur with the end of the JOBS program and the institution of TANF could be an important outcome for young people. A straightforward way to study this overlap and the changes in this population is to merge administrative data from community colleges and TANF programs.

JUVENILE JUSTICE

Although social competence and adjustment is a difficult dimension to study using administrative (or survey) data, one area that can be examined profitably is the involvement with the juvenile authorities that results when children and youth break adult laws. Parental welfare program participation has long been thought to be associated with criminal and juvenile justice involvement (e.g., Levinson, 1969). There are several reasons why changes in a parent's involvement with welfare could affect the likelihood of juvenile justice involvement by their children. Communities with high welfare participation also have high crime rates. In one study (Philips et al., 1999) these two factors were temporally linked, showing that mortality (particularly intentional mortality) was far higher during the first week of the month when welfare and other public assistance checks arrive. Some youth may be involved in such crimes. Households with parents who move off welfare into self-sufficiency will have additional resources that they could use to purchase a variety of services and activities that would occupy their children and help them avoid the hazards of "hanging out." At the same time, with parents working away from the home, there may be less supervision for those youth who do not become involved in other activities. Also, if families have their benefits cut, we know they often rely on "other family members" to assist them. Although this typically means other adult relatives, it is possible that youth would feel pressured to bring new resources into the household or to, at least, find resources that would allow them to be less dependent on their families for food, clothing, and entertainment.

The most common approach to assessing criminal justice involvement is to study "arrest records." This is the device used in most studies of the transition from child welfare programs to juvenile justice involvement (e.g., Widom, 1991; English and Widom, 1999). The potential drawback of arrest records is that they reflect the combined behaviors of juveniles *and* criminal justice systems. This is counterbalanced by the fact that they are generally considered to be more useful than conviction records because convictions or incarcerations are determined by so many other factors—especially for less violent crimes. Still, convictions or incarcerations can be used if the theoretical relationship between welfare participation and crime suggests there would be higher rates of major crimes. Incarcerations in state training programs have been shown to be sensitive enough to pick up differences between groups that did and did not obtain ongoing child welfare services following a child abuse investigation (Jonson-Reid and Barth, 2000).

Juvenile justice data also can be obtained from a variety of settings, depending on the geographic locus of the study. At the local level, youth often are remanded to juvenile detention and county camps and ranches. At the state level, they may attend a training school or youth authority program. In more populous counties, they generally have greater capacity to hold more youth who commit more serious offenses at the local level, whereas more rural areas may use the statewide facilities to a greater extent. Statewide facilities often have their own databases, which include substantial additional information collected about the child at intake. This makes such information particularly useful in trying to explain exit patterns and the path of services once in the training program.

Some juveniles are tried as adults and others may have their records sealed for a variety of offenses. Still, these remain the exception and they are unlikely to bias study results or affect interjurisdictional comparisons as long as reasonable sample sizes are maintained.

Although these authors were unable to identify any studies that have directly tested the relationship between parents' welfare participation and children's juvenile justice involvement, one important study matched juvenile justice data with survey data from the Moving to Opportunity (MTO) experiment. In the MTO, a total of 614 families living in high-poverty Baltimore neighborhoods were assigned into three different "treatment groups": *experimental group* families received housing subsidies, counseling, and search assistance to move to private-market housing in low-poverty census tracts (poverty rates under 10 percent); *Section 8-only group* families received private-market housing subsidies with no constraints on relocation choices; and a *control group* received no special assistance under the MTO. The impact of this "treatment" on juvenile *arrests* was then assessed (Ludwig et al., 1999). (The authors also tested models that used *convictions* instead of *arrests* and found similar results.)

The study also cast light on the utility of a variety of indicators of juvenile justice involvement, finding that false arrests are likely to be crime specific and disproportionately involve charges such as disorderly conduct, resisting arrest, and assaulting a police officer. Second, they replicated their analysis using convictions instead of arrests, assuming that these show less variation across neighborhoods in false convictions than arrests because juvenile prosecutions are handled at the county level and arrests are made by local police.

LINKING WELFARE AND CHILD WELL-BEING DATA

Despite the benefits of using linked longitudinal administrative data, the work is complex and the level of effort and skill required is easily underestimated. Linking across data systems poses many challenges. Linking is accomplished by matching unique identifying information such as Social Security numbers across data systems of interest. Even when "unique" identifiers exist in the data sources to be linked, probabilistic-matching software should be employed to link records across data systems to reduce matching errors. Readers should consult Lee and Goerge (1999) for an in-depth review of the advantages of probabilistic matching even when Social Security numbers are available in both data sets.

In addition to the complex logistics of linking files, new issues are posed by TANF reforms themselves. In particular, a model that thoroughly investigates the relationship between parental welfare paths and child well-being requires not only data on the timing of welfare receipt, but also an indication of the reason that aid ceased. Without an explanation of the reason for termination, it is difficult to distinguish between parents who left aid for gainful employment and those who were dropped from the rolls due to a sanction and/or failure to comply with regulations. In many cases, this information is lacking. Therefore, researchers may try to link welfare and child well-being data to parental employment data in an attempt to understand which families are leaving welfare for "positive" reasons.

Finally, most current evaluation efforts typically focus on examining the relationship between parental welfare careers and outcomes for children. Under TANF, however, children's and parents' welfare careers must be considered separately. In some states, such as California, sanctions and time limits will result in a decrease in only the parental portion of the welfare grant, with the child's portion maintained. Children might, then, move to another household assistance unit where the parent figure gets full benefits. Identifying and successfully tracking these parents and children may involve record linkage across cases and incorporate case flow dynamics that are quite complicated. Beyond receipt of TANF assistance, children's participation in other important programs such as Medicaid, the Food Stamp Program, and WIC also must be evaluated if we are to gain a comprehensive understanding of the impacts that reforms have on child well-being.

CONCLUSIONS

Using administrative data to evaluate welfare reform presents challenges and opportunities within each of the domains of child well-being. Child abuse and neglect data generally are available to the evaluation of welfare reform because both child welfare records and TANF data sets typically reside within the same governmental department at the local and state levels. However, developing appropriate measures of child well-being from administrative child welfare requires intricate programming of longitudinal data files: understanding of the differences between the child's experience and the system performance indicators; expertise with a range of sophisticated analysis methods; and understanding of many interpretations that administrative data might allow. In contrast, health measures of child well- being—for example, birthweight or immunization completeness—are more uniformly defined and there is more agreement about their implications. However, these data are less available to study welfare reform because they typically reside within government entities separate from departments where welfare data reside. When these data sources differ, issues of compatibility of data formats and definitions, linking of data, confidentiality, and ownership of data files call for collaborative efforts to evaluate welfare reform. Evaluation of impacts within juvenile justice and education include particularly acute challenges of data availability, as well as the need to create valid and reliable measures.

The authors of this paper have endeavored to increase readers' familiarity with needed indicators of child well-being and the administrative data sets that contain them. A secondary goal has been to alert readers to the ways that existing policies hamper access to the data necessary to make informed decisions. Obtaining permission to use administrative data for evaluation purposes is harder than it needs to be. Without substantial convergence around the purposes of using administrative data, this emerging technology is going to be a partial, piecemeal, and ephemeral aid to government. The technical solutions for linking are increasing (storage is more affordable, processing times are shorter, and matching software is better), but public support has not been built to encourage this linking. Issues of data access and confidentiality present the greatest barriers to full utilization of this resource.

Although the federal government is demanding more accountability from the states, and the states from the counties, there is little outcry from public officials to permit the broader use of administrative data to generate the information required to track the performance of human service agencies. Scandinavian countries are generating invaluable research using linked data across generations to understand, for example, the transmission of schizophrenia across generations and the likelihood that children born with birth defects will give birth to children with birth defects. Similarly, program participation data have been combined with information from driving records, educational attainment, military service, and marriage certificates to understand lifetime outcomes of family recomposition and participation in service programs. Researcher access to administrative data is beneficial, and more open access will permit individuals to educate themselves about what is contained in such databases, to use the information within those databases to conduct research for multiple purposes, and to reassure the public about the feasibility of using already gathered information for the public good.

Concerns over confidentiality continue to present a major barrier to linking administrative data to evaluate the effects of welfare reform on child well-being. Perhaps nowhere is there as much sensitivity concerning privacy and confidentiality as with records containing information about vulnerable children and parents who have been accused of violating social norms by abusing or neglecting their children. At the same time, electronic availability of information on individuals permits sophisticated research that was simply impossible in the past. How do we reconcile the need to provide privacy and confidentiality to individual patients while enabling public health researchers and policy makers to use available information to make the best decisions?

Although privacy and confidentiality of records about children's well-being are important, we suggest there are already adequate protections, incentives and disincentives, and policies and procedures, to preserve individual privacy. We already trust millions of individuals in our society to respect the confidentiality of information they encounter each day in the human services, child welfare, health care, law enforcement, juvenile justice, and education sysem, to name a few. We trust the individuals conducting research within each of these systems to maintain the confidentiality of records. Most of these data are collected without any explicit discussion of whether or how they will be used for research that might inform administration of the program. Yet we have generated the expectation that individuals not working for those institutions who obtain data from them in order to advance services research through data linking represent a risk to the confidentiality concerns of service recipients. The expectation that there is likely to be even a minimal risk of mishandling data lacks an evidentiary base. In our 10 years of experience using administrative data of the most sensitive kinds (including child abuse reports and juvenile justice records), we know of no violations of individual rights of persons in those data sets. Nor do we have any stories to tell about exceptional procedures we instituted to prevent such misuse. The handling of that information was simply very routine. Perhaps we need a more systematic effort to determine what real and imagined threats to confidentiality exist in data-linking efforts. Until we have evidence to the contrary, we should continue to maintain databases with adequate identifying information to support future research projects, and we should advocate for change in unwisely broad legislative or regulatory language that adversely affects interorganizational research.

We believe it is appropriate and indeed necessary to maintain personal identifying information on public health and child well-being databases, and that those identifiers should be available to facilitate linkage of electronic health databases to support research to improve the health of our population as well as to enhance the health of individuals. At the same time, we emphasize that availability of such identifiers is quite different from license to invade the privacy of individuals or disregard the need for strict confidentiality of the information held within medical records. We believe it is possible to reconcile all these goals.

We need to encourage constant conversation between investigators specializing in administrative data and those designing surveys so that the surveys can be used to help inform the interpretation of the administrative data. Survey researchers generally are not familiar with the needs for researchers to be provided with data that have adequate variables for matching. For example, data that tell us about the reasons why clients change service use patterns can be combined with information from administrative data about how often and when these service use patterns change. Furthermore, we must develop better strategies for making survey data available for linking with administrative data. A serious threat to this possibility is the assumption that if it is possible for the confidentiality of a data set to be compromised, it will. This leads to counterproductive strategies such as making it impossible to accurately match samples to their communities or counties of origin (thus obviating the possibility of exploring neighborhood or county effects).

Whereas linked administrative data can provide important information on the impact of welfare reform on child well-being, it is not a panacea and will not provide us with all the information we need to monitor welfare reform. We must be wary of the conclusions we draw from linked data because we often cannot determine whether an individual did not experience the outcome, was recorded as experiencing the outcome but could not be matched across data systems (e.g., if they moved across jurisdictional lines), or experienced the outcome but was not recorded as such. Even when the data are accurate, at best they help us monitor who appears to be affected by welfare reform, when those impacts occur, and where the impact is greatest or least. Sometimes we do not even know the direction of that change. For example, if more children per capita are reported for abuse and neglect under TANF than were reported under JOBS, this could mean that the smaller TANF caseloads have resulted in more opportunities for home visiting and better early identification of child abuse and neglect. As to why welfare reform affects children and families differentially, administrative data can only guide us as to the best places to look for those answers. Carefully designed representative samples can be drawn and subjected to other methods (e.g., surveys) that can build on the framework that a comprehensive administrative data analysis provides.

REFERENCES

Aber, J.L., J. Brooks-Gunn, and R. Maynard
  1995   The effects of welfare reform on teenage parents and their children. *The Future of Children* 5:53-71.
American Humane Association
  1984   *Highlights of Official Child Neglect and Abuse Reporting: 1982.* Denver. American Humane Association.
Ammerman, R.J., J.E. Cassissi, M. Hersen, and V.R. Van Hasselt
  1986   Consequences of physical abuse and neglect in children. *Clinical Psychology Review* 6:291-310.
Andrulis, D.P.
  1998   Access to care is the centerpiece in the elimination of socioeconomic disparities in health. *Annuals of Internal Medicine* 129(5):412-416.
Barnett, W.S.
  1998   Long-term cognitive and academic effects of early childhood education on children in poverty. *Preventive Medicine* 27:204-207.
Barth, R.P. and D. Blackwell
  1998   Death rates among California's foster care and former foster care population. *Children and Youth Services Review* 20:577-604.
Berrick, J.D., B. Needell, and M. Minkler
  1999   The policy implications of welfare reform for older caregivers, kinship care, and family configuration. *Children and Youth Services Review* 21(9/10):843-864.
Boots, S.W., and R. Green
  1999   Family care or foster care? How state policies affect kinship caregivers. In *New Federalism Issues and Options for States, Series A (A-34).* Washington, DC: The Urban Institute.
Boudett, K.P., and D. Friedlander
  1997   Does mandatory basic education improve achievement test scores of AFDC recipients? A reanalysis of data from California's GAIN program. *Evaluation Review* 21:568-588.
Brauner, S., and P. Loprest
  1999   Where Are They Now? What States' Studies of People Who Left Welfare Tell Us. *New Federalism: Issues and Options for States.* Series A. No. A-32. Washington, DC: The Urban Institute.
Card, D., and A.B. Krueger
  1998   School resources and student outcomes. *Annals of The American Academy of Political and Social Science* 559:39-53.
Chapin Hall Center for Children at the University of Chicago, Center for Social Services Research, University of California at Berkeley, University of North Carolina at Chapel Hill School of Social Work, and American Institutes for Research
  2000   *Dynamics of Children's Movement Among the AFDC, Medicaid, and Foster Care Programs Prior to Welfare Reform: 1995-1996.* Washington, DC: Office of the Secretary for Planning and Evaluation, U.S. Department of Health and Human Services. Available: http://aspe.hhs.gov/hsp/movement00/index.htm.
Child Trends
  1999   *Indicators of Children's Well-Being: From Construction to Application.* Washington, DC: Child Trends.
  2000a   *Children and Welfare Reform: A Guide to Evaluating the Effects of State Welfare Policies on Children.* Washington, DC: Child Trends.
  2000b   Indicators of Child and Family Well-Being: A Selected Inventory of Existing Projects. Available: http://childtrends.org. [September 30, 2000]

Children's Defense Fund
 1998   *Welfare to What? Early Findings on Family Hardship and Well-Being.* Washington, DC: Children's Defense Fund.
Collins, Anne
 1997   *Children and Welfare Reform Issue Brief 2: Anticipating the Effects of Federal and State Welfare Changes on Systems that Serve Children.* New York: National Center for Children in Poverty, School of Public Health, Columbia University. Available: http://cpmcnet.columbia.edu/dept/nccp/main10.html
Collins, Anne, and Lawrence Aber
 1996   *State Welfare Waiver Evaluations: Will They Increase Our Understanding of the Impact of Welfare Reform on Children?* Working paper prepared for the National Center for Children in Poverty, School of Public Health, Columbia University, New York. Available: http://cpmcnet.columbia.edu/dept/nccp/main10.html
Couch, J.L., and J.S. Milner
 1993   Effects of child neglect on children. *Criminal Justice and Behavior* 20(1):49-65.
Coulton, C., and R. Hollister
 1999   Measuring comprehensive community initiative outcomes using data available for small areas. In *New Approaches to Evaluating Community Initiatives. Volume 2: Theory, Measurement, and Analysis.* The Aspen Institute Roundtable on Comprehensive Community Initiatives. Available: http://www.aspenroundtable.org.
Coulton, C.J., J.E. Korbin, M. Su, and J. Chow
 1995   Community level factors and child maltreatment rates. *Child Development* 66:1262-1276.
Currie, J., and T. Duncan
 1995   *Could Subsequent School Quality Affect the Long Term Gains from Head Start.* Cambridge MA: National Bureau of Economic Research.
Darnell, J., and S. Rosenbaum
 1997   Welfare reform: Unanticipated but inevitable consequences for health insurance coverage for the poor. *Nutrition* 13(5):490-491.
Ellwood, M.
 1999   *The Medicaid Eligibility Maze: Coverage Expands, But Enrollment Problems Persist: Findings from a Five State Study.* Kaiser Commission on Medicaid and the Uninsured. Available: http:// www.kff.org [November 30, 1999]
Families USA
 1999   *One Step Forward, One Step Back,* Families USA. Available: http://www.familiesusa.org.
English, D., and C.S. Widom
 1999   *Childhood Victimization and Delinquency, Adult Criminality, and Violent Criminal Behavior.* Unpublished paper presented at the Child Welfare League of America National Conference on Research in Child Welfare. Seattle.
Gabor, V., A. Ben-Avi, and I. Hill
 1997   *Developing Performance Measures and Performance-Based Contracts for State and Local MCH Activities.* Washington, DC: Health Systems Research, Inc. Under contract to Health Resources and Services Administration, Maternal and Child Health Bureau.
Garfinkel, I., and S.S. McLanahan
 1986   Single mothers and their children: Summary and recommendations. In *Single Mothers and Their Children,* I. Garfinkel and S.S. McLanahan, eds. Washington, DC: The Urban Institute.
Geen, R., and S. Waters
 1997   *The Impact of Welfare Reform on Child Welfare Financing.* Washington, DC: The Urban Institute.

Gelles, R.J.
  1992   Poverty and violence toward children. *American Behavioral Scientist* 35(3):258-274.
Geltman, P.L., A.F. Meyers, J. Greenberg, and B. Zuckerman
  1996   Welfare reform and children's health. *Archives of Pediatric and Adolescent Medicine* 150:384-389.
Gil, D.G.
  1971   Violence against children. *Journal of Marriage and the Family* 33(4):637-648.
Giovannoni, J. M., and A. Billingsley
  1970   Child neglect among the poor: A study of parental adequacy in families of three ethnic groups. *Child Welfare* 49(4):196-204.
Gortmaker, S.L., and D.K. Walker
  1984   Monitoring child health in communities. In *Monitoring Child Health in the United States*, D.K. Walker and J.B. Richmond, eds. Cambridge, MA: Harvard University Press.
Grason, H., and N.E. Nachbar
  1997   *Developing MCH Systems Measures: A Process and Strategy in Kansas.* Washington, DC: Health Systems Research, Inc. Under contract to the Health Resources and Services Administration, Maternal and Child Health Bureau.
Gray, E.
  1988   The link between child abuse and juvenile delinquency: What we know and recommendations for policy and research. In *Family Abuse and its Consequences: New Directions in Research*, G.T. Hotaling, D. Finkelhor, J.T. Kirpatrick, and M.A. Straus, eds. Newbury Park, CA: Sage.
Greenberg, M.
  1998   *Participation in Welfare and Medicaid Enrollment.* Kaiser Commission on Medicaid and the Uninsured. Available: http://www.kff.org.
Haskins, R.
  1995   Losing ground or moving ahead? Welfare reform and children. Pp. 63-86 in *Escape from Poverty: What Makes a Difference for Children*, P. Chase-Lansdale and J. Brooks-Gunn, eds. New York: Cambridge University Press.
Jonson-Reid, M., and R.P. Barth
  2000   From maltreatment report to juvenile incarceration: The role of child welfare services. *Child Abuse and Neglect* 24:505-520.
Knitzer, J., and S. Bernard
  1997   *Children and Welfare Reform, Issue Brief I: The New Welfare Law and Vulnerable Families: Implications for Child Welfare and Child Protection Systems.* New York: National Center for Children in Poverty.
Koppelman, J., and J.G. Lear
  1998   The new child health insurance expansions: How will school-based health centers fit in? *Journal of School Health* 68(10):441-446.
Lee, B.J., & R.M. Goerge
  1999   Poverty, early childbearing, and child maltreatment: A multinomial analysis. *Children and Youth Services Review* 21(9/10):755-780.
Levinson, P.
  1969   The next generation: A study of children in AFDC families. *Welfare in Review* 7:1-9.
Ludwig, J., G.J. Duncan, and P. Hirschfield
  1999   Urban poverty and juvenile crime. Evidence from a randomized housing-mobility experiment. *American Journal of Epidemiology* 49(11):203-218.
Magura, S., and B.S. Moses
  1986   *Outcome Measures for Child Welfare Services: Theory and Applications.* Washington, DC: Child Welfare League of America.

Maine Department of Human Services
  1983   *Children's Deaths in Maine: 1976-1980 Final Report.* Augusta: Maine Department of Human Services.
Manpower Demonstration Research Corporation
  2000   *The Next Generation.* Available: http://www.mdrc.org/Families&Children/Next Generation.htm [July 19, 2000]
Margolis, L.H., G.P. Cole, and J.B. Kotch
  1997   Historical foundations in maternal and children's health. Chapter 2 in *Maternal and Child Health: Programs, Problems and Policy in Public Health*, Jonathan B. Kotch, ed. Gaithersburg, MD: Aspen Publishers, Inc.
Maternal and Child Health Bureau
  1996   *Maternal and Child Health Strategy Statement Data Utilization and Enhancement.* Washington, DC: U.S. Department of Health and Human Services.
Meezan, W., and J. Giovannoni
  1995   The current threat to protective services and the child welfare system. *Children and Youth Services Review* 17(4):567-574.
Moffitt, R.A., and E.P. Slade
  1997   Health care coverage for children who are on and off welfare. *Future of Children* 7(1):87-98.
National Center for Health Statistics
  1996   *Healthy People 2000 Review, 1995-96.* Hyattsville, MD: Public Health Service.
National Conference of State Legislators
  1999   *Tracking Welfare Reform: Designing Follow-up Studies of Recipients Who Leave Welfare*, National Conference of State Legislators. Available: http://www.ncsl.org/statefed/welfare/trackbrf.html. [November 1, 1999]
National Research Council
  1999   *Evaluating Welfare Reform: A Framework and Review of Current Work. Interim Report*, Robert A. Moffitt and Michele Ver Ploeg, eds. Committee on National Statistics, Panel on Data and Methods for Measuring the Effects of Changes in Social Welfare Programs, Washington, DC: National Academy Press.
Needell, B., S. Cuccaro-Alamin, A. Brookhart, and S. Lee
  1999   Transitions from AFDC to child welfare in California. *Children and Youth Services Review* 21(9/10):815-841.
O'Campo, P., and L. Rojas-Smith
  1998   Welfare reform and women's health: Review of the literature and implications for state policy. *Journal of Public Health Policy* 19(4):420-446.
Orthner, D.K., and K.A. Randolph
  1999   Welfare reform and high school dropout patterns for children. *Children and Youth Services Review* 21:881-900.
Pappas, G.
  1998   Monitoring the health consequences of welfare reform. *International Journal of Health Services* 23(4):703-713.
Philips, D. P., N. Christenfeld, and N.M. Ryan
  1999   An increase in the number of deaths in the United States in the first week of the month: An association with substance abuse and other causes of death. *New England Journal of Medicine* 341(2):93-98.
Reiss, J.
  1999   *Does Your State's Title XXI SCHIP Plan Promote the Development and Maintenance of Quality Systems of Care for Children with Special Health Needs, Issues and Criteria for SCHIP Plan Review and Analysis.* Available: http://www.ichp.edu/schip/materials/893253826.html

Research Forum on Children, Families, and the New Federalism
1999   Evaluating the effects of state welfare policies on children: The project on state level outcomes. *The Forum* 2(2):4-5.
Schorr, L.B.
1997   *Common Purpose: Strengthening Families and Neighborhoods to Rebuild America.* New York: Doubleday.
Shenkman, E.
1999   *Analysis of Pending Accounts in the Florida Healthy Kids Program: Executive Summary.* Prepared for the Healthy Kids Corporation. Available: http://www.ichp.edu/rmanaged/materials/896969477.html. [October 30, 1999]
Shook, K.
1998   Assessing the consequences of welfare reform for child welfare. *Poverty Research News* 11(1):8-12.
South Carolina Department of Social Services
1999   Welfare Reform/Child Well-Being Administrative Data Linking. South Carolina CHILD LINK. Available: http://aspe.hhs.gov/hsp/adminlink/sc/scfinal.htm. [November 13, 1999]
Starfield, B., M. Bergner, M. Ensminger, A. Riley, S. Ryan, B. Green, P. McGauhey, A. Skinner, and S. Kim
1993   Adolescent health status measurement: Development of the child health and illness profile. *Pediatrics* 91(2):430-435.
UC Data Archive and Technical Assistance
1999   *An Inventory of Research Uses of Administrative Data in Social Services Programs in the United States 1998.* Berkeley, CA: University of California. Available: http://ucdata.berkeley.edu/new_web/inventory/intro.html. [December 1, 1999]
Vermont Agency of Human Services
2000   *Community Profiles.* Available: http://www.ahs.state.vt.us.
Wells, K., and S. Guo
in press   Reunification of foster children under conditions of welfare reform. *Children and Youth Services Review.*
Widom, C.S.
1991   Avoidance of criminality in abused and neglected children. *Psychiatry* 54:162-174.
Willis, E., and R.M. Kleigman
1997   Wisconsin's welfare reform and its potential effects on the health of children. *Journal of Health Care for the Poor and Underserved* 8(1):25-35.
Wilson, J.B., D.T. Ellwood, and J. Brooks-Gunn
1995   Welfare-to-work through the eyes of children. Pp. 63-86 in *Escape from Poverty: What Makes a Difference for Children,* P. Chase-Lansdale and J. Brooks-Gunn, eds. New York: Cambridge University Press.
Wolock, I., and S. Magura
1996   Parental substance abuse as a predictor of child maltreatment re-reports. *Child Abuse & Neglect* 20(12):1183-1193.
Wulczyn, F.H., K. Brunner, and R.M. Goerge
1999   *A Report from the Multistate Foster Care Data Archive: Foster Care Dynamics, 1983-1997.* Chicago: Chapin Hall Center for Children at the University of Chicago.
Yaffe, A.
1998   Examining the Effects of Welfare Reform on Children: The project on state level outcomes. *Poverty Research News* 2(1), 1, 6.
Yoshikawa, H.
1999   Welfare dynamics, support services, mothers' earnings, and child cognitive development: Implications for contemporary welfare reform. *Child Development* 70(3):779-801.

Zaslow, M., K.A. Moore, D.R. Morrison, and M.J. Coiro
   1995   The family support act and children: Potential pathways of influence. *Children and Youth Services Review* 17(1,2):231-249.

Zaslow, M., K. Tout, C. Botsko, and K. Moore
   1998   Welfare reform and children: Potential implications. In *New Federalism: Issues and Options for States, Series A, No. A-23.* Washington, DC: The Urban Institute.

Zeller, D.E.
   1999   *Welfare Reform Impacts on Child Welfare Caseloads: A Research Agenda.* Troy, NY: Hornby Zeller Associates, Inc.

Zuravin, S.J., and F.A. DiBlasio
   1996   The correlates of child physical abuse and neglect by adolescent mothers. *Journal of Family Violence* 11(2):149-166.

Part III

Qualitative Data

11

The Right (Soft) Stuff: Qualitative Methods and the Study of Welfare Reform

Katherine S. Newman

Statistical trends are necessary but not sufficient. To me, statistical trends alone are like a canary in a coal mine—they yield life or death information on the "health" of an environment, but don't always lead to improvement, causes and corrective actions.

Dennis Lieberman, Director of the Office of Welfare-to-Work
U.S. Department of Labor

In the years to come, researchers and policy makers concerned with the consequences of welfare reform will dwell on studies drawn from administrative records that track the movement of Temporary Assistance for Needy Families (TANF) recipients from public assistance into the labor market and, perhaps, back again. Survey researchers with panel studies will be equally in demand as federal, state, and local officials charged with the responsibility of administering what is left of the welfare system come to grips with the dynamics of their caseloads. This is exactly as it should be, for the "poor support" of the future— whatever its shape may be—can only be fashioned if we can capture the big picture that emerges from the quantitative study of post-Aid to Families with Dependent Children (AFDC) dynamics when many of the nation's poor women have moved from welfare to work.

This research was supported by generous grants from the Foundation for Child Development, the Ford Foundation, the National Science Foundation, the Russell Sage Foundation, the MacArthur Foundation Network on Socio-Economic Status and Health, and the MacArthur Foundation Network on Inequality and Economic Performance.

Yet as the early returns tell us, the story that emerges from these large-scale studies contains many puzzles. The rolls have dropped precipitously nationwide, but not everywhere (Katz and Carnavale, 1998). TANF recipients often are able to find jobs, but many have trouble keeping them and find themselves back on the rolls in a pattern not unfamiliar to students of the old welfare system. Millions of poor Americans have disappeared from the system altogether: they are not on TANF, but they are not employed. Where in the world are these people? Welfare reform has pushed many women into the low-wage labor market, but we are only starting to understand how this trend has impacted their standard of living or the well-being of their children. Are they better off in terms of material hardship than they were before? Are the benefits of immersion in the world of work for parents—ranging from the psychological satisfaction of joining the American mainstream to the mobility consequences of getting a foot in the door—translating into positive trajectories for their children? Or are kids paying the price for the lift their mothers have experienced because they have been left behind in substandard childcare? And can their mothers stick with the work world if they are worried about what is happening to their kids?

These kinds of questions cannot be resolved through reliance on administrative records. Survey data can help answer some of these questions but without the texture of in-depth or ethnographic data collection. States and localities do not systematically collect data on mothers' social, psychological, or familial wellbeing. They will not be able to determine what has become of those poor people who have not been able to enroll in the system. They have little sense of how households, as opposed to individuals, reach collective decisions that deputize some members to head into the labor market, others to stay home to watch the kids, and yet others to remain in school. Problems like domestic abuse or low levels of enrollment in children's health insurance programs cannot be easily understood via panel studies that ask respondents to rate their lives on a scale of 1 to 10. Though one might argue that welfare reform was oriented toward "work first" and was not an anti poverty program per se, understanding the nature of material hardship is an important goal for any public official who wants to get to the bottom of the poverty problem. Trawling along the bottom of the wage structure, we are likely to learn a thing or two about recidivism as the burdens of raising children collide with the limitations of the low-wage labor market for addressing the needs of poor families.

If administrative records and panel studies cannot tell us everything we might want to know about the impact of welfare reform, what are the complementary sources of information we might use? I argue in this chapter that qualitative research is an essential part of the tool kit and that, particularly when embedded in a survey-based study, it can illuminate some of the unintended consequences and paradoxes of this historic about-face in American social policy.

From this vantage point, I argue that the "right soft stuff" can go a long way toward helping us to do the following:

• Understand subjective responses, belief systems, expectations, and the relationship between these aspects of world view and labor market behavior;
• Explore "client" understandings of rules, including the partial information they may have received regarding the intentions or execution of new policies;
• Uncover underlying factors that drive response patterns that are overlooked or cannot easily be measured through fixed-choice questionnaires;
• Explore in greater detail the unintended consequences of policy change; and
• Focus special attention on the dynamics shaping the behavior of households or communities that can only be approximated in most survey or administrative record studies that draw their data from individuals. This will be particularly significant in those domains where the interests of some individuals may conflict with others and hard choices have to be made.

The intrinsic value of qualitative research is in its capacity to dig deeper than any survey can go, to excavate the human terrain that lurks behind the numbers. Used properly, qualitative research can pry open that black box and tell us what lies inside. And at the end of the day, when the public and the politicians want to know whether this regime change has been successful, the capacity to illuminate its real consequences—good and bad—with stories that are more than anecdotes, but stand as representatives of patterns we know to be statistically significant, is a powerful means of communicating what the numbers can only suggest.

THE CONTENT OF THE TOOL KIT

A wide variety of methodologies come under the broad heading of qualitative methods, each with its own virtues and liabilities. In this section, I discuss some of the best known approaches and sketch out both what can be learned from each and where the limitations typically lie. I consider sequentially potential or actual studies of welfare reform utilizing:

• open-ended questions embedded in survey instruments
• in-depth interviews with subsamples, of survey respondents
• focus groups
• qualitative, longitudinal studies
• participant observation fieldwork

Where possible, I draw on ongoing research to illustrate the strengths and limits of these methods.

Open-Ended Questions Embedded in Survey Instruments

Obviously the great value of survey research is in its large sample size, its representativeness, and the capacity it provides for statistical analysis and causal inference. Typically the items on survey research instruments are close-ended questions based on fixed-choice response categories or questions that require respondents to rate their reactions on set scales. However, it is not uncommon for survey studies to include a limited number of items that are open ended, where respondents either write short responses in their own words with no guidance from the researcher or speak their minds into tape recorders that generate brief transcripts. Open-ended questions embedded in survey instruments typically follow more cut-and-dried queries (Were you "very happy, moderately happy, moderately unhappy, or very unhappy" with the quality of your child's care last week?) with "why?" questions designed to learn a bit more about the reasoning behind a respondent's answer. (What kinds of problems did you encounter with your child care last week?) The value of the follow-up question lies in the ability of the researchers to anticipate all the relevant fixed-choice categories. Where this is particularly vexing, open-ended questions can help to illuminate complex patterns while preserving the strength in numbers that survey research provides. They also sometimes have the secondary benefit of maintaining the engagement of subjects who may otherwise become bored and therefore less attentive to typical survey items.

At least two purposes can be served here. A key advantage to embedding qualitative research inside a survey design is that one benefits from the representativeness and sample size, while preserving the insights afforded by qualitative data. Second, open-ended responses (particularly in pilot studies) can be used to generate more nuanced fixed-choice questions for future surveys. Finally, open-ended responses can be coded and analyzed in much the same way that fixed choice questions are, but now with categories that essentially have been generated by the survey respondents rather than forced on them by the researcher. The new categories are more reflective of the experiences or views of interviewees as they see them. If the subjective understandings of respondents are the issue, this is an appropriate method for capturing them on a large scale.

Embedding open-ended questions has obvious limitations. Because of the expense involved in coding the material, open-ended questions are not always practical in large-scale surveys with thousands of respondents. If cost becomes a significant issue, it may be necessary to code a random subsample of the responses. Questionnaires administered face to face or over the telephone can still utilize open-ended items by having the interviewer record the responses or by using tape recorders. Problems of thoroughness can be minimized through careful training of interviewers. However, open-ended questions can be problematic in self-administered and mail questionnaires, particularly when one is dealing with respondents who have literacy problems.

Subsample and In-Depth Interviews

When one wants to collect more open-ended data from each subject, it may be appropriate to draw a smaller random subsample of a survey population for longer interviews designed to elicit information on a wide range of topics. A simple random sample or a stratified random sample may be used (assuming the appropriate demographic categories can be identified—for example, groups defined by race, age, family status, or those with children of particular ages) and can be interviewed in situ or in a central location. On the other hand, there may be situations for which it is helpful to select purposeful samples (that may or may not be selected randomly) for in-depth interviews. For example, among those leaving the welfare rolls, we may want to learn more about respondents who have never worked or who have not worked in many years. Pulling a subsample of this kind for an in-depth interview study can yield important insights. Of course, among respondents with literacy issues, using mail questionnaires is problematic anyways.

Studies of either kind can explore in some detail the experience "informants" are having in seeking a job, adjusting to employment, managing children's needs, coping with new expenses, finding transportation to work, relying on neighbors, and a host of other areas that may shed light on the TANF and post-TANF experience. As long as the subsample is representative, the researcher can extrapolate from it to the experience of the universe in the same way one would generalize from any representative group.

The advantage of the smaller subsample is that it solicits greater depth of knowledge on a larger number of subjects, yielding a more well-rounded perspective than is possible with only one or two open-ended questions. Such a methodology is appropriate when the study aims to understand the intricacies of subjective perspectives or the intertwined nature of family behavior when policy change impacts directly on one household member, but indirectly on other household members. Problems of this complexity can be understood only with a great deal of qualitative information.

The longitudinal study of the Milwaukee New Hope experiment is a good example of the value of this kind of research. New Hope provided low-income families in the experimental group with generous childcare, insurance supports, and earnings supplements to bring them above the poverty line to make it easier to remain in the labor force if they work at least 30 hours a week. Under the direction of Greg Duncan at Northwestern University and Tom Weisner at the

University of California, Los Angeles (UCLA), the New Hope research team developed both a longitudinal panel survey and an embedded ethnographic study[1] that drew mainly on (1) repeated interviews with a representative sample of participants and controls, as well as "outliers" chosen because they appeared to deviate from patterns observable in their data and (2) classical fieldwork (discussed in a later section). From Duncan's perspective, the blending of "hard" and "soft" data has been critical in understanding program impacts:

> New Hope's qualitative data proved indispensable for understanding the nature and meaning of program impacts. As simple as an experimental design may seem, analyses of experimental impacts are complicated by needs to quantify the key outcomes and isolate program impacts within important sample subgroups. Qualitative data are very helpful in both of these tasks.
>
> One of the most important—and initially puzzling—impacts of the New Hope experiment was on teacher-reported improvements in the behavior of preadolescent boys, but not girls. Boys but not girls in the experimental group were 0.3 to 0.5 standard deviations better behaved and higher achieving than their control-group counterparts. Based on the survey data alone, however, we were unable to account for this gender difference.
>
> Qualitative interviews suggested that interviewed mothers felt that gangs and other neighborhood pressures were much more threatening to their boys than girls. As a result, experimental group mothers channeled more of the program's resources (e.g. childcare subsidies for extended-day programs) to their boys than girls. Further quantitative analyses of both New Hope and national-sample survey data support this interpretation (Romich, 1999). It is unlikely that this important finding about family strategies in dangerous neighborhoods would have been discovered from the quantitative data alone (Greg Duncan, personal communication, 11/29/99).

The New Hope project also has provided useful analyses that separate the experiences of subgroups of participants who have responded differently to the same program opportunities. Because New Hope mirrors what some of the more generous states have tried to accomplish in their welfare-to-work programs, its experience is useful in parsing the differential impact of these supports for working families. As Duncan suggests in his comments on labor supply and earnings, without the qualitative component, it would have been harder to "unpack" the behavioral differences that distinguish subgroups:

> It was clear from the beginning of our quantitative work that program effects on work and earnings were heterogeneous. Roughly one-third of the families at-

---

[1]The design of the qualitative sample in New Hope took a random draw from all program and control cases that fell into the family and child sample (essentially, cases with at least one child aged 0-10 at the point of random assignment). The research team did some stratification before drawing the sample, sorting the list by program vs. control status, then by race. Thereafter, the sampling was random within these cells (see Weisner et al., 1999).

tracted to New Hope were already working more than 30 hours and viewed the program's benefits as a way of making work and family demands more manageable. If anything, experimental/control differences in the labor supply of these families were negative. In contrast, families not working full time at the start viewed New Hope as a way of facilitating a transition to full-time work. On balance, experimental/control impacts on labor supply were positive for these families, although stronger in the first than second year of the program.

Qualitative interviews pointed to important heterogeneity among this latter set of families. Some, perhaps one-fifth, had multiple problems (e.g., drug dependence, children with severe behavior problems, relatives in ill health) that New Hope's package of benefits were not designed to address. Others had no such apparent problems and, in these cases, both experimental and control families could be expected to do well in Milwaukee's job-rich environment.

But a third group, who were only one or two barriers away from making it, profited the most from the New Hope package of benefits (Weisner et al., 1999). Program impacts on the labor supply of families with a small number of barriers were large, and larger in the second than the first year. This key set of findings simply would not have been discovered were it not for the qualitative work (ibid.).

Focus Groups

A popular technique for exploratory research involves the use of focus groups, small gatherings of individuals selected for their demographic characteristics who engage in collective discussion following questions or prompts issued by a researcher acting as a facilitator. Focus groups operate in the native language of the participants and can last as long as 2 hours, providing an in-depth discussion of a topic. They can be used for a variety of purposes. Some researchers rely on focus groups as a means of generating questions they expect to ask in surveys. Others use focus groups as a primary means of data collection. Here the appeal usually lies in the modest expense involved: This is a "quick and dirty" method of gathering data on the subjective responses of program participants.[2] As a result, focus group studies can often be done on an ad hoc basis if they are not part of an initial evaluation design. A wide range of interested parties—from politicians to business firms—utilize focus groups as a means of "testing the market," particularly where public opinion is at issue.

Of course, the focus group approach has limitations. The contamination of opinion that occurs when individuals are exposed to the views of others can

---

[2]When one adds in the costs of transcription, this method may be more expensive than it first appears. However, because it involves a much smaller number of people gathered into one place, the logistics are less burdensome and the sheer amount of data probably more manageable than a large-scale survey.

render the data hard to interpret. When particularly forceful individuals dominate the discussion, the views of more passive participants can be easily squelched or brought into conformity in ways that distort their true reactions. Some people understandably are hesitant to air their opinions on sensitive subjects (e.g. domestic violence, employer misbehavior, criminal behavior) in these types of settings.

Moreover, it is hard to make focus groups representative of a population in any meaningful sense. They must therefore be used purposively or with caution. Focus groups are not a good tool for producing data that will withstand scrutiny for representativeness. What they do provide is a relatively inexpensive and rapid means of learning about underlying attitudes and reactions, an approach that may be informative for officials or scholars looking to design more nuanced research instruments. They are often used as an exploratory tool to help design survey or interview studies because they help to expose important problems that should be subjected to more systematic study. These are important goals for researchers. For program administrators looking for ways to give their staff members insight into the lives of those they may see only in "numerical form," focus groups can be a means of putting a human face on administrative records.

Some of the limitations of focus groups can be addressed to a modest degree through the careful selection of focus group members. Sensitive subjects may best be addressed by drawing together people who are as similar as possible, who have experienced a common dilemma, in the hopes that the similarities between them will lessen any discomfort. Hence investigators often construct focus groups along the lines of racial or ethnic groups, gender or age groups, or neighborhood groups. The "contamination" of forceful individuals can be limited by the guiding hand of a highly skilled facilitator who makes sure that others have a chance to participate. However, none of these approaches eliminates the difficulties inherent in public discussions of this kind.

Focus groups are therefore probably best used to gather data on community experience with and opinions toward public assistance programs rather than to gather systematic data on individual perspectives. For example, the problems associated with enrollment in children's health insurance systems probably could be well understood by convening focus groups. Indeed, one of the strengths of the method is that it prompts individuals who may not be able to express themselves easily in a one-on-one setting to recall and describe difficulties they have encountered. Information of this kind is far more textured and complete than fixed-choice questionnaires and can help public officials to address the deficiencies in outreach programs, for example.

Qualitative Longitudinal Studies

Welfare reform is a process unfolding over a number of years, where the before and the after may be widely separated and the "in between" states of at least as much interest as the ultimate outcomes. We have good reason to believe that families pass through stages of adaptation as their children age, new members arrive, people marry, jobs are won and lost, and the hold of new requirements (work hours, mandated job searches) exert their influences. For this reason, it will be critical that at least some of the nation's implementation research follow individuals and families over a period of years, rather than rest easy with cross-sectional studies. Indeed, one need only look at how the Panel Study of Income Dynamics, the National Longitudinal Study of Youth, or the Survey of Income and Program Participation have altered and enhanced our understanding of income over the lifespan or movements in and out of poverty over time to recognize the value of panel studies of this kind.

These longitudinal studies contain very little qualitative data. The number of sample members and broad coverage of information is expensive so that cost containment often means depth has been sacrificed in favor of coverage. However, anthropologists and sociologists have developed longitudinal interview studies in which the same participants are interviewed in an open-ended fashion at intervals over a long course of time. I have two studies in the field at the moment—one on the long-range careers of workers who entered the labor market in minimum-wage jobs in poor neighborhoods and the other on a sample of working poor families, intended to assess the impact of welfare reform on those who were not the targets of policy change—that utilize this approach. In each case, representative samples of approximately 100 subjects were drawn from larger samples of subjects who completed face-to-face surveys. Thereafter, the smaller subsamples were interviewed at 3-to 4-year intervals, for a total of 6-to 8-years' worth of data collection. Here it has proven possible to capture changes in perceptions of opportunity, detailed accounts of changing household composition, the interaction between children's lives and parents' lives, and the impact of neighborhood change on the fate of individual families. Although the samples are very small by the standards of survey research, the depth and nuance of the data that emerges from such an approach are of great value in opening the "black box" that may resist interpretation in studies based solely on administrative records or fixed-choice instruments.

Qualitative panel studies are, however, labor intensive and expensive for the number of respondents they generate. They ask a great deal from participants who typically have to give up several hours of their time for each wave. Given these high demands, providing honoraria of $50-100 to ensure participation in interviews is generally important to generate adequate response rates. Such generous honoraria would bankrupt a larger study. Longitudinal interview studies are typically done via the use of tape-recorded interviews, which must be transcribed and possibly translated. Given the nature of the data that studies of this kind are seeking, it is often helpful to employ interviewers who are matched by age, race, gender, and class. This process is not simple. For example, I have developed research teams that were closely matched along race and gender lines, only to discover that vast class differences became quite apparent between respondents who were poor and living in rundown neighborhoods and students who are clearly middle class in origin and living in far better circumstances.[3] Indeed class was often at least as important as race in making a match. The gulf between a professor in her forties and informants in their twenties can be quite substantial just because of the different worlds they inhabit because of their ages.

Not all studies attempt the matching process, and the question of whether it is necessary to find counterparts who are sociologically similar is controversial. For example, Edin and Lein, both white professional women, have done exquisite interview work with women of color on welfare and in low-wage jobs. Other white researchers (myself and some members of my research teams) have had good success despite racial differences. Indeed, it is sometimes easier for informants to reveal sensitive information to outsiders who are perceived as less likely to "spread their personal business" around town (Kathryn Edin, personal communication).

My experience has shown that long-term relationships are easier to develop when racial barriers are minimized and a comfort zone is reached based on perceived similarities.[4] It is imperative to have staff fluent in the languages of the subjects. It is even more important to invest in training the members of a research team: All the matching in the world will not make up for lack of training, and one should never assume that sharing skin color or gender is sufficient. These requirements add to the costs involved in research.

The quality of the data obtained through well-designed and well-executed qualitative, longitudinal studies can make them well worth the effort. This may be particularly true when one wants to go beyond a scholarly or policy audience to engage either the public or political figures in the exploration of welfare reform. Illustrating statistical trends with "real-life" examples of the dilemmas and success stories of former welfare recipients is of great value in this regard. Researchers should not cede to journalists the entire responsibility for telling the story of welfare reform "with a human face" because reporters rarely select their informants systematically and there is no guarantee that their accounts will be anything more than anecdotal.

Qualitative panel studies can be developed with an original sampling strategy that picks up a representative population based on neighborhood residence or participants and matched controls who participate in a social service program. However, they are probably most valuable when they are embedded in panel

---

[3]John L. Jackson's (2001) dissertation, "Doing Harlem," makes this point very forcefully as he negotiates the vast gulf that separated him as a black man in a doctoral program from his black informants who were far less well educated.

[4]One should not minimize the interference that class differences pose, even when interviewers are matched for race. Graduate students from research universities may have very little in common with welfare recipients, even when they share minority status. The class background gap can loom very large.

studies using a survey design and are therefore subsets of the much larger population of survey respondents that can serve as a better basis for statistical analysis.

This embedding strategy has one disadvantage: If the underlying survey is part of a longitudinal panel study, the selection of a subsample that will be accorded more attention may bias the responses of this group to succeeding waves of the survey. Researchers need to evaluate this possibility, though it need not be a serious flaw. Most surveys seeking to track the consequences of welfare reform are going to focus on "objective" and measurable outcomes: hours worked, income earned, jobs acquired, jobs lost, health insurance enrollment, and so forth. Qualitative studies may yield additional information on how these states of being were reached (job search strategies, barriers to insurance enrollment), but in most instances will not compromise the underlying information in a negative (concealing) direction. The experience of providing more information through open-ended interviews may, in fact, encourage greater revelation among the participants in the qualitative study. Researchers will want to check for any systematic biases that may be emerging and, for some purposes, exclude the subsample from statistical analyses of the survey population.

However, I would argue that the advantages of selecting the qualitative sample from an original panel population far outweigh the disadvantages. "Soft" studies of this kind are often suspect on grounds of representativeness and the value of their contribution dismissed as a result. Although one could, in theory, recruit participants in a qualitative study who are similar to those in the survey population, it is always possible that these "add ons" differ enough from the participants to raise doubt. Hence, in my view, it is a safer bet to draw the qualitative sample from the original research universe and risk the chances that their involvement may adversely alter their responses to a longitudinal study. (Obviously this is not a problem if the underlying survey is cross-sectional.)

Participant Observation Fieldwork

Anthropologists and qualitative sociologists often combine interviews with a large "N" with direct observation of behavior in order to fill in gaps that may emerge using other data collection methods. Fieldwork of this kind frequently involves day-in, day-out contact with a subset of a larger survey population, often resident in the same neighborhood or partaking of a common institutional setting (e.g., a welfare office, a job training program). Informal conversation between researchers and informants or between members of a community (with researchers "on the side") can be illuminating. Direct observation of behavior is often helpful as a check on what respondents (survey or interview) report about their state of mind or the actions they routinely take, as a fieldworker may see it differently when in situ.

Participant observation data are recorded in the form of daily fieldnotes that must be entered into a database then coded, sorted, and analyzed for patterns of recurrent behavior or illustrative instances of a pattern that might have popped up in another form (e.g., in a quantitative analysis). This data collection strategy is particularly helpful when researchers are dealing with behavior that might be concealed, easily forgotten, hard to elicit, or simply skewed by the desires informants often have to paint their behavior in a better light.

For some years now, for example, I have been conducting a study of the impact of welfare reform on the working poor in New York City. This is a longitudinal interview study involving 100 families in three ethnic groups across Manhattan, Brooklyn, and the Bronx. Three waves of interviews over a 6-year period provide a detailed sense of the difficulties these families have encountered securing childcare or finding work that dovetails with family responsibilities, even though these families were not the targets of reform per se (because they were already in the labor market prior to 1996). The two waves of interviews we have completed thus far indicate that although the availability of jobs has improved and wages are rising, problems remain for the working poor precisely because their wages do not push them above the poverty line. Improvements in their personal circumstances are, in many instances, offset by the extraordinary escalation in costs brought about by the same economic boom that is providing more employment opportunity. Rents are rising everywhere throughout the New York City area, dwarfing the gains these families have made, particularly for those who are not in rent-controlled or Section 8 housing. Family budgets are strained; relatives are doubling up; children are moving back and forth from New York to Puerto Rico because, as parents are preoccupied with work all day, some are having trouble supervising their children. These observations are clear enough in the interviews.

However, these data provide only a sketchy sense of how these dilemmas surface at the neighborhood level and how, in turn, that ecological context impacts the families in our study. Hence we developed a community study component of the project, a year's worth of intensive fieldwork in three New York neighborhoods—one primarily African American, one largely Dominican, and one with a large number of Puerto Ricans as well as other Latino immigrants from Mexico and Central America. For the past 7 months, we have been tagging along beside police officers, sitting in classrooms, visiting with congressmen and church leaders, talking with local employers, and devoting a lot of attention to 12 families drawn from our interview sample who live in these three communities.

Participant observation has been a valuable addition to what we know from the interview data. For example, we have been able to see for ourselves what the teen culture of the communities is like and the ways in which it is influencing the behavior of particular members of the households we study as the parents are occupied at work. We have witnessed the dilemmas of poor working mothers who cannot easily control their sons when they reach adolescence and we know how they adjust their work lives to try to provide more opportunity for surveillance. Having worked with these families over a long period of time—before and after their reentry into the labor force—we have learned that their capacity to steer their adolescents has declined sharply as the pressures for them to hold jobs increased.

For example, one family we have come to know quite well has a teenage son who is faring poorly in his middle school. When his mother was receiving public assistance, she was able to visit the school during the day to confer with his guidance counselors at length and to learn directly from them (as opposed to the filtered news from the son) that he was in danger of being held back a full year. Now that this mother is working full time, she is unable to exercise this level of involvement. Her family clearly benefits from her earnings: There is less tension over finances in the household and the departure of a paying boarder was less of a cataclysm than it might have been otherwise. However, the mother is worried about what will become of her teenage son in school and now depends on him for information on his progress. He is clearly at risk for dropping out altogether, which may impact his mother's employment stability and will surely influence his own trajectory into adulthood.

Our home-based and daycare based fieldwork also has helped us understand the dilemmas of poor working mothers who have been unable to afford or locate quality child care. The youngest children in some of these households are showing the effects of poor quality care, with some displaying seriously worrying behaviors that their mothers believe are the result of untrained or unconcerned childcare providers (including relatives pressed into service). When we compare these children to their older siblings, most of whom had more attention from their mothers when they were little, the differences are striking. This tells us there is a problem to be understood here, for the good fortune of mothers (most of whom report being happier because they are working) may be paralleled by the declining fortunes of their youngest children, an outcome many of Edin et al.'s (1999) interviewees worried about in advance. If suboptimal-quality childcare remains the lot of the working poor, we may come to understand welfare reform as a story with bifurcated outcomes within the same family: good news for Moms, bad news for kids.

The knowledge we have gained about the work lives of our main informants is complemented by the fieldwork we have done in the neighborhoods. We know, for example, that although opportunities for factory work are very limited in the city itself, that a whole private, off-the-books system of van pools carries Dominican workers out to New Jersey factories where they earn just above the minimum wage. Our observational data have shown that the van pools themselves have become a major source of information on job openings for low-skilled workers. The cost of this reverse commute is fairly onerous for low earners, however, amounting to more than 10 percent of take-home earnings for most users.

The perspectives of service providers, teachers, police officers, local politicians, and employers are equally valuable, for they are in a position to look beyond the immediate concerns of particular families to assess the consequences of welfare reform for neighborhoods and the institutions within them that must absorb the demands that policy change visits upon them. Service providers, particularly those in the child care and medical care fields, are concerned that they cannot respond adequately to the additional needs that have surfaced since time limits were imposed on federal cash assistance. Medical care personnel in poor neighborhoods continue to report that they have not been able to enroll enough children in Child Health Plus and that they are seeing a steady, and often overwhelming, demand in emergency rooms for treatment of conditions that should have been seen long before they reach this critical point.

Teachers and guidance counselors have noticed that they have a harder time getting parents to pay attention to children's school behavior or academic problems because they are not as available as they once were. The coincidence of welfare reform and the imposition of new state testing standards for children at all levels of the school system has ratcheted up the stakes in classrooms throughout New York City, leaving teachers and school principals even more concerned about bringing those with educational deficits up to speed. Without easy access to parents, this is proving a complex task. Ironically, however, this very demand has spurred the city to provide summer school classes, which have been an answer to many a working mother's prayers for childcare.

Police officers report steep declines in crime and much safer streets in the three neighborhoods we are studying. There is no evidence that this trend is related in any direct way to welfare reform, but it is instead part of a nationwide pattern that experts have yet to understand fully. In New York City, however, the move toward more aggressive policing in minority enclaves has met with mixed responses, as a number of notorious cases involving police violence have shown. On a day-to-day level, however, these pressures have surfaced in a higher level of street surveillance and some resentment of "police harassment" by youth in the families we study who report being told to "move on" when they are talking with friends on the corner. Young men, in particular, feel somewhat less welcome in their own neighborhoods than they once did.

For adults, particularly women and elderly men, these changes have been a blessing. They can pass without as much fear, walk to and from the subway without worrying about being harassed by drug dealers. Some report that the drug trade has moved indoors and off the streets, which makes them feel more vulnerable than before. But, on the whole, they approve of the changes or at least are willing to tolerate the increase in police aggression because it means fewer worries accompanying their ordinary movements.

It remains to be seen whether neighborhood safety will improve to the point where one of the chief worries of women moving off welfare and into work—that their children will not be safe if left unsupervised or will get into trouble in the absence of their mothers—will be assuaged (Edin and Lein, 1997, 1999; Newman,

1999; Anderson, 1999). This reservation has played a key role in the past in keeping mothers out of the labor market. Until now, crime rates seemed responsive mainly to levels of community social capital (Sampson, 1997) that could, in turn, be boosted through the deliberate efforts of stay-at-home mothers and elders. The absence of mothers from neighborhood streets as they head into the workplace renders this strategy less effective. In any case, if crime continues to decline, we may see that a key purpose of welfare reform (to get mothers into jobs) will be furthered by policy changes that had nothing to do with it (through policies such as increased community policing [Winship, in press] or the drive to lower crime rates).

Participant observation in TANF offices and in welfare-to-work programs is an important part of the picture as well. Rank's (1995) study is one of the few that attempted to get inside the culture of the old cash assistance system, and it was very valuable for understanding the perspective of welfare clients as they were processed by caseworkers. We shall have to await a new generation of organizational studies based on similar fieldwork methods in order to understand how the new goals of TANF offices—especially job placement—are being absorbed into a bureaucracy that was designed for entirely different purposes (Ellwood, 1988).

Qualitative research on welfare-to-work programs can tell us a great deal about the job retention problem as well. Watkins (1999) offers a compelling account of the disjuncture that plagues some programs that try to build self-esteem as a means of retaining participants, only to discover that graduates consequently expect much more from the labor market than they actually find. High job turnover rates follow as the frustration of discovering that an "I am somebody" campaign runs headlong into the low-wage labor market where the message may be something closer to "You are not important."

These examples are intended to illustrate the value of contextual information generated through the use of long-term fieldwork. Among other things, this approach provides something close to continuous monitoring of a small sample of families or participants in organizations. Rather than let weeks or years go by between short-term contacts, fieldwork permits ongoing contact and the capacity to check what informants say about their state of mind, their survival strategies, their relations with others, and their neighborhood or institutional conditions against what fieldworkers can observe for themselves and/or learn from "experts" situated in the community.

SAMPLING ISSUES IN QUALITATIVE RESEARCH

The data derived from interview and participant observation projects can be used in at least three ways: (1) to generate hypotheses that might be turned into survey research questions; (2) to complement research based on large-sample statistical analyses; or (3) as an end in and of themselves. These three aims are not mutually exclusive. The difficulty, of course, with the complementary research and "end in itself" approach is that questions of representativeness are always vexing with very small samples and for most research in this genre, small samples are the only affordable possibility.

My own approach has involved embedding the selection of informants within a larger survey design in order to respond to this concern. In 1995-96, we undertook a survey of 900 middle-aged African Americans, Dominicans and Puerto Ricans in New York City. They were chosen to be representative of ethnically diverse and ethnically segregated neighborhoods, with both high and low levels of household income. From this population, a random subsample of 100 respondents was chosen for in-depth interviews at 3-year intervals (1998 and again in 2001). Finally, 12 individuals—4 from each of the ethnic groups of central concern—living in the three neighborhoods described in the previous section were selected from this qualitative subsample. The choice of these particular 12 people was guided mainly by their employment status and family type, with a mix of single parents and intact couples. This nested design has enabled us to generalize from the families we have come to know best to the population as a whole with which we began.

A similar approach has been pursued by the Manpower Demonstration Research Corporation's "Urban Change" project, a study of the impact of devolution and the time limits of the TANF system on poor families in four cities: Philadelphia, Cleveland, Miami, and Los Angeles. A multidisciplinary team of social scientists are drawing on "administrative records; cross-sectional surveys of food stamp recipients; census tract-level neighborhood indicators; repeated interviews with Executive Directors of community-based social service organizations; repeated ethnographic interviews with welfare-reliant women in selected neighborhoods; and repeated interviews with and observations of welfare officials and line staff…" (Edin and Lein, 1999:6).[5]

The qualitative interview part of the Urban Change project has been following 80 families from high- and medium-poverty neighborhoods in Cleveland and Philadelphia. Under the direction of Edin at the University of Pennsylvania, this project has thus far collected a large amount of baseline information on a series of topics including:

> Aspirations for [women's lives] and their children; experiences with case workers and the welfare system; knowledge about and attitudes toward welfare reform; income and expenditure patterns; educational and work experiences; family life; attitudes toward marriage and future childbearing; health and caregiving; social support; material hardship; use of social service agencies; and perceptions of the quality of their neighborhoods (Edin and Lein, 1999:6).

---

[5]See Quint et al. (1999) for more detail on the methodology of the Urban Change project.

Families were chosen for this part of the study by selecting three neighbor-hoods[6] in each city with moderate to high concentrations of poverty (more than 30 percent living below the poverty line) and welfare receipt (20 percent or more of families receiving welfare). Ten to 15 families were recruited in each neighborhood by posting notices in the target neighborhoods, knocking on doors, and requesting referrals from community leaders and local institutions. They attempted to guard against the overrepresentation of any given social network by utilizing no more than two recruits through any of these sources. This strategy avoided the liabilities of drawing from lists provided by TANF offices (which would necessarily skew the research toward welfare recipients alone). The strategy also allowed the researchers to present a truly independent face to their informants, untainted by connection to enforcement agencies that could affect their cash benefits.

A strategy of this kind probably overrepresents people who are higher on social capital than some of their more isolated counterparts. They have connections. A strict sampling design from an established list may pick up people who are less "hooked in" to institutional resources or private safety nets and will therefore tell us something about people who confront welfare reform from a socially isolated vantage point as well as those who are more connected. However, the liabilities of this approach are considerable, for it is much harder to disassociate from official agencies when pursuing a sample generated randomly from, for example, a TANF office caseload.

The neighborhood strategy employed by the Urban Change project ensures that the qualitative study includes white, black, and Latino families who are particularly disadvantaged. As Edin and Lein (1999:7) have explained, the design will not pick up welfare recipients who live in mixed-income or more affluent neighborhoods. It is possible that this strategy yields a slightly more pessimistic perspective on the consequences of welfare reform as compared with what we would have seen had the study included the entire range of long term-recipients, many of whom moved off of the rolls with apparent ease as unemployment declined. These are the people whose human capital, including prior work experience, made them relatively easy to place. The Urban Change project will tell us how this transition affected those with less going for them, because their neighborhoods (and the contacts they derive from them) are less likely to provide useful information for job hunting. The communities selected as the focus neighborhoods undoubtedly present safety concerns that mothers will have to consider as they scramble to figure out how to care for their children. In the end, these are the more pressing questions in need of answers, hence the wisdom of the Urban Change project's approach.

---

[6]Neighborhoods are defined in terms of census tracts. Ranging in size from one to four contiguous tracts, these neighborhoods must meet the poverty, welfare receipt, and racial/ethnic composition (Edin and Lein, 1999:7)

Urban Change is not an ethnographic project in the strict sense of the term. Contact is maintained intermittently with the target families, often utilizing telephone interviews in place of face-to-face contact. Intervals of contact are approximately 6 weeks, though this varies by the informants' situation. Nonetheless, it will provide a very rich database, spanning the before and after of the imposition of time limits, that will tell us an enormous amount about the challenges women and their families have faced in transitioning from public assistance to the world of work. The size and ethnic diversity of the sample (including poor whites, often overlooked in studies of the poor), the multicity approach, and the fusion of administrative records, expert perspectives, and the inclusion of welfare-reliant families in communities with varying levels of poverty will help to address many of the more important theoretical questions before us, especially the consequences of race and ethnic differences, neighborhood effects, and human capital differences in the unfolding of welfare reform.

Angel, Burton, Chase-Landsdale, Cherlin, Moffitt and Wilson are in the midst of a similar study of welfare reform and its consequences, the Three-City Study. This project involves a survey, which began in 1999, of 2,800 households from poor and moderate income. The sample is divided between TANF recipients and those who do not receive these benefits. It is restricted to households with young children (younger than age 4) and those with children between 4 and 14. A developmental study of 800 of these families who have children ages 2-4 will be embedded in this larger design. This embedded study will include interviews with caretakers and the fathers of these children.

The Three-City Study also has an ethnographic component directed by Burton. The study will follow 170 families to track how welfare policies affect the daily lives and neighborhood resources of poor families. In-depth interviews will be conducted over the course of 2 years and will cover topics such as the respondent's life history and daily routines. This component also includes diary studies and observations of the participant when she goes to social service offices for assistance. (Winston et al., 1999). The great advantage of the three-city study is the way in which the ethnographic sample is nested inside a larger, more representative survey sample and contextual data set that can analyze neighborhood variables, state- and local-level employment data, and the repeated interviews and family assessments in the child development portion of the project.

This project has an enormous budget and is therefore the "Cadillac" model that few other studies of welfare reform will be able to match. Nonetheless, it is theoretically possible to use a rich fieldwork approach as long as the resources for this labor-intensive form of data gathering are available. Few social scientists would disagree that moving from macrolevel findings based on surveys to the most microlevel data drawn from fieldwork, with mid-range interviews and focus groups in between, is the best possible approach for preserving representativeness but building in the richness of qualitative research.

Few research projects will be able to match the scale of the Urban Change and the Three-city projects. Indeed, even my own more modest study of 100 families in one city required a substantial research budget and a rotating team of fieldworkers willing to commit a total of more than 6 years to the enterprise. Of course, not all studies of welfare reform need to be as long in duration as the ones described here. For state and local officials whose aim is less to explore the theoretical questions that motivated these studies and more to learn in depth about the family management problems of their caseloads, it may be possible to arrange with local universities to organize neighborhood-based research projects that will provide "snapshot" versions of the same kinds of questions.

Another sampling strategy involves the use of "snowball" samples that attempt to capture respondents who share particular characteristics (e.g., low-wage workers or welfare-reliant household heads) by asking those who meet the eligibility criteria to suggest friends or neighbors who do as well. Some classic studies in the annals of poverty research have used snowball samples to great effect (e.g., Lillian Rubin's *Worlds of Pain*, Elliot Liebow's *Tally's Corner*). More recently, Edin and Lein's *Making Ends Meet* relies on referrals from a variety of sources, including the personal contacts of individuals already in their study population, to build a sample in four cities. The defining feature of a snowball sample is that it gathers individuals into a sample that have some acquaintance with those who are already involved. Multiple snowball techniques seek to maximize the heterogeneity of the sample, while single snowballs maximize the homogeneity of the sample. Neither approach results in a sample that is genuinely random, though the former seeks diversity while the latter explicitly seeks purposive groups.

Snowballs can be bound tightly to a particular network, as was the case in Tally's Corner, or can guard against the possibility that membership will not represent truly independent cases. When the object of study is densely connected webs of friends and relatives, it is important to capture naturally occurring social networks. In this case, the initial selection of the key informant needs to pay attention to representativeness. Thereafter, however, there will be nothing random about the study participants: They will be selected members of the original informant's trusted associates.

For example, in my recent study of the working poor in central Harlem (Newman, 1999), a representative sample of workers in fast food restaurants formed the core of the research, but a selected subsample was central to a final phase of intensive participant observation that focused on the survival strategies of 10 households and the social networks attached to them. The ten key informants were selected to represent the racial and gender diversity of the universe of workers. Branching out from there, in concentric circles around the 10 key informants, we took in the friends, neighbors, schoolmates, teachers, preachers, distant relatives, and street contacts of these individuals. Hence, although the original subsample was representative, the snowballs grew around them because the purpose of the study was to learn about how these households managed the many challenges of low-wage work in naturally occuring contexts (school, home, church, extended family, etc.). Ultimately, perhaps as many as 500 additional people were included in this phase of the research, though they were hardly a random sample.

Others have used snowballs to generate the "master sample." However in this situation it is important to guard against the possibility that network membership is biasing the independence of each case. Some snowball samples are assembled by using no more than one or two referrals from any given source, for example. Edin and Lein's (1997), *Making Ends Meet* is a good example of a partial snowball strategy that has made independence of cases a high priority. Initially, they turned to neighborhood block groups, housing authority residents' councils, churches, community organizations and local charities to find mothers who were welfare reliant or working in the low-wage labor markets in Boston, Chicago, Charleston, and San Antonio. Concerned that they might miss people who were disconnected from organizations like those who served as their initial sources, Edin and Lein turned to their informants and tried to diversify:

> To guard against interviewing only those mothers who were well connected to community leaders, organizations and charities, we asked the mothers we interviewed to refer us to one or two friends whom they thought we would not be able to contact through other channels. In this way, we were able to get less-connected mothers. All in all we were able to tap into over fifty independent networks in each of the four cities (1997:12).

Using this approach, Edin and Lein put together a heterogeneous set of prospective respondents who were highly cooperative. Given how difficult it can be to persuade poor people who are often suspicious of researchers' motives (all the more so if they are perceived as working for enforcement agencies), working through social networks often can be the only way to gain access to a sample at all. Edin and Lein report a 90 percent response rate using this kind of snowball technique. Because this rate is higher than one usually expects, there may be less independence among the cases than would be ideal under random sample conditions, but this approach is far preferable to one that is more random but with very low response rates.

Sample retention is important for all panel studies, perhaps even more so for qualitative studies that begin with modest numbers. Experience suggests that studies that couple intensive interviews with participant observation tend to have the greatest success with retention because the ethnographers are "on the scene," and therefore have greater credibility in the neighborhoods from which the interview samples may be drawn. Their frequent presence encourages a sense of affiliation and participatory spirit into studies that otherwise might become a burden. However, my experience has shown that honoraria make a huge difference in sample retention when the subjects are poor families. I have typically offered honoraria of $25–$100, depending on the amount of time these interviewers require. Amounts of this kind would be prohibitive for studies involving thousands of respondents, but have proven manageable in studies of 100, tracked over time. The honoraria demonstrate respect for the time respondents give to the study.

Though design features make a difference, retention is a problem in all studies that focus on the poor, particularly those that aim at poor youth. The age range 16–25 is particularly complex because residential patterns are often unstable and connections between young adults and their parents often fray or become less intense. Maintaining contact with parents, guardians, or older relatives in any study dealing with poor youth is important because these are the people who are most likely to "stay put" and who have the best chance of remaining effective intermediaries with the targets of these longitudinal studies. Retention problems are exacerbated in all studies of the poor because of geographic mobility. One can expect to lose a good 25-40 percent of the respondents in studies that extend over a 5-year period. This may compromise the validity of the results, though it has been my experience that the losses are across the board where measurable characteristics are concerned. Hence one can make a reasonable claim to continued representativeness. Such claims will be disputed by those who think unmeasured characteristics are important and that a response rate of 60–75 percent is too low to use.

Coding Issues

Qualitative research of any kind—open-ended questions embedded in surveys, ethnographic interviews, long-term fieldwork with families or "neighborhood experts"—generates large volumes of text. Text files may derive from recorded interviews, which then must be transcribed verbatim (a costly and time-consuming proposition), or from field notes that represent the observer's account of events, conversations, or settings within which interactions of interest routinely occur. Either way, this material is generally voluminous and must be categorized to document patterns of note.

Anthropologists and qualitative sociologists accustomed to working with these kinds of data have developed various means for boiling them down in ways that make them amenable to analysis. At the simplest level, this can mean developing coding schemes that transform words into numeric representations that can be analyzed statistically, as one would do with any kind of close-ended survey data. Turning to the Urban Change project, for example, we find that initial baseline open-ended interviews show that respondents are hoping that going to work will enable them to provide a variety of opportunities for their children. Mothers also report that they expect their social status to rise as they depart welfare and note that their children have faced taunting because of their participation in AFDC; they trust the taunting will cease once they are independent of state support. These findings come from tape recorded interviews intended to capture their prospective feelings about moving into the labor market some 2 years before the imposition of time limits. These responses can be coded into descriptive categories that reflect the variety of expectations respondents have for the future, or the hopes they have expressed about how working will improve their lives.

Most qualitative interview instruments pose open-ended questions in a predefined order. They also may allow interviewers some latitude to permit informants to move the discussion into topic areas not envisioned originally. Within limits, this is not only acceptable, but it is desirable, for understanding the subjective perspectives of the respondents is the whole aim of this kind of research and the instrument may not effectively capture all the relevant points. However, to the extent that the original format is followed, the coding can proceed by returning to the responses that are contained in approximately the same "location" in each interview transcript. Hence, every participant in our study of the working poor under welfare reform was asked to talk about how their neighborhood has changed in the past 5 years. Their responses can be categorized according to the topics they generally raised: crime declining, gentrification reflected in rising rents, new immigrant groups arriving, and so forth. We develop codings that reflect these routine responses in order to be able to draw conclusions such as "50 percent believe that crime has declined precipitously in their neighborhood" or "20 percent object to police harassment of their teenage children."

However, we also want to preserve the nuances of their comments in the form of text blocks that are "dumped" into subject files that might be labeled "attitudes toward the police" or "comments on neighborhood safety." Researchers then can open these subject files and explore the patterned variety of perspectives on law enforcement or the ways in which increasing community safety have affected the patterns of movement out of the home or the hours that mothers feel comfortable commuting to work. When qualitative researchers report results, we typically draw on these blocks of text to illustrate the patterns we have discovered in the data, both to explore the nuances and to give the reader a greater feeling for the meaning of these changes for the informants. To have this material ready at hand, one need only use one of a variety of text-processing programs, including Atlas.ti, Nud.ist, and Ethnograph, each of which has its virtues.[7] Some proceed by using key words to search and then classify the text. Others permit the researcher to designate conceptual categories and then "block" the text with boundary markers on either side of a section so that the entire passage is preserved. It is even possible to use the indexing capacities of standard word-processing pro-

---

[7]For helpful reviews of these software packages, see Barry (1998) or "QDA Overview" on the web at http://www.quarc.de/body_overview.html.

grams, such as Microsoft Word 6.0 and above, which can "mark" the text and dump it into subject files for later retrieval.

Most qualitative projects require the analyst both to digest the interviews (which may be as long as 70 pages or more) into subject headings and to preserve the flow of a single informant's interview through summaries that are preserved by person rather than by topic. I typically maintain both kinds of qualitative databases, with person-based summaries that condense a 70-page text to 5–6 pages, offering a thumbnail sketch of each interview. This approach is of primary value to an academic researcher, but it may not be as important to practitioners who may be less interested in life histories for their own sake and more concerned with responses to welfare reform per se.

Practical Realities

Qualitative research is essential if we are to understand the real consequences of welfare reform. It is, however, a complex undertaking, one not responsive to the most pressing information needs of local TANF officials for whom documenting the dynamics of caseloads or the operation of programs in order to improve service is so critical. Yet the information gleaned from qualitative research may become critical to understanding caseloads or program efficiency, particularly if rolls continue to fall, leaving only the most disadvantaged to address. If the pressure to find solutions for this harder-to-serve population grows, it may become critical for administrators and policy makers to figure out new strategies for addressing their needs. This will not be easy to do if all we know about these people is that they have not found work or have problems with substance abuse or childcare. We may need to know more about how their households function, about where the gaps are in their childcare, about the successes or difficulties they have experienced in accessing drug treatment, or about the concerns they have regarding the safety of older children left unsupervised in neighborhoods with crime problems.

Is this information challenge one that federal and state officials should move to meet? Will they be able to use this information, above and beyond the more normative studies they conduct or commission on caseloads in their jurisdictions? To answer this question, I turn to several interviews with officials at the federal and state levels whom I've asked to comment on the utility of qualitative data in their domains. Their observations suggest that the range of methods described in this paper do indeed have a place in their world and that the investment required to have this material "at the ready" has paid off for them in the past. However, the timing of these studies has everything to do with the resources available for research and the information demands to which officials have to respond. For some, the time is right now. For others, qualitative work will have to wait until the "big picture" based on administrative records and surveys is complete.

Dennis Lieberman, Director of the Department of Labor's Office of Welfare to Work, is responsible for demonstrating to Congress and therefore to the public at large that the programs under his jurisdiction are making a significant difference. As is true for many public officials, Lieberman's task is one part politics and one part policy science: political in that he has to communicate the value of the work this program accomplishes in the midst of competing priorities, and scientific in that the outcomes that show accountability are largely "bottom line," quantitative measures. Yet, as he explains below, this is a complex task that cannot always be addressed simply by turning to survey or administrative records data:

> One of the major responsibilities I have is to demonstrate to the Congress and the American people that an investment of $3 billion (the size of the welfare to work grants program) is paying off. Numbers simply do not tell the story in its entirety or properly. Often times there are technical, law-driven reasons why a program may be expanding or enrolling slowly. These need to be fixed, most often through further legislative action by Congress.

> From a surface perspective a program may appear as a poor investment. Looking behind the numbers can illuminate correctable reasons and present success stories and practices whose promise may lie buried in a statistical trend. As an example: one of the welfare to work program criteria (dictated by statute) would not allow service providers to help those individuals who had a high school diploma. We were able to get that changed using specific stories of individuals who were socially promoted, had a high school diploma (but couldn't read it), and were in very great need. Despite all this, they were walled out of a program designed specifically for them. A high school diploma simply did not lift them out of the most in need category. The numbers showed only low enrollment, appearing at first glance like recruitment wasn't being conducted vigorously enough (Lieberman, 1999).

As this comment suggests, qualitative work is particularly useful for explaining anomalies in quantitative data that, left unsolved, may threaten the reputation of a program that officials have reason to believe is working well, but that may not be showing itself to best advantage in the standard databases.

These evaluations are always taking place in the context of debates over expenditures and those debates often are quite public. Whenever the press and the public are involved, Lieberman notes, qualitative data can be particularly helpful because they can be more readily understood and absorbed by nonspecialists:

> Dealing with the media is another occasion where numbers are not enough (although sought first). Being able to explain the depth of an issue with case histories, models, and simple, common-sense descriptions is often very helpful in helping the press get the facts of a program situation correct. There is a degree of "spin distrust" from the media, but the simpler and more basic the better. This, of course, also impacts on what Congress will say and do.

However, as Tom Moss, Deputy Commissioner of Human Services for the State of Minnesota, points out, the very nature of political debate surrounding welfare reform may raise suspicions regarding the objectivity of qualitative work or the degree to which the findings it contributes should be factored into the design of public policy:

> Many legislators would strenuously argue that we should not use public resources for this kind of exhaustive understanding of any citizen group, much less welfare recipients. They would be suspicious that perfect understanding is meant to lead to perfect acceptance—that this information would be used to argue against any sanctions or consequences for clients.

I would argue that qualitative data is no more subject to this objection than any other research method and that most officials recognize the value of understanding the behavior of citizen groups for designing more effective policies. Whether officials subsequently (or antecedently) decide to employ incentives or sanctions is generally guided by a theory of implementation, a view of what works. The subsequent research tells us whether it has worked or it hasn't, something that most administrators want to know regardless of the politics that lead to one policy design over another. If incentives produce bad outcomes, qualitative work will help us understand why. If sanctions backfire, leading to welfare recidivism, for example, even the most proreform constituencies will want to know how that comes about. Unintended consequences are hard to avoid in any reform.

For this reason, at least some federal officials have found qualitative data useful in the context of program design and "tinkering" to get the guidelines right. Focus groups and case studies help policy makers understand what has gone wrong, what might make a difference, and how to both conceptualize and then "pitch" a new idea after listening to participants explain the difficulties they have encountered. Lieberman continues:

> I personally have found qualitative data (aside from numbers) as the most useful information for designing technical assistance to help grantees overcome program design problems, to fix processes and procedures that "are broken," to help them enrich something with which they have been only moderately successful, and to try something new, which they have never done before.
>
> My office often convenes groups of similar-focus programs for idea sharing and then simply listens as practitioners outline their successes, failures, needs, and partnerships. We convene programs serving noncustodial fathers, substance abusers, employers and others. We have gotten some of the most important information (leading to necessary changes in regulation or law) this way.

Gloria Nagle, Director of Evaluation for the Office of Transitional Assistance in the State of Massachusetts, faces a different set of demands and therefore sees a slightly different place for qualitative work. She notes (personal communication, 11/30/99) that her organization must be careful to conduct research that is rigorous, with high response rates and large representative samples in order to be sure that the work is understood to be independent and scientific. Moreover, because collecting hard data on welfare reform is a high priority, her office has devoted itself primarily to the use of survey data and to the task of developing databases that will link various administrative records together for ongoing tracking purposes. However, she notes that the survey work the organization is doing is quite expensive (even if it is cost effective on a per-case basis) and that at some point in the future the funds that support it will dry up. At that point, she suggests, qualitative data of a limited scope will become important:

> Administrative data are like scattered dots. It can be very hard to tie the data together in a meaningful way. Quarterly Unemployment Insurance (UI) earnings data and information on food stamps might not give a good picture of how people are coping. For example, what about former welfare recipients who are not working and not receiving food stamps? How are they surviving? We can't tell from these data how they are managing. When we no longer can turn to survey data to fill in the gap, it would be very useful to be able to do selective interviews and focus groups.

Nagle sees other functions for qualitative research in that it can inform the direction of larger evaluations in an efficient and cost-effective fashion:

> Qualitative research can also be helpful in setting the focus of future evaluation projects. In this era of massive change, there are many areas that we would like to examine more closely. Focus groups can help us establish priorities.

Finally, she notes that focus groups and participant observation research is a useful source of data for management and program design purposes:

> I can also see us using qualitative research to better understand internal operations within the Department. For example, how well is a particular policy/program understood at the local level? With focus groups and field interviews we can get initial feedback quickly.

Joel Kvamme, Evaluation Coordinator for the Minnesota Family Investment Program, is responsible for the evaluation of welfare reform for the state's Department of Human Services. He and his colleagues developed a collaboration with the University of Minnesota's Center for Urban and Regional Affairs; together these groups designed a longitudinal study of cases converted from AFDC and new cases entering the state's welfare reform program. Kvamme found that resource constraints prevented a full-scale investment in a qualitative subsample study, but the groups did develop open-ended questions inside the survey that were then used to generate more nuanced close-ended items for future surveys in the ongoing longitudinal project. He notes the value of this approach:

> For the past 15 years, Minnesota really has invested in a lot of research and strategic analysis about what we should be doing to help families…. Yet, it is our most knowledgeable people who recognize that there is much that we do

not know and that we may not even know all the right questions. For example, we have much to learn about the individual and family dynamics involved in leaving welfare and the realities of life in the first year or so following a welfare exit. Consequently, in our survey work we are wary of relying exclusively on fixed-choice questions and recognize the usefulness of selective open-ended constructions.

Resource constraints alone were not the sole reason that this compromise was adopted. As Kvamme's colleague, Scott Chazdon (Senior Research Analyst on the Minnesota Family Investment Program Longitudinal Study), notes, the credibility of the research itself would be at stake if it privileged open-ended research over the hard numbers.

It is a huge deal for a government agency to strive for open-endedness in social research. This isn't the way things have historically been done.... We were concerned that the findings of any qualitative analyses may not appear "scientific" enough to be palatable. State agencies face somewhat of a legitimacy crisis before the legislature and I think that is behind the hesitance to rely on qualitative methods.

Between the reservations the research team had about qualitative work and the recognition they shared that close-ended surveys were not enough, was a compromise that others should bear in mind, as Chazdon explained:

We ended up with an extensive survey with quite a few open-ended questions and many "other" options in questions with specific answer categories. These "other" categories added substantial richness to the study and have made it easier for us to write answer codes in subsequent surveys.

"Other" options permit respondents to reject the close-ended categories in favor of a personally meaningful response. The Minnesota Family Investment Program (MFIP) Longitudinal Study made use of the patterns within the "other" responses to design questions for future close-ended studies that were more likely to capture the experiences of their subjects.

A more comprehensive opinion poll of federal and state officials on the program and on the research evaluation side would no doubt generate other perspectives. Suffice to say for the moment, there is potential for qualitative data to take their place in the arsenal of research approaches needed in order to understand what welfare reform has really meant over the long haul.

CONCLUSION: FORMING RESEARCH PARTNERSHIPS

Given the complexities of this style of research, it probably would be most effective for state agencies to provide requests for payments to which local universities can respond as part of their public service and training activities (as Minnesota already has). Students are a good source of research labor and often are very interested in the problems of the poor. Sociologists, demographers, political scientists, and anthropologists all can be drafted to assist state officials in understanding how welfare reform is unfolding. With proper planning, long-term panel studies that embed qualitative samples inside a large-scale survey design can be conducted in ways that will yield valuable information to policy makers and administrators. Whether these embedded subsamples are representative of the whole survey universe or purposive samples designed to understand one particular category (e.g., welfare leavers, single mothers with young children), these projects can be of great value. Utilizing this kind of partnership has the advantage of independence from the enforcement agencies with whom TANF participants may be reluctant to cooperate. Because most states have a network of public universities distributed throughout the territory, one can use their location to generate appropriately diverse research populations—urban/suburban/rural, multiple ethnic groups, neighborhoods with different levels of poverty, and areas with higher and lower levels of unemployment, could be among those most important to represent.

Research units of state agencies can also invest in in-house capacities for qualitative research. Even when research resources are tight, making sure that ethnographers and interviewers are part of the team is an important management decision. This may appear to be a "frill," but it actually may save the day when survey results cannot explain the findings on recidivism or childcare. The presence of ethnographers and interviewers in federal agencies is commonplace now. For example, the Census Bureau maintains a staff of anthropologists and linguists who study household organization in order to frame better census questions. In past years, the Bureau has employed teams of ethnographers to conduct multicity studies of homeless populations to check underrepresentation in the census. As devolution progresses, it will be important to replicate this expertise at the state level in the field of welfare reform.

Whether research partnerships or in-house teams are chosen, the greatest success undoubtedly will be achieved when qualitative research is embedded inside quantitative studies that are either cross-sectional or longitudinal panel studies. The fusion of the two approaches provides greater confidence in the representative nature of qualitative samples, and the capacity to move back and forth between statistical analyses and patterns in life histories renders either approach the richer for its partner.

REFERENCES

Anderson, Elijah
    1999   *Code of the Street.* New York: W.W. Norton.
Barry, Christine A.
    1998   Choosing qualitative data Analysis Software: Atlas/ti and Nudist compared. Sociological
            Research Online, 3. http//:www.socresonline.org/uk/socresonline/3/3/4.html
Edin, Kathryn, and L. Lein
    1997   *Making Ends Meet: How Single Mothers Survive Welfare and Low-Wage Work.* New
            York: Russell Sage Foundation.

1999   *My Children Come First: Welfare-Reliant Women's Post-TANF Views of Work-Family Tradeoffs, Neighborhoods and Marriage.* Paper presented at the Northwestern University/University of Chicago Joint Center for Poverty Research Conference, "For Better or Worse: State Welfare Reform and the Well-Being of Low-Income Families and Children, Washington, DC, September 16-17.

Ellwood, David
1988   *Poor Support.* New York: Basic Books.

Jackson, John L.
2001   *Harlemworld: Doing Race and Class in Contemporary America.* Chicago University of Chicago Press.

Katz, Bruce, and Kate Carnavale
1998   *The State of Welfare Caseloads in America's Cities.* Washington, DC: Brookings Institutions Center on Urban and Metropolitan Policy.

Newman, Katherine
1999   *No Shame in My Game: The Working Poor in the Inner City.* New York: Knopf/Russell Sage.

Quint, J., K. Edin, M.L. Buck, B. Fink, Y.C. Padilla, O. Simmons-Hewitt, and M.E. Valmont
1999   *Big Cities and Welfare Reform: Early Implementation and Ethnographic Findings for the Project on Devolution and Urban Change.* New York: Manpower Demonstration Research Corporation.

Rank, Mark
1995   *Living on the Edge: The Realities of Welfare in America.* New York: Columbia University Press.

Romich, Jennifer L.
1999   To Sons and Daughters: Bargaining, Child's Gender, and Resource Allocation in Low-Income Families. Presented at the annual meeting of the Midwest Economics Association, Nashville, TN.

Sampson, Robert, S., Raudenbush, and F. Earls
1997   Neighborhoods and Violent crime: A multilevel study of collective efficacy. *Science*, 277:918-924.

Watkins, Celeste
1999   Operationalizing the Welfare to Work Agenda: An Analysis of the Development and Execution of a Job Readiness Training Program. Unpublished manuscript. Department of Sociology, Harvard University.

Weisner, T.S., L. Bernheimer, C. Gibson, E. Howard, K. Magnuson, J. Romich, and E. Leiber
1999   From the Living Rooms and Daily Routines of the Economically Poor: An Ethnographic Study of the New Hope Effects on Families and Children. Presented at the biannual meetings of Society for Research in Child Development. Albuquerque, April.

Weisner, Thomas, et al.
1999   Getting closer to understanding the lives of economically poor families: Ethnographic and survey studies of the New Hope experiment. Poverty Research News. The Newsletter of the Northwestern University/University of Chicago Joint Center for Poverty Research. Based on the Joint Center's Workshop on Qualitative and Quantitative Methods, Chicago, June.

Winship, Christopher, and J. Berrien
in
press   Should we have faith in the churches? Ten Point Coalition's effects on Boston's youth violence. In *Managing Youth Violence*, Gary Katzmann, ed. Washington, DC: The Brookings Institution Press.

Winston, Pamela, Ronald J. Angel, Linda M. Burton, P. Lindsay Chase-Lansdale, Andrew J. Cherlin, Robert A. Moffitt, and William Julius Wilson
1999   *Welfare, Children, and Families: A Three City Study.* Baltimore, MD: Johns Hopkins University Press.

Part IV

Welfare Leavers and Welfare Dynamics

12

Studies of Welfare Leavers:
Data, Methods, and Contributions
to the Policy Process

Gregory Acs and Pamela Loprest

In August 1996, President Clinton signed the Personal Responsibility and Work Opportunity Reconciliation Act (PRWORA), making sweeping changes in the system of cash assistance for poor families and creating the Temporary Assistance for Needy Families (TANF) program. Four years after the passage of PRWORA, policy makers, practitioners, and the public continue to ask the ill-defined question, "Did welfare reform work?" Although cash assistance caseloads have dropped dramatically, from 4.4 million in August 1996 to 2.4 million in December, 1999, declining caseloads are not the sole criterion for a successful reform. Indeed, there is concern about the well-being of families who have left welfare: Are families leaving cash assistance postreform worse off than leavers prereform? Are they worse off than they were while receiving aid? To this end, many states and policy researchers, some with federal funding, have conducted and continue to conduct studies of families who have left the welfare rolls, often referred to as "leaver studies."

Given the proliferation of these studies, this paper attempts to provide guidance for authors and consumers of leaver studies on how to best use and create these studies. Our goals are threefold:

- To review the methods used in leaver studies;
- To identify preferred practices for those planning to conduct a leaver study; and
- To provide guidance to readers in assessing study results and making comparisons across studies.

To this end, we have examined 49 studies of welfare leavers, including 13 studies funded by the U.S. Department of Health and Human Services, Office of the Assistant Secretary for Planning and Evaluation (ASPE).[1] They are listed in Table 12-1. Although we have made every attempt to review the body of work on families leaving welfare, these studies are by no means an exhaustive list of research in this area. Although most are explicitly studies of welfare leavers, some are studies of specific state welfare programs and reforms. We include these latter studies because they provide significant amounts of information on welfare leavers. Several of the studies present ongoing work; their findings are preliminary.

This paper is organized into three sections. First, we discuss the value of leaver studies as well as their limitations. Next we discuss what leaver studies should measure, which addresses the question of how to measure economic well-being and how some studies have done so. Finally, we examine methods for conducting a leaver study. This section describes important issues around defining leavers, positives and limitations of administrative and survey data, and how to assess the quality of data used. We hope that information in all these sections will be valuable to both future authors of leaver studies and those who are using them to understand how former welfare recipients are faring.

THE VALUE OF LEAVER STUDIES

Leaver studies can be valuable tools for monitoring the well-being of families who have been exposed to TANF and have left the rolls. Indeed, they can tell policy makers if families who have left welfare are facing problems that can be addressed by policy changes regardless of whether these problems arose as the result of past reforms. Furthermore, although leaver studies may provide only limited information about welfare reform in 1996, the ongoing capacity built by states and the research community will provide a baseline for evaluating future reforms.

Policy researchers and some policy makers also may wish to compare findings across leaver studies; after all, it is tempting to compare the status of leavers across states taking different approaches to welfare reform in order to assess the relative effectiveness of various policies. However, any such comparisons should be made with great caution for two main reasons. First, as we discuss in detail, leaver studies can have important methodological differences. These differences

---

[1]Throughout this report, the term "welfare leaver" refers to someone exiting the Aid to Families with Dependent Children (AFDC) or TANF programs. Note that the 13 ASPE studies cover only 11 study locations because 2 of the locations report findings from different data sources in separate reports.

include the time period studied, the type of data used, the exact wording and ordering of survey questions, and even the definition of a leaver. Indeed, some leaver studies focus on families leaving welfare in the early to mid-1990s while other report findings from the late 1990s. Findings may differ or differences may be obscured simply because the studies analyze different historical periods. Similarly, some studies focus on the well-being of leavers shortly after they exit welfare while others examine their status several years later.

Second, differences between states, such as in economic opportunities or even the characteristics of welfare recipients themselves, may be even more important than policy differences in accounting for differences in the status of welfare leavers. It would not be surprising to find that leavers in areas where jobs are plentiful fare better than leavers in areas with slack economies regardless of the state's policy choices. Similarly, differences in the characteristics of state caseloads can affect the status of families leaving welfare. For example, if a state's welfare recipients are more disadvantaged than those in another state, then its leavers may be more likely to face difficulties after exiting. Finally, if a state pursues policies aimed at encouraging work among current welfare recipients rather than encouraging exits from welfare—for example, through generous earned-income disregards—then leaver studies could miss an important impact of reform: More families are mixing welfare and work. Such families would be ignored in leaver studies because they are still on welfare.

Nevertheless, as long as one keeps in mind these limitations in leaver studies, a well-done leaver study can help policy makers understand the process families go through as they leave welfare and the factors that help them make a successful and long-term transition. Furthermore, leaver studies can help identify challenges faced by leavers and the direction for subsequent policy interventions.

WHAT LEAVER STUDIES SHOULD MEASURE

The primary role of leaver studies is to assess and track the well-being of welfare leavers; associating changes in the well-being of welfare leavers to changes in welfare policy plays a secondary role. Thus, an assessment of leaver studies requires us to address the following questions:

- What do we mean by well-being?
- How do we measure well-being?

When assessing a family's overall well-being, policy makers and researchers generally consider five areas: (1) income security, (2) employment, (3) health, (4) living arrangements, and (5) quality of life or hardships. Although one can be "rich and miserable" or "poor and happy," a family's financial resources, especially a lack of resources, are an important indicator of well-being. Thus, leaver

TABLE 12-1 List of Leaver Studies by State

State	Title
General Leaver Studies	
Arizona-1*	Arizona Cash Assistance Exit Study: First Quarter 1998 Cohort-Final Report
Arizona-2*	Arizona Cash Assistance Exit Study: Cases Exiting Fourth Quarter 1996
California-Los Angeles County*	Employment and Earnings of Single-Parent AFDC Leavers: Quarter 3 1996 Leavers: PRELIMINARY REPORT
California-San Mateo County*	Examining Circumstances of Individuals and Families who Leave TANF: Assessing the Validity of Administrative Data
District of Columbia*	The Status of TANF Leavers in the District of Columbia—Final Report
Florida	The Family Transition Program: Implementation and Three-Year Impacts of Florida's Initial Time-Limited Welfare Program
Georgia-1	Transition from Welfare to Work: Findings for the First Year of Temporary Assistance for Needy Families
Georgia-2*	Outcomes for Single-Parent Leavers by Cohort Quarter for Jan-Mar 99: Quarterly Progress Report: PRELIMINARY REPORT
Idaho-1	Project Self-Reliance: TAFI Participant Closure Study (II)
Idaho-2	Differences Between a Surveyed Closed TAFI Case Population and Its "Unreachable" Subpopulation
Illinois-1	How are TANF Leavers Faring? Early Results from the Illinois TANF Closed Case Project
Illinois-2*	Illinois Study of Former TANF Clients: Interim Report
Indiana	The Indiana Welfare Reform Evaluation: Who is On and Who is Off? Comparing Characteristics and Outcomes for Current and Former TANF Recipients
Kentucky	From Welfare to Work: Welfare Reform in Kentucky
Maryland-1	Life After Welfare: An Interim Report
Maryland-2	Life After Welfare: Second Interim Report
Maryland-3	Life After Welfare Reform: Third Interim Report
Massachusetts	How are They Doing? A Longitudinal Study Tracking Households Leaving Welfare Under Massachusetts Reform
Mississippi	Tracking of TANF Clients: First Report of a Longitudinal Study
Missouri-1*	Preliminary Outcomes for 1996 Fourth Quarter AFDC Leavers: Revised Interim Report
Missouri-2*	Chapters 1-4: MRI Project No. 1033-1
Montana	Montana's Welfare Reform Project: Families Achieving Independence in Montana
New Mexico	Survey of the New Mexico Case Closed AFDC Recipients
New York-1	Leaving Welfare: Findings from a Survey of Former New York City Welfare Recipients
New York-2*	After Welfare: A Study of Work and Benefit in New York State After Case Closing

Author(s)	Date	Data Used
Karen L. Westra and John Routley	Jan-00	Survey/ Administrative
Karen L. Westra and John Routley	Jul-99	Administrative
	Jan-99	Administrative
Anne Moses and David Mancuso	May-99	Administrative
Gregory Acs and Pamela Loprest	Oct-99	Survey/ Administrative
Dan Bloom, Mary Farell, James J. Kemple, and Nandita Verma	Apr-99	Administrative
Georgia Department of Human Resources	Jan-98	Administrative
E. Michael Foster		Administrative
Idaho Department of Health and Welfare	Spring 1998	Survey
Idaho Department of Health and Welfare	Winter 1998	Survey
Steve Anderson, George Julnes, Anthony Halter, David Gruenenfelder, and Linda Brumleve	Aug-99	Survey
George Julnes and Anthony Halter	Mar 00	Survey/ Administrative
David J. Fein	Sep-97	Survey
Scott Cummings and John P. Nelson	Jan-98	Survey
University of Maryland- School of Social Work	Sep-97	Administrative
University of Maryland- School of Social Work	Mar-98	Administrative
University of Maryland- School of Social Work	Mar-98	Administrative
Massachusetts Department of Transitional Assistance	Apr-99	Survey
Jesse D. Beeler, Bill M. Brister, Sharon Chambry, and Anne L. McDonald	Jan-99	Survey/ Administrative
Sharon Ryan	Sep-99	Administrative
Midwest Research Institute	Jun-00	Survey
Montana Department of Public Health and Human Services	Feb-98	Survey
University of New Mexico-Bureau of Business and Economic Research	Sep-97	Survey
Andrew S. Bush, Swati Desai, and Lawrence M. Mead	Sep-98	Survey
Rockefeller Institute	Dec-99	Administrative

continues

TABLE 12-1 Continued

State	Title
North Carolina-1	Evaluation of the North Carolina Work First Program: Initial Analysis of Administrative Data
North Carolina-2	Evaluation of the North Carolina Work First Program: Status of Families Leaving Work First After Reaching the 24-Month Time Limit
Ohio-1 Cuyahoga County	Work After Welfare: Employment in the 1996 Exit Cohort, Cuyahoga County
Ohio-2 Cuyahoga County*	Employment and Return to Public Assistance Among Single, Female Headed Families Leaving AFDC in the Third Quarter, 1996, Cuyahoga County, Ohio
Oklahoma	Family Health and Well-Being In Oklahoma: An Exploratory Analysis of TANF Cases Closed and Denied October 1996-November 1997
Pennsylvania	TANF Closed-Case Telephone Survey
South Carolina-1	Former Clients of South Carolina's New Welfare Program: Trends and Issues in Surveys to Date
South Carolina-2	Survey of Former Family Independence Program Clients: Cases Closed During April Through June 1997
South Carolina-3	Survey of Former Family Independence Program Clients: Cases Closed During July Through September 1997
Tennessee	Summary of Surveys of Welfare Recipients Employed or Sanctioned for Noncompliance
Texas	Texas Families in Transition: The Impacts of Welfare Reform Changes in Texas: Early Findings
Virginia	Fairfax Welfare Reform Evaluation Study
Washington-1	Conversations with 65 Families
Washington-2	Washington's TANF Single-Parent Families Shortly After Welfare
Washington-3	Washington's TANF Single-Parent Families After Welfare
Washington-4*	A Study of Washington State TANF Leavers and TANF Recipients
Washington-5*	A Study of Washington State TANF Leavers and TANF Recipients
Wisconsin-1	Post-Exit Earnings and Benefit Receipt Among Those Who Left AFDC in Wisconsin
Wisconsin-2	Employment and Earnings of Milwaukee County Single Parent AFDC Families: Establishing Benchmarks for Measuring Employment Outcomes
Wisconsin-3	Survey of Those Leaving AFDC or W-2: January to March 1998 Preliminary Report
Wyoming	A Survey of Power Recipients
Sanctioned Leavers	
Iowa	Iowa's Limited Benefit Plan: Summary Report
Michigan	A Study of AFDC Case Closures Due to JOBS Sanctions: April 1996 AFDC Case Closures
New Jersey	Survey of WFNJ/TANF Case Closed to Sanction

*Assistant Secretary for Planning and Evaluation (ASPE) funded study.

Author(s)	Date	Data Used
Maximus	May-99	Administrative
Maximus	May-99	Survey
Claudia Coulton, Marilyn Su, Neil Bania, and Edward Wang		Administrative
Claudia Coulton and Nandita Verma	May-99	Administrative
Lynda Williams	Sep-98	Survey
Pennsylvania Bureau of Program Evaluation	Feb-98	Survey
Donald M. Klos		Survey
South Carolina Department of Social Services	12-Jun-98	Survey
South Carolina Department of Social Services	9-Oct-98	Survey
Center for Manpower Studies	Mar-98	Survey
Texas Department of Human Services	Dec-98	Survey
Carole Kuhns, Danielle Hollar, and Renee Loeffler		Survey
City of Seattle Department of Housing and Human Services	Mar-98	Survey
Washington Department of Social and Health Services	Jul-98	Survey
Washington Department of Social and Health Services	Jan-99	Survey
Jay Ahn	Feb-00	Administrative
Debra Fogerty and Shon Kraley	Feb-00	Survey
Marcia Cancian, Robert Haveman, Thomas Kaplan, and Barbara Wolfe	Oct-98	Administrative
University of Wisconsin- Milwaukee, Employment and Training Institute		Administrative
Institute for Research on Poverty- University of Wisconsin	13-Jan-99	Survey
Western Management Services	May-98	Survey
Thomas M. Fraker	May-97	Survey
Laura Colville, Gerry Moore, Laura Smith, and Steve Smucker	May-97	Survey
New Jersey Division of Family Development, Bureau of Quality Control	Mar-98	Survey

studies should collect and present information on a family's income.[2] In addition to earned income, the studies should consider cash from friends and family, including child support payments, as well as public assistance in the form of cash and near-cash aid such as food stamps.

Because a central goal of PRWORA is to move families from welfare to work, it is also important to consider their employment situation. Employment should be measured at a point in time as well as over a period of time. For example, there can be a great deal of difference in how many leavers are working in a specific month compared to how many have worked at any point over the past year. Having both sets of data allows for broader understanding of employment among leavers.

Leaver studies also should collect data on the number of hours that leavers work and how much their jobs pay. Additional information about jobs is also beneficial, including whether their jobs have regular hours or schedules, whether adult leavers hold multiple jobs, what noncash benefits they receive, what the costs of working are (transportation, child care, job-related expenses such as work clothes or uniforms), and what skills are required for their jobs.

Health status and access to health insurance and health care also are important indicators of well-being. In addition to ascertaining the health status of adult leavers and their children, it is also important to ask whether the members of a leaver's family have health insurance coverage and what the sources of that coverage are (public programs such as Medicaid, employer-sponsored health plans, or other sources). Although insurance is generally a good indicator of access to health care, it is also useful to directly determine if a leaver can obtain medical attention when needed.

One goal of welfare reform is to foster stable families, but the strain of balancing a job and child care may be profound on low-income single mothers. Thus, it is also important to understand if leavers' families are breaking up, with children being sent off to live with friends or relatives. Similarly, leavers may struggle to maintain independent households, so a leaver study also should determine whether leavers are "crowding in" with friends or relatives. Alternatively, leavers may be forming stable two-adult households either through marriage or cohabitation.

It is also important to assess if leavers are facing hardships that cannot be captured by examining income alone. Thus, leaver studies also should consider whether leavers must struggle to meet their families' nutritional needs, pay their bills, or live in substandard housing. In addition, policy makers are concerned

---

[2]Collecting reliable income information can be challenging. Generally the only way to obtain information on income is to ask people a detailed series of questions which was done for the March supplements to the Current Population Survey, and few leaver studies do this. In fact, only four of the studies we examine provide information on total family income (Arizona, Illinois, Missouri, and Washington).

about the impact of welfare reform on children. To assess child well-being, leaver studies could gather information about children's school performance and behavioral problems, for example. Some studies also have gathered information on leaver families' involvement in the child welfare system.

Furthermore, leaver studies can examine how a leaver's status changes over time. This information helps to answer the question of whether a leaver's situation is improving during the transition off welfare and whether he or she is achieving self-sufficiency. Specifically, studies should try to learn whether leavers experience earnings growth over time and whether their use of public program benefits wanes over time.

Finally, it is also useful for leaver studies to fit their findings into a broader context. For example, even if leavers report high incidences of hardships, it is important to be able to know whether they are worse off since leaving welfare than before leaving welfare. Another approach is to compare leavers' outcomes to other groups, such as current welfare recipients or other low-income families who never received welfare, to better interpret how well they are faring.

Taken together, these five areas—income security, employment, health, living arrangements, and quality of life or hardships—can describe the well-being of TANF leavers. In addition, states should think about how to tailor their leaver studies to garner information that is of specific interest to them.

LEAVER STUDY METHODS

Defining Welfare Leavers

The first issue all leaver studies must address is, "Who is a leaver?" A leaver clearly is someone who was receiving welfare and then stopped receiving welfare, but precisely how to define this term can vary.

It is not uncommon for a welfare case to be closed for administrative reasons—for example, the adult in the unit failed to appear for a recertification meeting. Sometimes cases closed for this reason reopen within a matter of weeks. These "leavers" were neither trying to exit welfare nor were they "forced off" by a formal sanction. To avoid including these "administrative closures," studies can require that a case remains closed for a certain period of time before the case is considered to be a leaver. Many studies follow a definition that requires closure for 2 months before inclusion in the sample of leavers. Others require only 1 month. One might expect that studies using a 1-month definition would have higher returns to welfare and lower employment than those using 2-month definitions, all else equal. Interestingly, we find no clear pattern across the two definitions, (as shown in Table 12-2). This could be because all else is not equal, and there are many other differences across these studies that could affect outcomes. Only Arizona-1 actually provides outcome numbers for both definitions in the same data. Although this is only one study, it does show that first-quarter returns

TABLE 12-2 Leaver Population Studied

State	Definition of Leaver[a]	All Leavers[b]	Continuous Leavers[c]	Sanctioned Leavers	Child Only Cases Excluded
Arizona-1	1 month	x		x	x
Arizona-2	2 months	x			x
California-Los Angeles Co.	2 months	x			
California-San Mateo Co.	2 months	x			
District of Columbia	1 month	x			
Florida		x			
Georgia-1	2 months	x			
Georgia-2	2 months	x			
Idaho-1		x			
Idaho-2		x			
Illinois-1	2 months	x			x
Iliinois-2	2 months	x			x
Indiana		x			
Iowa				x	
Kentucky		x			
Maryland-1		x	x	x	
Maryland-2		x	x	x	
Maryland-3		x	x	x	
Massachusetts		x			
Michigan	Sanctioned for 1 year			x	
Mississippi		x			
Missouri-1	2 months	x			
Missouri-2	2 months	x			x
Montana		x			
New Jersey				x	
New Mexico		x			
New York-1		x			
New York-2	2 months	x			x
North Carolina-1	1 month	x			
North Carolina-2		x			
Ohio-Cuyahoga Co. 1	2 months	x	x		x
Ohio-Cuyahoga Co. 2	2 months	x	x		x
Oklahoma		x	x	x	
Pennsylvania		x			
South Carolina-1			x		
South Carolina-2			x		
South Carolina-3			x		
Tennessee		x		x	
Texas	6 months	x			
Virginia		x			
Washington-1		x			
Washington-2			x		

continues

TABLE 12-2 Continued

State	Definition of Leaver[a]	All Leavers[b]	Continuous Leavers[c]	Sanctioned Leavers	Child Only Cases Excluded
Washington-3	1 month		x		
Washington-4	2 months	x	x		
Washington-5	2 months				x
Wisconsin-1	2 months	x	x		
Wisconsin-2		x			
Wisconsin-3	6 to 9 months		x		x
Wyoming		x			

NOTE: The notation x means that the study included a special focus on continuous or sanctioned leavers.

[a]If a cell in the leaver definition column is blank, then the study did not specifically define the term.

[b]If "all leavers" is marked, the study includes continuous leavers and sanctioned leavers. If the two subsequent categories are not marked, then the study does not include a special focus of either continuous or sanctioned leavers.

[c]Continuous leavers refers to individuals who did not return to cash assistance.

to welfare are higher using the 1-month definition of leaver. Employment is approximately the same.

In addition to defining the number of months a case is closed before being included as a leaver, studies must also define the period of time over which to "collect" the leaver sample. Studies usually include all who meet the leaver definition for a specific month, a quarter, or a longer period. Table 12-3 shows the specific calendar time period over which studies define their leaver sample, with results ranging up to a year. How the length of the time period chosen affects results depends on the extent to which the environment is changing. In an area where the context is rapidly changing, combining a group of leavers who left over a long time period can make results less easy to interpret. Many of the studies have chosen to define their leaver study cohort over a 3-month period.

The specific calendar time period chosen for defining the leaver sample also will likely affect results. Some of the studies examined here are based on cohorts from 1996 and others are based on cohorts from 1999. In addition to other differences across areas that make comparisons difficult, readers should keep in mind the specific time period the study is addressing.

Although most studies are interested in how all families that left welfare are faring, some studies also include information on families that remain off welfare for an extended period of time. We refer to such leavers as continuous leavers. For some studies, this is a subset of all leavers defined using a 1- or 2-month closure period. A few studies focus solely on leavers who remain off welfare for

TABLE 12-3 Time Period Covered by Leaver Studies

State/Study	Exit Cohort	Follow-up Period
Arizona-1	1Q98	Administrative: 1 year; Survey: 12-18 months
Arizona-2	4Q96	1 year
California-Los Angeles Co.	3Q96	1 year
California-San Mateo Co.	1997	1 year
District of Columbia	4Q97, 4Q98	Administrative data: 18 months; Survey: 1 year
Florida	*	3 years
Georgia-1	1997	1 year
Georgia-2	1Q97	1 yaer
Idaho-1	3rd and 4th Q97	6 months
Idaho-2	3rd and 4th Q97	10 months
Illinois-1	December1997 or June 1998	4-11 months
Illinois-2	Adminstrative: 3Q97-4Q98: Survey: Dec 1998	Administrative: One year; Survey: 6-8 months
Indiana	*	n.a.
Iowa	*	n.a.
Kentucky	January- November 1997	1-11 months
Maryland-1	October 1996-September 1997	One year
Maryland-2	October 1996-September 1997	Two years
Maryland-3	October 1996-March 1998	18 months
Massachusetts	1st and 2nd Q97	3 months**
Michigan	April 1996	12 months
Mississippi	1Q98	6 months
Missouri-1	4Q96	2 years
Missouri-2	4Q98	30 months
Montana	March 1996-September 1997	1-18 months
New Jersey	February-October 1998	n.a.
New Mexico	July 1996- June 1997	n.a.
New York-1	November 1997	6 months
New York-2	1Q97	One year
North Carolina-1	September 1996	30 months
North Carolina-2	July 1998	5 months
Ohio-Cuyahoga Co. 1	1996	One year
Ohio-Cuyahoga Co. 2	3Q96	One year
Oklahoma	October 1996-November 1997	2-20 months
Pennsylvania	March 1997-January 1998	1-11 months
South Carolina-1	n.a.	n.a.
South Carolina-2	2Q97	One year
South Carolina-3	3Q97	One year
Tennessee	n.a.	n.a.
Texas	November 1997	6 months
Virginia	n.a.	n.a.
Washington-1	n.a.	n.a.
Washington-2	December 1997-March 1998	12-18 months
Washington-3	*	n.a.

continues

TABLE 12-3 Continued

State/Study	Exit Cohort	Follow-up Period
Washington-4	4Q97	Two years
Washington-5	October 1998	6 months
Wisconsin-1	July 1995-1996	15 months
Wisconsin-2	n.a.	n.a.
Wisconsin-3	1Q98	6-9 months
Wyoming	n.a.	n.a.

*These studies took a random sample of people who began receiving benefits when Temporary Assistance for Needy Families (TANF) was implemented in the state. At the time of the survey, these recipients may or may not have been receiving TANF benefits. These are caseload tracking studies, not leaver studies.

**This study surveyed respondents every 3 months for a year. The study includes the results of the interviews at months 3 and 12.

a more extended period of time, defining leaver as a case being closed from 6 months to a year.

Information on continuous leavers is valuable because those who return to welfare most likely have lower rates of employment, and higher participation in other programs such as the Food Stamps Program and Medicaid. For example, if we examine all leavers, we might find that the share receiving food stamps remains constant over time. But this approach might mask two countervailing trends: As time goes by, one group of leavers returns to welfare, thereby increasing food stamp participation, while another group of leavers, continuous leavers, has declining food stamp participation. Consequently, examining continuous leavers can be extremely useful. Note, however, that presenting results solely for continuous leavers (without information on returns to welfare) biases results toward positive outcomes when a significant portion of the caseload returns. Indeed, results from the studies using administrative data reveal that returns to welfare 1 year after exit range from 13 percent to 40 percent. Thus, presentation of results for all leavers and continuous leavers is preferred.

Another important subgroup to consider is families that were terminated from welfare by a sanction. Nine of the studies reviewed examine sanctioned cases (see Table 12-2). Because sanctioned leavers may behave differently or have different characteristics than nonsanctioned leavers, separation of these results can be important, especially in areas where a significant portion of a given leaver group left due to sanctions. Results for all leavers in such an area could potentially mask negative results for the subset of sanctioned leavers.

Most studies are interested in how the adults in a welfare case fare after they leave welfare; however, a growing portion of welfare cases are "child only" cases. Ten of the studies we review explicitly exclude "child only" cases from their leaver studies. Because many of the outcomes examined in leaver studies involve parental employment, we suspect that most leaver studies, in fact, exclude such cases. Furthermore, when an adult leaves a welfare assistance unit but her children become a "child only" case, some studies consider that adult to be a welfare leaver while others consider the case to remain open. Finally, some studies focus exclusively on single parent cases while others combine information on one- and two-parent families. Providing information for all leavers as well as separately for one- and two-parent cases is preferred especially in locations with a high proportion of two-parent cases.

Data Used in Leaver Studies

Studies of welfare leavers rely heavily on two types of data: state administrative records and direct surveys of welfare leavers.[3] Each source can provide valuable but limited information about some aspects of the well-being of welfare leavers.

Administrative Data

Twenty-one of the 49 leaver studies we review use administrative data as shown in Table 12-4. States have data systems used in administering programs, such as TANF, and these databases can be used in conducting leaver studies. Typically state welfare program data can provide information on the timing of receipt of welfare benefits, the value of the grant, the number of people (adults and children) in the case, as well as some demographic characteristics of recipients, usually race, age, number and ages of children, and whether a case is single parent or two parent. Of course, availability of TANF data is critical to conducting a leaver study because the data allow one to define who is a leaver. In addition, this information can be used to determine who among a group of leavers returns to welfare and to develop some basic characteristics for conducting subgroup analysis. One also can examine records on participation prior to the month of exit to assemble a history of receipt.[4] This information also can be used to analyze subgroups based on being a long-term or short-term recipient, although none of the studies we review have carried out such a subgroup analysis.

---

[3]Ethnographic interviews and focus groups with welfare leavers also could provide valuable information on leavers; however, none of the studies reviewed here relied on this of type of data.

[4]In some states, the ability to assemble records of past welfare receipt may be limited because under AFDC, such information was not vital for program administration. Under TANF with its lifetime limit, it is imperative that state data systems contain lengthy historic information on receipt for each case.

TABLE 12-4 Studies Using Administrative Data

State	Exit Cohort	Period of Follow up After Exit	Programs Covered[a]
Arizona-1	1Q98	1 year	Employment, Temporary Assistance for Needy Families (TANF), Food Stamps, childcare subsidy, child support, child welfare
Arizona-2	4Q96	1 year	Employment, TANF, Food Stamps, Medicaid
California-Los Angeles Co.	3Q96	1 year	Employment
California-San Mateo Co.	1997	1 year	Employment, TANF, Food Stamps, Medicaid
District of Columbia	4Q98	18 months	TANF, Food Stamps, Medicaid
Florida	[c]	3 years	Employment, TANF, Food Stamps
Georgia-1	1997	1 year	Employment, TANF
Georgia-2	1Q97	1 year	Employment, TANF
Illinois-2	3Q97-4Q98	1 year	Employment, TANF, Food Stamps, Medicaid, the Special Supplemental Nutrition Program for Women, Infants, and Children (WIC), childcare subsidy, family case management services, drug and alcohol treatment services, child support, child welfare[b]
Maryland-1	October 1996-September 1997	1 year	Employment, TANF
Maryland-2	October 1996-September 1997	2 years	Employment, TANF
Maryland-3	October 1996-March 1998	18 months	Employment, TANF
Mississippi	1Q98	6 months	Employment, TANF
Missouri-1	4Q96	2 years	Employment, TANF, Food Stamps, Medicaid
New York-2	1Q97	1 year	Employment, TANF, Food Stamps, Medicaid
North Carolina-1	September 1996[d]	30 months	Employment, TANF, Food Stamps
Ohio-Cuyahoga Co. 1	1996	1 year	TANF
Ohio-Cuyahoga Co. 2	3Q96	1 year	Employment, TANF, Food Stamps, Medicaid
Washington-4	4Q97	2 years	Employment, TANF, Food Stamps, Medicaid, childcare subsidy, child support programs, child welfare[b]

continues

TABLE 12-4   Continued

State	Exit Cohort	Period of Follow up After Exit	Programs Covered[a]
Wisconsin-1	July 1995-1996	15 months	Employment, TANF, Food Stamps, Medicaid
Wisconsin-2	n.a.	n.a.	Employment, TANF, Food Stamps, Medicaid

[a]TANF refers to cash assistance. For studies that predate the implementation of TANF, the use of the term TANF in the table indicates Aid to Families with Dependent Children (AFDC) cash assistance.

[b]Child abuse and neglect referrals and out-of-home placements. Women, Infants, and Children (WIC).

[c]The AFDC Component exited in February 1995.

[d]Florida uses a TANF Cohort instead of an exit cohort. The study chose a random sample of people who began receiving TANF benefits with the implementation of TANF. The study tracks their employment, TANF, and Food Stamp history over three years.

State program data also can include information on participation in the Food Stamp and Medicaid programs linked to TANF program data. Table 12-4 shows that the majority of study areas (9 out of 15) have a study that includes both of these sources of data. Other types of program data also may be available to be linked to TANF data. Only three of the studies listed here have made use of additional program data. Examples of the types of data they examine include childcare subsidies, receipt of child support payments, and involvement in the child welfare system. Information from such programs provides a richer description of the well-being of leavers.

By their nature, program data do not contain information on families who no longer receive program benefits. Consequently, there is no way to determine if leavers who do not return to the caseload and are not participating in other programs from which data are available are finding jobs. To address this problem, many leaver studies use additional administrative data, linking their welfare program records to data from state unemployment insurance (UI) systems. If a leaver is working for an employer that reports wages to the state UI system, then these linked records can reveal whether a leaver is working in a given quarter and how much that leaver earned. Because the employment and earnings of welfare leavers are a key outcome for policy makers and researchers, linking administrative data from the welfare system with data from the state UI system is vital. Nineteen of the 21 studies link their program data with state UI data.

Note that using administrative data to assess the status of welfare leavers often requires researchers to link information across various data systems. In general, researchers use Social Security numbers to link information on welfare leavers with information from other sources such as UI earnings records. If there is a discrepancy in an individual's Social Security number across data systems, then no match can be made. Goerge and Lee (this volume: Chapter 7) provide a detailed discussion of techniques that can be used to improve the quality of matched data between administrative data systems.

Overall, the greatest strength of administrative data is that they provide accurate information on program participation for all leavers who continue to reside in the state. Information on employment and earnings from UI records also is reliable; however, leavers who work outside the state or in jobs that do not generate UI wage reports[5] will not be picked up in a state's UI system.[6] Thus, administrative data on employment probably understate employment among leavers. The greatest weakness of administrative data is their failure to provide information on many aspects of well-being and changes in family structure. Thus, they provide a limited picture of the status of TANF leavers.

Survey Data

Surveys of welfare leavers are particularly good at obtaining information that is beyond the scope of administrative data systems. For example, in addition to employment and wage information, a survey can obtain data on job characteristics—nonwage benefits, training, and work-related expenses. Surveys also can elicit information on changes in a leaver's personal characteristics and household composition as well as what sort of hardships the leavers have faced. Furthermore, leavers can be surveyed even if they have moved across state lines. Thirty-two of the 49 leaver studies we review use data collected from surveys of welfare leavers. Features of the 32 studies are listed in Table 12-5.

Surveys of welfare leavers generally collect information on a sample of families who left TANF during a specific timeframe by interviewing them months after their exit. The choice of how long after exit to interview respondents has advantages and disadvantages. The sooner the time period is to the exit from welfare, the more able a recipient is to recall information on the circumstances around leaving, such as reason for leaving and specifics of his or her first job. The later the interview takes place from the exit, the more information about a family's transition can be gathered. The actual range of time of the interview after exiting in these studies varies from 3 months (Massachusetts) to 30 months (Missouri).

Most studies gather survey information using telephone interviews, but many also conduct some in-person interviews. This combination method ensures that

---

[5]Most jobs are reported to a state's UI system. Some exceptions include certain jobs in agriculture, self-employed workers, and household employees whose employers often fail to meet reporting requirements.

[6]Missouri is the only study to examine UI data from a neighboring state (Kansas).

TABLE 12-5 Leaver Studies Using Surveys

State/Study	Exit Cohort	Timing of Survey Postexit	Sample Size	Response Rate (%)	Type of Survey	Respondents Paid
Leaver Studies:						
Arizona	1Q98	12-18 months	821	72	Phone/in person	Yes
District of Columbia	4Q98	1 year	277	61	Phone/in person	Yes
Idaho-1	3rd and 4th Q97	6 months	477	17	Mail	No
Idaho-2	3rd and 4th Q97	10 months	53	47	Mail	No
Illinois-1	December 1997 or June 1998	4-11 months	427	31	Phone	Yes
Illinois-2	December 1998	6-8 months	514	51	Phone/in person	Yes
Kentucky	January-November 1997	1-11 months	560	17	Phone	No
Massachusetts	1st and 2nd Q97	3 months[a]	341	53	In person	Yes
Michigan	July 1998	12 months	126	85	In person	No
Mississippi	1Q98	6 months	405	87	Phone/mail/in person	No
Missouri-2	4Q98	30 months	878	75	Phone/in person	Yes
Montana	March 1996- September 1997	1-18 months	208	[c]	Phone	No
North Carolina-2	July 1998	5 months	315	77	Phone	Yes
New Jersey	February-October 1998	n.a.	453	45	In person	No
New Mexico	July 1996-June 1997	n.a.	88	12	Mail	No
New York-1	November 1997	6 months	126	22	Phone	No
Oklahoma	October 1996-November 1997	2-20 months	292	53	Phone	Yes
Pennsylvania	March 1997-January 1998	1-11 months	169	47	Phone	No
South Carolina-1	n.a.	n.a.	2,002[b]	77	Phone/in person	No
South Carolina-2	2Q97	1 year	391	76	Phone/in person	No
South Carolina-3	3Q97	1 year	403	76	Phone/in person	No
Tennessee	n.a.	n.a.	2,500	51	Phone	No

Texas	November 1997	6 months	1,396	42	Phone/mail	No
Virginia	n.a.	n.a.	171	46	Phone	No
Washington-1	n.a.	n.a.	65	c	In person	No
Washington-2	December 1997-March 1998	12-18 months	560	31	Phone	No
Washington-5	October 1998	6 months	987	72	Phone/in person	Yes
Wisconsin-3	1Q98	6-9 months	375	69	d	No
Wyoming	n.a.	n.a.	200	32	Phone	No
Caseload Studies:[e]						
Indiana	n.a.	n.a.	847	71	Phone/in person	No
Iowa	n.a.	n.a.	162	85	In person	No
Washington-3	n.a.	n.a.	592	52	Phone	No

[a]This study surveyed respondents every 3 months for a year. The study includes the results of the interviews at months 3 and 12.

[b]This study is an analysis of five surveys performed in South Carolina. These five surveys have a total sample of 2002 cases. The overall response rate of these five surveys was 77 percent.

[c]Response rate not reported.

[d]Survey mode not described.

[e]These studies took a random sample of people who began receiving benefits when Temporary Assistance for Needy Families (TANF) was implemented in the state. At the time of the survey, these recipients may or may not have been receiving TANF benefits.

leavers without telephones are included in the study. Three studies (two from Idaho and one from New Mexico) used mail surveys; this method is not recommended because the common problems with all surveys (described as follows) are magnified in mail surveys.

Overall, the strength of survey data is the breadth of information they contain. However, survey data have their own shortcomings. First, surveys rely on respondents to answer questions accurately and truthfully.[7] Second, survey data are collected for only a sample of welfare leavers; therefore, any assessment of the well-being of leavers based on surveys is subject to sampling error. Finally, and potentially most seriously, even if the sample of leavers accurately reflects all leavers, not all sampled families will respond to the survey. That is, a researcher only will be able to contact and interview a subset of the original sample. If the leavers who respond to the survey are very different from the nonrespondents, then the survey data will suffer from nonresponse bias and not accurately represent the status of leavers. The best way to reduce nonresponse bias is to have a high response rate. A large literature is available on increasing response rates (see Cantor and Cunningham, this volume: Chapter 2; Singer and Kulka, this volume: Chapter 4, and Weiss and Bailar, this volume: Chapter 3). (See Table 12-5 for response rates in the leaver studies examined here.)

Getting the Most Out of a Leaver Study

Both administrative and survey data have their shortcomings, but combining data from these two sources provides a rich description of the overall well-being of leavers. As Table 12-1 shows, eight studies use both survey and administrative data to study the same cohort of leavers.[8] In the following sections, we describe steps researchers can take to examine the accuracy of employment information from administrative data and assess the accuracy and representativeness of survey data. None of these techniques can completely address the potential shortcomings in the data, but if they are employed, they can help readers weigh the findings reported in any given leaver study.

Do UI Records Understate Employment by Welfare Leavers?

With the exception of Missouri, all leaver studies using UI wage records to examine employment only link into a single state's UI system. Consequently, leavers that move out of state or work outside of their home state will not appear

---

[7]For a discussion of measurement in error in surveys of low-income populations, see Mathiowetz et al. (this volume: Chapter 6).

[8]Four states (Arizona, DC, Illinois, and Mississippi) present findings from both survey and administrative data in the same report; another four states (Missouri, North Carolina, Washington, and Wisconsin) present their findings from these two data sources in separate reports.

TABLE 12-6 Employment of Welfare Leavers: Comparison of Administrative and Survey Data

			Employment Rate (%)	
State/Study	Exit Cohort	Timing of Survey	Survey Data	Administrative Data*
Arizona	1Q98	12-18 months	57.0	50.0
District of Columbia	4Q98	12 months	60.3	n.a.
Illinois	December 1998	6-8 months	63.2	55.0
Missouri	4Q98	30 months	65.0	58.0
Washington	October 1998	6-8 months	59.0	57.0

*Based on employment rate from the fourth postexit quarter.
SOURCE: See Appendix B for a complete listing of the leavers studies referenced.

in the data.[9] Furthermore, not all jobs are covered by state UI systems so there will be no record of work for a leaver who works in an uncovered job. If a leaver study uses both administrative and survey data and has asked surveyed leavers about their employment status, one can assess the extent of this potential underreporting.

Five jurisdictions use surveys of TANF leavers to ask the leavers themselves about their current employment status. The responses of leavers generally refer to employment about 6 months to a year after exit. Table 12-6 compares these self-reported employment rates with fourth quarter post exit employment rates computed from administrative data. The surveys consistently find higher employment rates than those reported in UI wage records; in general they are about 7 percentage points higher. The Illinois survey presents some instructive information. In its administrative records, Illinois finds that 30 percent of leavers never worked over the first four postexit quarters. In its survey, Illinois finds that only 15 percent of leavers say they have never worked since exiting TANF.

Further, a supplemental study by Wisconsin's Department of Workforce Development (1998) examines how much employment is missed using UI wage records by comparing administrative and survey data on families leaving welfare in the first quarter of 1998. This study finds that out of the 375 surveyed leavers, 85 percent reported employment information consistent with administrative

[9]It may be possible to obtain employment and earnings information on leavers who work "out of state" by matching program data to UI data from neighboring states, but this may be too costly and time consuming for the expected benefit. Alternatively, several researchers and states have contemplated using data on the National Directory of New Hires maintained by the Office of Child Support Enforcement (OCSE) of the U.S. Department of Health and Human Services. This database contains information on the employment and earnings of all newly hired workers in the United States. To this date, however, OCSE has not allowed anyone to use these data for research purposes.

records. Among the leavers who reported that they had worked in the survey but did not show up in Wisconsin's UI data, 38 percent claimed to be working in temporary jobs that may not be reported to the UI system. Another 32 percent worked as housekeepers, childcare workers, farmhands, or in other jobs in which they may be considered self-employed and/or for which employers may not file UI reports. Ten percent explicitly stated they were self-employed and 17 percent had left the state.

Are Respondents Answering Survey Questions Accurately?

Survey data are based on self-reported information from respondents. If respondents intentionally or unwittingly provide inaccurate information, the survey findings may not reflect the well-being of leavers. When surveys gather information that duplicates information available through administrative sources, it is possible to compare a respondent's answer to the administrative report to assess accuracy. For example, a survey may ask, "In the year since you exited welfare, have you ever received food stamps?" Because this information is reported in administrative data, it is possible to see if survey respondents are providing reliable information. In general, studies that compare survey and administrative findings on common areas find fairly close agreement, as shown in Table 12-7. Finding similar results using survey and administrative data does not guarantee that all other survey responses are accurate; however, if the findings were different, it would undermine the confidence one would have in the survey results.

Of course, the real value of surveys is their ability to obtain information unavailable in administrative records, and for such items it is not possible to obtain external validation. This can be particularly challenging when trying to determine whether a leaver is better off since exit than before. For example, a welfare leaver interviewed 9 months after exit may not recall the trouble he or she had paying the rent prior to leaving welfare. One way to examine the importance of recall problems is to supplement a leaver study with a survey of families still on welfare. The Washington state study is the only study we review that conducts a "stayer" analysis. Surprisingly, while other surveys (Arizona and Illinois) that ask about food security find that leavers generally report the same or lower levels of insecurity prior to exit than after exiting, Washington finds that current recipients actually report higher rates of food insecurity than leavers.

How Representative Are Survey Respondents of Leavers in General?

As we discussed, nonresponse bias is a potentially significant problem for surveys of welfare leavers. Indeed, if the leavers who did not respond to the survey (either because they could not be located or because they refused to participate) are appreciably different from respondents, then survey data will

TABLE 12-7 Post-Temporary Assistance for Needy Families (TANF) Exit Program Participation: Comparing Administrative and Survey Data Findings

State	Point in Time		Since Exit	
	Administrative (%)	Survey (%)	Administrative (%)	Survey (%)
Welfare				
District of Columbia[a]	18.8	18.8	21.1	24.6
Illinois-2[c]	17.5	13.7	28.9	18.5
Missouri-1[b]	20.5	14.0	44.0	31.0
Washington-4[c]	16.0	19.0	23.4	n.a.
Food Stamps				
District of Columbia[a]	37.9	40.8	n.a.	55.2
Illinois-2[c]	34.2	32.9	56.0	44.1
Missouri-1[b]	40.1	47.0	81.0	83.0
Washington-4[c]	40.0	n.a.	n.a.	50.0
Medicaid[d]				
Arizona-1[a]	36.9	39.0	71.7	n.a.
District of Columbia[a]	47.5	53.8	n.a.	n.a.
Illinois-2[c]	47.4	46.9	68.8	n.a.
Missouri-1[b]	n.a.	33.0	n.a.	n.a
Washington-4[c]	39.6	53.3	n.a.	n.a.

[a]The periods of follow-up for Arizona and the District of Columbia's survey data are 12-18 months and 12 months, respectively. The administrative data are reported for the fourth quarter after exit.

[b]The period of follow-up for Missouri's survey is 30 months. However, only 12 months of administrative data are available. The administrative data reported are for the fourth quarter after exit.

[c]The period of follow-up for Illinois's and Washington's survey data is 6-8 months. The administrative data reported are for the third quarter after exit.

[d]Data reported for adults.

paint a misleading picture of the well-being of TANF leavers. In general, the higher the response rate to a survey, the less concerned one is about its representativeness. (Table 12-4 shows response rates.)

Differences in response rates can affect outcomes for welfare leavers as measured by surveys. We report these results separately for surveys with high, moderate, and low response rates. In general, we would expect respondents to lead more stable lives than nonrespondents and to be more eager to share good news with survey takers. To the extent that nonresponse bias is a problem in these surveys, we would expect surveys with lower response rates to generally show that welfare leavers are better off. Note, however, that even in a survey with a 75-percent response rate, the nonresponse bias may be profound.

Table 12-8 shows employment and earnings information from survey data by response rate. Out of the nine surveys with high response rates, seven report

TABLE 12-8 Employment Earnings of Employed Welfare Leavers: Survey Data Findings by Survey Response Rate

State	Hours Worked	Earnings
Panel A: Response Rate Greater Than 70%		
Arizona-1	#	Average wage: $7.52
Indiana	61% worked 35 or more hours a week	40.7% earned $7 or more an hour
Michigan	#	53.2% earned $400 or more a month
Mississippi	Average number of hours worked: 35	Average wage: $5.77
Missouri-2	Average number of hours worked: 39	##
North Carolina	37.9% worked 40 or more hours	Median monthly salary: $849.76
South Carolina-2	Average number of hours worked: 36	Average wage: $6.44
South Carolina-3	Average number of hours worked: 36	Average wage: $6.45
Washington-5	Average number of hours worked: 36	Average wage: $7.70
Panel B: Response Rate Between 50% and 70%		
District of Columbia	Average number of hours worked: 36	Average wage: $8.74
Illinois-2	Median number of hours worked: 37	Median wage: $7.42
Massachusetts	#	63.3% income $250 or more a week[a]
Oklahoma	Average number of hours worked: 34	Average wage: $6.15
Tennessee	35% worked full time	Average wage: $5.67
Washington-3	Average number of hours worked: 36	Average wage: $8.09
Wisconsin-3	57% worked 40 or more hours a week	Average wage: $7.42
Panel C: Response Rate Less Than 50%		
Idaho-1	40% worked 30 or more hours a week	21% earned $7 or more an hour
Illinois-1	Average number of hours worked: 35.8	Median wage: $7.11
Kentucky	73.5% worked 35 or more hours	40.9% earned $7 an hour or more
Montana	47% worked 21 or more hours	##
New Mexico	74.6% worked 30 or more hours	29% earned $7 or more an hour
New York-1	40% worked 35 or more hours	##
Pennsylvania	62% worked 30 or more hours	59% earned $6.50 or more an hour
Texas	Average numbers of hours worked: 34	Average wage: $6.28
Virginia	#	Median monthly salary: $1,160
Washington-2	Average hours worked: 34	Average wage: $8.42
Wyoming	#	83% earned $7.50 or more an hour

[a]Average weekly earning for full-time work is $305.
\# Hours worked not reported.
\## Earnings not reported.

information on hours worked, with five reporting the average number of hours worked by employed leavers. These five studies find that leavers work an average of 35 to 39 hours per week. Five studies report average hourly earnings: They range from $5.77 to $7.70. Among the studies with response rates of between 50 and 70 percent, four report average or median hours worked per week, and they show that employed leavers work between 34 and 37 hours per week. Among low-response-rate studies, three report average hours, and they, too, find an average of about 35 hours per week. The range of hourly wage rates reported in low- and moderate-response-rate studies runs from a low of $5.67 in Tennessee to a high of $8.74 in the District of Columbia.

Researches use two relatively straightforward techniques to assess the extent of nonresponse bias in surveys of welfare leavers. The first technique involves using administrative data on the entire survey sample and comparing respondents to nonrespondents. The second involves using the survey data to compare the characteristics of easily located and interviewed leavers with those of leavers that were "hard to find."[10]

First, consider how administrative data can help uncover potentially important non-response bias in survey data. Three studies, the District of Columbia (DC), Missouri, and South Carolina, have compared administrative information on survey respondents and nonrespondents to see if nonrespondents appear to be very different from respondents. Missouri (Dunton, 1999) finds that non-respondents tend to have less education and lower quarterly earnings than respondents. South Carolina (Edelhoch and Martin, 1999) compares the reasons for TANF exit for survey respondents and nonrespondents and finds that respondents are significantly less likely to have their cases closed because of a sanction and significantly more likely to have their cases closed because of earned income than nonrespondents. These comparisons suggest that findings from these studies may present too sunny a picture of the status of welfare leavers. On the other hand, DC's leaver study finds that nonrespondents are slightly younger, have younger children, and have had shorter spells of receipt than nonrespondents. Overall, however, DC finds that respondents are fairly similar to nonrespondents.

Another technique to gauge the importance and potential biases of non-response involves examining differences among respondents, comparing survey responses from respondents who were easy to contact and quickly agreed to be surveyed to the responses of hard-to-contact and reluctant responders.[11] This

---

[10]One also can attempt to do an ex post facto study of nonrespondents. This is rather costly and involves painstaking efforts to locate nonrespondents to the initial survey and interviewing them. None of the studies reviewed here attempt this; however, Mathematica Policy Research is conducting such a nonrespondent study in Iowa. The organization's goal is to locate and interview 15 nonrespondents.

[11]Groves and Wissoker (1999) use a similar approach for examining nonresponse bias in the National Survey of America's Families.

approach is based on the idea that "hard to interview" cases fall on a continuum between the "easy to interview" and nonrespondents. If the hard to interview are very different from the easy to interview in ways that are important to the study, it is likely that nonrespondents are even more different, and nonresponse bias is likely to be a big problem.

Only DC explicitly uses this technique. DC finds that hard-to-interview cases are neither clearly better nor worse off than the easy-to-interview cases; rather, their experiences are more diverse. For example, easy-to-interview cases are slightly more likely to work than hard-to-interview cases but among those who work, the hard-to-interview have higher hourly wages. In a supplementary study, Missouri (1999) compares employment and earnings among survey respondents in the Kansas City area based on the timing of response. Missouri finds that respondents among the final third of completed interviews are slightly less likely to work than respondents in the first two-thirds of completed interviews (88.5 versus 91.4 percent). The harder to interview also have lower monthly incomes ($935 versus $1,094).

Although we have described several techniques researchers can use to assess the potential for nonresponse bias in leaver studies, the best way to guard against nonresponse bias is to have a high response rate. Even though these techniques cannot rule out the possibility of significant nonresponse bias, they do provide readers with a sense of the potential size and direction of the bias. Interestingly, however, we find that surveys with moderate response rates (50 to 70 percent) report findings that are fairly similar to those with higher response rates (more than 70 percent).

CONCLUSION

Leaver studies are useful tools for monitoring the well-being of families that have been exposed to TANF and have left the rolls. They can help policy makers identify the problems that families who have left welfare are facing, and the ongoing capacity built by states and the research community will provide a baseline for formulating and evaluating future reforms.

This paper examines the methodologies used in a large set of leaver studies, identifies preferred practices for conducting such studies, and discusses the implications of research methods for the interpretations of the findings reported in these studies.

Leaver studies rely on two types of data: (1) linked administrative records from welfare programs, other low-income assistance programs, and state unemployment insurance systems, and (2) survey data. The quality of the information garnered from administrative data depends on how well the data systems are linked as well as the coverage of these systems. In general, leaver studies do not describe the methods they used to link data from multiple sources. Furthermore, although the employment of former welfare recipients is an important outcome, this information comes from state UI records. Even with a perfect match to welfare program data, state UI records will understate the level of employment of welfare leavers because a nontrivial portion of jobs are not reported to the state's UI system (jobs out of state, self-employment, as well as some domestic and agricultural work).

Surveys of leavers provide a broader set of information than administrative data on the well-being of families that have left welfare. However, the quality of survey data depend on the accuracy of the information garnered from respondents and the representativeness of the completed survey sample. Indeed, it is reasonable to expect that leavers who can be located and who choose to respond to a survey may be better off than other leavers.

Leaver studies that examine the same cohort of leavers using both administrative and survey data present a more complete picture of the status of leavers than studies that rely on only a single source. Although both sources have their limitations, combining information from the two sources can help researchers and policy makers to better assess the findings. For example, it is useful to obtain information on employment and program participation in surveys that is also available in administrative data. The survey data can be used to assess the extent of underreporting of employment in UI wage records, while the administrative data on program participation can be used to assess if respondents are responding accurately to survey questions.

In addition, nonresponse bias is potentially an important problem in leaver studies. By using administrative data available for both survey respondents and nonrespondents, researchers can gauge the extent to which respondents differ from leavers in general. In addition, one can also obtain a sense of the extent of nonresponse bias by comparing the responses of easily interviewed cases with those of cases that were hard to locate or initially refused to respond.

Finally, states can build on these studies by repeating them for new cohorts of leavers or by following existing cohorts over time. Studying new cohorts allows comparison of whether the status of leavers is changing as policies become more fully implemented and time limits are reached. Reinterviewing or analyzing administrative data for the same cohort of leavers as time passes provides information on whether employment is becoming more stable, earnings are rising, and economic hardship is decreasing—in short, whether the well-being of leavers is improving over time.

REFERENCES

Dunton, Nancy
    1999   Non-Response Analysis: Missouri Leavers Survey. Unpublished tables and presentation at the Fall 1999 Outcomes Grantee Meeting of the U.S. Department of Health and Human Services Office of the Assistant Secretary for Planning and Evaluation, Washington, DC, October 25-26.

Edelhoch, Marilyn, and Linda Martin
  1999   Analysis of Response Rates and Non-Response Bias in Surveys. Unpublished tables and presentation at the Fall 1999 Welfare Outcomes Grantee Meeting of the U.S. Department of Health and Human Services Office of the Assistant Secretary for Planning and Evaluation, Washington, DC, October 25-26.
Groves, Robert, and Douglas Wissoker
  1999   *No. 7: Early Nonresponse Studies of the 1997 National Survey of America's Families.* National Survey of America's Families Methodology Working Paper. Washington, DC: The Urban Institute.
Wisconsin Department of Workforce Development
  1998   *Differences between AFDC and W-W Leavers Survey Data for January–March 1998 and Wisconsin's UI Wage Records for 1998.* Department of Workforce Development MEP Folio Brief 09-99, October 19.

13

Preexit Benefit Receipt and Employment Histories and Postexit Outcomes of Welfare Leavers

Michele Ver Ploeg

The enactment of time limits, work requirements, and sanctions, among other rules of the Personal Responsibility and Work Opportunity Reconciliation Act of 1996 (PRWORA), caused many observers to wonder how welfare recipients would respond: Would they leave welfare? Would they find jobs? Would they face hardship or would their economic and family situations improve? These questions prompted numerous studies of "welfare leavers," or those who stopped receiving welfare benefits.

Most of these welfare leaver studies were conducted for monitoring purposes—to inform policymakers and program administrators about the needs and experiences of those who had left welfare. However, some were conducted with the goal of assessing the effectiveness of the reforms; that is, they intended to assess whether the reforms caused those who left welfare to be better off or worse off relative to a comparison group. To make this assessment, the studies usually employed a before-and-after research design, comparing outcomes of welfare leavers before they left welfare to outcomes after they left welfare, or a multiple-cohort design, comparing outcomes of a cohort of people who left welfare prior

The author is grateful to the Wisconsin State Department of Workforce Development and the Institute for Research on Poverty at the University of Wisconsin-Madison for making the data used in this paper available. Ingrid Rothe, Daniel Ross, and Allison Hales-Espeweth of the University of Wisconsin-Madison's Institute for Research on Poverty, and Barbara Wolfe, Director of IRP deserve special thanks for making the data available and assisting with use of the data. Thanks also to Karl Johnson, who provided research assistance from the project. Finally, the author is grateful to Robert Moffitt for valuable comments on the paper as it developed.

to the enactment of PRWORA to outcomes of a cohort of leavers who left welfare after enactment of PRWORA. Both of these designs have weaknesses in drawing causal conclusions.[1]

Factors outside of welfare, such as the economy, may also change and affect the outcomes of welfare leavers, making it difficult to assess whether outcome changes are due to the reforms or to the other factors using these methods. Another weakness of these methods is that the characteristics of the people leaving welfare at the time of the study, or at the time the cohorts are drawn, may be driving changes in outcomes. For example, if a cohort of leavers is drawn when the caseload is relatively small, the leavers may be comprised primarily of those who have the most barriers to leaving welfare, such as substance abuse, very young children, or little work experience. Their outcomes after leaving may be much different than the outcomes of a cohort of leavers drawn when the caseloads are relatively large, since this cohort may be composed of leavers with fewer barriers to self-sufficiency. This second problem of the composition of the caseload is also a problem even if the leaver studies are only used for monitoring, and not evaluation, purposes. For example, a monitoring study may be conducted to roughly quantify the need for child care services of those who leave welfare. Those who leave welfare in a time when caseloads are just beginning to drop may be able to leave because they had an easy time securing child care, while those who could not easily find childcare may not leave welfare until much later. It would be hazardous to base conclusions about the need for childcare from any single cohort of leavers if one does not know much about that cohort of leavers.

The National Research Council report (1999) suggested that as a crude means of standardizing descriptions of the caseload and the outcomes of leavers across time and across areas, outcomes could be stratified by the past welfare receipt history and past work experience of welfare leavers. Standardizing the composition of the caseload and the groups of the leavers would then make comparisons of outcomes of leavers across time and jurisdictions more credible because leavers with similar work and welfare receipt histories would be compared to each other. The purpose of this paper is to classify characteristics of welfare leavers and stayers and their outcomes by their preexit benefit receipt and employment experiences to illustrate one method the leaver studies might use to standardize their results to make comparisons across time and jurisdictions more credible. No attempts to make causal attributions are made in this study.

The second section of this study describes the data used. The third section examines the past welfare receipt, employment, and earnings histories of the caseload of AFDC recipients in 1995. Section 4 examines whether and how much welfare leavers work and earn after leaving, whether they return to welfare or use

---

[1]See NRC (1999, 2001) for a more detailed discussion of these weaknesses.

other public assistance after leaving, and how self-sufficient they are after they leave. In discussing each of these outcomes, results are presented separately across different types of welfare leavers based on their past welfare receipt and work histories. This section also examines the outcomes of cases classified as "high-barrier" leavers–that is, those who face multiple barriers to gaining self-sufficiency. The outcomes of this group are presented in an attempt to estimate a lower bound on outcomes of leavers. Section 5 examines the importance of past welfare receipt and work history measures in a multivariate setting. Probit models of the probability of leaving welfare and of being employed a year after leaving welfare, controlling for welfare and earnings histories, as well as demographic characteristics of leavers, are estimated. Tobit estimates of post-welfare earnings, controlling for welfare and work histories and demographic characteristics also are given. The coefficients from these models are then used to predict outcomes of different high-barrier groups to assess how cases with multiple barriers to self-sufficiency fare after leaving welfare.

This study was undertaken as part of a set of papers that explore the importance of caseload composition factors for outcomes of welfare leavers. Moffitt (this volume: Chapter 14) uses the National Longitudinal Survey of Youth data from 1979 to 1996 to describe the welfare receipt and employment experiences of young women ages 20-29. Stevens (2000) uses AFDC and Unemployment Insurance administrative records from Maryland and draws multiple cohorts of leavers across time periods. The past AFDC and work histories of these cohorts are described and employment outcomes after leaving welfare are compared across cases with different welfare receipt and work experience histories.

This study also builds on a series of papers on AFDC leavers in Wisconsin that has been conducted by researchers at the Institute for Research on Poverty at the University of Wisconsin-Madison.[2] These reports have examined employment, earnings, and benefit receipt after leaving welfare for a cohort of July 1995 AFDC recipients who left AFDC in the following year.

DESCRIPTION OF THE DATA AND KEY VARIABLE DEFINITIONS

Data for this study come from the Wisconsin Department of Workforce Development CARES system, which contains information collected through the administration of AFDC and other means-tested programs. These data were matched to earnings and employment data from the state's UI system. All persons in the data used in this study received AFDC benefits in Wisconsin in July 1995. These cases were tracked with linked administrative data from January 1989 until December 1997, providing up to 9 years of data for each case.

---

[2]See Cancian, M. et al. (1999); Cancian et al., (2000a); and Cancian, M., Haveman, R., Meyer, D.R., and Wolfe, B. (2000b).

Who Is in the Data Set?

Every observation in the data set received AFDC-Regular (for single-parent families) in July 1995. The entire caseload at the time numbered 65,017. The following types of cases were eliminated from the data, with the number of cases eliminated (nonsequentially) with the restriction in parentheses:

(1) Cases that were open in July 1995 but did not receive any benefits (n=397).

(2) Cases where there were no children 18 or younger in July 1995 (n=843).

(3) Cases where all eligible children in the case are being cared for by a not-legally responsible relative (n=6,101).

(4) Cases where there are two parents (n=907).

(5) Cases where a case head is a teen mom—meaning there is an eligible adult under the age of 18 (n=47), or there is no eligible adult and a child is the caretaker (n=254).

(6) Cases involving a large family or two conjoined families where a single case head is unidentifiable (n=138).

(7) Cases for which UI data were not requested (n=47).

(8) Cases where the case head is over 65 years old (n=83).

(9) Cases with a male case head (n=1,888).

After eliminating these cases, the data set contained 54,518 cases; this is the data set used by Cancian et al. (1999). We further eliminated cases under the age of 21 in 1995. Because we were able to obtain data on AFDC receipt back to July 1989 and UI earnings reports back to January 1989, those under age 21 were eliminated because they were under the age of 15 in 1989 and not reasonably expected to be on AFDC or working. After eliminating these cases, our final number of observations is 48,216.

Definition of a Leaver

A welfare "leaver" is defined as a case that received AFDC in July 1995 and, over the course of the next year (until August 1996), stopped receiving benefits for 2 consecutive months.[3] "Stayers" are those who did not stop receiving benefits for 2 consecutive months during the August 1995–August 1996 period. This period is referred to throughout the paper as the "exit period." The "preexit period" is between January 1989 and July 1995. The "postexit period" for a leaver begins in the quarter the leaver exited welfare and continues until the last

---

[3]This 2-month definition of a leaver was used in Cancian et al. (1999) and is being used by the leavers studies sponsored by the Office of the Assistant Secretary for Planning and Evaluation in the U.S. Department of Health and Human Services.

quarter of 1997. For a stayer, the postexit period is between July 1996 and the last quarter of 1997. Stayers may have left welfare after August 1996 but did not do so during the exit period.

Two alternative definitions of leavers were explored; first, only those who stopped receiving benefits for 3 consecutive months from August 1995 to September 1996 were considered leavers, and a more stringent definition of a leaver considered only those who stopped receiving benefits for 6 consecutive months from August 1995 to December 1996 to be leavers. Caseload composition and outcomes using these definitions are reported in Appendix 13-A. In general, we find only small changes in the demographic composition of the group of leavers under a more restrictive definition of a leaver, that is, one who has stayed off of welfare for 6 consecutive months. The differences in demographic composition between 2-month and 3-month leavers are negligible. Outcomes of leavers change slightly with the more restrictive definition of leavers, as 6-month leavers are less likely to return to welfare and have modestly higher earnings than 2-month and 3-month leavers.

Welfare History Variables

The cases were categorized into groups based on each case's past welfare receipt history. This was done as a means to characterize the welfare caseload at the time the sample of leavers was drawn and as a means to standardize comparisons of outcome measures across different types of leavers. Leavers were stratified into groups using monthly AFDC receipt data from July 1989 through December 1997.[4] From these data, spells of receipt were counted. A spell began with 1 month of receipt (preceded by a month of no receipt) and ended with 1 consecutive months of nonreceipt. Those enrolled in AFDC in July 1989 were counted as starting a spell, even though they may have already been enrolled in months prior to that. No adjustment was made for this censored data. A month of nonreceipt surrounded by two months of receipt was not counted as an end of a spell. Rather, it was counted as if the spell continued. We implemented this strategy to ensure that a spell actually ended and that the break in receipt was not the result of administrative churning or erroneous reporting. Some cases continued spells after July 1995 and are right censored. No adjustments for these censored data were made.

The total number of months on AFDC, the total number of spells, and the average spell length in months (total months of receipt divided by number of spells) were calculated for each observation. Using these measures, all leavers and stayers are classified as *short-termers*, *long-termers*, or *cyclers*. Short-termers have average spell lengths of less than 24 months and fewer than three total

---

[4]Data for November, 1992 are missing for all observations.

spells throughout the preexit period; long-termers have average spell lengths of 24 or more months and fewer than 3 total spells; and cyclers have three or more spells, regardless of average spell length. The exact cutoff points of these classifications are somewhat arbitrary, however, under this definition, long-termers are those who have spent at least a third of the time we observe them on welfare and short-termers are those who have spent less than one-third of the time on welfare.[5]

In general, we expect that short-termers face the fewest barriers to self-sufficiency. We expect that long-termers have the most barriers to self-sufficiency. Cyclers are expected to be somewhere between them. Therefore, we expect that short-termers will be less dependent on assistance and have better labor market outcomes after leaving than long-termers and we expect outcomes of cyclers to be somewhere between them.

The AFDC receipt data only include administrative records from the state of Wisconsin. Some cases may have moved to Wisconsin just before the exit period and started spells then. These may include a mix of long-term, cycler, and short-term welfare users. However, because we cannot track welfare receipt in other states, these cases are classified as short-termers. Similarly, the definitions do not account for the age of the case head (except that all were at least 15 in 1989). Those who are younger have fewer years of "exposure" to welfare and are likely to have fewer and shorter spells compared to older recipients.

Work History Variables

Earnings information from Unemployment Insurance records from first quarter 1989 to fourth quarter 1997 are used in this study. A variable for the percentage of quarters with any earnings in the preexit period was created and used to stratify outcomes (number of quarters from 1989 to 1995 with positive earnings divided by total number of quarters between first quarter 1989 and third quarter 1995). The percentage of quarters with earnings was divided into the following categories to make comparisons feasible: (1) those who had never worked in the preexit period; (2) those who had worked at least one quarter but no more than 25 percent of the quarters in the preexit period; (3) those who had worked more than 25 percent of the quarters but not more than 50 percent of the quarters; (4) those who had worked more than 50 percent of the quarters but not more than 75 percent of the quarters; and (5) those who had worked more than 75 percent of the quarters. Each outcome of interest is also stratified by these categories of work history. Again, earnings records from other states are not available for those who move into Wisconsin. Also, no standardization for the age of the case head was

---

[5]Alternative definitions were examined and the caseload compositions based on those definitions are reported in Table 13-B1 in Appendix 13-B.

made in this measure. The youngest welfare recipients in July 1995 are likely to have worked fewer quarters than older recipients. Thus, we expect the average age of groups with less work experience to be lower than the average age of groups with more work experience.

Postleaving Outcome Measures

Three types of outcomes for welfare leavers were examined: (1) public assistance receipt, such as whether the case returned to welfare and whether the case received other public assistance benefits (food stamps and medical assistance); (2) earnings and employment after leaving; and (3) total income, from earnings and public assistance benefits after leaving. The entire sample was tracked through administrative records through December 1997. For each leaver, there are at least five quarters of data on earnings and public assistance receipt after leaving.

Outcomes of both leavers and stayers are reported.[6] Some outcomes are reported relevant to the quarter the leaver stopped receiving AFDC, such as earnings in the first quarter after exit. For leavers, the actual calendar year quarter of these earnings will vary according to when the leaver stopped receiving welfare. For stayers, the first quarter after initial exit is the third quarter, 1996, the second quarter after exit is the fourth quarter 1996, and so on.

Data Limitations

This study relies solely on administrative records from the CARES system and matched UI records from the state of Wisconsin. These data have important limitations. First, only records from Wisconsin are included in this study. If a case moved into or out of Wisconsin, information about the case when not in the state is not available. Second, good information on how many of these movers might be in the data file at some point is not available. Administrative data are available on those in the case unit and not on others who might be living in the same household as the unit. For example, earnings of a cohabiting partner are not available, nor are data on living arrangements. Third, errors may occur during the process of matching the CARES data to the UI data may occur if Social Security numbers are reported erroneously or if there are duplications in the data reported to the UI system from employers. Finally, with specific regard to UI data, not all jobs are covered in the Unemployment Insurance system (for example, self-employed persons or federal government employees) or recorded

---

[6]Outcomes of leavers who did not return to AFDC in the follow-up period also were examined. As expected, these "continuous leavers" had better outcomes than those who returned to AFDC.

when they legally should be. As a result, some cases that appear to have no earnings may in fact have earnings from jobs. Hotz and Scholz (this volume: Chapter 9) review studies of underreporting in the UI system.

In the Wisconsin data, some cases cannot be tracked with the administrative records from the postexit period (for example, those who move into or out of the state as described). These cases, "disappearers," make up 3.7 percent of the total of 54,518 cases. Other cases appear in some but not all quarters. These "partial disappearers" make up 13.6 percent of the total caseload. Cases that disappear are used in the analysis unless otherwise noted. Cases not appearing in UI records for a quarter are assumed to have zero earnings for that quarter. Cases not appearing in public assistance records were assumed to not be receiving benefits.

THE WELFARE RECEIPT AND WORK HISTORIES

Because of dynamics in policy, economic conditions, and other social factors, the characteristics of those who receive welfare (and leave welfare) at one period may be quite different from the characteristics of those who receive (and leave welfare) at another time period. For example, during periods of high unemployment, the caseload may include many cases that have lots of work experience and have not received welfare very often, but who cannot find a job in a slack economy. On the contrary, during economic booms, these types will probably move into jobs and off welfare, leaving those with the most barriers to employment and self-sufficiency on the rolls. In this section, we describe the welfare receipt and work histories of the caseload of AFDC recipients with a sample of leavers drawn in July 1995.

Welfare Histories of the Caseload in July 1995

Table 13-1 provides the distribution of the total number of months of AFDC benefit receipt for the full caseload overall and separately by the number of spells of receipt during the time frame. (To abbreviate, we call this total-time-on, or TTO.) Column 1 shows TTO for the entire caseload. This column shows that a majority of the caseload in July 1995 received benefits for more than 2 years and that a large portion (nearly 38 percent) received benefits for at least 5 of the 6 years in the preexit period. This is not surprising given that at any point in time, the caseload will be made up disproportionately of long-term beneficiaries. (See Bane and Ellwood, 1994, for a discussion of welfare dynamics.)

The bottom row of Table 13-1 shows the overall distribution of the number of spells of the caseload in July 1995. The majority of cases had only one spell (57.2 percent) and just over a quarter had 2 spells (25.8 percent). The fraction of those with three or more spells is quite small; as only 14 percent fell into this category. Moffitt (this volume: Chapter 14) found that of those who were ever on AFDC of the 10 years of NLSY data used in the study, 48 percent had only one

TABLE 13-1 Distribution of Total-Time-On AFDC in Months Between 7/89 to 7/95 by Number of Spells of AFDC Receipt Over Entire Period (percent distribution)

Total-Time-On (months)	All	Number of Spells			
		0	1	2	3+
0	3.1	3.1	—	—	—
1-6	4.8	—	7.9	1.3	0.0
7-12	6.7	—	8.9	5.5	1.7
13-18	5.7	—	5.4	7.3	5.2
19-24	6.3	—	5.6	7.7	7.8
25-36	11.2	—	8.6	13.7	19.6
37-48	11.9	—	9.3	13.6	22.2
49-60	12.6	—	8.4	16.5	25.6
61+	37.7	—	46.0	34.4	17.9
Total percent with number of spells		3.1	57.2	25.8	13.9

NOTE: Total number of observations = 48,216.
Maximum number of months = 71.

spell of receipt and only 8 percent had 4 or more spells. Thus, both of these studies show a small amount of turnover in the caseload. Table 13-1 also reports the distribution of TTO by the number of spells of benefit receipt. Of those who had only one spell, 46 percent had a long spell of more than 5 years. The rest of those with only one spell are distributed fairly evenly across the TTO scale. For those with 2 spells, a smaller fraction received welfare for more than 5 years (34 percent). Those with two spells are, however, more concentrated in the categories of 2-6 years of benefit receipt than those with only one spell. Finally, those with three spells of receipt are concentrated primarily in the range of 2-5 years of benefit receipt. Two-thirds, 67 percent, of those with at least 3 spells received benefits for a total of 2-5 years.

Table 13-2 is a slight variation on Table 13-1. Instead of reporting the total number of months of benefit receipt, Table 13-2 reports the average spell length (ASL) of benefit receipt.[7] The first column gives the overall distribution of ASL. There is a cluster (26 percent) of the caseload with an ASL of more than 5 years. However, the majority of the caseload have ASLs of between half a year and 3 years.

The distribution of ASL for those with one spell is the same as in Table 13-1. For those with two spells of benefit receipt, more than half have ASLs of 2 to

[7]ASL was calculated as the TTO measure divided by the total number of spells.

TABLE 13-2 Distribution of Average AFDC Receipt Spell Length in Months Between 7/89 to 7/95 by Number of Spells of AFDC Receipt Over Entire Period (percent distribution)

Average Spell Length (months)	All	Number of Spells			
		0	1	2	3+
0	3.1	3.1	—	—	—
1-6	7.7	—	7.9	6.8	10.4
7-12	13.8	—	8.9	15.0	35.1
13-18	10.8	—	5.4	13.7	30.2
19-24	10.1	—	5.6	13.6	24.4
25-36	18.1	—	8.6	51.0	0.0
37-48	5.3	—	9.3	0.0	0.0
49-60	4.8	—	8.4	0.0	0.0
61+	26.3	—	46.0	0.0	0.0
Total percent with number of spells		3.1	57.2	25.8	13.9

3 years. For those with three spells, 11 percent have an ASL of less than half a year. An additional 35 percent have ASLs of less than a year. Thus, 45 percent of cases have short spells of benefit receipt on a relatively infrequent basis. However, 55 percent of those with three spells have ASLs of 1 to 2 years.

To capture the two concepts of average spell length and total number of spells in a less cumbersome way, three categories of welfare recipients were created: cyclers (more than two spells), short-termers (fewer than two spells and TTO of less than 2 years), and long-termers (fewer than two spells and TTO of 2 or more years). Table 13-3 illustrates the distribution of the caseload in July 1995 across these three categories. More than half the sample (55 percent) are long-term welfare users. Nearly a third (31 percent) are short-term users, and nearly 14 percent of the sample are cyclers.

Moffitt (this volume: Chapter 14) found about one-third of the women ever on AFDC were cyclers, between 37 and 58 percent were long-termers, and be-

TABLE 13-3 Long-termer, Short-termer, and Cycler Status (percent distribution)

	Overall	Leaver	Stayer
Long-termer	55.3	42.9	66.7
Short-termer	30.8	39.1	23.1
Cycler	13.9	18.0	10.2

tween 23 and 44 percent were short-termers, depending on how these two concepts were defined. Using Maryland administrative data on the AFDC/TANF caseload from 1985-1998 and linked UI data, Stevens (2000) disaggregated the AFDC/TANF caseload from Baltimore City into four birth cohorts and observed each of the cohorts for a ten-year period. He also divided the caseload into the long-termer, short-termer, and cycler distinctions and found more short-term welfare recipients than long-term welfare recipients. About 50 percent of those on welfare during the time span were short-termers while about one-third were long-termers, which is almost exactly the reverse of findings from the Wisconsin data. In another study that used the Maryland data and similar definitions of dependence, but that examined 11 birth cohorts of women, the percent of the caseload that was short-termers ranged between 44-67 percentage, the percent that was longer-termers ranged from 35 to 47 percent, and the percent that were cyclers ranged from 3-19 percent (Moffitt and Stevens, 2001). Except for two birth cohorts, the percent of short-termers was always greater than the percentage of long-termers. The results of the Maryland studies that show more short-termers than long-termers in the caseload compared to results from the Wisconsin data that show more long-termers illustrate the point about compositional factors of different caseloads at different times. Given these different compositions, we might expect Maryland leavers to have better postexit outcomes than Wisconsin leavers who have greater welfare dependency, with all, else being equal.

The Work Histories of the Caseload in July 1995

A principal emphasis of the 1996 welfare reforms was to push welfare recipients into work and work-related activities. Not surprisingly, most studies of welfare leavers focus on the work outcomes of leavers, whether they have and keep jobs, what their wages are, and how their wages change as they work more. As recipients leave welfare, we would expect those with more work experience to have better outcomes. To assess whether this hypothesis is correct, we have classified the entire caseload in July 1995, by the number and percentage of quarters between January 1989 and July 1995, in which the case had nonzero UI wage reports. Table 13-4 shows the distribution of prior work experience. We find that most of the caseload did not have much work experience during this time period. Less than a quarter of the caseload (21 percent) had worked more than half the quarters. Nearly 20 percent had no reported earnings during the time frame, 34 percent had earnings in less than 25 of the quarters, and 26 percent worked between 25 and 50 percent of the time between January 1989 and July 1995.

What is the relationship between work history and welfare receipt history? Table13-5 shows the distribution of work history across short-termer, long-termer, and cycler status. The table shows that those who cycle on and off welfare have the most work experience. Only 6 percent of cyclers had never worked in the

TABLE 13-4 Work Histories of Aid to Families with Dependent Children
Recipients (1/89–7/95)

Percent of Quarters with Nonzero Earnings	Number	Percent
No quarters with earnings	9,523	19.8
0 < x – 25% of quarters	16,369	34.0
25 < x – 50% of quarters	12,269	25.5
50 < x – 75% of quarters	6,770	14.4
More than 75% of quarters	3,285	6.8

preexit period. This is in comparison to 23 percent of long-termers and 21 percent of short-termers. Cyclers are also more concentrated at the higher end of the work experience distribution. A third of cyclers had worked between 26 and 50 percent of the quarters prior to the exit period, 24 percent had worked more than half but less than 75 percent of the quarters prior to exit and 13 percent had worked more than 75 percent of the quarters. Long-termers have the least work experience. Almost 63 percent of long-termers had worked fewer than 25 percent of the quarters. This is relative to 48 percent for short-termers and 30 percent for cyclers. To summarize, short-termers generally had less work experience than cyclers, but more than long-termers. Long-termers had the least amount of work experience. This is not surprising as we would expect those who are the most dependent on welfare to also be the least likely to hold jobs.

Throughout the rest of this paper, the short-term, long-term and cycler definitions of welfare receipt history and the categories of work history will be used to stratify outcomes of leavers and stayers. The distinctions are used to illustrate how the outcomes of leavers can vary by the characteristics of the people leaving the caseload at the time the welfare leaver sample is drawn. These categorizations are also given as an example of a crude means of standardizing outcomes across different leavers studies.

TABLE 13-5 Work Histories of AFDC Recipients by Short-Termer, Long-Termer, or Cycler Status

Welfare Receipt History	Percent of Quarters Worked 1/89 to 7/95				
	None	0 to 25%	26 to 50%	50 to 75%	More than 75%
Short-termer	20.9	27.3	21.8	18.4	11.5
Long-termer	22.5	40.2	25.5	9.1	2.7
Cycler	6.4	23.8	33.2	24.0	12.7

THE OUTCOMES OF WELFARE LEAVERS AND STAYERS

Who is a Leaver and Who is a Stayer

Table 13-6 describes characteristics of those who left welfare between July 1995 and July 1996 and those who did not leave during this time period. This time period coincides with the beginning of the very steep decline in the AFDC caseload in Wisconsin (see Cancian et al., 1999). During the exit period overall 48 percent of the caseload stopped receiving AFDC, and 52 percent remained on AFDC. This substantial decline continued through the end of 1997, the last year covered in these data, so that many of the stayers later left welfare.

As expected, leavers are more educated than stayers. About 64 percent of leavers had at least a high school diploma, but only 50 percent of stayers did. Leavers are more likely to be white than African Americans or Hispanic. Leavers are a bit younger than stayers. Stayers are more likely to live in Milwaukee, while leavers are more likely to live in rural and other urban areas of the state. Leavers are also less likely to have a child receiving Supplemental Security Income (SSI), payments as 8 percent of leavers had a child that received SSI compared to 13 percent of stayers. Again, this is not surprising given that having a child on SSI may make finding work or an alternative means of subsistence more of a burden. The youngest children of leavers are, in general, a little bit older than the youngest children of stayers.

In terms of welfare receipt history, as expected, leavers have shorter histories than stayers. Of leavers 39 percent were short-term welfare users in the preexit period compared to 23 percent of stayers. On the other hand, 67 percentage of stayers were long-termers compared to only 43 percent of leavers. Cyclers made up 17.9 percent of the leavers but 10 percent of the stayers. The total percentage of time spent on AFDC in the preexit period is also calculated for leavers and stayers. In general, stayers have spent more time on welfare than leavers. Seventy-four percent of stayers spent more than half of the preexit period on AFDC compared to 56 percent of leavers. As a final measure of welfare receipt history, the average length of AFDC receipt spells was calculated for both leavers and stayers. The mean spell length in the preexit period of leavers was about 28 months compared to 41 months for stayers. This is a substantial difference (46 percent).

Leavers also worked more quarters during the preexit period than stayers, as expected. Although about 25 percent of the stayers had never worked in the period prior to July 1995, only 14 percent of leavers had never worked. Twenty-eight percent of leavers worked for at least half the quarters prior to the preexit period compared to only 14 percent of stayers.

To summarize Table 13-6, as expected, those who left welfare had more education and more work experience than stayers. Over all four measures of prior AFDC receipt, we see that those who were on AFDC longer have substantially

TABLE 13-6 Characteristics of Welfare Leavers (full sample N=48,216)

Characteristics	Full Sample	Leaver	Stayer
Total number	48,216	23,207	25,009
Percent of sample	100.0	48.1	51.9
Race/ethnicity			
% black	43.0	32.2	48.1
% Hispanic	6.8	6.4	7.1
% white	50.2	61.4	44.8
Age of case head			
% <26 years old	36.3	37.1	35.5
% 27-31	24.4	25.2	23.7
% 32-41	31.6	30.9	32.2
% 42+	7.8	6.8	8.6
Education of case head			
% less than high school	43.4	36.1	50.2
% high school diploma	41.4	45.3	37.7
% some college	15.2	18.6	12.1
County of residence			
Milwaukee County	54.3	42.4	65.3
Other urban county	29.6	35.6	24.1
Rural	16.1	22.0	10.6
Percent with child on SSI	10.7	8.1	13.1
Age of youngest child			
% 0 to 1 year	28.2	27.1	29.2
% 2 to 4 years	31.2	31.4	31.0
% 5 to 11 years	29.8	29.7	29.9
% 12 or older	10.8	11.8	9.9
Welfare history (7/89 to 7/95)			
% Short-termer	30.8	39.1	23.1
% Long-termer	55.3	42.9	66.7
% Cycler	13.9	17.9	10.2
Percent of time on welfare (7/89 to 7/95)			
0 <= x < 25% of time	17.2	23.5	11.3
25 <= x < 50% of time	17.2	20.4	14.3
50 <= x < 100% of time	44.6	43.7	45.4
Always on	21.0	12.4	29.0
Mean AFDC spell length	34.6	27.5	41.23
7/89 to 7/95 (in months)	(25.2)	(23.2)	(25.2)
Median AFDC spell length	28	20	35
7/89 to 7/95 (in months)			
% of quarters with earnings (1/89 to 7/95)			
Never worked	19.8	14.0	25.1
0 < x <= 25%	34.0	30.0	37.6
25 < x <= 50%	25.5	28.0	23.1
50 < x <= 75%	14.0	17.7	10.6
More than 75% of quarters	6.8	10.3	3.6

lower exit rates. Leavers were also more likely to be non-minority and to come from counties other than Milwaukee. Leavers are also slightly younger than stayers. In general, leavers tend to be those who face fewer barriers to leaving than stayers do.

Table 13-7 shows the percentage of the caseload that left welfare by past AFDC receipt and past earnings histories. Again, we see that those who have received welfare for longer periods of time and those with the least work experience are the least likely to leave welfare. The percentage who left welfare by categories of the number of quarters with earnings prior to the exit period are also given. As expected, those who worked the least in the preexit period were the least likely to leave welfare. Of those with no earnings, only 34 percent left AFDC. This is in comparison to 73 percent of those with the most work experience—those with earnings in more than three-quarters of the preexit quarters. In general, the percentage who left welfare increases as the percentage of quarters with earnings increases.

Table 13-7 shows vast differences in the leaving rates for those with previous AFDC receipt and earnings histories. Long-term recipients are likely to be those who face the highest barriers to employment and self-sufficiency, which is probably why fewer leave welfare. Those who have worked little in the past are likely to have a harder time finding employment and are likely to earn less when they are employed. Employment, earnings, further public assistance receipt, and other outcomes of leavers will also vary widely across these AFDC receipt and work histories.

TABLE 13-7 Leaving Rates for Recipients with Different Recipiency and Work Histories

	Percent of Total Sample in Subgroup	Percent of Subgroup That Left Welfare
Past welfare receipt history		
Short-termer	30.8	61.1
Long-termer	55.3	37.4
Cycler	13.9	62.2
Percent of quarters with earnings (1/89–7/95)		
Never worked	19.8	34.2
0–25% of quarters	34.0	42.6
26–50% of quarters	25.5	52.9
51–75% of quarters	14.0	60.8
More than 75% of quarters	6.8	72.5

Public Assistance Usage After Leaving Welfare

A critical goal of welfare reform was to decrease dependency on public assistance. This section examines the use of public assistance by welfare leavers and stayers. Outcomes examined include the percentage who return to welfare and the percentage who receive food stamps and medical assistance after leaving welfare. Outcomes are stratified by past welfare receipt history and by past earnings receipt history.

Table 13-8 shows the percentage of leavers who returned to welfare by July 1997. This table also shows when, relative to leaving, the case returned to cash assistance. Overall, the majority of welfare leavers (71 percent) did not return to welfare within 16 months of leaving. A sizable proportion did not stay off welfare very long, as 20 percent returned within 6 months. Seven percent of the sample returned between 6 months and a year after leaving, and only 2 percent returned between 13 and 15 months after leaving. The percent returning to AFDC within 15 months (29 percent) is higher than what Blank and Ruggles (1994) found using national-level survey data from the late 1980s. They found that 20.5 percent returned to AFDC within 15 months of exiting. In a review of welfare leaver studies from 11 different states and counties sponsored by the Office of the Assistant Secretary for Planning and Evaluation (ASPE) of the Department of Health and Human Services (DHHS), Acs and Loprest (this volume: Chapter 12)

TABLE 13-8 Percent of Leavers Who Return to Welfare by Past Welfare Receipt and Past Earnings History (N=23,207)

	Never Return	Return Within 3–6 Months	Return Within 7–12 Months	Return Within 13–15 Months
Overall	70.9	20.1	7.0	1.9
Past welfare receipt				
Short-termer	76.9	15.4	5.9	1.8
Long-termer	66.5	23.8	7.7	2.1
Cycler	68.6	21.6	7.9	1.9
Past earnings receipt:				
Percentage of quarters with earnings > 0 prior to leaving				
Never worked	76.6	15.6	6.0	1.9
0 < x – 25%	68.6	22.0	7.5	1.9
25 < x – 50%	69.1	21.4	7.7	1.9
50 < x – 75%	72.5	18.9	6.5	2.1
More than 75% of quarters	72.6	19.3	6.1	2.0

found that between 18 to 35 percent of welfare leavers returned to TANF within a year after leaving.[8]

Table 13-8 also presents the percentage of leavers who returned to welfare by past welfare receipt history and by past earnings history. As expected, those with short receipt histories are the least likely to return to welfare in the 16 months following exit. Only 23 percent of short-termers returned to welfare compared to 33 percent of those with long-term welfare histories. Of those who cycle on and off welfare, 31 percent returned to welfare. Nearly a quarter of long-termers and about a fifth of cyclers were back on cash assistance within half a year after leaving. Only 15 percent of short-termers were back on welfare within 6 months of leaving. This table shows that there are considerable differences in the percentage of cases that return to AFDC across different welfare histories. Cancian et al. (1999) stratified the sample by the length of the case's current spell of AFDC usage, tracking receipt 2 years prior to the exit period and found small differences in AFDC return rates by the length of the current spell. Furthermore, they did not find a clear pattern between spell length and return rates. Cancian et al. (1999) also stratified return rates by the total number of months of AFDC receipt for 2 years prior to the exit period, and found that those who had received benefits for more months were more likely to return. These results are similar to results reported here.

Differences in return to AFDC across work histories are not as large. Surprisingly, cases with no prior work experience were the most likely to stay on welfare. Seventy-seven percent of cases that never worked did not return to cash assistance after leaving. Those who worked fewer than half the quarters before leaving were the most likely to return to welfare. About 69 percent of those who worked between zero and 50 percent of the quarters stayed off welfare. Of those who worked more than half the quarters before leaving, 73 percent stayed off of welfare. The composition of the group with no prior work experience is disproportionately made up of legal immigrants, Asians, Hispanics, and those without an eligible adult in the case. Cancian et al. (1999) found that legal immigrants were significantly less likely to return to welfare. Although no explanations were offered, it is possible that this group was particularly discouraged from returning to welfare by signals encouraging the end of welfare and emphasizing work that came out with the waiver and PRWORA legislation, along with real changes in how the Food Stamps Program treated legal immigrants. Most of the cases with no eligible adults are those where the AFDC case consists only of children, but the adult in the household is either on SSI or was sanctioned from AFDC. Matched UI earnings in these cases are those of the adult, not the child in the AFDC case.

---

[8]These studies used similar definitions of leavers and similar research designs, but covered different time periods and did not match methodologies exactly. Furthermore, the compositions of caseloads from each study area may be quite different although these compositional differences have not yet been explored.

The mixed composition of this group with no prior work experience as counted by UI records seems to produce other surprising outcomes across work experience as well, which we detail in the text that follows.

Food Stamps and Medical Assistance Receipt After Leaving by Quarters

Tables 13-9 and 13-10 examine food stamps and medical assistance benefit receipt among leavers and stayers. Welfare leavers may change their behaviors for a couple of reasons. Leavers' income also may increase after leaving if they earn more or if they marry, so much so that they are no longer eligible for food stamps. Leavers also may find jobs that provide health insurance. Alternatively, even though food stamp and medical assistance eligibility rules did not change much with waivers and PRWORA, recipients may be confused about the rules and think they are no longer eligible for food stamps or that work requirements and time limits for cash benefits also apply to food stamps and medical assistance receipt.

Table 13-9 shows the percentage of leavers and stayers that received food stamps on a quarterly basis after leaving welfare, or since the third quarter of 1996 for stayers. The first two columns show that the majority of the caseload (90 percent of leavers and 94 percent of stayers) received benefits in the quarter in which they exited. This does not vary greatly across past welfare receipt or work history. However, the percentage of leavers who received food stamps drops off dramatically in the first quarter after exit to 52 percent overall, and continues to drop such that only 37 percent received food stamps in the fifth quarter after exit. Although the number of stayers receiving food stamps also drops through the exit period, most stayers still receive food stamps.

These results show some clear differences between the leavers and stayers. Recall that the caseload in Wisconsin dropped dramatically during the years 1995–1997, when we observed leavers and stayers. Although many of the stayers may have left welfare after 1996, this table shows that despite this, most stayers continue to use food stamps while most leavers do not. Acs and Loprest (this volume: Chapter 12) found quite a bit of variation in food stamps receipt after leaving welfare for the 11 reviewed studies. They found that 45 to 100 percent of leavers received food stamps in the first quarter after exit and that between 24 and 67 percent received food stamps any time in the year after exit, although most studies found between 55 and 70 percent received food stamps at least once in the exit period. In a study based on survey data from three cities (Boston, Chicago, and San Antonio), Moffitt and Roff (2000) found that 38 percent of leavers (or those who were on TANF at some point 2 years before being interviewed but not at the time of the interview) received food stamps when interviewed, although this varied across the three cities.

Table 13-9 also shows food stamps receipt stratified by past welfare receipt history. Looking only at leavers, we see wide differences between short-termers

TABLE 13-9 Food Stamps Receipt After Leaving: Leavers versus Stayers

Percent Receiving Food Stamps by Quarter After Initial Exit (or since 3rd quarter 1996 for stayers)

	Exit Quarter		1st Q Postexit		2nd Q Postexit		3rd Q Postexit		4th Q Postexit		5th Q Postexit	
	S	L	S	L	S	L	S	L	S	L	S	L
Overall	94.3	90.3	93.4	52.0	87.1	46.2	81.7	43.0	77.2	40.3	72.6	37.4
By past welfare receipt history (7/89 to 7/95)												
Short-termer	93.9	89.4	92.9	45.4	82.9	39.1	75.0	35.6	69.2	32.7	63.6	30.3
Long-termer	94.6	91.3	93.7	57.8	89.1	52.0	84.8	48.6	81.0	46.6	76.8	43.3
Cycler	93.5	89.9	92.5	52.4	83.2	48.0	76.4	45.6	70.7	42.0	65.3	38.5
By past earnings history: Percent of quarters with earnings (1/89 to 7/95)												
Never worked	92.6	89.1	91.5	47.2	86.5	40.8	82.8	37.6	78.8	36.6	74.4	33.9
0 < x <= 25%	94.6	90.6	93.8	52.7	88.1	48.2	82.8	44.8	78.7	43.0	74.9	40.4
25 < x <= 50%	95.6	90.1	94.6	52.9	87.5	47.7	81.8	45.1	77.3	41.1	72.0	38.4
50 < x <= 75%	95.0	90.7	94.0	52.9	85.3	45.2	77.4	41.4	71.8	38.9	65.4	34.8
More than 75%	93.1	91.3	92.9	52.0	82.9	45.7	74.4	41.6	67.3	25.9	59.9	34.7

NOTE: S = Stayer.
　　　　L = Leaver.

TABLE 13-10 Quarterly Medical Assistance Receipt After Leaving: Leavers versus Stayers

Percent Receiving Medical Assistance by Quarter After Initial Exit (or since 3rd quarter 1996 for stayers)

	1st Q Postexit		2nd Q Postexit		3rd Q Postexit		4th Q Postexit		5th Q Postexit	
	S	L	S	L	S	L	S	L	S	L
Overall	99.1	75.7	96.6	69.1	93.0	65.7	90.1	63.0	86.5	54.5
By past welfare receipt history (7/89 to 7/95)										
Short-termer	99.8	71.5	94.5	64.0	89.1	60.2	84.7	57.0	80.2	48.9
Long-termer	100.0	79.5	97.6	73.8	94.7	70.5	92.4	68.0	89.4	59.2
Cycler	99.8	75.9	95.5	69.3	90.9	66.4	87.1	64.1	81.5	55.6
By past earnings history: percent of quarters with earnings (1/89 to 7/95)										
Never worked	99.8	62.6	96.6	56.3	93.5	53.3	90.6	51.0	87.3	45.5
0 < x <= 25%	99.9	74.5	96.7	68.0	93.2	65.0	90.5	62.7	87.5	56.0
25 < x <= 50%	100.0	79.3	96.9	73.0	93.3	69.5	90.6	66.3	86.6	57.4
50 < x <= 75%	100.0	80.4	95.9	73.0	91.2	68.7	87.7	65.1	82.8	55.5
More than 75% of qtrs	99.7	79.2	96.2	72.7	91.9	69.3	86.5	41.4	80.4	52.9

NOTE: S = Stayer.
L = Leaver.

and long-termers. In the first quarter after exit, 45 percent of short-termers received food stamps compared to 58 percent of long termers, which translates into a difference of nearly 30 percent. This gap persists throughout the postexit period. The percentage of cyclers who receive food stamps is consistently between the percentage of short-termers and long-termers who do. Moffitt and Roff (2000) divided their sample into "dependency" leavers and "non-dependency" leavers, where dependency leavers were dependent on welfare for part of the study period but were later off welfare, and nondependency leavers were either not dependent on welfare, or did not leave welfare. In contrast to findings here, they found few differences in usage of food stamps by dependency leavers, compared with nondependency leavers.

Those who never worked are the least likely to use food stamps after leaving. By the fifth quarter after exit, only 34 percent of those who had never worked received food stamps. This is in contrast to 40 percent of those who worked, up to 25 percent of the quarters prior to leaving. Again, this is a puzzling result that may be driven by the composition of the group that had never worked as described earlier. Excluding those who had never worked, more work experience is associated with less food stamps.

Medical assistance receipt by any member of the assistance unit after leaving is reported in Table 13-10.[9] Like food stamps usage, medical assistance usage by leavers declines steadily through the post-exit quarters, while stayers' usage decreases much less substantially. By the fifth quarter after exit, 55 percent of leavers still received medical assistance, while 87 percent of stayers did. Medical assistance receipt also varies substantially by past welfare receipt history. Short-termers are consistently less likely to receive medical assistance after leaving than long-termers and cyclers. By the fifth quarter after exit, 49 percent of short-termers receive medical assistance and 59 percent of long-termers did. Cyclers are between these two; 56 percent received medical assistance after leaving in the fifth quarter. Moffitt and Roff (2000) found that 69 percent of dependency leavers received medical assistance after leaving welfare and compared with 67 percent of nondependency leavers.

Those who never worked are the least likely to receive medical assistance compared to those with at least some work experience. Of those with some work experience, no clear pattern in medical assistance receipt and work experience emerges. In the first three quarters after exit, those who worked the least were the least likely to receive medical assistance. In the fourth and fifth quarters after exit, those with the most work experience were least likely to receive benefits.

Table 13-11 reports the percentage of stayers and leavers who received neither AFDC, food stamps, nor medical assistance in the first quarter after they left welfare and again in the fifth quarter after leaving. In the first quarter after

---

[9]Use of medical assistance in the quarter of exit is not available.

TABLE 13-11 Public Assistance Receipt After Leaving

	Stayers	Leavers
	Percent Not Receiving AFDC, Food Stamps or Medical Assistance in the First Quarter After Initial Exit (3rd quarter 1996 for stayers)	
Overall	0.0	22.2
By past welfare receipt history (7/89 to 7/95)		
Short-termer	0.0	26.8
Long-termer	0.0	18.2
Cycler	0.0	21.7
By past earnings history: Percent of quarters with earnings (1/89 to 7/95)		
Never worked	0.0	33.7
0 < x <= 25%	0.0	23.4
25 < x <= 50%	0.0	19.0
50 < x <= 75%	0.0	17.8
More than 75% of qtrs	0.0	19.0
	Percent Not Receiving AFDC, Food Stamps or Medical Assistance in the Fifth Quarter after Initial Exit (3rd quarter 1997 for stayers)	
Overall	27.3	43.2
By past welfare receipt history (7/89 to 7/95)		
Short-termer	18.5	49.3
Long-termer	9.7	38.3
Cycler	17.1	41.7
By past earnings history Percent of quarters with earnings (1/89 to 7/95)		
Never worked	11.4	51.0
0 < x <= 25%	11.5	41.8
25 < x <= 50%	12.9	40.6
50 < x <= 75%	15.9	42.7
More than 75% of qtrs	18.7	45.2
	Mean Number of Months Received Food Stamps After Leaving (or since July 1996 for stayers)	
Overall	10.29 (4.50)	7.03 (7.23)
By past welfare receipt history (7/89 to 7/95)		
Short-termer	9.35 (4.83)	5.76 (6.72)
Long-termer	10.76 (4.28)	8.04 (7.48)
Cycler	9.40 (4.67)	7.36 (7.27)
By past earnings history: Percent of quarters with earnings (1/89 to 7/95)		
Never worked	10.57 (4.63)	6.38 (7.24)
0 < x <= 25%	10.48 (4.38)	7.37 (7.30)
25 < x <= 50%	10.20 (4.39)	7.18 (7.19)
50 < x <= 75%	9.61 (4.63)	6.79 (7.14)
More than 75% of qtrs	9.07 (4.74)	6.90 (7.17)

NOTE: Standard deviations reported in parentheses.

leaving welfare, a large majority of cases still received food stamps or medical assistance benefits. Only 22 percent of leavers did not receive food stamps, medical assistance, nor AFDC. All those who stayed on welfare received at least one of these three benefits.

In the fifth quarter after leaving welfare, the percentage of leavers who no longer received benefits nearly doubled, as 43 percent received neither AFDC, food stamps, nor medical assistance. In contrast, of those who stayed on AFDC, only 27 percent were not receiving any of these three public assistance benefits. Cancian et al. (1999) found that only 11 percent of welfare leavers did not receive any of these benefits in the first quarter and that only 30 percent did not receive any benefits in the fifth quarter after exit. Differences between the Cancian et al. (1999) results and the results presented here probably can be attributed to the exclusion of disappearers in the Cancian study.

To summarize Tables 13-8 to 13-11, receipt of public assistance benefits after leaving varies substantially across welfare receipt history, although it does not vary as much across earnings history. Short-term welfare users seem to be more independent of public assistance after leaving than long-term users. Only 18 percent of long-termers did not receive public assistance in the first quarter after leaving welfare compared to 27 percent of short-termers. Again, cyclers were in between; 22 percent of cyclers did not receive assistance in the first quarter after leaving welfare. A similar pattern holds for the fifth quarter after leaving welfare, but the differences across short-term and long-term status are even more pronounced. There is nearly a 30-percent difference in the proportion who do not receive benefits (49 percent for short-termers and 38 percent for long-termers). Again, this table shows wide differences in outcomes across different types of leavers. Cancian et al. (1999) also found that those with shorter spells were significantly less likely to return to TANF after leaving. Moffitt and Roff (2000) found few differences in public assistance benefit receipt between dependency leavers and nondependency leavers, although their measures of dependency are quite different than that of the short-termer, long-termer, and cycler distinctions made here.

Public benefit receipt of those who left welfare is also reported by past earning histories. Results here are not as anticipated. It was expected that those who had the most work experience would have better labor market outcomes after leaving than those with less work experience, and subsequently, would be less likely to rely on public assistance benefits. Instead, results in Table 13-11 show that leavers who had never worked prior to July 1995 were the least likely to receive public assistance benefits after leaving. This is consistent with findings in Tables 13-9 and 13-10. Again, the mixed composition of this group with no prior work experience drives these unusual findings. In both the first quarter and the fifth quarter after exit, there is not a clear pattern in the percentage not receiving public benefits by work experience among those who had worked prior to exit. In the first quarter after exit, those who had worked the least (0–25 percent of the quarters) were the most likely to not receive benefits. Those who worked 50–75 percent of the quarters were the least likely to receive benefits. In the fifth quarter after exit, of those with prior work experience, those with the most work experience were the least likely to receive benefits. Those who worked 25-50 percent of the quarters prior to the exit period had the highest benefit receipt rates.

Employment, Earnings and Income Status After Leaving

A major goal of welfare reform was to increase employment and earnings of the low income and welfare populations. In this section, we examine common employment and earnings outcomes reported in studies of welfare leavers and stratify these outcomes by the past welfare receipt and past employment histories of the caseload. Employment rates, earnings, income, and a measure of dependency are reported in this section.

Employment Rates

The employment rates of welfare leavers and stayers are reported in Table 13-12, first on a quarter-by-quarter basis and overall for up to five quarters after each case left welfare, or since July 1996 for stayers. The table shows that two-thirds of the leavers were employed in the quarter in which they exited welfare while only one-third of stayers were employed in the third quarter of July 1996. Employment rates of leavers fell slightly after exit, but remained fairly consistent at just over 60 percent. The employment rates of stayers, however, grew over time (except in the third quarter after exit), until nearly half the stayers were employed in the fifth quarter after the exit period. The last column shows the percentage who were ever employed since leaving. Overall, of those who stayed on welfare, 65 percent of them were employed for at least one quarter. This is in comparison to 77 percent of leavers who were ever employed after leaving welfare.

Cancian et al. (1999) found that 82 percent of leavers were ever employed within a year after leaving and found quarter-by-quarter employment rates of between 72 and 75 percent.[10] Acs and Loprest found that employment rates in the first quarter after exit across 11 welfare leaver studies ranged between 47 and 64 percent. They also found that between 62 and 75 percent ever worked after leaving welfare, although the 11 studies reviewed followed the leavers for different lengths of time.

That the employment rates of leavers do not rise over time may be a point of concern if the 40 percent who are not working are looking for work and not

---

[10]The Cancian et al. (1999) figures exclude disappearers.

TABLE 13-12 Quarterly and Overall Employment Rates of Welfare Leavers and Stayers

| | | Percent Employed by Quarter After Initial Exit (or since 3rd quarter 1996 for stayers) | | | | | | | | | | | | | |
| | % Who Left Welfare | Exit Quarter | | 1st Quarter Postexit | | 2nd Quarter Postexit | | 3rd Quarter Postexit | | 4th Quarter Postexit | | 5th Quarter Postexit | | Ever Employed | |
		S	L	S	L	S	L	S	L	S	L	S	L	S	L
Overall	48.1	33.3	65.6	37.9	63.0	43.5	61.2	41.3	61.1	45.3	61.4	49.3	61.3	64.8	76.6
By past welfare receipt history (7/89 to 7/95)															
Short-termer	61.1	34.3	63.6	40.3	60.9	45.0	59.6	43.3	59.7	47.3	59.6	51.5	58.7	67.0	74.4
Long-termer	37.4	32.2	65.8	36.2	63.6	42.2	61.6	39.9	60.9	44.0	61.2	48.0	61.7	63.1	76.7
Cycler	62.2	38.4	69.2	43.5	66.1	48.2	64.1	46.5	64.5	49.0	65.7	53.1	65.9	70.5	81.3
By past earnings history: % of quarters with earnings (1/89 to 7/95)															
Never worked	34.2	14.5	31.0	18.6	29.7	22.7	29.1	23.1	29.9	26.2	30.1	29.9	30.2	40.0	41.6
0 < x <= 25%	42.6	31.3	58.6	35.0	54.4	41.4	52.9	38.5	52.1	42.4	52.4	47.0	52.3	65.4	70.9
25 < x <= 50%	52.9	44.4	72.8	50.7	70.4	56.0	68.3	52.1	68.4	57.6	68.8	61.4	68.6	78.3	85.3
50 < x <= 75%	60.8	49.7	79.8	54.8	77.8	61.3	75.5	60.0	75.1	63.7	76.0	66.9	75.6	82.4	89.7
More than 75%	72.5	65.7	88.9	70.4	87.5	76.2	85.7	73.9	85.8	75.8	85.0	79.7	85.3	91.4	95.0

NOTES: S = Stayer.
L = Leaver.

finding it, or if all leavers are having a hard time keeping jobs and are cycling between employment and unemployment. The 40 percent who are not working also could be relying on the income of a partner or spouse and not actively looking for work or not working for other reasons that cannot be uncovered with these data.

Employment rates by work history status vary widely. Those with the most work experience are nearly three times as likely to be employed as those with no work experience. A clear pattern between work experience and employment status emerges; those with more work experience are more likely to be employed. This is true for both leavers and stayers and in each quarter after the exit period. It is also the case that the group with no work experience is the least likely to work after exit. This group is disproportionately composed of legal immigrants, who may be less likely to work in jobs covered by the UI system, and cases without an eligible adult. When no eligible adults are in the AFDC case, reported earnings are those of an adult who lives with the child but who is not part of the AFDC case and who typically has been either sanctioned from AFDC or has a disability and receives SSI. Overall, although only about 40 percent of those who have never worked prior to the exit period were ever employed after the exit period, employment in the exit period was nearly universal for those with the most work experience, as 95 percent of leavers and 91 percent of stayers were ever employed.

Cancian et al. (1999) stratify the percentage of quarters worked in the postexit period by work experience in the 2 years prior to the exit period and also find wide variations in employment. These employment rates vary as expected; that is, those who worked the least in the preexit period also worked the least in the postexit period and those who worked the most in the preexit period worked the most in the postexit period. Those who had not worked in the 2 years prior to exit worked 56 percent of the quarters in the postexit period and those who worked every quarter in the 2 years prior to exit worked 93 percent of the quarters in the postexit period. If prior work experience is a determinant of the likelihood a leaver finds a job (and it seems to be), then we would expect that a caseload composed of those with more work experience to have better employment rates after leaving than a caseload composed of those with little work experience. Results here suggest how widely those employment rates may vary.

Differences in employment rates by past welfare receipt history are not as wide. However, the differences are somewhat surprising. Cyclers consistently have the highest employment rates. Long-termers have the next highest employment rates, and short-termers have the lowest employment rates, although they are usually very near the rates of long-termers. It is not so surprising that cyclers have the highest employment rates, because this group moves on and off welfare more frequently and may have employment experience from the times off welfare. It is somewhat surprising that long-termers have higher employment rates than short-termers, since long-termers had the least employment experience, as reported in Table 13-6. However, these descriptive statistics do not account for age, which is probably positively associated with being a long-termer and with higher employment rates.

Although Cancian et al. (1999) only tracked welfare receipt prior to the exit period for 2 years, they found similar results. For leavers who returned to welfare (they did not report employment rates for all leavers), employment rates of those who had received AFDC for 7-18 months before the exit period, 65 percent were employed. This is relative to 62 percent of those who had only received AFDC for 6 months prior to the exit period, and 63 percent of those who had received AFDC for more than 18 months before the exit period. For continuous leavers, Cancian et al. (1999) found that those who had received AFDC for more than 18 months had employment rates of 73 percent, but that those who received welfare between zero and 18 months prior to the exit period all had similar employment rates at 76 percent.

Earnings

The success of former welfare recipients in staying off welfare also depends on how much they can earn while working. Table 13-13 shows mean and median quarterly earnings of welfare leavers and stayers over the first four quarters after exiting welfare, or since the beginning of the third quarter of 1996 for stayers. Overall, the mean quarterly earnings of leavers in the first year after exit was $1,642 and the median was $1,311.[11] This translates into roughly $6,000 per year (using the median), which is still considerably below the poverty line for a family consisting of a mother and two children, which was $12,278 in 1996 and $12,641 in 1995. The mean quarterly earnings of stayers is $786 and the median is $199.

Breaking the caseload down by past welfare receipt, we see only small differences in earnings across short-termers, long-termers, and cyclers. Cyclers have the highest mean and median earnings ($1,663 for the mean and $1,374 for the median), which is in contrast to findings from survey data in Moffitt (this volume: Chapter 14), which found that cyclers had the lowest earnings off welfare compared to short-term and long-term welfare recipients. As Table 13-13 shows, long-termers earn nearly as much as cyclers on average ($1,657 for the mean and $1,330 for the median). Short-termers have the lowest earnings ($1,616 for the mean and $1,266 for the median). Stevens (2000) found that short-termers had the highest earnings over the decade for which earnings were observed, long-termers had the lowest earnings off welfare, and cyclers had earnings between the two groups. Stevens also notes that all three types of recipients have earnings that are well below a reasonable self-sufficiency level.

---

[11]Those who do not appear in UI records in a quarter are assumed to have no earnings. Therefore, many observations have zero earnings. The next table shows mean and median earnings, not including quarters in which the case does not appear in UI records.

TABLE 13-13 Mean and Median Quarterly Earnings Over the Year Following Exit

	Mean and Median Quarterly Earnings in the Year After Exiting Welfare (or since July 1996 for stayers)	
	Stayers	All Leavers
Overall		
Mean	786.1	1,642.1
Median	199.0	1,311.0
By past welfare receipt history (7/89 to 7/95)		
Short-termer		
Mean	870.8	1,616.2
Median	284.8	1,266.0
Long-termer		
Mean	741.0	1,657.0
Median	157.6	1,330.0
Cycler		
Mean	889.5	1,662.9
Median	325.7	1,373.5
By past earnings history: Percent of quarters with earnings (1/89 to 7/95)		
Never worked		
Mean	420.9	777.2
Median	0	0
$0 < x <= 25\%$		
Mean	673.1	1,293.1
Median	148.7	743.5
$25 < x <= 50\%$		
Mean	1,010.7	1,796.5
Median	577.2	1,565.1
$50 < x <= 75\%$		
Mean	1,219.6	2,086.2
Median	853.8	2,018.2
More than 75% of qtrs		
Mean	1,783.7	2,656.8
Median	1,552.8	2,537.9

Interestingly, of those who stay on welfare, long-termers have the lowest quarterly earnings of the three groups. The long-termers who leave welfare may be decidedly better off than the long-termers who stay on welfare in terms of employment and earnings potential.

Breaking the caseload down by past work experience again shows a clear distinction in earnings between those with no work experience and those with much work experience. For both leavers and stayers, those with no work experience had the lowest earnings. In fact, most were not working or at least not in jobs covered by UI, as the median earnings of this group are zero. On the other hand, those leavers who worked more than 75 percent of the quarters prior to the exit period had fairly high earnings ($2,657 for the mean and $2,538 for the median). In general, those with more experience had higher quarterly earnings.

Table 13-14 shows the same statistics, except that quarterly earnings are averaged only over quarters in which earnings were reported in the UI system (missing quarters were not counted as zeros). The mean quarterly earnings of leavers over quarters in which they were employed are $2,387 and the median

TABLE 13-14 Mean and Median Quarterly Earnings Over the Year Following Exit Only in Quarters When Leaver Worked

| | Mean and Median quarterly earnings in the year after exiting welfare (or since July 1996 for stayers). | |
	Stayers	All Leavers
Overall		
Mean	1,678.1	2,386.5
Median	1,449.8	2,225.8
By past welfare receipt history (7/89 to 7/95)		
Short-termer		
Mean	1,803.3	2,414.0
Median	1,559.2	2,244.4
Long-termer		
Mean	1,628.0	2,402.8
Median	1,411.8	2,271.0
Cycler		
Mean	1,701.7	2,295.2
Median	1,413.9	2,096.6
By past earnings history: Percent of quarters with earnings (1/89 to 7/95)		
Never worked		
Mean	1,611.3	2,175.3
Median	1,386.4	1,977.8
0 < x <= 25%		
Mean	1,484.7	2,100.7
Median	1,240.0	1,880.6
25 < x <= 50%		
Mean	1,733.0	2,348.5
Median	1,515.4	2,191.5
50 < x <= 75%		
Mean	1,930.3	2,548.6
Median	1,713.4	2,396.8
More than 75% of qtrs		
Mean	2,350.3	2,966.1
Median	2,109.3	2,782.3

was $2,226. This translates to around $9,500 per year, which is still below the poverty threshold for a family of three. The earnings of stayers are also much higher when we exclude those who do not have UI earnings reports. Overall, counting only the quarters in which stayers were employed, the mean quarterly earnings were $1,678 and the median was $1,450.

Cancian et al. (1999) also report median earnings across quarters worked after leaving welfare. Overall they find a median for all leavers of $2,417, which is higher than the median found here.[12] Findings from 11 leaver studies show mean quarterly earnings over the first year of between $2,300 and $3,600 (calculations based on data presented in Acs and Loprest, this volume: Chapter 12). Results from Wisconsin reported in this study are in the lower range of those found in Acs and Loprest. It is not clear if differences are due to regional variations in earnings, caseload composition differences across studies, or methodological differences.

Counting only quarters in which leavers worked, short-termers had the highest mean quarterly earnings ($2,414 for short-termers compared to $2,403 for long-termers and $2,295 for cyclers), but long-termers had the highest median quarterly earnings ($2,271 compared to $2,244 for short-termers and $2,097 for cyclers). The differences in earnings between long-termers and short-termers in quarters during which they worked (Table 13-14) are smaller than the differences across all quarters when disappearers are included (Table 13-13). Cancian et al. (1999) break out median quarterly earnings by the number of months of welfare receipt for 2 years prior to the exit period. In doing so, they find that those who had more months of benefit receipt in the preexit period had the highest median quarterly earnings. We find a similar result for median quarterly earnings of welfare leavers, but little difference between short-termers and long-termers. For mean quarterly earnings, short-termers had greater earnings. Earnings across past work history again show that those with more work experience have higher earnings. However, those who had never worked prior to the exit period had slightly higher earnings than those who had worked less than 25 percent of the time (a median of $1,978 for the never worked category compared to $1,881 for the more than zero but less than 25 percent category). Again, this group of leavers who have never worked seems to be an odd collection, as they have slightly higher earnings than other leavers who have a bit more work experience. Otherwise, the table shows that for both leavers and stayers, work experience before the exit period is associated with higher earnings after the exit period, and the differences are substantial.[13]

---

[12]Their figure includes a fifth quarter after exit. Furthermore, our figure includes only case heads over the age of 21 in 1995, while their figure includes case heads over the age of 18 in 1995.

[13]Earnings for those who returned in the months and quarters in which they received welfare will necessarily be lower because their eligibility for benefits is tied to earnings and income. Table 13-B2 in Appendix 13-B shows mean and median quarterly earnings for leavers during quarters in which no welfare benefits were received.

Income

Table 13-15 shows total income calculated on a quarterly basis as the sum of earnings, AFDC/TANF benefits, and food stamps benefits for leavers and stayers. This does not include any income from other household members, any income unreported to the UI system, nor any nonearned income. Mean and median quarterly income for leavers and stayers across past welfare and work receipt are examined in this table.

TABLE 13-15 Mean and Median Quarterly Income Over the Year Following Exit (income = AFDC benefits + food stamps + earnings in first four quarters after exit)

	Mean and median quarterly income in the year after exiting welfare (or since July 1996 for stayers).	
	Stayers	All Leavers
Overall		
Mean	2,301.5	2,003.6
Median	2,184.6	1,864.0
By past welfare receipt history (7/89 to 7/95)		
Short termer		
Mean	2,224.9	1,894.8
Median	2,072.8	1,720.8
Long termer		
Mean	2,339.7	2,088.7
Median	2,240.3	1,988.2
Cycler		
Mean	2,224.5	2,037.1
Median	2,070.7	1,903.0
By past earnings history: Percent of quarters with earnings (1/89 to 7/95)		
Never worked		
Mean	2,062.4	1,119.1
Median	1,914.9	509.5
$0 < x <= 25\%$		
Mean	2,260.6	1,702.8
Median	2,176.7	1,434.8
$25 < x <= 50\%$		
Mean	2,433.9	2,170.4
Median	2,328.1	2,065.2
$50 < x <= 75\%$		
Mean	2,498.9	2,393.7
Median	2,343.7	2,391.2
More than 75% of qtrs		
Mean	2,958.5	2,963.6
Median	2,728.8	2,918.1

Overall, stayers had higher income levels than leavers in the first year following exit. The median overall income of stayers was $2,185 compared to $1,864 for leavers, which is a 17-percent difference. Although stayers had lower earnings than leavers, stayers were more likely to receive AFDC/TANF and food stamps benefits than leavers. These benefits appear to be making the difference in overall income levels.

Long-termers had the highest median incomes over all leavers ($1,988). Median incomes of cyclers ($1,903) were only slightly lower than incomes of long-termers. Short-termers had the lowest overall median income ($1,721). Long-termers had higher average earnings than short-termers and also were slightly more likely to return to welfare. This probably explains the even wider difference in total incomes (as compared to differences in earnings) between these groups. Moffitt and Roff (2000) found that dependency leavers had lower household incomes than nondependency leavers, but that they received more income from child support and food stamps but less from earnings and income of other household members (data for this study were collected through surveys so measures of household income were collected).

The more work experience prior to the exit period, the higher the mean and median incomes of leavers and stayers were. Interestingly, leavers with the most work experience had higher overall mean and median incomes than stayers. This is the only subgroup for which leavers' incomes were higher than stayers' incomes. The earnings of this group of leavers were quite high and make up for the difference in benefit receipt of stayers with similar work experience.

Dependency

Table 13-16 attempts to measure dependency for leavers and stayers. The measure of dependency used in this case is the ratio of earnings to total income in the first year after leaving, or since July 1996 for stayers. Earnings over the year are summed and divided by total income (earnings + AFDC + food stamps) in the year to get an earnings-to-total-income ratio. Those with higher ratios are less dependent on government assistance.

Overall, the mean earnings-to-income ratio (ETI ratio) for leavers was nearly 70 percent compared to only 26 percent for stayers. This is a striking difference but not surprising given that stayers continued to receive benefits during the exit period, had lower overall earnings, and were more likely to receive food stamps throughout the year after the exit period. Looking at the subgroups of leavers by welfare receipt history, as expected, short-termers had the highest ETI ratios (73 percent) and long-termers have the lowest (66 percent), which is about a 10 percent difference. Cyclers are between long-termers and short-termers, with a mean ETI ratio of 70 percent.

ETI ratios vary significantly by past work experience. Again, those with the most work experience had higher ETI ratios (85 percent for those with the most

TABLE 13-16 Dependency After Leaving Welfare: Mean Ratio of Earnings to Total Income in the First Year After Exit by Leaver Status

	Mean Ratio of Earnings to Income Over the First Year After Initial Exit (from 3rd quarter 1996 to 3rd quarter 1997 for stayers)	
	Stayers	All Leavers
Overall	0.26 (0.31)	0.69 (0.37)
By past welfare receipt history (7/89 to 7/95)		
Short-termer	0.30 (0.33)	0.73 (0.36)
Long-termer	0.24 (0.29)	0.66 (0.38)
Cycler	0.31 (0.32)	0.70 (0.35)
By past earnings history: Percent of quarters with earnings (1/89 to 7/95)		
Never worked	0.14 (0.25)	0.44 (0.44)
0 < x <= 25%	0.23 (0.29)	0.62 (0.39)
25 < x <= 50%	0.34 (0.31)	0.73 (0.34)
50 < x <= 75%	0.40 (0.32)	0.80 (0.29)
More than 75% of qtrs	0.52 (0.31)	0.85 (0.23)

NOTES: Earnings from UI wage records. Total income = earnings + TANF benefits + food stamps. Standard deviations reported in parentheses.

work experience compared to 44 percent for those with no work experience). Also notable is the difference between leavers and stayers that had worked more than 75 percent of the quarters prior to the exit period. The difference in the ETI ratio of these two groups is very wide as only half of the incomes of the group of stayers with the most work experience came from earnings, while 85 percent of income from leavers with similar work experience came from earnings. Comparing stayers to leavers, only the group with no work experience had worse dependency ratios than even the group of stayers with the most work experience.

Cases With Multiple Barriers to Self-Sufficiency

In an attempt to estimate a lower bound on the outcomes of leavers, AFDC recipients that may face the most barriers to self-sufficiency were identified and their employment, earnings, and public assistance usage after leaving welfare were examined. High-barrier cases were identified by their education level, amount of time spent on welfare prior to the exit period, presence of young children, and employment experience prior to the exit period.[14] A case was clas-

───────────────

[14]Other characteristics, of course, could be used to identify high-barrier cases (SSI status for mother and child, for example). Different definitions were examined and are reported in the Table 13-B3 in Appendix 13-B.

sified as a "high-barrier" case if all of the following conditions applied: (1) no high school diploma; (2) presence of at least one child under the age of 5; (3) received welfare for more than 48 months in the period between July 1989 and July 1995; and (4) worked fewer than four quarters between January 1989 and July 1995. Of the total of 48,216 cases, 1,226 cases (or 2.5 percent) met each of these conditions and were classified as "high-barrier" cases. Of these 1,226 cases, only 307, or 25.1 percent, left welfare. This is in comparison to 48 percent of the entire caseload. Nearly 15 percent of high-barrier leavers were sanctioned from AFDC compared to 8 percent of all other leavers.[15] Table 13-17 shows the outcomes of those classified as high-barrier cases who left welfare and compares these outcomes to all other leavers. If these high-barrier cases are truly those who face the most barriers to self-sufficiency, then examining their outcomes can give us a sense of how bad the outcomes of some leavers may be, or in other words, a lower bound on outcomes of leavers.

The first five rows examine public assistance usage for leavers. In general, the high-barrier cases have higher levels of public assistance usage than all other leavers. For some public assistance receipt outcomes, the difference between high-barrier leavers and all other leavers are sizable. However, for most outcomes, the differences are not as bad as one might expect. The high-barrier leavers were much more likely to return to AFDC than all other leavers. Forty-three percent of high-barrier leavers returned to welfare after leaving compared to only 29 percent of all other leavers. This is a sizable difference of about 48 percent. About 20 percent of the worst off leavers received AFDC for three or more quarters after leaving. However, fewer than half of these high-barrier cases returned to AFDC in the exit period. This result is a favorable indicator in that even among the worst off cases, dependency on cash assistance decreased during this period.

However, this group of high-barrier cases still received public assistance from either food stamps, AFDC, or Medicaid. In the first quarter after exit, only 18 percent of high-barrier leavers did *not* receive public assistance. In the fifth quarter after exit, this grew to 30 percent. In both the first and fifth quarters, the percentage of high-barrier cases not receiving assistance was 13 percentage points lower than the percentage of all other leavers.

Food stamp usage after leaving is very high for the high-barrier cases. Eighty-one percent received food stamps for at least 1 month after leaving. This is, however, not greatly different from the percentage of all other leavers who received food stamps after leaving, which was 71 percent. High-barrier leavers

---

[15]In March 1996, Wisconsin's Pay for Performance policy went into effect, which included full-family sanctions for those who did not participate in 20-40 hours per week of the Job Opportunities and Basic Skills (JOBS) program (Cancian et al., 1999).

TABLE 13-17 A Comparison of Leavers With Multiple Barriers to All Other
Leavers

Outcomes	High-Barrier Leavers[a]	All Other Leavers
Total number of leavers	307	22,900
Percent of sample who are leavers	25.1[b]	48.7[c]
Percent of leavers who were sanctioned	14.7	7.8
Number of quarters received AFDC after leaving		
0	56.7	70.8
1-2	13.4	13.9
3-4	18.2	11.0
4+	11.7	4.4
Percent not receiving AFDC, food stamps, or medical assistance in the 1st quarter after exit	18.2	22.2
Percent not receiving AFDC, food stamps, or medical assistance in the 5th quarter after exit	30.3	43.4
Percent who ever received food stamps after leaving	80.5	70.7
Mean number of months received food stamps after leaving	9.7	7.0
# of quarters worked after leaving		
0	40.7	23.1
1-2	20.5	13.6
3-4	15.3	19.3
4+	23.5	44.0
Quarterly earnings over first year after exit (including quarters without earnings)		
Mean	819.7	1,653.8
Median	137.3	1,329.2
Quarterly earnings over first year after exit (excluding quarters without earnings)		
Mean	1,735.3	2,393.2
Median	1,593.5	2,235.2
Quarterly income from earnings, AFDC, and food stamps in the first year after exit		
Mean	1,523.2	2,010.0
Median	1,351.1	1,874.0

[a]High-barrier cases are those who, as of July, 1995: did not have a high school diploma, had at least one child under the age of 5, had received AFDC for more than 4 years between July 1989 and July 1995, and had worked four or fewer quarters between January 1989 and July 1989.

[b]Percent of all cases designated "high-barrier cases" who left AFDC.

[c]Percent of all cases not designated "high-barrier cases" who left AFDC.

received food stamps, on average, for nearly 3 more months than all other leavers (9.7 months compared to 7.0 months).

The employment and earnings status of high-barrier leavers is not as encouraging. Nearly 41 percent of high-barrier leavers did not have earnings in the quarters following the exit period. This is relative to only 23 percent of all other leavers who did not have earnings during the postexit period. In general, the high-barrier leavers worked fewer quarters than all other leavers. Twenty-one percent of high-barrier leavers worked only one or two quarters after leaving compared to only 14 percent for all other leavers. On the other hand, although 63 percent of all other leavers worked at least three quarters after leaving welfare, only 38 percent of the high-barrier leavers did.

The earnings and incomes of high-barrier leavers are substantially lower than those of all other leavers. Mean quarterly earnings in the year following exit for high-barrier leavers (including quarters in which the case did not work) were $820 and median quarterly earnings were $137. For all other leavers, mean quarterly earnings were $1,654 and median quarterly earnings were $1,329. Excluding quarters in which a case did not work, the mean quarterly earnings of high-barrier leavers are $1,735 and the median quarterly earnings are $1,593. This median translates into annual earnings of $6,372.

Mean and median total income from earnings, AFDC, and food stamps are also reported. Results show that combined income from public assistance and earnings of high-barrier leavers is not too low relative to all other leavers, but is still much below the poverty line. The mean income of high-barrier leavers in the first year after exit is $1,523 and the median is $1,351. This is relative to a mean of $2,010 for all other leavers and a median of $1,874. Annualized, these medians translate into $5,404 for high-barrier leavers and $7,496 for all other leavers.

Overall, the low earnings and employment rates of the group of high-barrier leavers are certainly of concern. However, this group is not, at least relative to all other leavers, extraordinarily different in terms of public assistance usage after leaving. In fact, most do not return to AFDC over the year to 2 years for which we observe them after leaving. It is important to note that these results are for welfare leavers and that 75 percent of high-barrier cases did not leave welfare. The outcomes of these high-barrier *stayers* are probably worse than the outcomes of high-barrier *leavers*.

MULTIVARIATE ANALYSIS OF THE PROBABILITY OF LEAVING AFDC, THE PROBABILITY OF EMPLOYMENT AFTER LEAVING AND EARNINGS AFTER LEAVING

The results presented thus far have only shown bivariate relationships between outcomes of welfare leavers and stayers and their past welfare receipt and work experience. This section assesses the importance of past welfare receipt and past earnings history, controlling for other demographic and economic variables on outcomes. The probability of leaving welfare and the probability of employment after leaving—controlling for programmatic, demographic, and economic factors—are estimated. Earnings of welfare leavers in the first year after exit are also estimated.

The Probability of Leaving Welfare

Table 13-18 shows probit estimates of the probability of leaving welfare for all July 1995 AFDC recipients. Estimates from two models that use different measures of past welfare receipt history are shown. The first model uses average spell length (ASL) and ASL-squared along with a series of dummy variables

TABLE 13-18 Probit Estimates of the Probability of Leaving Welfare (N = 48,213)

Independent Variable	Model 1 Sign	Model 1 m.e.	Model 2 Sign	Model 2 m.e.
Average spell length	$-^a$	−0.006		
Average spell length squared	$+^a$	0.000		
Total # of spells of AFDC receipt = 1	$-^a$	−0.05		
Total # of spells of AFDC receipt = 2 or 3	+	0.018		
Total # of spells of AFDC receipt= 4 or more	+	0.036		
(reference group is those with no spells of AFDC receipt)				
Long-termer			$-^a$	−0.104
Cycler (reference group is short-termers)			+	0.007
# quarters with earnings before leaving	$+^a$	0.011	$+^a$	0.012
Age of case head	$+^a$	0.008	$+^a$	0.008
Age of case head squared	$-^a$	−0.000	$-^a$	−0.000
Black	$-^a$	−0.058	$-^a$	−0.630
Hispanic (reference group is white)	+	0.008	+	0.009
No high school diploma	$-^a$	−0.037	$-^a$	−0.037
At least some college (reference group is high school diploma)	$+^a$	0.027	$+^a$	0.027
Age of youngest child	$+^a$	0.008	$+^a$	0.007
# of children under age 5	−	−0.038	$-^a$	−0.039
# of children over age 5	$-^a$	−0.021	$-^a$	−0.024
Legal immigrant	+	0.014	+	0.015
Other adult present in case	$+^a$	0.038	$+^a$	0.040
Milwaukee County resident	$-^a$	−0.194	$-^a$	−0.206
Resident of other urban county (reference group is rural county resident)	$-^a$	−0.057	$-^a$	−0.060
Child receives SSI	$-^a$	−0.025	$-^a$	−0.028
Mother receives SSI	$-^a$	−0.325	$-^a$	−0.326
Sanctioned case	$+^a$	0.029	$+^a$	0.030
Unemployment rate in county July 1995	$-^a$	−0.007	$-^a$	−0.006
Intercept	$+^b$		+	
Log likelihood (restricted log likelihood is −24,069.95)	−21,105.04		−21,203.53	
Likelihood ratio index		0.123		0.119
Percent of observations predicted correctly		67.4		67.1

^{a}Coefficient is statistically significant at the 5-percent level.
^{b}Coefficient is statistically significant at the 10-percent level.
m.e. = marginal effect

categorizing the number of spells of AFDC receipt the case had in the preexit period. The second model uses the long-termer, short-termer and cycler distinctions to synthesize the two concepts of spell length and number of spells. Both include a variable for the number of quarters for which the case had UI earnings during the preexit period, and controls for demographic characteristics of the case and for local economic conditions. The sign of the coefficient and the marginal effect of each variable on the probability of leaving welfare are given.

Model 1 uses ASL and its square and dummy variables for the number of spells of AFDC receipt to characterize past welfare receipt history.[16] The categories of number of spells are: zero spells (reference group), one spell, two to three spells, and four or more spells.

Results show that longer average spell lengths are negatively associated with the probability of leaving welfare, but the marginal effect of a 1 month change in ASL has a small effect on the probability of leaving. The relationship is nonlinear, however, as ASL gets longer, the rate at which the probability of leaving decreases starts to slow. Those who had one spell are significantly less likely to leave AFDC than those with no prior spell. However, the size of the marginal effect is small, as a shift from no spell to one spell decreases the probability of leaving by only 0.5 percentage points compared to 14 percentage points. Those with two or more spells are not significantly more or less likely to leave welfare than those with no prior spells. These results suggest that when the length of time on welfare is accounted for, the number of spells of receipt does not have a big impact on the probability of leaving welfare. Those with one spell of AFDC receipt are significantly less likely to leave welfare than those with no prior spells, but those with more than one spell are no more or less likely to leave welfare. Cancian et al. (1999) found consistent results. They found that those with spells of over two years long were significantly less likely to leave welfare and that those with more than one spell were significantly less likely to leave welfare than those with only one spell.

Results from the second model corroborate this conclusion. In the fourth model, the spell length and spell number concepts of welfare receipt are combined into the cycler, long-termer, and short-termer classifications. The short-termers are used as the reference group in this model. Results show that long-termers are significantly less likely to leave welfare than short-termers, but there are no differences between cyclers and short-termers in the probability of leaving welfare. Long-termer status decreases the probability of leaving welfare by 10 percentage points, which is a sizable reduction.

---

[16]Other explanatory variables will not be discussed. Their signs are consistent across all models. All are significant predictors of the probability of leaving welfare except for quadratic terms for the age of the case head in the second model, the dummy variable for Hispanic ethnicity (in all four models), the number of children under age 5 (in the third model), and the legal immigrant dummy variable (in the third and fourth models).

To summarize estimations of the probability of leaving welfare, the distinction between long-term AFDC recipients and other types of AFDC recipients is an important one as long-termers are significantly less likely to leave AFDC. The estimates also show that the number of preexit quarters with earnings is consistently a strong and positive predictor of the probability of leaving AFDC across all four models.

Probability of Employment After Leaving

Table 13-19 presents probit estimates of the probability of being employed for at least one quarter in the year after leaving welfare. Only those cases that left welfare are included. We expect that, controlling for all else, those with more work experience prior to leaving are more likely to be employed after leaving welfare. We also expect that those with shorter welfare receipt histories are more likely to be employed after leaving than those with longer welfare receipt histories.

Results presented in the first model are contrary to expectations in that both long-termers and cyclers are more likely to be employed after leaving welfare than short-termers. This controls for the age of the case head, the age and number of children, the SSI status of leavers, and other variables that also might be associated with employment. The results are, however, consistent with findings from Cancian et al. (1999).

In the next model, the long-term, short-term, and cycler distinctions were "unpacked"; that is, variables for ASL and ASL-squared along with the dummy variables for the number of spells were included. Results are similar to those in the first model in that longer spells of benefit receipt are positively associated with the probability of employment after leaving. However, the relationship is nonlinear as the coefficient on the variable for average spell length squared is negative and significant. As spell length increases, the marginal increase in the probability of employment gets smaller.

Instead of using the cycler distinction for measuring the frequency for which a case goes on and off AFDC, the second model includes a series of dummy variables for the number of spells of AFDC receipt, as explained earlier. In the first model, cyclers (three or more spells regardless of spell length) were significantly more likely to be employed within a year after leaving welfare than short-termers. In the second model, we see that relative to those with no prior AFDC spells, those with one to three spells of AFDC receipt are significantly less likely to be employed after leaving welfare. Those with more than three spells are no less likely to be employed than those with no prior AFDC spells. The results of the first two models do not conflict with each other because their reference groups are different. The reference group in the second model includes those with no prior AFDC receipt, which may include those who are slightly better off than short-termers because they have not had to rely on AFDC prior to July 1995 (the

TABLE 13-19 Probit Estimates of the Probability of Employment in the First Year After Leaving Welfare (N = 18,322)

Independent Variable	Model 1 Sign	m.e.	Model 2 Sign	m.e.	Model 3 Sign	m.e.
Long-termer	$+^a$	0.034				
Cycler (reference group is short-termers)	$+^a$	0.013				
Average spell length			$+^a$	0.002		
Average spell length squared			$-^a$	−0.000		
One spell of receipt			$-^a$	−0.040		
Two or three spells of receipt			$-^a$	−0.031		
Four or more spells of receipt (reference group is no prior spells)			−	−0.023		
No earnings prior to leaving & short-term welfare recipient					−	−0.006
Some earnings prior to leaving & long-term welfare recipient					$+^a$	0.034
No earnings prior to leaving & long-term welfare recipient					+	0.012
Some earnings prior to leaving & cycler					$+^a$	0.014
No earnings prior to leaving & cycler (reference group for this series is short-termers with earnings prior to leaving welfare)					−	−0.055
# quarters with earnings before leaving	$+^a$	0.010	$+^a$	0.011	$+^a$	0.010
Age of case head	$-^a$	−0.007	$-^a$	−0.007	$-^a$	−0.007
Age of case head squared	$-^a$	0.000	+	0.000	+	0.000
Black	+	0.004	−	0.002	+	0.004
Hispanic (reference group is white)	$+^a$	0.028	$+^a$	0.028	+	0.029
No high school diploma	−	−0.003	−	−0.003	−	−0.003
At least some college (reference group is high school diploma)	$+^a$	0.011	+	0.010	$+^b$	0.011
Age of youngest child	$+^a$	0.002	$+^a$	0.002	$+^a$	0.002
# of children under age 5	−	−0.003	−	−0.004	−	−0.003
# of children over age 5	$+^a$	0.012	$+^a$	0.011	$+^a$	0.012
Legal immigrant	+	0.001	+	0.002	+	0.002
Other adult present in household	−	−0.006	−	−0.005	−	−0.006
Milwaukee County resident	+	0.000	−	−0.002	+	0.000
Resident of other urban county (reference group is rural county resident)	−	−0.005	−	−0.005	−	−0.005
Child receives SSI	−	−0.007	−	−0.008	−	−0.007
Mother receives SSI	$-^a$	−0.219	$-^a$	−0.218	$-^a$	−0.219
Sanctioned case	$-^a$	−0.045	$-^a$	−0.044	$-^a$	−0.045
Unemployment rate in county in 1996	$-^a$	−0.010	$-^a$	−0.010	$-^a$	−0.010
Left AFDC 4th quarter 1995	+	0.009	+	0.008	+	0.009
Left AFDC 1st quarter 1996	+	−0.001	−	−0.002	−	−0.001
Left AFDC 2nd quarter 1996 (reference is left AFDC 3rd quarter 1995)	+	−0.004	−	−0.005	−	−0.004

continues

TABLE 13-19 Continued

Independent Variable	Model 1 Sign m.e.	Model 2 Sign m.e.	Model 3 Sign m.e.
Intercept	+[a]	+[a]	+[a]
Log likelihood (restricted log likelihood is −6,471.46)	−5,605.20	−5,597.75	−5,604.41
Likelihood ratio index	0.134	0.135	0.134
Percent of observations predicted correctly	88.4	88.4	88.4

[a]Coefficient is statistically significant at the 5-percent level.
[b]Coefficient is statistically significant at the 10-percent level.
m.e. = marginal effect.

short-termer group includes some with no prior AFDC receipt, but it also includes some with some prior AFDC receipt). The result that those with at least four prior spells of receipt are no less likely to find employment after leaving than those with no prior AFDC receipt and the positive and significant sign on the cycler variable in Model 1 are still a bit perplexing. One hypothesis is that those who cycle on and off welfare also cycle between employment and unemployment. Because this group has some work experience, its members may have a relatively easier time finding jobs after leaving. This hypothesis is only supported to the extent that those with many spells are more likely to be employed after leaving than those with a few spells. However, those with a few AFDC spells (between one and three) are less likely to find employment after leaving than those with no prior AFDC spells.

The third model attempts to flesh out the results in the first two models with respect to welfare receipt history. The model includes a series of dummy variables for the earnings and welfare receipt history of leavers. The third model combines the welfare receipt and work history variables. The sample is categorized into six groups: short-termers with no prior work experience, short-termers with at least one quarter of prior work experience, long-termers with no work experience, long-termers with some work experience, cyclers with no work experience, and cyclers with some work experience. The reference group consists of short-termers with some work experience.

Results from this model are useful in explaining the peculiar results in Models 1 and 2. Those with long-term welfare receipt histories and at least one quarter of work experience prior to leaving still have higher employment probabilities than short-termers with work experience. However, employment rates of long-termers with no prior work experience are not significantly different from the employment rates of short-term recipients with prior work experience. Likewise, cyclers with some prior work experience have higher probabilities of employment after leaving welfare than short-termers with some work experience. However, cyclers with no work experience do not have different employment rates than short-termers with some work experience. This group of leavers with long-term welfare receipt histories clearly have characteristics or faces economic or policy conditions that are associated with increased employment compared to those who have used welfare less. These results need further investigation.

For all three models of the probability of employment, those with more work experience are more likely to be employed after leaving welfare, as expected. The coefficient is positive and strongly significant. A one quarter increase in prior work experience increases the probability of employment after leaving by 1 percentage point. One other variable of interest is the dummy variable for whether or not a case was sanctioned from benefit receipt. In all three models, sanctioned cases were significantly less likely to be employed than nonsanctioned cases. The marginal effect of a sanctioned case decreases the probability of leaving welfare by more than 4 percentage points. This is as expected and is initial evidence that sanctioned cases may have a tough time finding employment.

Earnings in the Year After Welfare Exit

Table 13-20 presents Tobit estimates of leavers' earnings in the first year after exiting AFDC. Again, the relationship between preexit welfare receipt and preexit earnings on postexit earnings is of key interest. In these estimates, a measure of average quarterly earnings in the years prior to the exit period are included in this model as an additional measure of prior work history.

Results show that long-termers have higher earnings than short-termers even after controlling for other demographic, programmatic status, and local economic conditions. Status as a long-term AFDC user is positively associated with earnings after leaving and is statistically significant. This result holds even after controlling for the age of the leaver, prior work experience; and average quarterly earnings prior to leaving welfare, which is surprising because it is contrary to initial predictions that long-termers would have more barriers to self-sufficiency and have lower earnings after leaving. Further explanations for this result should be explored. It is possible that there are compositional differences in the welfare dependency groups that are not observed with these data. Cyclers, however, do not have higher earnings than short-termers. In combination with results from the first model in Table 13-19, although cyclers are more likely to be employed after leaving welfare than short-termers, they do not have earnings that are significantly different from short-termers.

The second model uses ASL and its square as measures of previous welfare benefit receipt history. It also uses the series of dummy variables for the number of prior welfare spells as measures of the degree of cycling on and off welfare. Results show that longer spells of benefit receipt are associated with higher earnings, but that the longer the spells of receipt, the slower the increase in

TABLE 13-20 Tobit Estimates of Earnings in the First Year After Leaving Welfare (N = 17,293)

Independent Variable	Model 1 β	m.e.	Model 2 β	m.e.
Intercept	1.85	0.29^a	2.00	0.29^a
Long-termer	0.31	0.03^a		
Cycler (reference group is short-termers)	0.03	0.04		
Average AFDC spell length			0.02	0.003^a
Average AFDC spell length squared			−0.00	0.000^a
Total # of spells =1			−0.34	0.08^a
Total # of spells=2 or 3			−0.36	0.08^a
Total # of spells=4 or more			−0.26	0.09^a
Average quarterly earnings before leaving	0.32	0.02^a	0.33	0.02^a
# Quarters with earnings before leaving	0.05	0.00^a	0.05	0.002^a
Age of case head	−0.03	0.02^b	−0.03	0.02^a
Age of case head squared	−0.001	0.002	−0.00	0.00
Black	0.04	0.04	0.03	0.04^a
Hispanic (reference group is white)	0.27	0.06^a	0.27	0.06^a
No high school diploma	−0.28	0.03^a	−0.27	0.03^a
At least some college (reference group is high school diploma)	0.39	0.03^a	0.39	0.03^a
Age of youngest child	0.00	0.00	0.002	0.005
# of children under age 5	−0.02	0.02	−0.02	0.02
# of children over age 5	0.14	0.02^a	0.13	0.02^a
Legal immigrant	0.51	0.19^a	0.53	0.19^a
Other adult present in household	−0.07	0.03^a	−0.07	0.03^a
Milwaukee County resident	0.45	0.04^a	0.43	0.04^a
Resident of other urban county (reference group is rural county resident)	0.08	0.04^b	0.07	0.04^a
Child receives SSI	−0.18	0.05^a	−0.18	0.05^a
Mother receives SSI	−1.89	0.09^a	−1.88	0.09^a
Sanctioned case	−0.52	0.05^a	−0.52	0.05^a
Unemployment rate in county in 1996	−0.10	0.02^a	−0.10	0.02^a
Left AFDC 4th quarter 1995	0.03	0.03	0.03	0.03
Left AFDC 1st quarter 1996	0.01	0.04	0.00	0.00
Left AFDC 2nd quarter 1996 (reference is left AFDC 3rd quarter 1995)	−0.14	0.03^a	−0.15	0.03^a
Scale parameter	1.64	0.01^a	1.64	0.01^a
Log likelihood	−30,993.14		−30,971.07	
Number of censored cases	2,227		2,227	

^{a}Coefficient is statistically significant at the 5-percent level.
^{b}Coefficient is statistically significant at the 10-percent level.
m.e. = marginal effect.

earnings. These results are consistent with the first model. The results are also consistent with findings from the 1995 cohort of leavers in Cancian et al. (1999), but not with earnings of the 1997 cohort of leavers from Cancian et al. (2000b).

Each of the coefficients on the dummy variables for the number of spells of benefit receipt are negative and statistically significant. Those with one spell of benefit receipt, those with two or three spells of benefit receipt, and those with four or more spells have significantly lower earnings than those with no prior spells of benefit receipt. The coefficient is the largest for those with two or three spells (-0.36).

The coefficients on average quarterly earnings and on total number of quarters worked in the years prior to leaving are positive and statistically significant. Those with higher average earnings in the preexit period had higher earnings after leaving. Likewise, those who worked more quarters prior to leaving welfare had higher earnings after leaving welfare, although the size of the coefficient is smaller than the size of the coefficient on average earnings prior to leaving welfare. Both results are as expected and indicate that a key component of labor market success after leaving welfare is work experience prior to leaving welfare.

Predictions of Outcomes for High-Barrier Cases

This section uses the coefficient estimates from the models predicting the probability of leaving welfare, the probability of employment after leaving, and earnings after leaving to predict each of these outcomes for different definitions of "high-barrier" cases.[17] Seven definitions of high-barrier cases are examined. The first is the same definition used earlier—cases that had no high school diploma, received welfare for at least 48 months in the preexit period, fewer than four quarters of earnings in the preexit period, and had at least one child under the age of 5. The rest of the definitions build this basic definition. They are:

Definition 2 = Definition 1 + the case head is on SSI.
Definition 3 = Definition 1 + the case includes a child on SSI.
Definition 4 = Definition 1 + the case lives in Milwaukee County.
Definition 5 = Definition 1 + the case head is black.
Definition 6 = Definition 1 + the case head is black and lives in Milwaukee County.
Definition 7 = Definition 1 + the case head was sanctioned from AFDC.

For each outcome, the coefficients from the model that uses the long-termer, short-termer and cycler distinction are used. Table 13-21 shows the mean predicted probability of the three outcomes computed for cases that qualify as high-

---

[17]Cancian et al. (2000b) conduct similar simulations, although definitions of high-barrier cases differ from those presented here.

TABLE 13-21 Predicted Outcomes for Cases That Face Multiple Barriers to Self-Sufficiency

	All Cases	High-Barrier Definition 1[a]	High-Barrier Definition 2[b]	High-Barrier Definition 3[c]	High-Barrier Definition 4[d]	High-Barrier Definition 5[e]	High-Barrier Definition 6[f]	High-Barrier Definition 7[g]
Number of cases	34,726	1,410	173	304	1,051	877	792	138
Percent of total sample	100.0	4.1	0.5	0.9	3.0	2.5	2.3	0.4
Number of leavers	17,294	344	26	65	192	150	125	45
Mean predicted probability of leaving welfare	48.7 (19.6)	23.9 (11.9)	7.5 (4.9)	21.5 (11.6)	19.0 (7.0)	18.9 (7.8)	17.5 (6.2)	28.7 (11.4)
Mean predicted probability of employment after leaving welfare	88.3 (11.2)	75.7 (15.0)	29.5 (9.5)	72.5 (16.5)	75.4 (15.8)	74.7 (16.2)	74.0 (17.0)	72.3 (7.1)
Mean predicted quarterly earnings after leaving welfare	1,929.9 (645.3)	1,224.1 (407.9)	293.5 (144.7)	1,046.0 (381.6)	1,329.0 (407.6)	1,246.2 (408.0)	1,276.7 (408.7)	953.5 (230.0)

NOTES: Cases with missing data for explanatory variables were eliminated. Predictions are based on the actual values of explanatory variables for each case. Standard deviations reported in parentheses.

[a]Definition 1 = No high school diploma; received AFDC for at least 4 years between 7/89 and 7/95; had fewer than four quarters with earnings between 1/89 and 7/95; had at least one child under the age of 5.

[b]Definition 2 = Definition 1 + case head is on SSI.

[c]Definition 3 = Definition 1 + case includes a child on SSI.

[d]Definition 4 = Definition 1 + case lives in Milwaukee County.

[e]Definition 5 = Definition 1 + case head is black.

[f]Definition 6 = Definition 1 + case head is black and lives in Milwaukee County.

[g]Definition 7 = Definition 1 + case head was sanctioned from AFDC.

barrier cases under these definitions. The first column shows the mean predicted outcomes for all cases in the sample as a reference.

Probability of Leaving Welfare for High-Barrier Cases

For the entire sample, the mean predicted probability of leaving welfare is nearly 49 percent. This is close to the 48 percent of the caseload that actually left welfare during the time period. Under different definitions of high-barrier cases, the probability of leaving welfare varies substantially. Under the basic high-barrier definition (Definition 1), the probability of leaving is 24 percent or about half the probability of leaving for the entire sample. Across different definitions of high-barrier cases, by far, cases that receive SSI have the lowest probability of leaving welfare. The mean predicted probability of leaving welfare for this group (Definition 2) is only 7.5 percent. For those high-barrier cases that include a child who receives SSI (Definition 3), the probability of leaving welfare is not as low as cases where the mother receives SSI. The mean predicted probability of leaving welfare for this group is 21.5 percent. For those who are high-barrier cases and who live in Milwaukee County the mean predicted probability of leaving welfare is 19 percent. This is nearly identical to the mean predicted probability of leaving for high-barrier cases that are also black (Definition 5). High-barrier cases that are black and live in Milwaukee County (Definition 6) have a slightly lower mean probability of leaving welfare, 17.5 percent.

These results suggest that high-barrier cases are much less likely to leave AFDC than those who do not face these barriers. This is especially true for those who receive SSI payments. High-barrier cases who are black and live in Milwaukee County also have a lower probability of leaving welfare than other high-barrier cases. Those high-barrier cases with a child who receives SSI payments are only slightly less likely to leave welfare than all high-barrier cases.

Probability of Employment in the First Year After Leaving

The next row shows the mean predicted probability of ever being employed in the first four quarters after leaving. These predictions are based on the coefficient estimates in Model 1 in Table 13-19, and are computed only for those who leave welfare. First, the overall mean predicted probability of employment after leaving is 88.3 percent. For the basic definition of high-barrier cases, the mean probability of employment is 75.7 percent, which is about a 14-percent difference from the overall mean probability. This is still a sizable difference, but not nearly as big as the difference in the mean predicted probabilities of leaving welfare for high-barrier and nonhigh-barrier cases. Furthermore, for nearly every additional definition of high-barrier cases, the mean probabilities of employment are approximately 75 percent. There are some exceptions. First, those high-barrier cases that receive SSI (Definition 2) have quite different mean predicted probabilities of employment than the overall sample and than the basic high-barrier definition. The mean predicted probability of employment after leaving for this group is only 29.5 percent.[18] Second, those with a child on SSI (Definition 3) and those who were sanctioned from AFDC (Definition 7) have slightly lower mean predicted probabilities of leaving (72.5 percent for Definition 3 and 72.3 percent for Definition 7). These results indicate that even sanctioned high-barrier cases and high-barrier cases with SSI-eligible children have fairly high employment rates after leaving welfare and do not appear to have trouble finding employment after leaving welfare.

Mean Predicted Quarterly Earnings After Leaving Welfare

The last row in Table 13-21 shows mean predicted quarterly earnings for leavers under the different definitions of high-barrier cases. These means are based on Tobit coefficient estimates from Model 1 of Table 13-20.

The mean predicted quarterly earnings of all leavers (column 1) in the first year after exit are $1,930. The mean quarterly earnings of high-barrier cases (Definition 1) are $1,224, which translates into a nearly 37-percent difference. Different high-barrier cases do better than this, however. The mean predicted earnings of those from Milwaukee County (Definition 4) are $1,329, higher than mean predicted earnings of the basic high-barrier cases. This result is probably a result of wage differences between Milwaukee and other areas of the state. High-barrier cases who are black (Definition 5) also have higher earnings ($1,246) than other high-barrier cases, although their means are not as high as the mean earnings for high-barrier cases from Milwaukee. Accordingly, those who are black and live in Milwaukee (Definition 6) have predicted earnings that fall between the predicted earnings of those from Milwaukee County (Definition 4) and those who are black (Definition 5). Their mean predicted earnings are $1,277.

The predicted earnings of those with other barriers are not as high, however. Again, those high-barrier cases that receive SSI (Definition 2) are the worst off. Their mean predicted earnings are just $293.5 per quarter. Again, only 26 observations fall into this category. High-barrier cases that have a child who is eligible for SSI also have low mean earnings, at $1046. Finally, sanctioned high-barrier cases have low mean earnings, too, at $953.5. Their mean is less than half of that for the entire sample of leavers and 22 percent lower than the basic high-barrier cases. So although the employment rates of sanctioned cases were not that different than other high-barrier cases, there are substantial earnings differences between sanctioned high-barrier cases and other high-barrier cases, and between sanctioned leavers and all other leavers.

Table 13-21 illustrates that it is likely that certain high-barrier cases will have a difficult time making it on their own. High-barrier cases in general are

---

[18]This mean is based on 26 observations, however.

much less likely to leave welfare than other cases. Although their employment rates are not vastly different from all other leavers, their earnings are substantially different. High-barrier cases that are eligible for SSI are likely to have even greater problems making it on their own, according to these predictions. For other types of high-barrier cases, employment may not be a significant problem for them; however, earnings do seem to be a problem.

Results found here should supplement similar simulations conducted in Cancian et al. (2000b), where much wider differences in predicted outcomes between high-barrier cases and low-barrier cases were found. The Cancian et al. definitions of high-barrier cases are more restrictive than definitions used here.

CONCLUSIONS

The purpose of this paper is to illustrate the importance of characterizing the composition of the caseload at the time the welfare leavers sample is drawn. The paper also aims to exemplify one method of standardizing results across different types of leavers with different benefit receipt and work histories in order to make the studies more comparable across time and across areas. In general, we find that past welfare receipt history matters a great deal for outcomes, but not always as expected. We also find that those with more work experience prior to leaving were more likely to leave welfare and were much more successful in gaining employment and earnings after leaving welfare.

We described the composition of the caseload during the time the leavers sample was drawn according to their prior work and benefit receipt. Results presented in that section show that a significant portion of the caseload received AFDC benefits for at least 5 of the 6 years in the preobservation period. Most of the cases on AFDC in 1995 had fewer than two spells of benefit receipt in the preexit period. Only 14 percent had three or more spells of receipt. The caseload was divided into three groups: long-termers, short-termers, and cyclers. Under these definitions, 55 percent of the caseload were long-termers, 31 percent were short-termers, and 14 percent were cyclers. The caseload was also broken down by past work experience, as measured by the percentage of quarters in the preexit period with UI earnings. Twenty percent of the caseload did not work at all in the preexit period, 60 percent worked at least one quarter but no more than half the quarters, and 25 percent worked for more than half the quarters. Crossing work history with welfare receipt history, we found that those who had received benefits the longest had the least amount of work experience. Short-termers had the most work experience. Cyclers had the least amount of work experience.

We also showed outcomes by past benefit receipt and work experience. The first outcome examined was the proportion of cases that left welfare. Results showed that higher percentages of cyclers and short-termers left welfare than long-termers. Results also showed that higher portions of leavers were found in the groups with the most work experience. For those who left welfare, two sets of outcomes were examined: benefit receipt after exit (return to AFDC, food stamps, or Medicaid) and employment status and earnings after exit. Results show that the cycler, short-termer, and long-termer distinction is an important distinction for benefit receipt outcomes. Long-termers were much more likely than short-termers and cyclers to return to welfare, and a higher proportion of long-termers continued to receive food stamps and Medicaid after leaving than short-termers. Benefit receipt outcomes after leaving did vary by work experience prior to leaving welfare, but the differences were not large. On the other hand, employment and earnings outcomes after leaving varied substantially across prior work experience strata. As expected, those who had worked more prior to leaving welfare had higher employment rates and higher earnings after leaving. Employment and earnings outcomes also varied by prior AFDC benefit receipt, but not as drastically. Surprisingly, long-termers had better employment outcomes than short-termers. Long-termers were more likely to be employed after leaving and their earnings were higher after leaving than short-termers. Cyclers' employment rates and earnings did not differ greatly from those of long-termers.

The final part of the paper examines how important past benefit receipt distinctions and work experience distinctions are for these outcomes when other background characteristics of the cases are controlled. The probability of leaving welfare and the probability of ever being employed in the year after leaving welfare were estimated. Earnings after leaving were also predicted for welfare leavers. The primary finding in this section is that prior work experience was a consistently strong predictor of success. The percentage of quarters worked in the preexit period was positively associated with the probability of leaving welfare and the probability of employment after leaving. Quarters worked and average wages in the preexit period were both positive and strong predictors of quarterly earnings after leaving welfare.

We also found that past welfare receipt distinctions were important predictors of the probability of leaving welfare. Short-termers were significantly more likely to leave welfare than long-termers and in general, results consistently show that those who had received AFDC longer were less likely to leave AFDC. The cycler distinction was not a strong predictor of the probability of leaving welfare, although there is some evidence that those with one spell of benefit receipt were less likely to leave welfare than those with no prior spells of receipt.

The probability of being employed after leaving is, surprisingly, positively related to the length of time spent on welfare prior to the preexit period. Average spell length and long-termer status were both positive and strong predictors of the probability of employment after leaving welfare. For this outcome, the cycler distinction was an important predictor of employment as cyclers were significantly more likely to be employed than short-termers.

Spell length is positively associated with earnings after leaving as well. Long-termer status is associated with higher earnings after leaving. Furthermore, average spell length is positively associated with earnings after leaving. The number of welfare receipt spells were significant predictors of earnings after leaving. The coefficient for each category of number of spells (one spell, two or three spells, or four or more spells) is negative and statistically significant compared to those with no prior spells.

The results that long-termers worked more quarters and had higher earnings after leaving than short-termers and cyclers is contrary to expectations that previous dependency levels would be negatively correlated with employment outcomes. A good explanation for these results is not clear.

In summary, we conclude that in examining the outcomes of welfare leavers, it is important to characterize the caseload by their past work experience and by their past benefit receipt history because outcomes vary widely across different work experience and benefit receipt backgrounds. Work history background is especially important, we find, as the outcomes vary greatly according to different work experience groups. In terms of past benefit receipt history, the long-term versus short-term distinction is an important one. Distinctions by the number of spells of receipt show mixed results—sometimes this distinction matters, sometimes it does not.

REFERENCES

Acs, G., and P. Loprest
2001   *Initial Synthesis Report of the Findings of ASPE's "Leavers" Grants.* Washington, DC: The Urban Institute. Available: http://aspe.hhs.gov/hsp/leavers99/synthesis01/
Bane, M.J., and D.T. Ellwood
1994   *Welfare Realities: From Rhetoric to Reform.* Cambridge, MA: Harvard University Press.
Blank, R.M., and P. Ruggles
1994   Short-term recidivism among public-assistance recipients. *American Economic Review* 84(2):49-53.
Cancian, M.R., Haveman, T. Kaplan, and B. Wolfe
1999   Post-Exit Earnings and Benefit Receipt Among Those Who Left AFDC in Wisconsin. Institute for Research on Poverty Special Report No. 75.
Cancian, M.R., Haveman, T. Kaplan, I. Rothe, and B. Wolfe
2000a   Before and After TANF: The Utilization of Noncash Public Benefits by Women Leaving Welfare in Wisconsin. Institute for Research on Poverty.
Cancian, M.R., Haveman, D.R. Meyer, and B. Wolfe
2000b   Before and After TANF: The Economic Well-Being of Women Leaving Welfare. Institute for Research on Poverty Special Report No. 77.
Moffitt, R.A.
1992   Incentive effects of the U.S. welfare system: A review. *Journal of Economic Literature* 30: 1-61.
Moffitt, R.A., and J. Roff
2000   The Diversity of Welfare Leavers. Background paper to Policy Brief 00-02. *Welfare, Children, and Families: A Three-City Study. Working Paper 00-01.* Baltimore, MD: Johns Hopkins University.

Moffitt, R. A., and D. Stevens
   2001   Changing Caseloads: Macro Influences and Micro Composition. Unpublished paper presented at conference, Welfare Reform Four Years Later: Progress and Prospects, Federal Reserve Bank of New York, November 17.
National Research Council
   1999   *Evaluating Welfare Reform: A Framework and Review of Current Work.* R. A. Moffitt and M.L. Ver Ploeg, eds. Commission on Behavioral and Social Sciences and Education. Committee on National Statistics. Washington, DC: National Academy Press.
   2001   *Evaluating Welfare Reform in an Era of Transition.* Panel on Data and Methods for Measuring the Effects of Changes in Social Welfare Programs, Robert A. Moffitt and Michele Ver Ploeg, Editors. Committee on National Statistics, Division of Behavioral and Social Sciences and Education. Washington, DC: National Academy Press.
Stevens, David W.
   2000   Welfare, Employment and Earnings. Memorandum prepared for the Panel on Data and Methods for Measuring the Effects of Changes in Social Welfare Programs, Committee on National Statistics. University of Baltimore, MD, October.

APPENDIX 13-A

DESCRIPTION OF LEAVERS AND OUTCOMES ACROSS
DIFFERENT DEFINITIONS OF LEAVERS

In this appendix, the definition of a leaver is modified to see how sensitive the composition and outcomes of leavers are to the definition used in the paper. Specifically, the requirement that a leaver must have stopped receiving AFDC for 2 consecutive months to be considered a leaver is made more restrictive. We try two additional definitions; first, that a leaver must have discontinued receiving benefits for 3 consecutive months to be considered a leaver, and second, that a leaver must have discontinued receiving benefits for 6 consecutive months to be considered a leaver. These definitions were operationalized as follows:

All cases received AFDC in July 1995. Leavers under the 2-month definition stopped receiving AFDC for 2 consecutive months between August 1995 and July 1996. (June 1996 was the last month a case may have received AFDC and still be considered a leaver if the case did not receive welfare in July and August of 1996.) Leavers under the 3-month definition stopped receiving AFDC for 3 consecutive months between August 1995 and July 1996. (June 1996 was the last month a case may have received AFDC and still be considered a leaver if the case did not receive welfare in July, August, and September of 1996.) Leavers under the 6-month definition stopped receiving AFDC for 6 consecutive months between August 1995 and July 1996. (June 1996 was the last month a case may have received AFDC and still be considered a leaver if the case did not receive welfare in July through December 1996.)

Using these definitions, Table 13-A1 shows how the composition of the leaver and stayer groups vary across the three definitions. Table 13-A2 shows how some key outcomes of leavers vary across the different definitions. A brief summary of these two tables is reported here.

With a more restrictive definition of a leaver, a smaller portion of the caseload, not surprisingly, qualifies as a leaver. With the 3-month definition, 45.1 percent are leavers compared to 48.1 percent for the 2-month definition. For the 6-month definition, only 41.1 percent are classified as leavers. The characteristics of leavers under the more restrictive definition change only slightly. There are few differences in the characteristics of 2-month leavers and 3-month leavers. The differences are very small across all the demographic and past work and welfare receipt history variables. There are small differences in the demographic composition of 6-month leavers and 2-month leavers. A higher proportion (2.5 percentage points) of 6-month leavers are white than 2-month leavers. Six-month leavers are slightly less likely to come from Milwaukee County than 2-month leavers (38.7 percent compared to 42.4 percent). Six-month leavers are slightly more likely to be short-termers than 2-month leavers (41.2 percent compared to 39.1 percent) and slightly less likely to be long-termers (40.7 percent compared to 42.9 percent). Six-month leavers have, in general, spent a little less time on

TABLE 13-A1 Characteristics of Welfare Leavers Under Different Definitions of "Leaver"

Characteristic	Leaver = 2 Months off		Leaver = 3 Months off		Leaver = 6 Months off	
	Leaver	Stayer	Leaver	Stayer	Leaver	Stayer
Total number	23,207	25,009	21,742	26,474	19,796	28,420
Percent of sample	48.1	51.9	45.1	54.9	41.1	58.9
Race/ethnicity						
% black	32.2	48.1	31.7	52.2	29.7	52.2
% Hispanic	6.4	7.1	6.5	7.1	6.4	7.1
% white	61.4	44.8	61.8	40.7	63.9	41.7
Age of case head						
% <26	37.1	35.5	37.1	35.6	37.1	35.7
% 27-31	25.2	23.7	25.1	23.8	25.1	23.9
% 32-41	30.9	32.2	30.8	32.2	30.8	32.1
% 42+	6.8	8.6	6.9	8.4	7.0	8.2
Education of case head						
% less than high school	36.1	50.2	35.4	50.0	34.4	49.7
% high school diploma	45.3	37.7	45.6	37.9	46.0	38.2
% some college	18.6	12.1	19.0	12.1	19.6	12.2
County of residence						
Milwaukee County	42.4	65.3	40.7	65.4	38.7	65.1
Other urban county	35.6	24.1	36.5	23.9	37.6	24.0
Rural	22.0	10.6	22.7	10.6	23.6	10.8
Percent with child on SSI	8.1	13.1	7.9	13.0	7.6	12.9
Age of youngest child						
% 0 to 1 years	27.1	29.2	27.2	28.9	27.4	28.7
% 2 to 4 years	31.4	31.0	31.2	31.2	31.1	31.3
% 5 to 11 years	29.7	29.9	29.6	30.0	29.4	30.0
% 12 or older	11.8	9.9	12.0	9.9	12.1	9.9

continues

TABLE 13-A1 Continued

Characteristic	Leaver = 2 Months off Leaver	Stayer	Leaver = 3 Months off Leaver	Stayer	Leaver = 6 Months off Leaver	Stayer
Total number	23,207	25,009	21,742	26,474	19,796	28,420
Percent of sample	48.1	51.9	45.1	54.9	41.1	58.9
Welfare History (7/89 to 7/95)						
% short-termer	39.1	23.1	40.0	23.2	41.2	23.6
% long-termer	42.9	66.7	41.9	66.3	40.7	65.4
% cycler	18.2	10.2	18.1	10.5	18.1	11.0
Percent of time on welfare (7/89 to 7/95)						
0 <= x <25% of time	23.5	11.3	24.3	11.3	25.3	11.5
25 <= x <50% of time	20.4	14.3	20.7	14.3	21.1	14.5
50 <= x <100% of time	43.7	45.4	43.2	45.7	42.3	46.2
Always on	12.4	29.0	11.8	28.6	11.3	27.8
Mean AFDC spell length 7/89 to 7/95 (in months)	27.5	41.2	26.9	40.9	26.3	40.4
	(23.2)	(25.2)	(23.0)	(25.2)	(22.8)	(25.2)
Percent of quarters with earnings (1/89 to 7/95)						
Never worked	14.0	25.1	14.2	24.3	14.4	23.5
0 < x <= 25%	30.0	37.6	29.6	37.5	29.3	37.2
25 < x <= 50%	28.0	23.1	27.9	23.4	27.7	23.9
50 < x <= 75%	17.7	10.6	17.9	10.8	18.2	11.2
More than 75% of quarters	10.3	3.6	10.3	3.9	10.5	4.2

TABLE 13-A2 Outcomes of Welfare Leavers Under Different Definitions of "Leaver"

Characteristic	Leaver = 2 Months off		Leaver = 3 Months off		Leaver = 6 Months off	
	Leaver	Stayer	Leaver	Stayer	Leaver	Stayer
Total number	23,207	25,009	21,742	26,474	19,796	28,420
Percent of sample	48.1	51.9	45.1	54.9	41.1	58.9
Number returned to AFDC	6,753		4,831		2,753	
Percent returned to AFDC	29.1	N/A	22.2	N/A	13.9	N/A
Average earnings over 4 quarters after leaving[a]	1,642.1	786.1	1,677.7	804.2	1,733.2	825.4
	(1,628.3)	(1,124.6)	(1,658.5)	(1,127.8)	(1,686.0)	(1,136.4)
Median earnings over 4 quarters after leaving[a]	1,311.0	199.0	1,371.9	226.5	1,459.9	259.8
Average income from earnings, AFDC, food stamps, over 4 quarters after leaving[a]	2,193.6	2,301.5	1,980.1	2,304.3	1,956.0	2,298.9
	(1,556.3)	(1,128.1)	(1,636.9)	(1,125.9)	(1,673.3)	(1,129.8)
Median income over 4 quarters after leaving[a]	1,864.0	2,184.6	1,817.1	2,189.1	1,761.6	2,180.3
Number of quarters with earnings after exit[b]						
% did not work	22.8	33.8	22.6	28.9	21.8	28.0
% worked 1-3 quarters	22.4	32.5	24.3	37.2	23.6	37.0
% worked 4+ quarters	54.7	37.7	53.1	33.9	54.6	35.0

NOTE: Standard deviations reported in parentheses.

[a]Does not include disappearers.

[b]Please note that one more quarter postexit is observed under the 2- and 3-month definitions than under the 6- month definition. The latest quarter a 2- or 3-month leaver could have exited would be third quarter 1996, whereas the latest quarter a 6-month leaver could have exited is fourth quarter 1996.

welfare prior to the exit period than 2-month leavers. This is as expected, because the group of 6-month leavers is probably composed of cases that are more self-sufficient than the group of 2-month leavers. There are only negligible differences in the work histories of 2-month, 3-month, and 6-month leavers.

As expected, 6-month leavers have better outcomes than 3-month and 2-month leavers. Only 13.9 percent of 6-month leavers returned to AFDC, compared to 22.2 percent of 3-month leavers and 29.1 percent of 2-month leavers. The mean and median earnings in the first year after exit of 6-month leavers are higher than those of 3-month and 2-month leavers. The mean and median earnings in the first year after exit for 6-month leavers are $1,733 and $1,460. For 3-month leavers, the mean and median are $1,678 and $1,372. For 2-month leavers, the mean and median are $1,642 and $1,311. Somewhat surprisingly, 6-month leavers did not work much more than 2-month leavers. However, one less quarter after exit is observed for 6-month leavers than for 2-month leavers, so little emphasis is put on this result.

APPENDIX 13-B

SUPPLEMENTARY TABLES

TABLE 13-B1 Distributions of Long-termer, Short-termer, and Cycler Welfare Histories by Alternative Definitions (percent distribution)

	Definition 1[a]	Definition 2[b]	Definition 3[c]	Definition 4[d]	Definition 5[e]
Full sample					
Long-termer	76.7	67.8	61.2	55.3	36.9
Short-termer	9.4	18.3	24.9	30.8	49.2
Cycler	13.9	13.9	13.9	13.9	13.9
By leaver status					
Stayers					
Long-termer	84.2	77.8	72.4	66.7	47.7
Short-termer	5.7	12.1	17.5	23.1	42.1
Cycler	10.2	10.2	10.2	10.2	10.2
Leavers					
Long-termer	68.7	57.0	49.1	42.9	25.2
Short-termer	13.3	25.0	32.9	39.1	56.8
Cycler	18.0	18.0	18.0	18.0	18.0

NOTE: All cyclers are those who have had three or more spells regardless of average spell length.

[a]Definition 1: Average spell length – 6 months=short-termer; average spell length >6 = long-termer.

[b]Definition 2: Average spell length –12 months=short-termer; average spell length >12 = long-termer.

[c]Definition 3: Average spell length –18 months=short-termer; average spell length >18 = long-termer.

[d]Definition 4: Average spell length –24 months=short-termer; average spell length >24 = long-termer.

[e]Definition 5: Average spell length –36 months=short-termer; average spell length >36 = long-termer.

TABLE 13-B2 Earnings of Leavers in Quarters Without AFDC Receipt (includes disappearers)

	1st Quarter After Exit	2nd Quarter After Exit	3rd Quarter After Exit	4th Quarter After Exit	5th Quarter After Exit
All leavers					
N	19,912	18,803	18,987	19,375	19,815
Mean earnings	1,370	1,656	1,745	1,827	1,860
Median earnings	1,245	1,381	1,290	1,385	1,382
Short-term welfare user					
N	8,610	7,766	7,832	7,955	8,113
Mean earnings	1,575	1,647	1,687	1,741	1,787
Median earnings	1,017	1,117	1,127	1,154	1,185
Long-term welfare user					
N	8,264	7,729	7,795	7,955	8,139
Mean earnings	1,697	1,762	1,801	1,893	1,927
Median earnings	1,399	1,408	1,421	1,524	1,528
Cycler					
N	3,545	3,308	3,360	3,465	3,563
Mean earnings	1,656	1,702	1,752	1,871	1,874
Median earnings	1,381	1,352	1,338	1,553	1,482

TABLE 13-B3 Different Definitions of High-Barrier Cases

	Definition 1[a]	Definition 2[b]	Definition 3[c]	Definition 4[d]	Definition 5[e]	Definition 6[f]
Number	1,410	421	1,723	361	2,484	3,292
Percent of total sample	2.9	2.1	3.6	0.7	5.2	6.8
Number of leavers	344	27	443	87	506	1,225
Percent in high-barrier definition who left AFDC	24.4	6.4	25.7	24.1	20.4	37.2

[a]Definition 1 = Basic high-barrier definition: Did not finish high school, received AFDC for more than 48 months in 72 months prior to exit, had at least one child under the age of 5, worked four or fewer quarters in the preexit period.

[b]Definition 2 = Same as #1 except did not work at all in the preexit period.

[c]Definition 3 = Same as #1 except worked fewer than eight quarters in the preexit period.

[d]Definition 4 = Same as #1 except had at least one child under the age of 1.

[e]Definition 5 = Only qualification is case head received SSI.

[f]Definition 6 = Only qualification is one child in case received SSI.

14

Experienced-Based Measures of Heterogeneity in the Welfare Caseload

Robert A. Moffitt

It has long been understood by welfare researchers that the welfare caseload is quite diverse. Many studies of the now-defunct Aid to Families with Dependent Children (AFDC) program demonstrated that some women on the welfare rolls were much worse off than women not on the rolls in terms of family background, educational attainment, labor market experience and skill, health problems, and many other indicators, and that different women might need different types of special assistance. This heterogeneity has assumed even greater importance in the welfare reform environment of the 1990s. The new reforms are, generally speaking, aimed at raising employment levels and promoting work, particularly off the welfare rolls. It is naturally to be expected that women with greater capabilities to respond to these policies will fare better than women with lesser capabilities.[1] In addition, from the program operator's viewpoint, heterogeneity is important because it implies that policies might be differentially targeted, or tailored, to different types of welfare recipients who have different needs and capabilities.

The author would like to thank Irwin Garfinkel, Karl Scholz, and the other members of the Panel for comments, and Eva Sierminska for research assistance.

[1]Whether this will turn out to be the case is an empirical matter. The evidence to date is not so clear that women with greater labor market skill have necessarily left the rolls. See Cancian et al. (2000), Danziger (2000), Loprest and Zedlewski (1999), Moffitt and Stevens (2001), Oellerich (2001), and Zedlewski and Alderson (2001).

Heterogeneity is also important in current discussions of so-called welfare leavers—women who have left the welfare rolls subsequent to welfare reform. The employment and other outcomes of welfare leavers are likely to differ according to their labor market skill and background. Women with greater labor market skills may be expected to fare better off the rolls than women with weaker labor market skills, for example. The existing studies on welfare leavers typically report only average outcomes for all leavers and hence do not attempt to detect differences arising from heterogeneity, but such heterogeneity is certain to be present.[2] Heterogeneity among leavers is also important because it may lead to differences in average outcomes of leavers across states, for different states have different mixes of recipient types. Hence surveys of how leaver outcomes vary in different states may be reporting differences that arise from differences in the types of women on the rolls in different states rather than the effects of different state welfare policies. The types of women who are on welfare also vary over time as the caseload shrinks and expands, as well for cyclical reasons, and this will cause the average outcomes of leavers to vary over time as well, depending on what types of women exit the rolls at different points in the cycle. Thus, for example, leaver outcomes before and after 1996 may differ because of the business cycle rather than because of welfare reform.[3]

Heterogeneity in the caseload can be characterized in many ways. A straightforward approach is simply to examine the distributions of characteristics thought to be related to labor market skill, income-generating potential, and general coping capabilities. Examining the distribution of recipients by education, work experience, health status, drug use and illegal activity, and similar variables, are typical for such an exercise. Many studies have examined these differentials. Another approach is simply to examine the labor market outcomes of those who have left the rolls, but this is not appropriate if the object of the analysis is to develop measures of heterogeneity that might be correlated with, or possibly determine or predict, those labor market outcomes.

The approach taken in this chapter instead examines heterogeneity as measured by the recipient's own welfare experience (hence "experienced-based" measures of heterogeneity). The most important aspect of that experience is the amount of time the recipient has received welfare benefits, which is also a measure of the individual's degree of welfare "dependence." The most common measure of this type is the "total-time-on" measure, which denotes the total amount of time within a fixed calendar time interval that the individual has

---

[2]See Brauner and Loprest (1999) and Acs and Loprest (2001) for reviews. For studies that examined heterogeneity among leavers, see Cancian et al. (1999), Moffitt and Roff (2000), and Ver Ploeg (this volume).

[3]See Moffitt and Stevens (2001) for a study of how the types of women on welfare have varied over the business cycle in the past, and whether the change in the types of women on welfare after 1996 was different than what would have been expected from the effects of the economy alone.

received welfare. Such total-time-on measures are, arguably, the best single measure of welfare dependence and have been assessed many times.[4]

However, the concept of total-time-on does not distinguish between short spells and long spells, or between larger and smaller numbers of spells within a given total. Most analyses of the dynamics of welfare participation treat the length of spells as the most important building block for an understanding of welfare participation, and treat the exit rate from a spell—which is an indirect indication of its length—as a key variable to be affected by welfare reform. The issue that this view raises is whether it is important or useful to know how a given total-time-on divides up into a number of spells and lengths of those spells. It might be hypothesized, for example, that women with long spells might be more disadvantaged than women with short spells, even though the latter has a higher rate of movement on and off the rolls and hence ends up with the same total length of time on welfare.

A related concept introduced by Ellwood and Bane (1994:40-41) consists of a three-fold classification of welfare recipients, dividing them into long-termers, short-termers, and cyclers. The first group is composed of recipients with long spells of receipt and hence heavy dependence on welfare; the second group is composed of recipients who have short spells and are on welfare infrequently, leading to relatively mild dependence; and the third group consists of women who frequently move on and off the rolls and may, in the end, accumulate enough total time on welfare that they should be classified as welfare dependent even though their spells are fairly short on average.[5] This view, again, suggests that the types of women who have high turnover and short spells are different than those who have low turnover and long spells, even though they might have the same total-time-on.

The reason that one might expect differences among recipients with different turnover rates will be discussed in the text of this paper. Perhaps the simplest economic model is one that presumes that the rate of going off the rolls is positively related to the level of an individual's labor market skill and experience. In this view, long-termers have the weakest labor market skills, short-termers have the strongest, and cyclers are somewhere in between, with stronger labor market skills than long-termers but not strong enough to stay off the rolls for long periods.

This chapter examines data on women on the welfare rolls and tests whether their labor market skills differ in these ways. Tests for whether total-time-on is

---

[4]See, for example, Ellwood (1986), Ellwood and Bane (1994), and Gottschalk and Moffitt (1994a). The U.S. Department of Health and Human Services (2000) uses a total-time-on definition of welfare dependence as well.

[5]In some of their discussion, Ellwood and Bane (1994:40) suggest that cyclers are a subset of long-termers rather than constituting a parallel category. This is a slightly different definition of what is meant by a "long-termer," as will be discussed in this chapter.

correlated with labor market skill are conducted, as well as whether the number of spells and their length is related to labor market skill on top of the total-time-on. The characteristics of long-termers, short-termers, and cyclers are examined to determine if their labor market skills are ordered in the ranking suggested by the simple theory just described, or not. Data from the National Longitudinal Survey over the 1979-96 period, covering monthly AFDC participation experiences, are used for the analysis.

STATISTICAL MODEL, MODELS OF TURNOVER, AND HETEROGENEITY DEFINITIONS

Statistical Model

The determinants of total-time-on, the number of spells, and the length of spells—as well as whether a recipient should be considered to be a short-termer, long-termer, or cycler—follows from the statistical features of her underlying time profile of participation. That time profile is generated mathematically by a discrete-time statistical process. The building blocks of any such process (in this case, moving on and off welfare) are a pair of hazard rates $p[i|t,X(i),Z(i,t),H(i,t)]$ and $q[i|t,X(i),Z(i,t),H(i,t)]$ for the probability that individual i moves onto the rolls at time t conditional on being off at t-1 and the probability that individual i moves off the rolls at time t conditional on being on at t-1, respectively. Here $X(i)$ denotes time-invariant characteristics (such as family background at age 16 and race), $Z(i,t)$ denotes the entire history of exogenous events that affect welfare transitions (such as business cycle and illnesses), and $H(i,t)$ denotes the individual's entire history of welfare recipiency up through t-1. The variable t is taken literally to denote age, with t=0 at some initial age like 16. The probability functions p and q are taken over all unobservables in all time periods, consisting of all random events and shocks in the period prior to t. Thus we conceptualize all individuals as starting off at the same age, with certain fixed initial background characteristics, and then proceeding period by period through their lifetimes, moving on and off the rolls according to their individual-specific transition rates p and q. This constitutes a complete model of the process.

We will be interested in this chapter not in these structural transition rates, but rather in the distributions of welfare participation outcomes—that is, the types of patterns of participation that occur—that result from them over a particular calendar interval. Nevertheless, that different women have different patterns over such an interval necessarily arises from differences in the underlying hazards, and those hazards are a function of the variables denoted. A mutually exclusive categorization of all possible sources of heterogeneity in welfare patterns across women is the following: (1) heterogeneity in background characteristics, $X(i)$; (2) heterogeneity in the vector of current and past time-varying exogenous events that differ across individuals, $Z(i,t)$; and (3) heterogeneity in unobserved differences across individuals with the same $X(i)$ and $Z(i,t)$, both those which arise from different time-invariant unobserved characteristics (unobserved heterogeneity) as well as differences in current and past random shocks.[6] Thus any measure y of welfare participation patterns over a given calendar period from, say, t_0 and t_1–such as total time on welfare, number of spells, average spell lengths—can be written as $y(t_0,t_1)=f(X,Z,e)$, where X, Z, and e represent the three components just listed, over the interval from t_0 to t_1.[7] Given the function f, we can ask what types of mean characteristics are observed for women who have a particular welfare participation pattern y. Mathematically, we can write this as $E[X|y(t_0,t_1)]$, and analogously for Z.

We will focus our empirical study below on X rather than Z. That is, we will examine the fixed, time-invariant characteristics (such as race, education, and average earnings and wages) of women with different welfare participation patterns. We will not examine time-varying characteristics, despite the fact that they presumably are important in explaining period-specific reasons for transitioning on and off the welfare rolls.

Models of Turnover

Given our interest in understanding why women with different labor market potential come to have different participation profiles, it is helpful to consider some alternative, stylized models of welfare turnover to fix ideas and establish intuition. One simple economic model presumes that the main reason for movement on and off welfare is fluctuation in job opportunities, as proxied by the level of earnings one can obtain off welfare. Because different women have different levels of labor market skill, they will have different quasi-permanent, mean earnings levels. Hence the existence of earnings fluctuations around each individual mean will lead to more movements on and off the rolls for those with mean earnings close to the cutoff point for leaving or entering the rolls than for those with mean earnings farther away from that cutoff, assuming that the variance of the fluctuations is the same for all. This simple model would lead to the presumption that short-termers have the highest labor market skill, with mean earnings sufficiently high that only significant negative earnings declines result in participation; long-termers have the lowest labor market skill, with mean earnings sufficiently low that only significantly positive earnings increases lead to an exit

---

[6]We do not list $H(i,t)$ as a source of heterogeneity because, at any point in time, it arises completely from the other three exogenous factors we have listed. There will be no need to distinguish between state dependence and heterogeneity here, given the goals of the analysis. Furthermore, we ignore initial conditions problems because the data will allow us to observe all women reasonably close to t=0, the start of the process.

[7]The initial conditions at t_0 also must be included but, as noted previously, the data will start reasonably close to $t_0=0$, so no conditioning is necessary.

from welfare; and cyclers have labor market skill in between, with mean earnings closest to the margin so that many modest fluctuations in earnings lead to entry or exit from the welfare rolls. This is the framework mentioned in the Introduction.[8]

A variant on this model, popular in some of the economics literature, holds that more time on welfare reduces the mean level of skill because women historically have not worked while on welfare, for the most part, and their labor market skills deteriorate.[9] The key issue for present purposes is whether it is time spent in the current spell, or in total over all past spells, that causes skills to deteriorate. If only total-time-on causes such deterioration, we should find that labor market skill—even though it is partly a result, not a cause, of welfare participation— should be negatively related to an individual's amount of total-time-on but not to turnover or spell lengths, holding total-time-on fixed.

A different model is one in which different individuals experience different degrees of fluctuation in earnings (i.e., different variances). In this case, it is possible that individuals with the same quasi-permanent, mean earnings will have different turnover rates, spell lengths, and total-time-on depending on the variance of their earnings. High-variance individuals will have the greatest turnover rates, for example. In this extreme model, one may find no differences in labor market skill among those with different amounts of turnover, unlike the first model we described.

One may ask why different individuals would have different variances of earnings. One possibility is that some individuals search harder for jobs because they have a stronger desire to leave welfare, but because their permanent skill levels are not very high, they can never succeed in achieving more than a temporary period of employment off the rolls. Another possibility is that some recipients have more turbulent personal lives (possibly including domestic violence or substance abuse, for example), have worse physical or mental health conditions that are episodic in their severity, or have other types of experiences that create instability and hence an inability to sustain a fixed status either on or off welfare.

A third model is one in which individuals differ both in their mean earnings and in their degrees of earnings instability, and the two are either positively or negatively correlated. Although a positive correlation is possible, it seems equally

---

[8]Mathematically, let $y(i,t) = m(i) + e(i,t)$, where $y(i,t)$ is earnings for individual i at time t, $m(i)$ is permanent earnings, and $e(i,t)$ is per-period transitory earnings. Assume that an individual goes off welfare in any period t if $y(i,t)>b$, the welfare benefit. If $e(i,t)$ has the same variance for all individuals but individuals differ in their level of $m(i)$, then the rate of turnover of an individual will be directly proportional to how close $m(i)$ is to b. Both those with very low $m(i)$ (relative to b) and those with very high $m(i)$ will have low turnover rates, while those with $m(i)$ close to b will have high turnover rates.

[9]Some argue that more time on welfare also increases the perception by employers that an individual has low job skills.

possible that they could be negatively correlated. That is, it is possible that those with the lowest labor market skills have the greatest degrees of instability as well.[10] Perhaps those with the lowest labor market skills are from the most disadvantaged family and neighborhood backgrounds where instability is high. Indeed, high levels of instability could lead to lack of investment in education and poor labor market experience and skills later. The implications of a negative correlation for how labor market skill is related to turnover are unclear, for high earnings instability should lead to high welfare turnover but low labor market skill leads to the opposite. Therefore, it is ambiguous in this model whether those with high welfare turnover will be revealed, on average, to have higher or lower labor market skill than those with low turnover.

A fourth and final model is one in which noneconomic considerations play a larger role in welfare turnover, unlike the models so far that tie welfare participation decisions closely to earnings levels. Noneconomic events like marriage, divorce, childbearing, and changes in personal situation, all can affect welfare turnover rates. Turnover also can be directly affected by welfare administration, through a process known as "administrative churning," which refers to frequent starts and stops in benefit payments because of temporary denials of eligibility, errors or delays in processing, or skipped payments for some other reason. Whatever the noneconomic cause of welfare turnover, the issue at hand is how each cause is related to labor market skill and mean earnings off welfare. This cannot be predicted in general, and hence leads to another source of possible ambiguity.

Heterogeneity Measures and Definitions

We will be interested in three summary statistics that describe an individual's welfare participation experiences over a fixed calendar interval:

(1) The total number of periods the individual is on welfare in the interval (T);
(2) The total number of welfare "spells" experienced by the individual within the interval (N); and
(3) The average length of these "spells" (L).

The first of these is the total-time-on measure mentioned previously. The second counts the number of separate welfare "spells" in the interval, where a welfare "spell" is defined as a sequence of consecutive periods on welfare. This is a measure of turnover, for it is closely related to the number of transitions on or off welfare that are experienced in the calendar interval. It should be noted that, here,

---

[10]Gottschalk and Moffitt (1994b:Table 1), indeed, found that the individual-specific level of permanent earnings is negatively correlated with the variance of earnings around that level.

a spell can be in progress at the beginning of the calendar interval or in progress at the end and still be counted as a spell. The third measure is the average length of these spells. Given these definitions, $T=N*L$. Consequently, any two of these measures for any individual determines the third.[11]

In addition to measuring T, N, and L themselves, we also define three combinations of these variables that together define long-termers, short-termers, and cyclers, the classification scheme proposed by Bane and Ellwood. The definitions we use are:

Long-termers:	$N < a$	and	$L > b$
Short-termers:	$N < a$	and	$L < b$
Cyclers:	$N > a$		

where "a" and "b" are some constants to be selected after an initial examination of the data, and which will be varied as part of a sensitivity analysis. Thus long-termers are defined as having relatively few spells but spells with long average lengths; short-termers are also defined as having relatively few spells but as having short average lengths; and cyclers are defined simply as those with a relatively high number of spells, regardless of their lengths (but, for a fixed interval length $[t_0,t_1]$, a high number of spells must necessarily ultimately lead to shorter average lengths).

Note that these groups are defined solely on the basis of N and L, not T. The total-time-on surely will be high for long-termers and surely will be low for short-termers, given the definitions provided, but whether T will be high or low (by some definition of those terms) for cyclers is ambiguous. There is no clear definition of these groups in the literature, so it is unclear whether this approach to the definition is the same or different as that used by others. Certainly some appear to use the term "long-termer" to refer to women who have high T per se, regardless of whether they have such a high T because of a small number of long spells or a large number of short spells (thereby using the word "long" to refer to the magnitude of total-time-on, not the length of spells).[12] In part this is just a

---

[11]The inclusion of both left-censored and right-censored spells, and the counting of their lengths as the lengths of a spell, is appropriate in the application here because such a spell concept is the appropriate one for a decomposition of a total-time-on measure defined over a fixed calendar interval. The only danger is that, because censored spells will be shorter than their completed counterparts, there will be an undercount of individuals with long completed spells. To the extent that the labor market skill measures that will be the main focus of our analysis are more weakly correlated with these censored spell lengths than their uncensored counterparts, our correlations of spell length with skill will be weakened. However, as we shall describe, our calendar interval is 10 years long and hence there are few censored spells relative to the total number of spells.

[12]As noted in the Introduction, Bane and Ellwood in some passages suggest that long-termers are those with high total-time-on, for example.

terminological matter, but defining "long-termer" in this way does have unsatisfactory aspects. It leaves as undefined women who have large numbers of spells but a modest level of T, for example, who do not fall into any category. Moreover, the literal interpretation of the verb "to cycle" implies a definition based purely on turnover rates and numbers of spells, not a total-time-on definition; hence it makes more sense in terms of language to let T be an outcome of a turnover definition of cycling, not as a definitional characteristic. One could stick with a T-defined classification scheme by parceling out cyclers to the long-termer and short-termer groups by saying that there are two types of cyclers—those with high T, whom we will call long-termers, and those with modest T, who will be called short-termers. But in this case, the latter group is lumped in with the more conventional short-termers with low turnover rates. The consequence would be that one would move from a definitional scheme that allows cyclers to be a heterogeneous group to one that allows long-termers and short-termers to each be heterogeneous, which would not appear to be a gain in terms of clarity. Alternatively, one could move to a classification scheme that has more than three groups, but then simplicity begins to be lost.

For all these reasons, we will use the three-fold classification based solely on N and L. However, we will examine the heterogeneity of the cycler group by examining their distributions of T and compare the different subgroups of cyclers so defined to short-termers and long-termers.

Past Work

There is surprisingly little evidence in the literature on the characteristics of individuals with different turnover rates and overall spell patterns, or on how groups of individuals defined by long-termer, short-termer, and cycler status differ by characteristics. The vast majority of studies of welfare dynamics present estimates of the determinants of exit from welfare spells or entry onto welfare or, sometimes, of rates of reentry onto welfare after an exit. These econometric models are not set up to distinguish the determinants of turnover per se from the determinants of total-time-on because they impose a restrictive relationship between the effects of the independent variables on turnover rates, total-time-on, and spell lengths. For example, it would not be possible in these models to find that some variable for labor market potential (e.g., mean potential earnings off welfare) could differ between short-termers and cyclers but not between cyclers and long-termers, to take one case. To distinguish these, a more sophisticated statistical specification would be required. Alternatively, and as a first step, it is more natural to simply examine the characteristics of individual recipients as ranked by their turnover rates, total-time-on, and spell lengths, or by their classification into short-termers, long-termers, or cyclers, as is done in this chapter.

A few recent studies have already attempted this, however. Stevens (2000:Table 4), in a study using administrative data from Maryland, found earnings of AFDC long-termers and cyclers to be not very different for white women. But cyclers had higher earnings than long-termers among the population of black women. In a study using administrative data from Wisconsin, Ver Ploeg (this volume: Table 13-5) examined employment rates of individuals on Temporary Assistance for Needy Families (TANF) and found them to be higher for cyclers than for long-termers. Cancian et al. (1999) also provided evidence on how leaver outcomes in Wisconsin vary with the amount of previous time on welfare.[13]

DATA AND RESULTS ON SPELL DISTRIBUTIONS

The data set used for the exercise is the 1979 National Longitudinal Survey of Youth, which is a nationally representative set of individuals who were 14 to 21 in 1979 and who were interviewed annually up to 1994 and biannually since then. We utilize the survey through the 1996 interview, which gives us a maximum of 18 years of data.[14] We select only women, given our interest in welfare participation. We focus on a 10-year period of each woman's life, from ages 20 to 29. We could examine the entire 18 years, but such a time period is so long that women might not be easily characterized as long-termers, short-termers, or cyclers for the entire period; they easily could have been long-termers for the first 10 years and cyclers for the second 8 years, for example. The shorter, 10-year time period is less likely to capture multiple stages in the life cycle where welfare participation behavior is markedly different.[15] The data give us monthly AFDC participation information (only receipt of AFDC benefits is examined, not other welfare programs), thereby providing us with $10*12=120$ months of observations with which to construct our measures of welfare experience. We have 2,763 women in our sample, 514 of whom experienced at least one month of AFDC receipt from ages 20 to 29.[16]

---

[13]A difference in the Ver Ploeg and Cancian studies, on the one hand, and the Stevens study and this study, on the other, is that the former were point-in-time samples composed of families on the rolls at a point in time, whereas this study and that by Stevens contain all women ever on welfare in a 10-year period. The former studies will omit short-term spells not in progress at the point in time at which the sample is drawn.

[14]The interviews gathered information on AFDC recipiency for the year prior to interview in a list format prior to 1993 and in an event-history format in 1993 and after, the latter format providing the start and end dates of all spells since the last interview. The calendar period for which recipiency is available is therefore January 1978 through the 1996 interview date. We use only 1978-95 calendar years.

[15]Despite this, all tables in this chapter were also estimated over the entire 18 years of data. With that longer period, there are a substantially greater number of cyclers than reported, and average spell lengths of long-termers are shorter. However, none of the critical results on the differences in labor market characteristics by T, N, L, and long-termer/short-termer/cycler status reported are different.

[16]We exclude women who have missing data for any of the 120 months (276 women are excluded for this reason).

Figure 14-1 shows the distribution of T in the sample for the 514 women with at least one month of receipt. About 81 percent of the population had no months of receipt—the exact numbers are given in Table 14-A1.[17] The distribution of total months of receipt declines with the number of months on welfare, on average, as is typical of these types of distributions. About one fifth (19 percent) received AFDC for only 1 to 6 months in the 10-year period; but, on the other hand, 9 percent received benefits for 8 or more years. The mean and median number of months of benefit receipt are 39 and 28, respectively.

Figure 14-2 shows how these T distributions differ for those with different numbers of spells over the period.[18] Not surprisingly, the distributions are shifted to the right for those with larger numbers of spells. The median T for those with one, two, or three spells are 12, 47, and 47, respectively.

Figures 14-3 and 14-4 show the distributions of N and L, respectively.[19] Of those ever on AFDC over the 10 years, about 48 percent had only one spell of receipt. The distribution rapidly declines and, in fact, there are relatively few women who had large numbers of spells in these data: Slightly more than 8 percent had four or more spells and only 2 percent had five or more spells. A 10-year period is a long time and offers the possibility of many more spells than this. Thus, even at this relatively young age, the sample shows relatively little turnover.[20]

Figure 14-4 shows that most recipients have relatively short spells: One-quarter had average spells on AFDC of shorter than 6 months, and 57 percent had average spells of 18 months or shorter. However, this distribution has a long right-hand tail, and a significant number of women have long average spell lengths. Nearly another 20 percent of the sample, for example, had average spells of 3 or more years in length (37 months and over). This skewness is reflected in the marked difference in the mean and median spell length (24 versus 15). Table 14-A3 shows how these average spell lengths differ by the number of spells in the period. Interestingly, those with larger numbers of spells tend to have larger numbers of medium spell lengths, but smaller numbers of both long and short spells. That those with many spells are less likely to have long spells is expected, but that they also have fewer shorter spells (1-6 months) is not. This suggests that those with greater number of spells—cyclers—may have greater welfare dependency than what might have been thought otherwise, a suggestion that will come up again in subsequent tables.

---

[17]The Appendix to this chapter is comprised of four tables with auxiliary data that will be referred to throughout the chapter.

[18]Exact figures are given in Table 14-A1.

[19]Exact figures are given in Tables 14-A2 and 14-A3. As noted in the last section, left-censored and right-censored spells are included as "spells" in these tabulations. However, only 3.4 percent of the sample was on AFDC in the first month of age 20 and only 2.6 percent were on in the last month of age 29.

[20]Administrative data may show more turnover because of administrative churning.

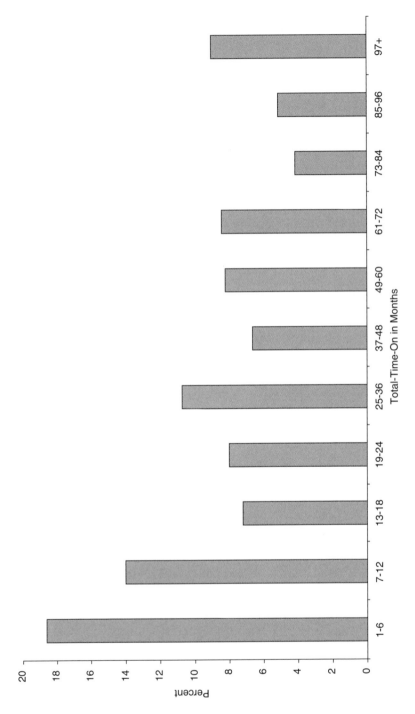

FIGURE 14-1 Distribution of total-time-on in months (T).

485

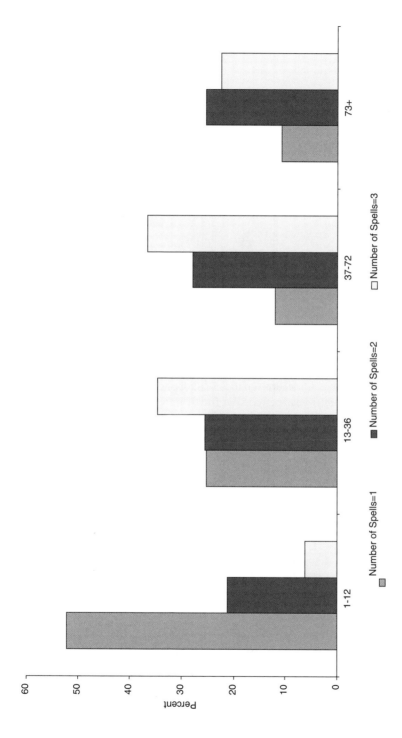

FIGURE 14-2 Distribution of total-time-on in months by number of spells.

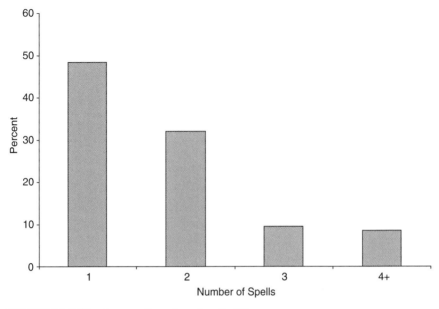

FIGURE 14-3 Distribution of number of spells (N).

Table 14-1 shows the characteristics of those women never on AFDC and those ever on in the 10-year period. We focus, in this table and all subsequent tables, on only a few fixed, unchanging background characteristics of individuals. These include education and race, but also employment status (whether worked at all during a year), annual earnings, weekly wages, and hourly wage rates, all measured only over periods off AFDC. The earnings and wages are measured only over periods off AFDC because they are intended to represent earning capability; including the AFDC periods would bias the measures in this sense, for earnings and wages are always lower on welfare than off.[21] In traditional economic analyses, an individual's potential hourly wage and weekly wage are usually considered to be the best indicators of labor market skill. Table 14-1 shows, as expected, that those ever on welfare have lower levels of education, are more likely black or Hispanic, and have lower mean earnings and wages than those never on welfare. Mean earnings and wages are, in addition, extremely low

---

[21]Because earnings and wages are measured only annually, the measures are all computed only over those years when the woman was not on AFDC at all (because otherwise, some of the earnings and wages might have been earned while on AFDC). For each woman, her mean employment (whether worked at all in the year), annual earnings, weekly wages, and hourly earnings are computed for each year she is off AFDC, then averaged to obtain a mean for her non-AFDC periods. The figures in Table 14-1 represent the means of these figures, taken over all women in the sample.

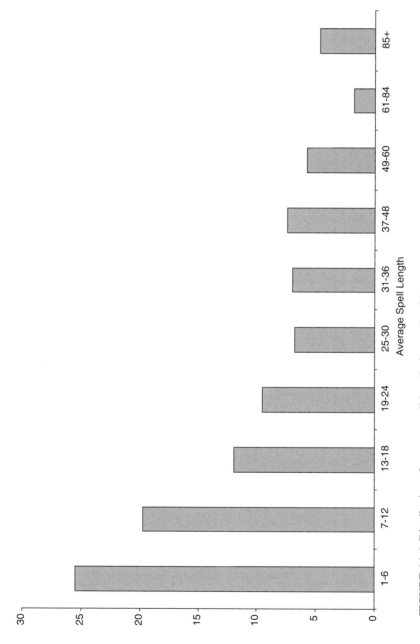

FIGURE 14-4 Distribution of average spell lengths in months (L).

TABLE 14-1 Characteristics of Population, by Welfare Recipiency Status

	Never On	Ever On
Education		
1979	10.7	9.7
1996	13.7	11.8
Race		
Non-Hispanic white	0.85	0.59
Non-Hispanic black	0.09	0.30
Hispanic	0.06	0.11
Employment rate off AFDC	0.98	0.86
Average annual earnings off AFDC (including zeroes)	$11,698	$5,179
Average annual earnings off AFDC (excluding zeroes)	$11,940	$5,997
Average weekly earnings (excluding zeroes)	$293	$193
Average hourly wage (workers only)	$7.95	$5.50

NOTE: Monetary figures are in real 1992 dollars.

in absolute terms for those women who have been on welfare in other periods. On the other hand, annual employment rates are moderately high (66 percent), on average—women work about two-thirds of the time that they are off AFDC.

Table 14-2 shows how these characteristics vary with T, N, and L. The variation in the characteristics with all three variables goes in the expected direction: Those with greater dependence, more spells, and longer average spell lengths tend to have lower levels of education, are more likely black (but not Hispanic), and have lower employment rates, earnings, and wages. A key additional question is whether there is any variation in characteristics by N and L, holding T fixed. We will consider this question using regression analysis.

LONG-TERMERS, SHORT-TERMERS, AND CYCLERS

Table 14-3 shows information from a classification of the population into the three groups discussed earlier—long-termers, short-termers, and cyclers. In all cases cyclers are defined as those with three or more spells. Any other cutoff would include either a much larger fraction of the sample in the cycler category or a much smaller fraction (see Figure 14-2 and Table 14-A2). Long-termers and short-termers are those with one or two spells, and with average spell lengths of half a year, a year, or a year and a half in length, depending on the definition.[22]

---

[22]Note that, in this classification, short-termers could have higher T than long-termers if a recipient in the former category has two spells and a recipient in the latter group has only one. This illustrates, once again, that this typology is not perfectly correlated with T (nor should it be, by concept, as discussed earlier). Nevertheless, despite this possibility, long-termers will be seen to have much larger T than short-termers on average.

TABLE 14-2 Characteristics of Population, by Time on Welfare and Spell Characteristics

	Total-Time-On (T)			Number of Spells (N)			Average Spell Lengths (L)		
	1-12 Months	13-60 Months	61-120 Months	1	2	3+	1-6	7-24	25+
Education									
1979	9.9	9.7	9.6	9.7	9.8	9.8	9.8	9.8	9.6
1996	12.1	11.7	11.6	11.9	11.6	11.8	12.0	11.9	11.6
Race									
Non-Hispanic white	0.71	0.59	0.43	.60	.59	.54	.77	.58	.45
Non-Hispanic black	0.21	0.27	0.47	.29	.32	.34	.15	.31	.42
Hispanic	0.08	0.14	0.10	.12	.09	.12	.08	.11	.12
Employment rate off AFDC	0.74	0.65	0.55	.65	.65	.65	.76	.67	.57
Average annual earnings off AFDC (including zeroes)	$6,672	$5,125	$2,911	$5,795	$5,066	$3,834	$6,360	$5,386	$3,811
Average annual earnings off AFDC (excluding zeroes)	$7,010	$5,794	$4,942	$6,484	$5,999	$4,641	$6,616	$6,156	$4,998
Average weekly earnings (excluding zeroes)	$210	$193	$155	$209	$186	$160	$205	$192	$179
Average hourly wage (workers only)	$5.80	$5.65	$4.41	$5.92	$5.43	$4.42	$5.52	$5.59	$5.30

NOTE: Monetary figures are in real 1992 dollars.

TABLE 14-3 Long-termer, Short-termer, and Cycler Distributions by Alternative Definitions (percent distribution)

	Definition 1[a]	Definition 2[b]	Definition 3[c]
Long-termer	57.6	43.8	36.8
Short-termer	23.0	36.8	43.8
Cycler	19.5	19.5	19.5
Total	100.0	100.0	100.0

NOTE: Numbers are rounded off, therefore totals will not add up to 100.
   [a]Definition 1: a=2 spells, b=6 months.
   [b]Definition 2: a=2 spells, b=12 months.
   [c]Definition 3: a=2 spells, b=18 months.

These classifications result in approximately one-fifth of the ever-on population assigned as cyclers, and more than one-third assigned to long-term status (from one-third to as high as 57 percent). Short-termers end up with a representation slightly above or slightly below one-third. Thus the division is not quite equal across the three groups, but deviates from an equal division only through a somewhat greater-than-one-third long-termer group and smaller-than-one-third cycler group. The percent of the population classified as long-termers may seem high, even for the 1.5-year spell definition, where more than one-third of ever-on recipients are so classified.[23] However, it should be noted that there have been no previous calculations of these distributions in the literature, and hence it is difficult to find comparisons in past work.[24] Still, a smaller fraction of long-termers clearly could be obtained by requiring longer average spell lengths than 1.5 years, but at the cost of including as short-termers those with such long average spell lengths; and a 1.5-year spell does not seem to fit the notion of a short-termer. These issues illustrate the problems with constraining the classification to only three categories, and there is clearly some arbitrariness involved in where to draw the various lines.

Figure 14-5 shows the distribution of T for each of the three groups, using Definition 2.[25] Short-termers are concentrated among the lowest values of total-time-on, as expected. However, the distributions for long-termers and cyclers are more mixed. Although long-termers are more commonly observed to have very

---

[23]This implies that an even larger percentage of the point-in-time caseload would be long-termers.

[24]See Stevens (2000) and Ver Ploeg (this volume: Chapter 3) for exceptions. Using Maryland administrative data, Stevens estimated a smaller fraction of cyclers (about 20 percent) and a larger fraction of short-termers (50 percent), but about the same fraction of long-termers (30 percent). Using Wisconsin data, Ver Ploeg finds that cyclers constitute 14 percent of the caseload, while long-termers constitute 55 percent and short-termers constitute 31 percent.

[25]Exact figures are given in Table 14-A4 as are the figures for Definitions 1 and 3.

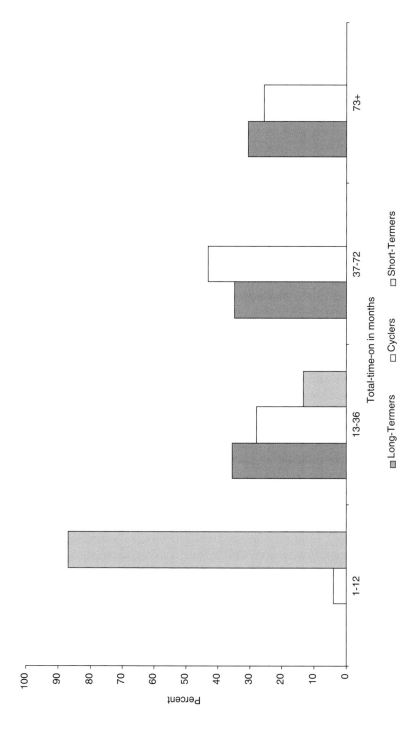

FIGURE 14-5 Distribution of total-time-on among long-termers, cyclers, and short-termers.

long total-time-on (e.g., 21 percent have more than 6 years of receipt in the 10-year period), cyclers are more likely to have total-time-on in the 3-to-5 year range. The differences are greater for Definition 3, that which defines long-termers as having longer average spells, where 37 percent have T greater than 6 years and 40 percent have T in the 3-to-5 year range (see Table 14-A4). However, despite these differences in the tails of the distribution, the median T is 56 months for cyclers and only 52 months for long-termers using Definition 2. The lower median T for long-termers reflects the fact that many long-termers by this type of definition have only a single spell that is below average in length and hence are on welfare for a shorter period in total than many cyclers, who, with three spells at minimum, commonly build up more total-time-on. However, for Definition 3, the median T for long-termers is 60 months, longer than that of cyclers. Still, the most appropriate conclusion from these calculations is that the typical experience of long-termers and cyclers in terms of total-time-on is not greatly different. Long-termers include more women with long total-time-on and more women with shorter total-time-on than cyclers, but on average they are not far different.[26]

Table 14-4 shows the characteristics of the three groups using Definition 2. As expected, short-termers are better off than long-termers and all cyclers in virtually every dimension. However, the table reveals that cyclers are also worse off than long-termers in nearly every labor market potential as well. Although the educational and racial distributions are approximately the same, and while employment rates off AFDC for long-termers are indeed somewhat lower than those for cyclers, cyclers have lower annual earnings, weekly earnings, and hourly wages than long-termers. This result is quite surprising in light of the conventional wisdom in the literature based on the model discussed earlier in the paper, which assumes that cyclers are somewhat better off than long-termers by virtue of having sufficiently greater earning power to leave the welfare rolls periodically to enter the labor market. A major conclusion of this chapter is the rejection of that model.

Because the cycler definition used here does not require T to be large (although, as noted, median T is about the same for cyclers and long-termers), the last two columns of Table 14-4 show the characteristics of cyclers with low T and high T.[27] Even the "better off" women among the cyclers—those with lower values of T—are substantially worse off than long-termers in earnings and wages. Hourly wages of these cyclers are $4.81 compared to $5.66 for long-termers, with similarly sized differences for unconditional earnings, conditional earnings, and

---

[26]See Table 14-A4. Cyclers have much shorter mean and median spell lengths than long-termers, as expected.

[27]The T cutoff was chosen to divide the cycler sample in half, that is, the approximate median T was used.

TABLE 14-4 Characteristics of Long-termers, Short-termers, and Cyclers

	Long-termers	Short-termers	Cyclers[a]		
			All	Low T	High T
Education					
1979	9.6	9.9	9.8	10.1	9.5
1996	11.6	12.1	11.8	11.9	11.7
Race					
Non-Hispanic white	0.51	0.70	0.54	0.65	0.44
Non-Hispanic black	0.36	0.22	0.34	0.23	0.44
Hispanic	0.12	0.08	0.12	0.13	0.12
Employment rate off AFDC	0.59	0.75	0.65	0.70	0.60
Average annual earnings off AFDC (including zeroes)	$4,976	$6,715	$3,649	$4,393	$2,539
Average annual earnings off AFDC (excluding zeroes)	$5,574	$7,055	$4,427	$4,802	$3,522
Average weekly earnings (excluding zeroes)	$192	$20	$157	$174	$125
Average hourly wage (workers only)	$5.66	$5,80	$4.34	$4.81	$3.45

NOTES: Monetary figures are in real 1992 dollars. Definition 2 used.

[a]Low T = 55 months total-time-on or less; High T = 56 months total-time-on or more.

weekly wages. In addition, the "worse off" cyclers are even worse off compared to long-termers than was true on average, necessarily. These results do not provide any evidence that there is a significantly better off subgroup of cyclers that is distorting their average representation. Instead, it appears that cyclers, like long-termers or perhaps even more than long-termers, are generally a very disadvantaged group as a whole.

Using Definition 3 instead of Definition 2, which applies a more stringent definition of long-termer, results in worsened characteristics of long-termers and hence a smaller gap between that group and cyclers. For example, mean wages of long-termers under Definition 3 are $5.31 and weekly earnings are $182. An even more stringent definition that included only long-termers with extremely long spells would no doubt result in worsened outcomes. Nevertheless, the same is true of cyclers, as already illustrated in the last column of Table 14-4. Moreover, even though the minimum spell length for long-termers used in Definitions 1, 2, and 3 is not large, the median and mean spell lengths are still in the range of 2- to 4 years (see Table 14-A4); so long-termers by these definitions typically indeed have very long spells. For all these reasons, it does not appear that any reasonable definition is likely to change the direction of differences in characteristics between long-termers and cyclers that has been found here.[28]

REGRESSION RESULTS

The final question of the chapter is whether characteristics of AFDC recipients vary significantly by N or L, holding T fixed—that is, those with high or low turnover differ in their characteristics if they have the same total-time-on—and whether the differences we have noted between short-termers, long-termers, and cyclers are statistically significant.

Table 14-5 shows the results. Each of the four key labor market characteristics—the employment rate, annual earnings, weekly wages, and the hourly wage, all measured only over periods off AFDC—is regressed, in the first case, on T and N, or on T and L (all three are not included in the same equation because they are definitionally related to each other) and, in the second case, on dummies for long-term and short-term status, with the cycler group omitted. The regressions involving T, N, and L show that T is a strong and statistically significant determinant of labor market characteristics, in the expected direction (higher T is associated with lower employment rates, earnings, and wages). However, the coefficients on N and L are mixed in their significance and their sign. Greater N and lower L are significantly correlated with higher employment rates off AFDC but lower wage rates. They are insignificantly related to earnings, which is the product of employment and wage rates, no doubt because the two operate in opposite directions and cancel out. The more appropriate indicators of earnings potential are the wage rate effects, and here the results change the impression taken from Table 14-2 that those with longer spells have lower wage rates; controlling for total-time-on, they have higher wage rates, an unexpected finding.

The regressions containing long-termer and short-termer dummies show that short-termers are always significantly better off than either long-termers or cyclers, as expected, but that long-termers and cyclers are not always statistically different and not always in the same direction. Again, long-termers appear to have slightly lower employment rates than cyclers (about 6 percentage points), insignificantly different earnings, but higher weekly and hourly wage rates. In fact, these results directly reflect the means shown in Table 14-4, but the regressions indicate statistical significance levels.

These findings show that the value of an individual's total-time-on, and whether she is or not a short-termer, are the most consistent predictors of labor market potential. The degree of turnover and whether a woman is a cycler or a long-termer are less consistently correlated with labor market performance.

---

[28]It is possible that selection bias is at work and that those long-termers who are observed to have worked have above-average wages. However, the employment rates of the two groups are not far different, suggesting that this justification is unlikely to be a major source of the explanation.

TABLE 14-5 Regressions of Labor Market Characteristics on Welfare Participation Indicators

	Employment Rate[a]			Annual Earnings (including zeroes)			Weekly Wages			Hourly Wages		
T	-.348*	-.173*	—	-48.0*	-53.1*	—	-.578*	-1.35*	—	-.012*	-.038*	—
	(.056)	(.083)		(8.4)	(12.6)		(.221)	(.32)		(.006)	(.009)	
N	2.94*	—	—	-169.7	—	—	-11.9	—	—	-.347*	—	—
	(1.45)			(219.5)			(5.14)			(.141)		
L	—	-.247*	—	—	5.2	—	—	1.13*	—	—	.039*	—
		(.119)			(18.0)			(.47)			(.013)	
LT	—	—	-6.16	—	—	768.3	—	—	35.6*	—	—	1.24*
			(4.37)			(656.6)			(15.5)			(.43)
ST	—	—	9.36*	—	—	3061.*	—	—	51.8*	—	—	1.38*
			(4.41)			(662)			(15.2)			(.41)

NOTES: All labor market characteristics measured over periods not on AFDC.

n = 514.

Standard errors in parentheses.

*: significant at the 10-percent level.

T = total-time-on; N = number of spells; L = average spell length; LT = dummy for long-termer, Definition 2;

ST = dummy for short-termer, Definition 2.

[a]All coefficients multiplied by 100.

Moreover, when they are, they indicate that cyclers are worse off than long-termers in terms of earnings potential, and no better off than long-termers in terms of overall earnings.

SUMMARY AND CONCLUSIONS

This chapter has explored measures of heterogeneity of the AFDC caseload in the 1980s and early 1990s based on patterns of AFDC participation and has investigated which of those measures are predictive of labor market potential and a few other sociodemographic characteristics. The analysis shows that the single most consistent predictor of those characteristics is the total amount of time a woman has been on welfare. However, whether that time arises from a larger number of shorter spells, or a smaller number of longer spells, is less consistently important; that is, neither turnover per se nor the length of individual spells of welfare receipt is always related to labor market characteristics holding constant the total time the individual has been on welfare. Relatedly, the analysis shows that classifying recipients into two groups is a useful predictor of labor market potential: short-termers who participate in welfare only occasionally and for short periods, and all others. However, among the latter group, whether an individual is a cycler who moves on and off the rolls frequently or a long-termer who has long, uninterrupted periods of welfare receipt, is not a consistent predictor of labor market potential. Further, when it is, it appears that cyclers have lower potential than long-termers.

The finding that mobility per se matters less than expected, and that recipients with high turnover and those with low turnover (but with the same total-time-on) either look the same or differ in unexpected ways, runs contrary to the conventional model in which mobility is taken as a sign of higher-than-average labor market skill and hence earnings potential. It suggests that there must be some other reason for high rates of mobility, perhaps related to more intrinsic, possibly noneconomic, sources of instability in individuals' lives, or in administrative practices that cause churning, or related to some other factor. More investigation into this question would be a fruitful area of future research.

For welfare reform studies, the implication of the analysis is that heterogeneity is important but that its most important measure is the total time a recipient has been on welfare. This suggests that studies which estimate the impact of welfare reform should do so separately for groups with different amounts of total-time-on, and should break out short-term recipients from others. Leaver studies are one type of welfare reform research that could benefit from a separation of leaver outcomes by such characteristics.

REFERENCES

Acs, G., and P. Loprest
  2001   *Initial Synthesis Report of the Findings from ASPE's "Leavers" Grants.* Washington, DC: Urban Institute.
Brauner, S., and P. Loprest
  1999   Where Are They Now? What States' Studies of Welfare Leavers Tell Us. Working Paper A-32. Washington, DC: Urban Institute.
Cancian, M., R. Haveman, T. Kaplan, and B. Wolfe
  1999   *Post-Exit Earnings and Benefit Receipt Among Those Who Left AFDC in Wisconsin.* Special Report #75. Madison: Institute for Research on Poverty, University of Wisconsin.
Cancian, M., R. Haveman, D. Meyer, and B. Wolfe
  2000   *Before and After TANF: The Economic Well-Being of Women Leaving Welfare.* Special Report #77. Madison: Institute for Research on Poverty, University of Wisconsin.
Danziger, S.
  2000   Approaching the Limit: Early Lessons from Welfare Reform. Unpublished paper presented at the conference on Rural Dimensions of Welfare Reform, Joint Center on Poverty Research, Washington, DC, May 4-5.
Ellwood, D.
  1986   *Targeting the "Would-Be" Long-Term Recipient: Who Should Be Served?* Princeton, NJ: Mathematica Policy Research.
Ellwood, D., and M.J. Bane
  1994   Understanding welfare dynamics. In *Welfare Realities: From Rhetoric to Reform*, M.J. Bane and D. Ellwood, eds. Cambridge, MA: Harvard University Press.
Gottschalk, P., and R. Moffitt
  1994a   Welfare dependence: Concepts, measures, and trends. *American Economic Review* 84:38-42.
  1994b   The growth of earnings instability in the U.S. labor market. *Brookings Papers on Economic Activity* 2:217-254.
Loprest, P., and S. Zedlewski
  1999   *Current and Former Welfare Recipients: How Do They Differ?* DP 99-17. Washington, DC: Urban Institute.
Moffitt, R., and J. Roff
  2000   *The Diversity of Welfare Leavers.* Baltimore: Johns Hopkins University.
Moffitt, R., and D. Stevens
  2001   Changing Caseloads: Macro and Micro Composition. *Economic Policy Review* 7:37-51.
Oellerich, D.
  2001   Welfare Reform: Program Entrants and Recipients. Unpublished paper. Washington, DC: U.S. Department of Health and Human Services.
Stevens, D.
  2000   Welfare, Employment and Earnings: Memorandum prepared for the Panel on Data and Methods for Measuring the Effects of Changes in Social Programs, Committee on National Statistics. University of Baltimore, MD.
U.S. Department of Health and Human Services
  2000   *Indicators of Welfare Dependence: Annual Report to Congress.* Washington, DC: U.S. Department of Health and Human Services.
Zedlewski, S., and D. Alderson
  2001   Do Families on Welfare in the Post-TANF Era Differ from Their Pre-TANF Counterparts? WP 01-03. Washington, DC: Urban Institute.

APPENDIX 14-A

AUXILIARY TABLES

TABLE 14-A1 Distribution of Total-Time-On in Months (T) (percent distribution)

		Ever On			
			No. Spells (N)		
	All	All	1	2	3
0	80.8	–	–	–	–
1-6	4.0	18.6	32.1	9.1	2.0
7-12	2.7	14.0	20.1	12.1	4.1
13-18	1.4	7.2	7.2	8.5	2.0
19-24	1.5	8.0	9.2	5.5	10.2
25-36	2.1	10.7	8.8	11.5	22.4
37-48	1.3	6.6	5.6	5.5	12.2
49-60	1.6	8.2	4.0	11.5	12.2
61-72	1.6	8.4	2.4	10.9	12.2
73-84	0.8	4.1	1.2	4.9	10.2
85-96	1.0	5.1	2.0	8.5	6.1
97+	2.0	9.0	7.6	12.0	6.1
Mean	7.6	39.2	27.2	48.3	50.7
Median	0	28.0	12.0	47.0	47.0

NOTES: Number of observations = 2,763 (all), 514 (ever on).
Maximum number of months = 120.

TABLE 14-A2 Distribution of Number of Spells (N) (percent distribution)

	All	Ever On
0	81.4	–
1	9.0	48.4
2	6.0	32.0
3	1.8	9.5
4	1.2	6.4
5	0.4	2.1
6	0.1	0.1
7	0.1	0.0
8+	0.3	0.0
Mean	0.4	1.9
Median	0	2.0

TABLE 14-A3 Distribution of Average Spell Lengths, in Months (L) (percent distribution)

	All Ever On	No. of Spells 1	2	3
1-6	25.5	32.1	21.2	12.2
7-12	19.7	19.7	13.9	28.6
13-18	11.9	7.2	11.5	16.3
19-24	9.5	9.2	5.5	20.4
25-30	6.8	2.4	11.5	14.3
31-36	7.0	2.4	10.9	5.6
37-48	7.4	5.6	13.3	5.3
49-60	5.8	4.0	12.1	0
61-84	1.8	3.6	0	0
85+	4.7	9.6	0	0
Mean	23.8	27.2	24.1	16.8
Median	14.9	12.0	23.5	15.7

TABLE 14-A4 Distribution of Total-Time-On and Spell Lengths Among Long-termers, Short-termers, and Cyclers

	Definition 1		Definition 2		Definition 3		
	Long-termer	Short-termer	Long-termer	Short-termer	Long-termer	Short-termer	Cycler
Total-Time-On:							
1-6	–	80.5	–	50.3	–	42.2	1.0
7-12	16.6	17.0	–	36.5	–	36.7	3.0
13-18	9.8	2.5	8.0	7.4	–	14.2	5.0
19-24	10.8	–	10.2	4.8	12.1	4.0	9.0
25-36	13.9	–	17.3	1.1	11.6	8.0	14.0
37-48	7.8	–	10.2	–	11.6	–	11.0
49-60	9.0	–	12.9	–	15.3	–	13.0
61-72	8.1	–	11.7	–	12.7	–	19.0
73-84	3.7	–	4.9	–	5.8	–	10.7
85-96	6.4	–	8.4	–	10.1	–	7.0
97+	13.1	–	17.3	–	20.6	–	8.0
Mean	47.9	4.8	58.8	8.0	65.5	10.5	54.5
Median	34.2	4.0	52.0	6.0	60.0	8.0	56.5
Spell Length:							
Mean	34.9	3.5	42.7	6.1	47.9	7.6	14.9
Median	26.5	3.5	35.0	5.5	38.0	6.0	13.5

Appendix

Panel on Data and Methods for Measuring the Effects of
Changes in Social Welfare Programs

AGENDA

Workshop on Data Collection for Low Income and Welfare Populations
December 16-17, 1999
Georgetown-Holiday Inn (Mirage I)
2101 Wisconsin Avenue, NW
Washington, D.C.

Thursday, December 16, 1999

8:30a.m.   Continental Breakfast

9:00a.m.   Welcome and Introduction
Robert Moffitt, Panel Chair, Johns Hopkins University
Andrew White, Acting Director, Committee on National
*   Statistics*
Patricia Ruggles, Office of the Assistant Secretary for
*   Planning and Evaluation, Department of Health and*
*   Human Services*

Session 1: Nonresponse in Surveys of the Low-Income Population
Chair: Richard Kulka, Research Triangle Institute
9:15a.m. - 10:10a.m.

9:15a.m.   Designing Surveys Acknowledging Nonresponse
                 Authors: Robert Groves and Mick Couper, Institute for
                 Survey Research, University of Michigan

9:45a.m.   *Discussant: Mike Brick, Westat*

9:55a.m.   Open Discussion Time

Session 2: Obtaining High Response Rates
Chair: John Adams, RAND
10:10a.m. - 11:40a.m.

10:10a.m.   Methods for Obtaining High Response Rates in Telephone
                 Surveys
                 Authors: David Cantor and Patricia Cunningham, Westat

10:40a.m.   High Response Rates for Low Income Population in In-
                 Person Surveys
                 Authors: Barbara Bailar and Charlene Weiss, National
                 Opinion Research Center, University of Chicago

11:10a.m.   *Discussant: Betsy Martin, Census Bureau*

11:25a.m.   Open Discussion Time

11:40a.m.   Break

11:50a.m.   Paying Respondents for Survey Participation
                 Authors: Eleanor Singer, University of Michigan and Richard
                 Kulka, Research Triangle Institute

12:20p.m.   *Discussant: Sandra Berry, RAND*

12:30p.m.   Open Discussion Time

Luncheon/Address (NAS Green Building Refectory)

12:45p.m.   Lunch

1:30p.m.   Luncheon Address: Data Federalism
                  Chair and Introductions: Eric Hanushek, University of
                      Rochester
                  Keynote Address: Janet Norwood, former Commissioner of
                      the Bureau of Labor Statistics

2:30p.m.   Break (Return to the Holiday Inn)

**Session 3: Measurement Error Issues on Surveys of the
Low Income Population**
Chair: John Czajka, Mathematica Policy Research
2:45p.m. - 3:40p.m.

2:45p.m.   Measurement Error in Surveys of the Low Income Population
                  Author: Nancy Mathiowetz, University of Maryland

3:15p.m.   *Discussant: Jeffrey Moore, Census Bureau*

3:25p.m.   Open Discussion Time

3:40p.m.   Break

Session 4: Obtaining Information on Eligible Non-Participants
Chair: Irwin Garfinkel, Columbia University
3:50p.m. - 5:00p.m.

3:50p.m.   Using Microsimulation and Administrative Data to Identify
                      the Eligible Nonparticipants in Safety Net Programs
                  Authors: Linda Giannarelli, Sheila Zedlewski, Joyce Merton
                      and Donald Alderson, The Urban Institute

4:20p.m.   *Discussant: Harold Beebout, Mathematica Policy Research*

4:30p.m.   Open Discussion Time

5:00p.m.   Reception (NAS Green Building, Room 130 and North
                      Lounge)

6:00p.m.   Adjourn

Friday, December 17, 1999

8:30a.m.   Continental Breakfast

Session 5: Administrative Data Topics
Chair: Joseph Hotz, University of California, Los Angeles
9:00a.m. - 10:30a.m.

9:00a.m.   Matching and Cleaning Administrative Data
                  Authors: Robert Goerge and Bong Joo Lee, Chapin Hall
                  Center for Children, University of Chicago

9:30a.m.   *Discussant: William Winkler, Census Bureau*

9:40a.m.   Access and Confidentiality Issues with Administrative Data
                  Authors: Henry Brady and Anne Powell, University of
                  California, Berkeley; and Werner Schink, California
                  Department of Social Services

10:10a.m.   *Discussant: Laura Zayatz, Census Bureau*

10:20a.m.   Open Discussion Time

10:40a.m.   Break

Session 6: Qualitative Data Sources
Chair: Kathryn Edin, University of Pennsylvania
11:00a.m. - 12:00p.m.

11:00a.m.   The Right (Soft) Stuff: Qualitative Methods and the Study of
                  Welfare Reform
                  Author: Katherine Newman, Harvard University

11:30a.m.   *Discussant: Rebecca Maynard, University of Pennsylvania*

11:40a.m.   Open Discussion Time

Luncheon Address (Holiday Inn)

12:00p.m.   Lunch

12:45p.m.   Lunch Address: Measuring Child Outcomes
                  Chair and Introductions: Suzanne Randolph, University of
                  Maryland Speaker: Kristin Moore, Child Trends

1:30p.m.   Break

Session 7: Measuring Outcomes Relevant for Welfare Reform Evaluations
Chair: Rebecca Maynard, University of Pennsylvania
1:45p.m. - 3:15p.m.

1:45p.m.   Measuring Employment Outcomes and Income with
           Administrative and Survey Data
           Authors: Joseph Hotz, University of California, Los Angeles;
           and Karl Scholz, University of Wisconsin-Madison

2:15p.m.   *Discussant: Howard Bloom, Manpower Demonstration*
           Research Corporation

2:25p.m.   Open Discussion Time

2:35p.m.   Administrative Data on the Well-Being of Children On and
           Off Welfare
           Author: Richard Barth and Eleanor Locklin, University of
           North Carolina,Chapel Hill; Barbara Needell and
           Stephanie Cuccaro-Alamin, University of California,
           Berkeley

3:05p.m.   *Discussant: Matt Stagner, Office of the Assistant Secretary*
           for Planning and Evaluation, Department of Health and
           Human Services

3:15p.m.   Open Discussion Time

3:30p.m.   Workshop Summary
           Robert Moffitt, Johns Hopkins University

           (Open discussion time and a summary of the workshop.)

4:00p.m.   Adjourn

Index

A

Access restrictions, *see* Confidentiality and privacy; Eligibility; Program participation; Sanctions; Time limits
Administration for Children and Families (ACF)
  well-being of children, 316-352
Administrative data and studies, 2, 6-7, 196-352
  see also Caseload measures; Program participation; Taxation
  access and confidentiality, *see* *"confidentiality" infra*
  AFDC, 6, 200, 202, 203-204, 214, 225, 249, 276, 278, 283, 300, 355, 418-427
    caseload heterogeneity, 473, 481-496
    child well-being, 318, 324, 326, 329-338 (passim)
    leavers, 8-9, 249, 388(n.1), 416, 417-472 (passim)
  alcohol and drug abuse, 199, 249
  birth certificates, 197, 202, 204, 221, 327
  child abuse and neglect, 318, 323, 327, 331-337, 344, 345, 346

child well-being, 7, 251, 316-352, 504, 505
  education, 316, 319, 328, 337-341, 344, 345
  eligibility, 318, 321, 323, 324-325, 326, 329, 331
  leaver studies, 324, 331
  state government role, 318, 327-331
  TANF, 316-317, 318, 324-325, 326, 327, 331-337 (passim), 343, 344, 346
children, data cleaning, 202-203
cleaning methods, 6, 197, 199-205, 211-212, 217, 304
confidentiality, 6-7, 220-274, 304, 305, 504
  adolescents, educational records, 339-340
  age factors, 228
  Assistant Secretary for Planning and Evaluation, 7, 238-239, 242
  children, 7, 339-341, 345-346
  cost factors, 222, 258, 263, 273-274
  criminal records, 238-239, 255-256, 263
  educational attainment, 228, 338-340
  food stamps, 225, 226-227, 240, 249
  funding, 236, 242, 246

legislation, 6-7, 222, 223-224, 232,
        233-241, 246, 247, 255-257,
        266-267, 268, 271-274
    criminal penalties for breeches,
        238-239, 254-256, 263, 268,
        274
    linkage of data and, 216-217, 220,
        222-223
    organizational factors, 243-254, 258-
        259, 262-264, 265, 266, 267-
        268
        Institutional Review Boards, 88,
            92, 125, 236-237, 266-267
    private contract researchers, 239, 241,
        243-254
    socially sensitive data, 221, 230-231
    standards, 233-237, 243-258
    state government role, 6-7, 222-223,
        238-258, 267-268, 271-274
    statistical analyses, 224-225, 255,
        258-262, 267
    tax records, 304, 305
    technical assistance, 256-257, 267
cost factors, 199, 200, 201, 278
    confidentiality, 222, 258, 263, 273-274
criminal records, 206, 238-239, 255-256,
        263
death certificates, 327, 328
defined, 197, 224-225
eligibility, general, 220-274, 304, 305, 504
    children, 318, 321, 323, 324-325, 326,
        329, 331
    linkage, 216-217, 220, 222-223
employment, 6, 7, 69, 228, 239, 275-279,
        287-288, 289, 290-315, 400-
        403, 406-408, 422-441
        (passim), 505
    Job Training Partnership Act, 246,
        278, 291, 295-302, 310-312
    leaver studies, 389, 394, 400-408, 412-
        413, 415, 416-443 (passim),
        448, 453-463, 464, 468
    survey data *vs* administrative data, 6,
        275-279, 287-288, 289, 295-
        303, 311
    unemployment insurance records, 7,
        69, 132, 203, 225, 249,
        276(n.3), 277, 278, 287, 290-
        312, 403, 406-408, 413, 417-
        422, 431-431, 442-445, 451,
        462

families and households, general, 278,
        317, 319, 320, 400, 473
food stamps, 283
    child well-being, 318, 320, 324, 331,
        343
    cleaning and matching of data, 197,
        203, 225, 226-227, 409
    confidentiality, 225, 226-227, 240, 249
    leaver studies, 401-402, 409, 432-435,
        445, 446, 448-449, 450, 463
funding, 207, 236, 242, 246
gender factors,
    caseload heterogeneity, 473, 474, 478,
        481, 482-499
    data matching, 204, 212
    linking, 25, 210, 212, 216, 229
geographic factors,
    cleaning of data, 202-203, 212
    confidentiality, 228, 261
    juvenile justice system, 342
    linkage of data, 207, 212, 216
incentives, survey data *vs*, 277
income and earnings, 7, 275, 329
    caseload heterogeneity, 474, 478-479,
        486, 488, 489, 492-496
        (passim)
    leaver studies, 389, 394, 409-411,
        413, 416-417, 432-436, 439,
        441-450, 454-464 (passim),
        468, 469, 470, 472
    survey data *vs* administrative data, 6,
        275-279, 287-288, 289, 295-
        303, 311
    unemployment insurance records, 7,
        69, 132, 203, 225, 249,
        276(n.3), 277, 278, 287, 290-
        312, 403, 406-408, 413, 417-
        422, 431, 442-445, 451, 462
in-person interviews and, 4, 89
leaver studies, 389, 390-393, 395-399,
        400-408, 411-443 (passim),
        448, 453-463, 464, 468
    AFDC data, 8-9, 249, 388(n.1), 416,
        417-472 (passim)
    child well-being, 324, 331
    employment and income, 389, 394,
        400-408, 412-413, 415, 416-
        443 (passim), 448, 453-463,
        464, 468
    food stamps, 401-402, 409, 432-435,
        445, 446, 448-449, 450, 463

linkage/matching of data, 6, 7, 41, 49, 60,
    93, 132, 134, 141, 143, 153,
    154, 167-168, 171, 173, 174,
    175, 197, 198, 204-219, 220,
    222-223, 224-227, 228-229,
    235-238, 241, 244, 252, 261,
    264, 268, 276, 287-288, 298,
    504
  child well-being, 336, 343, 344, 346
  gender factors, 210, 212, 216, 229,
    252
  leaver studies, 402-403, 408, 409,
    411, 412, 417-422
  longitudinal studies, 207, 336
  standards, 211-212, 235-237
  statistical analyses, 205(n.2), 206,
    209-211, 213-217
measurement error, 277, 292-295, 304-
    305
qualitative studies *vs*, 356, 357, 377, 378
race/ethnicity,
  caseload heterogeneity, 482, 486, 488,
    489, 493
  cleaning of data, 204, 212
  confidentiality and privacy, 228-229
  linking of data, 210, 212, 216, 228-
    229
sampling, 208, 261, 277, 278, 346
sharing of data, *see "linkage..." supra*
Social Security numbers, 58, 60, 69, 74,
    208, 209, 210, 211, 214-216,
    228, 238, 239, 287-288, 298,
    343, 402-403
standards, 211-212, 233-237, 243-258
state government role, 6-7, 56-58, 69,
    138-139, 142-143, 218, 222-
    223, 225-226, 292
  child well-being, 318, 327-331
  confidentiality issues, 6-7, 222-223,
    238-258, 267-268, 271-274
  statistical analyses, 224-225
    confidentiality, 224-225, 255, 258-
    262, 267
  linkage, 205(n.2), 206, 209-211, 213-
    217
survey data *vs* administrative data,
  child well-being, 324, 338, 346
  income and employment, 6, 275-279,
    287-288, 289, 295-303, 311
  leaver studies, 406-408
  taxation, 277, 278, 285-286

survey respondents, error of measurement,
    167-168, 171, 173, 174, 175,
    182
survey response and, 27, 50, 57, 132, 133-
    134, 142-143, 287-288, 411
TANF, 6, 134, 200, 201, 203, 204, 205,
    214, 224, 225, 249, 278, 283,
    355, 400-403, 431, 432, 437,
    445, 446
  child well-being, 316-317, 318, 324-
    325, 326, 327, 331-337
    (passim), 343, 344, 346
telephone surveys and, 57, 58, 60, 69, 70-
    71, 74
unemployment insurance records, 7, 69,
    132, 203, 225, 249, 276(n.3),
    277, 278, 287, 290-312, 403,
    406-408, 413, 417-422, 431-
    431, 442-445, 451, 462
vital statistics, 75, 225, 323, 327-331
Adolescents
  education, privacy rights, 339-340
  educational attainment, 228
  health status, 322, 323, 327
  incentives, surveys, 106-107, 121
  income and employment, 300-301
  in-person interviews, 90, 93
  juvenile justice system, 7, 75, 328, 341-
    343, 344, 345
  qualitative studies, 375
AFDC, *see* Aid to Families with Dependent
    Children
African Americans, *see* Black persons
Age factors
  *see also terms beginning "Child" and
    "Children"*
  caseload heterogeneity, 482
  confidentiality and privacy, 228
  elderly persons, 33, 111, 171, 368
  leaver studies, 428, 447-448, 451, 456,
    467
  survey respondents, error of measurement,
    167-168, 171, 176
  survey response, general, 29, 33, 37, 43,
    135-136, 137-138, 142, 167-
    168, 171, 176
Aggregation and disaggregation of data, 205,
    220, 252, 259, 260, 286
  see also Matching, administrative data
  child health status, 322, 329

Aid to Families with Dependent Children, 1, 220, 316
   see also Temporary Assistance for Needy Families
   administrative data, 6, 200, 202, 203-204, 214, 225, 249, 276, 278, 283, 300, 355, 418-427
      caseload heterogeneity, 473, 481-496
      child well-being, 318, 324, 326, 329-338 (passim)
      leavers, 8-9, 249, 388(n.1), 416, 417-472 (passim)
   income and employment data, 276, 278-283 (passim), 289, 300, 303, 306-310, 311, 418-427, 445-458, 462-463
   program participation, 276, 280
      leavers, 8-9, 249, 388(n.1), 416, 417-472 (passim), 481-496 (passim)
   qualitative studies, 375-376
   survey data, 276, 278-283 (passim), 289, 300
   survey respondents, error of measurement, 171-173
   waivers, 317
Alcohol and drug abuse
   administrative data, general, 199, 249
   Center for Substance Abuse Treatment, 134
   child well-being, 316, 323, 327
   qualitative studies, 368
   survey respondents, error of measurement, 177, 184-185
   survey sampling and, 93, 94
      state income tax records, 57-58
   Supplemental Security Income, 92, 134
American Association of Public Opinion Research, 86
Archives, *see* Data archives
Assistant Secretary for Planning and Evaluation (ASPE)
   access and confidentiality issues, 7, 238-239, 242
   child health status, 329-330
   leavers, 8, 9, 67, 238-239, 242, 388, 430-431
   telephone surveys, 67
Attitudes
   child well-being and, 319, 320
   interviewers, 95, 97, 99, 110-111

qualitative studies, 357, 378
Survey of Consumer Attitudes, 121
survey respondents, 30, 35, 36, 37, 39, 43, 96-97
   error of measurement, 157, 159, 164-165, 177-178, 194-186
   incentives and, 105-106, 110-111, 113-114, 116-119, 121
   socially sensitive questions, 5, 37, 66, 106, 157, 159, 164-165, 177-178, 184-186

B

Benefit penalties, *see* Sanctions
Best practices, 3, 9
   telephone surveys, 55, 56, 68, 72-75, 78, 79, 86
Best Practices Booklet, 86
Birth certificates, 197, 202, 204, 221, 327
Black persons, 21, 90, 91, 93, 115, 135, 136, 370, 371, 451, 454, 461, 486, 488, 493
Block grants, child health, 328-329
Bureau of the Census, 87, 88, 382
   see also Current Population Survey; Survey of Income and Program Participation
   Census of Population, 275
   data cleaning, 212
   data confidentiality, 262-263
   data linkage, 216

C

Case management, 48, 249, 369
Caseload measures, 3, 220, 276, 306, 311, 327, 355, 371, 377, 415-499
   child well-being, 324, 333-334, 335-336
   educational attainment, 473, 474-475, 478-479, 486, 488, 489, 493, 496
   heterogeneity of caseload, 473-499
      gender factors, 9, 473, 474, 478, 481, 482-499
   leaver studies, 387, 389, 415-473, 474, 477-478, 480
Census Bureau, *see* Bureau of the Census
Census of Population, 275
Center for Substance Abuse Treatment, 134

Child abuse and neglect, 199, 207-208, 226
    see also Child protective services
    administrative data, 318, 323, 327, 331-
        337, 344, 345, 346
    qualitative studies, 356
Child care services, 203, 204, 205, 206, 226,
        249, 319, 367, 368, 377, 416
Child protective services, 226, 318, 332, 333-
        334, 335-336, 345
    foster care, 26, 179, 182, 202-208
        (passim), 317, 318, 329, 333
Child support, 69, 74, 171-178, 225, 240, 249
Child well-being
    administrative data, 7, 251, 316-352, 504,
        505
        caseload measures, 324, 333-334,
            335-336
        education, 316, 319, 328, 337-341,
            344, 345
        eligibility, 318, 321, 323, 324-325,
            326, 329, 331
        leaver studies, 324, 331
        program participation, 324, 333, 337-
            338, 341, 342, 344-345
        state government role, 318, 327-331
        TANF, 316-317, 318, 324-325, 326,
            327, 331-337 (passim), 343,
            344, 346
    alcohol and drug abuse, 316, 323, 327
    attitudes, 319, 320
    health insurance, 318, 320, 321, 323, 329
        Medicaid, 318, 320, 321, 323, 324-
            326, 328, 329, 330, 331, 343
        mortality rates, 317, 320, 322, 323,
            327-328, 341
    health status, general, 318, 320, 321-331,
        344-345; *see also* Child abuse
        and neglect
    leaver studies, 8-9, 394-395, 396-397,
        399-400, 416, 427, 428, 431
    qualitative studies, 356, 366, 367
    sanctions and, 336, 343, 399-400
    waiver programs, 317
Children
    see also Aid to Families with Dependent
        Children; Juvenile justice
        system
    access to telephone by families with, 87
    administrative data cleaning, 202-203
    foster care, 26, 179, 182, 202-208
        (passim) 317, 318, 329, 333

in-person surveys, 90
    leavers studies, 8-9, 394-395, 396-397,
        399-400, 416, 427, 428, 447-
        448, 451, 454, 467
Children's Health Insurance Program (CHIP),
        318-326 (passim), 329
Cognitive factors, surveys
    see also Language factors
    comprehension of items, 5, 161, 173, 178-
        180, 189
    memory, 5, 159, 161, 162, 163-164, 168,
        175, 176-177, 180-184, 404,
        408
    respondents, error of measurement, 157,
        159, 160-164, 165, 167-168,
        174-175, 176-177, 178-184,
        187-189
    response rates, 37, 41-42
Cohort comparison studies
    child health status, 330-331
    income and employment, 279, 280, 406
    leavers, 8-9, 397, 398-399, 401-405, 406,
        407, 413, 415-416, 417-422
    National Longitudinal Surveys, 275, 476;
        see also National Longitudinal
        Survey of Youth
Community factors, *see* Local-level effects
Computer-assisted personal interviewing, 88,
        89, 90, 160, 177-178, 376-377
Computer-assisted telephone interview, 111
Computerized databases, *see* Databases
Confidentiality and privacy
    administrative data, 6-7, 220-274, 304,
        305, 504
        adolescents, educational records, 339-
            340
        Assistant Secretary for Planning and
            Evaluation, 7, 238-239, 242
        children, 7, 339-341, 345-346
        cost factors, 222, 258, 263, 273-274
        criminal records, 238-239, 255-256, 263
        educational attainment, other, 228
        food stamps, 225, 226-227, 240, 249
        funding, 236, 242, 246
        linkage, 216-217, 220, 222-223
        legislation, 6-7, 222, 223-224, 232,
            233-241, 246, 247, 255-257,
            266-267, 268, 271-274
        criminal penalties for breeches,
            238-239, 254-256, 263, 268,
            274

organizational factors, 243-254, 258-
    259, 262-264, 265, 266, 267-
    268
Institutional Review Boards, 88,
    92, 125, 236-237, 266-267
private contract researchers, 239, 241,
    243-254
socially sensitive data, 221, 230-231
standards, 233-237, 243-258
state government role, 6-7, 222-223,
    238-258, 267-268, 271-274
statistical analyses, 224-225, 255,
    258-262, 267
tax records, 304, 305
technical assistance, 256-257, 267
best practices, 86
computer-assisted questionnaires, 177-178
definitional issues, 228-231
homeless persons, 92
informed consent and notification, 4, 57-
    58, 68, 96, 125, 199, 231-232,
    237, 258, 266-267
in-person interviews, 86, 89, 92, 96
Internet, 265, 267
respondents' attitudes about, 106
school records, 339-341
tax records, 304, 305
Consent, see Informed consent and notification
Continuous welfare leavers, 183, 332, 396-
    397, 399, 421-422, 441
    see also Time limits
Cost and cost-effectiveness
    administrative data,
        cleaning, 200, 201
        confidentiality, 222, 258, 263, 273-274
        program participation studies, 199
        vs survey data, 278
    incentives, surveys, 117, 120-122, 124-125
    in-person interviews, 89, 91, 97, 100, 101,
        102-103
    mail, 59
    qualitative studies, 380-381
    survey response, general, 37, 39, 41, 46,
        49, 283
    telephone surveys, 56, 59-61, 78-83
    tracing and tracking, surveys, 30, 59-61,
        79-81, 101
    unemployment data, use of, 292
Council of Professional Associations on
    Federal Statistics, 115
CPS, see Current Population Survey

Crime and criminal justice system
    see also Alcohol and drug abuse; Child
        abuse and neglect; Sanctions
    administrative data confidentiality
        breeches, 238-239, 254-256,
        263, 268, 274
    administrative data linkage, 206
    caseload heterogeneity, 474
    income and employment, 300-301
    in-person interviews, 89, 93, 94
    juvenile, 7, 75, 328, 341-343, 344, 345
    qualitative studies, 368-369
    survey respondent incentives, interviewer
        at risk, 124
    survey respondent involvement in, 30, 36,
        86, 162, 164
Cultural factors, 4
    see also Language factors; Race/ethnicity;
        Social factors
    survey response, 36, 52
Current Population Survey (CPS)
    cognitive interviews, 281
    error of measurement, 158, 168, 169, 175
    income and employment data, 275, 277,
        279-290 (passim), 294, 310
    response rates, 21
Cyclic welfare users, 9, 89-91, 206, 396-397,
    399, 422-426, 430, 431, 433,
    434, 438-445, 451, 454, 456,
    457-459, 462-464, 468, 471,
    472, 478
    caseload heterogeneity, 474, 480, 481-
        482, 485-499 (passim)

D

Data archives
    cleaning methods, 6, 197, 199-205, 212
    confidentiality issues, 249-250, 268
    matching of data, 6, 7, 41, 49, 60, 93,
        132, 134, 141, 143, 153, 154,
        167-168, 171, 173, 174, 175,
        197, 205-218, 304
Data Matching and Privacy Protection Act,
    234, 235-236
Databases, 30
    see also Confidentiality and privacy
    child well-being, 328, 344-346
    cleaning methods, 6, 197, 199-205, 211-
        212, 217, 225, 226-227, 304,
        409

confidentiality and access, 57, 60
credit, 69
juvenile justice system, 342
mailing addresses, 91
matching/linking of data, 6, 7, 41, 49, 60,
    93, 132, 134, 141, 143, 153,
    154, 167-168, 171, 173, 174,
    175, 197, 205-218, 220, 222-
    223, 224-227, 228-229, 235-
    238, 241, 252, 261, 264, 268,
    276, 287-288, 298, 504
  child well-being, 336, 343, 344, 346
  leaver studies, 402-403, 408. 409,
    411, 412, 417-422
  longitudinal studies, 207, 336
  standards, 211-212, 235-237
  statistical analyses, 205(n.2), 206,
    209-211, 213-217
  sharing of data, 227-228, 241
  telephone surveys, 30, 57, 58, 59, 60, 69,
    70-71
Death certificates, 327, 328
Demographic factors
  see also Age factors; Gender factors;
    Geographic factors; Marriage
    and marital status; Race/
    ethnicity; Socioeconomic
    status
  administrative data cleaning, 200, 304
  error of measurement, 159
  heterogeneity of caseload, 473-499
    (passim)
  incentives for survey respondents, 105-
    106, 114, 115-116
  income and employment, survey data,
    282, 304, 305
  leaver, definition, 419
  qualitative studies, 359-361
  survey nonresponse, 37, 41, 42, 133, 135-
    140, 142, 143, 145, 146
Department of Health and Human Services
  see also Administration for Children and
    Families; Assistant Secretary
    for Planning and Evaluation
  child well-being, 322, 334
  privacy and confidentiality of data, 233,
    240
Department of Labor, 378-380
Diet, *see* Nutrition

Disaggregation, *see* Aggregation and
    disaggregation of data
Drug abuse, *see* Alcohol and drug abuse

E

Early Screening and Periodic Screening and
    Diagnostic Testing, 324
Earned Income Tax Credits (EITC), 275, 305-
    306, 446-447
Earnings, *see* Income and earnings, general
Econometric modeling, 481
  see also Caseload measures
Economic incentives, *see* Incentives, surveys
Education and training, 1
  adolescents, record confidentiality, 339-
    340
  child well-being,
    administrative data, 316, 319, 328,
      337-341, 344, 345
    qualitative studies, 356, 367
  Head Start, 329
  interviewers, 4, 5, 31-32, 40, 43-46, 47,
    51, 159-160
    in-person surveys, 92, 94-98, 99, 101,
      102-103
    telephone surveys, 63-64, 66, 67, 68
  Job Training Partnership Act, 246, 278,
    291, 295-302, 310-312
  qualitative studies, researchers, 381-382
Educational attainment
  caseload heterogeneity, 473, 474-475,
    478-479, 486, 488, 489, 493,
    496
  confidentiality and privacy, 228, 339-340
  incentives, surveys, 113, 114-115, 116
  leaver studies, 428, 447-448, 451, 454,
    467
  National Adult Literacy Survey, 121
  survey nonresponse, 24-25, 142, 151
  survey respondents, error of measurement,
    167-168, 173
Educational testing data, 338-339
Elderly persons, 33
  incentives, surveys, 111
  qualitative studies, 368
  survey respondents, error of measurement,
    171

Eligibility
    see also Leaver studies; Program
        participation; Sanctions; Time
        limits
    administrative data, 202, 226-227, 252,
        278-279
    administrative data, child well-being, 318,
        321, 323, 324-325, 326, 329,
        331
    caseload heterogeneity, 479
    income and employment data, 276
    survey response and, 113, 145, 154
    TANF, 113, 226-227
Employment, 5
    see also Income and earnings, general;
        Leaver studies
    access to telephone, 87
    administrative data, 7, 69, 228, 239, 275,
        290-312, 400-403, 406-408,
        422-441 (passim), 505
        child well-being and, 316-317, 319,
            321, 329, 332, 341, 343, 346
        leaver studies, 389, 394, 400-408,
            412-413, 415, 416-443
            (passim), 448, 453-463, 464,
            468
        unemployment insurance records, 7,
            69, 132, 203, 225, 249,
            276(n.3), 277, 278, 287, 290-
            312, 403, 406-408, 413, 417-
            422, 431, 442-445, 451, 462
    adolescents, 300-301
    caseload heterogeneity, 473, 475-476,
        478, 486, 488, 489, 492-496
    child well-being and, administrative data,
        316-317, 319, 321, 329, 332,
        341, 343, 346
    cohort comparison studies, 279, 280, 406
    Current Population Survey (CPS), 275, 277,
        279-290 (passim), 294, 310
    gender factors, 21, 173, 176, 280, 281,
        300-301, 473, 475-476, 478,
        486, 488, 489, 492-496
    health insurance, employer-provided, 321
    interviewer recruitment/supervision, 95-
        96, 98-100, 101, 102-103
    interviewer training, 4, 5, 31-32, 40, 43-
        46, 47, 51, 159-160
        in-person surveys, 92, 94-98, 99, 101,
            102-103
        telephone surveys, 63-64, 66, 67, 68

Job Training Partnership Act, 246, 278,
        291, 295-302, 310-312
    qualitative studies, 357, 359-361, 366-
        367, 378, 382
    survey data, 275, 277, 279-290, 295-303,
        403-408, 505
    survey nonresponse, 21, 22, 24-25, 30,
        138, 142, 159, 151
    survey respondents, error of measurement,
        7, 164-171, 173-177, 277, 282-
        290, 292-295, 304-305
    unemployment insurance records, 7, 69,
        132, 203, 225, 249, 276(n.3),
        277, 278, 287, 290-312, 403,
        406-408, 413, 417-422, 431,
        442-445, 451, 462
    welfare-to-work, see Personal
        Responsibility and Work
        Opportunity Reconciliation
        Act; Temporary Assistance for
        Needy Families; Time limits
Ethical issues, see Confidentiality and privacy
Ethnicity, see Race/ethnicity
Ethnographic studies, 90, 199, 356, 357, 359-
        360, 365-369, 375, 382
Experimental methods
    income and employment, 278
    juvenile justice system, 342-343
    qualitative, 360

                            F

Face-to-face interviews, see In-person
        interviews
Families and households
    see also Current Population Survey;
        Demographic factors; Marriage
        and marital status; Qualitative
        studies; Sampling and sample
        size; Single mothers;
        Socioeconomic status;
        Temporary Assistance for
        Needy Families; terms
        beginning "Child..."
    access to telephone, 87
    administrative data, general, 317, 319,
        320, 400, 473
    administrative vs survey data, 278
    heterogeneity of caseload, 473, 478

income and employment, survey data,
    general, 278, 280-282, 284,
    303, 304-305, 306-309
leaver studies, 388, 394, 400, 404, 415
qualitative studies, 8, 359-361, 363, 366-
    367, 371, 372-373, 382
survey respondents, error of measurement,
    171-173, 178
survey response, 30, 35, 37-43
Family Educational Rights and Privacy Act,
    339-341
Federal Communications Commission, 87
Fees for survey respondents, *see* Incentives,
    surveys
Females, *see* Gender factors
Focus groups, 8, 43, 52, 357, 361-362
Food stamps, 1, 69, 224
    administrative data, child well-being, 318,
        320, 324, 331, 343
    administrative data, general, 283
        cleaning and matching of, 197, 203,
            225, 226-227, 409
        confidentiality, 225, 226-227, 240,
            249
        leaver studies, 401-402, 409, 432-435,
            445, 446, 448-449, 450, 463
    income and employment, survey data,
        280, 283
    nonresponse to surveys, 26
Foster care, 26, 179, 182, 202-208 (passim),
    317, 318, 329, 333
Funding
    administrative data confidentiality and
        privacy and, 236, 242, 246
    administrative data linkage, 207
    block grants, child health, 328-329
    leaver studies, 9, 67, 242, 288

G

Gender factors, 355, 473
    administrative data cleaning, 204, 212
    administrative data linking, 210, 212, 216,
        229, 252
    caseload heterogeneity, 9, 473, 474, 478,
        481, 482-499
    doctor visits, 21
    incentives, surveys, 109

income and employment, 21, 173, 176,
    280, 281, 300-301, 473, 475-
    476, 478, 486, 488, 489, 492-
    496
in-person interviews, sample lists, 89, 90
qualitative studies, 363-364, 368, 373
survey respondents, error of measurement,
    173, 176
survey response, 21, 37, 41, 109, 135-136,
    137-138, 142, 143, 144, 146,
    151
Geographical factors
    see also Rural areas; State-level issues;
        Urban areas
    administrative data cleaning, 202-203,
        212
    administrative data confidentiality and
        privacy, 228, 261
    administrative data linkage, 207, 212, 216
    income and employment data, 312
    juvenile justice system, administrative
        data, 342
    leaver studies, 388(n.1), 428, 467
    survey respondent error of measurement,
        167-168
    survey response, 13, 29-31, 33, 57, 58-59,
        87, 91, 133, 142, 143

H

Head Start, 329
Health and Retirement Survey, 110
Health insurance
    see also Medicaid
    children, 318, 320, 321, 323, 329
    leaver studies, 394
Health status and care, 368
    see also Medicaid; Mental health and
        illness
    adolescents, 322, 323, 327
    caseload heterogeneity, 474
    child well-being, 318, 320, 321-331, 344-
        345
        mortality rates, 317, 320, 322, 323,
            327-328, 341
    death certificates, 327, 328
    leaver studies, 389, 394
    vital statistics, 75, 225, 323, 327-331
Healthy People 2000, 322

Hispanics, 56, 88, 91, 140, 370, 451, 454,
        486, 488, 489, 493
    Puerto Ricans, 90, 93, 370
Historical perspectives, 1, 275, 316, 371, 387,
        473
    caseload measures, 473-496
    income and employment data, 275, 276,
        286-287, 288
    in-person interviews, 90
    leaver studies, 387, 389, 472
Homeless persons, 92, 94
Households, *see* Families and households
Housing subsidies, 142, 143

I

Immigrants, 88, 90, 93, 366, 454, 457
    see also Hispanics; Language factors
Imputation, 3, 25-26, 28, 48, 52, 78, 131,
        154, 262, 277, 285
Incentives, surveys, 3, 4-5, 51, 105-128, 131,
        379
    administrative data *vs* survey data, 277
    adolescents, 106-107, 121
    cost factors, 117, 120-122, 124-125
    demographic factors, 105-106, 114, 115-116
    differential, 106, 117-120
    educational attainment, 113, 114-115, 116
    gifts *vs* money, 5, 38, 107, 108
    in-person interviews, 89, 90, 101, 108,
        110-111, 117-118, 120-121
    item nonresponse effects, 111-113
    local community level effects, 116-117,
        121
    lotteries as, 109, 124
    panel studies, 5, 109-110
    prepaid, 3-4, 59, 82, 105, 107, 108, 109,
        111, 112, 117, 118, 120-122,
        123-124
    response distribution effects, 113-115
    standards, 124-125
    telephone interviews, 4-5, 70-71, 72, 82-
        83, 106, 108, 110, 111
Income and earnings, general
    see also Aid to Families with Dependent
        Children; Earned Income Tax
        Credits; Supplemental Security
        Income; Taxation; Temporary
        Assistance for Needy Families;
        Unemployment insurance
        records

administrative data, 7, 275, 329
    caseload heterogeneity, 474, 478-479,
        486, 488, 489, 492-496
        (passim)
    leaver studies, 389, 394, 409-411,
        413, 416-417, 432-436, 439,
        441-450, 454-464 (passim),
        468, 469, 470, 472
adolescents, 300-301
AFDC, 276, 278-283 (passim), 289, 300,
        303, 306-310, 311, 418-427,
        445-458, 462-463
child well-being, 329
cohort comparison studies, 279, 280, 406
Current Population Survey (CPS), 275,
        277, 279-290 (passim), 294,
        310
gender factors, 21, 173, 176, 280, 281,
        300-301, 473, 475-476, 478,
        486, 488, 489, 492-496
historical perspectives, 275, 276, 286-287,
        288
leaver studies, 276, 389, 394, 400-413,
        416, 417-422, 426
local community effects, 275-276, 279,
        282
longitudinal studies, 275, 277, 279-280
national-level studies, general, 275, 277,
        279-290, 310, 311
Panel Study of Income Dynamics (PSID),
        275, 279, 280-281, 284, 288,
        289-290, 363
survey data, general, 275
survey design/response, 5, 30, 38, 86-87,
        138, 142, 143-144
Survey of Income and Program
        Participation (SIPP), 363
    incentives for respondents, 109-110
    income and employment data, 275,
        277, 279, 280-281, 284-290,
        310, 311
survey respondents, error of measurement,
        164-165, 166-171, 178
In-depth interviews, 77, 88, 93, 357, 359-361,
        370, 372
Informed consent and notification, 4, 57-58,
        68, 96, 125, 199, 231-232,
        237, 258, 266-267
In-person interviews
    adolescents, 90, 93
    children, 90

computer-assisted personal interviewing,
88, 89, 90, 160, 177-178, 376-377
confidentiality and privacy, 86, 89, 92, 96
cost factors, 89, 91, 97, 100, 101, 102-103
criminal histories, 89, 93, 94
focus groups, 8, 43, 52, 357, 361-362
gender factors, 89, 90
historical perspectives, 90
incentives, 89, 90, 101, 108, 110-111,
117-118, 120-121
interviewer training, 92, 94-98, 99, 101
leaver studies, 403-406
local community factors, 4, 91, 102
mail contacts and, 89, 91, 92, 102
organizational factors, 98-100, 101, 103
qualitative studies, 356, 357, 358-372,
375-377
ethnographic, 90, 199, 356, 357, 359-360, 365-369, 375, 382
focus groups, 8, 43, 52, 357, 361-362
respondents/interviewers, error of
measurement, 157-189
(passim)
response rates, 3, 4, 31-50, 69, 77, 78, 86-104, 502
tracing and tracking, 61, 74, 92-94,
96, 101, 102
sampling, 89-94, 100
state government role, 88, 93
teamwork, 100
tracking and tracing, 61, 74, 92-94, 96,
101, 102
urban areas, 87, 90, 93, 96, 97
Institutional factors, *see* Organizational factors
Institutional Review Boards, 88, 92, 125,
236-237, 266-267
Insurance, *see* Health insurance; Unemployment
insurance records
Internal Revenue Service (IRS), 7, 285-286,
302, 303-309, 312
Internet
child health status, 329, 330
data confidentiality, 265, 267
prison inmates, 93
Interviews, 3, 31-50, 69-73, 86-104
see also In-person interviews; Panel
studies; Response rates;
Telephone surveys; Tracing
and tracking
administrative data *vs*, 199

attitudes of interviewees, 30, 35, 36, 37,
39, 43, 96-97
error of measurement, 157, 159, 164-165, 177-178, 194-186
incentives and, 105-106, 110-111,
113-114, 116-119, 121
socially sensitive questions, 5, 37, 66,
106, 157, 159, 164-165, 177-178, 184-186
attitudes of interviewers, 95, 97, 99, 110-111
error of measurement, interviewers as
source of, 159-160, 161
focus groups, 8, 43, 52, 357, 361-362
followup, 4, 33, 48, 74, 75, 81, 88, 116,
131; *see also* Tracing and
tracking
incentives, general, 107, 110-111, 112,
113-114, 120, 122
protocols, standardized, 93, 96, 186
recruitment/supervision of interviewers,
95-96, 98-100, 101, 102-103
refusal conversion, 4, 5, 25, 36, 42, 50,
63, 64, 65, 66-67, 68, 75, 99
incentives, monetary, 107, 115-116,
124
training of interviewers, 4, 5, 31-32, 40,
43-46, 47, 51, 159-160
in-person surveys, 92, 94-98, 99, 101,
102-103
telephone surveys, 63-64, 66, 67, 68

J

Job Training Partnership Act, 246, 278, 291,
295-302, 310-312
Joint Center for Poverty Research, 225
Juvenile justice system, 7, 75, 328, 341-343,
344, 345

L

Language factors, 4, 56-57, 88, 130, 141-142
administrative data confidentiality
statutes, 257
error of measurement, 158-159, 160-161
focus groups, 361
National Adult Literacy Survey, 121
Law enforcement, *see* Crime and criminal
justice system

Leaver studies, 2, 8-9, 86, 356, 366-367, 382, 387-472
  see also Cyclic welfare users; Sanctions; Short-term welfare users; Time limits
  administrative *vs* survey data, 276, 278
  AFDC administrative data, 8-9, 249, 388(n.1), 416, 417-472 (passim)
  age factors, 428, 447-448, 451, 456, 467
  Assistant Secretary for Planning and Evaluation, 8, 9, 67, 238-239, 242, 388, 430-431
  caseload measures, 387, 389, 415-473, 474, 477-478, 480
  child well-being, administrative data, 324, 331
  children, 8-9, 394-395, 396-397, 399-400, 416, 427, 428, 447-448, 451, 454, 467
  cohort comparison studies, 8-9, 397, 398-399, 401-405, 406, 407, 413, 415-416, 417-422
  data access and confidentiality issues, 6-7, 230-231, 241-258
  definition of leavers, 395-400, 418-419, 460-462, 466-471, 472
  educational attainment, 428, 447-448, 451, 454, 467
  employment, administrative data, 389, 394, 400-408, 412-413, 415, 416-443 (passim), 448, 453-463, 464, 468
  food stamps, administrative data, 401-402, 409, 432-435, 445, 446, 448-449, 450, 463
  funding, 9, 67, 242, 288
  geographic factors, 388(n.1), 428, 467
  health status, 389, 394; *see also* "*Medicaid*" *infra*
  historical perspectives, 387, 389, 472
  homeless persons, 92
  incentives, 107
  income and earnings, administrative data, 389, 394, 409-411, 413, 416-417, 432-436, 439, 441-450, 454-464 (passim), 468, 469, 470, 472
  income and earnings data, 276, 389, 394, 400-413, 416, 417-422, 426
  mail contacts, 404-405
  matching of data, 402-403, 408, 409, 411, 412, 417-422
  Medicaid, 394, 401-402, 409, 432, 435-438, 448, 449, 463
  state government, 388, 395-407, 410, 413-431
  state-level factors, other, 388, 389, 390-393, 395-407, 410, 417-422
  statistical analysis, 450-464
  Supplemental Security Income (SSI), 427, 431, 451, 454, 460-461, 462
  survey nonresponse, 30, 406, 409-412, 413
  survey respondents, error of measurement, 170
  telephone surveys, 2, 3-4, 55, 57, 67-75, 78-79, 403-406
  urban areas, 427-472 (passim)
Leavers, *see* Continuous welfare leaver; Cyclic welfare users; Long-term welfare users; Short-term welfare users; Stayers
Legal issues, *see* Confidentiality and privacy
Legislation
  administrative data, confidentiality and access, 6-7, 222, 223-224, 232, 233-241, 246, 247, 255-257, 266-267, 268, 271-274
    criminal penalties for breeches, 238-239, 254-256, 263, 268, 274
  Data Matching and Privacy Protection Act, 234, 235-236
  educational testing, standardized, 338-339
  Family Educational Rights and Privacy Act, 339-341
  Freedom of Information Act, 233
  Job Training Partnership Act, 246, 278, 291, 295-302, 310-312
  Paperwork Reduction Act, 124-125
  Personal Responsibility and Work Opportunity Reconciliation Act (PRWORA), 1, 2, 8, 55, 275, 316-321, 330, 387, 394, 415-416, 431; *see also* Temporary Assistance for Needy Families; Time limits; Waiver programs; Work requirements
  Privacy Act, 233, 234-235, 237, 239, 240
Linguistic factors, *see* Language factors
Linkage, data, *see* Matching, administrative data

Local-level effects
   see also Qualitative studies
   child well-being, 322, 329, 343
   incentives, surveys, 116-117, 121
   income and employment data, 275-276,
      279, 282
   in-person surveys, 4, 91, 102
   survey nonresponse, 30
Longitudinal studies, 68, 103, 104-123
   see also Bureau of the Census; Cohort
      comparison studies; Panel
      studies; Survey of Income and
      Program Participation (SIPP)
   administrative data linkage, 207, 336
   child well-being, 324, 334, 335, 336
   data sets, 203
   error of measurement, 160
   income and employment, 275, 277, 279-280
   matching of data, 207, 336
   Panel Study of Income Dynamics (PSID),
      275, 279, 280-281, 284, 288,
      289-290, 363
   qualitative, general, 357, 360, 362-365
   telephone surveys, 55, 56
Long-term welfare users, 9, 163, 341, 371,
      400, 419-447 (passim), 451-
      458 (passim), 462-464, 466,
      471, 472, 475, 476, 477, 480-
      499 (passim)

M

Mail contacts, 131
   address databases, 91
   cost factors, 59
   incentives, 4-5, 70-71, 72, 82, 102, 106-
      109, 110-111, 112, 120, 122,
      123
   in-person interviews and, 89, 91, 92, 102
   leaver studies, 404-405
   telephone surveys and, 58-59, 66-73
      (passim), 82
Males, *see* Gender factors
Marriage and marital status
   see also Single mothers
   child well-being, 331, 336, 345
   leaver studies, 440
   qualitative studies, 356
   survey nonresponse, 30, 37, 142-143
   survey respondents, error of measurement,
      167-168

Matching, administrative data, 6, 7, 41, 49,
      60, 93, 132, 134, 141, 143,
      153, 154, 167-168, 171, 173,
      174, 175, 197, 198, 204-219,
      220, 222-223, 224-227, 228-
      229, 235-238, 241, 252, 261,
      264, 268, 276, 287-288, 298,
      504
   child well-being, 336, 343, 344, 346
   gender factors, 210, 212, 216, 229, 252
   leaver studies, 402-403, 408, 409, 411,
      412, 417-422
   longitudinal studies, 207, 336
   standards, 211-212, 235-237
   statistical analyses, 205(n.2), 206, 209-
      211, 213-217
Maternal and Child Health Block Grant, 328-
      329
Maternal and Child Health Bureau, 322
Measurement error, 3, 5, 157-194
   administrative data, 277, 292-295, 304-
      305
   alcohol and drug abuse, 177, 184-185
   autobiographical information, 160-171
   cognitive factors, 157, 159, 160-164, 165,
      167-168, 174-175, 176-177,
      178-184, 187-189
   Current Population Survey (CPS), 158,
      168, 169, 175
   definitional issues, 158
   employment and income data, 7, 164-171,
      173-177, 277, 282-290, 292-
      295, 304-305
   gender factors, 173, 176
   geographic factors, 167-168
   language of question, 158-159, 160-161
   survey data, 157-174, 277, 282-290
      (passim), 406, 408, 409
      AFDC, 171-173
      age factors, 167-168, 171, 176
      educational attainment, 167-168, 173
      race/ethnicity, 164, 171, 173, 176
   urban areas, 167-168
Medicaid, 26, 69, 197, 202, 203, 226-227, 249
   child well-being, 318, 320, 321, 323, 324-
      326, 328, 329, 330, 331, 343
   leaver studies, 394, 401-402, 409, 432,
      435-438, 448, 449, 463
Memory, survey respondents, 3, 5, 159, 161,
      162, 163-164, 168, 175, 176-
      177, 180-184, 404, 408

Men, *see* Gender factors
Mental health and illness
    see also Alcohol and drug abuse; Child
            abuse and neglect
    qualitative studies, 356
Minimum work requirements, *see* Work
            requirements
Minorities, *see* Race/ethnicity
Mortality rates, children, 317, 320, 322, 323,
            327-328, 341
Moving to Opportunity experiment, 342-343

N

National Adult Literacy Survey, 121
National Assessment of Educational Progress,
            121
National Association for the Advancement of
            Colored People, 91
National Change of Address, 91
National Health Interview Survey, 21
National Institute on Aging, 262
National-level studies
    see also Current Population Survey;
            National Longitudinal Survey
            of Youth; Survey of Income
            and Program Participation
    data sets, 203
    income and employment, 275, 277, 279-
            290, 311
    National Adult Literacy Survey, 121
    National Assessment of Educational
            Progress, 121
    National Health Interview Survey, 21
    National Survey of America's Families,
            50, 66-67
    National Survey of College Graduates, 116
    National Survey of Family Growth, 177
    Panel Study of Income Dynamics (PSID),
            275, 279, 280-281, 284, 288,
            289-290, 363
National Longitudinal Survey of Youth
            (NLSY), 363
    caseload heterogeneity, 482
    education, 338
    income and employment data, 279, 280,
            284, 289, 417, 422-423
National Opinion Research Center (NORC),
            4, 87, 88, 93, 96, 97, 98-99,
            101, 103

National Survey of America's Families
            (NSAF)
    interview techniques, 66-67
    response rate, 50
National Survey of College Graduates, 116
National Survey of Family Growth, 177
Noncash benefits
    see also Education and training; Food
            stamps
    child care services, 203, 204, 205, 206,
            226, 249, 319, 367, 368, 377,
            416
    housing subsidies, 142, 143
    transportation assistance, 367
Nonresponse adjustment, 3, 5, 13-54, 62, 86,
            129, 130-131, 132, 133, 134-
            154
    see also Response rates
    imputation and weighting, 25-28, 131,
            138-155
    leaver studies, 30, 406, 409-412, 413
    population-based, 147-152
    state government, 132, 138-139, 140, 142-
            143, 411
Nutrition, 197
    children, general, 322
    food stamps
    School Lunch Program, 203
    WIC, 203, 204, 214, 249, 318, 320, 324,
            343

O

Office of Management and Budget, 88, 92
    incentives, surveys, 123, 124-125
Old-Age and Survivors Insurance and
            Disability Insurance, 171
Open-ended questions, 357, 358-359, 375,
            376, 380, 381
Organizational factors
    administrative data, confidentiality issues,
            243-254, 258-259, 262-264,
            265, 266, 267-268
        Institutional Review Boards, 88, 92,
            125, 236-237, 266-267
    child well-being, services fragmentation,
            318
    error of measurement, 160
    in-person interviews, 98-100, 101, 103
    qualitative studies, 381-382

Outcome data, general, 416
Outcome measures, 276-277
    see also Caseload measures; Child well-
        being; Employment; Income
        and earnings; Leaver studies;
        Nutrition; Well-being
    administrative data confidentiality, 251-
        252
    administrative data linkage, general, 207
    caseload heterogeneity, 473, 474
    qualitative, 360, 365
    TANF administrative data linkage, 205

P

Panel studies
    see also National Longitudinal Survey of
        Youth (NLSY); Panel Study of
        Income Dynamics (PSID);
        Survey of Income and Program
        Participation (SIPP)
    incentives, 5, 109-110
    qualitative, 360, 363-365, 382
Panel Study of Income Dynamics (PSID),
        275, 279, 280-281, 284, 288,
        289-290, 363
Paper and pencil interviewing, 88, 89, 90,
        160
Participation, *see* Program participation;
        Response rates
Penalties, *see* Sanctions
Personal interviews, *see* In-person interviews
Personal Responsibility and Work
        Opportunity Reconciliation
        Act (PRWORA), 1, 2, 8, 55,
        275, 316-321, 330, 387, 394,
        415-416, 431
    see also Temporary Assistance for Needy
        Families; Time limits; Waiver
        programs; Work requirements
Postal surveys, *see* Mail contacts
Privacy, *see* Confidentiality and privacy
Privacy Act, 233, 234-235, 237, 239, 240
Private sector
    confidentiality issues, researchers, 239,
        241, 243-254
    contractor monitoring, survey response
        rates, 55, 81, 94

Program participation, 198, 229, 276, 277,
        356, 401-402
    see also Caseload measures; Cyclic
        welfare users; Eligibility;
        Leaver studies; Short-term
        welfare users; Stayers; Survey
        of Income and Program
        Participation
    AFDC, 276, 280
    leavers, 8-9, 249, 388(n.1), 416, 417-
        470 (passim)
    child well-being, administrative data, 324,
        333, 337-338, 341, 342, 344-
        345
    continuous welfare leavers, 183, 332,
        396-397, 399, 421-422, 441
    definitional issues, 479-480, 490, 492,
        493, 498-499
    income and employment data, 275, 276
    leaver studies, 399, 401-402
    long-term welfare users, 9, 163, 341, 371,
        400, 419-447 (passim), 451-
        458 (passim), 462-464, 466,
        471, 472, 475, 476, 477, 480-
        499 (passim)
PSID, *see* Panel Study of Income Dynamics
Puerto Ricans, 90, 93, 370

Q

Qualitative studies, 8, 355-383
    AFDC, 375-376
    alcohol and drug abuse, 368
    attitudes, 357, 378
    child abuse and neglect, 356
    child well-being, 356, 366, 367
    cost, 380-381
    employment, 357, 359-361, 366-367, 378,
        382
    ethnographic studies, 90, 199, 356, 357,
        359-360, 365-369, 375, 382
    focus groups, 8, 43, 52, 357, 361-362
    gender factors, 363-364, 368, 373
        single mothers, 366-367, 382
    panel studies, 360, 363-365, 382
    questionnaires, 337, 358-359, 375-377
    race/ethnicity, 363-364, 370, 371, 373,
        382
    researcher training, 381-382
    sampling, 359-361, 362, 369-375, 379-
        380, 382

sanctions, 379
single mothers, 366-367, 382
socioeconomic status, 363-364, 375-376
survey data and, 356, 357, 358-359, 377,
    378
TANF, 355, 356, 359, 369, 370, 371
urban areas, 359-360, 366, 368, 370-374,
    382
Questionnaires
computer-assisted personal interviewing,
    88, 89, 90, 160, 177-178
computer-assisted telephone interview,
    111
Current Population Survey (CPS), 281
error of measurement, 158-159, 160, 170-
    171, 177-180
language issues, 4, 56-57, 88, 158-159,
    170-171, 178-180, 184, 187
leaver studies, 389
open-ended questions, 357, 358-359, 375,
    376, 380, 381
qualitative items, 337, 358-359, 375-377
socially sensitive items, 5, 37, 66, 106,
    157, 159, 164, 174-175, 177-
    178, 184-186
standards, interviewing protocols, 93, 96,
    186
telephone interviews, 64-66, 68, 78

R

Race/ethnicity
see also Cultural factors; Language
    factors
administrative data cleaning, 204, 212
administrative data linking, 210, 212, 216,
    228-229
black persons, 21, 90, 91, 93, 115, 135,
    136, 370, 371, 451, 454, 461,
    486, 488, 493
caseload heterogeneity, 482, 486, 488,
    489, 493
confidentiality and privacy, 228-229
employment, 21, 24-25, 171, 176, 482,
    486, 488, 489, 493
focus groups, 362
Hispanics, 56, 88, 91, 140, 370, 451, 454,
    486, 488, 489, 493
immigrants, 88, 90, 93, 366, 454, 457
incentives, surveys, 111, 115, 123

leaver studies, 428, 451, 454, 457, 467
Puerto Ricans, 90, 93, 370
qualitative studies, 363-364, 370, 371,
    373, 382
survey respondents, error of measurement,
    164, 171, 173, 176
survey response, 21, 24-25, 41, 87, 111,
    115, 123, 135-136, 137-138,
    140, 142, 143, 144, 146, 151
Recall, survey respondents, *see* Memory,
    survey respondents
Referral and Monitoring Agencies, 134
Regression analysis, 3, 23-25, 152, 494-496
Reporting requirements
administrative data *vs* survey data, 277
TANF, 275
Response rates, 2, 3, 13-156
see also Incentives, surveys; Nonresponse
    adjustment
administrative data and, 27, 50, 57, 132,
    133-134, 142-143, 287-288,
    411
error of measurement, 167-168, 171,
    173, 174, 175, 182
age factors, 29, 33, 37, 43, 135-136, 137-
    138, 142
cognitive factors, 37, 41-42
cost factors, 37, 39, 41, 46, 49, 283
cultural factors, 36, 52
demographic factors, 37, 41, 42, 133,
    135-140, 142, 143, 145, 146
educational attainment, 24-25, 142, 151
employment information, 21, 22, 24-25,
    30, 138, 142, 159, 151
followup strategies, 4, 33, 48, 74, 75, 81,
    88, 116, 131
food stamp users, 26
gender factors, 21, 37, 41, 109, 135-136,
    137-138, 142, 143, 144, 146,
    151
geographic factors, 13, 29-31, 33, 57, 58-
    59, 87, 91, 133, 142, 143
income and employment data, 296, 297,
    410-411
in-person interviews, 3, 4, 31-50, 69, 77,
    78, 86-104, 502
tracing and tracking, 61, 74
item nonresponse effects, 111-113, 130
leaver studies, 30, 57, 67-75, 78-79, 86,
    92, 107, 404-405, 406, 408-412
locating sample persons, 29-31

marriage and marital status, 30, 37, 142-143
qualitative studies, 380
race/ethnicity, 21, 24-25, 41, 87, 111, 115, 123, 135-136, 137-138, 140, 142, 143, 144, 146, 151
refusal an refusal conversion, 4, 5, 25, 36, 42, 50, 63, 64, 65, 66-67, 68, 70-71, 75, 99, 408-409
rural areas, 3-4, 31, 32-33, 34, 37, 56-67, 70-75 (passim), 78-83, 87, 93, 141, 404-405, 502
social factors, 30, 35, 36, 37, 38, 39, 106
socioeconomic status, 37, 41, 50, 133, 142-143, 145
Supplemental Security Income (SSI), 26, 92, 94, 134-136
telephone interviews, 3-4, 31, 32-33, 34, 37, 56-67, 70-75 (passim), 78-83, 87, 93, 141, 404-405, 502
tracing and tracking, surveys, 30, 59-61, 68, 70-72, 73-75
urban areas, 21, 33, 36, 87, 142-143
welfare leavers, 3-4
Rural areas, nonresponse, surveys, 21, 33, 142

S

Sampling and sample size, 2, 3, 50, 86, 408-412
see also Caseload measures; Response rates
administrative data, child well-being, 346
administrative data confidentiality, 261
administrative data linking, 208
administrative data *vs* survey data, 277, 278
alcohol and drug abuse, 93, 94
state income tax records, 57-58
Supplemental Security Income, 92, 134
focus groups, 362
incentives, 115
income and employment data, 277-284 (passim), 290, 306
in-person interview surveys, 89-94, 100
leaver studies, 9, 396-397, 401-405, 406, 418

missing data, 3, 5, 129-156; *see also* Nonresponse adjustment
qualitative studies, 359-361, 362, 369-375, 379-380, 382
sample mean, 14-18
telephone surveys, 55-85
Sanctions, 395, 396-397, 399, 472, 448, 451, 454, 457, 461
child well-being and, 336, 343, 399-400
data confidentiality breaches, 238-239, 254-256, 263, 268, 274
income and employment data, 275
qualitative studies, 379
School Lunch Program, 203
Sensitivity analysis, 52
Short-term welfare users, 8, 176, 306, 400, 411, 419-420, 424-445 (passim), 456-459 (passim), 462, 466-470, 471, 472
see also Cyclic welfare users
caseload heterogeneity, 474, 480, 483-499 (passim)
Single mothers, 1, 317, 320
child abuse, administrative data, 331, 336
income, administrative data, 306-309
income, survey data, 280, 281
leaver studies, 394, 400
qualitative studies, 366-367, 382
SIPP, *see* Survey of Income and Program Participation
Social factors, 4
see also Attitudes; Cultural factors; Language factors; Local-level effects
child well-being, 316
confidentiality, sensitive data, 221, 230-231
qualitative studies, 356
survey nonresponse, 30, 35, 36, 37, 38, 39, 106
survey respondents, error of measurement, 157, 159, 160, 164, 174-175, 184-186
surveys, sensitive questions, 5, 37, 66, 106, 157, 159, 164, 174-175, 177-178, 184-186
Social Security Administration, 276, 288, 323
Social Security numbers, 58, 60, 69, 74, 208, 209, 210, 211, 214-216, 228, 238, 239, 287-288, 298, 343, 402-403

Socioeconomic status
    see also Educational attainment;
        Employment; Income and
        earnings, general
    error of measurement, 159, 164-171
    qualitative panel studies, 363-364, 375-376
    survey nonresponse, 37, 41, 50, 133, 142-
        143, 145
Soundex, 216-217
Spanish-speaking persons, see Hispanics
Special Supplemental Nutrition Program for
        Women, Infants and Children
        (WIC), 203, 204, 214, 249,
        318, 320, 324, 343
SSI, see Supplemental Security Income
State data
    administrative data, 6-7, 56-58, 69, 138-
        139, 142-143, 218, 222-223,
        225-226, 292
        child well-being, 318, 327-331
        confidentiality issues, 6-7, 222-223,
            238-258, 267-268, 271-274
        tax records, 57-58, 239, 293, 303-309,
            311, 312
    block grants, child health, 328-329
    child health care, 321, 322
    criminal justice system data, 93
    juvenile justice system, 7, 75, 328, 341-
        343, 344, 345
    leaver studies, 388, 395-407, 410, 413-431
    nonresponse adjustments, 132, 138-139,
        140, 142-143, 411
    qualitative studies, 382
    telephone surveys, 56-58, 69
    unemployment insurance records, 7, 69,
        132, 203, 225, 249, 276(n.3),
        277, 278, 287, 290-312, 403,
        406-408, 413, 417-422, 431,
        442-445, 451, 462
    waivers, 317
State-level issues, other, 2
    caseload heterogeneity, 474, 481-482
    income and employment data, 275-276, 279,
        282, 284, 290-309, 417-422
    leaver studies, 388, 389, 390-393, 395-
        407, 410, 417-422
Stayers, 9, 86, 424-429, 433-446 (passim),
        450-458 (passim), 463-464,
        466, 468, 471, 472
    caseload heterogeneity, 474, 480-499
        (passim)

Substance abuse, see Alcohol and drug abuse
Supplemental Security Income
    child health status, 323
    leaver studies, 427, 431, 451, 454, 460-
        461, 462
    response to surveys, 26, 92, 94, 134-136
Survey data, 1, 3-5, 13-194, 356
    see also Cognitive factors, surveys;
        Incentives, surveys; In-depth
        interviews; In-person
        interviews; Interviews; Mail
        contacts; National-level
        studies; Questionnaires;
        Response rates; Sampling and
        sample size; Telephone
        surveys; specific surveys
    administrative data vs,
        child well-being, 324, 338, 346
        error of measurement, 167-168, 171,
            173, 174, 175, 182
        income and employment, 6, 275-279,
            287-288, 289, 295-303, 311
        leaver studies, 406-408
        taxation, 277, 278, 285-286
    AFDC, 276, 278-283 (passim), 289, 300
    age factors, 29, 33, 37, 43, 135-136, 137-
        138, 142, 167-168, 171, 176
    best practices, surveys, 3, 9, 55, 56, 68,
        72-75, 78, 79, 86
    child well-being, 324
    employment and income, 6, 275, 276-290,
        295-303, 403-408, 409-411
    leaver studies, 2, 390-393, 403-412
    measurement error, 157-194, 277, 282-
        290 (passim), 406, 408, 409
        AFDC, 171-173
        age factors, 167-168, 171, 176
        educational attainment, 167-168, 173
    missing data, 3, 129-158
    paying respondents for participation, 105-
        128
    qualitative studies and, 356, 357, 358-
        359, 377, 378
    socially sensitive items, 5, 37, 66, 106,
        157, 159, 164, 174-175, 177-
        178, 184-186
    TANF, 6, 26-27, 134, 170, 278, 280, 282-
        283, 403, 409, 412
    telephone surveys, response rates, 55-85
Survey of Consumer Attitudes, 121

Survey of Income and Program Participation
(SIPP), 363
    incentives for respondents, 109-110
    income and employment data, 275, 277,
        279, 280-281, 284-290, 310,
        311

T

TANF, *see* Temporary Assistance for Needy
    Families
Taxation
    administrative data *vs* survey data, 277,
        278, 285-286
    Earned Income Tax Credits (EITC), 275,
        305-306, 446-447
    Internal Revenue Service (IRS), 7, 285-
        286, 302, 303-309, 312
    state income tax data, 57-58, 239, 293,
        303-309, 311, 312
Technical assistance, administrative data
    confidentiality, 256-257, 267
Telephone surveys, 31, 32-33, 34, 37, 49, 55-
        85, 90, 98-100, 101, 103
    access to telephones by householders, 87,
        98-100, 133
    answering machines, 4, 32, 48, 62-63
    best practices, 55, 56, 68, 72-75, 78, 79, 86
    computer-assisted telephone interview, 111
    cost factors, 56, 59-61, 78-83
    databases, 30, 57, 58, 59, 60, 69, 70-71
    incentives, 4-5, 70-71, 72, 82-83, 106,
        108, 110, 111
    interviewer training, 63-64, 66, 67, 68
    leaver studies, 2, 3-4, 55, 57, 67-75, 78-
        79, 403-406
    longitudinal, 55, 56
    mail contacts and, 58-59, 66-73 (passim),
        82
    questionnaires, 64-66, 68, 78
    random digit dialing (RDD) methods, 55-
        56, 63, 65, 76-78, 82-83, 106,
        111
    refusal conversion, 4, 5, 25, 36, 42, 50,
        63, 64, 65, 66-67, 68, 70-71,
        75, 99
    response rates, 3-4, 31, 32-33, 34, 37, 56-
        67, 70-75 (passim), 78-83, 87,
        93, 141, 404-405, 502

    sampling, 55-85
    state government, 56-58, 69
    tracing and tracking, 59-61, 68, 70-72, 73-
        75, 79-81, 98-99
Temporary Assistance for Needy Families
    (TANF), 1, 220, 275, 387
    administrative data, 6, 134, 200, 201, 203,
        204, 205, 214, 224, 225, 249,
        278, 283, 355, 400-403, 431,
        432, 437, 445, 446
    administrative data, child well-being, 316-
        317, 318, 324-325, 326, 327,
        331-337 (passim), 343, 344,
        346
    caseload heterogeneity, 482
    child well-being, qualitative data, 356
    income and employment data, 275, 276,
        278, 280, 282-283, 290, 310,
        311-312
    leaver studies, 8, 26-27, 72, 170, 205,
        249, 356, 359, 388-403
        (passim), 409, 412, 431, 432,
        437, 445, 446
    noncoverage, surveys, 134
    program participation, 276, 280
    qualitative studies, 355, 356, 359, 369,
        370, 371
    survey data, general, 278, 280, 282-283,
        403, 409, 412
    survey nonresponse, 6, 26-27, 134
    survey respondents, error of measurement,
        170
    waivers, 317
Three-City Study, 372-373
Time limits, 1, 6, 395, 472
    child well-being, 343
    income and employment data, 275
Time-use surveys, 32, 175
Tracing and tracking, 30
    cost factors, 30, 59-61, 79-81, 101
    followup, 4, 33, 48, 74, 75, 81, 88, 116,
        131
    in-person surveys, 61, 74, 92-94, 96, 101,
        102
    telephone surveys, 59-61, 68, 70-72, 73-
        75, 79-81, 98-99
Training, *see* Education and training
Transportation assistance, 367

U

Unemployment insurance records, 7, 69, 132, 203, 225, 249, 276(n.3), 277, 278, 287, 290-312, 403, 406-408, 413, 417-422, 431, 442-445, 451, 462
Urban areas
  in-person surveys, 87, 90, 93, 96, 97
  leaver studies, 427-472 (passim)
  nonresponse, surveys, 21, 33, 36, 87, 142-143
  qualitative studies, 359-360, 366, 368, 370-374, 382
  survey respondent error of measurement, 167-168
  Three-City Study, 372-373
  tracing and tracking, 75
Urban Change project, 371-372, 375-376
Urban Institute, *see* National Survey of America's Families

V

Vital statistics, 75, 225, 323, 327-331

W

Waiver programs, 317
Weighting, 25-28, 131, 138-155, 252, 290
Well-being, general, 389, 394-395, 406
  see also Child well-being; Health status and care; Income and earnings, general; Leaver studies
  administrative data, 197
  defined, 389, 394
  telephone surveys, 78
Welfare leavers, *see* Leaver studies
Welfare stayers, *see* Stayers
WIC, *see* Special Supplemental Nutrition Program for Women, Infants and Children
Women, *see* Gender factors
Work requirements, 1, 472
  child health status and, 321
World Wide Web, *see* Internet